The Art of
the Cake

OTHER BOOKS BY BRUCE HEALY AND PAUL BUGAT

The French Cookie Book
Mastering the Art of French Pastry

The Art of the Cake

MODERN FRENCH BAKING AND DECORATING

Bruce Healy and Paul Bugat

Illustrations by Paul Bugat

Photography by Pierre Ginet

WILLIAM MORROW AND COMPANY, INC. NEW YORK

Library of Congress Cataloging-in-Publication Data has been applied for.

ISBN 0-688-14199-4

Printed in the United States of America

First Edition

2 3 4 5 6 7 8 9 10

BOOK DESIGN BY ELLEN CIPRIANO

www.williammorrow.com

For
James and Margaret Healy
and in memory of
Marcel and Jeanne Bugat

Contents

Foreword by Shirley Corriher

. . . .

If you dare to dream of creating exquisitely beautiful French cakes—the unbelievably delicious *objets d'art* of the great pastry shops of Paris—Bruce Healy and Paul Bugat make it possible in *The Art of the Cake*. Whether you are a home cook or a master pastry chef, you want to own this book.

Here are the voluptuous classic cakes, many out of the pages of the history of France. Some are complex with multiple layers, luxurious fillings, and daring icings. Yet, Bruce and Paul make the seemingly impossible possible.

They break down these magnificent creations into manageable parts, starting with simple cakes. Slowly and surely, you master one phase after another, from sponge and meringue layers to buttercreams and mousses.

Bruce's writing is clear and vivid, giving exciting mental pictures of famous pastry chefs of the past and their shops. Paul, illustrator and collaborator, is from a family of pastry chefs who own many of the great shops in Paris. He contributes classic details and stories from his childhood, including the wonderful lemon cakes his grandmother took on road trips.

Bruce is very thorough. He explains every step, from preparing the pan to the final decorative touches. He never leaves you guessing about anything.

The Art of the Cake is the work of a true master's master. Bruce's information is as striking as his cakes. As much as I know about eggs and egg-white foams, I learned something new when I read this book.

Bruce goes to new depths in obtaining information, such as exactly which part of the three phases of creaming contributes to volume—creaming the butter; creaming the butter and sugar; or creaming the butter, sugar, and eggs. Of all of our great cake masters, I know of no one who has ever done this. Bruce's research indicates that creaming the butter and sugar is the most vital step in producing volume. Once you have added the eggs, there is no longer a major influence on the final volume, no matter how long you beat.

My respect and admiration for Bruce's work are enormous. He is a true leader in the field of baking and continually points out things that we thought we knew but do not know at all. Under his gentle tutelage, you will be able to create cakes of incredible beauty and taste. In the process, you will have had the advantage of learning from a great master.

The Art of the Cake is an invaluable book.

Acknowledgments

F rench cakes have evolved over centuries into a subject of enormous diversity, subtlety, and beauty. Yet in the French pastry chefs' way of thinking, they are so embedded in the larger subject of pastry that, until now, this glorious subdomain has not taken on a life of its own. I am indebted to the pioneering pastry chefs who, through their brilliant innovations and inexorable search for perfection, have developed and refined the art of the cake to its sophisticated and elegant modern form. At a more personal level, I am deeply indebted to the friends and colleagues who, through their generous consultation, encouragement, and support, have helped me to define the subject of French cakes in a way that brings out its inherent logic and to simplify and streamline the methods of the professional French pastry chef to the point where the most exquisite French gâteaux can be made in the American home kitchen. Among those friends and colleagues, I wish to thank especially:

My wife, Alice Fenvessy Healy, for her unfailing love and support, for a wealth of insightful criticism, and for her discerning assessment of every gâteau.

My daughter, Charlotte Alexandra Healy, for the joy she brings to life and the delight she brings to eating.

My parents, James and Margaret Healy, for their selfless generosity and enduring support, and for teaching me to strive for excellence in every endeavor.

Doris Fenvessy, my mother-in-law, for finding and sending me a steady stream of newspaper and magazine articles related to my work.

Shirley Corriher for numerous invaluable discussions on the science of baking and for her enthusiastic support; and Arch Corriher for providing technical literature searches to accompany Shirley's advice. Shirley's persistent urgings led me to a new level of understanding of the roles egg yolks, flour characteristics, and potato starch play in cake batters and opened the door to a systematic approach to improving many French cake recipes. Our discussions on chocolate have provided a deeper appreciation of the subtleties of that most sensuous and treacherous ingredient.

Peter and Nancy Kranz for their continued friendship and encouragement.

Kathryn Duffy, Gin Adlof, Nancy Zeff, and Linda Price for their capable and dependable assistance in the kitchen while I was developing the recipes. Kathryn and Gin were especially dedicated when the pressure was on to finish the manuscript. Kathryn also read much of the manuscript and contributed many useful suggestions.

Megan Newman for accepting the proposal for this book at Morrow five years ago, for her faith in the project, and for helpful discussions at the outset.

Pam Hoenig for her masterful editing and attention to every detail, for making it possible to have so many color photos, and for gently but persistently pointing me in the right direction.

Jennifer Herman for helping to coordinate the myriad logistical details required to get such a complicated manuscript safely through the copyediting process and into production.

Pierre Ginet for his ravishingly beautiful photography and his endless enthusiasm for making each photo even better than the previous one. And Christine Drin for her stylish and innovative prop styling.

Andrea Feldman for her expert consultation on the phonetic transcriptions of French cake names.

Judith Weber, our agent, for championing this project from start to finish.

Bernard Declos at Valrhona, Robin Long and John Vitagliano at Lindt, Tim Huff at Gold Medal, and P. J. Hamel at King Arthur for technical information about their products.

—BRUCE HEALY
Boulder

It is a pleasure to express my gratitude to my family and colleagues, in particular to:

My wife, Danielle Bugat, and our children, Isabelle, Nathalie, and Marc, for their unwavering love and encouragement. Danielle especially for her support and patience while I was working on the drawings.

My parents, Marcel and Jeanne Bugat, who guided me in my development as a pastry chef.

Charles and Jeannette Groscoeur, my parents-in-law, whose unfailing trust and generous support contributed greatly to my success both personally and professionally.

Pierre Ginet and Christine Drin for the pleasure of collaborating with them in styling the photographs, and for Pierre's consummate artistry.

Jean-Luc Augen for his loyal work as chef in my *pâtisserie* for many years and for his assistance in assembling the gâteaux for the photographs.

Guy Boileau, my cousin and fellow *pâtissier,* for sharing some secrets and tips on the preparation of several gâteaux that had been unfamiliar to me.

I am also grateful to the following boutiques in Paris for providing the beautiful tableware used in the color photos: Le Cèdre Rouge, Dehillerin, Geneviève Lethu, Siècle, Diners en Ville, and Deshoullieres.

—PAUL BUGAT
Paris

Preface

. . . .

In 1970 my wife, Alice, and I were graduate students at The Rockefeller University in Manhattan. One of her colleagues in psychology, Rich Shiffrin, got us interested in eating at French restaurants. Within a few months we had dined at some of the best restaurants in the city, and French food was becoming a favorite subject of conversation in The Rockefeller lunchroom. One of my fellow students in theoretical physics, Seth Putterman, had traveled to Europe and informed us that the New York restaurants could not hold a candle to the best in France, the restaurants rated 3 stars by the Guide Michelin. In the summer of 1972, the opportunity to verify his claims in person appeared. Alice and I would be attending conferences in Europe—mine in theoretical physics in the Black Forest in Germany, hers in psychology in The Hague. We arranged to spend ten days in France before our academic obligations, first in Paris and then a loop around the countryside from one obscure village or remote city to another. Obscure, that is, except that each one happened to be the location of a 3-star restaurant.

Dining at the great French restaurants—Laserre in Paris, Troisgros, Bocuse, Père Bise, and Auberge de l'Ill in the countryside—changed my life. I had never seen food like this before, or imagined that it could taste so good. Not only were the meals in the restaurants extraordinary, but it seemed that a pastry shop was located on every street corner. Especially in Paris.

Before we had left for Europe that summer, I had done a little cooking, mostly desserts. When we returned, I was inspired. I wanted to know everything about French food—how it developed and related to the rest of French culture, who the great chefs were, and most of all, how to make some of those incredible dishes we had tasted in France but could not obtain back home in New York. I read everything I could get my hands on and developed my cooking skills on the most challenging recipes I could manage. The books of Julia Child and Jacques Pépin became my guides, then Raymond Oliver and Henri-Paul Pellaprat.

Alice and I earned our Ph.D. degrees in 1973 and then found ourselves commuting between Yale University in New Haven, where she was Assistant Professor of Psychology, and The Institute for Advanced Study in Princeton, where I was doing research in physics. As our careers developed, we found an excuse to travel to France every year, attending conferences, dining in more great restaurants, exploring more glorious pastry shops. As a junior faculty member at The Institute and later at Yale, my burning interest in physics gradually began yielding to my growing passion for French food. At The Institute, I organized a dinner with my fellow young physicists. We set aside a week of preparation for the grandest dinner we could make: galantine of duck decorated with sliced vegetables and glazed with aspic; a ten-pound lobster sacrificed for *homard à l'armoricaine;* a great, domed *vol-au-vent* filled with veal sweetbreads, quenelles, and fluted mushroom caps in madeira sauce; a regal vanilla bavarian surrounded by caramel-dipped glacé chestnuts; plus salad, French wines and cheeses, petits fours, and cognac as digestif.

When I became J. Willard Gibbs Instructor in Physics at Yale in 1975, Alice and I could finally give up commuting and live together full-time, and formal dinners became a regular occurrence at our apartment. Reality also began to take hold. You can't become a first-class physicist if your passion lies elsewhere.

It was time to think about a career change from theoretical physics to writing about food and teaching cooking. To get my feet wet, I decided to write an article about a subject that, by now, I knew very well—the best pastry shops in Paris. So in June of 1977 Alice and I went to France with a mission—finish the research on Parisian pastry shops. André Neveu, a physicist friend from The Institute for Advanced Study, told me that I had to meet Paul Bugat. Paul's shop, Pâtisserie Clichy, near the *place de la Bastille,* was one of the best in Paris, renowned for Paul's painting on panels of marzipan and sculptures in blown sugar. What's more, Paul's father and brother owned Coquelin on the *place de Passy,* and his cousin owned Dalloyau-Gavillon on the *Faubourg St. Honoré.* His grandfather had been the original pastry chef at the Ritz in Paris under Escoffier. My friend André had grown up near the Bastille. His family had frequented Clichy for twenty years. An introduction to Paul was arranged, and soon I had interviewed not only Paul but also his brother and cousin, as well as several other pastry chefs. Paul is one of the great artists among pastry chefs, following a tradition that goes back to Carême. Sure his desserts look and taste great, but he also creates edible works of art that you could mistake for original masterpieces. So good, in fact, that when Paul has made edible copies of paintings in the Louvre to celebrate special exhibitions, the curator of paintings at the museum requested photos of Paul's copies for his files.

I returned home with voluminous tasting notes on the best pastries Paris had to offer, from every *arrondissement* in the city. A little distillation reduced my list of the finest shops to six extraordinary *pâtisseries:* Clichy, Dalloyau, and Coquelin, plus Millet, Fauchon, and Lenôtre. These six became the subject of an article I wrote for *Signature* magazine.

At the same time I started teaching French cooking in New Haven and soon developed a series of classes that I taught as a college seminar at Yale. I also began writing articles for a local travel magazine and reviewed restaurants for a newsletter in New York.

While I was in Paris, Paul Bugat and I had hit it off right away. We corresponded for a year or so and then decided we wanted to collaborate on a book on pastry. I arranged for him to visit the United States to teach a workshop on French pastry at Yale and to get a feel for how Americans cook. He arranged for me to work in his shop in Paris to become more familiar with professional pastry techniques. Then we set about redesigning the domain of the Parisian pastry chef to suit the logistics of the American home kitchen. I would use my teaching and science background to explain how and why everything in pastry worked; Paul would use his artistic skills to illustrate the pastry chef's techniques. Around the same time, Alice got an offer of a tenured professorship at the University of Colorado, and in 1980 we moved to Boulder.

The first book to come out of my collaboration with Paul was *Mastering the Art of French Pastry* (Barrons, 1984). Designed for serious amateur pastry cooks, it is now out of print and has become a much sought-after classic.

In Boulder, I opened a pastry business, Pâtisserie Healy, where I made classic French pastries and trained apprentices in the basics of the pastry chef's craft. People always wonder whether you can make authentic French pastries with American ingredients (not to mention American workers). Once when Paul was visiting, I asked him how he thought our pastries compared with the ones he made in Paris. He gave me a puzzled look and then with a French shrug of the shoulders replied, "But they are the same." So much for the authenticity question. Running the *pâtisserie* was a great experience for me, but I soon realized that the daily routine of pastry production was not what I wanted out of life. So I closed up shop and went back to teaching cooking, now specializing in pastry exclusively.

Meanwhile, Paul and I continued working together. In our second book, *The French Cookie Book* (Morrow, 1994), we explored the subject of French cookies in a more down-to-earth approach. That book turned out to be a fascinating project because, while the French pastry literature is rich in cookie recipes, the number of cookie recipes actually made in France today is quite small. Literally hundreds of great cookies have disappeared from the repertoire and exist today only as vague notes in nineteenth-century books. Much of the research for *The French Cookie Book* turned out to be a detective game of decoding and resuscitating these long-forgotten recipes.

Since *Mastering the Art of French Pastry* has been out of print, we often get calls from people who have seen or heard about the book but to their disappointment are unable to obtain a copy. We decided it was time to go back to the subject of French pastry, focusing this time on cakes and simplifying our approach to make these delectable desserts accessible to a wider audience. In *The Art of the Cake,* we have used modern techniques to make French cakes easier and manageable for anyone interested in preparing delicious and beautiful desserts. Not only are the modern techniques easier to learn than their classical counterparts, but many of them are really fun to use and produce startling results that elevate them beyond their simple mechanics. Fingerpainting in sheets of cake batter, forming ribbed ribbons of chocolate on strips of vinyl floormat, and caramelizing designs in sugar with a hobbyist's micro-torch or an electric charcoal lighter are just a few of the exciting decorative techniques available to the home cook.

Modern French cake making has entered a new era, and Paul and I are having more fun than ever sharing the excitement with you, our readers.

—BRUCE HEALY
Boulder

How and Why to Use This Book

To visit a great pastry shop in Paris is an overwhelming, sensual experience. The display cases are filled with row upon row of edible jewels, so exquisitely beautiful that we can scarcely believe they are actually desserts. The scent of baking pastries wafts in from the kitchen, as chefs wearing white tunics and tall toques occasionally glide in with trays of fresh treasures. The *salon de thé* beckons only a few feet away, and demure salesgirls stand ready to identify this gâteau or that *tarte*, then whisk our selections to a waiting table.

Seated at last, we take our first bite. Is it possible? The beautiful *objets d'art* on our plates taste even better than they look. Indeed, we are experiencing an art form designed to appeal to all of our senses, even our intellect. We begin to wonder what secrets lie behind the assembly of these magical creations, what science underwrites the pastry chef's craft.

WHAT ARE FRENCH CAKES?

Most beautiful and luscious of all the desserts in the *pâtissier*'s repertoire are the *entremets*, what we Americans would call French cakes. Gâteaux and charlottes, meringues and bavarians impress us with the precision and clarity of their design and execution at the same time as they lure us with their seductive charm. Tender cake layers enclose fillings ranging from light, soft fruit mousses to rich, firm buttercreams. Some glisten with satiny glazes of chocolate, fondant, or jelly. Others entrance us with rhythmic spirals of sliced jelly rolls encircling their plump bellies. Ripe red berries rest on pillows of whipped cream, while caramel chevrons stand against matte fields of confectioners' sugar. Chocolate curls and shavings and cigarettes festoon dark cylinders of decadence.

These desserts are truly unforgettable—and, outside the enchanted realm of the French pastry shop, unobtainable. Surely they are not desserts we Americans can make at home. Or are they?

Actually, most French cakes are not really difficult to prepare. They do take time, but so does preparing an "ordinary" American cake from scratch. In fact, French pastry chefs have worked very hard over the past few decades to streamline the techniques of cake making, modernizing their methods and making them less dependent on highly skilled labor. The result is that contemporary French cake making is now within reach of the home cook. The purpose of *The Art of the Cake* is to introduce you to this irresistible subject and teach you the techniques that will enable you to master it.

ANALYZING THE COMPONENTS

The only way to really understand French cakes is to break down the subject into manageable pieces. All cakes are made by putting together building blocks or components, so we will look at what the components are and how they are used.

In the most basic cakes there is only one component, the cake itself with, at most, a simple glaze. It can be a sponge cake, a pound cake, or a meringue. We call these "simple cakes." Since they are served solo, with no filling or frosting, they must have sufficient inherent character to carry their own weight.

The next step is to combine a simple cake with a filling and perhaps a frosting to make an assembled cake. The character of the cake component now recedes in importance. We use sponge cakes and meringues (almost always nut meringues because they are less sweet and have a more interesting texture than plain meringues) as components, but not pound cakes because they are already rich enough and would make an assembled cake too heavy.

The nature of an assembled cake is determined by the nature and relative importance of the cake component and the filling. In many assembled cakes the cake component supplies the bulk of the dessert, and the filling and frosting layers are thin, and usually rich. These cakes are built by sandwiching the filling between layers of the cake component. We Americans call them "layer cakes," and the French call them "*gâteaux*" (pronounced *ga-tō*). The singular of the French word is *gâteau*, which is pronounced the same because the final *x* used to form the plural is silent. Gâteaux can take almost any shape. Round and rectangular gâteaux are the most common, followed by logs and loaves; the layering is usually horizontal. The filling and frosting are most often buttercream or ganache (pronounced *gä-näsh*), the rich chocolate cream filling that is familiar from chocolate truffles. Jams, whipped cream, and light pastry creams are other possible fillings.

There is a totally different group of assembled cakes in which the filling supplies the bulk of the dessert and the cake layers are thin. In these desserts the filling is a mousse or bavarian cream.

These very light fillings are stabilized by gelatin, and the desserts containing them are almost always shaped in a mold. They are often glazed but never frosted. If the cake component is wrapped around the outside of the mousse, then we call the dessert a charlotte, a mousse cake, or a mousse log, depending on the shape and presentation. Charlottes and mousse cakes are round and deep, while mousse logs are log-shaped. On the other hand, if the cake component is embedded inside a bavarian cream, then the dessert is a bavarian.

Meringues (as opposed to simple cakes based on meringue or the plain meringue and nut meringue layers used in gâteaux) are a category of their own. Many of them are individual serving-sized desserts made by sandwiching a rich filling between two very light meringue domes or fingers. Others, called *vacherins* (pronounced *va-shrẽ*), are made by filling a large cylindrical shell of crisp meringue with ice cream or fresh berries in whipped cream.

Preparing and Assembling the Components—How the Recipes Are Organized and Structured

Now that we have analyzed French cakes by breaking them down into their component parts, we can begin to think about synthesizing French cakes by preparing these components and assembling them to build finished desserts. Our guiding organizational principle is that you build starting from the cake components. Then you select fillings and frostings as mortar to hold the cake components together, and decorations to embellish the exterior of the dessert.

Chapter 1 is devoted to the simple cakes. Each of the remaining six chapters in Part I of this book is centered around a particular type of cake component. We give recipes for the cake components first, followed by recipes for the desserts in which they are used. You will find the recipes for the other components you need (fillings and frostings, finishing touches, and some basic preparations) in Part II. For some components that are particularly simple or for which the preparation is integral to the recipe for the complete dessert, the recipe for the component is included as part of the dessert recipe. This organization makes the assembly process easy to understand and allows you to use the recipes for three or four cake components as a springboard from which to prepare dozens of different desserts. We have presented the material in sufficient detail and clarity that even a novice can be assured of success.

At the heart of our approach is the fact that an enormous variety of desserts can be prepared using a small number of basic components and techniques. This fact makes it possible to extract the detailed explanations of the techniques from the recipes and present them in a more general context at the beginning of each chapter. If you don't want or need the detailed hows and whys, you can simply follow the straightforward recipes. But if you want to improve your skills or acquire a better understanding of the subject, you can read the chapter introductions, then return to the recipes with an enlarged arsenal of techniques at your disposal. The general technique explanations are accompanied by Paul's line drawings to give you visual images that illustrate the essential features of each procedure.

Once you have assembled a dessert, the final step is to make it beautiful. Our approach to decoration is multi-faceted. We provide specific presentations in the recipes for the desserts, as well as general decorative techniques in Chapter 9, Finishing Touches. We include modern techniques in which the decoration becomes integral to the cake itself, as well as modern variations on the traditional methods of applied decoration. And we show you how to use some common household items, ranging from Lego assembly boards to electric charcoal lighters, to make cake decorating both easier and more exciting. The methods and results are illustrated with line drawings and color photographs.

The third part of this book is devoted to reference material. Here we describe the tools and ingredients important for cake making and tell you how to use them. We also list product sources and explain the different methods for measuring ingredients. And we provide a detailed explanation of some general techniques used throughout the book.

FITTING CAKE MAKING INTO YOUR SCHEDULE—HOW TO USE THE COMPONENT APPROACH TO YOUR ADVANTAGE

By now you know that making French cakes can be fun and rewarding. But perhaps you are still wondering how you can find the time for it. Luckily, the component structure of French cakes makes it very easy to integrate the preparation of even the most elaborate desserts into the hectic schedules of contemporary American life. Many of the components can be prepared most efficiently in quantities large enough for several desserts and then stored for future use as you need them to assemble each cake. Preparing each component requires a small amount of time and can be done at your leisure; and each component can be used in many different cakes. To help you coordinate the preparation of components with the desserts, we have included in the reference section a cross-index of components, listing the cakes in which each is used. With the bulk of the work done in advance, you will be amazed at the speed with which you can assemble desserts that will dazzle your family and friends.

HOW TO APPROACH EACH RECIPE

Your approach to a recipe will depend on your level of experience. Unless you are a real expert, you should start by reading the recipe you plan to use. As obvious as this advice may seem, we know almost no one who follows it. Yet, if there is one sure way to guarantee unfortunate suprises, frustration, and less than perfect results, launching into making a cake without reading the recipe carefully from beginning to end is it. Reading the recipe will tell you not only what special equipment and ingredients you need and which preparations you must do in advance but also it will alert you to any techniques that may be unfamiliar and where you can read about them in more detail. You can also turn it around and select the recipe you want to make based on what components you already have on hand and on what techniques you already know or want to learn.

Once you have read the recipe and done any advance preparation, it is time to get out your equipment and to measure your ingredients.

What Equipment Will You Need?

This question posed a dilemma for us. Some authors like to tell you every little tool you will need for each recipe. For cakes the result is a list that varies little from recipe to recipe and is so long that it becomes an impediment. On the other hand, there are some details of the equipment for each recipe that are easy to miss on first reading or get in the way of the flow of the recipe if they are buried in the instructions.

Our solution to this dilemma is to list at the beginning of each recipe only equipment in the following categories: tools special to the recipe; molds, baking sheets, and anything else that requires advance preparation; large pieces of equipment (especially electrical appliances) that may be awkward to pull out in the middle of the recipe; and anything (molds, pastry bags and tubes, cake cardboards) that requires a precise size specification. The result for each recipe is an equipment list that is concise and manageable.

In addition to the equipment specified for each individual recipe, here is a list of equipment that you should have at hand for every recipe:

- Set of stainless steel bowls in sizes ranging from ½ cup (1.2 dL) to 5 quarts (5 L)
- Saucepans in sizes ranging from 1 to 4 quarts (1 to 4 L)
- Butter melters, one 2-cup (5-dL) and at least one 1-cup (2.4-dL) or smaller
- If using a microwave for warming and melting, nonmetallic containers in a range of sizes including small custard cups or ramekins (in lieu of butter melters and small stainless steel bowls for many purposes)
- Rubber spatulas in small and large sizes
- Wooden spatulas in lengths ranging from 8 to 12 inches (20 to 30 cm)
- At least one wire batter whisk of medium size, preferably augmented by a small batter whisk and a medium-size balloon whisk
- Set of measuring implements for both dry and liquid ingredients, preferably including an accurate kitchen scale
- 10-inch (25-cm) chef's knife
- Paring knife
- Large icing spatula, with blade 10 to 12 inches (25 to 30 cm) long
- Small icing spatula, with blade about 4 inches (10 cm) long
- Wavy-edge bread knife with blade 10 to 12 inches (25 to 30 cm) long—the longer the better
- At least two bowl scrapers (or substitute rubber spatulas)
- Pastry brushes, preferably at least one small and one large

- Wire cooling racks
- Metal ruler or straightedge 12 to 18 inches (30 to 45 cm) long
- Flour sifter
- Fine stainless steel sieve
- Sugar dredge
- Blow dryer for most molded desserts
- Wax paper
- One or more trays for transporting and refrigerating cakes

All of the equipment used in this book is described in detail in the reference chapter on Equipment (page 460).

MEASURING THE INGREDIENTS

The ingredient lists for each recipe are broken down according to the way each cake is structured. This presentation makes it easy to see at a glance what the components and structure of each cake are and which ingredients will be used in each component. In fact, once you become familiar with some of our recipes and the techniques of cake making, you will find that the ingredient lists provide a convenient shorthand for many of the recipes and you can prepare them by following the ingredient lists alone. Of course that is precisely how skilled professional pastry chefs work, and in many cookbooks written for pastry chefs the "recipes" consist of little more than ingredient lists with a few notes to indicate when a preparation requires special attention or deviates from the standard procedures.

Carefully measure the quantities of ingredients called for in the recipe and lay them out in an organized fashion to avoid confusion in the heat of battle. All of the quantities are specified in both American and metric measures, with cup equivalents included for dry ingredients when appropriate. We like to measure liquid ingredients into small bowls or cups and dry ingredients onto sheets of wax paper. Always sift powdered ingredients onto sheets of wax paper. In many recipes, you will prepare the components one at a time, with plenty of time available in between if you need it. To minimize confusion, measure the ingredients for only the upcoming component or phase of the recipe to avoid a proliferation of ingredients on your countertop and the possibility that you may inadvertently use the wrong one. If you are measuring out the ingredients for more than one phase of a preparation, it helps to arrange the ingredients on trays (this is our favorite use for jelly roll pans), with a separate tray for each phase.

As with equipment, all of the ingredients used in this book are discussed in the reference section. However, one ingredient, namely flour, needs a special note here. We call for all-purpose flour in our recipes. We have developed our recipes using Gold Medal unbleached all-purpose flour. You can equally well use Gold Medal bleached all-purpose flour, which has comparable protein content to the Gold Medal unbleached, and expect comparable results, with only a very slight difference in taste and texture from the bleached flour. Other flours have very different protein contents, and as a result their baking characteristics can be very different. One that we want to single out is King Arthur flour because it is extremely high quality and is marketed throughout the country. King Arthur unbleached all-purpose flour has a significantly higher protein content than Gold Medal. We explain how to compensate for this high protein content in the reference chapter on Ingredients (page 513).

HAVE FUN

So much for the preliminaries. Now it is time to get into the kitchen and make some cakes. We hope you get as much enjoyment, enrichment, and satisfaction out of using this book as we did in writing it.

Happy baking.

Desserts

Simple Cakes

Here is a good place to begin. The cakes in this chapter are indeed simple—pound cakes, sponge cakes, and flans that are baked and cooled, then eaten as is, with, at most, a simple glaze or dusting of confectioners' sugar. No filling, no frosting, no fancy decoration. Among them are traditional regional cakes (*clafoutis* and *far*), old-fashioned cakes from the pastry shops of the early nineteenth century (*trois frères* and *croix de lorraine*), cakes that a Parisian housewife might make for the family (*quatre quarts* and *biscuit de savoie*), and cakes that, while easy to prepare, are so luxurious by virtue of their expensive ingredients that they are part of the repertoire of elegant pastry shops (*pain de gênes, week-end*, and *le cake*).

All of these cakes are leavened with eggs, with an occasional boost from a dash of baking powder. This mechanical leavening (as opposed to the chemical leavening of baking powder) is accomplished by beating air into the eggs to produce a mass of air bubbles called a foam. The expansion of the air bubbles during baking lightens the cake. Depending on the proportions of ingredients and method of preparing the cake batter, the cakes range from moist, dense, and rich (the pound cake end of the spectrum) to light and airy (the sponge cake end), or heavy and almost custardy (the flans).

POUND CAKE, SPONGE CAKE, OR FLAN

The essential ingredients for pound cake batters are butter, sugar, eggs, and flour. For the prototypical pound cake, *quatre quarts*, you use equal weights of these four ingredients. To prepare the batter, you cream the butter with the sugar, beat in the eggs, and fold in the flour. For other pound cakes, the proportions of the four essential ingredients vary and frequently they are augmented or replaced by almond-and-sugar powder, egg yolks (rather than whole eggs), potato starch, cream, and a variety of flavoring ingredients. Nonetheless, the method varies very little.

In contrast, the essential ingredients for sponge cakes are eggs, sugar, and flour, with little or no butter. In the separated-egg method, you whip the egg yolks with sugar and separately whip the egg whites, adding a little sugar at the end to produce a meringue. You then fold together the egg yolk and egg white mixtures with the flour. If there is any butter in the recipe, it is melted and folded in last. Whipping the egg whites and yolks separately aerates the eggs more than the pound cake method and, because there is little butter in the batter to deflate the eggs, sponge cakes are lighter and airier than pound cakes. Like pound cakes, sponge cake batters often have the basic ingredients augmented with almond-and-sugar powder, potato starch, and flavorings.

Actually, there is a continuous spectrum of batters that span the gap between pure pound cake and pure sponge cake. In the middle are some recipes that can be prepared by either method. Sometimes you can even use a hybrid pound cake method, beating only the egg yolks into the creamed butter and sugar and whipping the egg whites separately before folding the two mixtures together with the flour. There are also a few batters related to sponge cakes in which the egg yolk part of the batter is replaced by a sort of paste, typically containing some combination of almond-and-sugar powder, pureed fruit, unwhipped egg whites, and/or butter.

For all pound cake and sponge cake batters we recommend using an electric mixer, preferably a heavy-duty stand model, to prepare the batter. You can beat the batter by hand if you like, but that is hard work even for the small quantities in our recipes.

Flan batters are altogether different. Based on eggs, milk, sugar, and flour, they are aerated very little. The ingredients are just mixed together. Mixing these batters in an electric blender or food processor makes the process fast and foolproof. There isn't much more to say about the method except that in order to have a tender texture you should work the batter as little as possible after adding the flour to avoid developing gluten and making the batter elastic.

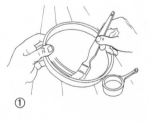

PREPARATION OF MOLDS

You will bake most of the cakes in this chapter in basic molds: loaf pans, round cake pans, or *tarte* rings. For a few of them, you will need a

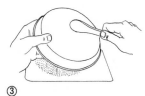

③

④

⑤

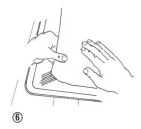

⑥

⑦

more unusual mold that is traditional for the particular cake, such as a *tarte* mold or deep quiche pan for *pain de gênes*, a brioche *parisienne* mold for *biscuit de savoie*, or a ring mold for *trois frères*. You will serve *clafoutis* and *far* directly from the baking dish, so for these an earthenware or porcelain pie pan or gratin dish is the best option. Of course, if you don't have the required mold and don't want to invest in one, you can always substitute another mold of the same volume and height.

You will coat the insides of loaf pans and round cake pans (as well as more elaborate molds) with butter to prevent sticking. For cakes that are especially fragile or likely to stick, clarified butter is preferable because it contains no milk solids that can adhere to the mold. The butter must be melted but not hot. Apply an even layer of butter on the bottom and sides of the mold using a pastry brush①. After brushing, let the butter set. For many cakes, you will then dust the mold with flour (or occasionally potato starch) to help keep the butter from running down the sides when it melts and to form a light crust when baked. Spoon some flour into the pan ②, and gradually tilt, rotate, shake, and tap the pan to distribute an even coating of flour over the butter on the bottom and sides of the pan. Turn the pan upside down and tap the bottom sharply with a wooden spatula to dislodge the excess flour ③. For the most fragile cakes, you can line the bottom of the pan with a sheet of parchment ④ after brushing with butter; then dust the sides of the pan with flour, and finally brush the parchment with melted butter ⑤.

You will bake some pound cakes in a loaf pan lined with brown wrapping paper or kitchen parchment. This heavy paper protects the surface of the cake from burning in the oven and keeps it fresh after baking by sealing out air. Brush the bottom and sides of the loaf pan with melted butter, line it with the brown wrapping paper (see page 544 for details), and then brush the paper with melted butter until it is thoroughly permeated.

For some thin round cakes a cake pan is too deep. To bake these cakes the best choice is a *tarte* ring (provided of course that the batter isn't at all runny). You will need a ring 1 inch (2.5 cm) deep, and you will place it on a heavy baking sheet to supply the bottom of the baking container. Cut a square of kitchen parchment a little wider than the diameter of the ring. On the baking sheet, brush either the outline or the diagonals of a similar square with melted butter, and place the parchment on the buttered square ⑥. The butter will hold the parchment in place. Brush the parchment with butter. (Using the parchment is easier than buttering and flour-

ing a circle on the baking sheet.) You can either butter and flour the ring or line it with parchment. Either way, brush the inside of the ring with melted butter ⑦, and let the butter set. To line it with parchment, cut a strip of parchment a little wider than the ring is high and a little longer than the circumference of the ring; place the ring on the baking sheet, centering it on the square of parchment, and wrap the strip of parchment around the inside of the ring, allowing the end of the strip to overlap the beginning ⑧; brush the parchment inside the ring with butter. To dust the ring with flour, hold it vertically and spoon some flour onto the inside of the ring at the bottom ⑨; gradually rotate and tap the ring, adding more flour as needed, to distribute an even coating of flour over the butter on the inside of the ring. Tap it on your countertop to dislodge the excess flour, then place the ring on the baking sheet, centering it on the square of parchment ⑩.

Preparing Pound Cake Batters

To get the best volume, the batter should stay between 60° and 65°F (just above 15°C) throughout the mixing process. If it gets warmer, the butter will melt, making the batter runnier and heavier. Since the mixer warms the butter as it works, we find it best to start with butter that is still cool (well below 60°F or 15°C), and in a warm kitchen you may even want to use butter straight from the refrigerator (if your mixer can handle it) and chill the sugar before adding it. Eggs, since they are added toward the end of the mixing, can be in the 60° to 65°F range (just above 15°C).

Cut the butter into pieces and beat it in your electric mixer, using the flat beater if your mixer has one ⑪, until smooth, white, and creamy. (If your mixer doesn't have a flat beater, then use the eggbeater attachment.) Add the sugar ⑫ (usually superfine or extra fine), along with almond-and-sugar powder if required. Continue beating at medium speed for 5 minutes, stopping the mixer and scraping down the sides of the bowl as needed, to make the mixture very smooth, light, and white. This step is very important, since it introduces air bubbles into the mixture. The sugar crystals break up the crystal structure of the butterfat, making way for tiny air cells between the fat crystals. Superfine or extra fine sugar is preferable to ordinary granulated sugar because it has a larger number of smaller crystals and thus more sharp edges to interrupt the crystals of butterfat; it also dissolves more quickly than ordinary granulated sugar after the eggs are added. Five minutes may seem like a long beating time, but if you compare the color of

⑬

⑭

⑮

⑯

the butter after 5 minutes of beating to what it was at 1 or 2 minutes, you will see that it is noticeably whiter. The whiter it is, the more air you have whipped in.

Now switch to the wire whip (if you aren't already using it) and beat in the first egg ⑬. When the first egg is completely incorporated, beat in the remaining eggs one by one at medium speed, being sure each egg is completely incorporated and the batter has lightened slightly before adding the next one. When all of the eggs have been added, continue beating a little longer to finish lightening the mixture and then beat in any flavorings ⑭. By now the air bubbles that had been incorporated in the butter will be transferred to the liquid supplied by the eggs. Don't worry if the mixture looks curdled at this point; when the flour is added, it will absorb the excess moisture and smooth the batter.

(Note that in a few cakes the quantity of sugar and/or almond-and-sugar powder is much greater than the quantity of butter. For these cakes, to effectively aerate the butter you should cream it with only part of the sugar and/or almond-and-sugar powder. Beat in the remainder after the butter mixture has been beaten for 5 minutes. The mixture will now be very thick. Beat in one of the eggs with the flat beater of the mixer, if your mixer has one, before switching to the wire whip to beat in the remaining eggs one by one.)

Remove the bowl from the mixer. Sift the flour ⑮ (with potato starch or baking powder if called for), and gently and gradually fold the flour into the batter ⑯. (Sometimes if the amount of liquid flavoring is large enough, it is better to add it to the batter after folding in the flour in order not to soften the batter too much.)

PREPARING SPONGE CAKE BATTERS

*B*iscuit is the French word for sponge cake. Its origin goes back at least as far as the thirteenth century, and it derives from the fact that the baked goods to which it was originally applied were cooked (*cuit*) twice (*bis*). *Biscuit* batters related to the recipes we use today were first developed in France around the beginning of the seventeenth century. However, the cakes made at that time were rather heavy. It was not until the beginning of the eighteenth century, contemporary with the development of meringue, that chefs began to beat the egg whites and yolks separately to achieve lighter cakes. At around the same time, they began to create sponge cakes enriched by the addition of melted butter. By the end of the nineteenth century, the introduction of mechanical whipping machines had made it very easy to prepare light sponge cake batters.

There are actually two distinct ways to prepare a sponge cake batter. One is the separated-egg method, in which you beat the yolks with sugar, whip the whites and then meringue them by adding a little more sugar, and finally fold the two together with the flour.

The other alternative is the whole-egg method. Here you beat whole eggs with sugar until the mixture becomes light and fluffy, then fold in the flour. This simple method produces cakes with a fine crumb and can easily accommodate a wide range of additions of butter or almond-and-sugar powder. The most refined form of this procedure is the génoise method, in which the eggs and sugar are warmed at the outset to make it possible to whip the mixture to greater volume. We take up the génoise method in Chapter 2, where génoise is used as the basis for a wide range of round gâteaux.

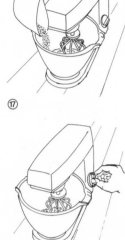

Separated-Egg Method

First separate the eggs and let them warm to room temperature. Combine the yolks with sugar ⑰ (preferably superfine or extra fine because it dissolves quickly), plus almond-and-sugar powder if required, and beat with an electric mixer ⑱ until the mixture whitens.

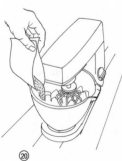

Place the egg whites in your electric mixer (in a clean bowl) and start whipping them at low speed to break up the whites. If you have a copper bowl for your mixer, use it; if not, then, when the whites start to froth, add a little cream of tartar ⑲, using ⅛ teaspoon (½ mL) for every 3 large egg whites. Gradually increase the whipping speed to medium-high and continue whipping. When you reach the "stiff-but-not-dry" stage, the whites will be thick and shiny, cling to the side of the bowl, and form stiff, unbending peaks if you lift the whip. As you continue whipping still more, the whites will become firmer, the surface will become a little duller, and the mass of egg whites will begin to slip on the side of the bowl, forming streaks as the wire whip drags it around. Never continue to whip the whites past this stage or they will give up too much moisture and become grainy. Depending on the amount of sugar that will be added to the whites and the texture of the egg yolk mixture, you may whip the whites all the way to the slip-and-streak stage or only to the stiff-but-not-dry stage.

As soon as the egg whites reach the appropriate stage, pour in the

sugar (preferably superfine) in a steady stream ⑳ and continue whipping at maximum speed for a few seconds to incorporate the sugar and tighten the meringue. The whites will become more cohesive almost immediately, and if enough sugar is whipped in, they will become shiny and totally smooth. Do not whip more than necessary to incorporate the sugar or the meringue will become too tough.

Sift the flour (with potato starch if called for) over the egg yolk mixture, add about one third of the meringue, and stir with a wooden spatula to mix quickly ㉑. Then gently fold in the remaining meringue.

When a small amount of butter is required in the recipe, it should be barely melted and not at all hot. Add it last, folding it in when the flour is completely incorporated ㉒. Do not add it earlier or you will risk deflating the batter.

Whole-Egg Method

As for the separated-egg method, the eggs should be at room temperature. Combine the eggs and sugar (usually superfine or extra fine is best because it dissolves quickly), plus almond-and-sugar powder if any, in your electric mixer. Start beating at low speed with the wire whip, and gradually increase the whipping speed to medium ㉓. (Beating at high speed would make the texture of the cake coarse by incorporating a relatively small number of large air bubbles rather than a large number of small ones.) The batter will become progressively paler and whiter in color and will begin to thicken. At the same time it will gain volume and become light. The color depends on the proportion of yolks in the batter as well as optional ingredients such as almond-and-sugar powder. In most cases the batter will start out yellow and eventually become cream-colored. A few batters will actually become thick enough to form slowly dissolving ribbons when dropped from the wire whip, but most will not thicken quite that much.

If the recipe calls for a small amount of liquid, beat it in after the batter becomes cream-colored, thick, and light. Then stop beating and remove the bowl from the mixer. Sift the flour and/or potato starch (occasionally with a little baking powder) onto a sheet of wax paper ㉔. Lift two opposite sides of the sheet of wax paper and use it as a funnel to gradually pour the flour mixture into the batter as you gently fold it in ㉕. On the other hand, if the recipe requires a large amount of liquid, it is better to add the liquid last, folding it in after the flour is completely incorporated.

When butter is included in the recipe, cream it (by beating with a wooden spatula, warming as needed, until smooth, white, and creamy) and add it last. When the flour is completely incorporated in the batter, stir a small portion of the batter into the creamed butter. Then gently fold this mixture back into the remaining batter. This procedure permits incorporating a large amount of butter without deflating the batter too much.

FILLING MOLDS AND RINGS

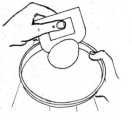

You can pour and scrape the batter from the mixing bowl into the mold or ring ㉖. Or, if the batter is thick, you can scoop up the batter with a bowl scraper and deposit it in the mold or ring a little at a time ㉗.

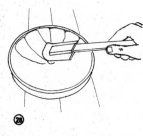

Ideally, you want the top surfaces of most cakes to be flat when they come out of the oven. To prevent the cake from forming a dome on top when it bakes, use the curved edge of a bowl scraper or rubber spatula to smooth the surface of the batter from the center out to the side of the pan, making a depression in the center ㉘. This technique works well for thick batters, but not for thin, runny batters, which won't retain a depression.

If you are using a bowl scraper to deposit the batter in a round cake pan, there is a more sophisticated way to fill the cake pan. Lift the cake pan with one hand and tilt it slightly toward you. With your other hand, scoop up some batter on the curved side of your bowl scraper and deposit it in the low side of the tilted pan, scraping the batter off the bowl scraper with the rim of the pan ㉙. Rotate the pan between each scoop. You will need about a half dozen scoops to work your way around the pan. Then deposit a small scoop of batter in the center of the mold ㉚. By controlling the amount of batter you take with each scoop, you can distribute the batter evenly and create a depression in the center without smoothing the surface afterward, thus reducing the chance of deflating the batter by manipulating it too much.

Usually the mold or ring should be filled to only about three quarters of its height so the batter has room to expand in the oven. Ideally, the mold or ring should not be filled much less than that because, if the mold or ring is too deep, the top of the cake will not bake and brown evenly. However, if you must bake the cake in a mold that is deeper than the one we suggest, naturally you should fill it to a lower proportion of its height.

Baking and Unmolding

Preheat the oven. If you don't, the cake will not bake properly.

If you are baking the batter in a cake pan or other mold, place the mold on a baking sheet to help distribute the heat evenly and protect the bottom of the cake. If you are baking the batter in a *tarte* ring, it will already be on a baking sheet.

In each recipe, we give a range of baking times for each cake. Do not open the oven door to check the cake until the beginning of the range of baking times or the cake may deflate. To test the cake, check the color and texture of the surface. When the cake is done, the top should be evenly browned and dry to the touch, and the sides of the cake should be just beginning to shrink away from the sides of the mold or ring. When you press the top gently with your fingertip, it should spring back to the touch. Insert the tip of a paring knife in the center of the cake ③. When the cake is done, the blade will come out clean, with no wet batter clinging to it. We do not recommend using a skewer or cake tester because it has so little surface area for batter to cling to that it can come out clean before the cake is done.

Remove the cake from the oven. If the top edge of the cake is clinging to the side of the mold or ring, slide the tip of a paring knife or small icing spatula between the edge of the cake and the mold or ring to loosen it. This helps prevent the cake from sticking to the mold. Most cakes are fragile when they first come out of the oven. Leave the cake in the ring (still on the baking sheet) or mold, place it on a wire rack, and allow to cool for a few minutes.

If the cake was baked in a mold, place a wire rack upside down on top and invert the mold and rack together ③. Carefully lift off the mold ③. If the cake doesn't slide out easily, invert the mold and wire rack together and loosen any spots where the cake is clinging to the side of the mold; then try again. Once the cake is unmolded on the wire rack, do not leave it upside down or the top surface can stick to the rack. If there is parchment on the bottom of the cake, carefully peel it off and place it clean side down on the cake ③. Place a second wire rack upside down on the cake and invert the cake together with the two racks. Lift off the first rack, and let the cake cool to room temperature.

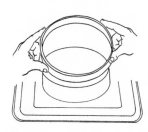

If the cake was baked in a *tarte* ring, you should be able to lift off the ring easily ③. Use a small icing spatula to loosen the cake from the side of

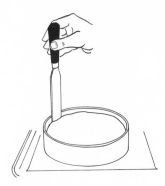

the ring if necessary ㊱. Slide the cake, with the parchment underneath, onto a wire rack using a large metal spatula, then let cool to room temperature. Place a second wire rack upside down on top ㊲ and invert the cake and two wire racks together. Lift off the first wire rack. Carefully peel off the square of parchment ㊳ and place it clean side down on the cake. Then place the first wire rack on top again and invert the cake once more. Lift off the second wire rack and let the cake cool to room temperature. If the ring was lined with a strip of parchment, carefully peel it off ㊴.

㊱

Top or Bottom?

Usually the side of the cake that was on the bottom in the oven becomes the top of the finished cake because it is perfectly flat with an evenly browned crust. If necessary, you can always trim the side that was on top in the oven to give the finished cake a flat bottom surface.

However, for a few cakes the side that was on top in the oven has a desirable appearance and remains on top in the finished cake. A good example is the classic pound cake, *quatre quarts*, which is baked in a loaf pan. The top domes and splits open down the center, and this feature is characteristic of its presentation.

㊲

Cardboard Cake-Decorating Circles

While they are sometimes not absolutely necessary for the simple cakes in this chapter, placing the cake on a cardboard cake-decorating circle will make it easier to handle and reduce the risk of damage. Use the foil board rounds sold as lids for aluminum foil take-out containers, or cut a round from a sheet of silver or gold matt board (see page 467 for details). In either case, cut the cardboard a little smaller than the bottom of the cake so that it won't show, and place it underneath the cake after it has cooled.

㊳

㊴

Dusting with Confectioners' Sugar

One of the simplest ways to finish a cake is to dust the top and sides with confectioners' sugar. This is easiest with a sugar dredge (see

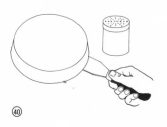

㊵

page 469). For most cakes you will dust both top and sides of the cake. For a few cakes, you dust only the top and leave the sides bare.

To dust the sides easily, first slide your icing spatula under the cake-decorating circle ㊵, lift the cake from your countertop, and support it on the fingertips of one hand ㊶. Tilt the cake away from you and dust the confectioners' sugar with the other hand ㊷, so it will coat the sides more effectively. Return the cake to the countertop and finish dusting the top.

When you want to dust only the top of the cake and not the sides, you should lift the cake on the fingertips of one hand and tilt it toward you ㊸. That way, nothing will land on the sides when you dust the confectioners' sugar on top with the other hand. For cakes baked in *tarte* rings, there is an even easier method: line the ring with a strip of parchment, and do not remove the parchment until after you have dusted the top of the cake ㊹. This trick produces a very sharp line between the white top and the browned sides of the cake.

GLAZING WITH APRICOT JAM AND CONFECTIONERS' SUGAR GLAZE

This is the easiest way to glaze a cake and it is used on many of the simple cakes.

Warm some strained apricot jam (page 412) in a butter melter or very small saucepan over low heat, stirring occasionally until melted. Brush the outside of the cake (top and sides or top only, depending on the cake) with the jam until lightly coated and glistening ㊺.

Sift confectioners' sugar into a small bowl and stir in enough cold water (or water and liqueur) to make a smooth, creamy paste that is just fluid enough to spread easily with a pastry brush. (Always add the specified amount of liqueur first to flavor the glaze, then finish thinning it with water to get the right consistency without shortchanging the flavor.) Lightly brush this confectioners' sugar glaze over the jam on the cake. Place the cake on a baking sheet and put it in a preheated 450°F (230°C) oven until the glaze turns from opaque white to translucent, about 1½ to 2 minutes. If the glaze starts to bubble around the edges, remove the cake from the oven immediately. Slide the cake onto a wire rack and let cool.

Glazing with Chocolate

U sually chocolate glaze works best over buttercream, but for some of the simple cakes you can glaze directly over the surface of the baked cake.

Place the cake right side up on a wire rack, with the side that was on the bottom in the oven on top. If necessary, trim the bottom of the cake with a long wavy-edge bread knife to make it flat ㊻. Place a large tray underneath the wire rack to catch the excess glaze.

The chocolate must be fluid enough to flow quickly and smoothly, producing a thin, even layer. It must not be too thin, however, or you will see too much of the surface texture of the cake through it; and it must not be so runny that it takes too long to set. Also, it should not be too brittle when set, or it will be difficult to cut and serve. We get the best results by thinning European bittersweet chocolate with clarified butter. Melt the chocolate and temper it ㊼ (see page 538 for a detailed discussion of tempering chocolate). The temperature of the chocolate must be between 86° and 91°F (30° to 33°C). The clarified butter must be at room temperature. Beat the clarified butter with a wooden spatula to make it smooth and creamy, then stir it into the chocolate.

Pour the chocolate glaze on top of the cake in a circle just inside the perimeter so that some of it flows naturally over the edges ㊽. Quickly smooth the top surface with the edge of a long icing spatula to cover the top with a thin, even layer of glaze and make the excess flow evenly down the sides ㊾. Try to make the glaze cover all sides of the cake. If there are any bare or uneven spots around the sides, smooth the glaze over them with the edge of the icing spatula. Work as quickly as you can because, once the glaze begins to thicken, you will no longer be able to spread it smoothly.

When the glaze has begun to thicken, clean off any excess around the base of the cake with a paring knife or small icing spatula ㊿. Then put the cake in a cool place (or in the refrigerator if necessary) and allow the glaze to set before serving.

Storage

N early all cakes are best when freshly made, but some deteriorate more quickly than others. As a general rule, all cakes should be stored in as airtight a fashion as possible without damaging their surfaces.

Of the cakes in this chapter, the sponge cakes with low butter content are the most perishable. To prevent them from drying out, they should be covered airtight with plastic wrap and kept in the refrigerator for up to 3 days. They do not freeze well.

Pound cakes and sponge cakes with relatively high butter content have more storage options. Before they are glazed or dusted with confectioners' sugar, cover them airtight with plastic wrap and keep at room temperature (in cool weather) or in the refrigerator (in hot weather) for up to 3 or 4 days. Or freeze for up to 3 months. If frozen, defrost overnight in the refrigerator and then unwrap the plastic wrap at least 2 hours before glazing, dusting, or serving to allow condensation produced by defrosting to evaporate.

Once glazed with apricot jam and confectioners' sugar glaze, the outsides of these cakes are well sealed and they can be kept at room temperature, uncovered or in a covered cake platter, for up to 4 days.

Cakes glazed with chocolate are best kept in a cool place—below 70°F (20°C)—to prevent fat bloom from forming on the chocolate. Under ideal conditions, these cakes will keep for up to 3 days. A warmer temperature will reduce the storage time, and in hot weather the chocolate will melt. You can keep chocolate-glazed cakes in the refrigerator for a day or so. Refrigerating them for longer can produce condensation on the chocolate that leads to sugar bloom.

Sponge cakes and pound cakes taste best when served at room temperature. They all go stale quickly when the interior is exposed to air. Once the cake is cut, the exposed surfaces of the cake will deteriorate more rapidly. To minimize this, cover any cut surfaces with a strip of plastic wrap.

The flans are best served while they are still warm from the oven. After cooling, you can cover them airtight with plastic wrap and keep them in the refrigerator for up to 3 days. Before serving, reheat in a 300°F (150°C) oven or in a microwave.

Quatre Quarts

(CLASSIC POUND CAKE)

The name *quatre quarts* derives from the proportions of the ingredients in the recipe for this cake: "four quarters," which is to say, equal weights of each of the four ingredients—butter, sugar, eggs, and flour. We have altered the recipe slightly, replacing about 10 percent of the flour with an egg yolk and a little potato starch to make the cake moister and more tender. The result is astonishingly successful.

Quatre quarts is delicious on its own, or if you prefer, you can serve it with jam, fruit salad (page 455), or stewed fruits.

For 8 servings

EQUIPMENT:
6-cup (1.5-L) loaf pan
• brush heavily with melted butter
Heavy baking sheet
Electric mixer, preferably a stand mixer with flat beater and wire whip

BATTER:

Unsalted butter, softened	8 ounces (225 g); 1 cup
Superfine or extra fine sugar, chilled in the refrigerator	8 ounces (225 g); 1 cup + 2 tablespoons
Large eggs, at room temperature	4
Large egg yolk, at room temperature	1
Pure vanilla extract	1 teaspoon (5 mL)
All-purpose flour	7 ounces (200 g); 1¼ cups + 3 tablespoons
Potato starch	⅓ ounce (10 g); 1 tablespoon

Preheat the oven to 350°F (175°C).

1. Cream the butter in the mixer, using the flat beater if your mixer has one. Beat in the sugar and continue whipping at medium-high speed for about 5 minutes to make the mixture very white and light.

2. One at a time, add each whole egg and beat it in with the wire whip. Continue whipping until the batter is smooth, light, and fluffy before adding the next egg. When all of the eggs have been added, add the egg yolk and continue whipping for a few seconds longer. Then beat in the vanilla.

3. Sift together the flour and potato starch onto a sheet of wax paper, and fold them into the batter using a wire whisk.

4. Scoop the batter into the prepared loaf pan and smooth the surface. The batter should fill the pan to about three fourths of its height. Place the loaf pan on the baking sheet.

5. Bake until the top of the cake is light brown and firm to the touch, about 1 hour and 15 to 20 minutes. The top surface of the cake will dome up and will probably split open down the center, revealing the yellow interior. When the cake is done, the tip of a paring knife inserted into the center will come out clean.

6. Unmold the cake, turn it right side up onto a wire rack, and let it cool. Serve at room temperature.

STORAGE: Covered airtight with plastic wrap, for up to 3 days at room temperature (or refrigerated in hot weather).

Or freeze for as long as 3 months. If frozen, defrost overnight in the refrigerator, then unwrap the cake and allow it to stand at room temperature for at least 2 hours before serving to allow condensation produced by defrosting to evaporate.

Le Cake

(FRENCH FRUIT CAKE)

What an odd name for a French cake! Its origin has to do with how this recipe and its name have evolved. There was an old English pound cake flavored with spices, loaded with prunes, and called plum cake. As time passed, the English replaced the prunes with sultana raisins and candied fruits, keeping the spices, and changed the name to fruit cake. The French, meanwhile, also adapted the recipe by replacing the prunes with raisins and glacé fruits (doesn't anyone like prunes?) but dropped the spices (which to them seemed alien in a dessert), continuing nonetheless to call their version *le plum cake*. Of course neither *plum* nor *cake* has any meaning in French (*prune* being the French word for plum), and eventually the combination was just too much, linguistically speaking. So *plum* got dropped, and *voilà*, the classic French cake named *le cake*.

For those who couldn't care less about history, evolution, or linguistics, here are the nuts and bolts. Our version of *le cake* is a butter-rich pound cake, studded with soft golden raisins and glacé fruits and doused with rum. Like the traditional American fruit cake, *le cake* is popular during the Christmas holiday season, but, unlike its English-speaking cousins, it requires no aging.

For 8 servings

EQUIPMENT:
6-cup (1.5-L) loaf pan
• brush with melted butter
• line with brown wrapping paper to extend about ½ inch (12 mm) above top of mold
• brush brown wrapping paper with melted butter
Heavy baking sheet
Electric mixer, preferably a stand mixer with flat beater and wire whip

BATTER:

Glacé fruits (cherries, pineapple, apricots)	6 ounces (170 g); 1 cup
Golden raisins	6 ounces (170 g); 1 cup + 1 tablespoon
Dark Jamaican or Haitian rum	⅓ cup (8 cL)
Unsalted butter, softened	6 ounces (170 g); ¾ cup
Confectioners' sugar	6 ounces (170 g); 1⅓ cups + 4 teaspoons

Large eggs, at room temperature	3
Large egg yolks, at room temperature	2
All-purpose flour	7 ounces (200 g); 1¼ cups + 3 tablespoons
Potato starch	½ ounce (15 g); 1 tablespoon + 1 teaspoon
Baking powder	½ teaspoon (3 mL)
Sliced almonds	⅓ ounce (10 g); 1 tablespoon

DOUSING:

Dark Jamaican or Haitian rum	2½ tablespoons (4 cL)

GLAZE:

Strained apricot jam (page 412), melted	1 ounce (30 g); 1½ tablespoons
Confectioners' sugar	⅔ ounce (20 g); 2 tablespoons + 2 teaspoons
Dark Jamaican or Haitian rum	1 teaspoon (5 mL)

DECORATION:

Glacé cherries or other glacé fruits

1. Cut the glacé fruits into ⅜-inch (1-cm) dice (except cherries, which you can leave whole). Combine the glacé fruits and raisins in a glass jar, pour the rum over them, and stir to mix. Cover airtight and let the fruits steep in the rum for 2 days, stirring two or three times so that they absorb the rum evenly. When ready to make the cake, drain the fruits thoroughly.

Preheat the oven to 350°F (175°C).

2. Cream the butter in the mixer, using the flat beater if your mixer has one. Beat in the confectioners' sugar and continue whipping at medium-high speed for about 5 minutes to make the mixture very white and light.

3. One at a time, add each whole egg and beat it in with the wire whip. Continue whipping until the batter is smooth, light, and fluffy before adding the next egg. When all of the whole eggs have been added, add the egg yolks one by one in the same manner and continue whipping for a few seconds longer.

4. Sift together the flour, potato starch, and baking powder onto a sheet of wax paper.

5. Combine about ¼ cup + 2 tablespoons (50 g) of the flour mixture with the raisins and glacé fruits and toss to coat them. Fold the rest of the flour mixture into the creamed butter mixture. When almost smooth, add the floured raisins and glacé fruits, and continue folding until uniformly mixed. Mix as gently and as little as possible so that you don't soften the batter.

6. Scoop the batter into the prepared loaf pan and smooth the surface. The batter should fill the pan to about three fourths of its height. Scatter the sliced almonds over the top of the batter. Place the loaf pan on the baking sheet.

continued

7. Bake until the top of the cake is a rich, deep brown and firm to the touch, 1 hour and 5 to 15 minutes. When done, the tip of a paring knife inserted into the center of the cake will come out clean.

8. Unmold the cake and turn it right side up on a wire rack. Sprinkle the top with the rum for dousing while the cake is hot. Then let it cool to room temperature.

Preheat the oven to 450°F (230°C).

9. Using a scissors, trim off the wrapping paper that extends above the top of the cake.

10. Brush the top of the cake with the melted apricot jam until lightly coated and glistening.

11. Sift the confectioners' sugar onto a sheet of wax paper. Pour it into a small bowl and stir in the rum. Then stir in enough cold water to make a smooth, creamy paste that is just fluid enough to spread easily with a pastry brush. Lightly brush this sugar glaze over the jam on top of the cake. Slide the cake onto a baking sheet and return it to the oven until the glaze turns from opaque white to translucent, about 1½ to 2 minutes. If the glaze starts to bubble around the edges, remove the cake from the oven immediately.

12. Decorate the top of the cake with a few glacé cherries cut in halves, or with other glacé fruits cut into decorative shapes (such as pineapple cut into thin triangles or diamonds).

13. Slide the cake onto a wire rack and let it cool. Do not remove the paper from the cake until ready to serve. Serve at room temperature.

VARIATION: You can trim the top of the paper in a saw-tooth or scalloped pattern, rather than cutting it off. In this case, use parchment paper to line the mold and let it extend about 1 inch (2.5 cm) above the top. Be careful not to get batter on the paper above the top of the mold. When the baked cake is cool, brush it with apricot jam and decorate with candied fruits, but omit the sugar glaze.

STORAGE: Uncovered, for up to 4 days at room temperature (or refrigerated in hot weather). The glaze on top and the paper around the sides and bottom prevent the cake from drying out.

Or, before glazing, cover the cake airtight with plastic wrap and freeze for as long as 3 months. If frozen, defrost overnight in the refrigerator; then proceed to glaze and decorate the cake following steps 9 through 13 above.

Cake au Citron

(LEMON POUND CAKE)

Paul has fond recollections of this cake from his childhood:

"For me it brings back memories of long lost times when I was a little boy and my grandmother took me with her to spend the good days in Corbigny [in the Morvan]. It was quite an adventure. We had to depart early in the morning because in those days it was a six-hour drive to get there from Paris in her old battered 201 Peugeot. We started to pack the car the evening before. Each time, she carried almost all of her belongings with her, as if she were embarking on an exodus—all the things she needed, and all the things she could need in a day. In addition, there were the food supplies, provided by my parents and my uncles. Among these were the *cake au citron* and *alhambra*. All this was crammed in the car and when the trunk was full, the rest went on the backseat, covered with a white cloth like a mysterious shroud. And then a roof rack was added, and more was added on the roof and tied with ropes.

"Of all the grandsons, I was the one who was going with *Her*. I could not sleep the night before, or at least I imagine I could not sleep; and when the day eventually came, I was awakened by the smell of the blend of chicory and coffee that was popular in those days.

"The journey was full of events. We had to stop every hour or so, due to the poor quality of the tires. A wheel went flat, just like that, and we had to stop in the middle of nowhere to repair it. Or the carburetor became obstructed by some filth, the car choked several times and stopped. The opportunity was seized to make a picnic on the roadside.

"Finally, the white gates of La Garenne [the country house] were in sight. It was spring, but the house was still damp from the winter. There was a musty smell in the air, overwhelmed by the perfume of the logs burning in a wild saraband in the fireplace.

"For dinner we usually had an omelet with eggs from the farm and the dessert came as a recompense. In the light of a single bulb, my grandmother ceremoniously unpacked the *cake au citron*, the *alhambra*, or the *polonaise*. Those three were among her favorites. But I keep a wonderful memory of the *cake au citron*—its taste, its texture, and especially this closeness with my grandmother."

continued

For 8 servings

EQUIPMENT:

6-cup (1.5-L) loaf pan
• brush with melted butter
• line with brown wrapping paper to extend about ½ inch (12 mm) above top of mold
• brush brown wrapping paper with melted butter
Heavy baking sheet
Electric mixer

BATTER:

Large eggs, at room temperature	3
Large egg yolks, at room temperature	2
Superfine or extra fine sugar	6½ ounces (185 g); ¾ cup + 3 tablespoons
Lemons, zest finely grated	3
Pure vanilla extract	1 teaspoon (5 mL)
Unsalted butter	6½ ounces (185 g); ¾ cup + 1 tablespoon
All-purpose flour	6½ ounces (185 g); 1⅓ cups

GLAZE:

Strained apricot jam (page 412), melted	1 ounce (30 g); 1½ tablespoons
Confectioners' sugar	⅔ ounce (20 g); 2 tablespoons + 2 teaspoons
Pure vanilla extract	¼ teaspoon (1 mL)

Preheat the oven to 450°F (230°C).

1. Combine two of the whole eggs with the yolks and sugar in the mixer and start beating at low speed with the wire whip. Gradually increase to medium speed, and continue whipping until the mixture whitens and forms slowly dissolving ribbons when dropped from the whip, about 10 minutes.

2. Beat in the lemon zest and vanilla followed by the third egg. Stop beating as soon as this egg is thoroughly incorporated.

3. Start heating the butter in a butter melter or small saucepan.

4. Sift the flour onto a sheet of wax paper. Gradually add it to the batter and gently fold it in.

5. Bring the butter to a simmer—about 180°F (80°C). Add the hot butter to the batter and continue folding until smooth.

6. Scoop the batter into the prepared loaf pan and smooth the surface. The batter should fill the pan to about three fourths of its height. Place the loaf pan on the baking sheet.

7. Bake until the top of the cake turns pale beige, about 10 minutes.

Reduce the oven temperature to 400°F (200°C).

8. Continue baking until the top of the cake is light brown and firm to the touch, about 30 to 35 minutes longer. The top of the cake will dome up slightly and split down the center, revealing the yellow interior. When the cake is done, the tip of a paring knife inserted into the center will come out clean.

9. Unmold the cake and turn it right side up on a wire rack. Let cool to room temperature.

Preheat the oven to 450°F (230°C).

10. Using a scissors, trim off the wrapping paper that extends above the top of the cake.

11. Brush the top of the cake with the melted apricot jam until lightly coated and glistening.

12. Sift the confectioners' sugar onto a sheet of wax paper. Pour it into a small bowl and stir in the vanilla. Then stir in enough cold water to make a smooth, creamy paste that is just fluid enough to spread easily with a pastry brush. Lightly brush this sugar glaze over the jam on top of the cake. Place the cake on a baking sheet and return it to the oven until the glaze turns from opaque white to translucent, about 1½ to 2 minutes. If the glaze starts to bubble around the edges, remove the cake from the oven immediately.

13. Slide the cake onto a wire rack and let it cool. Do not remove the paper from the cake until ready to serve. Serve at room temperature.

STORAGE: Uncovered, for up to 4 days at room temperature (or refrigerated in hot weather). The glaze on top and the paper around the sides and bottom prevent the cake from drying out.

Or, before glazing, cover the cake airtight with plastic wrap and freeze for as long as 3 months. If frozen, defrost overnight in the refrigerator; then proceed to glaze following steps 10 through 13 above.

Week-End

(WEEKEND LEMON CAKE)

• •

The Franglais name of this pound cake probably originated in the thirties to celebrate the introduction in France of the five-day workweek with a weekend holiday, which was dubbed the *semaine anglaise* (literally "English week").

The cake itself has undergone many transformations over the years. The version we offer here is quite modern, with crème fraîche added for moisture and flavor. Our *cake au citron* (previous recipe) is a more classic version. In contrast to *cake au citron,* which is glazed only on its domed top, *week-end* is turned upside down and glazed on its sides as well as its new, flat top surface.

For 8 servings

EQUIPMENT:

6-cup (1.5-L) loaf pan
• brush with melted butter
• line with kitchen parchment
• brush parchment heavily with melted clarified butter (page 449)
Heavy baking sheet
Electric mixer, preferably a stand mixer with flat beater and wire whip
Rectangle of silver or gold matt board or foil board (page 467)
• cut about ¼ inch (6 mm) smaller in length and width than the loaf

BATTER:

Unsalted butter, softened	3 ounces (85 g); 6 tablespoons
Superfine or extra fine sugar	9 ounces (225 g); 1 cup + 2 tablespoons
Lemons, zest finely grated	3
Large eggs, at room temperature	3
Large egg yolks, at room temperature	2
Crème fraîche (page 451)	½ cup (1.2 dL)
All-purpose flour	5 ounces (140 g); 1 cup
Potato starch	1 ounce (30 g); 2½ tablespoons
Baking powder	1 teaspoon (5 mL)
Dark Jamaican or Haitian rum	3 tablespoons (4.5 cL)

GLAZE:

Strained apricot jam (page 412), melted	3½ ounces (100 g); ¼ cup + 1 tablespoon
Confectioners' sugar	1¾ ounces (50 g); 2 tablespoons + 2 teaspoons
Dark Jamaican or Haitian rum	2 teaspoons (1 cL)

DECORATION:

Blanched almonds, chopped	1 ounce (30 g); 3 tablespoons
Raw pistachios, very coarsely chopped	A few

Preheat the oven to 350°F (175°C).

1. Cream the butter in the mixer, using the flat beater if your mixer has one. Beat in ½ cup (100 g) of the sugar and continue whipping at medium-high speed for about 5 minutes to make the mixture very white and light. Beat in the remaining sugar and the lemon zest.

2. Beat in one egg (still with the flat beater if you are using it). Then switch to the wire whip and beat in the remaining eggs one at a time, whipping until the batter is smooth, light, and fluffy before adding each successive egg. When all of the eggs have been added, continue whipping for a few seconds longer. Then whip in the crème fraîche.

3. Sift together the flour, potato starch, and baking powder onto a sheet of wax paper, and fold them into the batter using a rubber spatula. When completely incorporated, sprinkle the rum over the batter and fold it in very gently.

4. Scoop the batter into the prepared loaf pan. Smooth the surface, and spread the batter up the sides of the pan to make a depression down the center. The batter should fill the pan to about three fourths of its height. Place the loaf pan on the baking sheet.

5. Bake until the top of the cake is light brown and firm to the touch and the edges begin to shrink from the parchment lining the sides of the mold, about 50 minutes to 1 hour and 10 minutes. The top surface of the cake will probably split open down the center, revealing the yellow interior. When the cake is done, the tip of a paring knife inserted into the center will come out clean.

6. Let the cake cool in the mold for 5 minutes. Unmold it and turn it right side up on a wire rack. Then let it cool to room temperature.

7. Carefully peel the parchment away from the sides of the cake. Cut off the top of the cake with a wavy-edge bread knife to make a flat surface. Place the matt board or foil board rectangle upside down on top. Turn the cake upside down with the rectangle onto a wire rack. Remove and discard the parchment.

Preheat the oven to 450°F (230°C).

8. Brush the top and sides of the cake with the melted apricot jam until lightly coated and glistening.

continued

9. Sift the confectioners' sugar onto a sheet of wax paper. Transfer it to a small bowl and stir in the rum. Then stir in enough cold water to make a smooth, creamy paste that is just fluid enough to spread easily with a pastry brush. Lightly brush this confectioners' sugar glaze over the jam on the top and sides of the cake. Slide the cake onto a baking sheet. Spread the chopped almonds around the base of the cake on the baking sheet, and use a small icing spatula to press them against the sides of the cake to cover the bottom edge with a band of chopped almonds about ½ inch (12 mm) high. Scatter the chopped pistachios down the center of the top of the cake.

10. Return the cake to the oven until the glaze turns from opaque white to translucent, about 1½ to 2 minutes. If the glaze starts to bubble around the edges, remove the cake from the oven immediately.

11. Slide the cake onto a wire rack and let it cool. Serve at room temperature.

STORAGE: Uncovered (the glaze on the top and sides prevents the cake from drying out), for up to 4 days at room temperature (or refrigerated in hot weather).

Or, before glazing, cover the cake airtight with plastic wrap and freeze for as long as 3 months. If frozen, defrost overnight in the refrigerator; then proceed to glaze following steps 7 through 11 above.

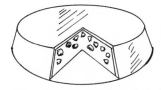

Colombier

This almond pound cake is served for Pentecoste in Provence. Flavored with anisette liqueur and enriched with glacé fruits, it is very moist and surprisingly subtle. Even people who dislike the flavor of anise are beguiled by the combination.

For 8 servings

EQUIPMENT:

9-inch (24-cm) round cake pan, 1½ inches (3½ to 4 cm) deep
• brush perimeter of bottom with melted clarified butter (page 449)
• line bottom with a circle of kitchen parchment
• brush sides heavily with melted clarified butter
• dust sides with potato starch
• brush parchment with melted clarified butter
Heavy baking sheet
Electric mixer
9-inch (24-cm) foil board or matt board cake-decorating circle (page 467)

BATTER:

Almond-and-sugar powder (page 442)	9½ ounces (270 g); 2 cups
Large eggs, at room temperature	2
Large egg yolks, at room temperature	2
Anisette liqueur (preferably French, such as Marie Brizard)	1 tablespoon + 1 teaspoon (2 cL)
Large egg whites, at room temperature	2
Cream of tartar (optional)	⅛ teaspoon (a pinch)
Superfine or extra fine sugar	1¾ ounces (50 g); ¼ cup
Potato starch	1½ ounces (40 g); 3 tablespoons + 2 teaspoons
Unsalted butter, barely melted	1¾ ounces (50 g); 3½ tablespoons
Glacé fruits (cherries, pineapple, apricot), cut into ¼-inch (6-mm) dice	2½ ounces (70 g); ¼ cup + 3 tablespoons

GLAZE:

Strained apricot jam (page 412), melted	3½ ounces (100 g); ⅓ cup
Confectioners' sugar	2⅔ ounces (75 g); ½ cup + 2 tablespoons
Anisette liqueur	1½ teaspoons (8 mL)

continued

Preheat the oven to 375°F (190°C).

1. Combine the almond-and-sugar powder with the whole eggs and yolks in the mixer and beat at medium speed with the wire whip until the mixture whitens and becomes glossy, about 5 minutes. Whip in the anisette liqueur.

2. Using a clean wire whip and bowl, whip the egg whites in the mixer at low speed until they start to froth. If you are not whipping the whites in a copper bowl, then add the cream of tartar. Gradually increase the whipping speed to medium-high, and continue whipping until the whites form very stiff peaks and just begin to slip and streak around the side of the bowl. Add the superfine sugar and continue whipping at high speed for a few seconds longer to incorporate the sugar and tighten the meringue.

3. Sift the potato starch over the whole-egg mixture, add about one third of the meringue, and stir with a wooden spatula to mix. Add the remaining meringue and fold it in, being careful not to deflate the batter. Then gently fold in the melted butter.

4. Scoop the batter into the cake pan, distributing it evenly. Smooth the batter from the center up the sides of the pan to make a slight depression in the center. Scatter the diced glacé fruits over the top.

5. Place the cake pan on the baking sheet and bake until the top of the cake is lightly browned and springs back to the touch, about 25 to 30 minutes. When done, the tip of a paring knife inserted into the center of the cake will come out clean.

6. Remove the cake from the oven and carefully slide the tip of a paring knife or small icing spatula between the edge of the cake and the pan to loosen the edges. Let the cake rest at room temperature for 5 minutes, then unmold it onto a wire rack. Carefully peel off the parchment and lay it clean side down against the top of the cake. Turn the cake upside down onto a second wire rack and allow it to cool to room temperature.

7. Trim off any uneven bumps on the bottom of the cake using a wavy-edge bread knife. Trim the cake-decorating circle slightly smaller than the bottom of the cake. Turn the cake right side up onto the cake-decorating circle and place it on a wire rack on your countertop.

Preheat the oven to 450°F (230°C).

8. Brush the top and sides of the cake with the melted apricot jam until lightly coated and glistening.

9. Sift the confectioners' sugar onto a sheet of wax paper. Pour it into a small bowl and stir in the anisette liqueur. Then stir in enough cold water to make a smooth, creamy paste that is just fluid enough to spread easily with a pastry brush. Lightly brush this sugar glaze over the jam on the top and sides of the cake. Slide the cake onto a baking sheet and return it to the oven until the glaze turns from opaque white to translucent, about 1½ to 2 minutes. If the glaze starts to bubble around the edges, remove the cake from the oven immediately.

10. Slide the cake onto a wire rack and let it cool. Serve at room temperature.

NOTE: Traditionally, *colombier* is decorated with *pralines de montargis*, which are made by mixing chopped almonds with hard-crack sugar syrup and then cooling to make small lumps of crunchy almonds and sugar. The *pralines* can be made in several colors, but for this cake they are tinted pink. *Pralines de montargis* are tricky and tedious to make, and while you could purchase them ready-made in France, they are not available in the United States. We have chosen to omit them in our recipe because the cake is very good, albeit not totally authentic, without them.

STORAGE: Uncovered, for up to 4 days at room temperature (or refrigerated in hot weather). The glaze prevents the cake from drying out.

Or, before trimming and glazing, cover the cake airtight with plastic wrap and freeze for as long as 3 months. If frozen, defrost overnight in the refrigerator; then proceed to trim and glaze following steps 7 through 10 above.

Pain de Gênes

(ALMOND POUND CAKE)

André Masséna was one of Napoleon's most important and trusted generals and a Marshal of France. He played a key role in the decisive defeat of the Austrians at Rivoli, in the Venetia, on January 15, 1797; for that service Napoleon would one day create for him the title Duke of Rivoli. Later, in the beginning of the year 1800, Napoleon sent Masséna to Genoa to command what was left of his Army of Italy. Masséna defended Genoa from February until June when, having survived for months on a diet of only rice and almonds, Masséna and his army were forced to surrender. However, by keeping the besieging troops occupied, Masséna gave Napoleon time to defeat the Austrians at the village Marengo (celebrated in a legendary chicken dish) in the Italian Piedmont, eventually leading to the Treaty of Luneville in February of 1801.

Pain de gênes was created in homage to André Masséna's courage and tenacity in adverse circumstances. The cake has a hefty dose of powdered almonds, and while it is customarily made with potato starch (and sometimes wheat flour) today, originally it was made with rice flour. At first it was called *gâteau d'ambroisie* because Napoleon had nicknamed Masséna "l'Ambroise," ambrosia being the food of the gods of Olympus, which, according to legend, rendered anyone who tasted it immortal. During the nineteenth century, the name of the cake was transformed to *gâteau de gênes* and eventually to *pain de gênes* (literally "Genoa loaf"), which has stuck.

Despite the circumstances which inspired its creation, *pain de gênes* is a very luxurious cake, with almonds making up one quarter of its weight and butter nearly the same proportion. It was invented by a pastry chef named Fauvel at the pâtisserie Chiboust, which was located on the rue St. Honoré in Paris.

For 6 to 8 servings

EQUIPMENT:
8-inch (20-cm) fluted *tarte* mold or deep quiche pan (or substitute a plain round cake pan)
• brush with melted butter
• sprinkle about 1 tablespoon (10 g) sliced almonds over the bottom of the mold
Heavy baking sheet
Electric mixer, preferably a stand mixer with flat beater and wire whip

BATTER:

Unsalted butter, softened	4½ ounces (125 g); ½ cup + 1 tablespoon
Almond-and-sugar powder (page 442)	12 ounces (340 g); 2½ cups
Large eggs, at room temperature	3
European kirsch or dark Jamaican or Haitian rum	2 tablespoons + 1 teaspoon (3.5 cL)
Potato starch	1½ ounces (45 g); ¼ cup + 2 tablespoons

Preheat the oven to 325°F (160°C).

1. Cream the butter in the mixer, using the flat beater if your mixer has one. Beat in half of the almond-and-sugar powder and continue whipping at medium-high speed for about 5 minutes to make the mixture very white and light. Beat in the remaining almond-and-sugar powder.

2. Beat in one egg (still with the flat beater if you are using it). Then switch to the wire whip and beat in the remaining eggs one at a time, whipping until the batter is smooth, light, and fluffy before adding each successive egg. When all of the eggs have been added, continue whipping for a few seconds longer, then gradually whip in the kirsch or rum.

3. Sift the potato starch onto a sheet of wax paper, and fold it into the batter using a wire whisk.

4. Scoop the batter into the prepared *tarte* mold. Smooth the surface from the center out to the sides of the pan, making a depression in the center. Place the *tarte* mold on the baking sheet.

5. Bake until the top of the cake is light brown and firm to the touch and the cake just begins to shrink from the sides of the mold, about 45 to 55 minutes. When the cake is done, the tip of a paring knife inserted into the center will come out clean.

6. Place the cake on a wire rack and let it rest for 5 minutes. Then unmold the cake onto a wire rack and let it cool right side up (that is, with the sliced almonds on top). Serve at room temperature.

STORAGE: Covered airtight with plastic wrap, for up to 3 days at room temperature (or refrigerated in hot weather).

Or freeze for as long as 3 months. If frozen, defrost overnight in the refrigerator, then unwrap the cake and let it stand at room temperature for at least 2 hours before serving to allow condensation produced by defrosting to evaporate.

Biscuit Chocolat

(CHOCOLATE ALMOND CAKE)

Dense, rich, moist, and chocolatey. Serve it in small portions to savor.

For 8 to 10 servings

EQUIPMENT:

9-inch (24-cm) round cake pan, 1½ inches (3½ to 4 cm) deep
• brush heavily with melted clarified butter (page 449)
Heavy baking sheet
Electric mixer, preferably a stand mixer with flat beater and wire whip
9-inch (24-cm) foil board or matt board cake-decorating circle (page 467)
Chocolate thermometer or digital pocket thermometer

BATTER:

Unsalted butter, softened	4½ ounces (125 g); ½ cup + 1 tablespoon
Raw-almond-and-sugar powder (page 442)	4½ ounces (130 g); ¾ cup + 3½ tablespoons
Superfine or extra fine sugar	1 ounce (25 g); 2 tablespoons
Large eggs, at room temperature	4
Large egg yolk, at room temperature	1
European bittersweet chocolate, melted	4½ ounces (125 g)
Pure vanilla extract	1 teaspoon (5 mL)
All-purpose flour	1 ounce (30 g); 3½ tablespoons

GLAZE:

European bittersweet chocolate, melted	9 ounces (250 g)
Clarified butter (page 449), at room temperature	1½ ounces (40 g); 3 tablespoons

DECORATION:

Raw almonds	12 to 15

Preheat the oven to 350°F (175°C).

1. Cream the butter in the mixer, using the flat beater if your mixer has one. Beat in the raw-almond-and-sugar powder and sugar and continue whipping at medium-high speed for about 5 minutes to make the mixture very white and light.

2. One at a time, add each whole egg and beat it in with the wire whip. Continue whipping until the batter is smooth, light, and fluffy before adding the next egg. After the whole eggs, add the egg yolk and continue whipping for a few seconds longer. Then whip in the melted chocolate, followed by the vanilla.

3. Sift the flour onto a sheet of wax paper, and fold it into the batter using a rubber spatula.

4. Scoop the batter into the prepared cake pan, distributing it evenly. Smooth the surface from the center out to the sides of the pan, making a depression in the center. Place the cake pan on the baking sheet.

5. Bake until the top of the cake is dry and springs back to the touch, about 25 to 30 minutes. The tip of a paring knife inserted in the middle of the cake should come out oily but with no specks of batter on it.

6. Remove the cake from the oven and carefully slip the tip of a paring knife or small icing spatula between the edge of the cake and the pan to loosen the edges. Let the cake rest at room temperature for about 5 minutes. Then unmold it onto a wire rack and invert it onto a second wire rack so that it will be flat side (i.e., top side) down. Let it cool to room temperature.

7. When ready to glaze, trim off any uneven bumps on the bottom of the cake using a wavy-edge bread knife. (The cake must have uniform thickness in order to have a flat top surface to coat with chocolate.) Trim the cake-decorating circle about ⅜ inch (1 cm) smaller in diameter than the bottom of the cake. Then turn the cake right side up onto the cake-decorating circle and place the cake on a wire rack on your countertop, with a large tray underneath.

8. If you did not melt the chocolate for the glaze in a stainless steel bowl, transfer it to one. Temper the chocolate as follows: Dip the bottom of the bowl of chocolate in a larger bowl of cold water and stir the chocolate until the temperature drops to between 80° and 84°F (26.5° to 29°C) and it begins to thicken. Immediately remove from the cold water and dip the bottom of the bowl of chocolate in a larger bowl of hot water. Stir over the hot water just long enough to warm the chocolate to between 86° and 91°F (30° to 33°C) and make it more fluid again. Then remove from the hot water immediately. Beat the clarified butter with a wooden spatula to make it smooth and creamy, then stir it into the chocolate.

9. Pour the chocolate on the top of the cake in a circle just inside the perimeter so that some of it flows naturally over the edges. Quickly smooth the top surface with the edge of a large icing spatula to cover the entire top with a thin layer of glaze and make the excess flow evenly down the sides. Touch up any uneven areas around the sides with the edge of the icing spatula. Let the chocolate thicken, then clean off any excess chocolate around the bottom edge.

10. Place the cake on a serving plate, and arrange the almonds in a decorative pattern on top of the cake before the chocolate sets. Put the cake in a cool place (or in the refrigerator if necessary) and let the chocolate set. Serve at room temperature.

STORAGE: Up to 3 or 4 days in a cool place—between 60° and 70°F (15° to 20°C)—to prevent fat bloom from forming on the chocolate glaze. Don't make this cake in hot weather.

Before glazing, the cake can be kept in the refrigerator, covered in plastic wrap, for up to 3 days.

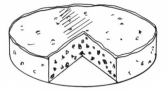

Gâteau Anglais

(ENGLISH CAKE)

This classic cake is baked in a wide, shallow *tarte* ring. According to Alexandre Dumas, the *gâteau anglais* is derived from the traditional English wedding cake, and the customs surrounding this wedding cake are described in the works of Charles Dickens.

    Gâteau anglais is moist, rich in butter, studded with currants and candied citron, and flavored with rum in both the batter and the sugar glaze on top.

For 6 to 8 servings

EQUIPMENT:

Heavy baking sheet
- brush a 9-inch (24-cm) square in the center with melted clarified butter (page 449)
- place a 9-inch (24-cm) square of kitchen parchment on the buttered square
- brush the parchment with melted clarified butter

8¾-inch (22-cm) *tarte* ring, 1 inch (2½ cm) deep
- brush inside with melted butter
- dust inside with flour
- place on baking sheet, centered on parchment square

Electric mixer

BATTER:

Currants	1¾ ounces (50 g); ⅓ cup
Candied citron	1¾ ounces (50 g); ¼ cup
Unsalted butter, softened	4½ ounces (125 g); ½ cup + 1 tablespoon
Large eggs, at room temperature	2
Superfine or extra fine sugar	4½ ounces (125 g); ½ cup + 2 tablespoons
All-purpose flour	4 ounces (110 g); ¾ cup + 2 teaspoons
Potato starch	⅔ ounce (17 g); 1½ tablespoons
Dark Jamaican or Haitian rum	2 teaspoons (1 cL)

DOUSING:

Dark Jamaican or Haitian rum	1 tablespoon + 1 teaspoon (2 cL)

GLAZE:

Strained apricot jam (page 412), melted	2 ounces (60 g); 3 tablespoons
Confectioners' sugar	1½ ounces (40 g); ⅓ cup
Dark Jamaican or Haitian rum	2 teaspoons (1 cL)

Preheat the oven to 425°F (220°C).

1. Place the currants in a strainer and steam them over simmering water until softened, about 5 minutes. Then lay them on a paper towel to absorb any excess moisture. Cut the citron into ¼-inch (6-mm) dice.

2. Place the butter in a small stainless steel bowl and warm it over low heat, beating with a wooden spatula until melted but still creamy.

3. Combine the eggs and sugar in the mixer and beat with the wire whip, starting at low and gradually increasing to medium speed, until light and cream-colored, about 5 minutes. The mixture will not quite reach the ribbon stage.

4. Sift together the flour and potato starch onto a sheet of wax paper. Combine about 2 tablespoons (15 g) of it with the citron and currants and toss to coat them.

5. Fold the rest of the flour and potato starch into the batter using a wire whisk. When completely incorporated, add about ½ cup (8 cL) of the batter and the rum to the butter and stir with a wooden spatula to mix thoroughly. Gently fold this mixture and the citron and currants into the remaining batter.

6. Pour and scrape the batter onto the baking sheet inside the *tarte* ring. Spread the batter evenly within the ring. Smooth the batter from the center up the sides of the ring, making a depression in the center.

7. Bake until the top of the cake is lightly browned and springs back to the touch, about 15 minutes. The sides of the cake should begin to shrink from the ring.

8. Remove the cake from the oven and carefully slide the tip of a paring knife or small icing spatula around the inside of the ring to loosen the edges of the cake. Let it set for a few minutes to allow the cake to shrink away from the ring. Then lift off the ring and slide the cake (with the parchment underneath) onto a wire rack. Turn it upside down onto a second rack. Carefully peel off the parchment, and lay it clean side down against the bottom of the cake. Turn the cake right side up onto the first rack. Brush the top of the cake with the rum for dousing. Then let the cake cool to room temperature.

Preheat the oven to 450°F (230°C).

9. Brush the top of the cake with the melted apricot jam until lightly coated and glistening.

10. Sift the confectioners' sugar into a small bowl, and stir in the rum. Stir in enough cold water to make a smooth, creamy paste that is just fluid enough to spread easily with a pastry brush.

continued

Lightly brush this sugar glaze over the jam on top of the cake. Slide the cake onto a baking sheet and return it to the oven until the glaze turns from opaque white to translucent, about 1½ to 2 minutes. If the glaze starts to bubble around the edges, remove the cake from the oven immediately.

11. Slide the cake onto a wire rack and let it cool. Serve at room temperature.

VARIATION: You can also bake the cake in a *tarte* ring 9½ inches (24 cm) wide and ¾ inch (2 cm) deep or in an 8-inch (20-cm) round cake pan with 1½-inch (4-cm) deep vertical sides. In the latter case, brush the sides and perimeter of the bottom of the pan with melted butter; line the bottom with parchment; dust the sides with flour; and brush the parchment with melted butter.

STORAGE: Uncovered, for up to 4 days at room temperature (or refrigerated in hot weather). The glaze on top and the paper around the sides and bottom prevent the cake from drying out.

Or, before glazing, cover the cake airtight with plastic wrap and freeze for as long as 3 months. If frozen, defrost overnight in the refrigerator; then proceed to glaze following steps 9 through 11 above.

Biscuit de Savoie

(SAVOY SPONGE CAKE)

This cake is a specialty of the Savoy region in the French Alps. Like the pound cakes, it is a simple, family-style dessert, complete in itself. However, it is much lighter and less rich than most of the cakes in this chapter, and it will be greatly enhanced if you serve it with jam, fruit salad (page 455), or stewed fruits.

While Savoy sponge cake can be baked in anything from a deep decorative tube pan (such as a kugelhopf mold) to an ordinary layer-cake pan, we think it is especially handsome when baked in a brioche *parisienne* mold (see page 465).

As a historical footnote, the origin of this cake is purported to go back to the fourteenth or fifteenth century when the chef of one of the counts of Savoy created a "*gâteau de savoie*" in the shape of a fortified castle. Perhaps with a little imagination that could explain why *biscuit de savoie* is baked in a brioche *parisienne* mold. However, even if the anecdote is true it is very unlikely that the original bore any resemblance to a modern sponge cake. The first known mention of *biscuit de savoie* in a cookbook appeared in 1654 in Nicolas de Bonnefons' *Les Délices de la Campagne*. Bonnefons, who was the valet of Louis XIV, alluded to its invention around the beginning of the seventeenth century but stopped short of giving a recipe. The first known recipe appeared in François Marin's *Le Dons de Comus ou les Delices de la Table* in 1739.

In 1805, the great culinary writer Grimod de la Reynière, remarking in his *Almanach des Gourmands* on the improvements made by the pastry chefs of the eighteenth century, observed that "when one compares the *biscuits de Savoie* of the old days with the ones made today, the first were heavy, massive. . . . Those of today are light, frothy, and in a way airy. One can eat them without risk, and they are still fresh at the end of three months . . . " Three *months*! Apparently, *biscuit de savoie* has changed every bit as much in the past two centuries as it did during the evolution noted by Grimod de la Reynière. Our modern version is light, frothy, and indeed airy, but it will be dry and stale long before three months.

For 6 servings

EQUIPMENT:
8-inch (20-cm) brioche *parisienne* mold, or other deep mold with 4- to 5-cup capacity
   (about 1 L)
• **brush with melted butter**
• **dust with ½ ounce (15 g) sliced almonds**

continued

Electric mixer

Heavy baking sheet

....

BATTER:

Superfine or extra fine sugar	3½ ounces (100 g); ½ cup
Large eggs, separated, at room temperature	3
Orange flower water,	½ teaspoon (3 mL)
or substitute pure vanilla extract	To taste
Cream of tartar (optional)	⅛ teaspoon (a pinch)
All-purpose flour	1¾ ounces (50 g); ⅓ cup + ½ tablespoon
Potato starch	1¾ ounces (50 g); ¼ cup + ½ tablespoon

DECORATION:

Confectioners' sugar for dusting

Preheat the oven to 325°F (160°C).

1. Set aside 1 tablespoon (15 g) of the superfine sugar. Combine the remaining superfine sugar with the egg yolks in the mixer and beat with the wire whip, starting at low and gradually increasing to medium speed, until light, thick, and smooth. Beat in the orange flower water.

2. Using a clean wire whip and bowl, whip the egg whites in the mixer at low speed until they start to froth. If you are not whipping the whites in a copper bowl, then add the cream of tartar at this point. Gradually increase the whipping speed to medium-high, and continue whipping until the whites form very stiff peaks and just begin to slip and streak around the side of the bowl. Add the reserved superfine sugar and continue whipping at high speed for a few seconds longer to incorporate the sugar and tighten the meringue.

3. Sift the flour and potato starch over the egg yolk mixture, add about a third of the meringue, and stir with a wooden spatula to mix quickly. Then gently fold in the remaining meringue.

4. Scoop the batter into the prepared brioche mold, distributing it evenly. Smooth the batter from the center up the sides of the pan to make a depression in the center.

5. Place the mold on the baking sheet, and bake until the top is a rich, uniform beige and firm to the touch, and the tip of a paring knife inserted in the center of the cake comes out clean, about 50 to 55 minutes.

6. Remove the cake from the oven and let it rest in the mold until it has cooled enough to handle, about 7 minutes. Then unmold it onto a wire rack, and let cool to room temperature.

7. When ready to serve, dust the cake with confectioners' sugar.

HOWS AND WHYS: We have given the recipe for *biscuit de savoie* using the classic separated-egg sponge cake method because is a prototypical example of this method. However, the batter can also be prepared by a variation of this method that is slightly simpler. For this variation, you do not whip the egg yolks with sugar. Instead, meringue the whipped egg whites with all of the superfine or extra fine sugar called for in the recipe. Then add the egg yolks one by one and fold them in gently with a wire whisk. When the yolks are completely incorporated, fold in the flour and potato starch with a rubber spatula. There are several points at which you can add the orange flower water, but the easiest is to whip it in right after the sugar.

STORAGE: Covered airtight with plastic wrap, for up to 3 days in the refrigerator.

Trois Frères

(THREE BROTHERS SPONGE CAKE)

During the eighteenth century, three brothers named Julien opened a pastry shop on the *place de la Bourse* in Paris. They began a dynasty of pastry chefs that lasted until the Second Empire. Alexandre Dumas dubbed them the "giants of pâtisserie," and among their creations were the rum-soaked savarin and the sponge cake called *trois frères*. Baked in a low, turban-shaped mold designed especially for the purpose, the *trois frères* sponge cake was the rage of Paris early in the nineteenth century. However, by the beginning of the twentieth century it was out of fashion, and in 1936 Henri-Paul Pellaprat (legendary chef and teacher at the École du Cordon Bleu in Paris) wrote in his *L'Art Culinaire Moderne* that "this ancient gâteau . . . is dethroned today by finer creations." Maybe so, but *today,* at the end of the twentieth century, we think this simple, old-fashioned cake is awfully nice.

What makes the *trois frères* sponge cake unique, other than its mold, is that the batter uses rice flour rather than ordinary wheat flour. The rice flour, which is available in natural foods markets, gives a special texture and tenderness. After baking, the cake is glazed with apricot jam and decorated with diced almonds and squares of candied angelica. In *Mémorial de la Pâtisserie*, pastry chef Pierre Lacam was emphatic in stating that, for the true *trois frères,* this is the only decor. We have taken the liberty of offering green glacé pineapple as an alternative to the rather esoteric angelica.

For 8 servings

EQUIPMENT:

5-cup (1.2- L) ring mold, either an 8¾-inch (22-cm) *trois frères* mold, or a savarin mold or
    American ring mold
• brush with melted butter
• dust with flour
Electric mixer
Heavy baking sheet

BATTER:

Superfine or extra fine sugar	4¼ ounces (120 g); ½ cup + 1⅔ tablespoons
Large eggs, separated at room temperature	4
Pure vanilla extract	1 teaspoon (5 mL)
or maraschino liqueur	1 tablespoon (1.5 cL)

Cream of tartar (optional)	⅛ teaspoon (a pinch)
Rice flour	4 ounces (115 g); ⅓ cup + ½ tablespoon
Unsalted butter, barely melted	3½ ounces (100 g); ¼ cup + 3 tablespoons

DECORATION:

Slivered almonds	1¼ ounces (35 g); ¼ cup
Heavy syrup (page 452)	1 teaspoon (5 mL)
Candied angelica or green glacé pineapple	About twenty-four ⅜-inch (1-cm) squares, sliced 1⁄16 inch (1½ mm) thick

GLAZE:

Strained apricot jam (page 412), melted	4¼ ounces (120 g); ¼ cup + 2 tablespoons

Preheat the oven to 375°F (190°C).

1. Set aside 2 tablespoons (25 g) of the sugar. Combine the remaining sugar with the egg yolks in the mixer and beat with the wire whip, starting at low and gradually increasing to medium speed, until light, thick, and smooth. Beat in the vanilla. Break up one of the egg whites by beating it with a fork, and stir it into the egg yolk mixture.

2. Using a clean wire whip and bowl, whip the remaining three egg whites in the mixer at low speed until they start to froth. If you are not whipping the whites in a copper bowl, then add the cream of tartar at this point. Gradually increase the whipping speed to medium-high, and continue whipping until the whites form very stiff peaks and just begin to slip and streak around the side of the bowl. Add the reserved sugar and continue whipping at high speed for a few seconds longer to incorporate the sugar and tighten the meringue.

3. Sift the rice flour over the egg yolk mixture, add about a third of the meringue, and stir with a wooden spatula to mix quickly. Then gently fold in the remaining meringue. When completely mixed, fold in the melted butter.

4. Scoop the batter into the prepared ring mold, distributing it evenly.

5. Bake until the cake is lightly browned and springs back to the touch, and the tip of a paring knife inserted in the center of the cake comes out clean, about 15 to 20 minutes.

6. Remove the cake from the oven and let it rest in the mold until it has cooled enough to handle, about 5 minutes. Then unmold it onto a wire rack, and let cool to room temperature.

Reduce the oven temperature to 350°F (175°C).

7. Cut the slivered almonds into dice. Toss them with the heavy syrup in a bowl. Spread them out on the baking sheet and roast them in the oven (stirring once or twice) until nicely browned, 6 to 7 minutes. Turn them out onto your countertop and let cool.

continued

8. Brush the surface of the cake with the melted apricot jam until evenly coated and glistening. Scatter the roasted almonds and squares of angelica (or pineapple) over the jam. Carefully transfer the cake to a serving plate.

HOWS AND WHYS: Traditionally, this cake is made by the génoise method in which the whole eggs are mixed with the sugar and warmed, then whipped until cool. Because the cake contains only rice flour, this produces a fragile cake that collapses easily. We prepare the batter using the separated-egg sponge cake method in which the egg yolks and whites are whipped separately, and then folded together. The result is much more stable.

The cake is not baked with a baking sheet underneath because a baking sheet would obstruct air flow through the center of the ring mold.

STORAGE: In a covered cake platter for up to 2 or 3 days at room temperature.

Biscuit aux Marrons
(CHESTNUT CAKE)

The French love chestnut desserts, and there are several cakes that use chestnut fillings. But cake batters using chestnuts are rare because these unusual, starchy nuts are difficult to incorporate in a way that retains their character. Here is the exception. Our opulent, heavenly chestnut cake is glazed with bittersweet chocolate. Fifty years ago it would have been glazed with vanilla or chocolate fondant, but the modern fashion is to use less fondant and more pure chocolate glazes. The thin, meltingly firm glaze is the perfect foil for the sumptuous chestnut flavor and the moist, delicate texture of the cake below.

For 8 to 10 servings

EQUIPMENT:

9-inch (24-cm) round cake pan, 1½ inches (3½ to 4 cm) deep
• brush perimeter of the bottom with melted clarified butter (page 449)
• line bottom with a circle of kitchen parchment
• brush sides heavily with melted clarified butter
• dust sides with flour
• brush parchment with melted clarified butter
Heavy baking sheet
Electric mixer
9-inch (24-cm) foil board or matt board cake-decorating circle (page 467)
Chocolate thermometer or digital pocket thermometer

BATTER:

Superfine or extra fine sugar	3½ ounces (100 g); ½ cup
Large eggs, separated at room temperature	3
Pure vanilla extract	1½ teaspoons (8 mL)
Chestnut spread (*crème de marrons*, page 498)	Two 8¾-ounce (250-g) cans, or one 17½-ounce (500-g) can
Unsalted butter, barely melted	2 ounces (60 g); ¼ cup
Cream of tartar (optional)	⅛ teaspoon (a pinch)
All-purpose flour	1¾ ounces (50 g); ⅓ cup + 1 teaspoon

continued

GLAZE:

European bittersweet chocolate, melted   9 ounces (250 g)
Clarified butter (page 449), at room temperature   1½ ounces (40 g); 3 tablespoons

Preheat the oven to 425°F (220°C).

1. Set aside 4 teaspoons (15 g) of the superfine sugar. Combine the remaining sugar with the egg yolks and vanilla in your electric mixer and beat with the wire whip, starting at low and gradually increasing to medium speed, until light, thick, and smooth. Beat in the chestnut spread, followed by the butter.

2. Whip the egg whites in the mixer at low speed until they start to froth. If you are not whipping the whites in a copper bowl, then add the cream of tartar at this point. Gradually increase the whipping speed to medium-high, and continue whipping until the whites are stiff but not dry. Add the reserved sugar and continue whipping at high speed for a few seconds longer to incorporate the sugar and tighten the meringue.

3. Sift the flour over the egg yolk mixture, add about a third of the meringue, and stir with a wooden spatula to mix quickly. Then gently fold in the remaining meringue.

4. Pour and scrape the batter into the cake pan, distributing it evenly. Smooth the surface from the center up the sides of the pan to make a depression in the center. Place the cake pan on the baking sheet.

5. Bake until the top of the cake is lightly browned and springs back to the touch, about 17 to 20 minutes.

6. Remove the cake from the oven and slide the tip of a paring knife or small icing spatula between the edge of the cake and the pan to loosen the edges. Let the cake rest at room temperature for about 5 minutes. Then unmold it onto a wire rack and invert it onto a second wire rack so that it is flat side (i.e., top side) down. Let it cool to room temperature.

7. When ready to glaze, trim off any uneven bumps on the bottom of the cake using a wavy-edge bread knife. (The cake must have uniform thickness in order to have a flat top surface to coat with chocolate.) Trim the cake-decorating circle about ⅜ inch (1 cm) smaller in diameter than the bottom of the cake. Then turn the cake right side up onto the cake-decorating circle and place the cake on a wire rack on your countertop, with a large tray underneath.

8. If you did not melt the chocolate for the glaze in a stainless steel bowl, transfer it to one. Temper the chocolate as follows: Dip the bottom of the bowl of chocolate in a larger bowl of cold water and stir the chocolate until the temperature drops to between 80° and 84°F (26.5° to 29°C) and it begins to thicken. Immediately remove from the cold water and dip the bottom of the bowl of chocolate in a larger bowl of hot water. Stir over the hot water just long enough to warm the chocolate to between 86° and 91°F (30° to 33°C) and make it more fluid again. Then remove from the hot water immediately. Beat the clarified butter with a wooden spatula to make it smooth and creamy, then stir it into the chocolate.

9. Pour the chocolate on the top of the cake in a circle just inside the perimeter so that some of it flows naturally over the edges. Quickly smooth the top surface with the edge of a large icing spatula to cover the entire top with a thin layer of glaze and make the excess flow evenly down the sides. Touch up any uneven areas around the sides with the edge of the icing spatula. Let the chocolate thicken, then clean off any excess chocolate around the bottom edge.

10. Place the cake on a serving plate. Put it in a cool place (or in the refrigerator if necessary) and let the chocolate set. Serve at room temperature.

HOWS AND WHYS: In this recipe we have used a separated-egg batter made by the traditional procedure. The whites are whipped only to the stiff-but-not-dry stage because they are meringued with very little sugar. If they were whipped to the slip-and-streak stage, the small amount of sugar would not make them cohesive enough and they would be difficult to incorporate into the batter.

STORAGE: Up to 3 or 4 days in a cool place—between 60° and 70°F (15° to 20°C)—to prevent fat bloom from forming on the chocolate glaze. Don't make this cake in hot weather.

Before glazing, the cake can be kept in the refrigerator, covered in plastic wrap, for up to 3 days.

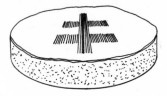

Croix de Lorraine

(CROSS OF LORRAINE)

Many different crosses are used as symbols. Some of the unusual ones, such as the triple Papal cross, are used in a religious context. Others, while they may originally have had religious connotations, became associated with secular institutions. The double cross of the dukes of Lorraine falls into the latter category. It is the classic decoration for this old-fashioned cake.

The batter for this cake is almost like a macaroon batter: powdered almonds and sugar, egg whites, flavored with praline powder and vanilla. Very moist and rich! The exterior is crusty. In his book *Mémorial de la Pâtisserie*, the pastry chef Pierre Lacam describes it as "very good and very fine . . . , can figure as the pinnacle among *gâteau de voyage* [a cake that isn't very perishable]." It was created by a pastry chef named M. Schwehr, who worked in Toul, on the outskirts of Nancy, and then quickly became popular all over Lorraine.

For 8 servings

EQUIPMENT:
Heavy baking sheet
• brush a 9-inch (24-cm) square in the center with melted butter
• place a 9-inch (24-cm) square of kitchen parchment on the buttered square
• brush the parchment with melted butter
8¾-inch (22-cm) *tarte* ring, 1 inch (2½ cm) deep
• brush inside with melted butter
• line with a strip of kitchen parchment 28 inches (70 cm) long and 1¼ inches (3 cm) wide
• place on baking sheet, centered on parchment square
Micro torch or propane torch with pinpoint tip (see page 479 for details and precautions)
Electric mixer

BATTER:

Almond-and-sugar powder (page 442)	13 ounces (370 g); 2¾ cups
Large egg whites, at room temperature	5, one of them lightly beaten
Pure vanilla extract	1 teaspoon (5 mL)
Cream of tartar (optional)	⅛ teaspoon (a pinch)
Superfine or extra fine sugar	1 ounce (30 g); 2½ tablespoons
Finely crushed *pralin* (page 446)	2⅔ ounces (75 g); ⅔ cup

DECORATION:

Confectioners' sugar for dusting

Preheat the oven to 375°F (190°C).

1. Combine the almond-and-sugar powder with half of the egg whites (two whole whites plus 1 tablespoon of the lightly beaten white) in a large mixing bowl and stir with a wooden spatula to mix. Stir in the vanilla.

2. Whip the remaining egg whites in the mixer at low speed until they start to froth. If you are not whipping the whites in a copper bowl, then add the cream of tartar. Gradually increase the whipping speed to medium-high, and continue whipping until the whites are stiff but not dry. Add the sugar and continue whipping at high speed for a few seconds longer to tighten the meringue.

3. Add the crushed *pralin* and about one third of the meringue to the almond-and-sugar mixture and stir with a wooden spatula to mix. Add the remaining meringue and carefully fold it in. Be very careful not to deflate the meringue. It is all right to have some streaks of meringue still visible.

4. Scoop the batter onto the baking sheet in the center of the ring. The batter will spread evenly, so you don't need to smooth it.

5. Bake until the top of the cake is richly browned and firm to the touch, about 30 minutes.

6. Remove the cake from the oven and lift off the ring. Then let it rest for a few minutes. Slide the cake (with the parchment underneath) onto a wire rack. Let cool to room temperature.

7. Turn the cake upside down and peel the parchment off the bottom. Then turn it right side up again. Dust the top with confectioners' sugar. Peel off the strip of parchment around the side.

8. Decorate the top of the cake with a Cross of Lorraine by using the micro torch to caramelize the design in the sugar on top. (Alternatively, you can stencil the design when you dust the confectioners' sugar on top.) If you prefer, you can substitute a design of your own choice.

STORAGE: Covered airtight with plastic wrap for up to 1 week at room temperature.

Le Saigon
(SAIGON CAKE)

Like the *croix de lorraine*, this cake is based on almond-and-sugar powder and egg whites, with no yolks. But the texture here is totally different because of a generous addition of apricot puree, chopped pineapple, and butter. None of the ingredients is characteristic of Vietnam, so we assume that the name of the cake was inspired by a distant, exotic, and little understood symbol of France's colonial power during the nineteenth century.

For 6 servings

EQUIPMENT:

Heavy baking sheet
• brush a 9-inch (24-cm) square in the center with melted clarified butter (page 449)
• place a 9-inch (24-cm) square of kitchen parchment on the buttered square
• brush the parchment with melted clarified butter
8¾-inch (22-cm) *tarte* ring, 1 inch (2½ cm) deep
• brush inside with melted clarified butter
• dust inside with potato starch
• place on baking sheet, centered on parchment square
Electric mixer

BATTER:

Large egg whites, at room temperature	3
Cream of tartar (optional)	⅛ teaspoon (a pinch)
Superfine or extra fine sugar	¾ ounces (20 g); 1 tablespoon + 2 teaspoons
Almond-and-sugar powder (page 442)	9 ounces (250 g); 1¾ cups + 2 tablespoons
Glacé pineapple, finely chopped	1¾ ounces (50 g)
Canned apricots in heavy syrup, drained, pureed in a blender, and forced through a fine sieve	2 ounces (60 g); ¼ cup
European kirsch	1 tablespoon (1.5 cL)
Pure vanilla extract	½ teaspoon (2.5 mL)
Unsalted butter, melted	1½ ounces (40 g); 3 tablespoons
Potato starch	1 ounce (30 g); 2 tablespoons + 2 teaspoons
All-purpose flour	1½ ounces (40 g); ¼ cup + 2 teaspoons

Sliced almonds   ⅓ ounce (10 g); 2 tablespoons

Confectioners' sugar for dusting

Preheat the oven to 325°F (160°C).

1. Whip the egg whites in the mixer at low speed until they start to froth. If you are not whipping the whites in a copper bowl, then add the cream of tartar. Gradually increase the whipping speed to medium-high, and continue whipping until the whites form very stiff peaks and just begin to slip and streak around the side of the bowl. Add the sugar and continue whipping at high speed for a few seconds longer to tighten the meringue.

2. Gradually fold the almond-and-sugar powder into the meringue with a rubber spatula.

3. In a large mixing bowl, stir together the chopped glacé pineapple, apricot puree, kirsch, and vanilla. Stir in the melted butter. Add about one third of the meringue mixture and stir with the spatula to mix. Add the remaining meringue mixture and fold it in gently.

4. Sift the potato starch and flour over the batter, and gently fold it in.

5. Pour and scrape the batter into the *tarte* ring and spread it evenly. Smooth the surface from the center up the sides of the ring, making a slight depression in the center. Scatter the sliced almonds over the top of the cake and dust it with confectioners' sugar.

6. Bake until the top of the cake is a uniform light brown and springs back to the touch, about 35 to 40 minutes. When the cake is done, the tip of a paring knife inserted into the center will come out clean.

7. Remove the cake from the oven and carefully slide the tip of a paring knife or small icing spatula around the inside of the ring to loosen the edges of the cake. Let it set for a few minutes to allow the cake to shrink away from the ring. Then lift off the ring and slide the cake (with the parchment underneath) onto a wire rack. Turn it upside down onto a second rack. Carefully peel off the parchment, and lay it clean side down against the bottom of the cake. Turn the cake right side up onto the first rack. Let the cake cool to room temperature.

STORAGE: In a covered cake platter for up to 3 days.

Clafoutis

(LIMOUSIN CHERRY FLAN)

Here is a rustic, simple dessert from the Limousin region in central France. *Clafoutis* is one of those dishes that inspires heated arguments among purists and local gastronomes from the Limousin about what is and is not authentic. Taking up the question in 1964, the Academie Française first defined it as a fruit flan, but then refined the definition to a black cherry flan. It was, of course, the abundance of superb black cherries in the Limousin that provided the impetus for *clafoutis* in the first place. Originally, it consisted of a plain crepe batter cooked with the cherries in a buttered skillet. In keeping with its peasant origins, the cherries were not pitted.

Today, *clafoutis* is more likely to be baked in a stoneware or porcelain gratin dish, flan dish, or pie plate that will look nice at the dinner table, but it is still traditional to leave the stones in the cherries. Some authors claim that the cherry stones add flavor to the dish, but that is hogwash. Try simmering cherry stones in milk and you will find that the flavor they give up is nil. The real reasons to leave the pits in the cherries are that pitting the cherries is time consuming, and once pitted they sit more on the surface of the batter and bleed too much, making the dish look sloppy. With the stones intact, the cherries sink into the batter just enough to leave little red spots peeking out all over the top of the flan, making a surprisingly attractive appearance for such a rustic dish.

We strongly recommend warning your dinner guests about the cherry stones. Anyone cooking for prissy guests may want to avoid the issue altogether by pitting the cherries and saying to hell with tradition. *Chacun à son gout.*

Whatever approach you take, be sure to choose the ripest, darkest, sweetest cherries you can find. When cherries are out of season, try the variations mentioned at the end of the recipe.

For 8 to 10 servings

EQUIPMENT:
10-inch (25-cm) porcelain or stoneware pie pan or deep gratin dish
• brush heavily with melted butter
Blender or food processor

BATTER:

Ripe, dark sweet cherries	1 pound (450 g)
Milk	¾ cup (1.8 dL)
Large egg, at room temperature	1
Large egg yolk, at room temperature	1
European kirsch	2 tablespoons (3 cL)
Granulated sugar	3½ ounces (100 g); ½ cup
All-purpose flour	4 ounces (115 g); ¾ cup + 1 tablespoon
Unsalted butter, softened	3 ounces (85 g); ¼ cup + 2 tablespoons

DECORATION:

Confectioners' sugar for dusting

Preheat the oven to 400°F (200°C).

1. Remove the stems from the cherries. Pit them if you must.

2. Combine the remaining ingredients for the batter in the blender or food processor. Process until smooth.

3. Pour the batter into the prepared pie pan or gratin dish. Scatter the cherries over the batter in a single layer.

4. Bake until the top of the *clafoutis* is puffed up, lightly browned on top, and set, about 45 to 50 minutes.

5. Place the pie pan on a wire rack until ready to serve. The *clafoutis* will sink as it cools. It is best served freshly baked and still warm. Dust the top with confectioners' sugar just before serving.

VARIATIONS: While not traditional, *clafoutis* is also excellent with fruits other than cherries. We like raspberries best of all. To make a raspberry *clafoutis*, substitute *framboise* (raspberry brandy) for kirsch in the batter, and set aside 2 tablespoons (25 g) of the sugar. Pour half of the batter into the pie pan, scatter the raspberries over it, and dust with the reserved sugar. Pour the remaining batter over the berries and proceed with the recipe as for ordinary *clafoutis*.

We are also very fond of *clafoutis* with blueberries and either kirsch or *myrtilles* brandy, a variation which you would never see in France.

STORAGE: Best served fresh from the oven, but can be kept in the refrigerator, covered airtight with plastic wrap, for up to 3 days. Before serving, reheat in a preheated 300°F (150°C) oven or in a microwave, then dust with confectioners' sugar.

After refrigeration, the bottom of the *clafoutis* sticks to the pie pan more than it does when freshly baked.

Far Breton

(BRETON PRUNE FLAN)

This flan from Brittany is very similar to *clafoutis*, but with prunes instead of cherries. However, the culinary traditions in Brittany are very different from the rest of France, and the origins of this particular dessert have nothing to do with the genesis of *clafoutis*.

Far originally referred to a porridge made from wheat flour with dried fruit. (*Far* is Latin for wheat and is the root of the word "farina," which means "flour" in Italian.) It was cooked in a linen bag and it could be sweet or savory, depending on whether it was served as a dessert or as an accompaniment to meat, soup, or vegetables.

The only dish in the *far* family that has gained renown outside of Brittany is the *far breton*. It is most often made with prunes, but muscat raisins are also traditional. Soaking the prunes in hot tea makes them softer and more tender.

For 8 servings

EQUIPMENT:

10-inch (25-cm) porcelain or stoneware pie pan or deep gratin dish
• brush heavily with melted butter
Blender or food processor

BATTER:

Pitted prunes	5¼ ounces (150 g)
Hot tea	1 cup (2.4 dL)
Unsalted butter, softened	1½ ounces (40 g); 3 tablespoons
Large eggs, at room temperature	2
All-purpose flour	3 ounces (85 g); ½ cup + 2 tablespoons
Milk	1¼ cups (3 dL)
Pure vanilla extract	1 teaspoon (5 mL)
Granulated sugar	3½ ounces (100 g); ½ cup

DECORATION:

Confectioners' sugar for dusting

1. Soak the prunes in the hot tea for about 2 hours. Then drain them.

Preheat the oven to 425°F (220°C).

2. Combine the butter and eggs in the blender or food processor and process until thoroughly mixed. Sift the flour and add it and the remaining ingredients for the batter to the butter and eggs. Process until smooth.

3. Pour the batter into the prepared pie pan or gratin dish. Scatter the prunes over the batter.

4. Bake for 10 minutes. The edges of the *far* will puff up.

Reduce the oven temperature to 350°F (175°C).

5. Continue baking until the top of the *far* is puffed up, lightly browned on top, and set, about 45 to 50 minutes longer.

6. Place the pie pan on a wire rack until ready to serve. The *far* will sink as it cools. It is best served freshly baked and still warm. Dust the top with confectioners' sugar just before serving.

VARIATION: *Far* can also be made with muscat raisins instead of prunes, or with a mixture of muscat raisins and prunes. If you prefer, the prunes and/or raisins can be soaked in dark pungent rum instead of tea, in which case the batter should be flavored with rum instead of vanilla.

STORAGE: Best served fresh from the oven, but can be kept in the refrigerator, covered airtight with plastic wrap, for up to 3 days. Before serving, reheat in a preheated 300°F (150°C) oven or in a microwave, then dust with confectioners' sugar.

After refrigeration, the bottom of the *far* sticks to the pie pan more than it does when freshly baked.

CHAPTER TWO

Round Sponge Cake Gâteaux

· ·

The gâteaux in this chapter are the elegant French counterparts to the pedestrian American layer cake. You make them from one round of sponge cake (usually génoise), cut in half to make two layers and sandwiched with one layer of filling. The sponge cake is brushed with a flavored syrup, and the top and sides of the cake are covered with some kind of frosting (such as buttercream). With good sponge cake, filling, and frosting, you already have a delicious cake at this point. To make it beautiful, you can decorate it in an infinite variety of ways, from a simple dusting of roasted sliced almonds to more elaborate glazes, piping, etc.

You can assemble these gâteaux in two ways. In the traditional method, you assemble the cake layers freehand, spreading the frosting over the outside using a long, flexible icing spatula. This technique requires practice, but once mastered it is quick and versatile.

The alternative is to assemble the gâteau in a cake ring. The ring does the work of smoothing the sides and serves as a guide for smoothing the top with your icing spatula. This second, more modern technique is much easier to learn than the traditional freehand technique, and it guarantees perfect results every time. It does require that you have a cake ring, but this is an affordable tool that you can use to bake cakes (and even some deep *tartes*) as well as to assemble a staggering variety of gâteaux. We highly recommend making this investment.

Up until the late 1970s, nearly all pastry shops in France assembled their gâteaux using the traditional method. But as labor costs in France have skyrocketed and skilled workers have become more and more scarce, many pastry shops have switched over to the modern method of assembling desserts in rings.

We will explain both methods thoroughly in this section. Then, in

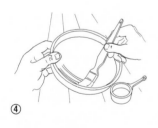

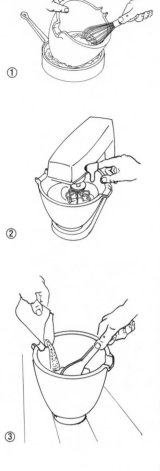

each recipe, we leave it to you to decide which method to use. Everything is designed to work equally well using the traditional method or the modern ring method. The only exceptions are gâteaux that are frosted with Italian meringue or whipped cream or brushed on the outside with apricot jam in lieu of frosting; these cakes cannot be assembled in a ring.

Making the Sponge Cake

All of the gâteaux in this chapter are based on sponge cakes baked in either round cake pans or cake rings. Of all the sponge cakes used in French gâteaux, génoise is the most versatile and widely used. The method of preparation is totally different from that used for the prototypical separated-egg sponge cake such as *biscuit de savoie* (page 45). For génoise, you mix whole eggs with sugar and stir over a hot water bath to warm the eggs to about 100°F (40°C) ①. (The heat produces thermal vibrations in the egg proteins, making them uncoil from their normal folded configuration so that they can cross-link with each other and give structure to the foam.) Then you remove the mixture from the heat and whip it until cool ②. Finally you fold in the flour ③. A hundred years ago, it was customary to incorporate a healthy amount of butter, but today the fashion is to include only a small addition of butter in order to enhance the flavor of the génoise without making it rich or heavy.

Génoise is intended to be used as a building block in assembling gâteaux. Part of the assembly procedure is to brush the génoise layers with a syrup flavored according to the gâteau in which it is used. This brushing also serves to moisten the génoise. In order to suit its destined role and to give it maximum versatility, the génoise is normally not flavored before baking and it must be sufficiently absorbent to accept the flavoring syrup. Some flavors (in particular almonds and chocolate) do not naturally lend themselves to incorporation in syrup form, so we prepare special almond and chocolate génoise recipes for use in cakes requiring these flavorings.

We recommend preparing two rounds of génoise at a time because this is easier and more efficient than preparing a single round, and the génoise can be frozen for up to 2 months so that you can have it on hand whenever you want to make a gâteau. Génoise is used in so many gâteaux that you will have a wide range of options to choose from. If you also happen to have some buttercream in your freezer, you will be able to put together an impressive gâteau for a party on short notice. However, if

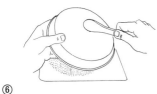
⑥

preparing two rounds of génoise at a time does not mesh with your kitchen logistics, you can simply cut the recipe in half and make a single round.

Whenever you are preparing two rounds of génoise, you can bake both in round cake pans, both in cake rings, or one in each. The sizes are chosen so that they are interchangeable.

Preparing Round Cake Pans

⑦

Brush the inside of the pan with melted butter ④, and let the butter set. Then spoon some flour into the pan ⑤, and gradually tilt, rotate, and shake the pan to distribute an even coating of flour over the butter on the bottom and sides of the pan. Invert the pan and tap it to dislodge the excess flour ⑥.

Preparing Cake Rings

⑧

Cut a square of kitchen parchment a little wider than the diameter of the ring. On a heavy baking sheet, brush either the outline or the diagonals of a similar square with melted butter, and place the parchment on the buttered square. The butter will hold the parchment in place. Brush the square of parchment with melted butter. Brush the inside of the ring with melted butter ⑦, and let the butter set. Then hold the ring vertically and spoon some flour onto the inside of the ring at the bottom. Gradually rotate and tap the ring to distribute an even coating of flour over the butter on the inside of the ring ⑧, adding more flour as needed. Tap the ring on your countertop to dislodge the excess flour. Finally, place the ring on the baking sheet, centering it on the square of parchment.

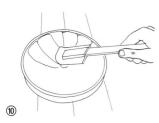
⑨

Filling Round Cake Pans and Cake Rings

Transfer the batter to the cake pan or ring by pouring and scraping it from the mixing bowl into the pan or ring or by scooping up the batter with a bowl scraper and depositing it in the pan or ring a little at a time ⑨. Using the curved edge of the bowl scraper or rubber spatula, smooth the surface of the batter from the center out to the side of the pan, making a depression in the center ⑩. This depression prevents the cake from forming a dome when baked. Ideally, you want the top surface of the cake to be flat when it comes out of the oven.

⑩

If you are using a bowl scraper to deposit the batter in a cake pan, there is a more sophisticated way to fill the cake pan. Lift the cake pan with

one hand and tilt it slightly toward you. With your other hand, scoop up some batter on the curved side of your bowl scraper and deposit it in the low side of the tilted pan ⑪, scraping the batter off the bowl scraper with the rim of the pan. Rotate the pan between each scoop. You will need about a half dozen scoops to work your way around the pan. Then deposit a small scoop of batter in the center of the mold ⑫. By controlling the amount of batter you take with each scoop, you can distribute the batter evenly and create a depression in the center without smoothing the surface afterward, thus reducing the chance of deflating the batter by manipulating it too much.

If you are baking the batter in a cake pan, place the cake pan on a baking sheet.

Usually the cake pan or ring should be filled to only about three quarters of its height so the batter has room to expand in the oven. Ideally, the pan or ring should not be filled much less than that because if the pan or ring is too deep the top of the cake will not bake and brown evenly. However, if you must bake the cake in a mold that is deeper than the one we suggest, naturally you should fill it to a lower proportion of its height.

Baking, Unmolding, and Cooling

Have the oven preheated to 375°F (190°C). Place the baking sheet with the cake pans or cake rings of batter on the middle rack in the oven and bake until the tops of the cakes are lightly browned and firm to the touch. This will take about 16 to 22 minutes. The top surface should be dry to the touch but not at all crusty, and the tip of a paring knife inserted in the center should come out clean ⑬. As soon as the cakes meet this test, remove them from the oven. Loosen the edges by sliding the tip of a paring knife or small icing spatula between the edge of each cake and the side of the pan or ring; this allows the cakes to settle evenly and makes them easier to unmold. If you are using cake pans, slide them onto a wire rack; if you are using cake rings, place the baking sheet on a wire rack. Let the cakes rest and begin to cool for 5 minutes.

If the cakes were baked in cake pans, place a wire rack upside down on top of each and invert the cake pan and rack together ⑭. Carefully lift off the cake pan ⑮. If the cake doesn't slide out easily, invert the cake pan and wire rack together and try to loosen any spots where the cake is clinging to the side of the pan, then try again. Once the cake is unmolded on the

⑯

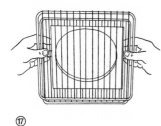

⑰

⑱

⑲

wire rack, do not leave it upside down or the top surface can stick to the rack. Place a second wire rack upside down on the cake and invert the cake together with the two racks. Lift off the first rack.

If the cakes were baked in cake rings, you should be able to lift off the rings easily ⑯. Use a small icing spatula to loosen the cakes from the side of the rings if necessary. Use a large metal spatula to slide the cakes, with the parchment underneath, onto a large wire rack. (Or slide each one onto its own round wire cake rack.) Place a second wire rack upside down on top ⑰ and invert the cakes (or each cake) and two wire racks together ⑱. Lift off the first wire rack. Carefully peel off the square of parchment ⑲ and place it clean side down on the cake. Then place the first wire rack on top again and invert the cakes (or each cake) once more. Lift off the second wire rack.

Let the cake rounds cool on the wire rack. They must cool flat side (the side that was on the bottom in the oven) down because this side will become the top of the finished gâteau and must remain flat. Also, the surface of the cake that was on top in the oven tends to stick to the wire rack if the cake is allowed to cool with that side down.

Storing the Cake Rounds

If you will not be using the cake rounds the day they are baked, then cover them airtight and store them in the refrigerator or freezer. They will dry out the least if you cover them while they are still barely warm. We find it best to cover each one in plastic wrap and then place it in an airtight plastic bag. Place them flat side down on a flat surface in the refrigerator or freezer. You can keep them for up to 2 days in the refrigerator or 2 months in the freezer. If frozen, defrost overnight in the refrigerator; and then unwrap the cake round at least 2 hours before using to allow condensation produced by defrosting to evaporate.

THE TRADITIONAL
FREEHAND ASSEMBLY METHOD

Cake Sizes

Bake the génoise in a 9-inch (24-cm) round cake pan with sloping sides 1½ inches (4 cm) deep. This is the standard size for all of the gâteaux in this chapter. A cake pan with vertical sides will work equally well, but will produce a gâteau with a different profile.

If you prefer to make another size, you can adjust our recipes accordingly. For an 8-inch (20-cm) cake, decrease the quantities of all ingredients by 20 percent. Or, for a 10-inch (25-cm) cake, increase the quantities of all ingredients by 25 percent.

Cardboard Bases

To properly assemble and decorate a round gâteau, you must have a cardboard cake-decorating circle. For this purpose we recommend the foil board lids made for aluminum foil take-out containers (and sold separately from the containers), or equivalently the cake-decorating circles imported from France. Both are a single layer of white cardboard with silver- or gold-colored foil on top. The available sizes include 9-inch (23-cm) diameter for the foil board lids and 9½-inch (24-cm) diameter for the French cake-decorating circles. (See pages 467 and 558 for details and sources.) Matt board, sold in 32×40-inch (80×100-cm) rectangular sheets at framing and art supply stores (see page 467), is also available with a silver or gold foil surface and is a good alternative. The matt board has the advantage that it is thicker and more rigid, but it is slightly less convenient because it is not precut. Do not use the corrugated cardboard cake-decorating circles sold in American cake supply shops; they are difficult to cut to size and they have all the elegance of a cardboard shipping box.

The cake-decorating circle must be cut to size, depending on how the outside of the gâteau will be finished. If the gâteau will simply be brushed with strained apricot jam, then the circle should be slightly smaller than the bottom of the gâteau so it won't show around the edge. If the outside of the gâteau will be spread with a frosting, such as buttercream, then the circle should be slightly larger than the bottom of the cake ⑳. It then serves as a guide and support for spreading and smoothing the frosting around the sides of the gâteau. Ideally, for buttercream or ganache frosting the circle should be about ¼ inch (6 mm) larger in diameter than the bottom of the cake; for lighter frostings (such as whipped cream, Italian meringue, or mousses), which are spread thicker than buttercream, the circle should be about ⅜ inch (1 cm) larger in diameter than the bottom of the cake.

Note that a 24-cm = 9½-inch French cake pan is slightly larger

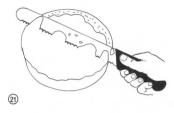

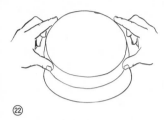

than a 9-inch = 23-cm American cake pan. The difference is so small that we treat them as identical, calling for a 9-inch (24-cm) round cake pan. If you are using a French cake pan, then for most gâteau assembled freehand you will want to have a 24-cm= 9½-inch cake-decorating circle, and a 9-inch = 23-cm foil board lid will not be quite large enough. For this reason we give American and metric dimensions for the cake-decorating circles that correspond, respectively, to the diameters of American and French cake pans.

Trimming and Slicing the Génoise

The bottom of the génoise round (which was the top side as it baked in the oven) must be flat and level, otherwise your finished gâteau will look saggy or lopsided. Unless your génoise round is already perfect, place it upside down on your countertop and trim off any uneven parts of the bottom crust with a wavy-edge bread knife . Then turn it right side up and center it on your cake-decorating circle.

Make a vertical slit in the side of the génoise so that you will be able to align the layers later. Then slice the génoise in half horizontally with your bread knife. To help guide the blade of your knife, hold one hand, palm down, on top of the génoise so you can feel the blade moving through the cake and detect any deviation from a straight horizontal cut.

Lift off the top layer of cake and turn it upside down on your countertop behind the bottom layer. Keep track of the alignment slits so that you don't have to worry about equalizing any unevenness in the two layers when you put them back together.

Brushing with Syrup

Génoise is brushed with a flavored syrup to moisten it and add flavor to the gâteau. The syrup is a standard heavy syrup (page 452) diluted with an equal volume of liqueur or coffee. We often replace part of the liqueur or coffee with water if this is an accent flavor (such as rum in a chocolate gâteau) or if the quantity of brushing required to moisten the génoise would make the flavor of the syrup oppressive. Diluting the heavy syrup makes it soak into the cake layers more easily and enables you to adjust the flavor to suit the gâteau. In our recipes we refer to this flavored syrup as the "brushing-syrup mixture."

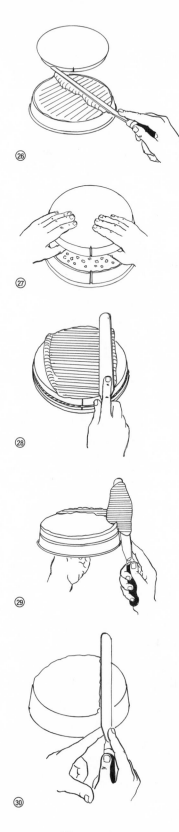

Brush the cut faces of both layers of génoise with most of the brushing-syrup mixture called for in the recipe ㉕. The cake should be very moist, but not soggy. Keep in mind that the quantity of brushing is a matter of taste. We prefer our cakes very moist. If you like drier cakes, you can reduce the quantities of syrup accordingly. On the other hand, if your génoise is a little dry, you may need to augment the quantity of brushing syrup (always in the proportions specified in the recipe) to moisten the cake sufficiently.

Filling the Génoise

Spread the filling in an even layer over the bottom layer of génoise using an icing spatula with a blade at least 10 inches (25 cm) long ㉖. Many recipes call for raisins, diced glacé fruits, or chopped nuts between the layers. Scatter them over the filling.

Place the top layer of génoise, cut side down, on the filling, remembering to align the slits in the sides of the cake ㉗. Press gently on top to eliminate any gaps between the layers and to be sure that the gâteau is even. Then lightly brush the top and sides of the génoise with the brushing-syrup mixture. Do not brush too much syrup on the outside of the cake or, when you spread the frosting over it, the frosting will not adhere well. If you have moistened the outside of the cake too much, blot it with paper towels to absorb the excess syrup.

Spreading and Smoothing the Frosting

Whatever the frosting, you will cover the cake with it following a three-stage process: Spreading the frosting over the entire outside of the gâteau, smoothing the top, and smoothing the sides.

First, spread an even layer of frosting over the top of the gâteau ㉘. Slide your icing spatula under the cake-decorating circle, lift the gâteau from the countertop, and transfer it to the fingertips of one hand. Scoop up some of the frosting with the tip of the icing spatula and scrape it off on the rim of the bowl. Slide the edge of the icing spatula under some of this frosting to pick it up about three quarters of the way up the face of the blade, near the tip. Spread this frosting on the side of the gâteau by moving the face of the icing spatula down and around the side, and leave a small rim of frosting extending above the top edge of the gâteau ㉙. Rotate the gâteau

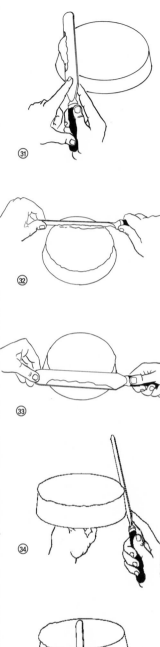

on your fingertips (use the tip of the icing spatula as an aid to avoid dropping it, if necessary), and repeat until you have covered all sides of the gâteau with the frosting and made a rim of frosting extending above the entire top edge. Slide the icing spatula under the gâteau and return it to the counter.

The second stage is to smooth the top surface of the gâteau. Start with the icing spatula at the right side of the gâteau, with the face of the blade at an angle of 30° relative to the top surface ③⓪. Sweep the blade a little more than halfway across the top ③①, keeping the edge of the blade at a fixed height and turning the face of the blade. As you sweep the blade across the center of the gâteau and lift it off the surface, the face of the blade should have rotated through about 90°. This motion spreads the rim of frosting across the gâteau and smooths half of the surface. Clean off the blade on the rim of the bowl of frosting. Next, sweep the blade from left to right across the left half of the gâteau, again keeping the edge of the blade at a fixed height and turning the face of the blade through about 90°. You should now have finished spreading the rim of frosting and the top of the gâteau should be almost smooth. Clean off the blade on the rim of the bowl again. To finish smoothing the top surface, grasp the ends of the blade of the icing spatula between the thumb and the index and middle fingers of each hand and place the edge of the blade on the far side of the gâteau. Starting with the face of the blade angled toward you ③②, sweep the entire top surface in one smooth, continuous motion. As you do so, keep the edge of the blade at a fixed height and gradually turn the edge first under and then up, so when it reaches the near side of the gâteau, the blade is angled away from you ③③. Take off just enough frosting to get a level surface.

Now you are ready to smooth the sides of the gâteau. Slide the icing spatula under the cake-decorating circle and lift the gâteau from the countertop. Transfer the gâteau to the fingertips of one hand. Place the bottom third of the blade of the icing spatula against the side of the gâteau, with the face of the blade nearly parallel to the surface ③④. Using the cake-decorating circle as a guide, sweep the edge of the blade around the side of the gâteau to smooth the surface and clean off the excess frosting. As you do so, draw the blade downward and turn the face of the blade toward you ③⑤. Clean off the blade on the rim of the bowl, rotate the gâteau on your fingertips, and repeat until you have smoothed the entire outside surface of the gâteau. Return the gâteau to the counter.

This completes the spreading and smoothing procedure. Do not expect to use all of the frosting, because a necessary part of the smoothing is sweeping excess frosting off the surface of the gâteau.

When you are covering a gâteau with Italian meringue, which is more sticky and viscous than the other frostings, you must make one alteration in the general procedure we have just described. When you are smoothing this frosting, keep the face of the icing spatula nearly perpendicular to the surface of the meringue. That will allow you to cut it cleanly, rather than having the meringue that clings to the blade drag the meringue on the surface of the gâteau.

Assembly in a Cake Ring

Cake Sizes

Bake the génoise in an 8¾-inch (22-cm) cake ring 1⅜ inches (3.5 cm) deep. This gives you a cake of precisely the right size to assemble in the same ring, which is the standard size for all of the gâteaux in this chapter. It produces a gâteau of almost identical size to one assembled freehand using a génoise round baked in a 9-inch (24-cm) cake pan, but with vertical rather than sloping sides.

If you prefer to make another size, you can adjust our recipes accordingly. Whatever size ring you choose, always bake the génoise in the same cake ring as you will use for the assembly and increase or decrease the quantities of filling and frosting according to the square of the diameter of the ring. In other words, if your ring has diameter D in cm, then you should multiply all of the quantities in the recipe by $(D/22)^2$. For example a 24-cm diameter ring requires about 20 percent more filling and frosting than a 22-cm ring, because $(24/22)^2 = 1.2$.

Cardboard Bases

As for the traditional freehand method, you will need a cardboard cake-decorating circle. You can use one of the foil board circles sold as lids for aluminum foil take-out containers or a cake-decorating circle imported from France (see pages 467 and 558 for details and sources). Or you can cut your own circles from a sheet of silver or gold matt board (available from framing and art supply stores, see page 467). Do not use the corrugated cardboard cake-decorating circles sold in American cake supply shops because they are too thick, difficult to cut, and make an unattractive presentation.

The cake-decorating circle must be cut to size so that it will just fit inside the cake ring.

Trimming and Slicing the Génoise

The bottom of the génoise round (which was the top side as it baked in the oven) must be flat and level, and it must be ¼ to 5⁄16 inch (6 to 8 mm) shorter than the cake ring to allow room for filling and frosting. Cutting the génoise to precisely the right height is foolproof if you create a thickness guide to support the génoise evenly. Use the removable bottom from a *tarte* pan or an American corrugated cardboard cake circle (5⁄32 inch=4 mm thick—perhaps they have some value after all); whichever you choose, it must be slightly smaller than the diameter of the génoise round. Then place under it a flat object smaller than the cake ring and of a thickness such that combined with the *tarte* pan bottom or corrugated cake circle you will raise the génoise round off the countertop ¼ to 5⁄16 inch (6 to 8 mm). Place your génoise round upside down on your thickness guide inside the cake ring, and trim off the bottom of the génoise level with the top of the ring using a wavy-edge bread knife ㊱. Then remove the thickness guide, and turn the génoise right side up.

Make a vertical slit in the side of the génoise round ㊲ so that you will be able to align the layers later. Then slice the génoise in half horizontally with your bread knife. To help guide the blade of your knife, hold one hand, palm down, on top of the génoise so you can feel the blade moving through the cake ㊳ and detect any deviation from a straight horizontal cut.

Lift off the top layer of cake and turn it upside down on your countertop behind the bottom layer. Keep track of the alignment slits so that you don't have to worry about equalizing any unevenness in the two layers when you put them back together.

Brushing with Syrup

Génoise is brushed with a flavored syrup to moisten it and add flavor to the gâteau. The syrup is a standard heavy syrup (page 452) diluted with an equal volume of liqueur or coffee. We often replace part of the liqueur or coffee with water if this is an accent flavor (such as rum in a chocolate gâteau), or if the quantity of brushing required to moisten the génoise would make the flavor of the syrup oppressive. Diluting the heavy syrup also makes it soak into the cake layers more easily and enables you to adjust the flavor to suit

(40)

(41)

(42)

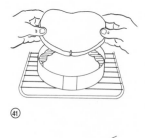

(43)

(44)

the gâteau. In our recipes we refer to this flavored syrup as the "brushing-syrup mixture."

Brush the cut faces of both layers of génoise with most of the syrup called for in the recipe ㊴. The cake should be very moist, but not soggy. Keep in mind that the quantity of brushing is a matter of taste. We prefer our cakes very moist. If you like drier cakes, you can reduce the quantities of syrup accordingly. On the other hand, if your génoise is a little dry, you may need to augment the quantity of brushing syrup (always in the proportions specified in the recipe) to moisten the cake sufficiently.

Filling the Ring

Place your cake-decorating circle on a baking sheet or wire rack. Choose an icing spatula with a blade at least 10 inches (25 cm) long. Grasp the side of the ring between the fingertips of one hand, lift the ring off the countertop, and hold it in a vertical position with your fingertips supporting it from the top. Scoop up some of the frosting on the tip of the icing spatula, and spread it inside the ring ㊵ near the lowest point on one side only—the side that will become the bottom when you put the ring back on the countertop. Rotate the ring and repeat until one half of the inside of the ring is coated all the way around with a layer of frosting about ¼ inch (6 mm) thick. Place the ring on the baking sheet or wire rack, centering it on the cake circle with the frosting-coated side on the bottom. Carefully lift the bottom layer of génoise and lower it into the ring ㊶, compressing the sides by pressing toward the center to make it fit inside the surrounding frosting. Spread an even layer of filling over the bottom layer of génoise using the icing spatula or a bowl scraper and spread frosting about ¼ inch (6 mm) thick over the upper half of the inside of the ring ㊷. If the recipe calls for it, scatter raisins, diced glacé fruits, or chopped nuts over the filling.

Place the top layer of génoise, cut side down, on the filling ㊸, remembering to align the slits in the sides of the cake and to center the génoise inside the frosting lining the ring, compressing the génoise as necessary to make it fit inside the frosting. Press gently on top to eliminate any gaps between the layers and to ensure that the top is below the top of the ring and there is room for a top layer of frosting ㊹. Then lightly brush the top of the génoise with the flavored syrup. Do not brush

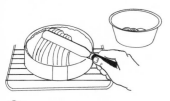

too much syrup on the top of the cake or, when you spread the frosting over it, the frosting will not adhere well. If you have moistened the top of the cake too much, blot it with paper towels to absorb the excess syrup.

Spread the remaining frosting over the top of the génoise to fill the ring ㊺. Grasp the ends of the blade of the icing spatula (or if it isn't long enough use a metal straightedge instead) between the thumb and the index and middle fingers of each hand and place the edge of the blade on the far side of the gâteau. Starting with the face of the blade angled toward you ㊻, sweep the entire top surface in one smooth, continuous motion. As you do so, keep the edge of the blade on the top edge of the ring and gradually turn the edge first under and then up, so when it reaches the near side of the gâteau, the blade is angled away from you ㊼. Take off just enough frosting to make it level with the top of the ring.

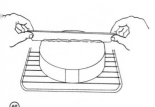

Refrigerate for at least 1 hour to make the frosting firm. Place the chilled gâteau on a bowl or cake pan taller and slightly smaller in diameter than the ring. Using a blow dryer, quickly and evenly warm the outside of the ring to just melt the frosting inside of the ring. Carefully slip the ring down off the gâteau ㊽. If the ring doesn't slip off easily, warm it a little more and try again.

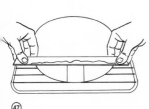

ADDING EXTRA LAYERS

Occasionally we like to make a taller gâteau with more layers by adding a round of French meringue plus an extra layer of filling in the center. The crisp meringue adds a note of textural contrast and lightness. The assembly of these gâteaux is not much more difficult than for the standard sponge cake gâteaux, but you will have the extra step of baking the meringue round. For the extra layer of filling you can repeat the filling or frosting already used in the gâteau, or you can add a different filling to complement the flavors already present.

Because these gâteaux typically require more components, and thus more time, than the basic round sponge cake gâteaux, we suggest them for readers who have more experience in making gâteaux. We offer two examples as variations on *délicieux* and *succulent*. If you like this type of gâteau, you can experiment with other combinations on your own.

We recommend that you assemble these gâteaux by the traditional freehand method. You can also assemble them in a deep cake ring, provided you can find one of just the right depth.

Using a *tarte* ring, a cake ring, a round mold, or a *vol-au-vent* disk as a guide, trim the round of meringue with a wavy-edge bread knife ㊾ to a circle the size of the top of the génoise round. To make the round more even in thickness, shave the top with the bread knife to take off any large bumps ㊿. Trim the bottom of the génoise round and slice it in half as usual. Brush the cut faces of both layers of génoise (but not the meringue) with flavored syrup. Spread a layer of filling on the bottom layer of génoise, then place the meringue round on top ㋱. Spread the second layer of filling over the meringue. Place the second layer of génoise cut side down on top, and finish assembling the gâteau as you would any round sponge cake gâteau.

GLAZING WITH CHOCOLATE OR FONDANT

You can use fondant or chocolate as a glaze over buttercream or ganache. In either case, you must first refrigerate the gâteau so the glaze won't melt the frosting. Slide your icing spatula under the cake-decorating circle, lift the gâteau from the countertop, and transfer it to a wire rack. Refrigerate for at least 1 hour to make the frosting firm. When ready to glaze, place the wire rack with the gâteau on your countertop, with a large tray underneath to catch the excess glaze.

If you are glazing with chocolate, it must be fluid enough to flow quickly and smoothly, producing a thin, even layer. But it must not be so runny that it takes too long to set. Also, it should not be too brittle when set, or it will be difficult to cut and serve. We get the best results by thinning European bittersweet chocolate with clarified butter. Melt the chocolate and temper it ㋲ (see page 538 for a detailed discussion of tempering chocolate). The temperature of the chocolate must be between 86° and 91°F (30° to 33°C). The clarified butter must be at room temperature. Beat the clarified butter with a wooden spatula to make it smooth and creamy, and then stir it into the chocolate.

If you are glazing with fondant, gently warm it, stirring constantly until melted ㋳. The temperature should be 100° to 105°F (38° to 40°C) and the fondant should be fluid, with about the same body as heavy cream or a light custard sauce. If necessary, add heavy syrup (page 452), a little at a time, until the fondant is thinned to the proper consistency. If the recipe calls for tinting the fondant, stir in a little food coloring to reach the required color.

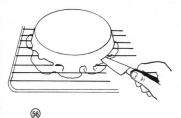

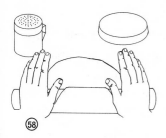

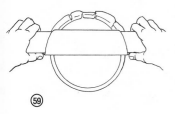

Pour the fondant or chocolate glaze on top of the gâteau in a circle just inside the perimeter so that some of it flows naturally over the edges ⑤④. Quickly smooth the top surface with the edge of a long icing spatula to cover the top with a thin, even layer of glaze and make the excess flow evenly down the sides ⑤⑤. Try to make the glaze cover all sides of the gâteau. If there are any bare or uneven spots around the sides, smooth the glaze over them with the edge of the icing spatula. Work as quickly as you can because, once the glaze begins to thicken, you will no longer be able to spread it smoothly.

When the glaze has begun to thicken, clean off any excess around the base of the gâteau with a paring knife or small icing spatula ⑤⑥. The glaze must be allowed to set before serving. However, if the base of the gâteau is to be coated with chopped nuts or chocolate sprinkles, this must be done before it sets so that they will adhere to the surface.

Put the gâteau in a cool place and let the glaze set. Then return the gâteau to the refrigerator.

Enrobing a Gâteau in Almond Paste

You can drape a thin sheet of almond paste over buttercream on the outside of a gâteau. Normally you will press the almond paste against the top and sides of the cake to make a smooth, flat surface, similar to a glaze but matte rather than shiny. In a few special gâteaux (in particular our *grand marnier*, page 118), you can drape a thin round of almond paste on the top of the gâteau in irregular, undulating folds to produce a very abstract and modern-looking dessert.

As for glazing, first transfer the gâteau to a wire rack and refrigerate for at least 1 hour to make the buttercream firm.

Work the almond paste on the countertop with the heel of your hand to smooth and soften it. If the recipe calls for it, tint the almond paste with a little food coloring, cutting the food coloring in with a dough scraper and then working it in with the heel of your hand until the color is uniform.

Dust your countertop and the almond paste with confectioners' sugar. Roll out the almond paste into a circle with your rolling pin ⑤⑦, dusting lightly with more confectioners' sugar as needed, to get an even, smooth sheet that doesn't stick to the counter or the rolling pin. Each time you dust with confectioners' sugar, wipe the sheet gently with the palm of your hand to spread the confectioners' sugar and elim-

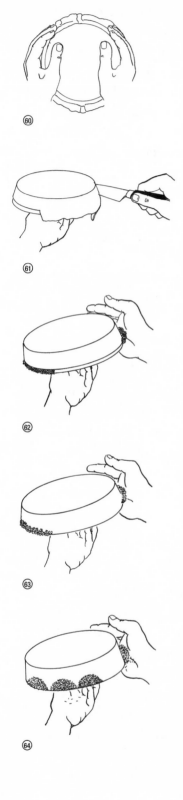

inate any white blotches of sugar. Roll out the almond paste into a sheet about 1/16 inch (1½ mm) thick and at least 4 inches (10 cm) larger in diameter than the gâteau.

Carefully roll or drape the sheet of almond paste over your rolling pin ⑤⑧ so it doesn't tear when you lift it. (Or fold it in half and lift it with your hands.) Then unroll ⑤⑨ (or unfold) it on the gâteau, centering the circle so that the edges hang over all sides and the sheet is flat against the top. Cup your hands around the sides of the gâteau and gently press the sheet of almond paste to make it lie flat against the sides ⑥⓪ with no folds or creases.

Trim the sheet of almond paste about ¼ to ⅜ inch (6 to 10 mm) above the bottom of the gâteau to leave a strip of buttercream exposed around the base ⑥①. This strip of buttercream will be coated with chopped nuts or chocolate sprinkles ⑥②.

FINISHING THE BOTTOM EDGE OF A GÂTEAU

You will coat the bottom edges of most round gâteaux with chopped nuts or chocolate sprinkles. You must do this while the topping or glaze is soft, so that the nuts or sprinkles will adhere.

Slide your icing spatula under the cake-decorating circle and lift the gâteau from the countertop. Support it on the fingertips of one hand. If the gâteau was glazed with fondant or chocolate, be careful to hold it straight so that cracks don't form in the glaze. Take the nuts or chocolate sprinkles in the palm of your other hand, and have more ready so you can refill your palm as you go along. Press the bottom edge of the gâteau against the nuts or sprinkles in your palm ⑥③ to make them adhere to the topping or glaze. Rotate the gâteau on your fingertips and press it against the nuts or sprinkles in your palm again. Continue until the entire bottom edge of the gâteau is coated with nuts or sprinkles.

For most gâteaux, you should coat the bottom edge with an even band of nuts or sprinkles ⅜ to ½ inch (10 to 12 mm) high. Sometimes you can be more fancy and make high arcs of chocolate sprinkles around the sides of the gâteau ⑥④ by taking more sprinkles in your hand and rotating the gâteau a little more each time you press it against the sprinkles. You can also coat the entire side of the gâteau with chopped nuts or sprinkles by taking a handful of them at a time, tilting the gâteau, and pressing the side of the gâteau against the nuts or sprinkles in your hand ⑥⑤. And you can substitute

fine chocolate shavings (page 423) for chocolate sprinkles provided you work quickly so they don't melt in your hand.

Another related technique is to decorate the sides of the gâteau with chocolate petals. We think this decoration looks especially beautiful on our *grand marnier* (page 118), but you can try it on any gâteau frosted with buttercream. You will form the petals directly on the sides of the gâteau using an icing spatula with a flexible blade 8 inches (20 cm) long. Chill the gâteau well. Melt 3 ounces (85 g) of European bittersweet chocolate, and temper it (see page 538 for details on tempering). Beat 1 teaspoon (5mL) of clarified butter (at room temperature) until smooth, then stir it into the chocolate. Place the bowl of chocolate on your counter and tilt it by placing a small mold under one side so you can easily dip the tip of the icing spatula in the chocolate. Lift the gâteau off the counter and support it on the fingertips of one hand. Lightly touch the face of the blade on the chocolate in the bowl , and clean any excess chocolate off the edges of the blade by wiping them on the edge of the bowl. Make a petal on the side of the gâteau by pressing the chocolate-coated face of the blade on it, bending the blade slightly and dragging it down the side of the gâteau . The petal should be about three quarters of the height of the gâteau and slightly wider than the blade of the icing spatula, with the center thinner than the edges. Rotate the gâteau on your fingertips, and repeat the procedure to make a second petal adjacent to the first one. Continue making petals all the way around the side, trying to make them as uniform in size as possible and adjusting the spacing as necessary to make the last petal end up adjacent to the first one. If the chocolate in the bowl begins to thicken while you are working, warm it gently to keep it fluid. When you have finished, place the gâteau on a tray and let the chocolate set. Then return the gâteau to the refrigerator.

DUSTING THE OUTSIDE OF A GÂTEAU

One of the simplest ways to finish a gâteau that has been frosted with buttercream is to cover the top and sides with sliced almonds, chocolate shavings, or pulverized nut-meringue (*dijonnaise* or *succès*) trimmings. Often the look of the cake will be enhanced if you add a final dusting of confectioners' sugar just before serving. You should always dust the gâteau lightly and evenly, and the only trick is in coating the sides.

To coat the sides easily, first slide your icing spatula under the cake-

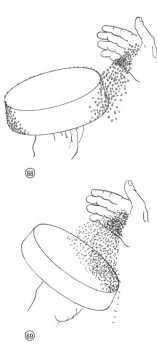

decorating circle, lift the gâteau from your countertop, and support it on the fingertips of one hand. Tilt the gâteau away from you and dust or sprinkle the sliced almonds, chocolate shavings, or nut-meringue trimmings with the other hand ⑥⑧, so they will coat the sides more effectively. When dusting with confectioners' sugar, use a sugar dredge (page 469).

On the other hand, if you want to dust only the top of the gâteau and not the sides, you should lift the gâteau and tilt it toward you ⑥⑨. That way, when you dust the sliced almonds or whatever with the other hand, nothing will land on the sides.

About Decorating Gâteaux

There are many ways to decorate the tops of round gâteaux. They include almond paste garnishes (vines, twigs, leaves, and berries, for example); inscriptions, scrolls, and borders in writing chocolate or royal icing; decorative patterns piped in buttercream or whipped cream; and designs stenciled in confectioners' sugar. The decoration depends on the flavors and the frosting on the gâteau and on your tastes and preferences.

One presentation can be used with different flavors. For example, whether it is flavored with coffee or chocolate, a *moka* is always decorated with piped buttercream. On the other hand, varying the way a particular gâteau is finished can produce strikingly different results. *Moka, mascotte café*, and *grenoblois* are all génoise filled and frosted with coffee buttercream, but their presentations are so dramatically different that they qualify as totally different gâteaux.

For each gâteau in this chapter, we give the presentation we like best. However, you can vary the decoration to suit your own tastes, the materials you have on hand, and the time available.

Keep in mind that if the surface of your gâteau has been swept perfectly smooth, it will look good no matter how simply you decorate it. A light sprinkling of roasted sliced almonds over buttercream or a geometric pattern made from a few strips of paper and stenciled in confectioners' sugar can be the perfect touch on a wide variety of gâteaux.

Finally, Mies van der Rohe's dictum that "less is more" is as valid in French pastry as it is in architecture. The one sure way to spoil the appearance of any gâteau is to cover it with an excess of piped flowers, almond paste fruits, or the like. So whatever you do, keep it simple!

STORAGE

Gâteaux filled and frosted with buttercream or ganache (chocolate cream filling) can be kept in the refrigerator (on a covered cake platter if you have one) for up to 2 days. These gâteaux can also be frozen before glazing, dusting with confectioners' sugar, chocolate sprinkles, nuts, etc., or decorating. When the gâteau has frozen, enclose it airtight with plastic wrap or in a plastic bag and store in the freezer for up to 3 weeks. The day before serving, remove the plastic wrap or bag and defrost the gâteau overnight in the refrigerator. Then finish the preparation.

Gâteaux that are filled with pastry cream or frosted with Italian meringue can be kept in the refrigerator (also on a covered cake platter, if available) for up to 1 day. They cannot be frozen. Those containing whipped cream should be kept in the refrigerator for no longer than 12 hours, and they are best eaten within 2 to 4 hours. On the other hand, gâteaux brushed with jam can be kept at room temperature, preferably in a covered cake platter, for up to 1 or 2 days.

Regardless of the filling and frosting, génoise (as well as other sponge cakes) goes stale quickly when exposed to air. So these storage times are applicable only if the génoise is completely enclosed in frosting. Once the gâteau is cut, the exposed surfaces of génoise will deteriorate more rapidly.

Génoise

. . . .

A good génoise should be fine-textured and tender, yet firm and of course not too moist. The classic génoise proportions are 9 ounces (250 g) each of sugar and flour for eight large eggs, plus 1 to 2 ounces (25 to 50 g) of butter. Unfortunately, when you prepare this recipe with American all-purpose flour, the resulting cake is rather coarse. Regardless of the flour, it has a tendency to be unnecessarily dry. We have chosen to remedy these shortcomings by replacing 20 percent of the flour with two egg yolks plus a little potato starch. The resulting cake is exquisitely fine, tender and moist, yet sufficiently absorbent.

For two 9-inch (24-cm) rounds baked in cake pans
  or two 8¾-inch (22-cm) rounds baked in cake rings

EQUIPMENT:
Large, heavy baking sheet
Either two 9-inch (24-cm) round cake pans, 1½ inches (4 cm) deep
• brush with melted butter
• dust with flour
or two 8¾-inch (22-cm) cake rings, 1⅜ inches (3.5 cm) deep
• brush with melted butter
• dust with flour
• brush outlines of two 9-inch (24-cm) squares on baking sheet with melted butter
• place a 9-inch (24-cm) square of kitchen parchment on each buttered square
• brush each square lightly with melted butter and place a cake ring on it
Electric mixer

BATTER:

Large eggs, at room temperature	7
Large egg yolks, at room temperature	2
Granulated sugar	8 ounces (225 g); 1 cup + 2 tablespoons
All-purpose flour	6¼ ounces (175 g); 1¼ cups
Potato starch	¾ ounce (20 g); 2 tablespoons
Unsalted butter, barely melted	1 ounce (30 g); 2 tablespoons

Preheat the oven to 375°F (190°C).

1. Combine the whole eggs, yolks, and sugar in a stainless steel mixing bowl, break up the yolks with a wire whisk, and beat until smooth. Set the bowl over a saucepan of simmering water, and stir with the whisk until warm (about 100°F = 40°C), frothy, and pale yellow.

2. Remove the bowl from the simmering water, and whip at medium speed in the mixer until the batter has risen and cooled, becoming light and thick and almost white in color. It should coat your finger very thickly and form very slowly dissolving ribbons when dropped from the whip.

3. Sift the flour with the potato starch onto a sheet of wax paper. A little at a time, dust the mixture over the batter and fold it in very gently but thoroughly. When the flour and potato starch are completely incorporated, slowly pour the melted butter over the batter and continue folding until the butter is uniformly mixed into the batter.

4. FOR CAKE PANS: Scoop the batter into the prepared cake pans, filling them to between **two thirds and three quarters** of their height. Smooth the surface of the batter and make a slight depression in the center. Place the cake pans on the baking sheet.

FOR CAKE RINGS: Scoop the batter into the prepared rings, filling them to between two thirds and three quarters of their height. Smooth the surface of the batter and make a slight depression in the center.

5. Bake until the top of the génoise is lightly browned and firm to the touch but not crusty, about 17 to 20 minutes. The tip of a paring knife inserted in the center of the cake should come out clean.

6. Remove the cakes from the oven and slide the tip of a paring knife or small icing spatula between the edge of each cake and the pan to loosen the edge. Let the génoise rest in the pans or rings for about 5 minutes.

FOR CAKE PANS: Unmold the cakes onto a wire rack, invert them onto another rack, and let cool there.

FOR CAKE RINGS: Lift off the rings. Use a metal spatula to slide each round of génoise onto a wire rack. Invert them onto another rack and peel off the parchment. Invert them again onto the first rack and let cool there.

HOWS AND WHYS: Adding the butter last, after the flour is completely incorporated, helps prevent the butter from deflating the foam.

STORAGE: Covered airtight with plastic wrap, for up to 2 days in the refrigerator.

Or freeze for as long as 2 months. If frozen, defrost overnight in the refrigerator, and unwrap the cake at least 2 hours before using to allow condensation produced by defrosting to evaporate.

Chocolate Génoise

. . . .

The best way to flavor your génoise with chocolate is to add cocoa powder to the batter. This method allows you to get a rich chocolate flavor without radically altering the texture of the génoise. You will sift the cocoa powder with the flour and potato starch before folding them into the egg-and-sugar batter.

Like plain génoise, chocolate génoise is intended to be used as a building block in assembling gâteaux. It is especially good in combination with ganache or chocolate buttercream, where it contributes a note of dark decadence, but at the other extreme it can provide a nice contrast in gâteaux filled and frosted with whipped cream.

For two 9-inch (24-cm) rounds baked in cake pans
   or two 8¾-inch (22-cm) rounds baked in cake rings

EQUIPMENT:
Large, heavy baking sheet
Either two 9-inch (24-cm) round cake pans, 1½ inches (4 cm) deep
• brush with melted butter
• dust with flour
or two 8¾-inch (22-cm) cake rings, 1⅜ inches (3.5 cm) deep
• brush with melted butter
• dust with flour
• brush outlines of two 9-inch (24-cm) squares on baking sheet with melted butter
• place a 9-inch (24-cm) square of kitchen parchment on each buttered square
• brush each square lightly with melted butter and place a cake ring on it
Electric mixer

BATTER:

Large eggs, at room temperature	7
Large egg yolks, at room temperature	2
Granulated sugar	8 ounces (225 g); 1 cup + 2 tablespoons
All-purpose flour	5¼ ounces (150 g); 1 cup + 1 tablespoon
Potato starch	⅓ ounce (10 g); 1 tablespoon
Unsweetened cocoa powder (Dutch processed)	1½ ounces (40 g); ¼ cup + 2 tablespoons
Unsalted butter, barely melted	1 ounce (30 g); 2 tablespoons

Preheat the oven to 375°F (190°C).

1. Combine the whole eggs, yolks, and sugar in a stainless steel mixing bowl, break up the yolks with a wire whisk, and beat until smooth. Set the bowl over a saucepan of simmering water, and stir with the whisk until warm (about 100°F = 40°C), frothy, and pale yellow.

2. Remove the bowl from the simmering water, and whip at medium speed in the mixer until the batter has risen and cooled, becoming light and thick and almost white in color. It should coat your finger very thickly and form very slowly dissolving ribbons when dropped from the whip.

3. Sift the flour with the potato starch and cocoa powder onto a sheet of wax paper. A little at a time, dust the mixture over the batter and fold it in very gently but thoroughly. When the flour, potato starch, and cocoa powder are completely incorporated, slowly pour the melted butter over the batter and continue folding until the butter is uniformly mixed into the batter.

4. FOR CAKE PANS: Scoop the batter into the prepared cake pans, filling them to between two thirds and three quarters of their height. Smooth the surface of the batter and make a slight depression in the center. Place the cake pans on the baking sheet.

FOR CAKE RINGS: Scoop the batter into the prepared rings, filling them to between two thirds and three quarters of their height. Smooth the surface of the batter and make a slight depression in the center.

5. Bake until the top of the génoise is firm to the touch but not crusty, about 16 to 20 minutes. The tip of a paring knife inserted in the center of the cake should come out clean.

6. Remove the cakes from the oven and slide the tip of a paring knife or small icing spatula between the edge of each cake and the pan to loosen the edge. Let the génoise rest in the pans or rings for about 5 minutes.

FOR CAKE PANS: Unmold the cakes onto a wire rack, invert them onto another rack, and let cool there.

FOR CAKE RINGS: Lift off the rings. Use a metal spatula to slide each round of génoise onto a wire rack. Invert them onto another rack and peel off the parchment. Invert them again onto the first rack and let cool there.

HOWS AND WHYS: The flour and potato starch in chocolate génoise are reduced slightly relative to plain génoise because the cocoa powder helps absorb the liquid in the batter. The color of this batter cannot be used as a guide in assessing when the baking is completed.

STORAGE: Covered airtight with plastic wrap, for up to 2 days in the refrigerator.

Or freeze for as long as 2 months. If frozen, defrost overnight in the refrigerator, and unwrap the cake at least 2 hours before using to allow condensation produced by defrosting to evaporate.

Almond Génoise

. . . .

Almond génoise is richer and a little heavier than ordinary génoise.

For two 9-inch (24-cm) rounds baked in cake pans
or two 8¾-inch (22-cm) rounds baked in cake rings

EQUIPMENT:
Large, heavy baking sheet
Either two 9-inch (24-cm) round cake pans, 1½ inches (4 cm) deep
• brush with melted butter
• dust with flour
or two 8¾-inch (22-cm) cake rings, 1⅜ inches (3.5 cm) deep
• brush with melted butter
• dust with flour
• brush outlines of two 9-inch (24-cm) squares on baking sheet with melted butter
• place a 9-inch (24-cm) square of kitchen parchment on each buttered square
• brush each square lightly with melted butter and place a cake ring on it
Electric mixer

BATTER:

Large eggs, at room temperature	7
Large egg yolks, at room temperature	2
Granulated sugar	4¾ ounces (135 g); ⅔ cup
All-purpose flour	3½ ounces (125 g); ¾ cup + 2 tablespoons
Potato starch	¾ ounce (20 g); 2 tablespoons
Almond-and-sugar powder (page 442)	7 ounces (200 g); 1½ cups
Unsalted butter, barely melted	1 ounce (30 g); 2 tablespoons

Preheat the oven to 375°F (190°C).

1. Combine the whole eggs, yolks, and sugar in a stainless steel mixing bowl, break up the yolks with a wire whisk, and beat until smooth. Set the bowl over a saucepan of simmering water, and stir with the whisk until warm (about 100°F = 40°C), frothy, and pale yellow.

2. Remove the bowl from the simmering water, and whip at medium speed in the mixer until the batter has risen and cooled, becoming light and thick and almost white in color. It

should coat your finger very thickly and form very slowly dissolving ribbons when dropped from the whip.

3. Sift the flour with the potato starch onto a sheet of wax paper, then mix in the almond-and-sugar powder. A little at a time, dust the mixture over the batter and fold it in very gently but thoroughly. When the flour, potato starch, and almond-and-sugar powder are completely incorporated, slowly pour the melted butter over the batter and continue folding until the butter is uniformly mixed into the batter.

4. FOR CAKE PANS: Scoop the batter into the prepared cake pans, filling them to between two thirds and three quarters of their height. Smooth the surface of the batter and make a slight depression in the center. Place the cake pans on the baking sheet.

FOR CAKE RINGS: Scoop the batter into the prepared rings, filling them to between two thirds and three quarters of their height. Smooth the surface of the batter and make a slight depression in the center.

5. Bake until the top of the génoise is lightly browned and firm to the touch but not crusty, about 18 to 22 minutes. The tip of a paring knife inserted in the center of the cake should come out clean.

6. Remove the cakes from the oven and slide the tip of a paring knife or small icing spatula between the edge of each cake and the pan to loosen the edge. Let the génoise rest in the pans or rings for about 5 minutes.

FOR CAKE PANS: Unmold the cakes onto a wire rack, invert them onto another rack, and let cool there.

FOR CAKE RINGS: Lift off the rings. Use a metal spatula to slide each round of génoise onto a wire rack. Invert them onto another rack and peel off the parchment. Invert them again onto the first rack and let cool there.

HOWS AND WHYS: The sugar content of almond génoise is reduced to compensate for the sugar in the almond-and-sugar powder, and the flour content is reduced relative to plain génoise because the almond-and-sugar powder helps absorb the liquid in the batter.

STORAGE: Covered airtight with plastic wrap, for up to 2 days in the refrigerator.

Or freeze for as long as 2 months. If frozen, defrost overnight in the refrigerator, and unwrap the cake at least 2 hours before using to allow condensation produced by defrosting to evaporate.

Moka

The first coffee beans that became popular in Europe were grown in the hills of what is now Yemen and shipped from the port of Al Mukha on the Red Sea. In France the word "moka" (usually spelled "mocha" in English) became a generic word for coffee. Later, when chocolate beans first arrived in Europe, they were imagined to be similar to coffee and moka also became associated with the combination of coffee and chocolate.

The gâteau called *moka* is one of the most fundamental gâteaux made from génoise and buttercream. It is just a round of génoise, filled and frosted with coffee buttercream, with chopped almonds around the bottom and coffee buttercream piped on top with a fluted pastry tube. Today it is difficult to imagine a time when the *moka* was a novel cake, and we are likely to underestimate its historical significance. A hundred years ago, pastry chef Pierre Lacam wrote in *Mémorial de la Pâtisserie*, "The *moka* is already a little old; but it will go very far. It is, along with the *gâteau d'amandes*, the brioche, and the *savarin*, the base of the edifice [i.e., the art of pastry]; one has created the *pralinés*, the *purée de marrons*, but all that is based on *crème au beurre* [buttercream] or [*crème à*] *moka*. We attribute the *moka* to [the pastry chef] Guignard, [whose shop was located] at the Odéon intersection; it dates to 1857."

Actually, in its most traditional form the sides of the *moka* were covered with large crystal sugar, which the French call "moka sugar." However, even Lacam mentioned the alternative of chopped toasted almonds. Lacam's contemporaries Émile Darenne and Émile Duval, authors of the classic book *Traité de Pâtisserie Moderne*, went so far as to say, "When the sale price permits, this gâteau is better with chopped grilled almonds." Then, as now, almonds were much more expensive than sugar.

Do not underestimate the *moka*. Well made, it is a beautiful and delicious gâteau, one of the great classics.

For 8 servings

EQUIPMENT:
9-inch (24-cm) foil board or matt board cake-decorating circle (page 467)
Optional: 8¾-inch (22-cm) cake ring (if the génoise was baked in one)
Small pastry bag fitted with
• fluted decorating tube (such as Ateco #17 open star tube)

CAKE:

Génoise (page 82)

One round baked in
- either a 9-inch (24-cm) cake pan
- or an 8¾-inch (22-cm) cake ring

FILLING, FROSTING, AND PIPING:

Coffee buttercream (page 390)

14 ounces (400 g); 2¼ cups

BRUSHING-SYRUP MIXTURE:

Heavy syrup (page 452)

⅓ cup (8 cL)

Double-strength brewed espresso (page 456)

⅓ cup (8 cL)

DECORATION FOR BOTTOM EDGE OF GÂTEAU:

Blanched almonds, roasted (page 444) and
    finely chopped

1 ounce (30 g); 3 tablespoons

1. Assemble the gâteau from the génoise round (cut into two layers), buttercream filling and frosting, and espresso brushing syrup either by the traditional freehand method (page 67) or by molding it (page 72) in the same ring in which the génoise was baked. Save at least ¼ cup (45 g) of excess buttercream for piping on top of the gâteau.

2. While the buttercream on the outside of the gâteau is still soft, lift the gâteau with a large icing spatula and support it on the fingertips of one hand. Take the chopped almonds in the palm of your other hand. Decorate the bottom edge of the gâteau with chopped almonds by pressing it against the almonds in your palm, then rotating the gâteau and repeating until you have covered the bottom edge with a band of nuts ⅜ to ½ inch (10 to 12 mm) high. Return the gâteau to the countertop.

3. Scoop the remaining buttercream into the pastry bag. Pipe the buttercream on the top of the gâteau in a decorative pattern. For example, make a lozenge pattern by piping one set of parallel lines separated by about 1 inch (2½ cm) and a second set of parallel lines on the diagonal with respect to the first set. Pipe tiny rosettes of buttercream at the intersections.

4. Refrigerate the gâteau until ready to serve.

VARIATION: Use chocolate buttercream instead of coffee but keep the coffee in the brushing syrup. Decorate the bottom edge of the gâteau with arcs of chocolate sprinkles (about ¼ cup = 35 g) instead of chopped almonds. To avoid any confusion, you can call the chocolate version *moka chocolat*.

STORAGE: In the refrigerator for up to 2 days.

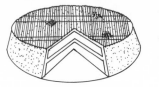

Fromage

Fromage is the French word for cheese, and this gâteau gets its name because it is decorated to look like a farmhouse Camembert. After frosting, you dust the outside of the gâteau with powdered roasted almonds or pulverized trimmings from one of the almond meringues, *succès* or *dijonnaise*. Then dust it all over with confectioners' sugar, and mark the top surface with the edge of an icing spatula to mimic the impression of a straw mat. Scatter some chopped pistachios in spots to simulate mold.

The presentation is very simple and very French. Today it is regarded as an old-fashioned, nostalgic cake, but at the end of the nineteenth century, it was considered radical. According to pastry chef Pierre Lacam in his *Mémorial de la Pâtisserie*, "This gâteau, which caused a furor, was created by a member of the association of *pâtissiers-cuisiniers* . . . In 1893, I could not imagine that it would last so long." So long indeed!

The allusion to cheese will probably be lost on most American guests, who are not likely to be so familiar with farmhouse Camembert that the image springs to mind. But it will certainly provide an opportunity for entertaining dinner table conversation.

We like to flavor the buttercream for *fromage* with *praliné*, and brush the génoise with kirsch. If you like anise flavor in your desserts, another good choice would be to flavor both buttercream and brushing syrup with anisette liqueur.

For 8 servings

EQUIPMENT:
9-inch (24-cm) foil board or matt board cake-decorating circle (page 467)
Optional: 8¾-inch (22-cm) cake ring (if the génoise was baked in one)

CAKE:

Génoise (page 82)	One round baked in • either a 9-inch (24-cm) cake pan • or an 8¾-inch (22-cm) cake ring

FILLING AND FROSTING:

Praliné buttercream (page 388)	12 ounces (340 g); 2 cups
Hazelnuts, finely chopped	1 ounce (25 g); 3 tablespoons

BRUSHING-SYRUP MIXTURE:

Heavy syrup (page 452)	⅓ cup (8 cL)
European kirsch	2 tablespoons + 2 teaspoons (4 cL)
Water	2 tablespoons + 2 teaspoons (4 cL)

DECORATION:

Either blanched almonds, roasted (page 444) and very finely chopped	1 ounce (30 g); ¼ cup
Or pulverized *dijonnaise* (page 146) or *succès* (page 148) trimmings	⅔ ounce (20 g); ¼ cup
Confectioners' sugar for dusting	
Finely chopped pistachios, or substitute chopped almonds tinted pale green with food coloring	1 teaspoon (4 g)

1. Assemble the gâteau from the génoise round (cut into two layers), buttercream filling and frosting, and kirsch brushing syrup either by the traditional freehand method (page 67) or by molding it (page 72) in the same ring in which the génoise was baked. Scatter the chopped hazelnuts over the layer of filling before placing the second layer of génoise on top.

2. While the buttercream on the outside of the gâteau is still soft, dust the top and sides of the gâteau with the powdered roasted almonds or pulverized nut-meringue trimmings.

3. Refrigerate the gâteau until ready to serve. Just before serving, lightly dust the top and sides of the gâteau with confectioners' sugar. Make a series of parallel lines on top by gently pressing the edge of an icing spatula on the surface of the buttercream; then make three pairs of lines in the perpendicular direction to complete the look of a straw mat. Finally, sprinkle the chopped pistachios in a few spots to simulate mold.

STORAGE: In the refrigerator for up to 2 days.

Mascotte

The *mascotte* is another of the classic génoise and buttercream gâteaux from the nineteenth century. It was created to honor the triumph of Audran's operetta *La Mascotte*, which opened in Paris in 1880. Here the buttercream is flavored with *praliné*, the génoise is brushed with kirsch syrup, and the top and sides of the gâteau are strewn with sliced almonds.

For 8 servings

EQUIPMENT:
Large heavy baking sheet
9-inch (24-cm) foil board or matt board cake-decorating circle (page 467)
Optional: 8¾-inch (22-cm) cake ring (if the génoise was baked in one)

DECORATION:

Sliced almonds	2 ounces (60 g); ½ cup + 2 tablespoons
Heavy syrup (page 452)	1 teaspoon (5 mL)
Confectioners' sugar for dusting	

CAKE:

Génoise (page 82)	One round baked in
or almond génoise (page 86)	• either a 9-inch (24-cm) cake pan
	• or an 8¾-inch (22-cm) cake ring

FILLING AND FROSTING:

Praliné buttercream (page 388)	12 ounces (340 g); 2 cups
Hazelnuts, finely chopped	1 ounce (25 g); 3 tablespoons

BRUSHING-SYRUP MIXTURE:

Heavy syrup	⅓ cup (8 cL)
European kirsch	2 tablespoons + 2 teaspoons (4 cL)
Water	2 tablespoons + 2 teaspoons (4 cL)

Preheat the oven to 350°F (175°C).

1. To prepare the sliced almonds for the decoration, toss them with the heavy syrup, spread them out on the baking sheet, and roast them in the preheated oven (stirring as needed after the first 5 minutes to prevent scorching), until lightly browned, about 10 minutes. Turn them out onto your countertop, and let cool.

2. Assemble the gâteau from the génoise round (cut into two layers), buttercream filling and frosting, and kirsch brushing syrup either by the traditional freehand method (page 67) or by molding it (page 72) in the same ring in which the génoise was baked. Scatter the chopped hazelnuts over the layer of filling before placing the second layer of génoise on top.

3. While the buttercream on the outside of the gâteau is still soft, lift the gâteau with a large icing spatula and support it on the fingertips of one hand. Take some roasted almonds in your other hand and scatter them over the sides of the gâteau, tilting the gâteau away from you and rotating it on your fingertips to coat the entire side evenly. If necessary, press the almonds against the side of the gâteau to make them adhere. Return the gâteau to the countertop and scatter the remaining roasted almonds over the top of the gâteau.

4. Refrigerate the gâteau until ready to serve. Just before serving, dust the top and sides of the gâteau lightly with confectioners' sugar.

VARIATION: Use coffee buttercream instead of *praliné*. Replace the kirsch and water in the brushing syrup with ⅓ cup (8 cL) double-strength brewed espresso (page 456). Call the gâteau *mascotte café*.

STORAGE: In the refrigerator for up to 2 days.

Succulent

Like *mascotte,* this gâteau is dusted with roasted sliced almonds. Here the buttercream is flavored with kirsch, and kirsch-soaked glacé fruits are embedded in the filling. For an even more luscious gâteau, you can add a layer of French meringue and a second layer of buttercream filling in the center.

For 8 servings

EQUIPMENT:

Large, heavy baking sheet
9-inch (24-cm) foil board or matt board cake-decorating circle (page 467)
Optional: 8¾-inch (22-cm) cake ring (if the génoise was baked in one)

FILLING AND FROSTING:

Glacé fruits, cut into ¼- to ⅜-inch (6- to 10-mm) dice	3 ounces (85 g)
European kirsch	3 tablespoons + 1 teaspoon (5 cL)
French buttercream (page 384)	13½ ounces (385 g); 2¼ cups

DECORATION:

Sliced almonds	2 ounces (60 g); ½ cup + 2 tablespoons
Heavy syrup (page 452)	1 teaspoon (5 mL)
Confectioners' sugar for dusting	

CAKE:

Génoise (page 82) or almond génoise (page 86)	One round baked in
	• either a 9-inch (24-cm) cake pan
	• or an 8¾-inch (22-cm) cake ring

BRUSHING-SYRUP MIXTURE:

Heavy syrup	⅓ cup (8 cL)
European kirsch	2 tablespoons + 2 teaspoons (4 cL)
Water	2 tablespoons + 2 teaspoons (4 cL)

1. Place the glacé fruits for the filling in a glass jar, pour 2 tablespoons (3 cL) of the kirsch over them, and stir to mix. Cover airtight and let steep in the kirsch for at least 2 hours and preferably overnight. When ready to make the gâteau, drain the fruits thoroughly.

Preheat the oven to 350°F (175°C).

2. To prepare the sliced almonds for the decoration, toss them with the heavy syrup, spread them out on the baking sheet, and roast them in the preheated oven (stirring as needed after the first 5 minutes to prevent scorching), until lightly browned, about 10 minutes. Turn them out onto your countertop, and let cool.

3. Flavor the buttercream with the remaining 4 teaspoons (2 cL) of kirsch for the filling and frosting. Assemble the gâteau from the génoise round (cut into two layers), kirsch buttercream filling and frosting, and kirsch brushing syrup either by the traditional freehand method (page 67) or by molding it (page 72) in the same ring in which the génoise was baked. Scatter the kirsch-soaked glacé fruits over the layer of filling before placing the second layer of génoise on top.

4. While the buttercream on the outside of the gâteau is still soft, lift the gâteau with a large icing spatula and support it on the fingertips of one hand. Take some roasted almonds in your other hand and scatter them over the sides of the gâteau, tilting the gâteau away from you and rotating it on your fingertips to coat the entire side evenly. If necessary, press the almonds against the side of the gâteau to make them adhere. Return the gâteau to the countertop and scatter the remaining roasted almonds over the top of the gâteau.

5. Refrigerate the gâteau until ready to serve. Just before serving, dust the top and sides of the gâteau lightly with confectioners' sugar.

VARIATION: To make a gâteau with more layers, you will need to add one 8¾-inch (22-cm) round of French meringue (page 190) and increase the quantities for the filling and frosting to:

Glacé fruits, cut into ¼- to ⅜-inch (6- to 10-mm) dice	5½ ounces (160 g)
European kirsch	¼ cup + 2 teaspoons (7 cL)
French buttercream	1 pound + 2 ounces (510 g); 3 cups

You can assemble the gâteau by the traditional freehand method; or if you have an extra-deep (5-cm) cake ring, you can assemble the gâteau in the ring.

Soak the glacé fruits in 3 tablespoons (4.5 cL) of the kirsch, and flavor the buttercream with the remaining kirsch. Carefully trim the round of meringue to a circle the size of the top of the génoise round. After you have spread buttercream over the bottom layer of génoise, scatter half of the kirsch-soaked glacé fruits over it and place the meringue round on top. Spread a layer of buttercream over the meringue, and scatter the remaining glacé fruits over the buttercream. Finish assembling the gâteau in the usual way.

continued

NOTE ON DECORATION: If you want a fancier decor, roll out some almond paste (page 428) about ³⁄₃₂ inch (2 mm) thick, and cut from it a writing card about 2 by 4 inches (5 by 10 cm). It can be a rectangle, a parallelogram, or some more fanciful shape. Place the writing card on the center of the gâteau. Make some writing chocolate (page 418) or royal icing (page 419), transfer about 1 tablespoon (1.5 cL) of it to a parchment decorating cone (page 416), and write an inscription (either the name of the gâteau or a message of your choice) on the writing card.

STORAGE: In the refrigerator for up to 2 days.

Thermidor

In the French Republican calendar, which replaced the Gregorian calendar during the Revolution, the eleventh month (which was actually in the summer) was called *Thermidor*. The Gregorian calendar was restored in 1806. Victorien Sardou's play *Thermidor* was even more short-lived; it closed immediately after its premiere in January 1894. Lobster thermidor was created for that opening night by either Maire's in the *boulevard St. Denis* or Leopold Mourier at the Café de Paris (both famous restaurants in Paris), depending on whom you believe. Whichever you choose, the lobster creation has had a substantially longer run than the play.

We aren't sure whether this gâteau was named for the month or the play, but its continued success is assured by a fortuitous choice of flavors: chocolate (génoise), chocolate (ganache filling and frosting), and more chocolate (glaze), highlighted with a double dose of rum (in the ganache and the brushing).

For 8 servings

EQUIPMENT:

9-inch (24-cm) foil board or matt board cake-decorating circle (page 467)
Optional: 8¾-inch (22-cm) cake ring (if the génoise was baked in one)
Chocolate thermometer or pocket digital thermometer
Parchment decorating cone (page 416)

CAKE:

Chocolate génoise (page 84)	One round baked in • either a 9-inch (24-cm) cake pan • or an 8¾-inch (22-cm) cake ring

FILLING AND FROSTING:

Rum ganache (page 400)	1 pound + 1¼ ounces (490 g); 2 cups

BRUSHING-SYRUP MIXTURE:

Heavy syrup (page 452)	⅓ cup (8 cL)
Dark Jamaican or Haitian rum	2 tablespoons + 2 teaspoons (4 cL)
Water	2 tablespoons + 2 teaspoons (4 cL)

continued

GLAZE:

European bittersweet chocolate, melted	9 ounces (250 g)
Clarified butter (page 449), at room temperature	1½ ounces (40 g); 3 tablespoons

DECORATION FOR BOTTOM EDGE OF GÂTEAU:

Chocolate sprinkles	1¼ ounces (35 g); ¼ cup

DECORATION FOR TOP OF GÂTEAU:

Heavy syrup, heated to lukewarm	1 tablespoon (1.5 cL)
Unsweetened chocolate, melted	½ ounce (15 g)

1. Assemble the gâteau from the chocolate génoise round (cut into two layers), ganache filling and frosting, and rum brushing syrup either by the traditional freehand method (page 67) or by molding it (page 72) in the same ring in which the génoise was baked.

2. Place the gâteau on a wire rack and chill in the refrigerator until the ganache is firm, at least 1 hour.

3. If you did not melt the chocolate for the glaze in a stainless steel bowl, transfer it to one. Temper the chocolate as follows: Dip the bottom of the bowl of chocolate in a larger bowl of cold water and stir the chocolate until the temperature drops to between 80° and 84°F (26.5° to 29°C) and it begins to thicken. Immediately remove from the cold water and dip the bottom of the bowl of chocolate in a larger bowl of hot water. Stir over the hot water just long enough to warm the chocolate to between 86° and 91°F (30° to 33°C) and make it more fluid again. Then remove from the hot water immediately. Beat the clarified butter with a wooden spatula until smooth and creamy, then stir it into the chocolate.

4. Pour the chocolate on the top of the gâteau in a circle just inside the perimeter so that some of it flows naturally over the edges. Quickly smooth the top surface with the edge of a large icing spatula to cover the entire top with a thin layer of glaze and make the excess flow evenly down the sides. Touch up any uneven areas around the sides with the edge of the icing spatula. Let the chocolate begin to thicken, then clean off any excess chocolate around the bottom edge.

5. Before the chocolate glaze sets, lift the gâteau from the wire rack with a large icing spatula and support it on the fingertips of one hand. Take the chocolate sprinkles in the palm of your other hand. Finish the bottom edge of the gâteau by pressing it against the sprinkles in your palm, then rotating the gâteau and repeating until you have covered the bottom edge with a band of sprinkles ⅜ to ½ inch (10 to 12 mm) high. Place the gâteau on a serving plate and let the chocolate glaze set.

6. Gradually stir the heavy syrup into the melted chocolate. The chocolate will thicken and will probably seize, becoming thick and granular. Keep adding heavy syrup until the chocolate becomes smooth and fluid again. Add only as much syrup as necessary to make this "writing chocolate" smooth and soft enough to pipe from a parchment decorating cone.

7. Spoon 1 tablespoon (1.5 cL) of the writing chocolate into the parchment decorating cone, fold over the back end to close it, and cut the tip. Pipe a scroll pattern around the rim of the gâteau, and write *Thermidor* across the center. Or, if you prefer, you can write another inscription on top of the gâteau.

8. Refrigerate the gâteau until ready to serve.

VARIATION: If you assemble the *thermidor* in a cake ring, then there is an alternative way to finish the gâteau. Glaze only the top before unmolding. Then after unmolding, coat the entire side of the gâteau with chocolate sprinkles or, better yet, chocolate shavings (page 423).

STORAGE: In the refrigerator for up to 2 days.

Délicieux

For this gâteau you need a well-stocked pantry, since it requires ganache for the filling and French buttercream for the frosting. You flavor both buttercream and ganache with Grand Marnier, and glaze the gâteau with chocolate. *Délicieux* indeed! If you are even more ambitious, add a round of French meringue and an extra layer of buttercream filling in the center.

For 8 servings

EQUIPMENT:

9-inch (24-cm) foil board or matt board cake-decorating circle (page 467)
Optional: 8¾-inch (22-cm) cake ring (if the génoise was baked in one)
Chocolate thermometer or pocket digital thermometer
Parchment decorating cone (page 416)
Small pastry bag fitted with
· ³⁄₁₆-inch (4-mm) plain pastry tube (Ateco #0)

FROSTING:

French buttercream (page 384)	9 ounces (250 g); 1½ cups
Grand Marnier	2½ teaspoons (1.3 cL)
Red food coloring	

CAKE:

Génoise (page 82)	One round baked in
	· either a 9-inch (24-cm) cake pan
	· or an 8¾-inch (22-cm) cake ring

FILLING:

Grand Marnier ganache (page 400)	5¾ ounces (165 g); ⅔ cup

BRUSHING-SYRUP MIXTURE:

Heavy syrup (page 452)	⅓ cup (8 cL)
Grand Marnier	2 tablespoons + 2 teaspoons (4 cL)
Water	2 tablespoons + 2 teaspoons (4 cL)

GLAZE:

European bittersweet chocolate, melted	9 ounces (250 g)
Clarified butter (page 449), at room temperature	1½ ounces (40 g); 3 tablespoons

DECORATION FOR BOTTOM EDGE OF GÂTEAU:

Chocolate sprinkles	1¼ ounces (35 g); ¼ cup

DECORATION FOR TOP OF GÂTEAU:

Heavy syrup, heated to lukewarm	1 tablespoon (1.5 cL)
Unsweetened chocolate, melted	½ ounce (15 g)

1. Flavor the buttercream with Grand Marnier, and tint it a pale pink color with a couple of drops of red food coloring. Assemble the gâteau from the génoise round (cut into two layers), ganache filling, Grand Marnier brushing syrup, and Grand Marnier buttercream frosting either by the traditional freehand method (page 67) or by molding it (page 72) in the same ring in which the génoise was baked. Save about ¼ cup (45 g) of excess buttercream for piping on top of the gâteau.

2. Place the gâteau on a wire rack and chill in the refrigerator until the buttercream is firm, at least 1 hour.

3. If you did not melt the chocolate for the glaze in a stainless steel bowl, transfer it to one. Temper the chocolate as follows: Dip the bottom of the bowl of chocolate in a larger bowl of cold water and stir the chocolate until the temperature drops to between 80° and 84°F (26.5° to 29°C) and it begins to thicken. Immediately remove from the cold water and dip the bottom of the bowl of chocolate in a larger bowl of hot water. Stir over the hot water just long enough to warm the chocolate to between 86° and 91°F (30° to 33°C) and make it more fluid again. Then remove from the hot water immediately. Beat the clarified butter with a wooden spatula until smooth and creamy, then stir it into the chocolate.

4. Pour the chocolate on the top of the gâteau in a circle just inside the perimeter so that some of it flows naturally over the edges. Quickly smooth the top surface with the edge of a large icing spatula to cover the entire top with a thin layer of glaze and make the excess flow evenly down the sides. Touch up any uneven areas around the sides with the edge of the icing spatula. Let the chocolate begin to thicken, then clean off any excess chocolate around the bottom edge.

5. Before the chocolate glaze sets, lift the gâteau from the wire rack with a large icing spatula and support it on the fingertips of one hand. Take the chocolate sprinkles in the palm of your other hand. Finish the bottom edge of the gâteau by pressing it against the sprinkles in your palm, then rotating the gâteau and repeating until you have covered the bottom edge with a band of sprinkles ⅜ to ½ inch (10 to 12 mm) high. Place the gâteau on a serving plate and let the chocolate glaze set.

continued

6. Gradually stir the heavy syrup into the melted chocolate. The chocolate will thicken and will probably seize, becoming thick and granular. Keep adding heavy syrup until the chocolate becomes smooth and fluid again. Add only as much syrup as necessary to make this "writing chocolate" smooth and soft enough to pipe from a parchment decorating cone.

7. Spoon 1 tablespoon (1.5 cL) of the writing chocolate into the parchment decorating cone, fold over the back end to close it, and cut the tip. Write *Délicieux* across the center of the gâteau. Or, if you prefer, you can write another inscription on top of the gâteau.

8. Transfer the reserved buttercream to the pastry bag and pipe a rope of buttercream about ¼ inch (6 mm) in diameter around the perimeter of the top of the gâteau.

9. Refrigerate the gâteau until ready to serve.

VARIATION: To make a gâteau with more layers, you will need to add one 8¾-inch (22-cm) round of French meringue (page 190) and increase the quantity of buttercream and liqueur for frosting and filling to:

French buttercream	15 ounces (425 g); 2½ cups
Grand Marnier	1 tablespoon + 1 teaspoon (2 cL)

Increase the amounts of chocolate and clarified butter for the glaze to:

European bittersweet chocolate, melted	12 ounces (350 g)
Clarified butter, at room temperature	1¾ ounces (50g); 3½ tablespoons

You can assemble the gâteau by the traditional freehand method; or if you have an extra-deep (5-cm) cake ring, you can assemble the gâteau in the ring.

Carefully trim the round of meringue to a circle the size of the top of the génoise round. Spread a layer of buttercream over the bottom layer of génoise and place the meringue round on top. Spread the ganache over the meringue, then finish assembling the gâteau in the usual way.

STORAGE: In the refrigerator for up to 2 days.

Caraïbe

If you like the combination of orange and chocolate, this gâteau is for you. The filling is Seville orange marmalade, the frosting is curaçao-flavored buttercream, and the glaze is chocolate. The bittersweet flavors and moist, rich textures conspire to produce a simple gâteau that is shockingly sensual.

The name *caraïbe*, which is French for Caribbean, refers to the origin of both curaçao liqueur and chocolate.

For 8 servings

EQUIPMENT:
9-inch (24-cm) foil board or matt board cake-decorating circle (page 467)
Chocolate thermometer or pocket digital thermometer
Optional: 8¾-inch (22-cm) cake ring (if the génoise was baked in one)
Parchment decorating cone (page 416)

FROSTING:

French buttercream (page 384)	9 ounces (250 g); 1½ cups
Curaçao liqueur	2½ teaspoons (1.3 cL)
Red and yellow food colorings	

CAKE:

Génoise (page 82)	One round baked in
	• either a 9-inch (24-cm) cake pan
	• or an 8¾-inch (22-cm) cake ring

FILLING:

Seville orange marmalade (thin cut)	6½ ounces (180 g); ½ cup + 1 tablespoon

BRUSHING-SYRUP MIXTURE:

Heavy syrup (page 452)	⅓ cup (8 cL)
Curaçao liqueur	2 tablespoons + 2 teaspoons (4 cL)
Water	2 tablespoons + 2 teaspoons (4 cL)

continued

GLAZE:

European bittersweet chocolate, melted	9 ounces (250 g)
Clarified butter (page 449), at room temperature	1½ ounces (40 g); 3 tablespoons

DECORATION FOR BOTTOM EDGE OF GÂTEAU:

Chocolate sprinkles	1¼ ounces (35 g); ¼ cup

DECORATION FOR TOP OF GÂTEAU:

Heavy syrup, heated to lukewarm	1 tablespoon (1.5 cL)
Unsweetened chocolate, melted	½ ounce (15 g)

1. Flavor the buttercream with the curaçao liqueur, and tint it a pale peach color with a couple of drops of red and yellow food colorings. Assemble the gâteau from the génoise round (cut into two layers), marmalade filling, curaçao buttercream frosting, and curaçao brushing syrup either by the traditional freehand method (page 67) or by molding it (page 72) in the same ring in which the génoise was baked.

2. Place the gâteau on a wire rack and chill in the refrigerator until the buttercream is firm, at least 1 hour.

3. If you did not melt the chocolate for the glaze in a stainless steel bowl, transfer it to one. Temper the chocolate as follows: Dip the bottom of the bowl of chocolate in a larger bowl of cold water and stir the chocolate until the temperature drops to between 80° and 84°F (26.5° to 29°C) and it begins to thicken. Immediately remove from the cold water and dip the bottom of the bowl of chocolate in a larger bowl of hot water. Stir over the hot water just long enough to warm the chocolate to between 86° and 91°F (30° to 33°C) and make it more fluid again. Then remove from the hot water immediately. Beat the clarified butter with a wooden spatula until smooth and creamy, then stir it into the chocolate.

4. Pour the chocolate on the top of the gâteau in a circle just inside the perimeter so that some of it flows naturally over the edges. Quickly smooth the top surface with the edge of a large icing spatula to cover the entire top with a thin layer of glaze and make the excess flow evenly down the sides. Touch up any uneven areas around the sides with the edge of the icing spatula. Let the chocolate begin to thicken, then clean off any excess chocolate around the bottom edge.

5. Before the chocolate glaze sets, lift the gâteau from the wire rack with a large icing spatula and support it on the fingertips of one hand. Take the chocolate sprinkles in the palm of your other hand. Finish the bottom edge of the gâteau by pressing it against the sprinkles in your palm, then rotating the gâteau and repeating until you have covered the bottom edge with a band of sprinkles ⅜ to ½ inch (10 to 12 mm) high. Place the gâteau on a serving plate and let the chocolate glaze set.

6. Gradually stir the heavy syrup into the melted chocolate. The chocolate will thicken and will probably seize, becoming thick and granular. Keep adding heavy syrup until the chocolate becomes smooth and fluid again. Add only as much syrup as necessary to make this "writing chocolate" smooth and soft enough to pipe from a parchment decorating cone.

7. Spoon 1 tablespoon (1.5 cL) of the writing chocolate into the parchment decorating cone, fold over the back end to close it, and cut the tip. Write *Caraïbe* across the center of the gâteau. Or, if you prefer, you can write another inscription on top of the gâteau.

8. Refrigerate the gâteau until ready to serve.

STORAGE: In the refrigerator for up to 2 days.

Ardechois

The Ardeche region in southeastern France is famous for chestnuts. This gâteau is filled and frosted with chestnut buttercream and glazed with chocolate. The classic accent flavor would be rum, but we recommend Kentucky bourbon as an even better choice to highlight the flavor of the chestnuts.

For 8 servings

EQUIPMENT:
9-inch (24-cm) foil board or matt board cake-decorating circle (page 467)
Optional: 8¾-inch (22-cm) cake ring (if the génoise was baked in one)
Chocolate thermometer or pocket digital thermometer
Parchment decorating cone (page 416)

CAKE:
Génoise (page 82)	One round baked in
	• either a 9-inch (24-cm) cake pan
	• or an 8¾-inch (22-cm) cake ring

FILLING AND FROSTING:
Chestnut buttercream flavored with bourbon (page 402)	12½ ounces (360 g); 2 cups

BRUSHING-SYRUP MIXTURE:
Heavy syrup (page 452)	⅓ cup (8 cL)
Kentucky bourbon	2 tablespoons + 2 teaspoons (4 cL)
Water	2 tablespoons + 2 teaspoons (4 cL)

GLAZE:
European bittersweet chocolate, melted	9 ounces (250 g)
Clarified butter (page 449), at room temperature	1½ ounces (40 g); 3 tablespoons

DECORATION FOR BOTTOM EDGE OF GÂTEAU:
Chocolate sprinkles	1¼ ounces (35 g); ¼ cup

DECORATION FOR TOP OF GÂTEAU:

Heavy syrup, heated to lukewarm	1 tablespoon (1.5 cL)
Unsweetened chocolate, melted	½ ounce (15 g)

1. Assemble the gâteau from the génoise round (cut into two layers), chestnut buttercream filling and frosting, and bourbon brushing syrup either by the traditional freehand method (page 67) or by molding it (page 72) in the same ring in which the génoise was baked.

2. Place the gâteau on a wire rack and chill in the refrigerator until the buttercream is firm, at least 1 hour.

3. If you did not melt the chocolate for the glaze in a stainless steel bowl, transfer it to one. Temper the chocolate as follows: Dip the bottom of the bowl of chocolate in a larger bowl of cold water and stir the chocolate until the temperature drops to between 80° and 84°F (26.5° to 29°C) and it begins to thicken. Immediately remove from the cold water and dip the bottom of the bowl of chocolate in a larger bowl of hot water. Stir over the hot water just long enough to warm the chocolate to between 86° and 91°F (30° to 33°C) and make it more fluid again. Then remove from the hot water immediately. Beat the clarified butter with a wooden spatula until smooth and creamy, then stir it into the chocolate.

4. Pour the chocolate on the top of the gâteau in a circle just inside the perimeter so that some of it flows naturally over the edges. Quickly smooth the top surface with the edge of a large icing spatula to cover the entire top with a thin layer of glaze and make the excess flow evenly down the sides. Touch up any uneven areas around the sides with the edge of the icing spatula. Let the chocolate begin to thicken, then clean off any excess chocolate around the bottom edge.

5. Before the chocolate glaze sets, lift the gâteau from the wire rack with a large icing spatula and support it on the fingertips of one hand. Take the chocolate sprinkles in the palm of your other hand. Finish the bottom edge of the gâteau by pressing it against the sprinkles in your palm, then rotating the gâteau and repeating until you have covered the bottom edge with a band of sprinkles ⅜ to ½ inch (10 to 12 mm) high. Place the gâteau on a serving plate and let the chocolate glaze set.

6. Gradually stir the heavy syrup into the melted chocolate. The chocolate will thicken and will probably seize, becoming thick and granular. Keep adding heavy syrup until the chocolate becomes smooth and fluid again. Add only as much syrup as necessary to make this "writing chocolate" smooth and soft enough to pipe from a parchment decorating cone.

7. Spoon 1 tablespoon (1.5 cL) of the writing chocolate into the parchment decorating cone, fold over the back end to close it, and cut the tip. Pipe a scroll pattern around the rim of the gâteau, and write *Ardechois* across the center. Or if you prefer, you can write another inscription on top of the gâteau.

8. Refrigerate the gâteau until ready to serve.

STORAGE: In the refrigerator for up to 2 days.

Noëlla

A very pretty chocolate gâteau, *noëlla* is topped with concentric circles of chocolate petals. The petals are labor intensive, but fun to make, and the finished product will definitely impress your friends.

Noëlla is a girl's Christian name in France, and we suspect that such a feminine gâteau was created for a special young lady.

For 8 servings

EQUIPMENT:

9-inch (24-cm) foil board or matt board cake-decorating circle (page 467)
Optional: 8¾-inch (22-cm) cake ring (if the génoise was baked in one)
Small pastry bag fitted with
• fluted decorating tube (such as Ateco #17 open star tube)

CAKE:

Génoise (page 82), or chocolate génoise (page 84)	One round baked in • either a 9-inch (24-cm) cake pan • or an 8¾-inch (22-cm) cake ring

FILLING, FROSTING, AND PIPING:

Chocolate buttercream (page 388)	13½ ounces (385 g); 2¼ cups

BRUSHING-SYRUP MIXTURE:

Heavy syrup (page 452)	⅓ cup (8 cL)
Pure vanilla extract	¾ teaspoon (4 mL)
Water	⅓ cup (8 cL)

DECORATION FOR SIDE OF GÂTEAU:

Chocolate sprinkles	1¼ ounces (35 g); ¼ cup

DECORATION FOR TOP OF GÂTEAU:

Petals for *noëlla* (page 426)	About 100
Confectioners' sugar for dusting	

1. Assemble the gâteau from the génoise round (cut into two layers), buttercream filling and frosting, and vanilla brushing syrup either by the traditional freehand method (page 67) or by molding it (page 72) in the same ring in which the génoise was baked. Save at least ¼ cup (45 g) of excess buttercream for piping on top of the gâteau.

2. While the buttercream on the outside of the gâteau is still soft, lift the gâteau with a large icing spatula and support it on the fingertips of one hand. Take the chocolate sprinkles in the palm of your other hand. Decorate the side of the gâteau with arcs of sprinkles by pressing it against the sprinkles in your palm, then rotating the gâteau and repeating until you have made adjacent arcs of sprinkles all the way around the gâteau. Return the gâteau to the countertop.

3. Scoop the remaining buttercream into the pastry bag. Pipe four concentric circles of buttercream on top of the gâteau, starting on the outside rim and separating the circles by about 1 inch (2.5 cm). Then arrange the *noëlla* petals on top in concentric pinwheel-like circles, propping them up against the buttercream circles and overlapping them slightly. Use the largest petals for the outer circle and the smallest ones for the inner circle. Pipe a rosette of buttercream in the center of the gâteau.

4. Refrigerate the gâteau until ready to serve. Then dust the top very lightly with confectioners' sugar.

STORAGE: In the refrigerator for up to 2 days.

Marguerite Cassis

. . . .

We rarely see black currant desserts in the United States, but in France they are very popular. This gâteau gets its black currant flavor from a combination of black currant preserves and crème de cassis liqueur. You will wrap the side of the gâteau in a wide strip of chocolate, and decorate the top with several slender chocolate strips to make a daisy shape.

For 8 servings

EQUIPMENT:

9-inch (24-cm) foil board or matt board cake-decorating circle (page 467)
8¾-inch (22-cm) cake ring
Large, heavy baking sheet, preferably black steel or stainless steel
Flexible drywall knife with 2-inch- (5-cm-) wide blade (page 469)

FILLING AND FROSTING:

Black currant preserves	4½ ounces (130 g); ¼ cup + 2½ tablespoons
French buttercream (page 384)	9½ ounces (270 g); 1⅔ cups
Crème de cassis liqueur	1 tablespoon + 1 teaspoon (2 cL)

CAKE:

Almond génoise (page 86)	One round baked in
	• an 8¾-inch (22-cm) cake ring

BRUSHING-SYRUP MIXTURE:

Heavy syrup (page 452)	¼ cup (6 cL)
Crème de cassis liqueur	¼ cup + 2 tablespoons (9 cL)
Water	2 tablespoons (3 cL)

DECORATION:

European bittersweet chocolate	Large bar or block weighing at least
	10½ ounces (300 g)
Confectioners' sugar for dusting	

1. Beat the black currant preserves into the buttercream. Then beat in the cassis liqueur. Assemble the gâteau from the génoise round (cut into two layers), flavored buttercream, and cassis brushing syrup by molding it (page 72) in the same ring in which the génoise was baked.

2. Place the gâteau on a tray and chill in the refrigerator until the buttercream is firm, at least 1 hour.

Preheat the oven to 250°F (120°C).

3. Put the baking sheet in the oven for about 10 minutes to heat it. Place the hot baking sheet on your countertop (with a kitchen towel underneath if necessary to protect your countertop) and rub the block of chocolate over it to melt the chocolate and cover the baking sheet evenly. Melt about 5¼ ounces (150 g) of the chocolate for a 12 × 16-inch (30 × 40-cm) baking sheet or 7 ounces (200 g) for a 13 × 20-inch (33 × 50-cm) baking sheet. When you have enough chocolate melted, smooth the surface with the edge of the block. Place the baking sheet in the refrigerator until the chocolate begins to set. Remove it from the refrigerator to allow the temperature of the chocolate to even out, then continue moving it in and out of the refrigerator until you can scrape chocolate off the baking sheet without it sticking to the drywall knife (indicating the chocolate is still too soft) or shattering (the chocolate is too hard).

4. Use the drywall knife to lift a 2-inch- (5-cm-) wide strip of chocolate off the baking sheet. (For more details on the procedure, see page 425.) Wrap the strip around the side of the gâteau. It will not be long enough to go all the way around, so lift off a second strip, wrap it around the remainder of the side of the gâteau, and trim it with a heated knife blade so the two strips just meet, with no overlap.

5. Now use the drywall knife to lift from the baking sheet a strip of chocolate about ¾ inch (2 cm) wide and 4 inches (10 cm) long. Bend this strip into a circle, and stand the circle on its edge on the center of the top of the gâteau. Finally, you will need five strips ¾ inch (2 cm) wide and 7 to 8 inches (18 to 20 cm) long. One at a time, lift off each strip, and form it into the outline of a teardrop-shaped petal standing on edge on the top of the gâteau, with the tip of the teardrop touching the chocolate circle in the center. Place each petal adjacent to the previous one so that when you are finished the petals form a flower on top of the gâteau.

6. Refrigerate the gâteau until ready to serve. Then dust the top lightly with confectioners' sugar.

STORAGE: In the refrigerator for up to 2 days.

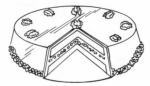

Grenoblois

The city of Grenoble in the French Alps is famous for walnuts. For this gâteau, you will fill and frost a génoise round with coffee buttercream, adding chopped walnuts to the filling. Then glaze the gâteau with coffee fondant and decorate it with walnut halves.

For 8 servings

EQUIPMENT:

9-inch (24-cm) foil board or matt board cake-decorating circle (page 467)
Optional: 8¾-inch (22-cm) cake ring (if the génoise was baked in one)
Small pastry bag fitted with
• fluted decorating tube (such as Ateco #17 open star tube)

CAKE:

Génoise (page 82)	One round baked in
	• either a 9-inch (24-cm) cake pan
	• or an 8¾-inch (22-cm) cake ring

FILLING AND FROSTING:

Coffee buttercream (page 390)	14 ounces (400 g); 2¼ cups
Walnuts, finely chopped	1 ounce (25 g); 3 tablespoons

BRUSHING-SYRUP MIXTURE:

Heavy syrup (page 452)	⅓ cup (8 cL)
Double-strength brewed espresso (page 456)	⅓ cup (8 cL)

GLAZE:

Fondant (page 408)	1 pound (450 g); 1⅓ cups
Double-strength brewed espresso	2 tablespoons (3 cL)
Caramel food coloring (page 457; optional)	1 tablespoon (1.5 cL)
Heavy syrup	As needed

DECORATION FOR BOTTOM EDGE OF GÂTEAU:

Walnuts, finely chopped	1 ounce (25 g); ¼ cup

DECORATION FOR TOP OF GÂTEAU:

Walnut halves	9

1. Assemble the gâteau from the génoise round (cut into two layers), buttercream filling and frosting, and espresso brushing syrup either by the traditional freehand method (page 67) or by molding it (page 72) in the same ring in which the génoise was baked. Scatter the chopped walnuts over the layer of filling before placing the second layer of génoise on top. Save about ¼ cup (45 g) of excess buttercream for piping on top of the gâteau.

2. Place the gâteau on a wire rack and chill in the refrigerator until the buttercream is firm, at least 1 hour.

3. Warm the fondant in a heavy 1-quart (1-L) saucepan over low heat, stirring constantly until melted. Mix in the espresso to flavor and color the fondant, and add the optional caramel food coloring to deepen the color. Stir in just enough heavy syrup to thin the fondant to the consistency of heavy cream. The temperature of the fondant must be between 100° and 105°F (38° to 40°C).

4. Pour the fondant on the top of the gâteau in a circle just inside the perimeter so that some of it flows naturally over the edges. Quickly smooth the top surface with the edge of a large icing spatula to cover the entire top with a thin layer of glaze and make the excess flow evenly down the sides. Touch up any uneven areas around the sides with the edge of the icing spatula. Let the fondant begin to thicken, then clean off any excess fondant around the bottom edge.

5. Before the fondant starts to set, lift the gâteau from the wire rack with a large icing spatula and support it on the fingertips of one hand. Take the chopped walnuts in the palm of your other hand. Finish the bottom edge of the gâteau by pressing it against the chopped nuts in your palm, then rotating the gâteau and repeating until you have covered the bottom edge with a band of chopped nuts ⅜ to ½ inch (10 to 12 mm) high. Place the gâteau on a serving plate and let the fondant set.

6. Scoop the excess buttercream into the pastry bag, and pipe eight rosettes of buttercream in a circle around the circumference of the gâteau. Pipe one rosette on the center. Place a walnut half on each rosette.

7. Refrigerate the gâteau until ready to serve.

STORAGE: In the refrigerator for up to 2 days.

Noisetier

True to its name (*noisetier* is the French word for a hazel tree), this gâteau is redolent of hazelnuts, from the *praliné* buttercream and chopped hazelnuts inside and around the bottom edge to the whole hazelnuts decorating the top. The gâteau is glazed with fondant.

For 8 servings

EQUIPMENT:

9-inch (24-cm) foil board or matt board cake-decorating circle (page 467)
Optional: 8¾-inch (22-cm) cake ring (if the génoise was baked in one)
Small pastry bag fitted with
• fluted decorating tube (such as Ateco #17 open star tube)

CAKE:

Génoise (page 82)	One round baked in
	• either a 9-inch (24-cm) cake pan
	• or an 8¾-inch (22-cm) cake ring

FILLING AND FROSTING:

Praliné buttercream (page 388)	13½ ounces (385 g); 2¼ cups
Hazelnuts, finely chopped	1 ounce (25 g); 3 tablespoons

BRUSHING-SYRUP MIXTURE:

Heavy syrup (page 452)	⅓ cup (8 cL)
European kirsch	2 tablespoons + 2 teaspoons (4 cL)
Water	2 tablespoons + 2 teaspoons (4 cL)

GLAZE:

Fondant (page 408)	1 pound (450 g); 1⅓ cups
Caramel food coloring (page 457)	1 tablespoon (1.5 cL)
Heavy syrup	As needed

DECORATION FOR BOTTOM EDGE OF GÂTEAU:

Hazelnuts, finely chopped	1 ounce (25 g); 3 tablespoons

DECORATION FOR TOP OF GÂTEAU:

Blanched (page 445) or raw hazelnuts	13

1. Assemble the gâteau from the génoise round (cut into two layers), buttercream filling and frosting, and kirsch brushing syrup either by the traditional freehand method (page 67) or by molding it (page 72) in the same ring in which the génoise was baked. Scatter the chopped hazelnuts over the layer of filling before placing the second layer of génoise on top. Save about ¼ cup (45 g) of excess buttercream for piping on top of the gâteau.

2. Place the gâteau on a wire rack and chill in the refrigerator until the buttercream is firm, at least 1 hour.

3. Warm the fondant in a heavy 1-quart (1-L) saucepan over low heat, stirring constantly until melted. Mix in the caramel food coloring to color the fondant. Stir in just enough heavy syrup to thin the fondant to the consistency of heavy cream. The temperature of the fondant must be between 100° and 105°F (38° to 40°C).

4. Pour the fondant on the top of the gâteau in a circle just inside the perimeter so that some of it flows naturally over the edges. Quickly smooth the top surface with the edge of a large icing spatula to cover the entire top with a thin layer of glaze and make the excess flow evenly down the sides. Touch up any uneven areas around the sides with the edge of the icing spatula. Let the fondant begin to thicken, then clean off any excess fondant around the bottom edge.

5. Before the fondant starts to set, lift the gâteau from the wire rack with a large icing spatula and support it on the fingertips of one hand. Take the chopped hazelnuts in the palm of your other hand. Finish the bottom edge of the gâteau by pressing it against the chopped nuts in your palm, then rotating the gâteau and repeating until you have covered the bottom edge with a band of chopped nuts ⅜ to ½ inch (10 to 12 mm) high. Place the gâteau on a serving plate and let the fondant set.

6. Scoop the excess buttercream into the pastry bag, and pipe twelve rosettes of buttercream in a circle around the circumference of the gâteau. Pipe one rosette on the center, and four teardrops pointing out from the center. Place a hazelnut on each rosette.

7. Refrigerate the gâteau until ready to serve.

STORAGE: In the refrigerator for up to 2 days.

Romeo

Raisins and rum make a perfect marriage in this romantic-sounding gâteau. Actually, the name derives from the French word for rum; it is spelled *rhum*, but pronounced *rome*.

For 8 servings

EQUIPMENT:

9-inch (24-cm) foil board or matt board cake-decorating circle (page 467)

Optional: 8¾-inch (22-cm) cake ring (if the génoise was baked in one)

FILLING AND FROSTING:

Seedless golden raisins	2½ ounces (70 g); ¼ cup + 3 tablespoons
Dark Jamaican or Haitian rum	3 tablespoons + 1 teaspoon (5 cL)
French buttercream (page 384)	12 ounces (340 g); 2 cups

CAKE:

Génoise (page 82)	One round baked in
	• either a 9-inch (24-cm) cake pan
	• or an 8¾-inch (22-cm) cake ring

BRUSHING-SYRUP MIXTURE:

Heavy syrup (page 452)	⅓ cup (8 cL)
Dark Jamaican or Haitian rum	2 tablespoons + 2 teaspoons (4 cL)
Water	2 tablespoons + 2 teaspoons (4 cL)

DECORATION FOR TOP OF GÂTEAU:

Seedless golden raisins	⅓ ounce (10 g); 1 tablespoon

GLAZE:

Fondant (page 408)	1 pound (450 g); 1⅓ cups
Heavy syrup	As needed

DECORATION FOR BOTTOM EDGE OF GÂTEAU:

Chocolate sprinkles	1½ ounces (35 g); 2 tablespoons

1. Place the raisins for the filling in a strainer and steam them over simmering water until they just begin to soften, about 5 minutes. Transfer the raisins to a glass jar, pour 2 tablespoons

(3 cL) of the rum over them, and stir to mix. Cover airtight and let steep in the rum for at least 2 hours and preferably overnight. When ready to make the gâteau, drain the raisins thoroughly.

2. Flavor the buttercream with the remaining 4 teaspoons (2 cL) of rum for the filling and frosting. Assemble the gâteau from the génoise round (cut into two layers), buttercream filling and frosting, and rum brushing syrup either by the traditional freehand method (page 67) or by molding it (page 72) in the same ring in which the génoise was baked. Scatter the rum-soaked raisins over the layer of filling before placing the second layer of génoise on top. Arrange the unsoaked raisins for decoration in a circle on top of the gâteau, and gently press them into the buttercream while it is still soft.

3. Place the gâteau on a wire rack and chill in the refrigerator until the buttercream is firm, at least 1 hour.

4. Warm the fondant in a heavy 1-quart (1-L) saucepan over low heat, stirring constantly until melted. Stir in just enough heavy syrup to thin the fondant to the consistency of heavy cream. The temperature of the fondant must be between 100° and 105°F (38° to 40°C).

5. Pour the fondant on the top of the gâteau in a circle just inside the perimeter so that some of it flows naturally over the edges. Quickly smooth the top surface with the edge of a large icing spatula to cover the entire top with a thin layer of glaze and make the excess flow evenly down the sides. Touch up any uneven areas around the sides with the edge of the icing spatula. Let the fondant begin to thicken, then clean off any excess fondant around the bottom edge.

6. Before the fondant starts to set, lift the gâteau from the wire rack with a large icing spatula and support it on the fingertips of one hand. Take the chocolate sprinkles in the palm of your other hand. Decorate the side of the gâteau with arcs of sprinkles by pressing it against the sprinkles in your palm, then rotating the gâteau and repeating until you have made adjacent arcs of sprinkles all the way around the gâteau. Place the gâteau on a serving plate and let the fondant set.

STORAGE: In the refrigerator for up to 2 days.

Grand Marnier

A sheet of almond paste draped in gently flowing asymmetrical folds gives this gâteau a very contemporary look. Paul Bugat devised the presentation around 1970, yet it still looks fresh and original today.

For 8 servings

EQUIPMENT:

9-inch (24-cm) foil board or matt board cake-decorating circle (page 467)
Optional: 8¾-inch (22-cm) cake ring (if the génoise was baked in one)
Chocolate thermometer or pocket digital thermometer
Icing spatula with very flexible blade 8 inches (20 cm) long
Rolling pin

FILLING AND FROSTING:

Glacé fruits, cut into ¼- to ⅜-inch (6- to 10-mm) dice	3 ounces (85 g)
Grand Marnier	3 tablespoons + 1 teaspoon (5 cL)
French buttercream (page 384)	12 ounces (340 g); 2 cups
Red and yellow food colorings	

CAKE:

Génoise (see page 82)	One round baked in
	• either a 9-inch (24-cm) cake pan
	• or an 8¾-inch (22-cm) cake ring

BRUSHING-SYRUP MIXTURE:

Heavy syrup (page 452)	⅓ cup (8 cL)
Grand Marnier	2 tablespoons + 2 teaspoons (4 cL)
Water	2 tablespoons + 2 teaspoons (4 cL)

DECORATION FOR SIDE OF GÂTEAU:

European bittersweet chocolate, melted	3 ounces (85 g)
Clarified butter (page 449), at room temperature	1 teaspoon (5 mL)

Almond paste (page 432)   4½ ounces (125 g)
Red food coloring
Confectioners' sugar for dusting

1. Place the glacé fruits for the filling in a glass jar, pour 2 tablespoons (3 cL) of the Grand Marnier over them, and stir to mix. Cover airtight and let steep in the Grand Marnier for at least 2 hours and preferably overnight. When ready to make the gâteau, drain the fruits thoroughly.

2. Flavor the buttercream with the remaining 4 teaspoons (2 cL) of Grand Marnier for the filling and frosting, and tint it a pale peach color with a couple of drops of red food coloring plus a drop of yellow food coloring. Assemble the gâteau from the génoise round (cut into two layers), Grand Marnier buttercream filling and frosting, and Grand Marnier brushing syrup either by the traditional freehand method (page 67) or by molding it (page 72) in the same ring in which the génoise was baked. Scatter the Grand Marnier–soaked glacé fruits over the layer of filling before placing the second layer of génoise on top.

3. Place the gâteau on a tray and chill in the refrigerator until the buttercream is firm, at least 1 hour.

4. If you did not melt the chocolate for decoration in a stainless steel bowl, transfer it to one. Temper the chocolate as follows: Dip the bottom of the bowl of chocolate in a larger bowl of cold water and stir the chocolate until the temperature drops to between 80° and 84°F (26.5° to 29°C) and it begins to thicken. Immediately remove from the cold water and dip the bottom of the bowl of chocolate in a larger bowl of hot water. Stir over the hot water just long enough to warm the chocolate to between 86° and 91°F (30° to 33°C) and make it more fluid again. Then remove from the hot water immediately. Beat the clarified butter with a wooden spatula to make it smooth and creamy, then stir it into the chocolate.

5. Place the bowl of chocolate on your counter and tilt it by placing a small mold or other prop under one side so you can easily dip the tip of the icing spatula in the chocolate. Lift the gâteau off the counter and support it on the fingertips of one hand. Take the very flexible icing spatula in the other hand, lightly touch the face of the blade on the chocolate in the bowl, and clean any excess chocolate off the edges of the blade by wiping them on the edge of the bowl. Make a vertical petal on the side of the gâteau by pressing the chocolate-coated face of the blade on it, bending the blade slightly, and dragging it down the side of the gâteau. The petal should be about three quarters of the height of the gâteau and slightly wider than the blade of the icing spatula, with the center thinner than the edges. Rotate the gâteau on your fingertips, and repeat the procedure to make a second petal adjacent to the first one. Continue making petals all the way around the side, trying to make them as uniform in size as possible and adjusting the spacing as necessary to make the last petal end up adjacent to the first one.

continued

6. On your countertop, work the almond paste with the heel of your hand to make it smooth, and then work in a drop or two of red food coloring to tint it a pale pink. Dust your countertop and the almond paste with confectioners' sugar and roll it out with the rolling pin into a rough circle about 10 inches (25 cm) in diameter. Cut a 9½-inch (24-cm) circle from the sheet of almond paste. Carefully lift the circle and drape it over the top of the gâteau in gentle, natural folds.

7. Return the gâteau to the refrigerator. When ready to serve, lightly dust the top of the gâteau with confectioners' sugar.

VARIATION: Decorate the bottom edge of the gâteau with arcs of chocolate sprinkles instead of chocolate petals.

STORAGE: In the refrigerator for up to 2 days.

Cherry

This gâteau contains glacé cherries steeped in a cherry liqueur and then embedded in a filling of buttercream flavored with the same liqueur. Like *framboisine*, it is enrobed in a sheet of almond paste.

The name "cherry" is traditional, despite the fact that it has no meaning in French. The French word for cherry is *cerise*. Around the middle of the twentieth century, when this gâteau originated, cherry liqueurs such as Cherry Rocher were popular in France. Cherry Marnier is a liqueur of this type that is widely available today. Maraschino liqueur is an altogether different type of cherry liqueur, but for our taste it is even better than the other cherry liqueurs in this gâteau. You can make your own choice depending on which you prefer or have on hand in your liqueur cabinet.

For 8 servings

EQUIPMENT:

9-inch (24-cm) foil board or matt board cake-decorating circle (page 467)
Optional: 8¾-inch (22-cm) cake ring (if the génoise was baked in one)
Rolling pin
Parchment decorating cone (page 416)

FILLING AND FROSTING:

Glacé cherries	1½ ounces (45 g)
Maraschino liqueur or Cherry Marnier	3 tablespoons (4.5 cL)
French buttercream (page 384)	12 ounces (340 g); 2 cups

CAKE:

Génoise (page 82)	One round baked in
	• either a 9-inch (24-cm) cake pan
	• or an 8¾-inch (22-cm) cake ring

BRUSHING-SYRUP MIXTURE:

Heavy syrup (page 452)	⅓ cup (8 cL)
Maraschino liqueur or Cherry Marnier	2 tablespoons + 2 teaspoons (4 cL)
Water	2 tablespoons + 2 teaspoons (4 cL)

continued

DECORATION FOR TOP OF GÂTEAU:

Almond paste (page 432)	4½ ounces (125 g)
Confectioners' sugar for dusting	
Green and yellow food colorings	
Glacé cherries	2 or 3
Granulated sugar	½ ounce (15 g); 1 tablespoon
Heavy syrup, heated to lukewarm	1 tablespoon (1.5 cL)
Unsweetened chocolate, melted	½ ounce (15 g)

DECORATION FOR BOTTOM EDGE OF GÂTEAU:

Chocolate sprinkles	1 ounce (25 g); 3 tablespoons

1. Place the glacé cherries for the filling in a glass jar, pour 1 tablespoon + 2 teaspoons (2.5 cL) of the maraschino liqueur or Cherry Marnier over them, and stir to mix. Cover airtight and let steep in the liqueur for at least 2 hours and preferably overnight. When ready to make the gâteau, drain the cherries thoroughly.

2. Flavor the buttercream with the remaining 4 teaspoons (2 cL) of liqueur for the filling and frosting. Assemble the gâteau from the génoise round (cut into two layers), buttercream filling and frosting, and liqueur brushing syrup either by the traditional freehand method (page 67) or by molding it (page 72) in the same ring in which the génoise was baked. Scatter the liqueur-soaked glacé cherries over the layer of filling before placing the second layer of génoise on top.

3. Place the gâteau on a tray and chill in the refrigerator until the buttercream is firm, at least 1 hour.

4. On your countertop, work the almond paste with the heel of your hand to make it smooth. Dust your countertop and the almond paste with confectioners' sugar and roll it out with the rolling pin into a rough circle 12 to 13 inches (30 to 33 cm) in diameter. Place the gâteau on your countertop. Carefully roll the sheet of almond paste over the rolling pin, then unroll it onto the gâteau, centering it so that the edges hang over the sides of the gâteau and the sheet is flat against the top. Gently press the almond paste against the sides so that it covers the entire surface of the gâteau with no creases. Using the tip of a paring knife, trim off the excess almond paste, leaving a strip of buttercream ¼ to ⅜ inch (6 to 10 mm) high showing around the bottom edge. Gather together the trimmings and work them into a smooth pad.

5. Lift the gâteau from the countertop with a large icing spatula and support it on the fingertips of one hand. Take the chocolate sprinkles in the palm of your other hand. Finish the bottom edge of the gâteau by pressing it against the sprinkles in your palm, then rotating the gâteau and repeating until you have covered the exposed strip of buttercream.

6. Work a drop each of green and yellow food coloring into the remaining almond paste to tint it a pale green. Dust your countertop and the almond paste with confectioners' sugar and roll it out into a sheet about ³⁄₃₂ inch (2 mm) thick. Cut out a few small leaf shapes from the sheet. Roll the glacé cherries in the granulated sugar to give them a frosted look.

7. Gradually stir the heavy syrup into the melted chocolate. The chocolate will thicken and will probably seize, becoming thick and granular. Keep adding heavy syrup until the chocolate becomes smooth and fluid again. Add only as much syrup as necessary to make this "writing chocolate" smooth and soft enough to pipe from a parchment decorating cone.

8. Spoon 1 tablespoon (1.5 cL) of the writing chocolate into the parchment decorating cone, fold over the back end to close it, and cut the tip. Pipe a scroll pattern or other border design around the rim of the gâteau. Then pipe a few cherry stems in writing chocolate around the center. Arrange the almond paste leaves and the frosted cherries with the stems to complete the motif. If you like, you can also pipe "Cherry" under the cherry and leaf decoration.

9. Refrigerate the gâteau until ready to serve.

STORAGE: In the refrigerator for up to 2 days.

Framboisine

The raspberry brandy, *framboise*, gives this gâteau a special flavor. The outside of the gâteau is covered with a smooth sheet of almond paste.

For 8 servings

EQUIPMENT:
9-inch (24-cm) foil board or matt board cake-decorating circle (page 467)
Optional: 8¾-inch (22-cm) cake ring (if the génoise was baked in one)
Rolling pin

FROSTING:
French buttercream (page 384)   9 ounces (250 g); 1½ cups
Framboise (raspberry brandy)   2½ teaspoons (1.3 cL)

CAKE:
Génoise (page 82)   One round baked in
                                             • either a 9-inch (24-cm) cake pan
                                             • or an 8¾-inch (22-cm) cake ring

FILLING:
Raspberry jam   6¼ ounces (180 g); ½ cup + 1 tablespoon

BRUSHING-SYRUP MIXTURE:
Heavy syrup (page 452)   ⅓ cup (8 cL)
Framboise (raspberry brandy)   2 tablespoons + 2 teaspoons (4 cL)
Water   2 tablespoons + 2 teaspoons (4 cL)

DECORATION FOR TOP OF GÂTEAU:
Almond paste (page 432)   9 ounces (250 g)
Confectioners' sugar for dusting
Green and yellow food colorings
Fresh raspberries, or substitute German   A few
    raspberries (raspberry jelly candies)

DECORATION FOR BOTTOM EDGE OF GÂTEAU:
Chocolate sprinkles   1 ounce (25 g); 3 tablespoons

1. Flavor the buttercream with the *framboise*. Assemble the gâteau from the génoise round (cut into two layers), raspberry jam filling, *framboise* buttercream frosting, and *framboise* brushing syrup either by the traditional freehand method (page 67) or by molding it (page 72) in the same ring in which the génoise was baked.

2. Place the gâteau on a tray and chill in the refrigerator until the buttercream is firm, at least 1 hour.

3. On your countertop, work the almond paste with the heel of your hand to make it smooth. Dust your countertop and the almond paste with confectioners' sugar and roll it out with the rolling pin into a rough circle 12 to 13 inches (30 to 33 cm) in diameter. Place the gâteau on your countertop. Carefully roll the sheet of almond paste over the rolling pin, then unroll it onto the gâteau, centering it so that the edges hang over the sides of the gâteau and the sheet is flat against the top. Gently press the almond paste against the sides so that it covers the entire surface of the gâteau with no creases. Using the tip of a paring knife, trim off the excess almond paste, leaving a strip of buttercream ¼ to ⅜ inch (6 to 10 mm) high showing around the bottom edge. Gather together the trimmings and work them into a smooth pad.

4. Lift the gâteau from the countertop with a large icing spatula and support it on the fingertips of one hand. Take the chocolate sprinkles in the palm of your other hand. Finish the bottom edge of the gâteau by pressing it against the sprinkles in your palm, then rotating the gâteau and repeating until you have covered the exposed strip of buttercream.

5. Work a drop each of green and yellow food coloring into the remaining almond paste to tint it a pale green. Take half of this almond paste and roll it under your palms into a long thin rope, about 3⁄16 inch (5 mm) in diameter. Arrange this rope as a meandering, vine-like decoration around the top of the gâteau. Dust your countertop and the remaining almond paste with confectioners' sugar and roll it out into a sheet about 3⁄16 inch (2 mm) thick. Cut out small leaf shapes from the sheet. Arrange the leaves with the vine on the gâteau. Finally, add a few raspberries around the vine to complete the motif. If you are using German raspberries, stick them in place with a dab of buttercream.

6. Refrigerate the gâteau until ready to serve.

VARIATION: For a more formal decoration, you can arrange the vines, leaves, and raspberries around the perimeter of the top, and pipe *Framboisine* across the center in writing chocolate (page 418). If you prefer, you can also pipe the vines and leaves in writing chocolate instead of making them from almond paste. In this case, you can stick the German raspberries on top with a dab of writing chocolate.

STORAGE: In the refrigerator for up to 2 days.

Marquis

Filled and frosted with whipped cream and fresh peaches, this is a delightful gâteau for the height of the peach season in late summer. It was created by Bernard Desbois, who was chef at the pastry shop Le Canigou on the *rue de la Convention* in Paris when Paul Bugat purchased it from Jean Cassadessus in 1966. At the time, Cassadessus was hospitalized and Michel Guérard was running the business for him. After Paul took over Le Canigou, Michel Guérard opened his famous bistrot Le Pot au Feu in Asnières, the Parisian suburb where Paul's father, Marcel, once owned yet another pastry shop called Janou-Michou.

For 8 servings

EQUIPMENT:

Electric mixer
9-inch (24-cm) foil board or matt board cake-decorating circle (page 467)
Small pastry bag fitted with
• small fluted pastry tube (Ateco #1)

FILLING AND FROSTING:

Ripe medium-size freestone peaches, poached in light syrup (page 454) if they are too firm	3 or 4
Confectioners' sugar	1¾ ounces (50 g); ⅓ cup + 4 teaspoons
Heavy cream	2 cups (5 dL)
Vanilla bean	¼

CAKE:

Chocolate génoise (page 84)	One round baked in • a 9-inch (24-cm) cake pan

BRUSHING-SYRUP MIXTURE:

Heavy syrup (page 452)	⅓ cup (8 cL)
European kirsch	2 tablespoons + 2 teaspoons (4 cL)
Water	2 tablespoons + 2 teaspoons (4 cL)

DECORATION FOR BOTTOM EDGE OF GÂTEAU:

Chocolate sprinkles	1 ounce (25 g); 3 tablespoons

1. If the peaches were poached, drain them thoroughly.

2. Peel and stone the peaches. Cut them into slices ¼ inch (6 mm) thick. If the peaches have not been poached, dip them in acidulated water to prevent discoloration.

3. Sift the confectioners' sugar into the bowl of the mixer, stir in the cream, and refrigerate for about an hour. Chill the wire whip or beater of the mixer as well.

4. Slit the vanilla bean lengthwise and scrape out the seeds into the cream. (Reserve the pod for another purpose.) Whip the cream at medium speed in the mixer. When the cream holds soft peaks, slow down to avoid overbeating. Continue whipping until the cream is light and thick and holds stiff peaks.

5. Assemble the gâteau from the génoise round (cut into two layers), whipped cream and sliced peach filling, whipped cream frosting, and kirsch brushing syrup by the traditional freehand method (page 67). The filling requires a little extra explanation: Use about ⅔ cup (85 g) of the whipped cream on the bottom layer of génoise, and arrange the peach slices over this whipped cream filling in concentric circles, starting from the outside and overlapping the slices slightly like the blades of a fan. Save eight of the slices for decorating the top of the gâteau. Spread another ⅔ cup (85 g) of whipped cream over the cut surface of the top layer of génoise, and place this layer, cut side down, on the peaches so that the peaches are completely enclosed in whipped cream. Frost the outside of the gâteau as usual, saving about ½ cup (65 g) of whipped cream for decorating the top.

6. Lift the gâteau with a large icing spatula and support it on the fingertips of one hand. Take the chocolate sprinkles in the palm of your other hand. Decorate the side of the gâteau with arcs of sprinkles by pressing it against the sprinkles in your palm, then rotating the gâteau and repeating until you have made adjacent arcs of sprinkles all the way around the gâteau.

7. Transfer the remaining whipped cream to the pastry bag. Pipe a circle of teardrops around the rim of the gâteau. Pipe a large rosette of whipped cream in the center and arrange the reserved peach slices around it like a pinwheel. Pipe a rosette of whipped cream between each pair of peach slices.

8. Place the gâteau on a serving plate and refrigerate until ready to serve.

VARIATIONS: For a more flavorful whipped cream, substitute 1¾ cups (4.2 dL) crème fraîche thinned with ¼ cup (6 cL) crushed ice or cold water for the heavy cream.

If you prefer, you can substitute fresh raspberries for the peaches, and use *framboise* (raspberry brandy) instead of kirsch in the brushing.

STORAGE: In the refrigerator for up to 12 hours, but best eaten within 4 hours.

Abricotine

Filled and glazed with apricot jam, *abricotine* is especially easy to make. The jam is applied to the outside of the cake using a pastry brush, so you don't need an icing spatula or a cake ring.

For 8 servings

EQUIPMENT:

9-inch (24-cm) foil board or matt board cake-decorating circle (page 467)
Rolling pin

CAKE:

Génoise (page 82)	One round baked in • a 9-inch (24-cm) cake pan

BRUSHING-SYRUP MIXTURE:

Heavy syrup (page 452)	⅓ cup (8 cL)
European kirsch	2 tablespoons + 2 teaspoons (4 cL)
Water	2 tablespoons + 2 teaspoons (4 cL)

FILLING:

Whole apricot jam	8 ounces (225 g); ⅔ cup

GLAZE:

Strained apricot jam (page 412), melted	3½ ounces (100 g); ⅓ cup

DECORATION FOR BOTTOM EDGE OF GÂTEAU:

Blanched almonds, roasted (page 444) and finely chopped	1 ounce (30 g); 3 tablespoons

DECORATION FOR TOP OF GÂTEAU:

Almond paste (page 432)	1 ounce (30 g)
Green and yellow food colorings	
Confectioners' sugar for dusting	
Glacé apricot (page 516)	1

1. Cut the cardboard cake-decorating circle slightly smaller than the bottom of the génoise round.

2. If the bottom of the génoise is not flat, slice off the bottom to give a flat surface. Slice the génoise in half horizontally. Place the bottom layer on the cake-decorating circle and brush the cut faces of both layers with most of the kirsch brushing syrup. Spread the whole apricot jam over the bottom layer of génoise. Add the second layer, cut side down, and lightly brush the top and sides with kirsch syrup.

3. Brush the top and sides of the gâteau with the melted apricot jam until lightly coated and glistening.

4. Lift the gâteau from the countertop with a large icing spatula and support it on the fingertips of one hand. Take the chopped almonds in the palm of your other hand. Finish the bottom edge of the gâteau by pressing it against the chopped nuts in your palm, then rotating the gâteau and repeating until you have covered the bottom edge with a band of chopped nuts ⅜ to ½ inch (10 to 12 mm) high. Place the gâteau on a serving plate.

5. On your countertop, work the almond paste with the heel of your hand to make it smooth. Then work in a drop each of green and yellow food colorings to tint it a pale green. Take half of the almond paste and roll it under your palms into a thin string about ⅛ inch (3 mm) in diameter. Cut the string into short stems. Dust your countertop and the remaining almond paste with confectioners' sugar. Roll out the remaining almond paste with the rolling pin into a sheet about 3/32 inch (2 mm) thick, and cut from it a few leaf shapes. Slice the glacé apricot in half horizontally to make two thin, round slices. Arrange the almond paste leaves and stems and the apricot halves (cut side down) on the center of the gâteau.

STORAGE: At room temperature, preferably in a covered cake platter, for 1 to 2 days.

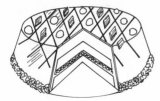

Napolitain

This gâteau gets its name (which is French for "Neapolitan") from its frosting of Italian meringue and its colorful and unusual decoration. You burn a design into the surface of the meringue using a red-hot wire or skewer or an electric charcoal lighter, and garnish the top of the gâteau with glacé cherries and angelica (or green pineapple).

For 8 servings

EQUIPMENT:
9-inch (24-cm) foil board or matt board cake-decorating circle (page 467)
Heavy baking sheet
Electric charcoal lighter (page 468),
    or straight steel wire or very slender skewer about 8 inches (20 cm) long

FILLING:

Pineapple slices in heavy syrup	One 8-ounce (225-g) can
Strained apricot jam (page 412)	¼ cup + 2 tablespoons (120 g)

CAKE:

Génoise (page 82)	One round baked in
	• a 9-inch (24-cm) cake pan

BRUSHING-SYRUP MIXTURE:

Heavy syrup (page 452)	⅓ cup (8 cL)
European kirsch	2 tablespoons + 2 teaspoons (4 cL)
Water	2 tablespoons + 2 teaspoons (4 cL)

FROSTING:

Italian meringue (page 184)	9½ ounces (270 g); 4½ cups

GLAZE:

Strained apricot jam, melted	3½ ounces (100 g); ⅓ cup

DECORATION FOR BOTTOM EDGE OF GÂTEAU:

Blanched almonds, roasted (page 444) and finely chopped	1 ounce (30 g); 3 tablespoons

DECORATION FOR TOP OF GÂTEAU:

Glacé cherries   5 to 7

Candied angelica or green glacé pineapple

1. Drain the canned pineapple. Cut it into ¼- to ⅜-inch (6- to 10-mm) dice and place the dice on a paper towel to drain off as much moisture as possible. Mix the dice with the apricot jam to make a *salpicon* filling.

2. Assemble the gâteau from the génoise round (cut into two layers), *salpicon* filling, kirsch brushing syrup, and Italian meringue frosting by the traditional freehand method (page 67). Make the layer of Italian meringue on top of the gâteau about 1 inch (2.5 cm) thick. Remember that the meringue is sticky, so you should hold the face of your icing spatula almost perpendicular to the surface of the gâteau when you sweep the top and sides to smooth it. Place the gâteau on the baking sheet.

Preheat the oven to 175°F (80°C).

3. Put the gâteau in the oven and let the meringue dry until it is crusty outside but still soft inside, 2 to 3 hours. Slide it onto a wire rack and let cool.

4. Preheat the electric charcoal lighter, or heat the wire or skewer on your cooktop until red-hot. Using one side of the loop of the charcoal lighter or the wire or skewer, burn six parallel straight lines in the surface of the meringue on top of the gâteau by gently pressing on the surface just long enough to caramelize the sugar in the meringue. Space the lines evenly about 1½ inches (4 cm) center to center. (If you are using a wire or skewer, reheat it between making each line.) Then caramelize a second set of six parallel lines on the diagonal with respect to the first six. This will make a lozenge pattern on top of the gâteau. Finally, continue the lines about one quarter of the way down the sides of the gâteau.

5. Brush the top and sides of the gâteau with the melted apricot jam until lightly coated and glistening.

6. Lift the gâteau from the wire rack with a large icing spatula and support it on the fingertips of one hand. Take the chopped almonds in the palm of your other hand. Finish the bottom edge of the gâteau by pressing it against the chopped nuts in your palm, then rotating the gâteau and repeating until you have covered the bottom edge with a band of chopped nuts ⅜ to ½ inch (10 to 12 mm) high. Place the gâteau on a serving plate.

7. Cut the glacé cherries in half. Slice some angelica or green glacé pineapple about ⅛ inch (3 mm) thick and cut it into ½-inch (12-mm) diamonds. Arrange alternating rows of half cherries and green diamonds in the lozenges on top of the gâteau.

VARIATION: If you are using a steel wire or skewer, you can make a more sophisticated design on top by replacing each line by a pair of lines spaced about ¼ inch (6 mm) apart.

STORAGE: In the refrigerator for up to 1 day.

Génoise Polonaise

There is a grande luxe gâteau called *brioche polonaise* made by layering slices of brioche with pastry cream to make a beehive shape, frosting the beehive with Italian meringue, and browning the surface of the gâteau in a hot oven. The pastry cream is laced with curaçao liqueur and studded with curaçao-soaked glacé fruits, the brioche is soaked with curaçao syrup, and—well, you get the idea, this isn't really a dessert for kids. It also requires leftover brioche. However, some people like this dessert so much that they want to be able to make it even when there just isn't any leftover brioche in the pantry. The solution is *génoise polonaise*, which transposes the same filling, frosting, and flavors into the context of a round sponge cake gâteau.

For 8 servings

EQUIPMENT:
9-inch (24-cm) foil board or matt board cake-decorating circle (page 467)
Heavy baking sheet

FILLING:

Glacé fruits, cut into ¼- to ⅜-inch (6- to 10-mm) dice	3 ounces (85 g)
Curaçao liqueur	3 tablespoons (4.5 cL)
French pastry cream (page 394), very thick and thoroughly chilled	12 ounces (340 g); 1⅓ cups

CAKE:

Génoise (page 82)	One round baked in • a 9-inch (24-cm) cake pan

BRUSHING-SYRUP MIXTURE:

Heavy syrup (page 452)	⅓ cup (8 cL)
Curaçao liqueur	2 tablespoons + 2 teaspoons (4 cL)
Water	2 tablespoons + 2 teaspoons (4 cL)

FROSTING:

Italian meringue (page 184)	3¼ ounces (90 g); 1½ cups

DECORATION:

Sliced almonds   1 ounce (30 g); ⅓ cup

Confectioners' sugar for dusting

1. Place the glacé fruits for the filling in a glass jar, pour 2 tablespoons (3 cL) of the curaçao liqueur over them, and stir to mix. Cover airtight and let steep in the curaçao for at least 2 hours and preferably overnight. When ready to make the gâteau, drain the fruits thoroughly.

2. Flavor the pastry cream with the remaining 1 tablespoon (1.5 cL) of curaçao for the filling. Assemble the gâteau from the génoise round (cut into two layers), pastry cream filling, curaçao brushing syrup, and Italian meringue frosting by the traditional freehand method (page 67). Scatter the curaçao-soaked glacé fruits over the layer of filling before placing the second layer of génoise on top. Remember that the meringue is sticky, so you should hold the face of your icing spatula almost perpendicular to the surface of the gâteau when you sweep the top and sides to smooth it.

Preheat the oven to 500°F (260°C).

3. Lift the gâteau with a large icing spatula and support it on the fingertips of one hand. Take some sliced almonds in your other hand and scatter them over the sides of the gâteau, tilting the gâteau away from you and rotating it on your fingertips to coat the entire side evenly. If necessary, press the almonds against the side of the gâteau to make them adhere. Return the gâteau to the countertop and scatter the remaining sliced almonds over the top of the gâteau. Lightly dust the top and sides of the gâteau with confectioners' sugar. Place the gâteau on the baking sheet.

4. Put the gâteau in the oven until a crust forms on the surface of the meringue and it browns lightly, about 2 to 3 minutes. Then slide it onto a wire rack and let cool to room temperature.

STORAGE: In the refrigerator for up to 1 day.

CHAPTER THREE

Round Nut Meringue Gâteaux

You can use rounds of the nut meringues *dijonnaise* and *succès* to make round gâteaux in the same styles as you can with sponge cakes. Of course, the taste and texture will be totally different. As with sponge cakes, the typical format is two layers of nut meringue with one layer of filling. In contrast to the sponge cake gâteaux, where you use a single round of sponge cake, cutting it in half to make the two layers for the gâteau, for the nut meringues you need to bake two separate rounds for the two layers of each gâteau. Like sponge cakes, *succès* is usually moistened by brushing it with a flavored syrup, but *dijonnaise* is never brushed because the syrup would destroy its crisp texture.

The top and sides of the gâteau are usually frosted with buttercream, but for some gâteaux (notably *progrès*), there is no frosting at all. And some gâteaux (*chocolatine, noisettine, and marie stuart*) are assembled in a cake ring with a single layer of *dijonnaise* topped by a thick layer of very light buttercream.

The decoration of the nut meringue gâteaux is usually very simple. Most often you just scatter chocolate shavings, roasted almonds, or pulverized nut meringue trimmings over the frosting. You can stencil some of them with a dusting of confectioners' sugar. A few old-fashioned gâteaux with *succès* layers are glazed with fondant. At the other extreme there are very modern presentations, with ribbons of chocolate wrapped around the side.

You can assemble most of these gâteaux using essentially the same two methods as for sponge cakes, namely: the traditional method of assembling the cake layers and filling freehand and spreading the frosting over the outside using a long, flexible icing spatula; or the more modern alternative of molding the gâteau in a cake ring. As with sponge cakes, the cake ring method is easier to learn, and here it has the additional advantage that some gâteaux made with a single layer of nut meringue can be assembled only in a ring. Also, there are a few gâteaux for which only the top (not the side) is glazed or dusted, and this is difficult, or impossible, without a ring.

While the basic methods are the same as those explained in the previous chapter on sponge cake gâteaux, there are some significant differences because of the nature of the nut meringue rounds. In the interest of clarity, we will repeat both methods here, with the modifications required for nut meringue rounds. As before, we leave it to you to decide which method to use in each recipe. Whenever possible, each recipe is designed to work equally well using the traditional method or the modern ring method. Gâteaux that are not frosted or that have only a single nut meringue round require special (and very simple) assembly procedures, so for these we give the detailed instructions in each recipe.

Making the Nut Meringue Rounds

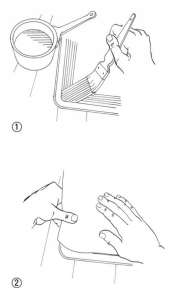

All of the gâteaux in this chapter are based on two nut meringues, *dijonnaise* and *succès*, which are piped on a baking sheet in rounds using a pastry bag. You can pipe two rounds, enough for one gâteau, on a large baking sheet.

Preparing the Baking Sheet

The baking sheet can be either lined with kitchen parchment or buttered and floured. The two methods are essentially equivalent, the only significant difference being how the rounds are removed after baking. We prefer the parchment-lined baking sheet for both *dijonnaise* and *succès* because it is easier to peel the parchment off the backs of the rounds without breaking them than it is to lift the rounds off a buttered and floured baking sheet. However, if you are out of parchment, you can always switch to butter and flour.

To line the baking sheet with parchment, first brush a band 1½ to 2 inches (3 to 5 cm) wide around the edge and down the diagonals of the baking sheet with melted butter 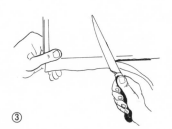 so that the paper will stick to the baking sheet. Then line the baking sheet with a sheet of kitchen parchment ②. The parchment can be precut to the size of the baking sheet. Or, if you have a French black steel baking sheet with a low, turned-up lip around the edge, you can trim off the excess paper by running the back edge of your chef's knife over the paper around the edge of the baking sheet ③.

To butter and flour the baking sheet, first brush the entire top surface

of the baking sheet with melted butter ④, then let it set so you won't get too much flour adhering to the butter. Sprinkle flour over the butter ⑤, using more flour than you will need in the end. Tilt, shake, and tap the sheet to distribute the flour and coat the sheet evenly. Then invert the baking sheet and tap it with a wooden spatula or the handle of a dough scraper to dislodge the excess flour ⑥. The purposes of the flour are to prevent the batter from slipping as you pipe it and to prevent the undersides of the nut-meringue rounds from deflating because of direct contact with the butter.

Marking the Circles

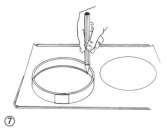

Mark two circles of the size you need to pipe on the baking sheet using a *tarte* ring, cake ring, *vol-au-vent* disk, round mold, or bowl as a guide. If the baking sheet is lined with parchment, draw the circles with a pencil ⑦. On a buttered-and-floured baking sheet, just tap the ring, disk, mold, or bowl on the baking sheet ⑧ to mark the circles in the flour.

Piping the Batter in Rounds

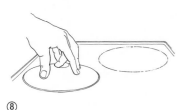

Choose a large (18-inch= 45-cm) pastry bag and fit it with a large plain pastry tube. Fill the pastry bag with the batter.

Hold the pastry bag almost vertical, with the tip of the pastry tube 1 to 1½ inches (2½ to 3½ cm) above the baking sheet. Pressing steadily on the pastry bag, and starting from the center of each circle, pipe the batter in a continuous spiral that completely fills the circle ⑨. Move the tip of the pastry tube in a smooth and continuous motion and let the batter drop over the outside third of the previous arc of the spiral. The batter will fall down onto the baking sheet, leaving no gaps in the final round of batter. (If there are any gaps after you have finished piping the rounds, fill them by piping in a little more batter.) When you have filled the circle, release the pressure on the pastry bag and quickly flick the tip of the pastry tube horizontally along the outside of the round to terminate the spiral.

All of the batter must be piped out and baked right away or it will deflate. If there is a little extra batter, you can pipe it in domes about 1¼ inches (3 cm) wide ⑩. These small domes are useful for assessing how the almond meringue is baking without damaging the large rounds.

As the rounds bake, the batter will expand beyond the circles marked on the baking sheet. This doesn't matter because when you are ready to make a gâteau you will trim them to the precise size. Once the rounds have cooled, turn them upside down and carefully peel off the parchment; or, if you used a buttered-and-floured baking sheet, carefully slide the blade of a large icing spatula or pancake turner under each round to loosen it and then lift or slide the rounds off the baking sheet. If you will not be using the rounds the same day, store them in a tin cookie box (the best because it protects them) or sealed airtight in plastic wrap. Keep them in a dry place for up to 2 weeks. Do not put them in the refrigerator, which would produce condensation and soften them.

Cake Sizes, Trimming the Rounds, Cardboard Bases, and Brushing with Syrup

Cake Sizes

For both assembly methods (traditional freehand and molding in a ring), pipe the nut meringue in rounds about 8¾ inches (22 cm) in diameter. Remember that the rounds will expand, so the exact size isn't crucial. However, the baking sheet must be large enough to accommodate two rounds of this size. If you don't have a baking sheet this large, then use two sheets and pipe one round on each.

After baking and cooling, you will trim the rounds to circles of identical size. The standard we have chosen is to make the gâteaux 8¾ inches (22 cm) in diameter, which is the same as the standard size of cake ring we use in Chapter 2. If you are using a cake ring, the nut meringue rounds must be cut about ⅜ inch (1 cm) smaller in diameter than the ring, which is to say about 8⅜ inches (21 cm) in diameter for an 8¾-inch (22-cm) ring. For both methods, the gâteau will have a profile with vertical sides rather than the sloping sides of a sponge cake gâteau produced by the traditional method.

If you prefer to make another size, you can adjust our recipes accordingly. For an 8-inch (20-cm) gâteau, decrease the quantities of all ingredients by 20 percent. Or, for a 9½-inch (24-cm) gâteau, increase the quantities of all ingredients by 20 percent.

Trimming the Nut Meringue Rounds

Using a *tarte* ring, a cake ring, a round mold, or a *vol-au-vent* disk as a guide, trim the two rounds with a wavy-edge bread knife ⑪ to make two circles

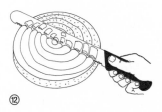

of about 8⅜ inches (21 cm) in diameter. Cut carefully so that you don't crack the rounds. If one does crack, piece it back together; the filling in the gâteau will eventually hold the pieces together.

Dijonnaise and *succès* have a tendency to rise a bit unevenly when baked, with some arcs of the spiral you piped bulging up above the rest. To make the baked rounds more even in thickness, shave the top of each with the bread knife ⑫, taking off just a little at a time. Shave off only the tops of the highest bumps. If you shave off too much, you may uncover large air pockets in the rounds, making them more, rather than less, uneven.

Save the trimmings from *dijonnaise* and *succès*, and store them airtight in a plastic bag for up to 1 month. Pulverize them in a blender, food processor, or mortar and pestle to use for decorating or in place of chopped nuts to finish the bottom edges of gâteaux. Pulverized *succès* trimmings can also be used in place of part of the almond-and-sugar powder the next time you make *succès*.

Cardboard Bases

To properly assemble and decorate a round gâteau, you must have a cardboard cake-decorating circle. You can use the foil board circles sold as lids for aluminum foil take-out containers (and sold separately from the containers) or the cake-decorating circles imported from France. (See pages 467 and 558 for details and sources.) Or you can cut your own circles from a sheet of gold or silver matt board (available from framing and art supply stores, page 467). Do not use the corrugated cardboard cake-decorating circles sold in American cake supply shops because they are difficult to cut to size, they make frosting cumbersome, and they look tacky when you cut and serve the gâteau.

The cake-decorating circle must be cut to size, depending on how the outside of the gâteau will be finished. If the gâteau will be molded in a cake ring, the cake-decorating circle must be cut to just fit inside the ring. For the traditional method, the circle should be slightly larger than the nut meringue rounds ⑬ in order to serve as a guide and support for spreading and smoothing the frosting around the sides of the gâteau. Ideally, for buttercream or ganache frosting the circle should be about ¼ inch (6 mm) larger in diameter than the nut meringue round; and for lighter frostings, such as whipped cream or a mousse (which are spread thicker than buttercream), the circle should be about ⅜ inch (1 cm) larger in diameter than the bottom of the nut-meringue rounds.

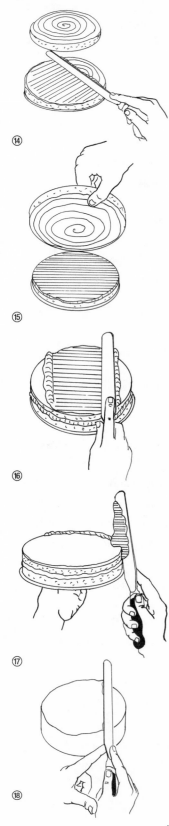

Brushing with Syrup

Succès can be brushed with a flavored syrup to add flavor to the gâteau. The syrup, which we call the "brushing-syrup mixture," is a standard heavy syrup (page 452) diluted with an equal volume of liqueur or coffee. Brush the tops of both rounds of *succès* with most of the syrup called for in the recipe, being careful not to make the *succès* soggy. The *succès* will absorb much less syrup than does génoise, so you don't need to worry about the flavor of the syrup becoming overpowering. Never brush *dijonnaise* with syrup; it would destroy the crisp texture of the *dijonnaise*.

THE TRADITIONAL FREEHAND ASSEMBLY METHOD

Choose the less perfect or less even round of *dijonnaise* or *succès* for the bottom layer and place it flat side (the side that was on the baking sheet) down on your cake-decorating circle.

Filling the Gâteau

Spread the filling in an even layer over the bottom nut meringue round ⑭ using an icing spatula with a blade at least 10 inches (25 cm) long. Many recipes call for raisins, diced glacé fruits, or chopped nuts between the layers. Scatter them over the filling.

Turn the second nut meringue round upside down to get a flat top surface, and place it on the filling ⑮. Press gently on top to eliminate any gaps between the layers and to be sure that the gâteau is even. For *succès,* lightly brush the top of the round with the brushing-syrup mixture.

Spreading and Smoothing the Frosting

Whatever the frosting, you will cover the cake with it following a three-stage process: Spreading the frosting over the entire outside of the gâteau, smoothing the top, and smoothing the sides.

First spread an even layer of frosting over the top of the gâteau ⑯. Slide your icing spatula under the cake-decorating circle, lift the gâteau from the countertop, and transfer it to the fingertips of one hand. Scoop up some of the frosting with the tip of your icing spatula and scrape it off on the rim of the bowl. Slide the edge of your icing spatula under some of this

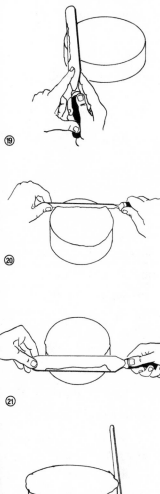

frosting to pick it up about three quarters of the way up the face of the blade near the tip. Spread this frosting on the side of the gâteau by moving the face of the icing spatula down and around the side, and leave a small rim of frosting extending above the top edge of the gâteau ⑰. Rotate the gâteau on your fingertips (use the tip of your icing spatula as an aid to avoid dropping it, if necessary), and repeat until you have covered all sides of the gâteau with the frosting and made a rim of frosting extending above the entire top edge. Slide your icing spatula under the gâteau and return it to the counter.

The second stage is to smooth the top surface of the gâteau. Start with your icing spatula at the right side of the gâteau, with the face of the blade at an angle of 30° relative to the top surface ⑱. Sweep the blade a little more than halfway across the top ⑲, keeping the edge of the blade at a fixed height and turning the face of the blade. As you sweep the blade across the center of the gâteau and lift it off the surface, the face of the blade should have rotated through about 90°. This motion spreads the rim of frosting across the gâteau and smooths half of the surface. Clean off the blade on the rim of the bowl of frosting. Next, sweep the blade from left to right across the left half of the gâteau, again keeping the edge of the blade at a fixed height and turning the face of the blade through about 90°. You should now have finished spreading the rim of frosting and the top of the gâteau should be almost smooth. Clean off your blade on the rim of the bowl again. To finish smoothing the top surface, grasp the ends of the blade of the icing spatula between the thumb and the index and middle fingers of each hand and place the edge of the blade on the far side of the gâteau. Starting with the face of the blade angled toward you ⑳, sweep the entire top surface in one smooth, continuous motion. As you do so, keep the edge of the blade at a fixed height and gradually turn the edge first under and then up, so when it reaches the near side of the gâteau, the blade is angled away from you ㉑. Take off just enough frosting to get a level surface.

Now you are ready to smooth the sides of the gâteau. Slide your icing spatula under the cake-decorating circle and lift the gâteau from the countertop. Transfer the gâteau to the fingertips of one hand. Place the bottom third of the blade of the icing spatula against the side of the gâteau, with the face of the blade vertical and nearly parallel to the surface ㉒. Using the cake-decorating circle as a guide, sweep the edge of the blade around the side of the gâteau to smooth the surface and clean off the excess frosting. As you do so, draw the blade downward and turn the face of the blade toward you ㉓. Clean off the blade on the rim of the bowl, rotate the gâteau

on your fingertips, and repeat until you have smoothed the entire outside surface of the gâteau. Return the gâteau to the counter.

This completes the spreading and smoothing procedure. Do not expect to use all of the frosting, because a necessary part of the smoothing is sweeping excess frosting off the surface of the gâteau.

ASSEMBLY IN A CAKE RING

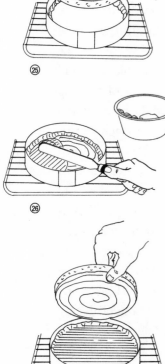

Filling the Ring

Place your cake-decorating circle on a baking sheet or wire rack. Choose an icing spatula with a blade at least 10 inches (25 cm) long. Grasp the side of the ring between the fingertips of one hand, lift the ring off the countertop, and hold it in a vertical position with your fingertips supporting it from the top. Scoop up some of the frosting on the tip of the icing spatula, and spread it inside the ring ㉔ near the lowest point on one side only—the side that will become the bottom when you put the ring back on the countertop. Rotate the ring and repeat until one half of the inside of the ring is coated all the way around with a layer of frosting about ¼ inch (6 mm) thick. Place the ring on the baking sheet or wire rack, centering it on the cake circle with the frosting-coated side on the bottom.

Choose the less perfect or less even round of *dijonnaise* or *succès* for the bottom layer and lower it into the ring ㉕, flat side (the side that was on the baking sheet) down. Center the round of nut meringue in the frosting lining the ring.

Spread an even layer of filling over the bottom layer of nut meringue ㉖ using the icing spatula, the flat side of a bowl scraper, or a rubber spatula, and spread frosting about ¼ inch (6 mm) thick over the upper half of the inside of the ring. If the recipe calls for it, scatter raisins, diced glacé fruits, or chopped nuts over the filling.

Turn the second nut meringue round upside down to get a flat top surface, and place it on the filling ㉗, centering the round inside the frosting lining the ring. Press gently on the nut meringue round to eliminate any gaps between the layers and to ensure that there is room at the top of the ring for a final layer of frosting ㉘. For *succès*, lightly brush the top of the round with the brushing-syrup mixture.

Spread the remaining frosting over the top of the nut meringue round to fill the ring ㉙. Grasp the ends of the blade of the icing spatula (or if it

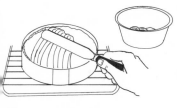

isn't long enough, use a metal straightedge) between the thumb and the index and middle fingers of each hand and place the edge of the blade on the far side of the gâteau. Starting with the face of the blade angled toward you ㉚, sweep the entire top surface in one smooth, continuous motion. As you do so, keep the edge of the blade on the top edge of the ring and gradually turn the edge first under and then up, so when it reaches the near side of the gâteau, the blade is angled away from you ㉛. Take off just enough frosting to get a level surface.

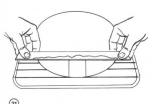

Refrigerate for at least 1 hour to make the frosting firm.

Glazing or Dusting the Top

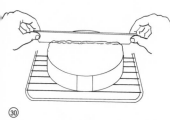

If the top of the gâteau is to be glazed with chocolate or dusted with chocolate shavings, nuts, etc., then do this before unmolding ㉜ to get a very clean demarcation between the top and sides.

For glazing with chocolate, the procedure is the same as described on page 76 for round sponge cake gâteaux, except that you simply allow the excess glaze to flow down the sides of the ring without worrying about coating the sides evenly ㉝. Clean the excess chocolate off the ring with a spatula, and put the gâteau in a cool place while the glaze sets. Then return the gâteau to the refrigerator until you are ready to unmold it.

Unmolding

Place the chilled gâteau on a bowl or cake pan taller and slightly smaller in diameter than the ring. Using a blow dryer, quickly and evenly warm the outside of the ring to just melt the frosting inside the ring. Carefully slip the ring down off the gâteau. If the ring doesn't slip off easily, warm it a little more and try again.

ADDING EXTRA LAYERS

Occasionally we like to make a taller gâteau with more layers by adding a round of French meringue plus an extra layer of filling in the center. The crisp meringue adds a note of textural contrast and lightness. We especially like this addition for gâteaux containing *dijonnaise*. The assembly of these gâteaux is not much more difficult than for the standard round nut meringue gâteaux, but you will have the extra step of baking the meringue round. For the extra layer of filling you can repeat the filling or frosting already used in the gâteaux or you can add a different filling to complement the flavors already in the gâteau.

Because these gâteaux typically require more components, and thus more time, than the basic round nut meringue gâteaux, we suggest them for readers who have more experience in making gâteaux. We offer one example as a variation on *stanislas*. If you like this type of gâteau, you can experiment with other combinations on your own.

We recommend that you assemble these gâteaux by the traditional freehand method. You can also assemble them in a deep cake ring, provided you can find one of just the right depth.

Using a *tarte* ring, a cake ring, a round mold, or a *vol-au-vent* disk as a guide, trim the round of meringue with a wavy-edge bread knife to a circle of the same size as the *dijonnaise* rounds. To make the round more even in thickness, shave the top with the bread knife to take off any large bumps. Spread a layer of filling on the bottom layer of *dijonnaise*, then place the meringue round on top. Spread the second layer of filling over the meringue. Turn the second layer of *dijonnaise* upside down to get a flat top surface, and place it on the second layer of filling. Finish assembling the gâteau as you would any round nut meringue gâteau.

GLAZING WITH CHOCOLATE OR FONDANT

Glazing the entire outside of the gâteau with fondant or chocolate glaze is done in precisely the same way as described in Chapter 2 for round sponge cake gâteau (page 76).

FINISHING THE BOTTOM EDGE OF A GÂTEAU

You will coat the bottom edges of many round nut-meringue gâteaux with chopped nuts or chocolate sprinkles. You must do this while the topping or glaze is soft, so that the nuts or sprinkles will adhere.

Slide your icing spatula under the cake-decorating circle and lift the gâteau from the countertop. Support it on the fingertips of one hand. If the gâteau was glazed with fondant or chocolate, be careful to hold it straight so that cracks don't form in the glaze. Take the nuts or chocolate sprinkles in the palm of your other hand, and have more ready so you can refill your palm as you go along. Press the bottom edge of the gâteau against the nuts or sprinkles in your palm to make them adhere to the topping or glaze.

Rotate the gâteau on your fingertips and press it against the nuts or sprinkles in your palm again. Continue until the entire bottom edge of the gâteau is coated with nuts or sprinkles. For most gâteaux, you should coat the bottom edge with an even band of nuts or sprinkles ⅜ to ½ inch (10 to 12 mm) high.

DUSTING AND DECORATING THE OUTSIDE OF A GÂTEAU

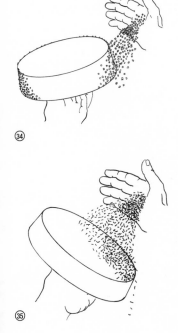

③④

③⑤

Many round nut-meringue gâteaux are finished by covering the top and sides with sliced almonds, chocolate shavings, or pulverized nut-meringue (*dijonnaise* or *succès*) trimmings. Often the look of the cake will be enhanced if you add a final dusting of confectioners' sugar just before serving; and stencilling a design on top in confectioners' sugar can provide a very simple and elegant decoration.

You should always coat the gâteau lightly and evenly, and the only trick is in coating the sides. To coat the sides easily, first slide your icing spatula under the cake-decorating circle, lift the gâteau from your countertop, and support it on the fingertips of one hand. Tilt the gâteau away from you and dust or sprinkle the sliced almonds, chocolate shavings, or nut-meringue trimmings with the other hand ③④, so they will coat the sides more effectively. When dusting with confectioners' sugar, use a sugar dredge (page 469).

On the other hand, if you want to dust only the top of the gâteau and not the sides, you should lift the gâteau and tilt it toward you ③⑤. That way, when you dust the sliced almonds or whatever with the other hand, nothing will land on the sides.

STORAGE

Gâteaux that are filled and frosted with buttercream or ganache (chocolate cream filling) can be kept in the refrigerator (on a covered cake platter if you have one) for up to 2 days. Gâteaux made from *succès* rounds (but not *dijonnaise*) can also be frozen before glazing, dusting with confectioners' sugar, chocolate sprinkles, nuts, etc., or decorating. When the gâteau has frozen, cover it airtight with plastic wrap or in a plastic bag and store in the freezer for up to 3 weeks. The day before serving, remove the plastic wrap or bag and defrost the gâteau overnight in the refrigerator. Then finish the preparation.

Dijonnaise

. . . .

Here is a light, crisp almond meringue that offers a beautiful textural contrast when paired with French buttercream. *Dijonnaise* is less sweet and much more flavorful than ordinary French meringue.

For two 8¾-inch (22-cm) rounds

EQUIPMENT:
One or two large, heavy baking sheets
• brush edges and diagonals with melted butter
• line with kitchen parchment
Electric mixer
Large pastry bag fitted with
• ¹¹⁄₁₆-inch (18-mm) plain pastry tube (Ateco #9)

BATTER:

Confectioners' sugar	3¼ ounces (90 g); ¾ cup
Almond-and-sugar powder (page 442)	5¾ ounces (165 g); 1 cup + 3½ tablespoons
Large egg whites, at room temperature	5
Cream of tartar (optional)	¼ teaspoon (1 mL)
Superfine or extra fine sugar	2¼ ounces (65 g); ¼ cup + 1 tablespoon
Milk	3 tablespoons (4.5 cL)

Preheat the oven to 275°F (135°C).

1. Draw two circles, each about 8¾ inches (22 cm) in diameter, on the parchment on the baking sheet (or sheets if you can't fit them both on one), leaving space between the circles and the edges of the baking sheet as well as each other.

2. Sift the confectioners' sugar and combine it with the almond-and-sugar powder in a large mixing bowl.

3. Whip the egg whites in the mixer at low speed until they start to froth. If you are not whipping the whites in a copper bowl, then add the cream of tartar at this point. Gradually increase the whipping speed to medium-high and continue whipping until the whites form very stiff peaks and just begin to slip and streak around the side of the bowl. Add the superfine sugar and continue whipping for a few seconds longer, then stop whipping immediately.

4. Stir the milk into the confectioners' sugar and almond-and-sugar powder. Add about one third of the meringue and quickly mix it in. Then add the remaining meringue and fold it in gently.

5. Scoop the batter into the pastry bag. Starting from the center of each circle, pipe the batter in a continuous spiral that completely fills the circle. All of the batter must be piped out and baked right away or it will deflate. If there is a little extra batter, you can pipe it in domes about 1¼ inches (3 cm) wide; these small domes are useful for assessing how the *dijonnaise* is baking without damaging the large rounds.

6. Bake until the *dijonnaise* is puffed up, dry, firm to the touch, and a uniform light brown, about 1 hour and 30 to 45 minutes. (If you piped the rounds on two baking sheets and must bake them in one oven, place one sheet on a lower oven rack and one on an upper oven rack for half of the baking period. Reverse the positions of the two baking sheets for the second half of the baking period.) If you have piped some small test domes, you can lift one off the baking sheet, let it cool for a few minutes, and cut it in half to see if the *dijonnaise* is cooked through. Otherwise, to be sure they are dry, carefully lift the edge of the parchment and feel the underside of one of the rounds.

7. Place the baking sheet on a wire rack and let cool. Then carefully remove the rounds of *dijonnaise* from the parchment.

STORAGE: Up to 2 weeks in a very dry place, either in a tin cookie box (the best) or covered airtight in plastic wrap.

If the *dijonnaise* rounds soften, transfer them to a baking sheet and place them in a preheated 250°F (120°C) oven for 10 to 15 minutes to crisp them, then cool on a wire rack before using.

Succès

Compared with *dijonnaise*, this nut meringue has a much higher nut content, and a lower sugar content. While it is crisp, it is not as light as *dijonnaise*, but much more flavorful. Here the nuts are raw rather than blanched. We recommend preparing the *succès* with half almonds and half hazelnuts, but you can alter that ratio to suit your own taste. The higher the percentage of hazelnuts, the more intense the flavor of the *succès*.

For two 8¾-inch (22-cm) rounds

EQUIPMENT:
One or two large, heavy baking sheets
• brush edges and diagonals with melted butter
• line with kitchen parchment
Electric mixer
Large pastry bag fitted with
• ⅝-inch (16-mm) plain pastry tube (Ateco #8)

BATTER:

Confectioners' sugar	1½ ounces (40 g); ⅓ cup
Raw-nut-and-sugar powder (page 442), made with half almonds and half hazelnuts	7 ounces (200 g); 1½ cups
Pulverized *succès* or *dijonnaise* (page 146) trimmings,	1½ ounces (40 g); ½ cup
or almond-and-sugar powder (page 442)	1½ ounces (40 g); ¼ cup + 2 teaspoons
Large egg whites, at room temperature	5
Cream of tartar (optional)	⅛ teaspoon (a pinch)
Superfine or extra fine sugar	1¾ ounces (50 g); ¼ cup

Preheat the oven to 300°F (150°C).

   1. Draw two circles, each about 8¾ inches (22 cm) in diameter, on the parchment on the baking sheet (or sheets if you can't fit them both on one), leaving space between the circles and the edges of the baking sheet as well as each other.
   2. Sift the confectioners' sugar and combine it with the raw-nut-and-sugar powder and the pulverized *succès* or *dijonnaise* trimmings or almond-and-sugar powder.

3. Whip the egg whites in the mixer at low speed until they start to froth. If you are not whipping the whites in a copper bowl, then add the cream of tartar at this point. Gradually increase the whipping speed to medium-high, and continue whipping until the whites form very soft peaks. Gradually add the superfine sugar and continue whipping until the meringue is very stiff, smooth, and shiny. It should form sharp peaks but not slip or streak around the side of the bowl.

4. Gradually fold the mixture of confectioners' sugar, raw-nut-and-sugar powder, and pulverized nut-meringue trimmings into the meringue.

5. Scoop the batter into the pastry bag. Starting from the center of each circle, pipe the batter in a continuous spiral that completely fills the circle. All of the batter must be piped out and baked right away or it will deflate. If there is a little extra batter, you can pipe it in domes about 1¼ inches (3 cm) wide; these small domes are useful for assessing how the *succès* is baking without damaging the large rounds.

6. Bake until the *succès* is puffed up, dry, firm to the touch, and a uniform medium brown, about 50 minutes. (If you piped the rounds on two baking sheets and must bake them in one oven, place one sheet on a lower oven rack and one on an upper oven rack for half of the baking period. Reverse the positions of the two baking sheets for the second half of the baking period.) If you have piped some small test domes, you can lift one off the baking sheet, let it cool for a few minutes, and cut it in half to see if the *succès* is cooked through. Otherwise, to be sure they are dry, carefully lift the edge of the parchment and feel the underside of one of the rounds.

7. Place the baking sheet on a wire rack and let cool. Then carefully remove the rounds of *succès* from the parchment.

STORAGE: Up to 2 weeks in a very dry place, either in a tin cookie box (the best) or covered airtight in plastic wrap.

If the *succès* rounds soften, transfer them to a baking sheet and place them in a preheated 250°F (120°C) oven for 10 to 15 minutes to crisp them, then cool on a wire rack before using.

Succès Kirsch

This is a rather sweet and old-fashioned gâteau with two layers of *succès*, kirsch buttercream filling and frosting, kirsch-soaked glacé fruits in the middle, and fondant glaze.

For 8 servings

EQUIPMENT:
9-inch (24-cm) foil board or matt board cake-decorating circle (page 467)
Optional: 8¾-inch (22-cm) cake ring

FILLING AND FROSTING:

Glacé fruits (cherries, pineapple, apricots), cut into ¼- to ⅜-inch (6- to 10-mm) dice	3 ounces (85 g)
European kirsch	3 tablespoons + 1 teaspoon (5 cL)
French buttercream (page 384)	14 ounces (400 g); 2⅓ cups

CAKE:

Succès (page 148)	Two 8¾-inch (22-cm) rounds

BRUSHING-SYRUP MIXTURE:

Heavy syrup (page 452)	2 tablespoons (3 cL)
European kirsch	2 tablespoons (3 cL)

GLAZE:

Fondant (page 408)	1 pound (450 g); 1⅓ cups
Heavy syrup	As needed

DECORATION FOR BOTTOM EDGE OF GÂTEAU:

Blanched almonds, roasted (page 444) and finely chopped	1 ounce (25 g); 3 tablespoons

DECORATION FOR TOP OF GÂTEAU:

Glacé fruits	
Granulated sugar	½ ounce (15 g); 1 tablespoon

1. Place the glacé fruits for the filling in a glass jar, pour 2 tablespoons (3 cL) of the kirsch over them, and stir to mix. Cover airtight and let steep in the kirsch for at least 2 hours and preferably overnight. When ready to make the gâteau, drain the fruits thoroughly.

2. Flavor the buttercream with the remaining 4 teaspoons (2 cL) of kirsch for the filling and frosting. Assemble the gâteau from the *succès* rounds, kirsch buttercream filling and frosting, and kirsch brushing syrup either by the traditional freehand method (pages 138 and 140) or by molding it (pages 138 and 142) in the cake ring. Scatter the kirsch-soaked glacé fruits over the layer of filling before placing the second round of *succès* on top.

3. Place the gâteau on a wire rack and chill in the refrigerator until the buttercream is firm, at least 1 hour.

4. Warm the fondant in a heavy 1-quart (1-L) saucepan over low heat, stirring constantly until melted. Stir in just enough heavy syrup to thin the fondant to the consistency of heavy cream. The temperature of the fondant must be between 100° and 105°F (38° to 40°C).

5. Pour the fondant on the top of the gâteau in a circle just inside the perimeter so that some of it flows naturally over the edges. Quickly smooth the top surface with the edge of a large icing spatula to cover the entire top with a thin layer of glaze and make the excess flow evenly down the sides. Touch up any uneven areas around the sides with the edge of the icing spatula. Let the fondant begin to thicken, then clean off any excess fondant around the bottom edge.

6. Before the fondant starts to set, lift the gâteau from the wire rack with a large icing spatula and support it on the fingertips of one hand. Take the chopped almonds in the palm of your other hand. Finish the bottom edge of the gâteau by pressing it against the chopped nuts in your palm, then rotating the gâteau and repeating until you have covered the bottom edge with a band of chopped nuts ⅜ to ½ inch (10 to 12 mm) high. Place the gâteau on a serving plate and let the fondant set.

7. For decoration, thinly slice some glacé fruits and cut geometric shapes from the slices. Toss the slices with the granulated sugar to give them a frosted look. Arrange them in a floral pattern on the center of the gâteau. Place the gâteau on a serving plate and let the fondant set.

8. Refrigerate the gâteau until ready to serve.

STORAGE: In the refrigerator for up to 2 days.

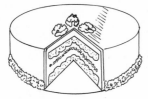

Café Noix

Did you ever peruse the pastries in the display case at a *pâtisserie* in France, select one that looked interesting, and then ask the salesperson behind the counter what it was? The response for this gâteau might well be *café noix*, or "coffee walnut," which would tell you the flavors involved but not much else. What the salesperson didn't bother to say was that it is made from *succès* and coffee-flavored buttercream, and glazed with fondant. The chopped walnuts are inside, as well as around the bottom edge of the gâteau.

For 8 servings

EQUIPMENT:
9-inch (24-cm) foil board or matt board cake-decorating circle (page 467)
Optional: 8¾-inch (22-cm) cake ring

CAKE:
Succès (page 148)	Two 8¾-inch (22-cm) rounds

FILLING AND FROSTING:
Coffee buttercream (page 390)	15 ounces (425 g); 2⅓ cups
Chopped walnuts	1 ounce (25 g); 3 tablespoons

BRUSHING-SYRUP MIXTURE:
Heavy syrup (page 452)	2 tablespoons (3 cL)
Double-strength brewed espresso (page 456)	2 tablespoons (3 cL)

GLAZE:
Fondant (page 408)	1 pound (450 g); 1⅓ cups
Double-strength brewed espresso	1 tablespoon (1.5 cL)
Caramel food coloring (page 457), optional	
Heavy syrup	As needed

DECORATION FOR BOTTOM EDGE OF GÂTEAU:
Chopped walnuts	1 ounce (25 g); 3 tablespoons

DECORATION FOR TOP OF GÂTEAU:
Walnut halves	3 or 4

1. Assemble the gâteau from the *succès* rounds, buttercream filling and frosting, and espresso brushing syrup either by the traditional freehand method (pages 138 and 140) or by molding it (pages 138 and 142) in the cake ring. Scatter the chopped walnuts over the layer of filling before placing the second layer of *succès* on top.

2. Place the gâteau on a wire rack and chill in the refrigerator until the buttercream is firm, at least 1 hour.

3. Warm the fondant in a heavy 1-quart (1-L) saucepan over low heat, stirring constantly until melted. Mix in the espresso to flavor and color the fondant, and add the optional caramel food coloring to deepen the color. Stir in just enough heavy syrup to thin the fondant to the consistency of heavy cream. The temperature of the fondant must be between 100° and 105°F (38° to 40°C).

4. Pour the fondant on the top of the gâteau in a circle just inside the perimeter so that some of it flows naturally over the edges. Quickly smooth the top surface with the edge of a large icing spatula to cover the entire top with a thin layer of glaze and make the excess flow evenly down the sides. Touch up any uneven areas around the sides with the edge of the icing spatula. Let the fondant begin to thicken, then clean off any excess fondant around the bottom edge.

5. Before the fondant starts to set, lift the gâteau from the wire rack with a large icing spatula and support it on the fingertips of one hand. Take the chopped walnuts in the palm of your other hand. Finish the bottom edge of the gâteau by pressing it against the chopped nuts in your palm, then rotating the gâteau and repeating until you have covered the bottom edge with a band of chopped nuts ⅜ to ½ inch (10 to 12 mm) high.

6. Place the gâteau on a serving plate, and arrange the walnut halves on top around the center to finish decorating it. Let the fondant set.

7. Refrigerate the gâteau until ready to serve.

STORAGE: In the refrigerator for up to 2 days.

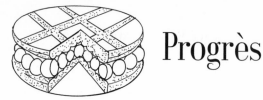

Progrès

The appearance of this gâteau is unique. You sandwich *praliné* buttercream between two layers of *succès* and stencil the top with confectioners' sugar. The special feature is that the buttercream is piped from a pastry bag, so that what shows around the circumference is a circle of buttercream balls. It is an easy and striking gâteau.

For 8 servings

EQUIPMENT:

9-inch (24-cm) foil board or matt board cake-decorating circle (page 467)
Medium-size pastry bag fitted with
• ⁷⁄₁₆- to ½-inch (11- to 12-mm) plain pastry tube (Ateco #5 or #6)

CAKE:

Succès (page 148)   Two 8¾-inch (22-cm) rounds

FILLING:

Praliné buttercream (page 388)   14 ounces (400 g); 2⅓ cups

DECORATION FOR TOP OF GÂTEAU:

Confectioners' sugar for dusting

1. Using a cake ring, a round mold, or a *vol-au-vent* disk as a guide, carefully trim each round of *succès* into a circle 8¾ inches (22 cm) in diameter with a wavy-edge bread knife. Shave the tops of both circles of *succès* to eliminate any large bumps.

2. Cut the cardboard cake-decorating circle slightly smaller than the circles of *succès*.

3. Place one circle of *succès* on the cake-decorating circle. Scoop the buttercream into the pastry bag. Starting from the center, pipe a continuous spiral of buttercream over this circle of *succès*, leaving a border 1 inch (2.5 cm) wide around the circumference uncovered. Fill the border by piping 1-inch (2.5-cm) balls of buttercream around the circumference. Pipe the balls adjacent to each other and about ½ inch (12 mm) thick.

4. Invert the second circle of *succès* to get a flat top surface, place it on the buttercream, and press down very gently.

5. Cut some strips of paper about ⅜ inch (1 cm) wide and arrange them on top of the gâteau in a decorative geometric pattern. (For example, arrange a few strips parallel to each other and equally spaced across the top, then arrange an equal number of strips on the diagonal with respect to the first set to create a pattern of diamonds between the strips.) Dust the top heavily with confectioners' sugar. Then carefully remove the paper strips.

VARIATION: For a more assertive hazelnut taste, use all hazelnuts in the nut-and-sugar powder for the *succès*.

STORAGE: In the refrigerator for up to 2 days. Do not dust the top with confectioners' sugar until shortly before serving.

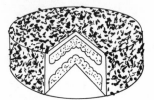

Janou and Michounnet

Janou-Michou was a pastry shop in the Parisian suburb of Asnières. The owner named the shop and these two gâteaux after his twin sons. Paul's father, Marcel Bugat, obtained the recipes when he purchased that shop many years ago, then took them with him when he went to Pâtisserie Clichy in 1955. Paul took over Clichy in 1970 and is still making *janou* and *michounnet*.

You will make both gâteaux from two layers of *dijonnaise* filled and frosted with buttercream—chocolate for *janou*, coffee for *michounnet*. Scatter chocolate shavings or roasted sliced almonds over the top, and finish with a light dusting of confectioners' sugar. Ideally, you should assemble these gâteaux in a cake ring, because the decoration was designed for this method. If you don't have the ring, then increase the quantities of chocolate shavings or sliced almonds and scatter them over the sides as well as the top of the gâteaux.

For 8 servings

EQUIPMENT:
Large, heavy baking sheet
9-inch (24-cm) foil board or matt board cake-decorating circle (page 467)
Optional: 8¾-inch (22-cm) cake ring

DECORATION FOR TOP OF MICHOUNNET:
Sliced almonds	1¼ ounces (35 g); ⅓ cup
Heavy syrup (page 452)	½ teaspoon (3 mL)

CAKE:
Dijonnaise (page 146)	Two 8¾-inch (22-cm) rounds

FILLING AND FROSTING:
Either chocolate buttercream (page 388) for *janou,*	14 ounces (400 g); 2⅓ cups
or coffee buttercream (page 390) for *michounnet*	15 ounces (425 g); 2⅓ cups

DECORATION FOR TOP OF JANOU:
Chocolate shavings (page 423)	1¾ ounces (50 g); ¼ cup
Confectioners' sugar for dusting	

For michounnet, *preheat the oven to 350°F (175°C).*

1. To prepare the sliced almonds for decorating the *michounnet*, toss them with the heavy syrup, spread them out on the baking sheet, and roast them in the preheated oven (stirring as needed after the first 5 minutes to prevent scorching), until lightly browned, about 10 minutes. Turn them out onto your countertop, and let cool.

2. Assemble the gâteau from the *dijonnaise* rounds and the buttercream filling and frosting, preferably by molding it (pages 138 and 142) in the cake ring or, if necessary, by the traditional freehand method (pages 138 and 140).

3. Scatter the chocolate shavings or roasted sliced almonds over the top of the gâteau before unmolding the cake ring. Or, if you aren't using a ring, scatter them over the entire outside of the gâteau before chilling the gâteau.

4. Refrigerate the gâteau until ready to serve. Dust the top of *janou* very lightly with confectioners' sugar.

VARIATION: If you are pressed for time, or if you are preparing *janou* for kids who love chocolate sprinkles, you can substitute chocolate sprinkles for the chocolate shavings in the decoration. Since you will need a lot of sprinkles, it is especially important to have really good-quality chocolate sprinkles for this gâteau.

STORAGE: In the refrigerator for up to 2 days.

Stanislas

This gâteau is the *dijonnaise* analog to the sponge cake gâteau *délicieux* (page 100), and like *succulent* it requires a well-stocked pantry. You will need ganache for the filling and coffee buttercream for the frosting, and you will glaze the gâteau with chocolate. Adding a round of French meringue and an extra layer of buttercream filling in the center will make it even better.

For 8 servings

EQUIPMENT:

9-inch (24-cm) foil board or matt board cake-decorating circle (page 467)
Optional: 8¾-inch (22-cm) cake ring
Parchment decorating cone (page 416)
Small pastry bag fitted with
• fluted decorating tube (such as Ateco #17 open star tube)

CAKE:

Dijonnaise (page 146)	Two 8¾-inch (22-cm) rounds

FILLING:

Ganache *clichy* (page 400)	5¾ ounces (165 g); ⅔ cup

FROSTING:

Coffee buttercream (page 390)	10½ ounces (300 g); 1⅔ cups

GLAZE:

European bittersweet chocolate, melted	9 ounces (250 g)
Clarified butter (page 449), at room temperature	1½ ounces (40 g); 3 tablespoons

DECORATION FOR BOTTOM EDGE OF GÂTEAU:

Chocolate sprinkles	1¼ ounces (35 g); ¼ cup

DECORATION FOR TOP OF GÂTEAU:

Heavy syrup, heated to lukewarm	1 tablespoon (1.5 cL)
Unsweetened chocolate, melted	½ ounce (15 g)
Chocolate espresso beans	12

1. Assemble the gâteau from the *dijonnaise* rounds, ganache filling, and buttercream frosting either by the traditional freehand method (pages 138 and 140) or by molding it (pages 138 and 142) in the cake ring. Save about ¼ cup (45 g) of excess buttercream for piping on top of the gâteau.

2. Place the gâteau on a wire rack and chill in the refrigerator until the buttercream is firm, at least 1 hour.

3. If you did not melt the chocolate for the glaze in a stainless steel bowl, transfer it to one. Temper the chocolate as follows: Dip the bottom of the bowl of chocolate in a larger bowl of cold water and stir the chocolate until the temperature drops to between 80° and 84°F (26.5° to 29°C) and it begins to thicken. Immediately remove from the cold water and dip the bottom of the bowl of chocolate in a larger bowl of hot water. Stir over the hot water just long enough to warm the chocolate to between 86° and 91°F (30° to 33°C) and make it more fluid again. Then remove from the hot water immediately. Beat the clarified butter with a wooden spatula to make it smooth and creamy, then stir it into the chocolate.

4. Pour the chocolate on the top of the gâteau in a circle just inside the perimeter so that some of it flows naturally over the edges. Quickly smooth the top surface with the edge of a large icing spatula to cover the entire top with a thin layer of glaze and make the excess flow evenly down the sides. Touch up any uneven areas around the sides with the edge of the icing spatula. Let the chocolate begin to thicken, then clean off any excess chocolate around the bottom edge.

5. Before the chocolate glaze sets, lift the gâteau from the wire rack with a large icing spatula and support it on the fingertips of one hand. Take the chocolate sprinkles in the palm of your other hand. Finish the bottom edge of the gâteau by pressing it against the sprinkles in your palm, then rotating the gâteau and repeating until you have covered the bottom edge with a band of sprinkles ⅜ to ½ inch (10 to 12 mm) high. Place the gâteau on a serving plate and let the chocolate glaze set.

6. Gradually stir the heavy syrup into the melted chocolate. The chocolate will thicken and will probably seize, becoming thick and granular. Keep adding heavy syrup until the chocolate becomes smooth and fluid again. Add only as much syrup as necessary to make this "writing chocolate" smooth and soft enough to pipe from a parchment decorating cone.

7. Spoon 1 tablespoon (1.5 cL) of the writing chocolate into the parchment decorating cone, fold over the back end to close it, and cut the tip. Write *Stanislas* across the center of the gâteau. Or, if you prefer, you can write another inscription on top of the gâteau.

8. Scoop the reserved buttercream into the pastry bag and pipe twelve rosettes in a circle around the circumference of the gâteau. Place a chocolate espresso bean on top of each rosette.

9. Refrigerate the gâteau until ready to serve.

VARIATIONS: To make a gâteau with more layers, you will need to add one 8¾-inch (22-cm) round of French meringue (page 190) and increase the quantity of buttercream for frosting and filling to:

Coffee buttercream	1 lb 1½ ounces (500 g); 2¾ cups

continued

Increase the quantities of chocolate and clarified butter for the glaze to:

European bittersweet chocolate	**12 ounces (350g)**
Clarified butter, at room temperature	**1¾ ounces (50g); 3½ tablespoons**

You can assemble the gâteau by the traditional freehand method; or if you have an extra-deep (5-cm) cake ring, you can assemble the gâteau in the ring.

Carefully trim the round of meringue to a circle the same size as the *dijonnaise* rounds. Spread a layer of buttercream over the bottom layer of *dijonnaise* and place the meringue round on top. Spread the ganache over the meringue, then finish assembling the gâteau in the usual way.

To vary the decoration on top of the gâteau, instead of rosettes of buttercream topped with chocolate espresso beans you can pipe a scroll pattern in writing chocolate around the perimeter using the parchment decorating cone.

STORAGE: In the refrigerator for up to 2 days.

Chanteclair

Rum-soaked raisins add a dash of excitement to the *praliné* buttercream filling and frosting in this *dijonnaise* gâteau. The classic decoration is a rooster stenciled on top in confectioners' sugar. *Chanteclair* in French, or chanticleer in English, is an old-fashioned word for a rooster. Remember Chaucer's tale of *Chanticleer and the Fox*?

For 8 servings

EQUIPMENT:

9-inch (24-cm) foil board or matt board cake-decorating circle (page 467)
Optional: 8¾-inch (22-cm) cake ring
Foil board or other lightweight cardboard for making stencil

FILLING AND FROSTING:

Golden raisins	2½ ounces (70 g); ¼ cup + 3 tablespoons
Dark Jamaican or Haitian rum	2 tablespoons (3 cL)
Praliné buttercream (page 388)	14 ounces (400 g); 2⅓ cups

CAKE:

Dijonnaise (page 146)	Two 8¾-inch (22-cm) rounds

DECORATION FOR TOP OF GÂTEAU:

Confectioners' sugar for stenciling

1. Place the raisins in a strainer and steam them over simmering water until they just begin to soften, about 5 minutes. Transfer the raisins to a glass jar, pour the rum over them, and stir to mix. Cover airtight and let steep in the rum for at least 2 hours and preferably overnight. When ready to make the gâteau, drain the raisins thoroughly.

2. Assemble the gâteau from the *dijonnaise* rounds and the buttercream filling and frosting either by the traditional freehand method (pages 138 and 140) or by molding it (pages 138 and 142) in the cake ring. Scatter the rum-soaked raisins over the layer of filling before placing the second layer of *dijonnaise* on top. Save the trimmings from the *dijonnaise*, and pulverize them in a blender, food processor, or mortar and pestle.

3. Sprinkle the top and sides of the gâteau with about ¼ cup (20 g) of the pulverized *dijonnaise* trimmings. Then refrigerate the gâteau until shortly before serving.

4. If you don't already have a stencil, cut one from a piece of foil board. Make a rooster, or a design of your own choice. Place the stencil on top of the gâteau and dust it heavily with confectioners' sugar. Then carefully remove the stencil.

STORAGE: In the refrigerator for up to 2 days.

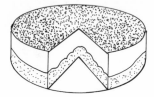

Chocolatine and Noisettine

Here are two of the simplest gâteaux to assemble. For both, you cover a single round of *dijonnaise* with a thick layer of very light buttercream—flavored with chocolate for *chocolatine* and with *praliné* (which contains hazelnuts, or *noisette* in French) for *noisettine*. You must form them in a cake ring, which does all the work, and the only decorations are chocolate sprinkles or pulverized *dijonnaise* trimmings scattered over the top.

For 8 servings

EQUIPMENT:
8¾-inch (22-cm) cake ring
9-inch (24-cm) foil board or matt board cake-decorating circle (page 467)
• cut to just fit inside the cake ring
Blender, food processor, or mortar and pestle

CAKE:

Dijonnaise (page 146)	One 8¾-inch (22-cm) round

FILLING:

Unsalted butter, softened	5¼ ounces (150 g); ⅔ cup
Praliné (page 446), for *noisettine*	1¼ ounces (35 g); ⅓ cup
Italian meringue (page 184)	9½ ounces (270 g); 4½ cups
Unsweetened chocolate, melted, for *chocolatine*	1½ ounces (45 g)

DECORATION FOR TOP OF CHOCOLATINE:

Chocolate shavings (page 423), or substitute chocolate sprinkles	1¼ ounces (35 g); 3 tablespoons
Confectioners' sugar for dusting	

1. Trim the round of *dijonnaise* with a wavy-edge bread knife so it just fits inside the cake ring. Shave the top of the *dijonnaise* to eliminate any large bumps. For *noisettine*, pulverize the *dijonnaise* trimmings in the blender, food processor, or mortar and pestle.

2. Place the softened butter in a stainless steel bowl and beat it with a wooden spatula until very soft, warming it over low heat if necessary.

FOR NOISETTINE: Transfer the *praliné* to a small mixing bowl and gradually beat in the butter with a wire whisk to make it smooth, with no lumps of *praliné*.

3. Add about one third of the Italian meringue to the butter (or butter and *praliné*), and mix thoroughly with a rubber or wooden spatula. Then gently fold in the remaining meringue.

FOR CHOCOLATINE: Add the melted chocolate when the mixture is almost smooth, and continue folding until completely mixed.

The result is a very light buttercream.

4. Place the *dijonnaise* round inside the cake ring, with the cake-decorating circle underneath. Scoop the buttercream into the ring, and sweep the surface level with the rim using a large icing spatula.

5. Scatter the chocolate shavings (for *chocolatine*) or 2 tablespoons (10 g) of the *dijonnaise* trimmings (for *noisettine*) over the top of the gâteau.

6. Refrigerate the gâteau until the buttercream is set, at least 1 hour.

7. Place the chilled gâteau on a bowl or cake pan taller and slightly smaller in diameter than the ring. Using a blow dryer, quickly and evenly warm the outside of the ring to just melt the buttercream inside the ring. Carefully slip the ring down off the gâteau. If the ring doesn't slip off easily, warm it a little more and try again.

8. Place the gâteau on a serving plate, and refrigerate until ready to serve. Lightly dust the top of *chocolatine* with confectioners' sugar.

STORAGE: In the refrigerator for up to 2 days.

Marie Stuart

This gâteau is very similar to *chocolatine* and *noisettine*, but here you fill it with an extravagantly rich chestnut buttercream instead of the very light chocolate or *praliné* buttercream, then glaze the top with chocolate. Bourbon-soaked *marrons glacés* (candied chestnuts) in the filling and a single *marron glacé* decorating the top make this gâteau the pinnacle of decadent luxury.

For 8 servings

EQUIPMENT:
8¾-inch (22-cm) cake ring
9-inch (24-cm) foil board or matt board cake-decorating circle (page 467)
• cut to just fit inside the cake ring
Chocolate thermometer or pocket digital thermometer

FILLING:

Marrons glacés (page 497)	3½ ounces (100 g)
Bourbon	¼ cup (6 cL)
Chestnut buttercream flavored with bourbon (page 402)	1 pound + 3 ounces (540 g); 3 cups

CAKE:

Dijonnaise (page 146)	One 8¾-inch (22-cm) round

GLAZE:

European bittersweet chocolate, melted	3½ ounces (100 g)
Clarified butter (page 449), at room temperature	½ ounce (15 g); 1 tablespoon

1. Set aside one *marron glacé* to decorate the top of the gâteau. Place the remaining *marrons* in a bowl, pour the bourbon over them, and cover airtight. Let steep overnight, then drain thoroughly.

2. Trim the round of *dijonnaise* with a wavy-edge bread knife so it just fits inside the cake ring. Shave the top of the *dijonnaise* to eliminate any large bumps.

3. Place the *dijonnaise* round inside the cake ring, with the cake-decorating circle underneath. Spread a thin layer of chestnut buttercream over the *dijonnaise* and arrange the bourbon-soaked *marrons* on it. Fill the ring with the remaining chestnut buttercream, covering the *marrons glacés*, and smooth the surface level with the rim using a large icing spatula.

4. Refrigerate the gâteau until the buttercream is firm, at least 1 hour.

5. If you did not melt the chocolate for the glaze in a stainless steel bowl, transfer it to one. Temper the chocolate as follows: Dip the bottom of the bowl of chocolate in a larger bowl of cold water and stir the chocolate until the temperature drops to between 80° and 84°F (26.5° to 29°C) and it begins to thicken. Immediately remove from the cold water and dip the bottom of the bowl of chocolate in a larger bowl of hot water. Stir over the hot water just long enough to warm the chocolate to between 86° and 91°F (30° to 33°C) and make it more fluid again. Then remove from the hot water immediately. Beat the clarified butter with a wooden spatula to make it smooth and creamy, then stir it into the chocolate.

6. Pour the chocolate glaze over the top of the gâteau and spread it with the edge of the icing spatula, smoothing the top surface and making the excess flow down the sides of the ring. Place the reserved *marron glacé* on the center of the gâteau. Let the chocolate glaze set, then chill the gâteau in the refrigerator.

7. Place the chilled gâteau on a bowl or cake pan taller and slightly smaller in diameter than the ring. Using a blow dryer, quickly and evenly warm the outside of the ring to just melt the chestnut buttercream inside the ring. Carefully slip the ring down off the gâteau. If the ring doesn't slip off easily, warm it a little more and try again.

8. Place the gâteau on a serving plate, and refrigerate until ready to serve.

STORAGE: In the refrigerator for up to 2 days.

Chocorêve

The word *rêve* means dream in French, and this chocolate gâteau certainly qualifies as a chocolate dream. It pairs two layers of crisp *dijonnaise* with a dark, rich chocolate mousse. You wrap a ribbed ribbon of chocolate around the side and cover the top with chocolate curls. Making the ribbon is a quick and easy trick accomplished using ribbed vinyl floor mat. The curls are more time consuming, but really fun to make. Be sure to make the curls very large—1¼ to 1½ inches (3.5 to 4 cm) long and ¾ to 1 inch (2 to 2.5 cm) in diameter. The larger the curls, the fewer of them you will need, and the more spectacular the gâteau will be.

For 8 servings

EQUIPMENT:
Chocolate thermometer or pocket digital thermometer
Electric mixer
8¾-inch (22-cm) cake ring
9-inch (24-cm) foil board or matt board cake-decorating circle (page 467)
Strip of ribbed vinyl floor mat (page 480)
• cut about 1⅝ inches (4 cm) wide and 28 inches (71 cm) long

FILLING AND FROSTING:
European bittersweet chocolate, melted	5¼ ounces (150 g)
Unsalted butter, melted	2⅔ ounces (75 g); 5 tablespoons + 1 teaspoon
Reconstituted powdered egg whites (page 511)	½ cup (1.2 dL)
Cream of tartar (optional)	⅛ teaspoon (a pinch)
Superfine sugar	1½ ounces (40 g); 3 tablespoons

CAKE:
Dijonnaise (page 146)	Two 8¾-inch (22-cm) rounds

CHOCOLATE RIBBON:
European bittersweet chocolate	3 ounces (85 g)

DECORATION FOR TOP OF GÂTEAU:
Large chocolate curls (page 424)	About 8 ounces (225 g)
Confectioners' sugar for dusting	

1. If you did not melt the chocolate for the filling and frosting in a stainless steel bowl, transfer it to one. Temper the chocolate as follows: Dip the bottom of the bowl of chocolate in a larger bowl of cold water and stir the chocolate until the temperature drops to between 80° and 84°F (26.5° to 29°C) and it begins to thicken. Immediately remove from the cold water and dip the bottom of the bowl of chocolate in a larger bowl of hot water. Stir over the hot water just long enough to warm the chocolate to between 86° and 91°F (30° to 33°C) and make it more fluid again. Then remove from the hot water immediately.

2. Stir the melted butter into the chocolate with a wire whisk. When smooth, stir in 2 tablespoons (3 cL) of the reconstituted egg whites.

3. Whip the remaining reconstituted egg whites in the mixer at low speed until they start to froth. If you are not whipping the whites in a copper bowl, add the cream of tartar at this point. Gradually increase the whipping speed to medium-high, and continue whipping until the whites form very stiff peaks and just begin to slip and streak around the side of the bowl. Add the superfine sugar and continue whipping at high speed for a few seconds longer to incorporate the sugar and tighten the meringue.

4. Transfer the chocolate mixture to a medium-size mixing bowl and thoroughly mix in about one third of the meringue. Then gently fold in the remaining meringue to finish the chocolate mousse.

5. Assemble the gâteau from the *dijonnaise* rounds and chocolate mousse filling and frosting by molding it (pages 138 and 142) in the cake ring. If possible, let the gâteau rest in a cool place, rather than the refrigerator, both before and after unmolding in order not to deflate the mousse.

6. If you did not melt the chocolate for the ribbon in a stainless steel bowl, transfer it to one. Temper the chocolate following the instructions in step 1.

7. Lay the strip of vinyl floor mat on your countertop, ribbed side up. Pour the tempered chocolate down the center of the strip of vinyl, and spread it with your icing spatula to cover the strip in an even layer. Carefully lift the ribbon, bend it into a gentle arc, and stand it on edge on a tray. Let it rest in a cool place or in the refrigerator until the chocolate thickens. While the chocolate is still flexible, wrap the vinyl strip around the side of the gâteau, pressing gently to make the chocolate adhere to the mousse and overlapping the ends. Let the chocolate set. Then carefully peel off the vinyl strip, and cut off the overlapping pieces of chocolate with a hot knife blade.

8. Cover the top of the gâteau with the chocolate curls, placing them on end and arranging them adjacent to each other.

9. Place the gâteau on a serving plate, and keep cool until ready to serve. Then dust the top lightly with confectioners' sugar

STORAGE: In a cool place, for up to 1 day. Chilling in the refrigerator tends to make the mousse heavier, but if no cool place is available, then refrigerate the gâteau for as short a time as possible.

Paris

Mound a light chocolate mousse on a round of *dijonnaise*, and top it with a sheet of pure chocolate draped in undulating folds. The chocolate sheet is easier than you might think, and both fun and satisfying to make.

Louis Clichy created the *paris* nearly a hundred years ago, but even today it seems strikingly modern, a stunning piece of abstract sculpture in chocolate.

For 8 servings

EQUIPMENT:
Chocolate thermometer or pocket digital thermometer
Electric mixer
8¾-inch (22-cm) *tarte* ring, ¾ inch (2 cm) deep
9-inch (24-cm) foil board or matt board cake-decorating circle (page 467)
• cut to just fit inside the *tarte* ring
Large baking sheet, preferably black steel or stainless steel
Drywall taping knife, with flexible blade 5 to 6 inches (12.5 to 15 cm) wide (page 469)

CAKE:

Dijonnaise (page 146)	One 8¾-inch (22-cm) round

FILLING:

European bittersweet chocolate, melted	7 ounces (200 g)
Unsalted butter, melted	3½ ounces (100 g); 7 tablespoons
Reconstituted powdered egg whites (page 511)	½ cup + 2 tablespoons (1.5 dL)
Cream of tartar (optional)	⅛ teaspoon (a pinch)
Superfine sugar	1¾ ounces (50 g); ¼ cup

DECORATION FOR TOP OF GÂTEAU:

European bittersweet chocolate	Large bar or block weighing at least 10½ ounces (300 g)

Confectioners' sugar for dusting.

1. Trim the round of *dijonnaise* with a wavy-edge bread knife so it just fits inside the *tarte* ring. Shave the top of the *dijonnaise* to eliminate any large bumps.

2. If you did not melt the chocolate for the filling in a stainless steel bowl, transfer it to one.

Temper the chocolate as follows: Dip the bottom of the bowl of chocolate in a larger bowl of cold water and stir the chocolate until the temperature drops to between 80° and 84°F (26.5° to 29°C) and it begins to thicken. Immediately remove from the cold water and dip the bottom of the bowl of chocolate in a larger bowl of hot water. Stir over the hot water just long enough to warm the chocolate to between 86° and 91°F (30° to 33°C) and make it more fluid again. Then remove from the hot water immediately.

3. Stir the melted butter into the chocolate with a wire whisk. When smooth, stir in 2 tablespoons (3 cL) of the reconstituted egg whites.

4. Whip the remaining reconstituted egg whites in the mixer at low speed until they start to froth. If you are not whipping the whites in a copper bowl, add the cream of tartar at this point. Gradually increase the whipping speed to medium-high, and continue whipping until the whites form very stiff peaks and just begin to slip and streak around the side of the bowl. Add the superfine sugar and continue whipping at high speed for a few seconds longer to incorporate the sugar and tighten the meringue.

5. Transfer the chocolate mixture to a medium-size mixing bowl and thoroughly mix in about one third of the meringue. Then gently fold in the remaining meringue to finish the chocolate mousse.

6. With the tip of a large icing spatula, coat the inside of the *tarte* ring with mousse, and place it on the countertop with the cake-decorating circle underneath. Press the *dijonnaise* round down inside the ring, centering it carefully. Scoop the remaining mousse over the *dijonnaise* and smooth it into a low conical mound using the icing spatula.

7. Slide the gâteau onto a tray. Put it in a cool place (or the refrigerator if necessary), and let the mousse set.

8. Place the gâteau on a bowl or cake pan taller and slightly smaller in diameter than the ring. Using a blow dryer, quickly and evenly warm the outside of the ring to just melt the mousse inside the ring. Slip the ring down off the gâteau. Let the gâteau rest in a cool place.

Preheat the oven to 250°F (120°C).

9. Put the baking sheet in the oven for about 10 minutes to heat it. Place the hot baking sheet on your countertop (with a kitchen towel underneath if necessary to protect your countertop) and rub the long edge of the block of chocolate over it to melt the chocolate. As it melts, use the edge of the chocolate to spread the melted chocolate in a thin, even layer over the entire surface of the baking sheet. Melt about 5¼ ounces (150 g) of chocolate for a 12 × 16-inch (30 × 40-cm) baking sheet or 7 ounces (200 g) of chocolate for a 13 × 20-inch (33 × 50-cm) baking sheet.

When you have enough chocolate melted, smooth the surface with the edge of the chocolate. Place the baking sheet in the refrigerator until the chocolate begins to set. Remove it from the refrigerator to allow the temperature to even out, then continue moving it in and out of the refrigerator until you can scrape chocolate off the baking sheet without it sticking to the drywall knife (meaning the chocolate is still too soft) or shattering (the chocolate is too hard). If the chocolate gets too hard, use a blow dryer briefly on the back of the baking sheet to rewarm it evenly and quickly.

10. Slide the drywall knife under the chocolate with one hand to lift up a wide sheet of chocolate, and use the fingertips of your other hand to hold the free end of the sheet. Work crosswise on the baking sheet to get a sheet of chocolate as long as the baking sheet is wide. Quickly and carefully carry the sheet of chocolate to the top of the gâteau and drape it on top in smooth, dramatic folds. Press the sheet against the side of the gâteau. Repeat twice more with the remaining chocolate on the baking sheet to entirely cover the top of the gâteau. Trim the chocolate at the bottom edge of the gâteau with the tip of your paring knife to remove the excess.

11. Place the gâteau on a serving plate, and keep cool until ready to serve. Then dust the top lightly with confectioners' sugar.

STORAGE: In a cool place, for up to 1 day. Chilling in the refrigerator tends to make the mousse heavier, but if no cool place is available, then refrigerate the gâteau for as short a time as possible.

Meringues

· ·

A meringue is simply a mixture of stiffly whipped egg whites and sugar. When baked, it is very light, sweet, and usually crisp.

There are three distinct methods of preparing meringue batters (called French, Italian, and Swiss), depending on how the sugar is incorporated. For French (or "ordinary") meringue, sugar is beaten into the whipped whites, while for Italian meringue hot sugar syrup is used instead of dry sugar. For Swiss meringue, egg whites and sugar are combined at the outset and whipped over low heat.

You will use French meringue to make individual-serving-size desserts, decorations, rounds for layers in gâteaux, and shells that are filled with ice cream or whipped cream and fruits to become the classic desserts called *vacherins*. You will also make French meringue as part of the preparation of separated-egg sponge cake batters.

You will use Italian meringue for some decorations and individual-serving-size desserts and as part of the preparation of *vacherin* shells, and you will use it as a frosting on some gâteaux. It is not used in sponge cake batters, but some chefs like to include it in mousses to give them extra lightness and stability.

Swiss meringue is much heavier than French and Italian meringues. At one time it was considered quite versatile, and some chefs preferred it over French and Italian meringues for many purposes because it is very stable. However, today the fashion is for meringues to be as light as possible. Consequently, Swiss meringue is used very little in modern cake making. We will not discuss it any further.

History of Meringue

The first known mention of meringues in a cookbook was in François Massialot's *Le Cuisinier Roïal et Bourgeois*, published in 1691. At least two credible explanations have been proposed for the origin of the word meringue. It may derive from Mieringen (also spelled Mehrinyghen), a small town south of Lucerne in the Swiss alps. A Swiss pastry chef of Italian descent named Gasparini, who worked in that town, has been credited with the invention of the meringue near the end of the seventeenth century. However, some culinary historians believe that meringues were created even earlier. A second hypothesis relates meringue to the low Latin "meringa," a corruption of the word "merenda," which refers to an afternoon snack.

Meringues were introduced into France in the eighteenth century by Stanislaus Leszczynski, the deposed king of Poland and father-in-law of the French King Louis XV. When Stanislaus abdicated the Polish throne for the second time in 1735, King Louis did a bit of diplomatic maneuvering to give him the dukedom of Lorraine. Stanislaus was a noted gourmet, and meringues quickly became the rage among royalty after he began serving them to his entourage at the court in Luneville. Toward the end of the century they were a favorite of Queen Marie Antoinette, who prepared them herself at the Trianon.

Understanding Egg White Foams

Whipping egg whites properly is essential to making any kind of meringue. The delicate stability of the whipped egg whites depends on several factors. By understanding and controlling these factors, you can make whipping egg whites a trouble-free procedure.

The egg white, or albumen, is a solution of several proteins in water. At the outset, the egg white has a cohesiveness that is a result of a layered structure among its component molecules. Beating the white with a wire whisk or beater quickly breaks up this structure and makes the whites more fluid.

When you whip the whites, the whisk or beater drags air into them, dispersing air bubbles throughout the liquid to produce a mass of bubbles that we call a foam. At the same time, whipping gradually stabilizes the foam by altering the physical configuration of the proteins and linking them to each other and to water molecules. This combination of effects makes the whites become thicker and less fluid. We say they become more viscous.

Continued whipping incorporates more air in the foam and divides large bubbles into smaller ones. It also builds up a loosely connected network of protein and water molecules. The foam grows in volume and becomes more stable. Eventually, when the foam is baked (whether in a meringue or a cake batter), the air in the bubbles expands and the proteins coagulate (meaning they bond together chemically), replacing the loosely connected network of the foam with a more tightly connected structure that doesn't collapse when the bubbles in the foam burst and the air escapes.

If the egg whites are whipped more before baking, the protein molecules link together progressively more tightly. There is less room in the network for water molecules to connect to the proteins, and eventually some water will be released and the foam will become drier.

When sugar is added to an egg white foam, it dissolves in the water in the bubble walls to become a sugar syrup that makes the bubble walls thicker and more elastic. As a result, bubbles slide past each other rather than breaking and coalescing, and the foam holds together rather than separating into fluffy, semi-solid masses. The syrup also coats the protein molecules so that continued whipping will not tighten their connections and squeeze out water from the interconnecting network. Thus the addition of sugar prevents water from being released and keeps the foam moist. When the foam bakes, the greater elasticity of the bubbles helps prevent them from expanding too much and bursting too early. The sugar also contributes to the foam's stability during baking by delaying the evaporation of water from the foam, giving the proteins more time to coagulate.

WHIPPING EGG WHITES— SOME PRELIMINARIES

①

First, the eggs should be separated carefully ①, so that no yolk gets in the whites. Fats, particularly egg yolks (which contain emulsifiers as well as fats), interfere with the development of the egg white foam. The presence of even a speck of egg yolk will drastically increase the amount of energy required to produce the foam and will reduce the foam's stability. For this reason, you should always use a very clean bowl and whisk (or beater) to whip egg whites. (Never use plastic bowls because the plastic retains traces of fat on its surface, even after a thorough cleaning.) After the whites have been whipped, ingredients containing fats can be added without damaging the foam.

The fresher the eggs, the more viscous (thicker) the egg whites. The whites of eggs that are at least three days old can actually be whipped to slightly greater volume than those of very fresh eggs. This is an advantage for making soufflés, where maximum volume is highly desirable. In pastry making, stability is more important than maximum volume, and whipping fresh whites makes the foam more stable.

While it is easiest to separate eggs when they are cold, it is easier to whip air into warm whites. For this reason the egg whites should be allowed to warm to room temperature before whipping.

You can whip the whites using a flexible wire whisk or the wire whip of an electric mixer. The whisk gives you tremendous control, but whisking even two or three egg whites for a meringue takes a lot of energy. We strongly recommend using a heavy-duty electric stand mixer with planetary action. An eggbeater-type electric mixer is very efficient for the early stages of whipping the whites, but when the whites become thick, it whips them unevenly if the beater stays in one place. With a handheld electric mixer, you can remedy that problem by continually moving the beaters around the bowl. If you have an eggbeater-type stand mixer, use it to whip the whites until they start to become thick, and then finish with a wire whisk.

Use a copper, stainless steel, glass, or glazed ceramic bowl to whip egg whites. Do not use aluminum, which discolors the whites. A good rule of thumb is that the bowl should have a volume at least 32 times that of the initial volume of the whites. Since the volume of eight large egg whites is about 1 cup (2.4 dL) before whipping, you will need a bowl with a capacity of at least 1 quart (1 L) for every two large whites. We recommend whipping a minimum of two large egg whites when making a meringue. The volume of one large egg white is only 2 tablespoons (3 cL) before whipping, and most whisks and beaters are too large to whip air into so small a quantity of albumen effectively.

Copper bowls are the best choice for whipping egg whites. The advantage of the copper bowl is that atoms of copper bind with parts of the egg white proteins. The result is an egg white foam that is creamier and less easy to overwhip than one whipped in a stainless steel bowl. To keep the copper bowl absolutely free of fats or detergents, follow these steps: After each use, wash the bowl thoroughly with hot water; clean the surface with a mixture of coarse salt (such as coarse kosher salt) and distilled white vinegar

→ Le Cake page 26 →

→ Week-End page 32 →

→ Biscuit de Savoie page 45 ←

→ Biscuit Chocolat page 40 ←

✣ Croix de Lorraine page 54 ✣

✣ Clafoutis page 58 ✣

✦ Moka page 88 ✦

→ Nöella page 108 →

→ Marguerite Cassis page 110 →

↦ Succulent page 94 ↤

↦ Grenoblois page 112 ↤

→ Framboisine page 124 →

→ Marquis page 126 →

➢ Abricotine page 128 ➢

Succès Kirsch page 150

→ Progrès page 154 →

❖ Chanteclair page 161 ❖

❖ Chocolatine and Noisettine page 162 ❖

→ Marie Stuart page 164 →

Chocorêve page 166

→ Truffes Praliné and
Truffes Chocolat page 192 →

→ Fromage Citron page 196 →

→ Meringues Café and
Meringues Chocolat page 200 →

❖ Paris page 168 ❖

→ Vacherin Glacé page 206 →

Ray Ventura page 230

Clichy page 239

❖ Ébéniste page 236 ❖

→ Lucifer page 242 →

✦ Russe au Chocolat page 248
and Russe Praliné page 250 ✦

✦ Chocomel page 256 ✦

→ Mango Charlotte page 312 →

→ Java page 324 →

→ Gâteau au Fromage Blanc page 318 →

❖ Romanov page 288 ❖

❖ Raspberry Charlotte page 294 ❖

⇢ Alhambra page 369 ⇢

✦ Chocolate Yule Log page 351 ✦

→ Lemon Meringue Yule Log page 354 →

➔ Trianon Montmorency page 375 ➔

(or other inexpensive white vinegar), which removes oxidation as well as fats and detergents; rinse it out with cold water; and leave it upside down to drain and air dry.

If you do not have a copper bowl, add some cream of tartar to the whites shortly after you begin whipping them. The cream of tartar is a mildly acidic salt that lowers the initially alkaline pH of the whites and also reduces the risk of overwhipping them. While the mechanism is totally different (and not well understood), the end result is similar to that produced by whipping in a copper bowl.

WHIPPING EGG WHITES—THE PROCEDURE

Now you are ready to whip the whites. Start at low speed to break up the whites. At the beginning, the albumen is so cohesive that there is a tendency to whip large bubbles into the whites. By starting slowly, you get smaller bubbles and a finer texture.

If you are whipping by hand with a wire whisk, tilt the bowl and move the whisk in a rhythmic circular motion ②. Sweeping the whisk around the bottom of the bowl, in and out of the mass of egg whites (which will actually lift with each stroke of the whisk at the beginning), is the most efficient way to break up the whites and drag the maximum amount of air into them.

If you are whipping with an eggbeater-type electric mixer, constantly move it around the bowl to beat the whites evenly.

Soon the whites will begin to froth. If you are not whipping the whites in a copper bowl, add a little cream of tartar at this point ③. The amount of cream of tartar required is about ⅛ teaspoon (a pinch) for three large egg whites. (If you use much more than that, it will be impossible to determine when the whites have been beaten to the optimal degree.)

Now gradually increase the whipping speed. In a planetary-action electric mixer, we find that medium-high speed works best ④. If you are whipping by hand using a wire whisk, do most of the beating at medium speed so you can save your energy for a burst of high speed whipping at the end.

As progressively more air is whipped into the egg whites, new air bubbles are created and large air bubbles are divided into progressively finer ones. The whites will increase in volume and change from a slightly yellowish, clear liquid to an opaque white foam that soon becomes thick enough to hold soft, bending peaks as you lift the whisk. When you tilt the bowl at this "soft peaks" stage, the mass of egg whites will slide around in it and will not cling to the side of the bowl. If you are whipping with an egg-beater-type stand mixer, quickly switch to a wire whisk when you reach the soft peaks stage. (If you were to stop whipping at the soft peaks stage, the foam would not be sufficiently light, firm, or fine, and there would not be enough proteins linked together to support it. The result would have low volume and be unstable.)

Continue whipping. The whites will become stiffer and will begin to cling to the side of the bowl so that the mass of whites will not slip when the bowl is tipped. Lifting the whip will produce stiff, unbending peaks, and the whites will still be moist and shiny. This is the "stiff-but-not-dry" stage. For soufflés you will get the best results (maximum expansion and optimal moisture inside when baked) by whipping the whites to this point. However, for pastry making most batters will be too soft and will spread too much when baked if you stop at this point.

As you whip the whites still more, the surface of the whites will become a little duller, and the whites around the side of the bowl (where whipping applies the greatest force on the albumen) will just begin to release a little moisture. This allows the mass of egg whites to slip on the side of the bowl, forming streaks as the whisk drags the mass around. This "slip-and-streak" stage is the crucial stage to look for. It gives a sharp, well-defined test for the point at which the optimal texture is reached. (If you use too much cream of tartar, the whites will not slip and streak around the side of the bowl.)

If you whip the whites more than this, the egg white proteins will gradually lose their ability to hold water. The foam will release liquid, become grainy, and lose volume. At this point the whites are overwhipped. They cannot be rescued, but, fortunately, egg whites are cheap. Discard the overwhipped whites and start again.

So far you have only whipped egg whites. They do not become a meringue until the sugar is added. For French and Italian meringues, you add the sugar or hot sugar syrup at the end of the whipping, usually at the slip-and-streak stage. You then whip the whites at maximum speed for a few seconds to incorporate the sugar and "tighten" the meringue. The sugar makes the foam smoother and more cohesive almost instantly. The extent of the change depends on the quantity of sugar used. Tightening the meringue by whipping it briefly at high speed after adding the sugar helps prevent the meringue from expanding too much in the oven and then deflating, which would cause the meringue to be too dry inside and tacky on the surface. The sugar is added at the end of the whipping, rather than at the beginning, because once the sugar has been added it requires much more energy to create new air bubbles in the foam and the structure that supports the foam develops more slowly.

FRENCH MERINGUE

French meringue (or ordinary meringue) is the simplest type of meringue to prepare. It is always baked, and it is the most widely used meringue in cake making. When used alone, it is baked crisp and dry. The texture is very fine, crumbly, and fragile. When eaten, it is tender and melting.

On the average it is also the least sweet type of meringue. For plain meringues the amount of sugar used ranges from 4½ to 9 ounces (125 to 250 g) for three large egg whites. The more sugar, the firmer the batter and the crisper the baked meringue.

The whites are usually whipped to the slip-and-streak stage and then "meringued" by whipping in part of the sugar called for in the recipe ⑤. The remaining sugar, as well as other ingredients, are folded in after the completion of the whipping. Whipping in too much sugar, or whipping for too long after adding the sugar, would make the baked meringue tough and chewy. Folding in part of the sugar produces a more tender meringue.

⑤

The sugar used to tighten the meringue is always superfine or extra fine sugar because these fine-textured sugars dissolve quickly. They are preferable to confectioners' sugar because they don't require sifting and mix in readily without clinging to the side of the bowl or forming dust in the air as confectioners' sugar is prone to do. The sugar that is folded in after the whites are meringued is most often confectioners' because it dissolves even more quickly than does superfine.

The proportion of the sugar whipped in depends partly on how the meringue is baked, and partly on the other ingredients included in the recipe. For plain meringues, typically half the sugar is whipped in. This makes the whipped whites very shiny, smooth, firm, and cohesive, enabling you to pipe very precise forms that hold their shapes. Since the meringue is normally baked crisp, the result is a desirable brittleness rather than an undesirable chewiness. These meringues are tolerant of slight overwhipping before adding the sugar because the high amount of sugar used to tighten the meringue can bind water released by the egg white proteins. However, it is especially important that after adding the sugar they be whipped only the minimum necessary to incorporate the sugar and make the meringue smooth and shiny. Otherwise the baked meringue will be tough.

ITALIAN MERINGUE

Italian meringue is the lightest and, on average, the sweetest of all the meringues.

When Italian meringue is baked alone, the result can be similar to that produced with French meringue, but there are important differences. If baked dry, the Italian meringue is also quite crisp but not as fragile. However, Italian meringue bakes faster than ordinary meringue, and it can be baked crisp on the outside but still be soft and creamy inside, whereas plain French meringue does not normally produce a successful result unless crisp throughout. Italian meringue is most often flavored with chocolate or coffee to offset its sweetness.

The amount of sugar used in Italian meringue is typically 6 to 9 ounces (175 to 250 g) for three large egg whites. The sugar is moistened with water and cooked to the high end of the firm-ball stage (about 248°F = 120°C). Then the hot syrup is added to egg whites that have been whipped to the slip-and-streak stage. The syrup and whites must be ready simultaneously, so these meringues can be a little tricky to prepare.

⑥

To prepare the syrup, combine the granulated sugar with a little water in a small, heavy saucepan or caramel pot. Ideally the saucepan should have a spout for pouring the syrup in a thin stream, and the level of the sugar syrup in the pot should be high enough so that you can easily measure its temperature. Use about ¼ cup (6 cL) of water for each 7 ounces (200 g), or 1 cup, of sugar. Stir to thoroughly moisten the sugar ⑥, then bring to a boil over medium heat. Do not stir while you are cooking the sugar because syrup splashed on the sides of the saucepan dries and produces unwanted sugar crystals.

⑦

Right after the syrup comes to a boil, some sugar crystals will form on the sides of the saucepan. Dissolve these crystals by washing down the sides with a moistened pastry brush ⑦, using as little water as possible so that you don't slow the cooking.

Start whipping the egg whites after the syrup comes to a boil. We strongly recommend using a planetary-action electric mixer to prepare Italian meringue. It is almost impossible to whisk the egg whites by hand (or even to whip them with a handheld electric mixer) while you assess the progress of the sugar syrup, and pouring hot sugar syrup with one hand while you whisk it into the whites with the other is dangerous, even for an experienced professional. If you must whisk the whites by hand, then have a second person cook the syrup and pour it into the whites.

⑧

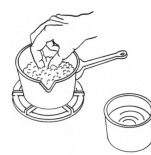

⑨

⑩

⑪

As you continue to boil the syrup, you will evaporate water and raise the temperature of the syrup, making it more viscous. You can check the temperature of the syrup either with a candy thermometer or by testing its viscosity.

To test the viscosity of the syrup, pluck out a little syrup and plunge it into a bowl of cold water. (Professionals use their fingertips, moistened first in cold water to protect them and keep them cool ⑧ ⑨, but most amateurs prefer a spoon.) Feel the cooled syrup between your thumb and index finger. At the beginning it will dissolve immediately in the water, but as the syrup becomes more viscous it will dissolve more slowly. When the syrup reaches the soft-ball stage, or 234° to 239°F (113° to 115°C), you will be able to roll it between your fingertips into a small, very soft and sticky ball that will flatten as you lift it. As you continue to raise the temperature of the sugar you will be able to form the cooled syrup into a larger, firmer ball that will hold its shape. When you reach the high end of the firm-ball stage—about 248°F (120°C)—the ball will be a little larger than a pea and will no longer stick to your moistened fingertips ⑩, but will still be firm and malleable rather than hard. This is the temperature you need for the Italian meringue.

(If you are cooking a sugar syrup at high altitude, remember to adjust the temperature to compensate for the change in the boiling point of water. For all stages of sugar cooking up to and including the soft-crack stage, reduce the temperature specified by 1.8°F (1°C) for each 1,000 feet (300 m) above sea level.)

Gradually increase the speed at which you whip the whites as the temperature of the syrup increases, so that the whites reach the slip-and-streak stage at the same time as the sugar reaches the upper-firm-ball stage. If you find that the whites are progressing too rapidly, then reduce the whipping speed. If the syrup is heating too rapidly, lower the heat under it.

When the sugar reaches the high end of the firm-ball stage, pour the hot syrup into the whites in a thin stream while you whip the whites at high speed ⑪. The meringue will rise and become very light. Avoid pouring the syrup onto the wire whip or it will splatter around the sides of the bowl. Try to pour the syrup directly into the whites. The problem is that in a planetary-action mixer the bowl has very steep sides, which make this impossible unless you are whipping a large volume of meringue. For the small volume of meringue in our recipes, you will probably need to pour the syrup down the side of the bowl in order to avoid pouring it onto the whip.

After all of the syrup has been added, continue whipping for a few seconds at high speed to make the meringue smooth and shiny. Quickly reduce the mixer to the lowest speed and continue stirring to prevent a crust from forming on top of the meringue while you finish any final mixing of the other ingredients in the recipe. Then turn off the machine, and remove any syrup that has solidified on the side of the bowl using a bowl scrapper. For baking, the meringue must be used while it is still hot.

BAKING

Batters based on French meringue should be baked as soon as possible after they are prepared. If you let them wait too long before baking, they begin to deflate. Also, some sugar syrup can separate from the batter, drip onto the baking sheet, and make it difficult to remove the meringues after baking.

While Italian meringue is more stable than French meringue, it will also deteriorate with time. We recommend the same precautions be followed as for French meringue.

You will pipe meringue batters onto a baking sheet with a pastry bag and tube. To prevent the meringues from sticking to the baking sheet, brush the baking sheet with melted butter ⑫ and let the butter set. (The butter does not need to be clarified.) Sprinkle flour over the butter ⑬, using more flour than you will need in the end. Tilt, shake, and tap the sheet to distribute the flour and coat the sheet evenly. Then invert the baking sheet and tap it with a wooden spatula ⑭ or the handle of a dough scraper to dislodge the excess flour. The flour prevents the batter from slipping around as you pipe it, and it keeps the butter separate from the batter so that the fat in the butter doesn't damage the structure of the bottom of the meringues. In rare instances, you can pipe meringue batter onto a moistened plank of wood covered with a sheet of newsprint to produce meringues (in particular, our chocolate meringue corkscrews, page 202) that are moist and custardy inside rather than crisp throughout.

Plain meringues are most often baked at a low oven temperature, 250° to 325°F (120° to 160°C). If the oven temperature is too high, the meringues expand too much and the outsides color too quickly while the insides are insufficiently baked and become tough and chewy. But if the oven temperature is too low, the meringues don't expand enough and are too dry, hard, and heavy.

Since the baking temperature is low, it is often possible to bake two

⑫

⑬

⑭

sheets of meringues on two oven racks simultaneously. Place one sheet on the bottom oven rack and the other on an upper oven rack, being sure there is plenty of space between them. Then reverse the positions of the two sheets about halfway through the baking period. A good rule of thumb is that this will always work if the oven temperature is 300°F (150°C) or lower. If the oven temperature is much higher, then bottom heat is too important a factor for this procedure to be successful.

STORAGE

Unfilled meringues should be kept enclosed airtight in a tin cookie box, a plastic storage container, or (for large meringues) a plastic bag. They should not be exposed to high humidity. In fact, meringues are so adversely affected by high humidity that it is better not to make them at all in humid weather.

Crisp meringues can last for up to 1 or 2 weeks. Italian meringues that are baked on a moistened plank will last only for a day or two.

Meringues filled with buttercream can be kept, uncovered, in the refrigerator for 1 or 2 days. Those filled with whipped cream should be eaten within 2 to 4 hours. Meringues with ice cream should be filled and decorated shortly before serving so that the whipped cream decoration will be tender, the ice cream soft, and the meringue crisp.

Italian Meringue

· ·

This meringue, prepared by whipping hot sugar syrup into stiffly beaten egg whites, is incredibly light and extremely versatile. Not only can you pipe it from a pastry bag and tube and bake it like ordinary meringue but you can also use it as for a frosting or as the basis for a filling (such as our new French buttercream, page 384), or fold it into other fillings to lighten them.

For 9½ ounces (270 g); about 4½ cups

EQUIPMENT:
Large bowl of cold water or candy thermometer
Electric mixer, preferably a stand mixer equipped with wire whip

BATTER:

Granulated sugar	7 ounces (200 g); 1 cup
Water	¼ cup (6 cL)
Large egg whites (see note), at room temperature	3
Cream of tartar (optional)	⅛ teaspoon (a pinch)

   1. Combine the sugar and water in a heavy 1-quart (1-L) saucepan or caramel pot and stir to thoroughly moisten the sugar. Bring to a boil over medium heat. Moisten a pastry brush with cold water and wash down the sides of the saucepan to dissolve any sugar crystals that form there. Continue boiling over medium heat without stirring, washing down the walls of the saucepan as needed to dissolve sugar crystals, until the sugar reaches the high end of the firm-ball stage (see page 181). When you pluck a little syrup from the saucepan and immerse it in the bowl of cold water, you will be able to roll the syrup into a firm ball that holds its shape and is no longer sticky. The temperature of the syrup will measure 248°F (120°C) on the candy thermometer.

   2. Meanwhile, when the sugar comes to a boil, start whipping the egg whites in the mixer at low speed until they start to froth. If you are not whipping the whites in a copper bowl, add the cream of tartar at this point. Gradually increase the whipping speed and continue whipping at medium to high speed until the whites form very stiff peaks and just begin to slip and streak around the side of the bowl. Adjust the speed at which you whip the whites (lowering the speed if necessary) and the rate at which you cook the sugar so that they are ready simultaneously.

3. Pour the syrup into the egg whites in a steady stream while you whip the whites at high speed. Try to pour the syrup directly into the whites, but in an electric mixer with a steep-sided bowl you will probably need to pour the syrup down the side of the bowl in order to avoid pouring it onto the whip and spattering syrup around the inside of the bowl. The meringue will rise and become very light.

4. After all of the syrup has been added, continue whipping briefly until the meringue is smooth and shiny.

5. If you are making the meringue to be piped and baked or as a frosting, then use it while still hot. Otherwise, let the meringue cool to room temperature, stirring at very low speed in the electric mixer, or gently stirring occasionally with a wire whisk, to prevent it from forming a skin on top.

6. Before using, remove any sugar syrup that has solidified on the side of the bowl using a bowl scraper.

STORAGE: For piping from a pastry bag and then baking or for frosting, the meringue should be used within an hour after it is prepared. It will always have the best consistency and lightness when freshly made, but for other purposes it can be kept in the refrigerator, covered airtight, for up to 2 days if necessary.

NOTE: If the meringue will not be baked and if salmonella in eggs is a problem in your area, then it is important to pasteurize the egg whites. The egg whites in Italian meringue are partially cooked by the heat of the sugar syrup. Unfortunately, while the heat of the syrup is, in principle, sufficient to raise the temperature of the egg whites above 160°F (71°C) and pasteurize them instantly, the mixing bowl quickly absorbs heat from the meringue and (depending on the size of the bowl, number of whites, and speed of adding the syrup) may prevent the temperature of the meringue from actually reaching the pasteurization point.

There are two easy solutions to this problem. One is to avoid it altogether by using reconstituted powdered egg whites (such as Just Whites, page 511) in our Italian meringue recipe. The other is to warm the mixer bowl and the egg whites before whipping. We prefer the second technique because it is more versatile.

To warm the bowl and egg whites, first turn the mixer bowl upside down in your sink and run hot tap water over it to heat it quickly. While the bowl is being warmed, pour some hot tap water into a bowl or saucepan large enough to set your mixer bowl in. Adjust the temperature of the water in the bowl to 120°F (50° C), and adjust the level of the water so that it is high enough to surround the bottom of the mixer bowl but not so high that the mixer bowl will float and tip over. Set the heated mixer bowl in the hot water bath, be sure that it is dry inside, and pour in the whites. Stir the whites occasionally with a wire whisk while you are bringing the sugar syrup to a boil. If the temperature of the hot water bath starts to drop below 120°F (50°C), add more hot water to keep the temperature there. When the syrup comes to a boil, remove the mixer bowl from the hot water bath and whip the whites as instructed in the recipe. When you pour the hot sugar syrup into the whipped whites, do it quickly so that the heat of the syrup will raise the temperature of the whites all at once, before too much heat drains off into the mixer bowl.

French Meringue

· ·

French meringue can be piped in an infinite variety of shapes.

For 15½ ounces (440 g); about 4 cups

EQUIPMENT:
Electric mixer

BATTER:

Confectioners' sugar	5¼ ounces (150 g); 1¼ cups
All-purpose flour	⅓ ounce (10 g); 1 tablespoon + ½ teaspoon
Large egg whites, at room temperature	4
Cream of tartar (optional)	⅛ teaspoon (a pinch)
Superfine or extra fine sugar	5¼ ounces (150 g); ¾ cup

1. Mix the confectioners' sugar and flour and sift them together on a sheet of wax paper.

2. Whip the egg whites in the mixer at low speed until they start to froth. If you are not whipping the whites in a copper bowl, then add the cream of tartar at this point. Gradually increase the whipping speed to medium-high, and continue whipping until the whites form very stiff peaks and just begin to slip and streak around the side of the bowl. Add the superfine sugar and continue whipping at high speed for a few seconds longer to make the meringue smooth and shiny.

3. Gently fold the confectioners sugar' and flour into the meringue. The meringue is now ready to pipe and bake following one of the recipes for meringue desserts in this chapter.

STORAGE: None. The batter must be piped and baked soon after it is prepared or it will deflate.

Vacherin Shells

. . . .

A *vacherin* is a shell of meringue filled with either ice cream or whipped cream and fresh fruits. It is named for the French *vacherin* cheeses from Savoy and the Franche-Comte, which it is thought to resemble.

Vacherins require no mold, so you can make them in any size you like. We give the recipes for a shell 9½ inches (24 cm) in diameter.

The preparation is done in two stages. Stage 1: Pipe a round of meringue with a rim around the circumference, and a ring of meringue of the same diameter, and bake the round and the ring. Stage 2: Glue the ring on top of the rim on the round of meringue with more meringue batter, cover the outside with a smooth layer of meringue, and pipe meringue in a decorative pattern around the outside; then bake again to dry out the meringue glue, coating, and decoration.

For one 9½-inch (24-cm) shell

EQUIPMENT, STAGE 1:
2 heavy baking sheets
• brush with melted butter
• dust with flour
Medium-size pastry bag fitted with
• ½-inch (12-mm) plain pastry tube (Ateco #6)
Second medium-size pastry bag fitted with
• ⅝-inch (16-mm) plain pastry tube (Ateco #8)

EQUIPMENT, STAGE 2:
Heavy baking sheet
Medium-size pastry bag fitted with
• ½-inch (12-mm) plain pastry tube (Ateco #6)
Small pastry bag fitted with
• medium-small fluted pastry tube (Ateco #3)
9-inch (24-cm) foil board or matt board cake-decorating circle (page 467)

continued

BATTER, STAGE 1:

French meringue (page 186)   15½ ounces (440 g);
                                                4 cups

BATTER, STAGE 2:

Italian meringue (page 184), or substitute   6½ ounces (180 g);
   an equal volume of French meringue   3 cups

Stage 1.
Preheat the oven to 275°F (135°C).

1. Mark one 9½-inch (24-cm) circle on each baking sheet by tapping the baking sheet with a cake ring, *tarte* ring, round mold, or *vol-au-vent* disk ①. Leave space between the circles and the edges of the baking sheet.

2. Scoop half of the French meringue into the first pastry bag. Starting from the center of one of the circles, pipe a continuous spiral of meringue ② that fills the circle.

3. Scoop the remaining French meringue into the second pastry bag. Pipe a ring of meringue ¾ inch (2 cm) wide on the perimeter of the round you have already piped ③ to finish the base. Pipe a second ring of meringue ¾ inch (2 cm) wide just inside the second circle marked on the baking sheet.

4. Bake, using a wooden spatula to hold the oven door ajar, until the meringue is set, dry, and firm to the touch, about 40 to 60 minutes.

5. Place the baking sheet on a wire rack and let the meringue cool to room temperature.

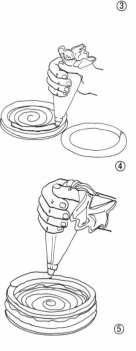

Stage 2.
Preheat the oven to 200°F (100°C).

6. Place the meringue base on the cake-decorating circle on your countertop.

7. Scoop half of the Italian meringue into the first pastry bag. Pipe a strip of meringue on the rim on the meringue base ④. Turn the baked ring of meringue upside down and place it on top of the rim. Pipe a strip of meringue over the top of the ring ⑤. Slide a large icing spatula under the cake-decorating circle, lift the *vacherin* shell from the countertop, and transfer it to the fingertips of one hand. With the icing spatula in the other hand, spread meringue over the sides of the shell ⑥, leaving a rim of meringue extending above the top edge. Return the shell to the countertop.

Smooth the top surface of the *vacherin* shell by sweeping the edge of the blade of the icing spatula across the top to take off excess meringue. Start with the icing spatula at one side of the shell, with the face of the blade at an angle of 30° relative to the top surface, and rotate the face of the blade through about 90° as you sweep across the top so that when the blade reaches the opposite side the excess meringue is lifted on top of the face of the blade. Depending on how much excess meringue is on top, it may take a second sweep in the opposite direction to get the top surface flat.

⑥

When you are ready to smooth the side of the *vacherin* shell, slide the icing spatula under the cake-decorating circle and lift the shell from the countertop again. Transfer the shell to the fingertips of one hand and take the icing spatula in the other hand. Smooth the side by sweeping the edge of the blade of the icing spatula over the side to take off excess meringue. Start with the bottom third of the blade against the side of the shell, with the face of the blade nearly parallel to the surface, and sweep the edge of the blade around the side, drawing the blade downward and turning the face of the blade toward you. Clean off the blade on the rim of the bowl of meringue, rotate the shell on your fingertips, and repeat until you have smoothed the entire outside surface.

8. Place the *vacherin* shell on a round wire rack so you can rotate it easily. Scoop the rest of the meringue into the second pastry bag. Pipe a simple scroll pattern around the sides of the *vacherin* ⑦.

⑦

9. Place the *vacherin* shell on the baking sheet and bake until the outside of the shell is dry and firm to the touch but still white, about 1 hour or longer if necessary. The surface of the meringue should stay white. If it begins to color before it is dry, reduce the oven temperature to 175°F (80°C).

10. Place the baking sheet on a wire rack, and let the *vacherin* shell cool on the baking sheet.

NOTE: The technique for spreading and smoothing the meringue on the *vacherin* shell is essentially the same as for frosting a round nut meringue gâteau by the traditional freehand method. See page 140 for more details.

STORAGE: At room temperature in a very dry place, either in a tin cookie box or covered airtight in a plastic bag, for up to 2 weeks.

Meringue Rounds

. . . .

You can use rounds of French meringue as layers in gâteaux just as you do with *dijonnaise* and *succès*. The meringue rounds are very light and sweet. They are usually most successful when you use them as a third cake layer between two layers of génoise or *dijonnaise* in a taller gâteau.

For two 8¾-inch (22-cm) rounds

EQUIPMENT:

1 or 2 large, heavy baking sheets
• brush with melted butter
• dust with flour
Large pastry bag fitted with
• ½-inch (12-mm) plain pastry tube (Ateco #6)

BATTER:

French meringue (page 186)   15½ ounces (440 g); 4 cups

Preheat the oven to 275°F (135°C).

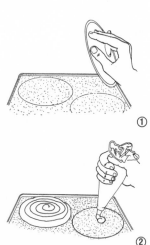

1. Mark two 8¾-inch (22-cm) circles on the baking sheet (or sheets if you can't fit them both on one) by tapping the baking sheet with a cake ring, *tarte* ring, round mold, or *vol-au-vent* disk ①. Leave space between the circles and the edge of the baking sheet as well as each other.

2. Scoop the meringue batter into the pastry bag. Starting from the center of each circle, pipe the batter in a continuous spiral ② that completely fills the circle. All of the batter must be piped out and baked right away or it will deflate. If there is a little extra batter, you can pipe it in domes about 1¼ inches (3 cm) wide; these small domes are useful for assessing how the meringue is baking without damaging the large rounds.

3. Bake, using a wooden spatula to hold the oven door ajar, until the meringue is set, dry, and firm to the touch, about 40 to 60 minutes. (If you piped the rounds on two baking sheets and must bake them in one oven, place one sheet on a lower oven rack and one on an upper oven rack for half of the baking period. Reverse the positions of the two baking sheets for the second half of the baking period.) If you have piped some small test domes, you can lift one off the baking sheet, let it cool for a few minutes, and cut it in half to see if the meringue is cooked through.

4. Place the baking sheet on a wire rack and let the meringue cool to room temperature. Then slide the blade of a large icing spatula or pancake turner under each round and carefully lift it off the baking sheet.

STORAGE: At room temperature in a very dry place, either in a tin cookie box or covered airtight in a plastic bag, for up to 2 weeks.

Truffes Praliné and Truffes Chocolat

These meringue truffles are made by sandwiching two domes of French meringue together with *praliné* or chocolate buttercream, then coating the outside with the buttercream and either chocolate shavings or roasted sliced almonds.

For 10 truffles

EQUIPMENT:

2 large, heavy baking sheets
• brush with melted butter
• dust with flour
Large pastry bag fitted with
• ⅝-inch (16-mm) plain pastry tube (Ateco #8)

BATTER:

French meringue (page 186)	15½ ounces (440 g); 4 cups

FILLING:

Chocolate buttercream or *praliné* buttercream (page 388)	1 pound + 2 ounces (510 g); 3 cups
For *truffes praliné*	
Either coarsely crushed *pralin* (page 446) Or raw almonds, roasted (page 444) and chopped	1¼ ounces (35 g); ¼ cup

DECORATION:

For *truffes praliné*	
Sliced almonds, roasted (page 444)	10½ ounces (300 g); 2½ cups
For *truffes chocolat*	
Chocolate shavings (page 423)	9 ounces (250 g)
Confectioners' sugar for dusting	

Preheat the oven to 250°F (120°C).

1. Scoop the meringue into the pastry bag. Pipe the meringue onto the prepared baking sheets in twenty domes ①, each 2½ inches (6 cm) in diameter and ¾ to 1 inch (2 to 2½ cm) high. Arrange the domes in staggered rows and separate them by 1 to 1½ inches (2½ to 4 cm).

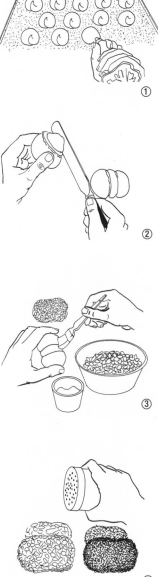

2. Place one baking sheet on a lower oven rack and one on an upper oven rack, and bake for 25 minutes, using a wooden spatula to hold the oven door ajar. Reverse the positions of the two baking sheets, and continue baking with the oven door ajar until the meringues barely begin to color and are dry inside, about 30 to 40 minutes longer.

3. Place each baking sheet on a wire rack and let the meringues cool to room temperature.

4. Separate 1 cup (170 g) of the *praliné* buttercream, and mix the crushed *pralin* or chopped almonds into it.

5. Spread 5 teaspoons (20 g) of the chocolate or *praliné*-and-crushed-*pralin* buttercream on the center of the flat side of one of the meringue domes ②, and press a second dome against it back to back, cementing the two together with the buttercream to make a rough sphere. Repeat with the remaining domes of meringue. Place the spheres or a tray and refrigerate to set the filling.

6. Put the sliced almonds or chocolate shavings in a wide, shallow bowl. Transfer the remaining buttercream to a small stainless steel bowl and warm it over low heat, stirring constantly with a wooden spatula until it is soft enough to spread easily with a pastry brush. Thoroughly brush the outside of one meringue sphere with buttercream to coat the surface heavily ③, place it in the bowl of almonds or chocolate shavings, and shake the bowl back and forth to roll the sphere around and coat it with the almonds or shavings on all sides. Then return it to the tray. Repeat with the remaining spheres of meringue. Refrigerate to set the buttercream.

7. When ready to serve, lightly dust the top of each truffle with confectioners' sugar ④.

STORAGE: Before filling, keep the meringue domes for up to 2 weeks at room temperature in a very dry place, either in a tin cookie box or covered airtight in a plastic bag.

After filling keep, uncovered, in the refrigerator for up to 1 or 2 days.

Meringues Chantilly

Fat fingers of meringue, piped from a plain pastry tube, start out seeming dull and clunky. But sandwich them with whipped cream (*crème chantilly*, which gives them their name), and pipe a swath of whipped cream down the side using a fluted pastry tube, and they take on an entirely different character. Place a crystallized violet on top and they are elegant enough for a *salon de thé* on the *faubourg Saint Honoré*.

Perhaps we should note that the crystallized violets (page 508) are rather expensive. Half of a glacé cherry may not look as ethereal, but it is a perfectly acceptable alternative.

For 10 filled meringues

EQUIPMENT:
2 large, heavy baking sheets
• brush with melted butter
• dust with flour
Large pastry bag fitted with
• ⅝-inch (16-mm) plain pastry tube (Ateco #8)
Electric mixer
Large pastry bag fitted with
• medium-size fluted pastry tube (Ateco #4)

BATTER:	
French meringue (page 186)	15½ ounces (440 g); 4 cups

FILLING:	
Confectioners' sugar	1¾ ounces (50 g); ⅓ cup + 4 teaspoons
Heavy cream	2 cups (5 dL)
Vanilla bean	½

DECORATION:	
Crystallized violets,	10
or substitute glacé	
cherries, cut in halves	5

Preheat the oven to 250°F (120°C).

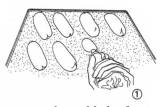

1. Scoop the meringue into the pastry bag with the plain tube. Pipe the meringue onto the prepared baking sheets in twenty fingers ①, each 3½ inches (9 cm) long and 2 inches (5 cm) wide. Pipe the fingers on the diagonal in staggered rows, separating them by 1 to 1½ inches (2½ to 4 cm).

2. Place one baking sheet on a lower oven rack and one on an upper oven rack, and bake for 25 minutes, using a wooden spatula to hold the oven door ajar. Reverse the positions of the two baking sheets, and continue baking with the oven door ajar until the meringues barely begin to color and are dry inside, about 30 to 40 minutes longer.

3. Place each baking sheet on a wire rack and let the meringues cool to room temperature.

4. Sift the confectioners' sugar into the bowl of the mixer, stir in the heavy cream, and refrigerate for about an hour. Chill the wire whip or beater of the mixer as well.

5. Slit the vanilla bean lengthwise and scrape out the seeds into the cream. (Reserve the pod for another purpose.) Whip the cream at medium speed in the mixer. When the cream holds soft peaks, slow down to avoid overbeating. Continue whipping until the cream is light and thick and holds stiff peaks.

6. Scoop the whipped cream into the pastry bag with the fluted tube. Pipe a thick strip of whipped cream down the center of the flat side of one of the meringue fingers ②. Press a second finger against it back to back, cementing the two together with the whipped cream. Place this sandwich of meringue fingers on its side and cover the crack between them by piping whipped cream down the center, using a repeated back-and-forth figure-eight motion as you move from one end to the other. Pipe a rosette of whipped cream on the center, and top it with a crystallized violet or half of a glacé cherry. Repeat with the remaining meringues.

STORAGE: Before filling, keep the meringue fingers for up to 2 weeks at room temperature in a very dry place, either in a tin cookie box or covered airtight in a plastic bag.

After filling keep, uncovered, in the refrigerator for no more than 2 to 4 hours.

Fromage Citron

These meringue sandwiches are filled and frosted with a mixture of lemon curd and buttercream. The tart, velvety filling makes a nice contrast to the sweet, crisp meringue. The shape is reminiscent of a small, soft-ripened cheese such as Camembert. To enhance the image, you dust the outside with confectioners' sugar, then make a crosshatched design on top to mimic the impression of the straw mats on which farmhouse Camemberts are aged. The name translates literally as "lemon cheese."

For 12 or 13 filled meringues

EQUIPMENT:

2 large, heavy baking sheets
• brush with melted butter
• dust with flour
Large pastry bag fitted with
• ⅜-inch (1-cm) plain pastry tube (Ateco #4)
12 or 13 circles of foil board or matt board (page 467), each 3 inches (7 cm) in diameter

BATTER:

French meringue (page 186)	15½ ounces (440 g); 4 cups

FILLING AND FROSTING:

French buttercream (page 384)	9 ounces (260 g); 1½ cups
Lemon curd (page 393)	9 ounces (260 g); 1 cup

GLUE:

Honey

DECORATION:

Confectioners' sugar for dusting

Preheat the oven to 250°F (120°C).

1. Mark twenty-six 3-inch (7-cm) circles on the baking sheets by tapping each sheet with a round cookie cutter or mold ①. Arrange the circles in staggered rows, separating them by about 1 inch (2½ cm).

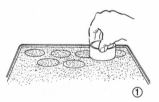

2. Scoop the meringue into the pastry bag. Starting from the center of each circle, pipe the batter in a continuous spiral that completely fills the circle ②. All of the batter must be piped out and baked right away or it will deflate.

3. Place one baking sheet on a lower oven rack and one on an upper oven rack, and bake for 30 minutes, using a wooden spatula to hold the oven door ajar. Reverse the positions of the two baking sheets, and continue baking with the oven door ajar until the meringues barely begin to color and are dry inside, about 35 to 45 minutes longer.

4. Place each baking sheet on a wire rack and let the meringues cool to room temperature. Then loosen the meringues by sliding an icing spatula underneath and remove them from the baking sheet.

5. Combine the buttercream and lemon curd in a mixing bowl and beat with a wooden spatula until smooth. Continue beating with the spatula or with an electric mixer to make this lemon buttercream lighter.

6. Put a dab of honey on each foil board or matt board circle and place a round of meringue on each. Spread about 2 tablespoons (25 g) of the lemon filling on each of these rounds ③. Place one of the remaining meringue rounds upside down on top of the lemon buttercream on each. Press gently to flatten the filling slightly and stick the top and bottom meringues together in a sandwich.

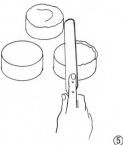

7. Spread lemon buttercream on the top and sides of each meringue sandwich with a medium-size icing spatula ④. Hold each sandwich in one hand with the thumb on the bottom and the index and middle fingers on top, and smooth the side with the icing spatula. Then place them on the countertop and sweep the icing spatula across the top of each to take off excess buttercream and make the top smooth ⑤.

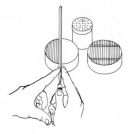

8. Place the sandwiches on a tray and refrigerate until ready to serve.

9. Dust the top and sides of each sandwich heavily with confectioners' sugar. Then make a crosshatched design on top of each by pressing with the edge of an icing spatula ⑥.

NOTE: The dab of honey on the foil board circle will keep the meringue round from sliding around on the circle. Having the foil board circle underneath makes it easier to handle the sandwiches without damaging them when you are spreading and smoothing the frosting around the sides.

STORAGE: Before filling, keep the meringue rounds for up to 2 weeks at room temperature in a very dry place, either in a tin cookie box or covered airtight in a plastic bag.

After filling keep, uncovered, in the refrigerator for up to 1 or 2 days.

Meringues Curaçao

Here is an altogether different meringue sandwich. For this one, the bottom is a plain round of meringue, but the top is piped in the shape of a daisy. The filling is an ultralight buttercream based on Italian meringue and flavored with curaçao liqueur. It is very sweet and very tasty.

For 12 filled meringues

EQUIPMENT:
2 large, heavy baking sheets
• brush with melted butter
• dust with flour
Large pastry bag fitted with
• ⅜-inch (1-cm) plain pastry tube (Ateco #4)
Medium-size pastry bag fitted with
• ½-inch (12-mm) plain pastry tube (Ateco #6)

BATTER:

French meringue (page 186)	15½ ounces (440 g); 4 cups

DECORATION:
Confectioners' sugar for dusting

FILLING:

Unsalted butter, softened	2 ounces (60 g); ¼ cup
Almond-and-sugar powder (page 442)	2 ounces (60 g); ¼ cup + 3 tablespoons
Italian meringue (page 184)	4¼ ounces (120 g); 2 cups
Curaçao liqueur	2½ teaspoons (1.2 cL)
Red food coloring	

Preheat the oven to 250°F (120°C).

1. Mark twenty-four 3-inch (7-cm) circles on the baking sheets by tapping each sheet with a round cookie cutter or mold ①. Arrange the circles in staggered rows, separating them by about 1 inch (2½ cm).

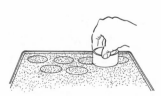

①

2. Scoop the meringue into the pastry bag. For half the circles, pipe a plain round of meringue: Starting from the center of each circle, pipe the batter in a continuous spiral that completely fills the circle ②. For the other half of the circles, pipe a decorative round of meringue: In the center of each circle, pipe a dome 1 inch (2.5 cm) in diameter, then surround it with seven adjacent domes, each ¾ inch (2 cm) in diameter, to fill the circle with a daisy-shaped round of meringue ③. All of the batter must be piped out and baked right away or it will deflate. Dust all of the rounds of meringue heavily with confectioners' sugar.

3. Place one baking sheet on a lower oven rack and one on an upper oven rack, and bake for 30 minutes, using a wooden spatula to hold the oven door ajar. Reverse the positions of the two baking sheets, and continue baking with the oven door ajar until the meringues barely begin to color and are dry inside, about 35 to 45 minutes longer.

4. Place each baking sheet on a wire rack and let the meringues cool to room temperature. Then loosen the meringues by sliding an icing spatula underneath and remove them from the baking sheet.

5. Place the softened butter in a small stainless steel bowl and beat it with a wooden spatula, warming it over low heat if necessary, until it is smooth and creamy. Add the almond-and-sugar powder and beat a little longer. Add about one third of the Italian meringue and mix it in quickly and thoroughly. Stir in the curaçao liqueur and a drop or two of red food coloring to tint it pink. Then gently fold in the remaining meringue to make a very light buttercream filling.

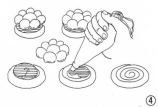

6. Scoop the buttercream filling into the medium-size pastry bag, and pipe a lump of meringue about 3 tablespoons (20 g) in size on each of the plain rounds ④. Place a daisy-shaped meringue round right side up on top of the curaçao buttercream on each plain round. Press gently to flatten and spread the filling and stick the top and bottom meringues together in a sandwich.

7. Place the sandwiches on a tray and refrigerate until ready to serve.

8. Serve the meringues as is; or, if the daisy-shaped meringues on the tops of the sandwiches took on some color when they were baked, then you can dust the tops lightly with confectioners' sugar.

NOTE: Dusting the tops of the meringue rounds with confectioners' sugar before baking gives them a dimpled surface.

STORAGE: Before filling, keep the meringue rounds for up to 2 weeks at room temperature in a very dry place, either in a tin cookie box or covered airtight in a plastic bag.

After filling keep, uncovered, in the refrigerator for up to 1 or 2 days.

Meringues Café
and Meringues Chocolat

. . . .

You can flavor Italian meringue with coffee or chocolate and bake it just like French meringue in finger shapes to make crisp individual desserts that are left unfilled. The meringues are very light and sweet. Typically they crack around the base as they bake.

For about 16 meringues

EQUIPMENT:
Large, heavy baking sheet
• brush with melted butter
• dust with flour
Large pastry bag fitted with
• medium-size fluted pastry tube (Ateco #4)

BATTER:

Confectioners' sugar	3½ ounces (100 g); ¾ cup + 4 teaspoons
Italian meringue (page 184), still warm	9½ ounces (270 g); 4½ cups

COFFEE FLAVORING:

Freeze-dried instant coffee	2 tablespoons (3 cL)
Boiling water	4 teaspoons (2 cL)

CHOCOLATE FLAVORING:

Large egg white, at room temperature	1
Red food coloring	
Unsweetened chocolate, melted	1½ ounces (40 g)

Preheat the oven to 275°F (135°C).

1. Sift the confectioners' sugar.

2. FOR COFFEE: Dissolve the instant coffee in the boiling water and stir in half the confectioners' sugar.

FOR CHOCOLATE: Mix half the confectioners' sugar with the egg white and a drop of red food coloring using a wooden spatula. Stir this mixture into the melted chocolate all at once.

3. Gently fold the remaining confectioners' sugar into the meringue. Stir a little of the meringue into the coffee or chocolate mixture. Then gently fold the flavored mixture back into the rest of the meringue.

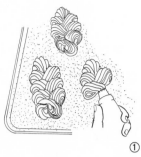

4. Scoop the meringue into the pastry bag. Hold the tip of the pastry tube about ¼ inch (6 mm) above the baking sheet. Press on the pastry bag, and when the batter starts to spread around the tip of the pastry tube, draw the tube toward you in a repeated side-to-side figure-eight motion to pipe a broad finger ① of meringue 1½ inches (4 cm) wide and 3½ inches (9 cm) long. Terminate by releasing the pressure on the bag and cutting the meringue with a quick flick of the tip of the pastry tube through the final loop of the figure eight. Pipe about sixteen fingers, arranging them on the diagonal in staggered rows and separating them by about 1 inch (2½ cm).

5. Bake until set, dry, and firm to the touch, 40 to 60 minutes.

6. Place the baking sheet on a wire rack and let the meringues cool to room temperature.

HOWS AND WHYS: The cracking around the base of these cookies is due to the high sugar content of the meringue batter. There is a slight imbalance between the sugar and egg whites which allows some of the sugar syrup to melt and bubble during the baking. Since the high sugar content is also the source of the unique crisp yet tender texture of these cookies, the cracking is regarded as normal rather than as a defect.

While we don't usually like to use instant coffee, in *meringues café* it is unavoidable.

STORAGE: At room temperature, covered airtight in a tin cookie box or a cookie jar, for up to 1 week if they are not in a humid place.

Chocolate Meringue Corkscrews

The batter for this meringue is very similar to that for *meringues chocolat*. In fact you can use the same Italian meringue batter (either the one in *meringues chocolat*, page 200, or the one below) for both desserts. But unlike *meringues chocolat*, you will bake chocolate meringue corkscrews on a moistened sheet of plywood so that the insides of the meringues are steamed and remain soft and creamy while the outsides become crisp. Then sandwich the corkscrews back to back in pairs. The luscious, velvety interiors are totally unexpected for a meringue.

The Italian meringue for these corkscrews should be prepared with slightly less sugar than usual—only 6 ounces (175 g) instead of the usual 7 ounces (200 g), for three egg whites.

For 8 meringue sandwiches

EQUIPMENT:
Sheet of plywood ⅜ inch (1 cm) thick, cut to fit on a large baking sheet (see notes)
• **soak in cold water until thoroughly moistened**
• **cover top side with a sheet of newsprint (see notes)**
• **place on the baking sheet**
Large pastry bag fitted with
• **medium-size fluted pastry tube (Ateco #4)**

BATTER:
Red food coloring	
Italian meringue (page 184), made with 6 ounces (175 g) sugar and still hot	**8¾ ounces (245 g); 4½ cups**
Confectioners' sugar	**3½ ounces (100 g); ¾ cup + 4 teaspoons**

FLAVORING:
European bittersweet chocolate, finely grated	**3½ ounces (100 g)**

Preheat the oven to 300°F (150°C).

1. Whip two drops of red food coloring into the hot meringue.

2. Sift the confectioners' sugar over the meringue and gently fold it in. When almost completely incorporated, gently fold in the grated chocolate.

3. Scoop the meringue into the pastry bag. Hold the tip of the pastry tube about ¼ inch (6 mm) above the newsprint-covered sheet of plywood. Press on the pastry bag, and when the batter starts to spread around the tip of the pastry tube, draw the tube toward you in a spiral motion ① to pipe a corkscrew-shaped swath of meringue 1½ inches (4 cm) wide and 3½ inches (9 cm) long. Terminate the spi-

ral by releasing the pressure on the bag and cutting the meringue with a quick flick of the tip of the pastry tube through the final loop of the spiral. Pipe about sixteen corkscrews, arranging them on the diagonal in staggered rows and separating them by about 1 inch (2½ cm).

4. Bake until the meringues are dry and crusty outside and still soft but no longer runny inside, about 30 minutes. The base of each meringue will bubble up during baking, and when they are ready the surface will just begin to become crusty at the base. Do not overbake or the insides of the meringues will shrink.

5. Place the baking sheet on a wire rack and let the meringues cool until they can be moved without breaking. Then carefully slide (don't lift) each warm meringue corkscrew off the paper and sand-wich it back to back with a second one ②. The bottoms of the corkscrews will be soft and sticky and they will stick together. Place the sandwiched meringue corkscrews on a wire rack and let cool to room temperature.

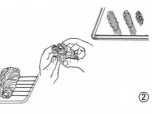

NOTES: Choose plywood with at least one smooth side. Bake the meringues on the smooth side.

Newsprint is the paper that newspapers are printed on, as opposed to the printed newspaper. Many newspapers sell their end rolls of unused newsprint at nominal charge. You can also purchase pads of artists' newsprint in art supply stores.

STORAGE: At room temperature, covered airtight in a tin cookie box or a cookie jar, for up to 1 or 2 days.

Meringue Mushrooms

You will use these whimsical mushrooms for decorating yule logs (pages 348–356). Unless you are churning out yule logs as holiday presents, you won't need more than a dozen or so mushrooms for the entire Christmas season; and this requires only a fraction of a recipe of French meringue. So make the mushrooms at the same time as you are preparing another meringue dessert.

There are two methods for piping the mushrooms. The easiest to learn is to pipe the stems and caps separately and glue them together after baking. When you become more expert, you can try piping a more stylized mushroom in one piece.

For about 12 mushrooms

EQUIPMENT:
Large, heavy baking sheet
• brush with melted butter
• dust with flour
Pastry bag fitted with
• ⅜-inch (1-cm) plain pastry tube (Ateco #4)

BATTER:
French meringue (page 186)   4 ounces (110 g); 1 cup

DECORATION:
Unsweetened cocoa powder (Dutch processed),
    sifted with a little confectioners' sugar,
    for dusting

Preheat the oven to 275°F (135°C).

1. Scoop the meringue into the pastry bag.
    METHOD 1. First pipe the stems. Hold the pastry bag vertical, with the tip of the pastry tube just above the baking sheet. Gently press on the pastry bag, and when the batter spreads around the tip of the tube to a width of about ¾ inch (2 cm), decrease the pressure on the bag, and gradually lift the pastry tube straight up to make a cone-shaped stem about ¾ inch (2 cm) high.

Release the pressure on the pastry bag and continue lifting the tube straight up to draw out a pointed vertical tail at the top of the cone ①. Repeat until you have piped more stems than you will need to be sure you get enough attractive ones. For the caps, pipe at least a dozen domes 1¼ inches (3 cm) in diameter and ¾ inch (2 cm) high ②. Arrange both stems and caps on the baking sheet in staggered rows and separate them by 1 to 1½ inches (2½ to 4 cm).

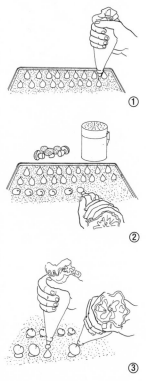

METHOD 2. Your batter must be very stiff or it won't maintain the shape. Hold the pastry bag nearly vertical, with the tip of the pastry tube just above the baking sheet. Press gently on the bag. When the batter spreads around the pastry tube to a width of about ¾ inch (2 cm), decrease the pressure on the pastry bag and slowly lift the tube straight up to make a cone-shaped stem about ¾ inch (2 cm) high. Momentarily stop moving the tip of the pastry tube and gently increase the pressure on the pastry bag to enlarge the top of the stem and make an hourglass shape. Then drop the tip of the tube slightly, tilt the pastry bag, and press firmly on the bag to inflate the upper part of the hourglass into a cap 1¼ inches (3 cm) wide ③. The cap will be tilted, with the far side extending a little beyond the stem and the near side resting on the baking sheet. To finish the cap, release the pressure on the pastry bag and cut the batter with a quick, semi-circular flick of the tip of the pastry tube.

2. Dust the tops of the mushroom caps very lightly with the cocoa powder.

3. Bake, using a wooden spatula to hold the oven door ajar, until the mushrooms are set, dry, and firm to the touch, about 30 to 40 minutes.

4. Place the baking sheet on a wire rack and let the mushrooms cool to room temperature.

5. If the stems and caps were piped separately, when you are ready to use the mushrooms, scrape out a small indentation in the center of the underside of each cap using the tip of a paring knife. Fill the indentation with a little filling or frosting (such as buttercream or Italian meringue) from the dessert you are decorating, and insert the tip of the stem into the indentation to cement the stem and cap together ④.

HOWS AND WHYS: We have suggested gluing together the separately piped caps and stems with filling or frosting because this doesn't require any additional preparation. If you prefer to assemble the mushrooms in advance, you can use a little French or Italian meringue batter as the glue (piping it into the indentation in the underside of the caps using a pastry bag with a small plain tube). Then place the assembled mushrooms on a baking sheet in a preheated 200°F (100°C) oven for 20 or 30 minutes to set the meringue used for glue.

STORAGE: At room temperature in a very dry place, either in a tin cookie box or covered airtight in a plastic bag, for up to 2 weeks.

Vacherin Glacé

The *vacherin* you are most likely to encounter is the *vacherin* filled with ice cream. Indeed, it is not unusual for chefs to think of the *vacherin* solely as a frozen (*glacé* in French) dessert.

The choice of ice cream is up to you. We suggest that you avoid vanilla or other ice creams white in color purely because they provide no visual contrast to the white meringue shell.

For 10 to 12 servings

EQUIPMENT:
Electric mixer or wire whisk
Large pastry bag fitted with
• medium-small fluted pastry tube (Ateco #3)

MERINGUE:

Vacherin shell (page 187)	One 9½-inch (24-cm) shell

FILLING:

Ice cream (preferably two flavors such as chocolate and coffee, chocolate and butter pecan, or coffee and *praliné*), softened	2 quarts (2 L)

DECORATION:

Confectioners' sugar	1 ounce (25 g); 3 tablespoons
Heavy cream	1 cup (2.4 dL)
Vanilla bean	¼
Chocolate espresso beans, chocolate cigarettes (page 424), pecan halves, raw almonds or hazelnuts, etc.	

1. Fill the *vacherin* shell to the rim with the ice cream ①, in two layers if you are using two flavors. Keep the *vacherin* in the freezer while you prepare the whipped cream.

2. Sift the confectioners' sugar into the bowl of the mixer or a stainless steel mixing bowl, stir in the heavy cream, and refrigerate for about an hour. Chill the wire whisk or the whip or beater of the mixer as well.

3. Slit the vanilla bean lengthwise and scrape out the seeds into the cream. (Reserve the pod for another purpose.) Whip the cream with the wire whisk or at medium speed in the mixer. When the cream holds soft peaks, slow down to avoid overbeating. Continue whipping until the cream is light and thick and holds stiff peaks.

4. Scoop the whipped cream into the pastry bag. Cover the top of the ice cream in the *vacherin* with adjacent rosettes of whipped cream, starting at the perimeter and working to the center in concentric circles. Pipe a large rosette on top of the center, and pipe a circle of overlapping teardrops on top of the rim of the *vacherin* shell ②.

5. Finish decorating the top of the *vacherin* according to the ice cream flavors. For example, if you chose chocolate and butter pecan ice creams, you might place a pecan half on the rosette in the center, and arrange about six chocolate cigarettes (each 1½ to 2 inches or 4 to 5 cm long) radiating out from the center. If you included coffee ice cream, use a few chocolate espresso beans for decoration, and with *praliné* ice cream use a few raw almonds or hazelnuts. Keep the garnish to a minimum, just enough to prevent the pure white exterior of the *vacherin* from becoming monotonous.

STORAGE: Best served shortly after assembling.

Vacherin Chantilly

In summer, a *vacherin* shell filled with whipped cream (*crème chantilly* in French) and fresh berries is a refreshing treat.

For 10 to 12 servings

EQUIPMENT:
Electric mixer
Large pastry bag fitted with
• medium-small fluted pastry tube (Ateco #3)

FILLING AND DECORATION:

Confectioners' sugar	2¾ ounces (80 g); ⅔ cup
Heavy cream	3 cups (7.2 dL)
Vanilla bean	½
Fresh raspberries, hulled strawberries, or blueberries	2 pounds (900 g); 2⅔ pints

MERINGUE:

Vacherin shell (page 187)	One 9½-inch (24-cm) shell

1. Sift the confectioners' sugar into the bowl of the mixer, stir in the heavy cream, and refrigerate for about an hour. Chill the whip or beater of the mixer as well.

2. Slit the vanilla bean lengthwise and scrape out the seeds into the cream. (Reserve the pod for another purpose.) Whip the cream at medium speed in the mixer. When the cream holds soft peaks, slow down to avoid overbeating. Continue whipping until the cream is light and thick and holds stiff peaks.

3. Set aside 2 cups (250 g) of the whipped cream and some fresh berries for decorating the top of the *vacherin*. (If you are using strawberries, select small- to medium-size ones for decorating.) Fill the *vacherin* shell to the rim with alternating layers of the remaining whipped cream and fresh berries, starting and finishing with layers of whipped cream ①.

①

4. Scoop the reserved whipped cream into the pastry bag. Cover the top of the *vacherin* with adjacent rosettes of whipped cream, starting at the perimeter and working to the center in concentric circles. Pipe a large rosette on top of the center, and pipe a circle of overlapping teardrops on top of the rim of the *vacherin* shell ②.

②

5. Place one berry on the rosette on the center and eight to twelve berries on teardrops around the perimeter. If you are using strawberries, small ones work best for decoration. If they are a bit larger, cut them in half.

STORAGE: Best served shortly after assembling.

Vacherin Chantilly Glacé

Here you get the best of both worlds—sorbet or ice cream on the bottom of the *vacherin*, then whipped cream, and finally fresh berries. Freshly assembled, with the soft sorbet or ice cream and light, delicate whipped cream contrasting with the crisp meringue and luscious berries, it is a sensual extravaganza.

For 10 to 12 servings

EQUIPMENT:

Electric mixer

Large pastry bag fitted with

• medium-small fluted pastry tube (Ateco #3)

FILLINGS AND DECORATION:

Confectioners' sugar	1¾ ounces (50 g); ¼ cup + 3 tablespoons
Heavy cream	2 cups (4.8 dL)
Vanilla bean	¼
Raspberry or strawberry sorbet, or vanilla ice cream, softened	1 quart (1 L)
Fresh rasberries, hulled strawberries, or blueberries, or a mixture	1 pound (450 g); 1⅓ pints

MERINGUE:

Vacherin shell (page 187)	One 9½-inch (24-cm) shell

1. Sift the confectioners' sugar into the bowl of the mixer, stir in the heavy cream, and refrigerate for about an hour. Chill the whip or beater of the mixer as well.

2. Slit the vanilla bean lengthwise and scrape out the seeds into the cream. (Reserve the pod for another purpose.) Whip the cream at medium speed in the mixer. When the cream holds soft peaks, slow down to avoid overbeating. Continue whipping until the cream is light and thick and holds stiff peaks.

3. Fill the *vacherin* shell about halfway with the sorbet or ice cream. Smooth the surface with an icing spatula ① or the flat side of a bowl scraper.

①

4. Set aside 1½ cups (190 g) of the whipped cream and one whole berry for decorating the top of the *vacherin*. (If you are using strawberries, select a small- to medium-size one for decorating.) Scoop the rest of the whipped cream on top of the sorbet or ice cream in the *vacherin* shell and smooth the surface. Fill the shell to the rim with the fresh berries.

5. Scoop the reserved whipped cream into the pastry bag. Pipe about eight large teardrops on top of the berries, radiating out from the center of the *vacherin*, and then pipe a large rosette on top of the center ②. Pipe a circle of overlapping teardrops on top of the rim of the *vacherin* shell.

6. Place one berry on the rosette on the center. For strawberries, use a small berry or half a medium-size one.

STORAGE: Best served shortly after assembling.

②

Rectangular Gâteaux

T o make rectangular gâteaux you will layer thin sheets of sponge cake (génoise, chocolate génoise, *joconde*, or diagonally piped sponge cake) or almond meringue (*russe*) with buttercream or other fillings. These gâteaux include some of the most elegant desserts in the French pastry chef's repertoire, yet they are relatively easy to assemble and decorate because the sides of the rectangular gâteaux are not coated with frosting. Instead, they are simply trimmed to reveal their multi-layered structure.

Preparing the Baking Sheet

The baking sheet on which you prepare a rectangular sheet of cake can be either lined with kitchen parchment or buttered and floured. The two methods are essentially equivalent, the only significant difference being how the sheets are removed after baking. We prefer the parchment-lined baking sheet for sponge cakes because it is easier to peel the parchment off the back of a sheet of sponge cake without breaking it than it is to slide the sponge cake off a buttered and floured baking sheet. However, if you are out of parchment, you can always switch to butter and flour. For *russe* we prefer a buttered and floured sheet.

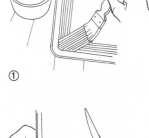

To line the baking sheet with parchment, first brush a band 1½ to 2 inches (3 to 5 cm) wide around the edge and down the diagonals of the baking sheet with melted butter ① so that the paper will stick to the baking sheet. Then line the baking sheet with a sheet of kitchen parchment. The parchment can be precut to the size of the baking sheet. Or, if you have a French black steel baking sheet with a low, turned-up lip around the edge, you can trim off the excess paper by running the back-edge of your chef's

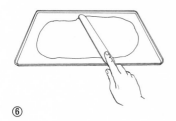

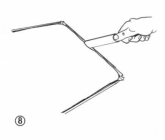

knife over the paper around the edge of the baking sheet ②. For génoise and *joconde*, brush the parchment with melted butter to eliminate any possibility of sticking.

To butter and flour the baking sheet, first brush the entire top surface of the baking sheet with melted butter ③, then let it set so you won't get too much flour adhering to the butter. Sprinkle flour over the butter ④, using more flour than you will need in the end. Tilt, shake, and tap the sheet to distribute the flour and coat the sheet evenly. Then invert the baking sheet and tap it with a wooden spatula or the handle of a dough scraper to dislodge the excess flour ⑤. The purpose of the flour is to prevent the batter from slipping as you spread it.

SPREADING BATTER ON A BAKING SHEET

Regardless of how the baking sheet is prepared, the method for spreading the batter on the baking sheet is always the same.

To minimize the amount of spreading you must do, first distribute the batter evenly over the baking sheet by scooping it from the mixing bowl onto the baking sheet using a bowl scraper or by pouring and scraping the batter from the mixing bowl. This will reduce the risk of deflating the batter by manipulating it too much. If you have a French-style baking sheet, finish spreading the batter using the largest icing spatula you have ⑥. With the rim of the baking sheet as a guide, use the edge (rather than the face) of the blade to move the batter where needed. Work from one side of the baking sheet at a time, and scrape off the batter sticking to the face of the blade on the rim of the baking sheet as needed. If you must use an American jelly roll pan rather than a French baking sheet, spread the batter with the flat edge of a bowl scraper ⑦ or an offset spatula. The sides of most jelly roll pans are much taller than the thickness of our cake layers and make it awkward to produce an even layer using an icing spatula.

REMOVING THE CAKE FROM
THE BAKING SHEET

Because the sheets of cake are thin, they must be baked quickly to prevent them from drying out. Sheets of sponge cake bake in a 375° to

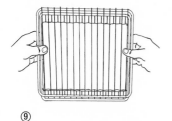

425°F (190° to 220°C) oven for between 6 and 10 minutes. *Russe*, which is an almond meringue, bakes for 25 to 35 minutes in a 350°F (175°C) oven.

When the sheet of cake has finished baking, remove it from the oven and loosen the edges of the cake from the parchment or the baking sheet underneath using a small icing spatula ⑧.

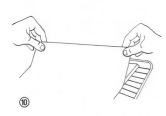

If the cake was baked on parchment, slide a large metal spatula under the parchment to loosen it, and transfer the cake (with the parchment underneath) from the baking sheet to a wire rack. When it is no longer hot but still warm enough that the butter between the parchment and cake hasn't solidified, place a second wire rack upside down on top of the sheet of cake ⑨ and turn the cake upside down with both racks to transfer it to the second rack. Lift off the first wire rack. Carefully peel the parchment away from the back of the cake ⑩, and place it clean side down against the cake to protect the cake. Place the first wire rack back on the sheet of cake and turn it right side up again. Lift off the second wire rack, and allow the cake to finish cooling. (Note that some cakes can be allowed to cool completely before you turn them upside down and remove the parchment.)

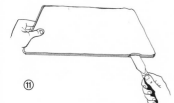

If the cake was baked on a buttered and floured baking sheet, then, after loosening the edges, place the baking sheet on a wire rack and let rest until it is no longer hot (but still warm). Slide a large icing spatula or pancake turner under the cake to loosen it ⑪ and transfer it to a wire rack. Then let it finish cooling to room temperature.

Cake Sizes and Trimming Cake Layers

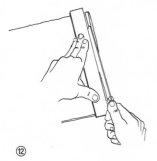

For all of our rectangular gâteaux, we give recipes using both 13 × 20-inch (33 × 50-cm) and 12 × 16-inch (30 × 40-cm) sheets of cake. Most baking sheets and jelly roll pans are close enough to one of these standard sizes that you can use them in our recipes without altering the quantities of ingredients.

Cut the sheet of cake into two, three, or four rectangles, depending on the number of layers in the gâteau you are making. Always cut the cake with a wavy-edge bread knife using a straightedge as a guide. Usually it is best to trim the short ends from the sheet of cake ⑫ before cutting it ⑬. To minimize waste, for most gâteaux we recommend trimming the long ends after they are assembled.

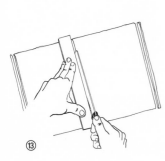

To make larger gâteaux, you can use whole sheets of cake for each layer, multiplying our recipes by two, three, or four to reach the required quantities. This is a simple way to make a dessert for a large party. And rectangular gâteaux have the added advantage that they are very easy to cut and serve.

CARDBOARD BASES

Assembling the gâteau on a cardboard base will make it easier to decorate and move without damage. The best cardboard for this purpose is matt board with a silver or gold foil surface (available from framing and art supply stores, page 467). Although not as stiff as matt board, the foil board lids made for aluminum foil take-out containers (and sold separately, page 467) are a good alternative if you can get a large enough size. The lid for a 5-pound (2.3-kg) loaf pan is the largest standard size and measures 7 × 9½ inches (17.5 × 24 cm)—large enough for some, but not all, of our rectangular gâteaux. Do not use the corrugated cardboard cake-decorating rectangles sold in cake supply shops because they are difficult to cut to size and make an unattractive presentation.

BRUSHING WITH SYRUP

Before assembling the gâteau, always brush sponge cake layers with a flavored syrup to make the cake layers more moist and flavorful. *Russe* is often brushed with syrup as well. Since all of these cake layers are thin, you often need to brush only one side of each layer with syrup.

The syrup you will use for brushing is a standard heavy syrup (page 452), diluted with an equal volume of liqueur or coffee. Part of the liqueur may be replaced with water if the liqueur is only a flavor accent or if the quantity of brushing required to moisten the cake would make the flavor of the syrup oppressive. Diluting the heavy syrup makes it soak into the cake layers more easily and enables you to adjust the flavor to suit the gâteau. In our recipes we refer to this flavored syrup as the "brushing-syrup mixture."

ASSEMBLING THE GÂTEAU

Cut a rectangle of matt board about 1 inch (3 cm) smaller in length and width than the rectangles of cake so that it won't extend beyond the sides of the finished dessert. Place the first layer of cake on the cardboard.

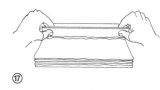

Brush the top of the cake with syrup ⑭, as called for, and spread the filling over it in an even layer using a large icing spatula ⑮. Place the second layer of cake on the filling; brush it with syrup, and spread a layer of filling over it. Continue stacking layers of cake and filling until all of the cake layers are used. Make the top of each layer of filling as flat as you can before placing the next rectangle of cake on top, and use the filling to compensate for any unevenness in the cake layers. To help make the layers more even, after adding each cake layer you can place a flat tray on top of the gâteau and press firmly and evenly to be sure the top is level. Then remove the tray.

To finish the tops of some rectangular gâteaux, you will simply dust the top layer of cake with confectioners' sugar. However, most gâteaux are topped with a layer of buttercream or other frosting; and occasionally the top can be glazed with fondant or chocolate as well. In this case, spread the final layer of frosting on the top of the gâteau using a large icing spatula ⑯. Then smooth it using either the icing spatula (if its edge is as long as the gâteau is wide) or a metal straightedge. Grasp the ends of the blade between the thumb and the index and middle fingers of each hand. Start with the edge of the blade on the far side of the gâteau and the face of the blade angled toward you ⑰. In one continuous motion, pull the edge of the blade toward you across the surface of the gâteau, gradually turning the face of the blade so that when it reaches the near side of the gâteau, the face of the blade is angled away from you ⑱. Keep the edge of the blade at a fixed height as you sweep it across the gâteau, and take off just enough frosting to get a level surface.

Before glazing or trimming the gâteau, slide it onto a tray (page 487) or wire rack and refrigerate it until the filling and frosting are firm so that the glaze won't melt the frosting and the edges can be cut evenly. Chill it for at least 1 hour.

Glazing with Fondant or Chocolate

If you will be glazing the gâteau with fondant or chocolate over the top layer of buttercream, then refrigerate it on a wire rack until the buttercream is firm. When ready to glaze, place the wire rack with the gâteau on your countertop, with a large tray underneath to catch the excess glaze.

If you are glazing with chocolate, it must be fluid enough to flow quickly and smoothly, producing a thin, even layer, but it must not be so runny that it takes too long to set. In addition, it should not be too brittle

(19)

(20)

(21)

when set, or it will be difficult to cut and serve. We get the best results by thinning European bittersweet chocolate with clarified butter. Melt the chocolate and temper it (see page 538 for a detailed discussion of tempering chocolate). The temperature of the chocolate must be between 86° and 91°F (30° to 33°C). The clarified butter must be at room temperature. Beat the clarified butter with a wooden spatula to make it smooth and creamy, then stir it into the chocolate.

If you are glazing with fondant, gently warm it, stirring constantly until melted. The temperature should be 100° to 105°F (38° to 40°C) and the fondant should be fluid, with about the same body as heavy cream or a light custard sauce. If necessary, add heavy syrup (page 452), a little at a time, until the fondant is thinned to the proper consistency.

Pour the fondant ⑲ or tempered chocolate ⑳ over the top of the gâteau, covering the area inside the perimeter so that the glaze flows evenly over the entire top of the gâteau. Quickly smooth the top surface with the edge of a large icing spatula ㉑ or a metal straightedge ㉒ to cover the top with a thin, even layer of glaze and push the excess over the edges. Work as quickly as you can, because once the fondant or chocolate begins to thicken, it will no longer flow smoothly.

Put the gâteau in a cool place and allow the fondant or chocolate to set. Then refrigerate the gâteau until you are ready to trim it.

DECORATING THE TOP

Usually the decoration top of the gâteau should be kept quite simple to avoid detracting from the ordered beauty of the sides. The rippled surface of a diagonally piped sheet of sponge cake needs nothing more than a light dusting of confectioners' sugar. Many gâteaux made with sheets of *russe* are just stencilled with a geometric design in confectioners' sugar or strewn with chocolate shavings or nuts. For gâteaux glazed with chocolate or fondant, a simple inscription in writing chocolate or royal icing is all that is needed. And for gâteaux filled with mousse, often a few rosettes piped in whipped cream can be the perfect accent. Let restraint be your guiding principle.

TRIMMING THE SIDES

About half an hour before serving, remove the gâteau from the refrigerator and place it on a flat cutting surface. Cut a slice ¼ to ⅜ inch (6

(22)

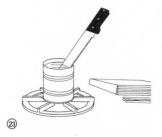

to 10 mm) thick from each side of the gâteau using a wavy-edge bread knife. If the gâteau is glazed with fondant or chocolate, heat the blade before making each cut so the blade will melt through the glaze without cracking it. To heat the blade, dip it in boiling water ㉓ (and wipe it dry) or hold it over the burner on your cooktop. When you are finished, all four sides of the gâteau should be perfectly flat and vertical ㉔. If there are any gaps in the layers of filling, you didn't trim off enough of the side.

Storage

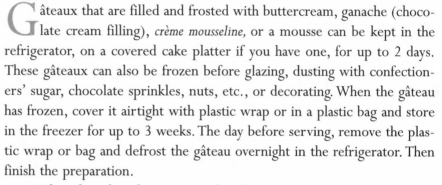

Gâteaux that are filled and frosted with buttercream, ganache (chocolate cream filling), *crème mousseline,* or a mousse can be kept in the refrigerator, on a covered cake platter if you have one, for up to 2 days. These gâteaux can also be frozen before glazing, dusting with confectioners' sugar, chocolate sprinkles, nuts, etc., or decorating. When the gâteau has frozen, cover it airtight with plastic wrap or in a plastic bag and store in the freezer for up to 3 weeks. The day before serving, remove the plastic wrap or bag and defrost the gâteau overnight in the refrigerator. Then finish the preparation.

When the sides of any rectangular gâteau are trimmed, the trimmings should be saved to pack against the exposed sides of the gâteau and prevent the sides from drying out during storage. If you don't have enough trimmings to cover the exposed sides, use strips of plastic wrap.

Génoise Sheets

. . . .

The same génoise batter that we used for round cakes in Chapter 2 can be baked in a large, thin rectangle on a baking sheet. As with the round cakes, we brush these sheets of génoise with flavored syrups after baking.

EQUIPMENT:

Heavy 12 × 16-inch (30 × 40-cm) or 13 × 20-inch (33 × 50-cm) baking sheet
• brush edges and diagonals with melted butter
• line with kitchen parchment
• brush parchment with melted butter
Electric mixer

	For one 12 × 16-inch (30 × 40-cm) sheet	For one 13 × 20-inch (33 × 50-cm) sheet
BATTER:		
Large eggs, at room temperature	4	6
Large egg yolk, at room temperature	1	1
Granulated sugar	4½ ounces (125 g); ½ cup + 2 tablespoons	6½ ounces (185 g); ¾ cup + 3 tablespoons
All-purpose flour	3½ ounces (100 g); ½ cup + 3½ tablespoons	5¾ ounces (160 g); 1 cup + 2 tablespoons
Potato starch	⅓ ounce (10 g); 1 tablespoon	⅓ ounce (10 g); 1 tablespoon
Unsalted butter, melted	½ ounce (15 g); 1 tablespoon	¾ ounce (20 g); 1½ tablespoons

Preheat the oven to 375°F (190°C).

1. Combine the whole eggs, yolk, and sugar in a stainless steel mixing bowl, break up the yolks with a wire whisk, and beat until smooth. Set the bowl over a saucepan of simmering water, and stir with the whisk until warm (about 100°F=40°C), frothy, and pale yellow.

2. Remove the bowl from the simmering water, and whip at medium speed in the mixer until the batter has risen and cooled, becoming light and thick and almost white in color. It should coat your finger very thickly and form very slowly dissolving ribbons when dropped from the whip.

3. Sift the flour with the potato starch onto a sheet of wax paper. A little at a time, dust the mixture over the batter and fold it in very gently but thoroughly. When the flour and potato starch are completely incorporated, slowly pour the melted butter over the batter and continue folding gently until the butter is uniformly mixed with the batter.

4. Scoop the batter from the mixing bowl onto the prepared baking sheet, distributing it evenly. Spread and smooth the batter with a large icing spatula to completely cover the baking sheet in an even layer about ⅜ inch (1 cm) thick.

5. Bake until the top of the génoise is lightly browned and firm to the touch but not crusty, about 6 to 10 minutes.

6. Remove from the oven and loosen the edges of the génoise from the parchment using a small icing spatula. Slide the génoise off the baking sheet onto a wire rack. When it is no longer hot but still warm enough that the butter between the parchment and génoise hasn't solidified, place a second wire rack upside down on top of the sheet of génoise and turn the génoise upside down with both racks to transfer it to the second rack. Lift off the first wire rack. Carefully peel the parchment away from the back of the génoise, and place it clean side down against the génoise to protect the cake. Place the first wire rack back on the sheet of génoise and turn it right side up again. Lift off the second wire rack, and allow the génoise to finish cooling.

NOTE: We obtain the proportions for the génoise batter by scaling a basic eight egg/250 g sugar/250 g flour génoise recipe to the quantity required and then substituting egg yolk plus potato starch for part of the flour. While this is not as direct as simply rescaling the génoise recipe from Chapter 2, it allows us to give quantities of ingredients that are easy to measure.

STORAGE: When baked in a thin sheet, the génoise dries very quickly. It is best used the same day as it is prepared.

Chocolate Génoise Sheets

As for plain génoise, we use essentially the same chocolate génoise batter for thin sheets as we used for round cakes in Chapter 2.

EQUIPMENT:

Heavy 12 × 16-inch (30 × 40-cm) or 13 × 20-inch (33 × 50-cm) baking sheet
• brush edges and diagonals with melted butter
• line with kitchen parchment
• brush parchment with melted butter
Electric mixer

	For one 12 × 16-inch (30 × 40-cm) sheet	For one 13 × 20-inch (33 × 50-cm) sheet
BATTER:		
Large eggs, at room temperature	4	6
Large egg yolk, at room temperature	1	1
Granulated sugar	4½ ounces (125 g); ½ cup + 2 tablespoons	6½ ounces (185 g); ¾ cup + 3 tablespoons
All-purpose flour	3 ounces (85 g); ½ cup + 2 tablespoons	5 ounces (145 g); 1 cup + 2 teaspoons
Potato starch	¼ ounce (5 g); 1½ teaspoons	¼ ounce (5 g); 1½ teaspoons
Unsweetened cocoa powder (Dutch processed)	1 ounce (25 g); ¼ cup	1½ ounces (40 g); ¼ cup + 2 tablespoons
Unsalted butter, melted	½ ounce (15 g); 1 tablespoon	¾ ounce (20 g); 1½ tablespoons

Preheat the oven to 375°F (190°C).

1. Combine the whole eggs, yolk, and sugar in a stainless steel mixing bowl, break up the yolks with a wire whisk, and beat until smooth. Set the bowl over a saucepan of simmering water, and stir with the whisk until warm (about 100°F = 40°C), frothy, and pale yellow.

2. Remove the bowl from the simmering water, and whip at medium speed in the mixer until the batter has risen and cooled, becoming light and thick and almost white in color. It should coat your finger very thickly and form very slowly dissolving ribbons when dropped from the whip.

3. Sift the flour, potato starch, and cocoa powder onto a sheet of wax paper. A little at a time, dust the mixture over the batter and fold it in very gently but thoroughly. When the flour, potato starch, and cocoa powder are completely incorporated, slowly pour the melted butter over the batter and continue folding gently until the butter is uniformly mixed with the batter.

4. Scoop the batter from the mixing bowl onto the prepared baking sheet, distributing it evenly. Spread and smooth the batter with a large icing spatula to completely cover the baking sheet in an even layer about ⅜ inch (1 cm) thick.

5. Bake until the top of the génoise is firm to the touch but not crusty, about 6 to 10 minutes.

6. Remove from the oven and loosen the edges of the génoise from the parchment using a small icing spatula. Slide the génoise off the baking sheet onto a wire rack. When it is no longer hot but still warm enough that the butter between the parchment and génoise hasn't solidified, place a second wire rack upside down on top of the sheet of génoise and turn the génoise upside down with both racks to transfer it to the second rack. Lift off the first wire rack. Carefully peel the parchment away from the back of the génoise, and place it clean side down against the génoise to protect the cake. Place the first wire rack back on the sheet of génoise and turn it right side up again. Lift off the second wire rack, and allow the génoise to finish cooling.

HOWS AND WHYS: Because it contains cocoa powder, the color of the cake cannot be used as a guide in assessing when the baking is completed.

STORAGE: When baked in a thin sheet, the génoise dries very quickly. It is best used the same day as it is prepared.

Joconde

. . . .

Leonardo da Vinci's extraordinary masterpiece, the *Mona Lisa*, was the portrait of the third wife of a Florentine merchant, Francesco di Bartolommeo del Giocondo. The painting, which is also referred to as *La Gioconda,* was completed sometime around 1503. Later, when Leonardo arrived at the royal castle at Amboise in 1516 or 1517 as the guest of the young French King François I, the Mona Lisa was one of only three paintings still in his possession. Leonardo spent the remaining years of his life at the nearby manor house of Cloux, and as a result this painting, one of the greatest achievements of the Italian Renaissance, found permanent residence in France. The French call it *La Joconda*.

The name *joconde* gives an indication of how highly regarded this sponge cake is among pastry chefs. In addition to containing powdered almonds, it differs from other sponge cakes by having whole eggs (rather than just the yolks) beaten with the sugar and powdered almonds before the meringue is folded in. *Joconde* is thin and rich, and we use it in such sumptuous, multi-layered gâteaux as the *clichy* (page 239). We also use *joconde* in Chapter 6 to make the spongecake-and-jam rolls and sandwiches that line our royal charlottes.

EQUIPMENT:

Heavy 12 × 16-inch (30 × 40-cm) or 13 × 20-inch (33 × 50-cm) baking sheet
• brush edges and diagonals with melted butter
• line with kitchen parchment
• brush parchment with melted butter
Electric mixer

	For one 12 × 16-inch (30 × 40-cm) sheet	For one 13 × 20-inch (33 × 50-cm) sheet
BATTER:		
Large eggs, at room temperature	2	3
Almond-and-sugar powder (page 442)	5½ ounces (150 g); 1 cup + 2 tablespoons	8 ounces (230 g); 1¾ cups
All-purpose flour	1 ounce (25 g); 3 tablespoons	1¼ ounces (35 g); ¼ cup
Large egg whites, at room temperature	2	3
Cream of tartar (optional)	⅛ teaspoon (a pinch)	⅛ teaspoon (a pinch)
Superfine or extra fine sugar	1 ounce (25 g); 2 tablespoons	1¼ ounces (35 g); 3 tablespoons
Unsalted butter, melted	½ ounce (15 g); 1 tablespoon	¾ ounce (20 g); 1½ tablespoons

Preheat the oven to 425°F (220°C).

1. Combine the whole eggs with the almond-and-sugar powder, and beat at medium speed in the mixer until cream-colored and light.

2. Sift the flour over the beaten eggs.

3. Using a clean wire whip and bowl, whip the egg whites in the mixer at low speed until they start to froth. If you are not whipping the whites in a copper bowl, add the cream of tartar at this point. Gradually increase the whipping speed to medium-high, and whip until the whites form very stiff peaks and just begin to slip and streak around the side of the bowl. Add the superfine sugar and continue whipping at high speed for a few seconds to incorporate the sugar and tighten the meringue.

4. Scoop about one third of the meringue into the bowl with the beaten eggs and flour, and stir with a wooden spatula to mix quickly. Add the remaining meringue and gently fold it into the batter. When completely incorporated, slowly pour the melted butter over the batter and continue folding gently until the butter is uniformly mixed with the batter.

5. Scoop the batter from the mixing bowl onto the prepared baking sheet, distributing it evenly. Spread and smooth the batter with a large icing spatula to completely cover the baking sheet in an even layer about ⅜ inch (1 cm) thick.

6. Bake until the cake is lightly browned and firm to the touch but not dry, about 6 to 8 minutes.

7. Remove from the oven and loosen the edges of the *joconde* from the parchment using a small icing spatula. Slide the *joconde* off the baking sheet onto a wire rack. When it is no longer hot but still warm enough that the butter between the parchment and *joconde* hasn't solidified, place a second wire rack upside down on top of the sheet of *joconde* and turn the *joconde* upside down with both racks to transfer it to the second rack. Lift off the first wire rack. Carefully peel the parchment away from the back of the *joconde*, and place it clean side down against the *joconde* to protect the cake. Place the first wire rack back on the sheet of *joconde* and turn it right side up again. Lift off the second wire rack, and allow the *joconde* to finish cooling.

STORAGE: Covered airtight with plastic wrap, for up to 2 days in the refrigerator. Or freeze for as long as 3 months. If frozen, defrost overnight in the refrigerator before using.

Russe

. . . .

Before the Bolshevik revolution so abruptly ended their grand lifestyle, the Russian nobility liked to employ French chefs. As a result, much of the cooking we associate with Russia is actually French, and many creations in French cuisine and *pâtisserie* bear Russian names. While some can be traced to a particular nobleman or his chef, or to a location or historical event, others, like this almond meringue, are of unknown lineage.

In contrast to other nut meringues and to ordinary meringue, which are piped from a pastry bag, *russe* is always spread in a thin layer on a baking sheet. And unlike its crisp meringue cousins, it is soft, and just a little bit chewy.

EQUIPMENT:

Heavy 12 × 16-inch (30 × 40-cm) or 13 × 20-inch (33 × 50-cm) baking sheet
• brush with melted butter
• dust with flour
Electric mixer

	For one 12 × 16-inch (30 × 40-cm) sheet	For one 13 × 20-inch (33 × 50-cm) sheet
BATTER:		
Large egg whites, unbeaten, at room temperature	6	8
Cream of tartar (optional)	¼ teaspoon (1 mL)	⅜ teaspoon (2mL)
Superfine or extra fine sugar	1¾ ounces (50 g); ¼ cup	2¾ ounces (75 g); ¼ cup + 2 tablespoons
Almond-and-sugar powder (page 442)	8 ounces (230 g); 1 cup + 2 tablespoons	10½ ounces (300 g); 1½ cups
Large egg whites, lightly beaten, at room temperature	1½; 3 tablespoons (4.5 cL)	2
All-purpose flour	¾ ounce (20 g); 2⅓ tablespoons	1 ounce (30 g); 3 tablespoons

DECORATION (EXCEPT FOR *RUSSE PRALINÉ*, PAGE 250):
Confectioners' sugar for dusting

DECORATION (FOR *RUSSE PRALINÉ* ONLY):

Blanched almonds,	1 ounce (30 g);	1½ ounces (40 g);
chopped	3 tablespoons	¼ cup
Granulated sugar	1 ounce (25 g);	1¼ ounces (35 g);
	2 tablespoons	3 tablespoons

Preheat the oven to 350°F (175°C).

1. Whip the unbeaten egg whites in the mixer at low speed until they start to froth. If you are not whipping the whites in a copper bowl, add the cream of tartar at this point. Gradually increase the whipping speed to medium-high, and whip until the whites form soft peaks. Add the sugar very gradually and continue whipping until the meringue is very stiff.

2. In a large mixing bowl, mix the almond-and-sugar powder with the lightly beaten egg whites. Stir about one third of the meringue into this mixture using a wooden spatula. When smooth, sift the flour over it, add the remaining meringue, and gently fold until thoroughly mixed. Be very careful not to deflate the batter.

3. Scoop the batter from the mixing bowl onto the prepared baking sheet, distributing it evenly. Spread and smooth the batter with a large icing spatula to completely cover the baking sheet in an even layer about ⁹⁄₁₆ inch (14 mm) thick.

4. Dust the top of the sheet of batter with confectioners' sugar ①; or, if the *russe* will be used for a *russe praliné*, sprinkle the chopped almonds ② and sugar over the sheet of batter.

①

5. Bake until the top of the *russe* is dry, firm to the touch, and a uniform light brown, about 25 to 35 minutes. The *russe* should still be soft inside.

6. Remove from the oven and loosen the edges of the *russe* using a small icing spatula. Place the baking sheet on a wire rack, and let rest until it is no longer hot but still warm. Then slide a large icing spatula or pancake turner under the *russe* to loosen it and transfer it to a wire rack. Allow the *russe* to finish cooling on the wire rack.

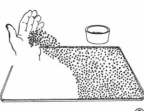

②

STORAGE: *Russe* dries out quickly, so if possible, use it the day it is made. Otherwise, cover it airtight with plastic wrap and keep for up to 2 days in the refrigerator.

Diagonally Piped Sponge Cake Sheets

· ·

Sheets of ladyfinger sponge cake piped on the diagonal are very easy to make and have a striking appearance when used as the top layer of a rectangular gâteau. Strips cut from a sheet of the sponge cake can also be used to line a ring in making a mousse cake for another intriguing presentation (see the recipe for *nelusko*, page 321). In either case, you can also use part of the same sheet of sponge cake for the bottom and interior layers of the gâteau or mousse cake.

EQUIPMENT:

Heavy 12 × 16-inch (30 × 40-cm) or 13 × 20-inch (33 × 50-cm) baking sheet
• brush edges and diagonals with melted butter
• line with kitchen parchment
Electric mixer
Large pastry bag fitted with
• ⅜-inch (1-cm) plain pastry tube (Ateco #4)

	For one 12 × 16-inch (30 × 40-cm) sheet	For one 13 × 20-inch (33 × 50-cm) sheet
BATTER:		
Large eggs, separated, at room temperature	3	5
Cream of tartar (optional)	⅛ teaspoon (a pinch)	¼ teaspoon (1 mL)
Superfine or extra fine sugar	1 ounce (30 g); 2 tablespoons + 1 teaspoon	1¾ ounces (50 g); ¼ cup
Confectioners' sugar	1½ ounces (40 g); ⅓ cup	2½ ounces (70 g); ½ cup + 1 tablespoon
All-purpose flour	1¾ ounces (50 g); ¼ cup + 2 tablespoons	3 ounces (85 g); ½ cup + 2 tablespoons
Potato starch	½ ounce (15 g); 1⅓ tablespoons	1 ounce (25 g); 2¼ tablespoons

DECORATION:

Confectioners' sugar for dusting

Preheat the oven to 425°F (220° C).

1. Whip the egg whites in the mixer at low speed until they start to froth. If you are not whipping the whites in a copper bowl, add the cream of tartar at this point. Gradually increase the whipping speed to medium-high, and whip until the whites form very stiff peaks and just begin to slip and streak around the side of the bowl. Add the superfine sugar and continue whipping at high speed for a few seconds to incorporate the sugar and tighten the meringue. Turn down the whipping speed to medium, pour in the egg yolks, and whip for a few seconds longer.

2. Sift the confectioners' sugar over the whipped eggs and gently fold it in. Sift the flour with the potato starch onto a sheet of wax paper and gradually fold the mixture into the batter.

3. Scoop the batter into the pastry bag. Starting from the upper left corner of the baking sheet, and pressing firmly on the pastry bag, pipe a thick rope of batter on the diagonal down the baking sheet ①. Pipe a second rope of batter adjacent to the first one. Continue piping adjacent ropes of batter on both sides of the first rope until you have filled the entire baking sheet with diagonal ropes of batter. Don't worry if there are some small gaps between the ropes of batter; they will fill in as the batter expands in the oven.

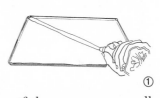

4. Dust the piped batter heavily with confectioners' sugar ② until the surface is white. Wait for 2 minutes to let the sugar dissolve. Then dust with confectioners' sugar a second time. Quickly turn the baking sheet upside down, tap it firmly with a wooden spatula to remove the excess sugar ③, and turn the baking sheet right side up again before the batter has a chance to move.

5. Place the baking sheet in the preheated oven and splash about ⅓ cup (8 cL) of water on the bottom of the oven. Bake until the sponge cake is nicely colored and crusty outside but still soft inside and not dry, about 7 to 9 minutes.

6. Remove from the oven and loosen the edges of the sponge cake from the parchment using a small icing spatula. Slide the sponge cake off the baking sheet onto a wire rack and let it cool to room temperature.

7. Place a second wire rack upside down on top of the sponge-cake, and turn the sponge cake upside down with both racks to transfer it to the second rack. Lift off the first wire rack. Carefully peel the parchment away from the back of the sponge cake, and place it clean side down against the sponge cake to protect the cake. Place the first wire rack back on the sheet of sponge cake, turn it right side up again, and lift off the second wire rack.

HOWS AND WHYS: Splashing water on the oven floor produces steam, which dissolves the sugar on top of the batter and gives the baked sponge cake a pearly look.

STORAGE: Best used the day it is made. If necessary, cover airtight with plastic wrap, and keep for up to 1 day at room temperature.

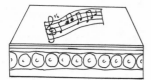

Ray Ventura

The top of this voluptuous gâteau, filled with kirsch-flavored *crème mousseline* and fresh strawberries, is glazed with fondant and decorated by writing a couple of bars of a musical score in chocolate. It is named for a French bandleader who was very popular in France right after World War II. Some chefs prefer to call this gâteau *fraisier*, for the strawberries (*fraises* in French) that provide its distinctive appearance.

EQUIPMENT:

Silver or gold matt board (page 467), at least as large as half of the génoise sheet
Parchment decorating cone (page 416)

	For 8 to 10 servings	For 12 to 15 servings
CAKE LAYERS:		
Génoise (page 220)	One 12 × 16-inch (30 × 40-cm) sheet	One 13 × 19-inch (33 × 50-cm) sheet
BRUSHING-SYRUP MIXTURE:		
Heavy syrup (page 452)	¼ cup (6 cL)	⅓ cup (8 cL)
European kirsch	2 tablespoons (3 cL)	2 tablespoons + 2 teaspoons (4 cL)
Water	2 tablespoons (3 cL)	2 tablespoons + 2 teaspoons (4 cL)
FILLING AND FROSTING:		
Small- to medium-size fresh strawberries	1 pound + 5 ounces (600 g); 1⅓ pints	1 pound + 12 ounces (800 g); 1¾ pints
European kirsch	2 tablespoons (3 cL)	2 tablespoons + 2 teaspoons (4 cL)
Crème mousseline (page 396)	1 pound + 5 ounces (600 g); 3 cups	1 pound + 12 ounces (800 g); 4 cups
GLAZE:		
Fondant (page 408)	12 ounces (340 g); 1 cup	1 pound (450 g); 1⅓ cups
Green food coloring		
Heavy syrup		

DECORATION:

Heavy syrup, heated to lukewarm	1 tablespoon (1.5 cL)	1 tablespoon (1.5 cL)
Unsweetened chocolate, melted	½ ounce (15 g)	½ ounce (15 g)

1. Trim the short ends from the sheet of génoise with a wavy-edge bread knife and cut it in half crosswise to make two equal rectangles. Brush the tops of both rectangles of génoise heavily with the kirsch brushing syrup. Cut from the matt board a rectangle about 1 inch (2.5 cm) smaller in each dimension than the rectangles of génoise.

2. Hull the strawberries. If they are small, leave them whole. Otherwise, cut them in half.

3. Beat the kirsch into the *crème mousseline* with a wooden spatula. Place one rectangle of génoise on your countertop, with the rectangle of matt board underneath. Spread a thin layer of kirsch-flavored *crème mousseline* over this rectangle of génoise using a large icing spatula. Arrange the strawberries over the *crème mousseline*, with a row of strawberries in a straight line down each edge of the cake ①. Spread *crème mousseline* over the strawberries ②, filling the gaps between them and just covering them to make a layer of uniform thickness. Turn the second rectangle of génoise upside down and place it on top. Brush the top of the gâteau lightly with the kirsch brushing syrup. Spread a thin layer of *crème mousseline* over it, and smooth the *crème mousseline* with the icing spatula or a metal straight-edge to give the gâteau a flat top surface.

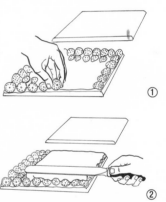

4. Slide the gâteau onto a wire rack and refrigerate for at least 1 hour to make the *crème mousseline* firm.

5. Warm the fondant in a heavy 1-quart (1-L) saucepan over low heat, stirring constantly until melted. Tint it a very pale green with a drop of green food coloring, and stir in just enough heavy syrup to thin the fondant to the consistency of heavy cream. The temperature of the fondant must be between 100° and 105°F (38° to 40°C).

6. Pour the fondant over the top of the gâteau. Quickly smooth the top surface with the edge of a large icing spatula or metal straight-edge to cover the entire top with a thin layer of glaze, letting the excess flow off the edges of the gâteau ③. Let the fondant set.

7. Gradually stir the heavy syrup into the melted chocolate. The chocolate will thicken and will probably "seize," becoming thick and granular. Keep adding heavy syrup until the chocolate becomes smooth and fluid again. Add only as much syrup as necessary to make this "writing chocolate" smooth and soft enough to pipe from a parchment decorating cone.

continued

8. Spoon 1 tablespoon (1.5 cL) or less of the writing chocolate into the parchment decorating cone, fold over the back end to close it, and cut the tip. Decorate the top of the gâteau by writing a couple of bars of a musical score or a design and/or inscription of your own choice.

④

9. Refrigerate the gâteau until 30 minutes before serving. Using a wavy-edge bread knife, cut a thin slice from each side of the gâteau, through the center of the row of strawberries on each edge, to make the sides flat with the cut strawberries showing down the center ④. Before making each cut, heat the blade so it will cut through the fondant without cracking it. Slide the gâteau onto a serving platter, being careful not to crack the fondant.

STORAGE: In the refrigerator (on a covered cake platter if you have one) for up to 2 days. If already cut, pack the trimmings against the sides of the gâteau to prevent the sides from drying out.

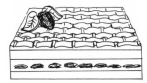

Pavé aux Pruneaux

Prunes. The very thought will cause some readers to pause. High in fiber, yes. Good for your regularity, yes. But a gourmet treat? Think again. Soak those prunes in Armagnac, embed them in a *crème mousseline* filling between layers of Armagnac-brushed génoise, and add a decorative (and luxurious) layer of almond paste. The result is definitely not for children or geriatrics.

EQUIPMENT:

Silver or gold matt board (page 467), at least as large as half of the génoise sheet
Rolling pin
Decorative rolling pin (page 480) with basketweave, checkerboard, or ribbed texture,
  or sheet of ribbed vinyl floor mat (page 480) a little larger than the size of the gâteau

	For 8 to 10 servings	For 12 to 15 servings
FRUIT:		
Pitted prunes	18; about 6 ounces (170g)	24; about 8 ounces (225 g)
Armagnac	¼ cup + 2 tablespoons (9 cL)	½ cup (1.2 dL)
CAKE LAYERS:		
Génoise (page 220)	One 12 × 16-inch (30 × 40-cm) sheet	One 13 × 19-inch (33 × 50-cm) sheet
BRUSHING-SYRUP MIXTURE:		
Heavy syrup (page 452)	¼ cup + 2 tablespoons (9 cL)	½ cup (1.2 dL)
Armagnac	3 tablespoons (4.5 cL)	¼ cup (6 cL)
Water	3 tablespoons (4.5 cL)	¼ cup (6 cL)
FILLING AND FROSTING:		
Armagnac	2 tablespoons (3 cL)	2 tablespoons + 2 teaspoons (4 cL)
Crème mousseline (page 396)	1 pound + 5 ounces (600 g); 3 cups	1 pound + 12 ounces (800 g); 4 cups

continued

Almond paste (page 432)   9 ounces (250 g)   12 ounces (340 g)
Green food coloring
Confectioners' sugar for dusting

1. Set aside one prune for decoration. Place the remaining prunes in a strainer and set the strainer over a saucepan of simmering water. Cover and steam for 5 minutes. Pour the steamed prunes into a glass jar, pour the Armagnac over them, and stir to mix. Cover airtight and let steep in the Armagnac for at least 24 hours, and for as long as several weeks. When you are ready to make the gâteau, drain the prunes thoroughly, and cut them into quarters.

2. Trim the short ends from the sheet of génoise with a wavy-edge bread knife and cut it in half crosswise to make two equal rectangles. Brush the tops of both rectangles of génoise heavily with the Armagnac brushing syrup. Cut from the matt board a rectangle about 1 inch (2.5 cm) smaller in each dimension than the rectangles of génoise.

3. Beat the Armagnac into the *crème mousseline* with a wooden spatula. Place one rectangle of génoise on your countertop, with the rectangle of matt board underneath. Spread a thin layer of *crème mousseline* over this rectangle of génoise using a large icing spatula. Arrange the quartered prunes over the *crème mousseline*. Spread *crème mousseline* over the prunes, filling the gaps between them and just covering them to make a layer of uniform thickness. Turn the second rectangle of génoise upside down and place it on top. Brush the top of the gâteau lightly with the Armagnac brushing syrup. Spread a thin layer of *crème mousseline* over it, and smooth the *crème mousseline* with the icing spatula or a metal straightedge to give the gâteau a flat top surface.

4. Slide the gâteau onto a tray and refrigerate for at least 1 hour to make the *crème mousseline* firm.

5. On your countertop, work the almond paste with the heel of your hand to make it smooth, then work in a drop or two of green food coloring to tint it a pale green. Dust your countertop and the almond paste with confectioners' sugar and roll it into a rough rectangle a little wider and shorter than the top of the gâteau. Then roll your textured rolling pin lengthwise down the sheet of almond paste to impress the texture in the sheet and elongate it so that it is a little longer than the top of the gâteau. (Or place the sheet of almond paste on the sheet of ribbed vinyl floor mat and roll your plain rolling pin over it to impress the texture in the sheet.) Trim off the ragged edges of the sheet of almond paste to get a clean rectangle a little larger than the top of the gâteau. Carefully roll the sheet of almond paste over your plain rolling pin, then unroll it onto the gâteau, centering it so that the edges hang over the sides.

6. Gather together the almond paste trimmings into a pad, and roll it out into a sheet about ⅛ inch (3 mm) thick. Cut out two leaf shapes 1 to 1¼ inches (2.5 to 3 cm) long. Impress them with veins using the side of a small icing spatula or the back edge of a paring knife. Place the reserved prune on top of the gâteau near one of the corners. Place a leaf on each side of the prune, arching the leaves and arranging them so that they touch near the end of the prune closest to the corner of the gâteau and open around the prune.

7. Refrigerate the gâteau until 30 minutes before serving. Then cut a thin slice from each side of the gâteau with a wavy-edge bread knife, carefully cutting through the almond paste on top, to make the sides of the gâteau flat.

STORAGE: In the refrigerator (on a covered cake platter if you have one) for up to 2 days. If already cut, pack the trimmings against the sides of the gâteau to prevent the sides from drying out.

Ébéniste

For centuries, the French have elevated both cabinetry and pastry to an art form. The name of this gâteau, which means "cabinetmaker," refers to its appearance. You will decorate the top surface with imitation wood grain in dark and white chocolate, and pipe the filling in alternating ropes of ganache and coffee buttercream to give the cut sides of the gâteau the look of marquetry. The cake itself is a dark chocolate génoise.

EQUIPMENT:

Sheet of clear polyester (page 483) slightly larger than half of the chocolate génoise sheet
Painter's wood grain tool (page 490)
Two medium-size pastry bags, each fitted with
• ³⁄₁₆-inch (11-mm) plain pastry tube (Ateco #5)
Silver or gold matt board (page 467), at least as large as half of the chocolate génoise sheet

	For 8 to 10 servings	For 12 to 15 servings
DECORATION:		
Heavy syrup (page 452), heated to lukewarm	2 tablespoons (3 cL)	2 tablespoons (3 cL)
Unsweetened chocolate, melted	1 ounce (30 g)	1 ounce (30 g)
European white chocolate, melted	4 ounces (115 g)	5¼ ounces (150 g)
FILLING AND FROSTING:		
Coffee buttercream (page 390)	12 ounces (340 g); 2 cups	1 pound (450 g); 2⅔ cups
Ganache *clichy* (page 400)	9 ounces (250 g); 1 cup	12 ounces (340 g); 1⅓ cups
CAKE LAYERS:		
Chocolate génoise (page 222)	One 12 × 16-inch (30 × 40-cm) sheet	One 13 × 19-inch (33 × 50-cm) sheet
BRUSHING-SYRUP MIXTURE:		
Heavy syrup	¼ cup + 2 tablespoons (9 cL)	½ cup (1.2 dL)
Double-strength brewed espresso (page 456)	¼ cup + 2 tablespoons (9 cL)	½ cup (1.2 dL)

1. You will assemble the gâteau upside down, starting with the wood grain decoration. Gradually stir the heavy syrup into the melted unsweetened chocolate. The chocolate will thicken and will probably seize, becoming thick and granular. Keep adding heavy syrup until the chocolate becomes smooth and fluid again and looks satiny. This is "writing chocolate," but for the wood grain it must be softer than for piping from a parchment decorating cone.

2. Place the sheet of polyester on the countertop with the long sides of the sheet on the left and right. Dab a bit of writing chocolate under each corner to hold it in place. Spread the writing chocolate over the sheet of polyester. Place the wood grain tool on the far left side of the sheet. Pressing evenly, draw the wood grain tool toward you across the chocolate, slowly rocking it first toward you and then away from you, to make a heart-grain pattern in the chocolate. Clean off the tool, go back to the top of the sheet to the right of the first swath of wood grain, and repeat to make a second swath of wood grain. Repeat a third time if necessary. Place the sheet of polyester on a flat tray (see page 487) and set it aside in a cool place, or in the refrigerator if necessary, until the chocolate sets.

3. If you did not melt the white chocolate in a stainless steel bowl, transfer it to one. Temper the white chocolate as follows: Dip the bottom of the bowl of chocolate in a larger bowl of cold water and stir the chocolate until the temperature drops to between 77° and 80°F (25° to 26.5°C) and it begins to thicken. Immediately remove from the cold water and dip the bottom of the bowl of chocolate in a larger bowl of hot water. Stir over the hot water just long enough to warm the chocolate to between 84° and 86°F (29° to 30°C) and make it more fluid again. Then remove from the hot water immediately.

4. Slide the sheet of polyester onto your countertop. Spread the tempered white chocolate evenly over the dark chocolate wood grain on the polyester sheet, being careful not to damage the dark chocolate. You can do this with the flat side of a bowl scraper or with a large icing spatula. Return the sheet to the tray and set it aside again in a cool place or in the refrigerator until the white chocolate is set but not brittle.

5. Put the tray with the sheet of polyester on your countertop. Using a large icing spatula, spread about one third of the coffee buttercream in an even layer over the white chocolate.

6. Trim the short ends from the sheet of génoise with a wavy-edge bread knife and cut it in half crosswise to make two equal rectangles. Turn one of the rectangles upside down and brush the flat side heavily with espresso brushing syrup. Carefully lift this rectangle, turn it flat (brushed) side down, and place it on the buttercream layer on the polyester sheet, centering it carefully. Brush the top of this rectangle heavily with the espresso syrup.

7. Scoop the remaining coffee buttercream into one pastry bag and the ganache into the other pastry bag. Pipe a ⅜-inch (1-cm) rope of coffee buttercream crosswise down the center of the first layer of génoise. Pipe a similar rope of ganache on either side of the first rope of coffee buttercream. Continue, alternating ropes of buttercream and ganache, until you reach the short sides of the cake. Finish with a double rope of ganache on each side so that when you trim the edges of the gâteau, you will see only ganache on the short sides.

continued

8. Brush the top of the second rectangle of génoise heavily with espresso syrup. Turn it upside down and place it on top of the filling, centering it carefully so that you don't disturb the alternating ropes of filling.

9. Cut from the matt board a rectangle about 1 inch (2.5 cm) smaller in each dimension than the rectangles of génoise. Place this rectangle on top of the génoise. Place a second flat tray on top and press firmly and evenly to be sure the gâteau has an even thickness. Lift the gâteau between the two trays and quickly turn the gâteau right side up. Lift off the tray on top.

10. Refrigerate for at least 1 hour to make the fillings and the chocolate firm. Then carefully peel off the sheet of polyester.

11. Refrigerate the gâteau until 30 minutes before serving. Then cut a thin slice from each side of the gâteau with a wavy-edge bread knife to make the sides flat. Before making each cut, heat the blade so that it will melt through the chocolate layer on top of the gâteau.

STORAGE: In the refrigerator (on a covered cake platter if you have one) for up to 2 days. If already cut, pack the trimmings against the sides of the gâteau to prevent the sides from drying out.

Clichy

Louis Clichy premiered his now famous gâteau at the Exposition Culinaire of 1903 in Paris. The gâteau won a silver medal, and it became the signature cake of Clichy's shop on the *boulevard Beaumarchais*. It is composed of four layers of *joconde* separated by alternating layers of coffee buttercream and ganache and the top is glazed with pure chocolate.

Over the years, the *clichy* has inspired many imitations, but none has ever equaled the sumptuous quality of the original. To this day, Paul Bugat continues to make the *clichy* according to the original recipe in the same location where Louis Clichy established his *pâtisserie* in 1892.

EQUIPMENT:

Silver or gold matt board (page 467), at least as large as one quarter of the *joconde* sheet
Parchment decorating cone (page 416)

	For 6 to 8 servings	For 8 to 10 servings
CAKE LAYERS:		
Joconde (page 224)	One 12 × 16-inch (30 × 40-cm) sheet	One 13 × 19-inch (33 × 50-cm) sheet
BRUSHING-SYRUP MIXTURE:		
Heavy syrup (page 452)	1 tablespoon (1.5 cL)	1½ tablespoons (2.3 cL)
Double-strength brewed espresso (page 456)	1 tablespoon (1.5 cL)	1½ tablespoons (2.3 cL)
FILLING AND FROSTING:		
Coffee buttercream (page 390)	6¼ ounces (180 g); 1 cup	9½ ounces (270 g); 1½ cups
Ganache *clichy* (page 400)	3 ounces (85 g); ⅓ cup	4½ ounces (125 g); ½ cup
GLAZE:		
European bittersweet chocolate	4½ ounces (130 g)	6 ounces (170 g)
Clarified butter (page 449), at room temperature	¾ ounce (20 g); 1½ tablespoons	1 ounce (25 g); 2 tablespoons

continued

Heavy syrup, heated to lukewarm	1 tablespoon (1.5 cL)	1 tablespoon (1.5 cL)
Unsweetened chocolate, melted	½ ounce (15 g)	½ ounce (15 g)

1. Trim all four edges from the sheet of *joconde* with a wavy-edge bread knife and cut it in half crosswise and lengthwise to make four equal rectangles. Brush the tops of all four rectangles heavily with the espresso brushing syrup. Cut from the matt board a rectangle about 1 inch (2.5 cm) smaller in each dimension than the rectangles of *joconde*.

2. Place one rectangle of *joconde* on your countertop, with the rectangle of matt board underneath. Spread one third of the buttercream over this rectangle of *joconde* with a large icing spatula. Place a second rectangle of *joconde* on the layer of buttercream, and spread the ganache over it. Place a third rectangle of *joconde* on the layer of ganache, and spread half of the remaining buttercream over it. Turn the fourth layer of *joconde* upside down and place it on top. Brush the top lightly with espresso syrup. Spread the remaining buttercream over it and smooth the buttercream with the icing spatula or a metal straightedge to give the gâteau a flat top surface.

3. Slide the gâteau onto a wire rack, and refrigerate for at least 1 hour to make the buttercream firm.

4. If you did not melt the chocolate for the glaze in a stainless steel bowl, transfer it to one. Temper the chocolate as follows: Dip the bottom of the bowl of chocolate in a larger bowl of cold water and stir the chocolate until the temperature drops to between 80° and 84°F (26.5° to 29°C) and it begins to thicken. Immediately remove from the cold water and dip the bottom of the bowl of chocolate in a larger bowl of hot water. Stir over the hot water just long enough to warm the chocolate to between 86° and 91°F (30° to 33°C) and make it more fluid again. Then remove from the hot water immediately. Beat the clarified butter with a wooden spatula to make it smooth and creamy, then stir it into the chocolate.

5. Pour the chocolate over the top of the gâteau. Quickly smooth the top surface with the edge of a large icing spatula or metal straightedge to cover the entire top with a thin layer of glaze, letting the excess flow off the edges of the gâteau. Let the chocolate set.

6. Gradually stir the heavy syrup into the melted chocolate. The chocolate will thicken and will probably seize, becoming thick and granular. Keep adding heavy syrup until the chocolate becomes smooth and fluid again. Add only as much syrup as necessary to make this "writing chocolate" smooth and soft enough to pipe from a parchment decorating cone.

7. Spoon 1 tablespoon (1.5 cL) or less of the writing chocolate into the parchment decorating cone, fold over the back end to close it, and cut the tip. Write *Clichy* on the diagonal across the top of the gâteau. Or write a design and/or inscription of your own choice.

8. Refrigerate the gâteau until 30 minutes before serving. Then cut a thin slice from each side of the gâteau with a wavy-edge bread knife to make the sides flat. Before making each cut, heat the blade so it will cut through the chocolate without cracking.

STORAGE: In the refrigerator (on a covered cake platter if you have one) for up to 2 days. If already cut, pack the trimmings against the sides of the gâteau to prevent the sides from drying out.

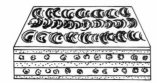

Lucifer

Here is a pyromaniac's delight. Brush three layers of *joconde* with raspberry brandy and fill them with a light pastry cream and fresh raspberries. Pretty conventional so far. But then dust the top of the gâteau with sugar and caramelize it with an electric charcoal lighter. (Or you can dust it with sanding sugar and lightly caramelize the sugar with a propane torch—see precautions on page 480.) Hence the name *lucifer*. While this technique is definitely not play for children, it does make the finishing touch on *lucifer* child's play for adults. If you don't have a charcoal lighter or propane torch, you can finish the (well-chilled) gâteau by running it under the broiler to lightly caramelize the sugar.

EQUIPMENT:

Silver or gold matt board (page 467), at least as large as one third of the *joconde* sheet
Electric mixer
Electric charcoal lighter (page 468) or propane torch (page 479)

	For 6 to 8 servings	For 8 to 10 servings
CAKE LAYERS:		
Joconde (page 224)	One 12 × 16-inch (30 × 40-cm) sheet	One 13 × 19-inch (33 × 50-cm) sheet
BRUSHING-SYRUP MIXTURE:		
Heavy syrup (page 452)	2 tablespoons + 2 teaspoons (4 cL)	3½ tablespoons (5.3 cL)
Framboise (raspberry brandy)	2 tablespoons + 2 teaspoons (4 cL)	3½ tablespoons (5.3 cL)
FILLING:		
Unflavored gelatin	1 teaspoon (5 mL)	1½ teaspoons (7.5 mL)
Cold water	1 tablespoon (1.5 cL)	1½ tablespoons (2.3 cL)
French pastry cream (page 394), preferably still hot	13 ounces (370 g); 1¼ cups + 3 tablespoons	1 pound + 2 ounces (500 g); 1¾ cups + 3 tablespoons
Heavy cream, well chilled	1 cup + 2 tablespoons (2.7 dL)	1½ cups (3.6 dL)
Framboise (raspberry brandy)	2 tablespoons (3 cL)	2 tablespoons + 2 teaspoons (4 cL)
Fresh raspberries	9 ounces (250 g); ¾ pint	12 ounces (340 g); 1 pint

French pastry cream	4¾ ounces (135 g); ½ cup	6¼ ounces (180 g); ⅔ cup

DECORATION:

Either granulated sugar (for charcoal lighter)	2⅔ ounces (75 g); ¼ cup + 2 tablespoons	3½ ounces (100 g); ½ cup
Or sanding sugar (for propane torch)	1¼ ounces (35 g); 3 tablespoons	1¾ ounces (50 g); ¼ cup

1. Trim the short ends from the sheet of *joconde* with a wavy-edge bread knife and cut it cross-wise into three equal rectangles. Brush the tops of all three rectangles heavily with the *framboise* brushing syrup. Cut from the matt board a rectangle about 1 inch (2.5 cm) smaller in each dimension than the rectangles of *joconde*.

2. Stir the gelatin into the water and let it soften. If the pastry cream has already cooled, transfer it to a heavy 1-quart (1-L) saucepan and bring it back almost to a simmer over low heat, stirring constantly with a wooden spatula.

3. Pour the hot pastry cream into a stainless steel mixing bowl and stir in the softened gelatin to dissolve it. Place the bowl of pastry cream on a wire rack and allow the pastry cream to cool, stirring occasionally. Do not allow it to set. While the pastry cream is cooling, chill the bowl and the wire whip or beater of the mixer in the refrigerator.

4. Pour the heavy cream into the chilled mixer bowl and whip the cream at medium speed with the chilled wire whip or beater until it is light and thick and holds soft peaks. Stop whipping.

5. Stir the *framboise* into the pastry cream. Dip the bottom of the bowl of pastry cream in a larger bowl of ice water, and stir with a rubber spatula until it just begins to thicken. Immediately remove the bowl from the ice water.

6. Continue whipping the cream at medium speed until it holds stiff peaks, then whip in the pastry cream to finish the filling.

7. Place one rectangle of *joconde* on your countertop, with the rectangle of matt board underneath. Spread a thin layer of the filling over this rectangle of *joconde* using a large icing spatula. Scatter half of the raspberries over the filling, and then spread more filling over the raspberries, using altogether about half of the filling. Turn the second rectangle of *joconde* upside down and place it on top. Brush it heavily with *framboise* syrup. Spread a thin layer of filling on the second rectangle, scatter with the remaining raspberries, and cover the berries with the rest of the filling. Turn the third rectangle of *joconde* upside down and place it on top. Brush the top lightly with *framboise* syrup.

8. Slide the gâteau onto a tray and chill the gâteau in the refrigerator to firm the filling.

9. Spread a thin layer of pastry cream frosting over the top layer of *joconde*. Carefully smooth the pastry cream with the icing spatula or a metal straightedge to give the gâteau a flat top surface. Slide the gâteau onto a tray and refrigerate for at least 1 hour to make the frosting firm.

continued

10. Shortly before serving, sprinkle the granulated or sanding sugar evenly over the top of the gâteau. Cut a thin slice from each side of the gâteau with a wavy-edge bread knife to make the sides flat.

11. TO CARAMELIZE THE GRANULATED SUGAR ON TOP USING THE CHAR-COAL LIGHTER: Starting from the far left of the gâteau, touch the loop of the charcoal lighter to the top surface to caramelize the sugar, lift it, move it toward you, and repeat until you reach the near side of the gâteau. This will make a swath of caramelized arcs down the left side of the top of the gâteau. Rotate the gâteau 180 degrees so the caramelized side is on the right. Repeat this procedure, starting from the far side and working to the side nearest you to produce a second swath of caramelized arcs adjacent to the first swath, but with the arcs in the opposite direction. Rotate the gâteau a second time, and make a third swath of caramelized arcs adjacent to the second one. If you have not yet caramelized the entire top of the gâteau, rotate it one more time and repeat the procedure to make a final swath of caramelized arcs on the left side of the gâteau. You will now have caramelized the entire top surface of the gâteau in three or four adjacent swaths.

TO CARAMELIZE THE SUGAR USING THE PROPANE TORCH: Sweep the cone of the flame back and forth over the surface, working on a small area of the cake at a time. To avoid burning the sugar, never hold the flame in a fixed spot, and as soon as sugar begins to melt in the area you are working on, move to another area. Return to areas where the sugar has begun to melt as needed to produce a light caramel color. When you are finished, there should be no unmelted sugar crystals remaining, and the top of the cake should be covered with golden beads of caramel.

STORAGE: Before caramelizing the top, in a covered cake platter for up to 2 days in the refrigerator. The gâteau is best served within 1 or 2 hours after caramelizing the top to avoid having the caramel dissolve. If already cut, pack the trimmings against the sides of the gâteau to prevent the sides from drying out.

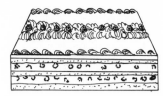

Pavé Framboise

For a light, fruit-flavored gâteau, you can fill layers of *russe* with fruit mousse instead of buttercream. We especially like raspberry mousse in this gâteau, and we add whole fresh berries to the layers of mousse. The gâteau is topped and decorated with whipped cream, plus a handful of fresh raspberries. If you prefer, you can vary the flavor of the gâteau by substituting any of the fruit mousses that we use for charlottes in Chapter 6.

The word *pavé* means paving stone and refers to the shape of the gâteau.

EQUIPMENT:

Silver or gold matt board (page 467), at least as large as one third of the *russe* sheet
Blender or food processor
Electric mixer
Large pastry bag fitted with
• small fluted pastry tube (Ateco #1)

	For 6 servings	For 8 servings
CAKE LAYERS:		
Russe (page 226)	One 12 × 16-inch (30 × 40-cm) sheet	One 13 × 19-inch (33 × 50-cm) sheet
FILLING:		
Fresh raspberries for puree	9 ounces (250 g); ¾ pint	12 ounces (340 g); 1 pint
Superfine or extra fine sugar	2 ounces (60 g); ¼ cup + 1 tablespoon	3 ounces (85 g); ¼ cup + 3 tablespoons
Fresh orange juice	1½ tablespoons (2.3 cL)	2 tablespoons (3 cL)
Unflavored gelatin	2 teaspoons (1 cL)	1 tablespoon (1.5 cL)
Heavy cream, well chilled	1 cup + 2 tablespoons (2.7 dL)	1½ cups (3.6 dL)
Fresh raspberries (optional) to leave whole	4¼ ounces (120 g); ⅓ pint	5¾ ounces (160 g); ½ pint
BRUSHING-SYRUP MIXTURE:		
Heavy syrup (page 452)	1 tablespoon (1.5 cL)	1 tablespoon + 1 teaspoon (2 cL)
Framboise (raspberry brandy)	1 tablespoon (1.5 cL)	1 tablespoon + 1 teaspoon (2 cL)

continued

FROSTING AND DECORATION:

Confectioners' sugar	⅔ ounce (17 g); 2 tablespoons	1 ounce (25 g); 3 tablespoons
Heavy cream	⅔ cup (1.6 dL)	1 cup (2.4 dL)
Fresh raspberries	8	12

1. Trim the short ends from the sheet of *russe* with a wavy-edge bread knife and cut it cross-wise into three equal rectangles. Cut from the matt board a rectangle about 1 inch (2.5 cm) smaller in each dimension than the rectangles of *russe*.

2. Puree the raspberries with the sugar and orange juice in the blender or food processor. Strain through a fine sieve to eliminate the seeds.

3. Combine the brushing-syrup mixture with an equal volume of the raspberry puree—2 tablespoons (3 cL) for a small gâteau or 2 tablespoons + 2 teaspoons (4.5 cL) for a large gâteau—to make a raspberry brushing syrup.

4. Pour about one third of the remaining raspberry puree into a heavy 2-cup (5-dL) butter melter and stir in the gelatin. Let the gelatin soften, then warm over low heat, stirring constantly, until the gelatin dissolves. Remove from the heat and pour into a stainless steel mixing bowl. Stir in the rest of the raspberry puree, and allow to cool, stirring occasionally. Do not allow it to set. While the raspberry puree is cooling, chill the bowl and the wire whip or beater of the mixer in the refrigerator.

5. Pour the heavy cream into the chilled mixer bowl and whip the cream at medium speed with the chilled wire whip or beater until it is light and thick and holds soft peaks. Stop whipping.

6. Dip the bottom of the bowl of raspberry puree in a larger bowl of ice water, and stir with a rubber spatula until it just begins to thicken. Immediately remove the bowl from the ice water.

7. Continue whipping the cream at medium speed until it holds stiff peaks, then whip in the raspberry puree to make the mousse. Gently fold in the optional raspberries, if you are using them. The mousse should be very thick. If necessary, chill the mousse until it is almost about to set so that it won't be runny when you fill the cake.

8. Brush the tops of all three rectangles of *russe* with the raspberry brushing syrup.

9. Place one rectangle of *russe* on your countertop, with the rectangle of matt board underneath. Spread half of the mousse over it using a large icing spatula. Place a second rectangle of *russe* on the layer of mousse, and spread the remaining mousse over it. Turn the third rectangle of *russe* upside down and place it on top.

10. Slide the gâteau onto a tray and chill in the freezer for several hours so the mousse will be firm when you trim the edges. If you will not be cutting it the same day, cover the frozen gâteau airtight with plastic wrap.

11. Cut a thin slice from each edge of the gâteau with a wavy-edge bread knife to make the sides flat. Then defrost in the refrigerator for several hours or overnight.

12. Sift the confectioners' sugar into the bowl of the mixer, stir in the heavy cream, and refrigerate for about an hour. Chill the wire whip or beater of the mixer as well. Whip the cream at medium speed in the mixer. When the cream holds soft peaks, slow down to avoid overbeating. Continue whipping until the cream is light and thick and holds stiff peaks.

13. Spread half of the whipped cream on top of the gâteau in a layer ¼ inch (6 mm) thick. Carefully smooth the whipped cream with the icing spatula or a metal straightedge to give the gâteau a flat top surface.

14. Scoop the remaining whipped cream into the pastry bag. Pipe a swath of whipped cream 2 inches (5 cm) wide lengthwise down the center of the gâteau, using a back-and-forth figure-eight motion. Pipe a row of teardrops down the center of the swath, then pipe a row of teardrops down each long edge of the gâteau. Arrange the fresh raspberries between the teardrops down the center.

HOWS AND WHYS: If fresh raspberries are unavailable, you can use unsweetened frozen raspberries in the puree for the mousse and brushing syrup. Defrost the berries before using. Do not use frozen raspberries for decoration. Either omit the raspberries in the decoration altogether or substitute German raspberries.

STORAGE: In the refrigerator for up to 12 hours. Best eaten within 2 to 4 hours. If already cut, pack the trimmings against the sides of the gâteau to prevent the sides from drying out. Before covering the top with whipped cream, the gâteau can be covered airtight with plastic wrap and kept in the refrigerator for up to 2 days.

Before trimming, the gâteau can be covered airtight with plastic wrap and kept frozen for up to 2 weeks.

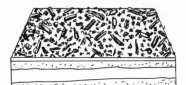

Russe au Chocolat

This gâteau is unusually light, thanks to the addition of Italian meringue to the chocolate buttercream filling. The decoration is an abstract expressionist composition of chocolate cigarettes and shavings, with a dusting of confectioners' sugar.

EQUIPMENT:

Silver or gold matt board (page 467), at least as large as half of the *russe* sheet

	For 6 to 8 servings	For 8 to 10 servings
CAKE LAYERS:		
Russe (page 226)	One 12 × 16-inch (30 × 40-cm) sheet	One 13 × 19-inch (33 × 50-cm) sheet
BRUSHING-SYRUP MIXTURE:		
Heavy syrup (page 452), mixed with an equal volume of water	As needed	As needed
FILLING AND FROSTING:		
Italian meringue (page 184)	3¼ ounces (90 g); 1½ cups	4¼ ounces (120 g); 2 cups
Chocolate buttercream (page 388)	7 ounces (200 g); 1 cup + 3 tablespoons	9½ ounces (270 g) 1½ cups + 1 tablespoon
DECORATION:		
Chocolate shavings (page 423)	About ⅓ ounce (10 g)	About ½ ounce (15 g)
Chocolate cigarettes (page 424)	A few	A few
Confectioners' sugar for dusting		

1. Trim the short ends from the sheet of *russe* with a wavy-edge bread knife and cut it in half crosswise to make two equal rectangles. If the *russe* is too dry and cracks easily, brush both rectangles with the syrup to soften them. Cut from the matt board a rectangle about 1 inch (2.5 cm) smaller in each dimension than the rectangles of *russe*.

2. Gently fold the Italian meringue into the chocolate buttercream to make a very light chocolate buttercream.

3. Place one rectangle of *russe* on your countertop, with the rectangle of matt board underneath. Spread about two thirds of the light chocolate buttercream over this rectangle of *russe* using a large icing spatula. Turn the second rectangle of *russe* upside down and place it on the buttercream. Spread the remaining buttercream in a thin, even layer on top. Carefully smooth the buttercream with the icing spatula or a metal straightedge to give the gâteau a flat top surface.

4. Scatter the chocolate shavings and chocolate cigarettes over the top of the gâteau. Slide the gâteau onto a tray and refrigerate until 30 minutes before serving.

5. Lightly dust the top of the gâteau with confectioners' sugar. Then cut a thin slice from each edge of the gâteau with a wavy-edge bread knife to make the sides flat.

STORAGE: In the refrigerator (on a covered cake platter if you have one) for up to 2 days. If already cut, pack the trimmings against the sides of the gâteau to prevent the sides from drying out.

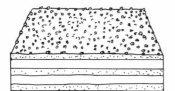

Russe Praliné

The flavor of *praliné* (roasted-nut-and-caramel paste) contributes a sensual note to this gâteau. If you already have some *praliné* on hand, *russe praliné* is particularly easy to prepare. The decoration is a simple dusting of confectioners' sugar.

EQUIPMENT:

Silver or gold matt board (page 467), at least as large as one third of the *russe* sheet

	For 6 servings	For 8 servings
CAKE LAYERS:		
Russe (page 226), dusted with chopped almonds and granulated sugar before baking	One 12 × 16-inch (30 × 40-cm) sheet	One 13 × 19-inch (33 × 50-cm) sheet
BRUSHING-SYRUP MIXTURE:		
Heavy syrup (page 452) mixed with an equal volume of water	As needed	As needed
FILLING:		
Praliné buttercream (page 388)	9½ ounces (270 g); 1½ cups + 1 tablespoon	12¾ ounces (360 g); 2 cups + 2 tablespoons
DECORATION:		
Confectioners' sugar for dusting		

1. Trim the short ends from the sheet of *russe* with a wavy-edge bread knife and cut it cross-wise into three equal rectangles. If the *russe* is too dry and cracks easily, brush all three rectangles with the syrup to soften them. The rectangle that will be the top of the finished gâteau should be brushed on the underside, but the other two rectangles should be brushed on top. Cut from the matt board a rectangle about 1 inch (2.5 cm) smaller in each dimension than the rectangles of *russe*.

2. Place one rectangle of *russe* on your countertop, with the rectangle of matt board underneath. Spread half of the *praliné* buttercream over this rectangle of *russe* using a large icing spatula. Place a second rectangle of *russe* on the buttercream, and spread the remaining buttercream over it. Place the third rectangle of *russe* right side up on top.

3. Slide the gâteau onto a tray and refrigerate until 30 minutes before serving.

4. Lightly dust the top of the gâteau with confectioners' sugar. Then cut a thin slice from each edge of the gâteau with a wavy-edge bread knife to make the sides flat.

STORAGE: In the refrigerator (on a covered cake platter if you have one) for up to 2 days. If already cut, pack the trimmings against the sides of the gâteau to prevent the sides from drying out.

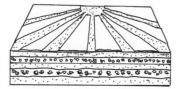

Dauphinois

Before the Revolution, the Dauphiné was the province in southeast France between Savoie and Provence. The name is still used today for the region encompassing the *départements* of Isère, the Drome, and the Haute Alpes. It derived from the title Dauphin given to the eldest sons of the kings of France. The Dauphiné province was first presented by Charles of Valois to his eldest son in 1364 when Charles became King Charles V, and it remained the semi-independent domain of the king's eldest son until 1456, when it was annexed to the crown by Louis XI.

The Dauphiné has long been famous for its walnuts. In this cake, three layers of *russe* are filled with coffee buttercream and chopped walnuts, which account for the name. The top of the gâteau is stenciled with confectioners' sugar.

EQUIPMENT:

Silver or gold matt board (page 467), at least as large as one third of the *russe* sheet

	For 6 servings	For 8 servings
CAKE LAYERS:		
Russe (page 226)	One 12 × 16-inch (30 × 40-cm) sheet	One 12 × 19-inch (33 × 50-cm) sheet
BRUSHING-SYRUP MIXTURE:		
Heavy syrup (page 452)	2 teaspoons (1 cL)	1 tablespoon (1.5 cL)
Double-strength brewed espresso (page 456)	2 teaspoons (1 cL)	1 tablespoon (1.5 cL)
FILLING:		
Coffee buttercream (page 390)	8 ounces (225 g); 1¼ cups	10½ ounces (300 g); 1⅔ cups
Walnuts, chopped	1 ounce (25 g); 3 tablespoons	1¼ ounces (35 g); ¼ cup
DECORATION:		
Confectioners' sugar for dusting		

1. Trim the short ends from the sheet of *russe* with a wavy-edge bread knife and cut it crosswise into three equal rectangles. Brush the tops of all three rectangles of *russe* with the espresso brushing syrup. Cut from the matt board a rectangle about 1 inch (2.5 cm) smaller in each dimension than the rectangle of *russe*.

2. Place one rectangle of *russe* on your countertop, with the rectangle of matt board underneath. Spread half of the coffee buttercream over this rectangle of *russe* using a large icing spatula. Scatter half of the chopped walnuts over the buttercream. Place a second rectangle of *russe* on the layer of buttercream, spread the remaining buttercream over it, and scatter the remaining walnuts over the buttercream. Turn the third rectangle of *russe* upside down and place it on top.

3. Slide the gâteau onto a tray and refrigerate until 30 minutes before serving.

4. Cut some strips of heavy paper about ½ inch (12 mm) wide and arrange them on top of the gâteau in a decorative geometric pattern, for example diagonal stripes, lozenges, or a sunburst. Dust the top of the gâteau with confectioners' sugar. Carefully remove the paper strips.

5. Cut a thin slice from each edge of the gâteau with a wavy-edge bread knife to make the sides flat.

STORAGE: In the refrigerator (on a covered cake platter if you have one) for up to 2 days. If already cut, pack the trimmings against the sides of the gâteau to prevent the sides from drying out.

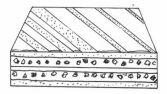

Russe Grand Marnier

This gâteau is quite similar to *dauphinois* (page 252) in structure, but the flavor is totally different. Here three layers of *russe* are filled with Grand Marnier–flavored buttercream and glacé fruits soaked in Grand Marnier. As for *dauphinois*, the top of the gâteau is stenciled with confectioners' sugar. A very heady dessert! You won't want to be the designated driver when *russe grand marnier* is on the menu.

EQUIPMENT:

Silver or gold matt board (page 467), at least as large as one third of the *russe* sheet

	For 6 servings	For 8 servings
FRUIT GARNISH:		
Glacé fruits (cherries, pineapple, apricots), cut into ¼-inch (6-mm) dice	5 ounces (150 g)	7 ounces (200 g)
Grand Marnier	3 tablespoons (4.5 cL)	¼ cup (6 cL)
CAKE LAYERS:		
Russe (page 226)	One 12 × 16-inch (30 × 40-cm) sheet	One 13 × 19-inch (33 × 50-cm) sheet
BRUSHING-SYRUP MIXTURE:		
Heavy syrup (page 452)	2 teaspoons (1 cL)	1 tablespoon (1.5 cL)
Grand Marnier	2 teaspoons (1 cL)	1 tablespoon (1.5 cL)
FILLING:		
Grand Marnier	2¼ teaspoons (1.1 cL)	1 tablespoon (1.5 cL)
French buttercream (page 384)	7½ ounces (215 g); 1¼ cups	10 ounces (285 g); 1⅔ cups
Red and yellow food colorings		
DECORATION:		
Confectioners' sugar for dusting		

1. Place the glacé fruits in a glass jar, pour the Grand Marnier over them, and stir to mix. Cover airtight and let steep for at least 24 hours. When ready to make the gâteau, drain the glacé fruits thoroughly.

2. Trim the short ends from the sheet of *russe* with a wavy-edge bread knife and cut it crosswise into three equal rectangles. Brush the tops of all three rectangles of *russe* with the Grand Marnier brushing syrup. Cut from the matt board a rectangle about 1 inch (2.5 cm) smaller in each dimension than the rectangle of *russe*.

3. Beat the Grand Marnier into the buttercream with a wooden spatula, and tint it a pale peach color with a couple of drops of red and a drop of yellow food coloring.

4. Place one rectangle of *russe* on your countertop, with the rectangle of matt board underneath. Spread half of the Grand Marnier buttercream over this rectangle of *russe* using a large icing spatula. Scatter half of the glacé fruits over the buttercream. Place a second rectangle of *russe* on the layer of buttercream, spread the remaining buttercream over it, and scatter the remaining glacé fruits over the buttercream. Turn the third rectangle of *russe* upside down and place it on top.

5. Slide the gâteau onto a tray and refrigerate until 30 minutes before serving.

6. Cut some strips of heavy paper about ½ inch (12 mm) wide and arrange them on top of the gâteau in a decorative geometric pattern, for example diagonal stripes, lozenges, or a sunburst. Dust the top of the gâteau with confectioners' sugar. Carefully remove the paper strips.

7. Cut a thin slice from each edge of the gâteau with a wavy-edge bread knife to make the sides flat.

STORAGE: In the refrigerator (on a covered cake platter if you have one) for up to 2 days. If already cut, pack the trimmings against the sides of the gâteau to prevent the sides from drying out.

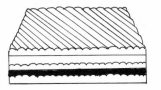

Chocomel

. . . .

One of the easiest ways to finish the top of a rectangular gâteau is to use diagonally piped sheets of sponge cake, and let the piping itself supply the decoration. In this gâteau, we divide a sheet of sponge cake in three and fill it with layers of chocolate and caramel mousses. Brushing the sponge cake with Drambuie liqueur provides a mysterious accent.

EQUIPMENT:

Silver or gold matt board (page 467), at least as large as one third of the sponge cake sheet
Electric mixer

	For 6 servings	For 8 servings
CAKE LAYERS:		
Diagonally piped sponge cake sheets (page 228)	One 12 × 16-inch (30 × 40-cm) sheet	One 13 × 19-inch (33 × 50-cm) sheet
FLAVORINGS:		
Granulated sugar	2¾ ounces (75 g); ¼ cup + 2 tablespoons	3½ ounces (100 g); ½ cup
Heavy cream, heated almost to a simmer	3 tablespoons (4.5 cL)	¼ cup (6 cL)
Heavy cream, heated to lukewarm	2 tablespoons (3 cL)	3 tablespoons (4.5 cL)
European bittersweet chocolate, melted	1¾ ounces (50 g)	2½ ounces (70 g)
FILLING:		
Unflavored gelatin	¾ teaspoon (4 mL)	1 teaspoon (5 mL)
Cold water	2 teaspoons (1 cL)	1 tablespoon (1.5 cL)
Milk	¼ cup + 2 tablespoons (9 cL)	½ cup (1.2 dL)
Superfine or extra fine sugar	3½ ounces (100 g); ½ cup	4¾ ounces (135 g); ⅔ cup
Large egg yolks	3	4
Heavy cream, well chilled	1 cup + 2 tablespoons (2.7 dL)	1½ cups (3.6 dL)
BRUSHING-SYRUP MIXTURE:		
Heavy syrup (page 452)	¼ cup (6 cL)	¼ cup + 2 tablespoons (9 cL)
Drambuie liqueur	¼ cup (6 cL)	¼ cup + 2 tablespoons (9 cL)

1. Trim the short ends from the sheet of sponge cake with a wavy-edge bread knife and cut it crosswise into three equal rectangles. Cut from the matt board a rectangle about 1 inch (2.5 cm) smaller in each dimension than the rectangles of sponge cake.

2. To make the caramel, put the granulated sugar in a heavy 2-cup (5-dL) butter melter or 3-cup (8-dL) caramel pot and cook it over medium to high heat, without stirring. As soon as the sugar begins to melt around the sides of the pot, begin stirring with a wooden spatula. When the sugar becomes fluid, with small white lumps floating in the syrup, reduce the heat to low and continue cooking, stirring constantly and crushing the solid lumps with the wooden spatula, until the sugar is completely melted and turns a medium amber. Remove from the heat and add the hot heavy cream a little at a time, stirring constantly to keep the caramel smooth. The cream must be added very gradually to the caramel at the beginning or it will splatter. When all of the cream has been incorporated, let cool, stirring occasionally to prevent a crust from forming on top.

3. Stir the gelatin into the cold water and let it soften. In a heavy 1-quart (1-L) saucepan, combine the milk with about one third of the superfine sugar—3 tablespoons (35 g) for a small gâteau or ¼ cup (50 g) for a large gâteau. Bring the milk and sugar to a simmer. Combine the remaining superfine sugar with the egg yolks in a small mixing bowl and beat with a wire whisk until lemon-colored. Whisk in the simmering milk. Strain the mixture through a fine sieve back into the saucepan and cook over low to medium heat, beating constantly with the wire whisk, until the mixture thickens and barely comes to a simmer. Remove it from the heat and stir in the softened gelatin. Pour into the bowl of the mixer, and whip at medium speed until light, thick, and cool. This is a bombe batter.

4. Whip the heavy cream in the mixer, using a clean (and chilled if you have two sets) bowl and wire whip or beater until it is light and thick and holds stiff peaks. Then whip in the bombe batter to make the mousse. Stop whipping as soon as the bombe batter and cream are uniformly mixed.

5. Divide the mousse in half.

Gradually stir the lukewarm heavy cream into the melted chocolate. Scoop about ¼ cup (6 cL) of mousse from one half into a small mixing bowl and beat in the melted chocolate. Fold the chocolate mixture back into the remainder of this half of the mousse using a wire whisk.

Scoop about ¼ cup (6 cL) of mousse from the other half into the small mixing bowl (you can use the same one as for the chocolate) and beat in the caramel. Fold the caramel mixture back into the second half of the mousse using the wire whisk (again, you can use the same one as for the chocolate).

6. Set the bowl of chocolate mousse over a bowl of ice water, and gently fold the mousse, repeatedly scraping it off the sides of the bowl, until it is almost about to set. Repeat this procedure with the caramel mousse.

7. Place one rectangle of sponge cake on your countertop, with the rectangle of matt board underneath. Brush this layer of sponge cake heavily with the Drambuie brushing syrup. Spread the chocolate mousse over it in an even layer using a large icing spatula. Brush one side of the second rectangle of sponge cake heavily with Drambuie syrup, turn it upside down, and place it on the chocolate mousse. Brush the top of this layer of sponge cake heavily with Drambuie syrup, and spread the caramel mousse over it in an even layer. Turn the third layer of sponge cake upside down and brush the bottom side with Drambuie syrup. Turn it right side up again, and place it on top of the caramel mousse.

8. Slide the gâteau onto a tray and chill in the freezer for several hours so the mousses will be firm when you trim the edges. If you will not be cutting it the same day, cover the frozen gâteau airtight with plastic wrap.

9. Cut a thin slice from each edge of the gâteau with a wavy-edge bread knife to make the sides flat. Then defrost in the refrigerator for several hours or overnight.

STORAGE: In the refrigerator (on a covered cake platter if you have one) for up to 2 days. If already cut, pack the trimmings against the sides of the gâteau to prevent the sides from drying out. Before trimming, the gâteau can be kept frozen for up to 2 weeks.

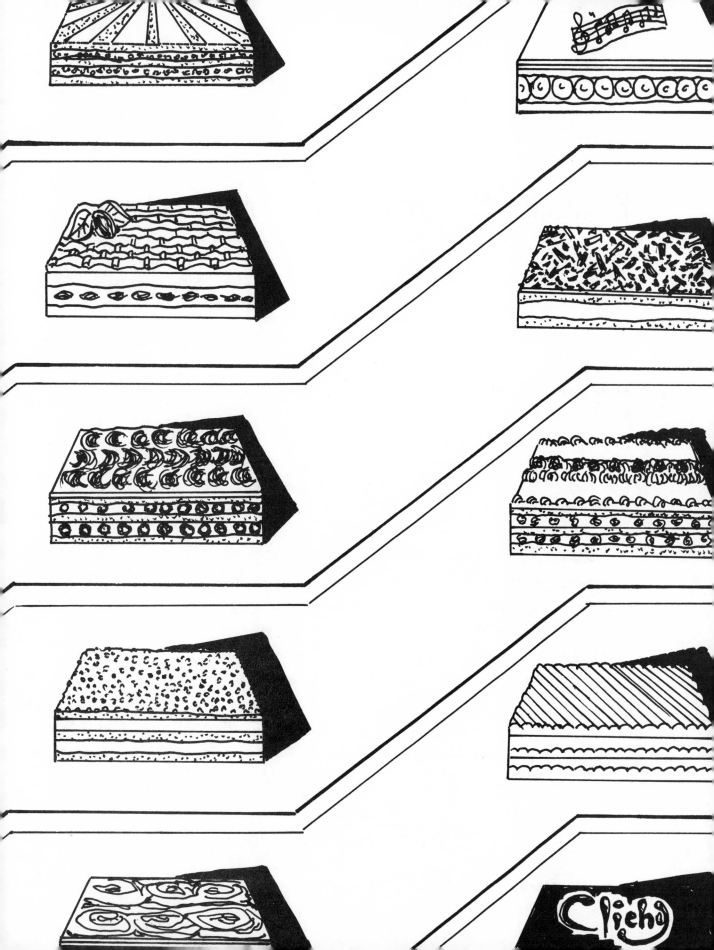

CHAPTER SIX

Bavarians, Charlottes, and Mousse Cakes

Bavarians, charlottes, and mousse cakes are molded desserts that get their lightness from whipped cream and their stability from gelatin. They are very different from the other desserts in this book because here the filling becomes the essential element, with the mold defining the shape of the dessert.

BAVARIANS

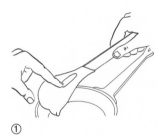

Bavarians are the simplest molded desserts. The mousse in these desserts, called a bavarian cream, is based on *crème anglaise* (custard sauce) ① with gelatin added while it is still hot. (For a detailed discussion of *crème anglaise*, see the recipe on page 436.) After cooling, you whip the *crème anglaise* into whipped cream.

In their most basic form, bavarians are just bavarian cream poured into a mold, refrigerated until set, and then unmolded onto a serving plate. To add variety of texture and flavor, we embed layers of liquor-soaked fruit and sponge cake in the bavarian cream.

You can mold bavarians in just about any shape, and some very elaborate molds have been created for them. We like our bavarians creamy, with just enough gelatin to hold their shape. This makes them somewhat delicate, and you will find them easier to handle if you choose molds that aren't too deep. We have based the quantities in our recipes on a 5- to 6-cup (1.2- to 1.5-L) ring mold. If you have a more elaborate mold, increase or decrease the quantities in the recipe according to its volume.

Whatever mold you choose, trim the crust from a round of sponge cake (we usually use génoise) and cut it in a way suitable to the shape of the

mold. For example, you can cut strips and arrange them in a circle around a ring mold; or for a round mold without a central tube you can cut a round of sponge cake a little smaller in diameter than the mold. Mix heavy syrup with an equal volume of liqueur and brush the sponge cake strips with this syrup.

To make unmolding easier, rinse the mold with cold water and shake it out. Pour about one third of the bavarian cream into the mold ②. Arrange the fruit (cut in pieces, slices, or segments when appropriate) over the bavarian cream ③. Pour in half of the remaining bavarian cream to cover the fruit. Place the sponge cake in the mold and press it gently into the bavarian cream. Pour in the remaining bavarian cream to cover the sponge cake and fill the mold. Smooth the surface and sweep off any excess bavarian cream with a large icing spatula or a metal straightedge ④.

Chill the molded bavarian in the refrigerator for 3 or 4 hours to set the bavarian cream.

Run the tip of a small icing spatula around the rim of the mold to loosen the top edge of the bavarian cream. Place a round serving plate upside down on top of the mold and invert the plate and mold together. Warm the outside of the mold with a blow dryer until the bavarian slides out easily and you can lift off the mold ⑤. Refrigerate again to chill the surface of the bavarian.

After unmolding a ring-shaped bavarian, fill the center with whipped cream using a pastry bag ⑥. We recommend decorating the bavarian with glacé fruits for a very classic and formal presentation. Serve a *crème anglaise* sauce or fruit sauce with the bavarian for maximum decadence.

We have also included a recipe for a bavarian called *romanov* with a very unconventional presentation. This one is molded in a cake ring, and the top surface is embedded with a flat layer of cut strawberries.

HISTORY OF CHARLOTTES

The original charlotte—an apple compote baked in a mold lined with toast slices—was created at the end of the eighteenth century and named for the wife of King George III of England. In the nineteenth century, the French chef Marie-Antoine Carême adopted the name and radically refined the concept in response to a kitchen disaster. At a banquet to celebrate the return to Paris of Louis XVIII in 1815, the supply of gelatin was insufficient for the bavarian creams Carême was preparing. To solve the problem, the great chef buttressed the sides of his sagging desserts with ladyfingers. Carême named it *charlotte parisienne*, but it got changed to *charlotte russe* (Russian charlotte) during the Second Empire when the Russian style of table service was introduced to the French aristocracy by Prince Alexander Kourakine, the ambassador of Tzar Alexander I, and then popularized by the chef Urbain Dubois. In an even fancier version, called *charlotte royale* (royal charlotte), the ladyfingers are replaced by slices of a jelly roll or a multi-layered sponge cake and jam sandwich.

In the past, bavarian creams were the traditional fillings for charlottes. However, we prefer light, intensely flavored fruit mousses made by dissolving the gelatin in warm fruit puree, then whipping the cooled fruit puree into whipped cream. The vivid colors of the fruit mousses provide added visual excitement to the presentations. Fruits with strong distinctive flavors give the best results. We give recipes for nine charlottes, with a different presentation for each. Since the quantities of mousse required for each charlotte are about the same (6½ to 7 cups, or 1.5 to 1.7 L), you can mix and match mousses with presentations according to your own fancy. You can also use the mousse recipes from the log presentations in Chapter 7 in any of the charlotte presentations in this chapter.

Classically, charlottes are molded upside down, in deep molds with sloping sides for Russian charlottes or in deep, dome-shaped molds for royal charlottes. These molds were fine when the charlottes were prepared for banquets, but for pastry shops they proved awkward and inefficient. In the middle of the twentieth century, pastry chefs in Paris developed adaptations of the classic presentations using deep rings, called *vacherin* rings, that had first been used for frozen desserts. With these rings, the delicate operation of unmolding the fragile charlottes is replaced by the trivial step of sliding off the *vacherin* ring. We use an 8¾-inch (22-cm) *vacherin* ring in nearly all of our charlotte recipes. Like the cake rings we use for gâteaux, the *vacherin* rings are a modest and worthwhile investment since they make assembling charlottes so easy. If you want to use a slightly smaller or larger *vacherin* ring, you need only adjust the quantities in the recipe for the mousse. For an 8-inch (20-cm) *vacherin* ring, decrease the quantity of mousse by 20 percent; for a 9½-inch (24-cm) ring, increase the quantity by 20 percent. A springform pan can be substituted for the *vacherin* ring, but it is more cumbersome. If you must use a springform pan, remove the bottom; you need only the ring.

RUSSIAN CHARLOTTES

If you have ever lined a traditional charlotte mold with ladyfingers to make an old-fashioned *charlotte russe*, you will understand why French pastry chefs wanted an easier presentation. Trimming the ladyfingers to angle their sides so that they mesh around the sloping sides of the mold and cutting pieces to fit together like a jigsaw puzzle on the bottom of the mold is finicky (and tedious) work.

In the modern method, you line the sides of the *vacherin* ring with ladyfingers. Since the sides of the ring are vertical, there is no angled trimming. To make handling the ladyfingers even easier, you pipe the ladyfingers adjacent to each other so that, when baked, they hold together in a long band. Pipe the ladyfingers about 2¾ inches (7 cm) long and 1 inch (2½ cm) wide, either vertically for a classic look or at an angle for a more modern presentation. In a home oven, you will need to bake two bands of ladyfingers, each as long as a large baking sheet, to get the length necessary to line one 8¾-inch (22-cm) *vacherin* ring.

You will also need two 8¾-inch (22-cm) rounds of sponge cake, one for the bottom of the charlotte and the other for a layer in the center. In our recipe for ladyfingers and sponge cake rounds, we give a quantity sufficient for the bands of ladyfingers and the two rounds. However, if you happen to have an extra round of génoise on hand, you can cut it into thin rounds to substitute for the sponge cake rounds. Cut a round of génoise 1½ inches (4 cm) thick into four slices ⅜ inch (1 cm) thick—enough for two Russian charlottes. If you want to minimize waste, a third alternative is to replace the round of sponge cake in the middle of the charlotte with trimmings from the round of sponge cake on the bottom and from the band of ladyfingers on the side.

Trim off one side of each band of ladyfingers with a wavy-edge bread knife ⑦ to make the ladyfingers the same height as the ring (about 2⅜ inches = 6 cm) and give the band a straight bottom edge. Brush the back side of the ladyfingers with a syrup flavored according to the charlotte you are making. Place the *vacherin* ring on a tray (page 487) so that it will be easy to move in and out of the refrigerator. Cut a foil board or matt board (page 467) cake-decorating circle to fit inside the ring and place it at the bottom of the ring on the tray. Line the inside of the ring with the bands of ladyfingers, trimming the ends of the bands so they don't overlap ⑧.

Trim the rounds of sponge cake to fit inside the lined ring. Place one

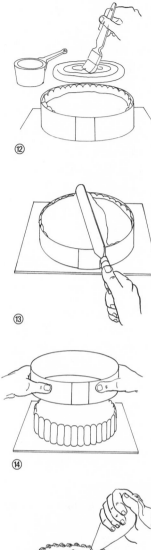

⑫

⑬

⑭

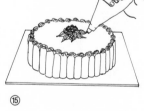

⑮

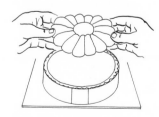

⑯

round inside the ring ⑨ on the cake-decorating circle. Brush it heavily with the flavored syrup ⑩.

You are now ready to fill the ring. Scoop about half of the mousse into the lined ring and smooth the surface using an icing spatula or the flat side of a bowl scraper ⑪. Brush the second sponge cake round heavily with the flavored syrup ⑫, turn it upside down, and place it on top of the mousse inside the ring. Brush the top of the second round heavily with the syrup. Scoop in the remaining mousse to fill the charlotte to the top of the ladyfingers, and smooth the surface with the icing spatula or bowl scraper ⑬.

Chill the charlotte in the refrigerator for several hours to set the mousse. Then you can unmold the charlotte by simply lifting off the ring ⑭. Decorate the top of the charlotte with fresh fruit and whipped cream ⑮, depending on the fruit in the mousse.

The presentation we have just described is especially beautiful when the fruit mousse has a vibrant color to show off. For pale-colored fruits (pears, in particular), we offer an alternative presentation that omits the sponge cake round in the middle of the charlotte and replaces it with a decorative round on top ⑯. (This second presentation also happens to be closer in appearance to Russian charlottes made in the traditional charlotte mold.) In this case, you must trim both top and bottom of the bands of ladyfingers in straight lines so the ladyfingers are precisely the height of the ring. To make the decorative round, you will pipe adjacent teardrops from the circumference of a circle to the center, working all the way around the circle and then finishing with a small dome of batter on the center. You will pipe the decorative round in a size such that after baking it just covers the top of the charlotte.

Royal Charlottes

The modern version of the royal charlotte is totally analogous to the modern Russian charlotte, with the ladyfingers around the side replaced by slices of a sponge cake and jam roll or a multi-layered sponge cake and jam sandwich. We especially like the royal charlotte presentation on the one hand for fruits like lemon and sour cherry, where the sweetness of raspberry jam in the lining slices balances the tartness of the fruit in the filling; and on the other hand for very sweet fruits like mango, with Seville orange marmalade in the lining slices to give a hint of bitterness as a highlight for the lusciousness of the fruit. The sponge cake we use for the lining

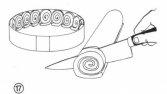

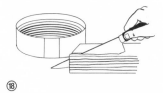

is *joconde*, which, since it contains ground almonds, adds another dimension of flavor and textural contrast.

The *joconde*-jam sandwiches and *joconde*-jam rolls that will be used to line the rings must be prepared in advance and frozen so that you can cut slices without deforming them. The sandwich you will make from one sheet of *joconde* provides enough slices to line two or three royal charlottes. For *joconde*-jam rolls, the number of charlottes you can make depends on the presentation. For our mango charlotte, the rolls you will make from one large sheet or two small sheets of *joconde* will provide enough slices to line two or three charlottes, respectively. For comparison, our blood orange charlotte requires only half as many slices of a *joconde*-jam roll for lining as the mango charlotte.

As for Russian charlottes, you will also need two 8¾-inch (22-cm) rounds of sponge cake, one for the bottom of the charlotte and the other for a layer in the center. If you happen to have an extra round of génoise on hand, you can slice the génoise ⅜ inch (1 cm) thick and substitute two slices of the génoise for the sponge cake rounds.

Place the *vacherin* ring on a tray so that it will be easy to move in and out of the refrigerator. Cut a foil board or matt board (page 467) cake-decorating circle to fit inside the ring and place it at the bottom of the ring on the tray.

Lining with Slices of a Joconde-Jam Roll

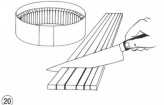

Cut the roll into slices ⅜ inch (1 cm) thick using a chef's knife ⑰. Arrange a single row of slices, pressed tightly against each other, around the inside of the ring with the the spirals all running the same way and their tail ends at the bottom.

Lining with Slices of a Joconde-Jam Sandwich

The *joconde*-jam sandwich will be 11½ to 12½ inches (29 to 32 cm) long and 1¾ to 2 inches (4.5 to 5 cm) high. The thickness will depend both on the size of the sheet of *joconde* from which the sandwich was made and on how many slices you have already cut from it. Using a 10-inch (25-cm) chef's knife, cut from the sandwich ⑱ three lengthwise slices ⅜ inch (1 cm) thick, two of them 11½ to 12½ inches (29 to 32 cm) long and the third one half that length. Do not let the slices warm up or they will soften and become limp and difficult to handle. Trim off the ends of the slices to make them straight.

You can line the *vacherin* ring with the layers of the sandwich running horizontally or vertically. For horizontal stripes the height of the slices will be about ½ inch (12 mm) shorter than the height of the ring, so a narrow band of fruit mousse will show at the top of the finished charlotte. Line the inside of the ring with the slices, trimming the end of one of them ⑲ so they form a continuous band around the ring with three tight seams and no overlap.

For vertical stripes cut each slice into rectangles 2 inches (5 cm) long ⑳. Arrange the rectangles adjacent to each other around the inside of the ring, with the jam stripes vertical. As for horizontal stripes, the rectangles will be a little shorter than the height of the ring to let a narrow band of fruit mousse show around the top. Trim the last rectangle so the slices don't overlap.

Filling the Ring

Trim the rounds of sponge cake to fit inside the lined ring. Place one round inside the ring on the cake-decorating circle, and brush it heavily with a syrup flavored according to the charlotte you are making. Brush the inside of the *joconde*-jam lining slices lightly with the syrup.

Scoop about half of the mousse into the lined ring ㉑ and smooth the surface using an icing spatula or the flat side of a bowl scraper. Brush the second sponge cake round heavily with the flavored syrup ㉒, turn it upside down, and place it on top of the mousse inside the ring ㉓. Brush the top of the second round heavily with the syrup ㉔. Scoop in the remaining mousse to fill the charlotte to the top of the ring, and smooth the surface. Sweep the edge of a large icing spatula or a metal straightedge across the top surface, using the ring as a guide, to scrape off the excess mousse. Start with the face of the blade angled down toward the top of the charlotte at the beginning ㉕, and gradually rotate the face of the blade as you move it across the top until it is angled away from the top of the charlotte at the end of the sweep to lift the excess mousse that has been taken off ㉖.

Chill the charlotte in the refrigerator or freezer for several hours to set the mousse.

Glazing

For some royal charlottes, you will glaze the top with jelly. Apply the glaze before unmolding, while the charlotte is at refrigerator temperature. (If the

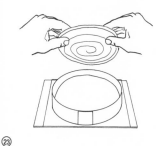
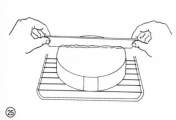
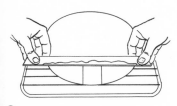

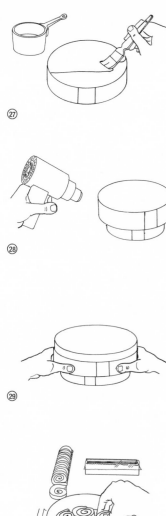

charlotte is frozen, the jelly sets too quickly and is difficult to apply in an even layer.) Cool the melted glaze until it just begins to thicken; it must be able to flow, but should not be too runny. Pour the jelly on top of the charlotte and brush it over the top surface using a soft pastry brush ㉗, being careful not to damage the surface of the mousse. Distribute the glaze evenly and brush gently to eliminate any flow lines and get a uniformly thick, mirror-like surface. Return the charlotte to the refrigerator until the glaze has set.

Unmolding

Place the chilled charlotte on a bowl or round mold taller and slightly smaller in diameter than the ring. Using a blow dryer, quickly and evenly warm the outside of the ring ㉘ to just melt the mousse inside the ring. Carefully slip the ring down off the charlotte ㉙. If the ring doesn't slip off easily, warm it a little more and try again.

If you have not glazed the top of the charlotte, then decorate it with fresh fruit and whipped cream, depending on the flavor of the mousse.

Other Related Presentations

You can make several simple variations on the royal charlotte theme using slices of a *joconde*-jam roll.

Still molding the charlotte in a *vacherin* ring, one of the simplest is to omit the slices from the sides of the charlotte, and use them on top instead. In this case, you must assemble the charlotte upside down on a tray covered with plastic wrap. Place the *vacherin* ring on the tray and arrange slices of the roll tight against each other inside on the tray ㉚. Brush the slices very lightly with flavored syrup ㉛, and fill the ring halfway with mousse. Cut a round of sponge cake about ¾ inch (2 cm) smaller than the ring, brush heavily with syrup, and place it upside down on the mousse in the ring. Brush heavily with syrup on the second side, and fill the ring almost to the rim with mousse. Cut a second round of sponge cake ⅜ inch (1 cm) smaller than the ring, brush the top heavily with syrup, and place it upside down on the mousse in the ring. Press it down firmly to make it level with the top of the ring and push out any excess mousse ㉜. Cut a foil board cake-decorating circle to fit inside the ring, place it on top, and refrigerate to set the mousse. Turn the charlotte upside down onto a second tray, lift off the first tray, and peel off the plastic wrap on top. Brush the top with a jelly glaze and let it set before unmolding.

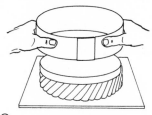

Another easy alternative is to mold the charlotte in a round cake pan. Brush the inside of the cake pan with melted butter and dust it with granulated sugar. Arrange slices of a *joconde*-jam roll around the sides of the cake pan, and then on the bottom of the cake pan ㉝. Fill the pan to the rim with mousse ㉞. (You don't need any sponge cake rounds for this presentation.) Refrigerate the charlotte until the mousse is set. Cut a foil board cake-decorating circle to fit the cake pan and place it on top. Place a round wire rack upside down on top and turn the cake pan and rack upside down together to unmold the charlotte onto the wire rack. The cake pan will lift off easily. Brush the outside of the charlotte with a jelly glaze ㉟.

Finally, you can use slices of *joconde*-jam rolls or sandwiches to line a yule log mold and fill the log with mousse. This presentation is covered in Chapter 7 (pages 336 to 338).

MOUSSE CAKES

You can also make charlottes with non-fruit flavors such as chocolate, *praliné*, coffee, or fresh cheese in the mousse. To simplify our terminology, we have refered to these non-fruit charlottes as mousse cakes. We often use a bombe batter as the base for the mousse in these mousse cakes. The bombe batter is related to a *crème anglaise*, but after cooking it is whipped until cool to make it light and thick. Then the bombe batter is whipped into whipped cream.

In addition to making a different type of mousse for mousse cakes, we choose presentations appropriate to their non-fruit flavors. In these presentations, you will line the *vacherin* rings with bands cut from a decorative sheet of sponge cake.

One approach, which is a direct descendent of the Russian charlotte presentation, is to pipe the sponge cake on the diagonal in adjacent ribbons to cover an entire baking sheet. When you have a band of this sponge cake wrapped around the side of the mousse cake, the diagonal ribbing creates a very dynamic effect ㊱. We use this method in the mousse cake called *nelusko* (page 321).

A second option is to create a design on a sheet of Silpat or other reusable pan liner (page 484) in tinted cigarette cookie batter, freeze it, then place it on a baking sheet and cover with a layer of *joconde* batter. When baked, the design becomes embedded in the sheet of *joconde*. (Unfortunately, while you can use the same technique on ordinary kitchen parchment, moisture in the batter makes the parchment wrinkle. So the result isn't as pretty as it is when baked on a reusable pan liner.) The options here are very diverse. You can easily make rhythmic wavy or diagonally banded designs by spreading the cigarette batter with a cake comb or a notched trowel or glue spreader (page 487). Or you can create more open designs by piping the cigarette batter with a pastry bag; anything that will fit in a band 2 inches (5 cm) wide can work. Perhaps most fun of all (especially if you are baking with the kids) is to finger paint the design.

Whichever method you choose, cut the bands of sponge cake or *joconde* 2 inches (5 cm) wide so that when you line the *vacherin* ring, you will leave about ⅜ inch (1 cm) uncovered at the top. That way there will be a band of mousse showing around the top to give a preview of what is inside.

The method of assembling the mousse cakes is precisely the same as for the charlottes. See the instructions above.

STORAGE

Bavarians can be kept in the refrigerator, covered airtight with plastic wrap, for up to 2 or 3 days before unmolding. After unmolding, they should be kept refrigerated (on a covered cake platter if you have one), and they should be served within an hour or two after being filled with whipped cream.

Charlottes can be stored in the refrigerator for 2 or 3 days before unmolding and decorating or glazing. It is best to unmold and glaze or decorate them the day they will be served. Whether before or after unmolding, the surface of the charlotte will dry out less if it is kept on a covered cake platter. Charlottes decorated with whipped cream should be served within an hour or two after decorating.

Charlottes can also be frozen for up to 15 days in the mold. Enclose the frozen charlotte airtight in a plastic bag, being careful not to damage the top surface. The day before serving, remove the frozen charlotte from the plastic bag and defrost overnight in the refrigerator before glazing (if required), unmolding, and decorating.

Mousse cakes are stored in the same way as charlottes.

Ladyfingers and Sponge Cake Rounds

. . . .

For each charlotte, you will need two sponge cake rounds 8¾ inches (22 cm) in diameter. For a Russian charlotte you will also need about 28 ladyfingers piped adjacent to each other in two long bands. In the special presentation we use for our pear charlotte, one of the sponge cake rounds should be a decorative one made by piping teardrops radially from the circumference to the center.

EQUIPMENT:

One (for rounds only) or two (for rounds and ladyfingers) large, heavy baking sheets
• brush with melted butter
• dust with flour
Electric mixer
Medium-size pastry bag fitted with
• ¹¹⁄₁₆-inch (18-mm) plain pastry tube (Ateco #9) for ladyfingers
Large pastry bag fitted with
• ⁹⁄₁₆-inch (14-mm) plain pastry tube (Ateco #7) for rounds

	For two 8¾-inch (22-cm) plain rounds or one plain round plus one decorative round	For two 8¾-inch (22-cm) rounds plus 28 ladyfingers
BATTER:		
Large eggs, separated, at room temperature	4	6
Cream of tartar (optional)	⅛ teaspoon (a pinch)	¼ teaspoon (1 mL)
Superfine or extra fine sugar	1½ ounces (40 g); 3 tablespoons	2 ounces (60 g); ¼ cup + 2½ teaspoons
Confectioners' sugar	2 ounces (55 g); ¼ cup + 3 tablespoons	3 ounces (80 g); ⅔ cup
All-purpose flour	2¼ ounces (65 g); ½ cup	3½ ounces (100 g); ¾ cup
Potato starch	¾ ounce (20 g); 2 tablespoons	1 ounce (30 g); 3 tablespoons
Confectioners' sugar for dusting		

continued

Preheat the oven to 425° F (220° C).

1. To make piping easier, mark some guides on the baking sheets. Mark two circles in the flour on one baking sheet for the two rounds of sponge cake. For each plain round, mark an 8¾-inch (22-cm) circle by tapping a *vacherin* ring (the one you will use to assemble the charlotte) on the baking sheet ①. For a decorative round, tap an 8-inch (20-cm) ring, round mold, or *vol-au-vent* disk on the baking sheet. (Remember that it will expand when it bakes, and, unlike plain rounds, decorative rounds are not trimmed to size after baking.) As a guide for piping two bands of ladyfingers, mark two pairs of straight lines lengthwise down one of the baking sheets by tapping the side of a straightedge on the flour. Separate each pair of lines by 2¾ inches (7 cm).

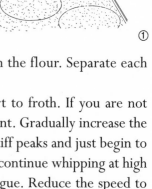

2. Whip the egg whites in the mixer at low speed until they start to froth. If you are not whipping the whites in a copper bowl, add the cream of tartar at this point. Gradually increase the whipping speed to medium-high, and whip until the whites form very stiff peaks and just begin to slip and streak around the side of the bowl. Add the superfine sugar and continue whipping at high speed for a few seconds to incorporate the sugar and tighten the meringue. Reduce the speed to medium, pour in the yolks, and continue whipping for a few seconds longer.

3. Sift the confectioners' sugar over the whipped eggs and gently fold it in. Sift the flour with the potato starch onto a sheet of wax paper and gradually fold them into the batter.

4. For piping ladyfingers, scoop about one third of the batter into the medium-size pastry bag. Starting at the left side of the baking sheet, pipe fingers 1 inch (2½ cm) wide and ½ inch (12 mm) thick in the space between one pair of guidelines. Pipe them adjacent to each other so that they will hold together in a long band when baked. Depending on the presentation you want to make, you can pipe the fingers perpendicular to the guidelines ②, or on a diagonal ③. Repeat by piping a band of ladyfingers between the second pair of lines. Don't worry if there are some small gaps between the fingers of batter; they will fill in as the batter expands in the oven.

5. Scoop the remaining batter into the large pastry bag for piping rounds.

For plain rounds, start at the center of each circle ④ and pipe the batter in a continuous spiral that completely fills the circle.

For decorative rounds, start from the perimeter of the far side of the circle and pipe a teardrop ending with the tip at the center of the circle. Rotate the baking sheet and pipe another teardrop adja-

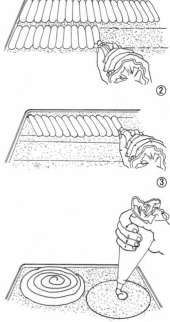

cent to the first one. Repeat until you have piped ten to twelve adjacent teardrops that fill the circle with their tips meeting at the center. Finally, pipe a 1¼-inch (3-cm) dome of batter on the center ⑤.

6. Dust the piped batter on one baking sheet heavily with confectioners' sugar until the surface is white. Wait for 2 minutes to let the sugar dissolve. Then dust with confectioners' sugar a second time. Quickly turn the baking sheet upside down, tap it firmly with a wooden spatula to remove the excess sugar, and turn the baking sheet right side up again before the batter has a chance to move.

7. Place the baking sheet in the preheated oven and splash about ⅓ cup (8 cL) of water on the bottom of the oven. Bake until the sponge cake is nicely colored and crusty outside but still soft inside and not dry, about 8 to 9 minutes.

8. Meanwhile, if you are baking two sheets of sponge cake, repeat step 6 on the second baking sheet, and bake following step 7 as soon as the oven is available.

9. Place the baking sheet on a wire rack and let cool to room temperature. Then slide a metal spatula under the sponge cake rounds and bands of fingers and slide them off the baking sheet.

HOWS AND WHYS: Splashing water on the oven floor produces steam, which dissolves the sugar on top of the batter and gives the baked sponge cake a pearly look.

Since the baking time is very short, if you are baking two sheets and don't have two ovens, there is no harm in baking one sheet after the other.

STORAGE: Best used the day it is made. If necessary, store rounds covered airtight in a tin cookie box or with plastic wrap for up to 1 day at room temperature. If you must cover decorative rounds or bands of ladyfingers in plastic wrap, protect the surface by placing a sheet of wax paper between the top of the sponge cake and the plastic wrap.

Joconde-Jam Sandwiches

The sandwich you make with this recipe will supply more than enough slices for lining either two or three 8¾-inch (22-cm) royal charlottes, depending on the size sheet of *joconde* you are using. To minimize the number of seams in the lining slices for each charlotte, you want to make the sandwich (and the slices you cut from it) as long as possible without becoming unwieldy. Given the logistics of home kitchens, the width of a baking sheet is about the longest practical length.

	For one sandwich 11½ inches (29 cm) long, 1¾ to 2 inches (4.5 to 5 cm) high, and 2½ inches (6.3 cm) wide	For one sandwich 12½ inches (32 cm) long, 1¾ to 2 inches (4.5 to 5 cm) high, and 3 inches (8 cm) wide
Joconde (page 224)	One 12 × 16-inch (30 × 40-cm) sheet	One 13 × 20-inch (33 × 50-cm) sheet
Heavy syrup (page 452)	**As needed**	**As needed**
Either raspberry jam (with seeds)	**5¾ ounces (160 g); ½ cup**	**7½ ounces (215 g); ⅔ cup**
Or orange marmalade (thin cut), melted		

1. Trim the edge of each sheet of *joconde* with a wavy-edge bread knife. If the *joconde* is dry and cracks easily, brush it with a little heavy syrup to moisten and soften it. Cut the sheet of *joconde* crosswise into three equal rectangles 11½ to 12½ inches (29 to 32 cm) long ①.

2. Set aside about one fifth of the jam or marmalade—a little more than 1½ tablespoons (30 g) for a small sheet of *joconde* or 2 tablespoons (40 g) for a large sheet. For raspberry jam, spread the rest of the jam evenly over two of the rectangles of *joconde* using a large icing spatula ②. For orange marmalade, spread the rest of the

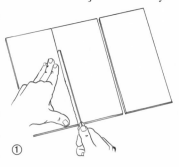

melted marmalade evenly over two of the rectangles of *joconde* using a pastry brush.

3. Neatly stack the rectangles one on top of the other, placing the rectangle without jam or marmalade on top ③. Slice this three-layer sandwich in half lengthwise ④. Spread the reserved raspberry jam or melted orange marmalade on top of one half ⑤, and stack the other half on top ⑥. You will now have a sandwich 11½ to 12½ inches (29 to 32 cm) long, with 6 layers of *joconde* and 5 layers of jam or marmalade.

4. Wrap the *joconde*-jam or *joconde*-marmalade sandwich in a sheet of wax paper, cover it airtight in plastic wrap, and then enclose it in a plastic bag to ensure that the plastic wrap stays tightly sealed. Freeze the sandwich so you will be able to slice it cleanly and evenly without distorting its shape.

STORAGE: Up to 2 months in the freezer.

②

③

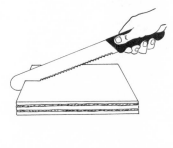

④

⑤

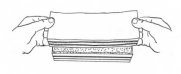

⑥

Joconde-Jam Rolls and *Joconde*-Marmalade Rolls

. . . .

For our mango charlotte (page 312) and cranberry mousse log (page 363), you will need one roll 10 inches (25 cm) long or two rolls 6 inches (15 cm) long. Our blood orange charlotte (page 315) requires only one 6-inch (15-cm) roll, or half of a 10-inch (25-cm) roll.

	For two rolls 10 inches (25 cm) long plus two rolls 6 inches (15 cm) long	For two rolls 10 inches (25 cm) long
Joconde (page 224)	Two 12 × 16-inch (30 × 40-cm) sheets	One 13 × 20-inch (33 × 50-cm) sheet
Heavy syrup (page 452),	As needed	As needed
Either raspberry jam (with seeds)	11¼ ounces (320 g); 1 cup	7½ ounces (215 g); ⅔ cup
Or Seville orange marmalade (thin cut), melted		

1. Trim the long edges of each sheet of *joconde* with a wavy-edge bread knife and place it, top side up, on a sheet of wax paper. If the *joconde* is dry and cracks easily, brush it with a little heavy syrup to moisten and soften it.

2. For raspberry jam, spread the jam evenly over the sheet (or sheets) of *joconde* using a large icing spatula. For orange marmalade, spread the melted marmalade evenly over the sheet (or sheets) of *joconde* using a pastry brush ①.

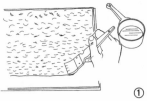

①

3. Use the end of the sheet of wax paper to lift the long edge of each sheet of *joconde* and begin rolling the *joconde* ②. Once the roll is started, let go of the wax paper and finish rolling the *joconde* ③ into a cylinder—the *joconde*-jam or *joconde*-marmalade roll—approximately 16 inches (40 cm) or 20 inches (50 cm) long, depending on which size sheet of *joconde* you started with.

4. To make the rolls more manageable and to correlate them with the quantities required for individual charlottes: cut each 20-inch (50-cm) cylinder in half to make two rolls, each 10 inches (25 cm) long; and cut each 16-inch (40-cm) roll into two rolls, one 10 inches (25 cm) long and the other 6 inches (15 cm) long.

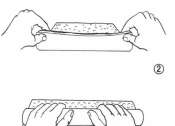

5. Wrap each cylinder of joconde in the sheet of wax paper, cover it airtight in plastic wrap, and then enclose it in a plastic bag to ensure that the plastic wrap stays tightly sealed. Freeze the rolls so you will be able to slice them cleanly and evenly without distorting their shape.

STORAGE: Up to 2 months in the freezer.

Joconde Sheets with Combed, Piped and Finger-Painted Designs

· ·

Make a design in cigarette cookie batter (tinted with food coloring or cocoa powder, depending on the color required by the specific mousse cake you plan to make) on a sheet of Silpat or other reusable pan liner (page 484) and freeze it. Then spread *joconde* batter on top and bake. The design will be embedded in the sheet of *joconde*, which you can cut into bands to line the sides of charlottes and mousse cakes. The technique is very versatile and easy, since the design can be produced by combing the cigarette batter with a notched trowel or glue spreader, piping it from a pastry bag, or even finger painting.

We highly recommend a Silpat pan liner becase it is easier to use than a lightweight Teflon pan liner. On the other hand, Teflon pan liners can be cut to size whereas Silpat cannot.

Since the available sizes of Silpat are limited, you will probably have to choose one slightly smaller than your baking sheet. We suggest lining the baking sheet with parchment before placing the Silpat on top so that the batter will not stick on the area of the baking sheet not covered by the Silpat.

EQUIPMENT:

Either a heavy 12 × 16-inch (30 × 40-cm) or 13 × 20-inch (33 × 50-cm) baking sheet
• brush edges and diagonals with melted butter
• line with Teflon pan liner cut to fit the baking sheet
• brush pan liner with melted butter
Or a half-size sheet of Silpat
** and a heavy 13 × 20-inch (33 × 50-cm) baking sheet**
• brush edges and diagonals of baking sheet with melted butter
• line with kitchen parchment
• brush a wide band around all four sides of the parchment with melted butter
For combed designs, a notched trowel or glue spreader with blunt teeth (page 487)
For piped designs, a small pastry bag fitted with
• 5/32-inch (4-mm) plain pastry tube (Ateco #0)
Electric mixer
Sheet of kitchen parchment

CIGARETTE COOKIE BATTER:

Unsalted butter, softened	1 ounce (25 g); 2 tablespoons
Superfine or extra fine sugar	1 ounce (25 g); 2 tablespoons
Almond-and-sugar powder (page 442)	⅔ ounce (17 g); 2 tablespoons
Large egg white, at room temperature	1
All-purpose flour	⅓ ounce (10 g); 1 tablespoon + ½ teaspoon
Unsweetened cocoa powder (Dutch processed) or food coloring paste	⅓ ounce (10 g); 1 tablespoon + 2 teaspoons
	As needed

	For one 12 × 16-inch (30 × 40-cm) sheet	For one 13 × 20-inch (33 × 50-cm) sheet
JOCONDE BATTER:		
Large eggs, at room temperature	2	3
Almond-and-sugar powder (page 442)	5½ ounces (150 g); 1 cup + 2 tablespoons	8 ounces (230 g); 1¾ cups
All-purpose flour	1 ounce (25 g); 3 tablespoons	1¼ ounces (35 g); ¼ cup
Large egg whites, at room temperature	2	3
Cream of tartar (optional)	⅛ teaspoon (a pinch)	⅛ teaspoon (a pinch)
Superfine or extra fine sugar	1 ounce (25 g); 2 tablespoons	1¼ ounces (35 g); 3 tablespoons
Unsalted butter, melted	½ ounce (15 g); 1 tablespoon	¾ ounce (20 g); 1½ tablespoons

1. Place the butter for the cigarette cookie batter in a small stainless steel bowl and beat with a wooden spatula, warming the butter over low heat as needed to make it smooth, white, and creamy. Beat in the sugar and almond-and-sugar powder. When smooth, beat in the egg white. Sift the flour (with the cocoa powder if you want a dark brown design) over the batter and mix it in with the spatula. Tint the batter with food coloring paste if you want a color other than dark brown.

2. Place the sheet of Silpat or the lined baking sheet on your countertop.

FOR COMBED DESIGNS: Spread an even layer of cigarette batter on the lined baking sheet or the sheet of Silpat, using a large icing spatula or the flat side of a bowl scraper. Draw the notched trowel or glue spreader across the sheet ① to make a design on the sheet and to remove excess batter. For example, make a wavy pattern across the sheet from left to right, or make a straight diagonal pattern. Repeat as many times as necessary in adjacent bands to make the design cover the entire sheet, scraping the excess batter off the trowel or glue spreader between each pass.

①

FOR PIPED DESIGNS: Mark the width of the bands of *joconde* you will need for the desserts you plan to make on the lined baking sheet or the sheet of Silpat. Scoop the cigarette batter into the pastry bag, and pipe a repeating design down the length of each band.

FOR FINGER PAINTING: Spread a thin even layer of cigarette batter on the lined baking sheet or the sheet of Silpat using a large icing spatula or the flat side of a bowl scraper. Use your fingertips to make a tight, small-scale swirling design ② on the sheet and to remove excess batter.

3. If you are using Silpat, slide it onto a tray. Place the lined baking sheet or the tray with the Silpat in the freezer to freeze the cigarette cookie batter.

Preheat the oven to 425° F (220°C).

②

4. Combine the whole eggs with the almond-and-sugar powder, and whip at medium speed in the mixer until cream-colored and light.

5. Sift the flour over the beaten eggs.

6. Using a clean wire whip and bowl, whip the egg whites in the mixer at low speed until they start to froth. If you are not whipping the whites in a copper bowl, add the cream of tartar at this point. Gradually increase the whipping speed to medium-high, and whip until the whites form very stiff peaks and just begin to slip and streak around the side of the bowl. Add the superfine sugar and continue whipping at high speed for a few seconds to incorporate the sugar and tighten the meringue.

7. Scoop about one third of the meringue into the bowl with the beaten eggs and flour, and stir with a wooden spatula to mix quickly. Add the remaining meringue and gently fold it into the batter. When completely incorporated, slowly pour the melted butter over the batter and continue folding gently until the butter is uniformly mixed with the batter.

8. Take the sheet of Silpat from the freezer and line the baking sheet with it, being sure that any parchment not covered by the Silpat is coated with butter. Or, take the lined baking sheet from the freezer.

9. Scoop the batter from the mixing bowl onto the prepared baking sheet, distributing it evenly. Spread and smooth the batter with a large icing spatula ③ to completely cover the baking sheet in an even layer about ⅜ inch (1 cm) thick.

10. Bake until the cake is lightly browned and firm to the touch, but not dry, about 7 to 9 minutes.

11. Loosen the edges of the *joconde* with a small icing spatula. Slide the *joconde* with pan liner or the parchment and Silpat off the baking sheet onto a wire rack. Let cool for 5 minutes. Place the clean sheet of parchment on top of the *joconde* and place a second wire rack upside down on top of the sheet of parchment. Turn the *joconde* upside down with both racks to transfer it to the second rack. Lift off the first wire rack, and carefully peel the pan liner or the

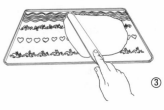

③

parchment and Silpat away from the back of the *joconde*. Allow the *joconde* to finish cooling with the design side up.

HOWS AND WHYS: Having a sheet of parchment under the *joconde* while it cools prevents it from sticking to the wire rack.

STORAGE: Covered airtight with plastic wrap for up to 2 days in the refrigerator. Or freeze for as long as 3 months. If frozen, defrost overnight in the refrigerator before using.

Peach Bavarian

Luscious ripe peaches embedded in a heady kirsch bavarian cream make this dessert a special summer treat.

For 6 to 8 servings

EQUIPMENT:
5- or 6-cup (1.5-L) ring mold
Electric mixer
Pastry bag fitted with
• medium-small fluted pastry tube (Ateco #3)

FRUIT:

Fresh, ripe freestone peaches	2 or 3 medium-size
Fresh lemon juice, strained	1 tablespoon (1.5 cL)
Cold water	1 cup (2.4 dL)
European kirsch	3 tablespoons (4.5 cL)

CAKE:

Génoise (page 82)	Half a 9-inch (24-cm) round

BRUSHING-SYRUP MIXTURE:

Heavy syrup (page 452)	2 tablespoons (3 cL)
Kirsch reserved from steeping peaches	2 tablespoons (3 cL)

BAVARIAN CREAM:

Unflavored gelatin	2¼ teaspoons (1.1 cL)
Cold water	1 tablespoon (1.5 cL)
Milk	1 cup (2.4 dL)
Large egg yolks	4
Granulated sugar	2¾ ounces (75 g); ¼ cup + 2 tablespoons
European kirsch	3 tablespoons (4.5 cL)
Heavy cream, well chilled	1¼ cups (3 dL)

Confectioners' sugar	1½ ounces (40 g); ⅓ cup
Heavy cream	1½ cups (3.6 dL)
Glacé fruits	

ACCOMPANIMENT:

Crème anglaise (page 436)	1½ cups (3.5 dL)
European kirsch	1 tablespoon + 1 teaspoon (2 cL)

1. Peel and stone the peaches, then cut them into wedges ¼ inch (6 mm) thick. Mix the lemon juice with the cold water in a bowl and dip the wedges in it to prevent them from discoloring. Combine the peach wedges with the kirsch in a small mixing bowl and let steep, covered, for 2 to 3 hours. Drain well, reserving the kirsch.

2. Trim the crust from the génoise and cut it into strips 2 to 2½ inches (5 to 6 cm) long and about 1 inch (2.5 cm) square. Mix the heavy syrup with 2 tablespoons (3 cL) of the kirsch reserved from steeping the peaches and brush the génoise strips with this syrup.

3. Chill the bowl and the wire whip or beater of the mixer in the refrigerator. Stir the gelatin into the cold water and let it soften.

4. Bring the milk to a simmer in a heavy 1-quart (1-L) saucepan. Beat together the egg yolks and sugar until smooth and lemon-colored, then slowly pour in the simmering milk, stirring constantly with a wire whisk. Pour the mixture back into the saucepan. Cook over low heat, stirring constantly with a wooden spatula, until this *crème anglaise* coats the back of the spatula and the bubbles formed when you stirred the milk into the yolks have disappeared. Do not allow to boil.

Remove the saucepan from the heat, add the softened gelatin, and stir to dissolve. Strain through a fine sieve into a stainless steel bowl. Dip the bottom of the bowl of *crème anglaise* in a larger bowl of ice water, and stir to cool the *crème anglaise* quickly. When it has reached room temperature, remove from the ice water and stir in the kirsch. Do not let the *crème anglaise* set.

5. Pour the heavy cream into the chilled mixer bowl and whip the cream at medium speed in the mixer using the chilled wire whip or beater until it is light and thick and holds soft peaks. Stop whipping.

6. Dip the bottom of the bowl of *crème anglaise* in the bowl of ice water again and stir with a rubber spatula until it just begins to thicken. Immediately remove the bowl from the ice water.

7. Continue whipping the cream at medium speed until it holds stiff peaks, then whip in the *crème anglaise* to finish the bavarian cream.

8. Rinse the ring mold with cold water and shake it out. Pour about one third of the bavarian cream into the mold. Arrange the peach wedges over the bavarian cream. Pour in half of the remaining bavarian cream to cover the fruit. Arrange the génoise strips in a continuous circle in the mold and press them gently into the bavarian cream. Pour in the remaining bavarian cream to cover the génoise strips and fill the mold. Smooth the surface.

9. Chill in the refrigerator for 3 or 4 hours to set the bavarian cream.

10. Run the tip of a small icing spatula around the rim of the mold to loosen the top edge of the bavarian cream. Place a round serving plate upside down on top of the mold and invert the plate and mold together. Warm the outside of the mold with a blow dryer until the bavarian slides out easily and you can lift off the mold. Refrigerate again to chill the surface of the bavarian.

11. Sift the confectioners' sugar into the bowl of the mixer, stir in the heavy cream, and refrigerate for about an hour. Chill the wire whip or beater of the mixer as well. Whip the cream at medium speed in the mixer. When the cream holds soft peaks, slow down to avoid overbeating. Continue whipping until the cream is light and thick and holds stiff peaks.

12. Scoop the whipped cream into the pastry bag and pipe it into the center of the bavarian, mounding the whipped cream slightly. Pipe rosettes of whipped cream to cover the mound.

13. Cut a few glacé cherries in half. Cut thin slices of larger glacé fruits (such as pineapple, apricots, or pears) and cut from the slices a few triangles or diamonds. Decorate the bavarian with the glacé fruits, arranging them around the top of the ring.

14. Serve the bavarian accompanied by the *crème anglaise*, flavored with the kirsch.

STORAGE: Serve the bavarian within an hour or two after filling with whipped cream.

Before unmolding, cover airtight with plastic wrap and keep for up to 2 or 3 days in the refrigerator.

Orange Bavarian

Aromatic orange zest combined with dark pungent rum, rather than the more obvious choice of an orange liqueur, gives this bavarian cream an entrancing flavor.

For 6 to 8 servings

EQUIPMENT:
5- or 6-cup (1.5-L) ring mold
Electric mixer
Pastry bag fitted with
• medium-small fluted pastry tube (Ateco #3)

FRUIT:

Large navel oranges	2
Dark Jamaican or Haitian rum	3 tablespoons (4.5 cL)

CAKE:

Génoise (page 82)	Half a 9-inch (24-cm) round

BRUSHING-SYRUP MIXTURE:

Heavy syrup (page 452)	2 tablespoons (3 cL)
Liqueur reserved from steeping oranges	2 tablespoons (3 cL)

BAVARIAN CREAM:

Unflavored gelatin	2¼ teaspoons (1.1 cL)
Cold water	1 tablespoon (1.5 cL)
Milk	1 cup (2.4 dL)
Large egg yolks	4
Granulated sugar	2¾ ounces (75 g); ¼ cup + 2 tablespoons
Dark Jamaican or Haitian rum	3 tablespoons (4.5 cL)
Heavy cream, well chilled	1¼ cups (3 dL)

DECORATION:

Confectioners' sugar	1½ ounces (40 g); ⅓ cup
Heavy cream	1½ cups (3.6 dL)
Glacé fruits	

continued

Créme anglaise (page 436)   1½ cups (3.5 dL)

Dark Jamaican or Haitian rum   1 tablespoon + 1 teaspoon (2 cL)

1. Grate the aromatic zest from the outside of one of the oranges and set it aside. Peel the oranges, removing all of the bitter white pith and the outer membrane surrounding the flesh of the oranges. Remove each segment of orange flesh by cutting down to the core along the membranes that separate the segments. Combine the nude orange segments with the rum in a small mixing bowl and let steep, covered, for 2 to 3 hours. Drain well, reserving the rum.

2. Trim the crust from the génoise and cut it into strips 2 to 2½ inches (5 to 6 cm) long and about 1 inch (2.5 cm) square. Mix the heavy syrup with 2 tablespoons (3 cL) of the rum reserved from steeping the orange segments and brush the génoise strips with this syrup.

3. Chill the bowl and the wire whip or beater of the mixer in the refrigerator. Stir the gelatin into the cold water and let it soften.

4. Combine the milk with the reserved orange zest in a heavy 1-quart (1-L) saucepan and bring to a simmer. Beat together the egg yolks and sugar until smooth and lemon-colored, then slowly pour in the simmering milk, stirring constantly with a wire whisk. Pour the mixture back into the saucepan. Cook over low heat, stirring constantly with a wooden spatula, until this *crème anglaise* coats the back of the spatula and the bubbles formed when you stirred the milk into the yolks have disappeared. Do not allow to boil.

Remove the saucepan from the heat, add the softened gelatin, and stir to dissolve. Strain through a fine sieve into a stainless steel bowl. Dip the bottom of the bowl of *crème anglaise* in a larger bowl of ice water, and stir to cool the *crème anglaise* quickly. When it has reached room temperature, remove from the ice water and stir in the rum. Do not let the *crème anglaise* set.

5. Pour the heavy cream into the chilled mixer bowl and whip the cream at medium speed in the mixer using the chilled wire whip or beater until it is light and thick and holds soft peaks. Stop whipping.

6. Dip the bottom of the bowl of *crème anglaise* in the bowl of ice water again and stir with a rubber spatula until it just begins to thicken. Immediately remove the bowl from the ice water.

7. Continue whipping the cream at medium speed until it holds stiff peaks, then whip in the *crème anglaise* to finish the bavarian cream.

8. Rinse the ring mold with cold water and shake it out. Pour about one third of the bavarian cream into the mold. Arrange the orange segments over the bavarian cream. Pour in half of the remaining bavarian cream to cover the fruit. Arrange the génoise strips in a continuous circle in the mold and press them gently into the bavarian cream. Pour in the remaining bavarian cream to cover the génoise strips and fill the mold. Smooth the surface.

9. Chill in the refrigerator for 3 or 4 hours to set the bavarian cream.

10. Run the tip of a small icing spatula around the rim of the mold to loosen the top edge of the bavarian cream. Place a round serving plate upside down on top of the mold and invert the plate and mold together. Warm the outside of the mold with a blow dryer until the bavarian slides out easily and you can lift off the mold. Refrigerate again to chill the surface of the bavarian.

11. Sift the confectioners' sugar into the bowl of the mixer, stir in the heavy cream, and refrigerate for about an hour. Chill the wire whip or beater of the mixer as well. Whip the cream at medium speed in the mixer. When the cream holds soft peaks, slow down to avoid overbeating. Continue whipping until the cream is light and thick and holds stiff peaks.

12. Scoop the whipped cream into the pastry bag and pipe it into the center of the bavarian, mounding the whipped cream slightly. Pipe rosettes of whipped cream to cover the mound.

13. Cut a few glacé cherries in half. Cut thin slices of larger glacé fruits (such as pineapple, apricots, or pears) and cut from the slices a few triangles or diamonds. Decorate the bavarian with the glacé fruits, arranging them around the top of the ring.

14. Serve the bavarian accompanied by the *crème anglaise,* flavored with the rum.

STORAGE: Serve the bavarian within an hour or two after filling with whipped cream.

Before unmolding, cover airtight with plastic wrap and keep for up to 2 or 3 days in the refrigerator.

Romanov

Here is a pretty presentation to use when fresh strawberries are in season. *Romanov* is molded in a cake ring, rather than a ring mold like our other bavarians, in order to provide the perfect balance between the berries and a curaçao liqueur mousse. You will assemble it upside down, with strawberry halves arranged in a single layer on the bottom to make a flat surface, then cover them with bavarian cream and finally a sponge cake round. After the bavarian cream sets, turn it right side up and glaze the top with clear jelly before unmolding the ring to produce a glistening, flat layer of strawberries. If you happen to have a heart-shaped cake ring, you can assemble the *romanov* in it to make a very romantic and luscious treat for Valentine's Day.

    Romanov descends from *fraises romanov*, a classic dessert named for the Russian imperial family. In the original dessert strawberries are steeped in orange juice and curaçao liqueur, then served with sweetened whipped cream. Here the flavor combination is the same, but the conception and presentation are totally different—and, if anything, more splendid.

For 6 to 8 servings

EQUIPMENT:

8¾-inch (22-cm) cake ring, 1⅜ inches (3.5 cm) deep

Electric mixer

9-inch (24-cm) foil board or matt board cake-decorating circle (page 467)
• cut to fit inside the cake ring

CAKE:

| Sponge cake (page 271) | One 8¾-inch (22-cm) round |

FRUIT:

| Small- to medium-size fresh strawberries, hulled and cut in half | 12 ounces (340 g); 1 pint |

BAVARIAN CREAM:

Unflavored gelatin	1¼ teaspoons (6 mL)
Cold water	1 tablespoon (1.5 cL)
Egg yolks, lightly beaten	1½ tablespoons (2.3 cL); about 1⅓ large yolks
Superfine or extra fine sugar	1¼ ounces (35 g); 2½ tablespoons

Dry white wine	3 tablespoons (4.5 cL)
Curaçao liqueur	⅓ cup (8 cL)
Heavy cream, well chilled	1 cup + 2 tablespoons (2.7 dL)

BRUSHING-SYRUP MIXTURE:

Heavy syrup (page 452)	1 tablespoon (1.5 cL)
Curaçao liqueur	1 tablespoon (1.5 cL)

GLAZE:

Unflavored gelatin	¾ teaspoon (4 mL)
Cold water	3 tablespoons + 1 teaspoon (5 cL)
Fresh orange juice, strained	3 tablespoons + 1 teaspoon (5 cL)
Superfine or extra fine sugar	1½ ounces (40 g); 3 tablespoons + 1 teaspoon

1. Cut the sponge cake round to fit neatly inside the cake ring.

2. Place the cake ring on a tray, with a sheet of plastic wrap underneath. Arrange the strawberries cut side down in a tightly spaced single layer inside the ring, starting at the outside and working to the center in concentric circles.

3. Chill the bowl and the wire whip or beater of the mixer in the refrigerator. Stir the gelatin into the cold water and let it soften.

4. In a 2-cup (5-dL) butter melter, whisk together the egg yolks and superfine sugar until lemon-colored. Whisk in the white wine and 1 tablespoon (1.5 cL) of the curaçao liqueur. Bring just to a simmer, whisking constantly. Remove from the heat, add the softened gelatin, and stir until dissolved. Strain through a fine sieve into a small stainless steel bowl and let cool. Stir in the remaining curaçao.

5. Pour the heavy cream into the chilled mixer bowl and whip the cream at medium speed in the mixer using the chilled wire whip or beater until it is light and thick and holds stiff peaks. Then whip in the curaçao-flavored custard to finish the bavarian cream.

6. Scoop the bavarian cream into the ring and spread it to fill the spaces between the strawberries. Smooth the top surface and leave just enough space for the round of sponge cake.

7. Brush the sponge cake round heavily with the curaçao brushing syrup. Turn it upside down and place it on the mousse at the top of the ring. Place the cake-decorating circle upside down on top.

8. Chill the *romanov* in the refrigerator for several hours or overnight to set the mousse. Then turn it right side up onto a wire rack, remove the tray, and peel off the plastic wrap.

9. For the glaze, stir the gelatin into the cold water and let it soften. Heat the orange juice and sugar in a butter melter, stirring occasionally, until the sugar is dissolved in the orange juice. Add the softened gelatin and stir until the gelatin dissolves. Pour into a small stainless steel bowl and let cool. Dip the bottom of the bowl in a larger bowl of ice water and stir until it begins to thicken very lightly. Remove the bowl from the ice water immediately.

continued

10. Pour the glaze over the top of the *romanov* and spread it quickly with a soft pastry brush to cover the berries and the mousse showing through, fill any gaps, and make a thick, even coating of glaze. Let the excess glaze flow over the sides of the ring. Be careful not to damage the surface of the bavarian cream. Refrigerate to set the glaze.

11. Place the chilled *romanov* on a bowl or cake pan taller and slightly smaller in diameter than the ring. Using a blow dryer, quickly and evenly warm the outside of the ring to just melt the bavarian cream, touching the ring. Carefully slip the ring down off the *romanov*. Then place the *romanov* back on the tray and return it to the refrigerator.

12. Refrigerate until ready to serve.

NOTE: The filling we use in *romanov* is a little different from a standard bavarian cream because the custard base is made with white wine and curaçao liqueur instead of milk. However, we still refer to it as a bavarian cream.

STORAGE: In the refrigerator for up to 1 or 2 days.

Strawberry Bavarian

Fresh strawberries with curaçao-flavored bavarian cream are a natural combination.

For 6 to 8 servings

EQUIPMENT:
5- or 6-cup (1.5-L) ring mold
Electric mixer
Pastry bag fitted with
• medium-small fluted pastry tube (Ateco #3)

FRUIT:

Fresh strawberries, hulled and cut into halves, quarters, or even slices if they are large	7 to 8 ounces (200 to 225 g); 1¼ cups
Curaçao liqueur	3 tablespoons (4.5 cL)

CAKE:

Génoise (page 82)	Half a 9-inch (24-cm) round

BRUSHING-SYRUP MIXTURE:

Heavy syrup (page 452)	2 tablespoons (3 cL)
Liqueur reserved from steeping strawberries	2 tablespoons (3 cL)

BAVARIAN CREAM:

Unflavored gelatin	2¼ teaspoons (1.1 cL)
Cold water	1 tablespoon (1.5 cL)
Milk	1 cup (2.4 dL)
Large egg yolks	4
Granulated sugar	2¾ ounces (75 g); ¼ cup + 2 tablespoons
Curaçao liqueur	3 tablespoons (4.5 cL)
Heavy cream, well chilled	1¼ cups (3 dL)

continued

Confectioners' sugar	1½ ounces (40 g); ⅓ cup
Heavy cream	1½ cups (3.6 dL)
Glacé fruits	

1. Combine the strawberries with the curaçao liqueur in a small mixing bowl and let steep, covered, for 2 to 3 hours. Drain well, reserving the curaçao liqueur.

2. Trim the crust from the génoise and cut it into strips 2 to 2½ inches (5 to 6 cm) long and about 1 inch (2.5 cm) square. Mix the heavy syrup with 2 tablespoons (3 cL) of the curaçao liqueur reserved from steeping the strawberries and brush the génoise strips with this syrup.

3. Chill the bowl and the wire whip or beater of the mixer in the refrigerator. Stir the gelatin into the cold water and let it soften.

4. Bring the milk to a simmer in a heavy 1-quart (1-L) saucepan. Beat together the egg yolks and sugar until smooth and lemon-colored, then slowly pour in the simmering milk, stirring constantly with a wire whisk. Pour the mixture back into the saucepan. Cook over low heat, stirring constantly with a wooden spatula, until this *crème anglaise* coats the back of the spatula and the bubbles formed when you stirred the milk into the yolks have disappeared. Do not allow to boil.

Remove the saucepan from the heat, add the softened gelatin, and stir to dissolve. Strain through a fine sieve into a stainless steel bowl. Dip the bottom of the bowl of *crème anglaise* in a larger bowl of ice water, and stir to cool the *crème anglaise* quickly. When it has reached room temperature, remove from the ice water and stir in the curaçao liqueur. Do not let the *crème anglaise* set.

5. Pour the heavy cream into the chilled mixer bowl and whip the cream at medium speed in the mixer using the chilled wire whip or beater until it is light and thick and holds soft peaks. Stop whipping.

6. Dip the bottom of the bowl of *crème anglaise* in the bowl of ice water again and stir with a rubber spatula until it just begins to thicken. Immediately remove the bowl from the ice water.

7. Continue whipping the cream at medium speed until it holds stiff peaks, then whip in the *crème anglaise* to finish the bavarian cream.

8. Rinse the ring mold with cold water and shake it out. Pour about one third of the bavarian cream into the mold. Arrange the strawberries over the bavarian cream. Pour in half of the remaining bavarian cream to cover the fruit. Arrange the génoise strips in a continuous circle in the mold and press them gently into the bavarian cream. Pour in the remaining bavarian cream to cover the génoise strips and fill the mold. Smooth the surface.

9. Chill in the refrigerator for 3 or 4 hours to set the bavarian cream.

10. Run the tip of a small icing spatula around the rim of the mold to loosen the top edge of the bavarian cream. Place a round serving plate upside down on top of the mold and invert the plate and mold together. Warm the outside of the mold with a blow dryer until the bavarian slides out easily and you can lift off the mold. Refrigerate again to chill the surface of the bavarian.

11. Sift the confectioners' sugar into the bowl of the mixer, stir in the heavy cream, and refrigerate for about an hour. Chill the wire whip or beater of the mixer as well. Whip the cream at medium speed in the mixer. When the cream holds soft peaks, slow down to avoid overbeating. Continue whipping until the cream is light and thick and holds stiff peaks.

12. Scoop the whipped cream into the pastry bag and pipe it into the center of the bavarian, mounding the whipped cream slightly. Pipe rosettes of whipped cream to cover the mound.

13. Cut a few glacé cherries in half. Cut thin slices of larger glacé fruits (such as pineapple, apricots, or pears) and cut from the slices a few triangles or diamonds. Decorate the bavarian with the glacé fruits, arranging them around the top of the ring.

14. Serve the bavarian accompanied by the strawberry sauce.

STORAGE: Serve the bavarian within an hour or two after filling with whipped cream.

Before unmolding, cover airtight with plastic wrap and keep for up to 2 or 3 days in the refrigerator.

Raspberry Charlotte

The beautiful, deep color of raspberry mousse makes the *charlotte russe* presentation ideal for this charlotte. If you want a sauce with it, try a *crème anglaise* flavored with *framboise* (raspberry brandy) or, for an overwhelming raspberry assault, raspberry sauce.

For 8 to 10 servings

EQUIPMENT:

Electric blender or food processor

8¾-inch (22-cm) *vacherin* ring, 2⅜ inches (6 cm) deep

9-inch (24-cm) foil board or matt board cake-decorating circle (page 467)

• cut to fit inside the ring

Electric mixer

Pastry bag fitted with

• small fluted pastry tube (Ateco #1)

FILLING:

Fresh raspberries for puree	1 pound + 2 ounces (500 g); 1½ pints
Superfine or extra fine sugar	4½ ounces (125 g); ½ cup + 2 tablespoons
Fresh orange juice	3 tablespoons (4.5 cL)
Unflavored gelatin	3½ teaspoons (1.8 cL)
Heavy cream, well chilled	2¼ cups (5.3 dL)
Fresh raspberries (optional) to leave whole	7 to 8 ounces (200 to 225 g); 1¼ cups

BRUSHING-SYRUP MIXTURE:

Heavy syrup (page 452)	3 tablespoons (4.5 cL)
Framboise (raspberry brandy)	3 tablespoons (4.5 cL)

CAKE:

Ladyfingers (page 271), piped adjacent to each other	About 28, in two bands totaling at least 28 inches (70 cm) long
Sponge cake (page 271)	Two 8¾-inch (22-cm) rounds

DECORATION:

Confectioners' sugar	½ ounce (12 g); 2 tablespoons
Heavy cream	½ cup (1.2 dL)
Fresh raspberries	A few

ACCOMPANIMENT:

Either raspberry sauce (page 438)	1½ cups (3.5 dL)
Or *crème anglaise* (page 436)	1½ cups (3.5 dL)
and *framboise* (raspberry brandy)	1 tablespoon + 1 teaspoon (2 cL)

1. Puree the raspberries with the sugar and orange juice in the blender or food processor. Strain through a fine sieve to eliminate the seeds.

2. Combine the brushing-syrup mixture with ¼ cup (6 cL) of the raspberry puree to make a raspberry brushing syrup.

3. Pour about one third of the remaining raspberry puree into a heavy 2-cup (5-dL) butter melter and stir in the gelatin. Let the gelatin soften, then warm over low heat, stirring constantly, until the gelatin dissolves. Remove from the heat and pour into a stainless steel mixing bowl. Stir in the rest of the raspberry puree, and allow to cool, stirring occasionally. Do not allow it to set. While the raspberry puree is cooling, chill the bowl and the wire whip or beater of the mixer in the refrigerator.

4. Pour the heavy cream into the chilled mixer bowl and whip the cream at medium speed in the mixer using the chilled wire whip or beater until it is light and thick and holds soft peaks. Stop whipping.

5. Dip the bottom of the bowl of raspberry puree in a larger bowl of ice water, and stir with a rubber spatula until it just begins to thicken. Immediately remove the bowl from the ice water.

6. Continue whipping the cream at medium speed until it holds stiff peaks, then whip in the raspberry puree to make the mousse. Gently fold in the optional raspberries, if you are using them.

7. Using a wavy-edge bread knife, trim off one side of each band of ladyfingers to make them exactly as high as the ring and to give them a straight bottom edge. Brush the backs of the bands of ladyfingers with some of the raspberry brushing syrup.

8. Place the *vacherin* ring on a tray, with the cake-decorating circle on the bottom. Line the ring with bands of ladyfingers, trimming the ends so they fit tightly together with no overlap. Trim the sponge cake rounds to fit neatly inside the lined ring. Place one round on the bottom inside the lined ring, and brush it heavily with the raspberry syrup.

9. Scoop half of the raspberry mousse into the ring, spread it evenly, and smooth the surface. Heavily brush the second round of sponge cake with the raspberry syrup, turn it upside down, and place it on top of the mousse. Heavily brush the top side with raspberry syrup as well. Scoop more raspberry mousse on top of the second sponge cake round to fill the ring to the top of the ladyfingers and smooth the surface.

10. Chill the charlotte in the refrigerator for several hours or overnight to set the mousse.

11. Lift the ring off the charlotte and transfer the charlotte to a serving plate.

12. Sift the confectioners' sugar into the bowl of the mixer, stir in the heavy cream, and refrigerate for about an hour. Chill the wire whip or beater of the mixer as well. Whip the cream at medium speed in the mixer. When the cream holds soft peaks, slow down to avoid overbeating. Continue whipping until the cream is light and thick and holds stiff peaks.

13. Scoop the whipped cream into the pastry bag and pipe rosettes in a decorative pattern on top of the charlotte. Place fresh raspberries on top of some of the rosettes. You can also pipe rosettes of whipped cream between the ladyfingers around the base of the charlotte.

14. Serve the charlotte accompanied by either the raspberry sauce or the *crème anglaise* flavored with the *framboise*.

NOTES: If you want to make the charlotte without the *framboise*, substitute 1 tablespoon (1.5 cL) each of raspberry puree, heavy syrup, and cold water for the 3 tablespoons (4.5 cL) of *framboise* in the brushing-syrup mixture.

If fresh raspberries are unavailable, you can use unsweetened frozen raspberries in the puree for the mousse and brushing. Defrost the berries before using. Omit the optional whole berries in the filling.

STORAGE: In the refrigerator for up to 2 or 3 days.

Or, before glazing and unmolding, freeze for up to 2 weeks. Once frozen, cover the top of the charlotte airtight with plastic wrap. Remove the plastic wrap and the *vacherin* ring, then defrost overnight in the refrigerator before decorating.

Strawberry Charlotte

This charlotte, filled with the lush taste of the fresh berries, reminds us of William Butler's assessment of strawberries quoted in Izaak Walton's *The Compleat Angler:* "Doubtless God could have made a better berry, but doubtless God never did."

Diagonally piped ladyfingers around the sides of the charlotte add interest to the presentation and differentiate it from our raspberry charlotte.

For 8 to 10 servings

EQUIPMENT:

Electric blender or food processor
8¾-inch (22-cm) *vacherin* ring, 2⅜ inches (6 cm) deep
9-inch (24-cm) foil board or matt board cake-decorating circle (page 467)
• cut to fit inside the ring
Electric mixer
Pastry bag fitted with
• small fluted pastry tube (Ateco #1)

FILLING:

Fresh strawberries for puree	1 pound + 4 ounces (570 g); 1⅔ pints
Superfine or extra fine sugar	3½ ounces (100 g); ½ cup
Fresh orange juice	3 tablespoons (4.5 cL)
Unflavored gelatin	3½ teaspoons (1.8 cL)
Heavy cream, well chilled	2 cups (4.8 dL)
Fresh strawberries (optional) to leave whole or cut in halves or quarters if large	7 to 8 ounces (200 to 225 g); 1¼ cups

BRUSHING-SYRUP MIXTURE:

Heavy syrup (page 452)	3 tablespoons (4.5 cL)
European kirsch	3 tablespoons (4.5 cL)

CAKE:

Ladyfingers (page 271), piped adjacent to each other on the diagonal	About 28, in two bands totaling at least 28 inches (70 cm) long
Sponge cake (page 271)	Two 8¾-inch (22-cm) rounds

continued

DECORATION:

Confectioners' sugar	½ ounce (12 g); 2 tablespoons
Heavy cream	½ cup (1.2 dL)
Fresh strawberries	A few

ACCOMPANIMENT:

Strawberry sauce (page 438)	1½ cups (3.5 dL)

1. Puree the strawberries with the sugar and orange juice in the blender or food processor. Strain through a fine sieve to eliminate any hard, unripe pieces of strawberry.

2. Combine the brushing-syrup mixture with ¼ cup (6 cL) of the strawberry puree to make a strawberry brushing syrup.

3. Pour about one third of the remaining strawberry puree into a heavy 2-cup (5-dL) butter melter and stir in the gelatin. Let the gelatin soften, then warm over low heat, stirring constantly, until the gelatin dissolves. Remove from the heat and pour into a stainless steel mixing bowl. Stir in the rest of the strawberry puree, and allow to cool, stirring occasionally. Do not allow it to set. While the strawberry puree is cooling, chill the bowl and the wire whip or beater of the mixer in the refrigerator.

4. Pour the heavy cream into the chilled mixer bowl and whip the cream at medium speed in the mixer using the chilled wire whip or beater until it is light and thick and holds soft peaks. Stop whipping.

5. Dip the bottom of the bowl of strawberry puree in a larger bowl of ice water, and stir with a rubber spatula until it just begins to thicken. Immediately remove the bowl from the ice water.

6. Continue whipping the cream at medium speed until it holds stiff peaks, then whip in the strawberry puree to make the mousse. Gently fold in the optional strawberries, if you are using them.

7. Using a wavy-edge bread knife, trim off one side of each band of ladyfingers to make them exactly as high as the ring and to give them a straight bottom edge. Brush the backs of the bands of ladyfingers with some of the strawberry brushing syrup.

8. Place the *vacherin* ring on a tray, with the cake-decorating circle on the bottom. Line the ring with bands of ladyfingers, trimming the ends so they fit tightly together with no overlap. Trim the sponge cake rounds to fit neatly inside the lined ring. Place one round on the bottom inside the lined ring, and brush it heavily with the strawberry syrup.

9. Scoop half of the strawberry mousse into the ring, spread it evenly, and smooth the surface. Heavily brush the second round of sponge cake with the strawberry syrup, turn it upside down, and place it on top of the mousse. Heavily brush the top side with strawberry syrup as well. Scoop more strawberry mousse on top of the second sponge cake round to fill the ring to the top of the ladyfingers and smooth the surface.

10. Chill the charlotte in the refrigerator for several hours or overnight to set the mousse.

11. Lift the ring off the charlotte and transfer the charlotte to a serving plate.

12. Sift the confectioners' sugar into the bowl of the mixer, stir in the heavy cream, and refrigerate for about an hour. Chill the wire whip or beater of the mixer as well. Whip the cream at medium speed in the mixer. When the cream holds soft peaks, slow down to avoid overbeating. Continue whipping until the cream is light and thick and holds stiff peaks.

13. Scoop the whipped cream into the pastry bag and pipe rosettes in a decorative pattern on top of the charlotte. If you have small strawberries, place them on top of some of the rosettes. Otherwise, cut the strawberries in halves or slice them, and decorate the top of the charlotte by placing them directly on the surface of the mousse. Sliced strawberries look nice arranged in a circle on the center of the charlotte, with the slices overlapping like the blades of a fan. You can also pipe rosettes of whipped cream between the ladyfingers around the base of the charlotte.

14. Serve the charlotte accompanied by the strawberry sauce.

NOTES: If you want to make the charlotte without the kirsch, substitute 1 tablespoon (1.5 cL) each of strawberry puree, heavy syrup, and cold water for the 3 tablespoons (4.5 cL) of kirsch in the brushing-syrup mixture.

If fresh strawberries are unavailable, you can use unsweetened frozen strawberries in the puree for the mousse and brushing. Defrost the berries before using. Omit the optional whole berries in the filling.

STORAGE: In the refrigerator for up to 2 or 3 days.

Or, before glazing and unmolding, freeze for up to 2 weeks. Once frozen, cover the top of the charlotte airtight with plastic wrap. Remove the plastic wrap and the *vacherin* ring, then defrost overnight in the refrigerator before decorating.

Pear Charlotte

For pear charlotte we recommend a special presentation, in which you will use ladyfingers to line the sides of the *vacherin* ring and a decorative round made from the same sponge cake batter on top. To enhance the delicate pear flavor, serve this charlotte with chocolate sauce.

For 8 to 10 servings

EQUIPMENT:
Electric blender or food processor
8¾-inch (22-cm) *vacherin* ring, 2⅜ inches (6 cm) deep
9-inch (24-cm) foil board or matt board cake-decorating circle (page 467)
• cut to fit inside the ring
Electric mixer

FILLING:

Fresh pears, peeled and poached in light syrup (page 454)	1 pound + 10 ounces (750 g); 5 to 7 pears
Superfine or extra fine sugar	1 ounce (25 g); 2 tablespoons
Fresh lemon juice, strained	2 teaspoons (1 cL)
Unflavored gelatin	3½ teaspoons (1.8 cL)
Poire william (pear brandy)	2 tablespoons (3 cL)
Heavy cream, well chilled	1¾ cups + 2 tablespoons (4.4 dL)

CAKE:

Ladyfingers (page 271), piped adjacent to each other	About 28, in two bands totaling at least 28 inches (70 cm) long
Sponge cake (page 271)	One 8¾-inch (22-cm) plain round and one decorative round

BRUSHING-SYRUP MIXTURE:

Syrup from poaching the pears	2 tablespoons + 2 teaspoons (4 cL)
Heavy syrup (page 452)	2 tablespoons + 2 teaspoons (4 cL)
Poire william (pear brandy)	1 tablespoon + 1 teaspoon (2 cL)

ACCOMPANIMENT:

Chocolate sauce (page 435)	1½ cups (3.5 dL)

1. Drain the poached pears, cut them in half, and core them. Puree 1 pound 5 ounces (600 g) of the pears with the superfine sugar and lemon juice in the blender or food processor. Strain the puree through a fine sieve. Cut the remaining pears into slices ¼ inch (6 mm) thick.

2. Pour about one third of the pear puree into a heavy 2-cup (5-dL) butter melter and stir in the gelatin. Let the gelatin soften, then warm over low heat, stirring constantly, until the gelatin dissolves. Remove from the heat and pour into a stainless steel bowl. Stir in the remaining pear puree and the *poire william,* and allow to cool, stirring occasionally. Do not allow it to set. While the pear puree is cooling, chill the bowl and the wire whip or beater of the mixer in the refrigerator.

3. Pour the heavy cream into the chilled mixer bowl and whip the cream at medium speed in the mixer using the chilled wire whip or beater until it is light and thick and holds soft peaks. Stop whipping.

4. Dip the bottom of the bowl of pear puree in a larger bowl of ice water, and stir with a rubber spatula until it just begins to thicken. Immediately remove the bowl from the ice water.

5. Continue whipping the cream at medium speed until it holds stiff peaks, then whip in the pear puree to make the mousse.

6. Using a wavy-edge bread knife, trim off both sides of each band of ladyfingers to make them exactly as high as the ring and to give them straight top and bottom edges. Brush the backs of the bands of ladyfingers with some of the *poire william* brushing syrup.

7. Place the *vacherin* ring on a tray, with the cake-decorating circle on the bottom. Line the ring with bands of ladyfingers, trimming the ends so they fit tightly together with no overlap. Trim the plain round of sponge cake to fit neatly inside the lined ring. Place it on the bottom inside the lined ring, and brush it heavily with the *poire william* syrup.

8. Scoop half of the pear mousse into the ring, spread it evenly, and smooth the surface. Arrange the pear slices over the mousse in the ring. Then scoop the remaining mousse into the ring to fill the ring to the top of the ladyfingers. Smooth the top of the mousse and sweep off any excess with a large icing spatula or metal straightedge to make a flat top surface.

9. Brush the back of the decorative round of sponge cake with *poire william* syrup and place it on top of the charlotte.

10. Chill the charlotte in the refrigerator for several hours or overnight to set the mousse.

11. Place the chilled charlotte on a bowl or cake pan taller and slightly smaller in diameter than the ring and carefully slip the ring down off the charlotte. Then transfer the charlotte to a serving plate.

12. Serve the charlotte accompanied by the chocolate sauce.

STORAGE: In the refrigerator for up to 2 or 3 days.

Or, before unmolding, freeze for up to 2 weeks. Once frozen, cover the top of the charlotte airtight with plastic wrap, being careful not to damage the decorative sponge cake round. Remove the plastic wrap and defrost overnight in the refrigerator before unmolding.

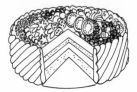

Mixed Fruit Charlotte

For a totally different look, you can make a Russian charlotte with a curaçao liqueur mousse and cover the top with an assortment of fresh fruits. The mousse is actually the same bavarian cream as we use in *romanov* (page 288).

For 8 to 10 servings

EQUIPMENT:

8¾-inch (22-cm) *vacherin* ring, 2⅜ inches (6 cm) deep
9-inch (24-cm) foil board or matt board cake-decorating circle (page 467)
• cut to fit inside the ring
Electric mixer

FILLING:

Unflavored gelatin	2½ teaspoons (1.3 cL)
Cold water	2 tablespoons (3 cL)
Egg yolks, lightly beaten	3 tablespoons (4.5 cL); about 2⅔ large yolks
Superfine or extra fine sugar	2½ ounces (70 g); ¼ cup + 2 tablespoons
Dry white wine	¼ cup + 2 tablespoons (9 cL)
Curaçao liqueur	⅔ cup (1.6 dL)
Heavy cream, well chilled	2¼ cups (5.4 dL)

CAKE:

Ladyfingers (page 271), piped adjacent to each other on the diagonal	About 28, in two bands totaling at least 28 inches (70 cm) long
Sponge cake (page 271)	Two 8¾-inch (22-cm) rounds

BRUSHING-SYRUP MIXTURE:

Heavy syrup (page 452)	¼ cup (6 cL)
Curaçao liqueur	¼ cup (6 cL)
Fresh orange juice	2 tablespoons (3 cL)

FRUIT:

Assorted fresh fruits, such as blueberries, grapes, slices of banana or kiwi, peeled pineapple wedges, and small- to medium-size strawberries	Enough to cover top of charlotte in one layer

GLAZE:

Unflavored gelatin	¾ teaspoon (4 mL)
Cold water	3 tablespoons + 1 teaspoon (5 cL)
Fresh orange juice, strained	3 tablespoons + 1 teaspoon (5 cL)
Superfine or extra fine sugar	1½ ounces (40 g); 3 tablespoons + 1 teaspoon

1. Chill the bowl and the wire whip or beater of the mixer in the refrigerator. Stir the gelatin into the cold water and let it soften.

2. In a 2-cup (5-dL) butter melter, whisk together the egg yolks and superfine sugar until lemon-colored. Whisk in the white wine and 2 tablespoons (3 cL) of the curaçao liqueur. Bring just to a simmer, whisking constantly. Remove from the heat, add the softened gelatin, and stir until dissolved. Strain through a fine sieve into a small stainless steel bowl and let cool. Stir in the remaining curaçao.

3. Pour the heavy cream into the chilled mixer bowl and whip the cream at medium speed in the mixer using the chilled wire whip or beater until it is light and thick and holds stiff peaks. Then whip in the curaçao-flavored custard to finish the bavarian cream.

4. Using a wavy-edge bread knife, trim off one side of each band of ladyfingers to make them just a little higher than the ring and give them a straight bottom edge. Lightly brush the backs of the strip of ladyfingers with the curaçao brushing syrup.

5. Place the *vacherin* ring on a tray, with the cake-decorating circle on the bottom. Line the ring with bands of ladyfingers, trimming the ends so they fit tightly together with no overlap. Trim the sponge cake rounds to fit neatly inside the lined ring. Place one round on the bottom inside the lined ring, and brush it heavily with the curaçao syrup.

6. Scoop half of the curaçao bavarian cream into the ring, spread it evenly, and smooth the surface. Heavily brush the second round of sponge cake with the curaçao syrup, turn it upside down, and place it on top of the bavarian cream. Heavily brush the top side with curaçao syrup as well. Scoop the remaining bavarian cream on top of the second sponge cake round to fill the ring almost to the top of the ladyfingers and smooth the surface.

7. Chill the charlotte in the refrigerator for several hours or overnight to set the mousse.

8. Arrange the fresh fruit in a single layer on top of the mousse, covering the surface.

9. For the glaze, stir the gelatin into the the cold water and let it soften. Heat the orange juice and sugar in a butter melter, stirring occasionally, until the sugar is dissolved in the orange juice. Add the softened gelatin and stir until the gelatin dissolves. Pour into a small stainless steel bowl and let cool. Dip the bottom of the bowl in a larger bowl of ice water and stir until it begins to thicken very lightly. Remove the bowl from the ice water immediately. Brush the glaze on the fruits until they are lightly coated and glistening. Then refrigerate to set the glaze.

10. Lift the ring off the charlotte and transfer the charlotte to a serving plate.

11. Refrigerate until ready to serve.

STORAGE: In the refrigerator for up to 1 or 2 days.

Lemon Charlotte

The mousse for this lemon charlotte is based on lemon curd. Lining the *vacherin* ring with a multi-layered *joconde*-raspberry jam sandwich makes a nice contrast to the tartness of the mousse, and serving the charlotte with a raspberry or strawberry sauce provides a beautiful complement of flavor and color.

For 8 to 10 servings

EQUIPMENT:

8¾-inch (22-cm) *vacherin* ring, 2⅜ inches (6 cm) deep
9-inch (24-cm) foil board or matt board cake-decorating circle (page 467)
• cut to fit inside the ring
Electric mixer

FILLING:

Fresh lemon juice, strained	3 tablespoons (4.5 cL)
Heavy syrup (page 452)	3 tablespoons (4.5 cL)
Unflavored gelatin	1½ teaspoons (8 mL)
Heavy cream, well chilled	2¼ cups (5.4 dL)
Lemon curd (page 393), at room temperature	9¼ ounces (260 g); 1 cup

CAKE:

Joconde-raspberry jam sandwich (page 274)	Three slices 1¾ to 2 inches (4.5 to 5 cm) high, ⅜ inch (1 cm) thick, and with combined length at least 28 inches (72 cm)
Sponge cake (page 271)	Two 8¾-inch (22-cm) rounds

BRUSHING-SYRUP MIXTURE:

Lemon syrup (page 453)	3 tablespoons (4.5 cL)
Heavy syrup	2 tablespoons (3 cL)
Water	5 tablespoons (7.5 cL)

DECORATION:

Candied lemon slices (page 453)	3 or 4

ACCOMPANIMENT:

Raspberry or strawberry sauce (page 438)	1½ cups (3.5 dL)

1. Chill the bowl and the wire whip or beater of the mixer in the refrigerator. Combine the lemon juice and heavy syrup in a butter melter, and stir in the gelatin. Let the gelatin soften, then warm over low heat, stirring constantly, until the gelatin dissolves. Remove from the heat and pour into a stainless steel mixing bowl.

2. Pour the heavy cream into the chilled mixer bowl and whip the cream at medium speed in the mixer using the chilled wire whip or beater until it is light and thick and holds soft peaks. Stop whipping.

3. Stir the lemon curd into the dissolved gelatin with a wire whisk to mix thoroughly.

4. Continue whipping the cream at medium speed until it holds stiff peaks, then whip in the lemon curd mixture to finish the lemon mousse.

5. Cut the slices of the *joconde*-jam sandwich into rectangles 2 inches (5 cm) long. Place the *vacherin* ring on a tray, with the cake-decorating circle on the bottom. Line the ring with rectangles of the *joconde*-jam sandwich, arranging them with the jam stripes running vertically. Using a wavy-edge bread knife, trim the sponge cake rounds to fit neatly inside the lined ring. Place one round on the bottom inside the lined ring, and brush it heavily with the lemon brushing syrup. Lightly brush the inside of the *joconde*-jam lining slices with the lemon syrup.

6. Scoop half of the lemon mousse into the ring, spread it evenly, and smooth the surface. Heavily brush the second round of sponge cake with the lemon syrup, turn it upside down, and place it on top of the mousse. Heavily brush the top side with lemon syrup as well. Scoop the remaining lemon mousse on top of the second sponge cake round and spread it to fill the ring. Smooth the top of the mousse and sweep off any excess with a large icing spatula or a metal straightedge to make a flat top surface.

7. Chill the charlotte in the refrigerator for several hours or overnight to set the mousse.

8. Place the chilled charlotte on a bowl or cake pan taller and slightly smaller in diameter than the ring. Using a blow dryer, quickly and evenly warm the outside of the ring to just melt the mousse touching the ring near the top. Carefully slip the ring down off the charlotte. Transfer the charlotte to a serving plate.

9. Cut the candied lemon slices in half and arrange them like a pinwheel on the center of the charlotte.

10. Serve the charlotte accompanied by the raspberry or strawberry sauce.

STORAGE: In the refrigerator for up to 2 or 3 days.

Or, before unmolding, freeze for up to 2 weeks. Once frozen, cover the top of the charlotte airtight with plastic wrap. Remove the plastic wrap and defrost overnight in the refrigerator before unmolding.

Sour Cherry Charlotte

Sour cherries are one of the ephemeral pleasures of summer. If you are fortunate enough to have a montmorency cherry tree, put your harvest to good use in this creamy charlotte.

There is no need to pit the cherries. You break up the cherries coarsely in the blender, bring them to a simmer to set their color and extract flavor from the skins, then strain out the pits and skins. Simmering destroys natural enzymes that would oxidize the pureed cherries and turn them brown easily.

For 8 to 10 servings

EQUIPMENT:

Electric blender or food processor
8¾-inch (22-cm) *vacherin* ring, 2⅜ inches (6 cm) deep
9-inch (24-cm) foil board or matt board cake-decorating circle (page 467)
• cut to fit inside the ring
Electric mixer

FILLING:

Unflavored gelatin	1 tablespoon + ½ teaspoon (1.8 cL)
Cold water	2 tablespoons (3 cL)
Fresh sour cherries	1 pound + 12 ounces (800 g)
Superfine or extra fine sugar	4½ ounces (125 g); ½ cup + 2 tablespoons
Fresh orange juice	3 tablespoons (4.5 cL)
Heavy cream, well chilled	2 cups (4.8 dL)
European kirsch (optional)	1 tablespoon (1.5 cL)

BRUSHING-SYRUP MIXTURE:

Water	⅓ cup (8 cL)
Heavy syrup (page 452)	⅓ cup + 3 tablespoons (12.5 cL)
European kirsch	3 tablespoons (4.5 cL)

CAKE:

Joconde-raspberry jam sandwich (page 274)	Three slices 1¾ to 2 inches (4.5 to 5 cm) high, ⅜ inch (1 cm) thick, and with combined length at least 28 inches (72 cm)
Sponge cake (page 271)	Two 8¾-inch (22-cm) rounds

GLAZE:

Unflavored gelatin	¾ teaspoon (4 mL)
Cold water	¼ cup (6 cL)
Sour cherry jelly or red currant jelly	3 ounces (80 g); ¼ cup

ACCOMPANIMENT:

Crème anglaise (page 436)	1½ cups (3.5 dL)
European kirsch	1 tablespoon + 1 teaspoon (2 cL)

1. Stir the gelatin into the cold water and let it soften.

2. Combine the cherries with the sugar and orange juice in the blender or food processor and process briefly to break up the cherries without chopping the pits. Pour the mixture into a heavy 2-quart (2-L) saucepan and bring to a simmer, stirring constantly with a wooden spatula. Remove from the heat and strain through a fine sieve into a stainless steel bowl to eliminate the cherry skins and pits.

3. Stir the softened gelatin into the hot cherry puree, and allow to cool, stirring occasionally. Do not allow it to set. While the cherry puree is cooling, chill the bowl and the wire whip or beater of the mixer in the refrigerator.

4. Combine the skins and pits strained out of the puree with the water and ⅓ cup (8 cL) of the heavy syrup in a small saucepan and bring to a simmer. Reduce the heat to very low and cook 5 minutes. Strain through a fine sieve, pressing down firmly to extract as much syrup as possible, then discard the skins and pits. Mix ¼ cup (6 cL) of strained syrup with the rest of the heavy syrup and the kirsch to make the cherry brushing syrup.

5. Pour the heavy cream into the chilled mixer bowl and whip the cream at medium speed in the mixer using the chilled wire whip or beater until it is light and thick and holds soft peaks. Stop whipping.

6. Stir the optional kirsch into the cherry puree. Dip the bottom of the bowl of cherry puree in a larger bowl of ice water, and stir with a rubber spatula until it just begins to thicken. Immediately remove the bowl from the ice water.

7. Continue whipping the cream at medium speed until it holds stiff peaks, then whip in the cherry puree to finish the mousse.

8. Place the *vacherin* ring on a tray, with the cake-decorating circle on the bottom. Line the ring with slices of the *joconde*-jam sandwich, arranging them with the jam stripes running horizontally and trimming the ends so they fit tightly together with no overlap. Using a wavy-edge bread knife, trim the sponge cake rounds to fit neatly inside the lined ring. Place one round on the bottom inside the lined ring, and brush it heavily with the cherry brushing syrup. Lightly brush the inside of the *joconde*-jam lining slices with the cherry syrup.

9. Scoop half of the cherry mousse into the ring, spread it evenly, and smooth the surface. Heavily brush the second round of sponge cake with the cherry syrup, turn it upside down, and place it on top of the mousse. Heavily brush the top side with cherry syrup as well. Scoop the remaining cherry mousse on top of the second sponge cake round and spread it to fill the ring. Smooth the top of the mousse and sweep off any excess with a large icing spatula or a metal straightedge to make a flat top surface.

10. Chill the charlotte in the refrigerator for several hours or overnight to set the mousse.

11. For the glaze, stir the gelatin into the cold water and let it soften. Heat the jelly in a butter melter, stirring occasionally until melted. Add the softened gelatin and stir until the gelatin dissolves. Pour into a small stainless steel bowl and let cool. Dip the bottom of the bowl in a larger bowl of ice water and stir until it begins to thicken very lightly. Remove the bowl from the ice water immediately. Pour the glaze on the top of the mousse and spread it quickly with a soft pastry brush to make a thick, even coating of glaze, letting the excess flow over the sides of the ring and being careful not to damage the surface of the mousse. Refrigerate to set the glaze.

12. Place the chilled charlotte on a bowl or cake pan taller and slightly smaller in diameter than the ring. Using a blow dryer, quickly and evenly warm the outside of the ring to just melt the mousse touching the ring near the top. Carefully slip the ring down off the charlotte. Transfer the charlotte to a serving plate.

13. Serve the charlotte accompanied by the *crème anglaise* flavored with the kirsch.

NOTE: If you want to make the charlotte without the *kirsch*, substitute 1 tablespoon (1.5 cL) each of cherry puree, heavy syrup, and cold water for the 3 tablespoons (4.5 cL) of kirsch in the brushing-syrup mixture and omit the kirsch from the *crème anglaise*.

STORAGE: In the refrigerator for up to 2 or 3 days.

Or, before glazing and unmolding, freeze for up to 2 weeks. Once frozen, cover the top of the charlotte airtight with plastic wrap. Remove the plastic wrap and defrost overnight in the refrigerator, then glaze and unmold as usual.

Blackberry Charlotte

Imagine how fabulous blackberries would be if they didn't have those big, hard seeds. Then try this blackberry charlotte to make your fantasy come true. The mousse has an extraordinary deep color and reverberates with the rich flavor of the berries. Try it with a curaçao-flavored *crème anglaise* sauce for maximum drama.

For 8 to 10 servings

EQUIPMENT:

Electric blender or food processor

8¾-inch (22-cm) *vacherin* ring, 2⅜ inches (6 cm) deep

9-inch (24-cm) foil board or matt board cake-decorating circle (page 467)

• cut to fit inside the ring

Electric mixer

FILLING:

Fresh blackberries	1 pound (450 g); 1⅓ pints
Superfine or extra fine sugar	3½ ounces (100 g); ½ cup
Fresh orange juice	¼ cup (6 cL)
Unflavored gelatin	1 tablespoon + ½ teaspoon (1.8 cL)
Heavy cream, well chilled	2 cups (4.8 dL)

BRUSHING-SYRUP MIXTURE:

Fresh orange juice	3 tablespoons (4.5 cL)
Heavy syrup (page 452)	3 tablespoons (4.5 cL)

CAKE:

Joconde-raspberry jam sandwich (page 274)	Three slices 1¾ to 2 inches (4.5 to 5 cm) high, ⅜ inch (1 cm) thick, and with combined length at least 28 inches (72 cm)
Sponge cake (page 271)	Two 8¾-inch (22-cm) rounds

GLAZE:

Gelatin	¾ teaspoon (4 mL)
Cold water	¼ cup (6 cL)
Black currant jelly or elderberry jelly	3 ounces (80 g); ¼ cup

continued

ACCOMPANIMENT:

Crème anglaise (page 436)	1½ cups (3.5 dL)
Curaçao liqueur	1 tablespoon + 1 teaspoon (2 cL)

1. Puree the blackberries with the sugar and orange juice in the blender or food processor. Strain through a fine sieve to eliminate the seeds.

2. Combine the brushing-syrup mixture with ¼ cup (6 cL) of the blackberry puree to make a blackberry brushing syrup.

3. Pour about one third of the remaining blackberry puree into a heavy 2-cup (5-dL) butter melter and stir in the gelatin. Let the gelatin soften, then warm over low heat, stirring constantly, until the gelatin dissolves. Remove from the heat and pour into a stainless steel mixing bowl. Stir in the rest of the blackberry puree, and allow to cool, stirring occasionally. Do not allow it to set. While the blackberry puree is cooling, chill the bowl and the wire whip or beater of the mixer in the refrigerator.

4. Pour the heavy cream into the chilled mixer bowl and whip the cream at medium speed in the mixer using the chilled wire whip or beater until it is light and thick and holds soft peaks. Stop whipping.

5. Dip the bottom of the bowl of blackberry puree in a larger bowl of ice water, and stir with a rubber spatula until it just begins to thicken. Immediately remove the bowl from the ice water.

6. Continue whipping the cream at medium speed until it holds stiff peaks, then whip in the blackberry puree to finish the mousse.

7. Place the *vacherin* ring on a tray, with the cake-decorating circle on the bottom. Line the ring with slices of the *joconde*-jam sandwich, arranging them with the jam stripes running horizontally and trimming the ends so they fit tightly together with no overlap. Using a wavy-edge bread knife, trim the sponge cake rounds to fit neatly inside the lined ring. Place one round on the bottom inside the lined ring, and brush it heavily with the blackberry brushing syrup. Lightly brush the inside of the *joconde*-jam lining slices with the blackberry syrup.

8. Scoop half of the blackberry mousse into the ring, spread it evenly, and smooth the surface. Heavily brush the second round of sponge cake with the blackberry syrup, turn it upside down, and place it on top of the mousse. Heavily brush the top side with blackberry syrup as well. Scoop the remaining mousse on top of the second sponge cake round and spread it to fill the ring. Smooth the top of the mousse and sweep off any excess with a large icing spatula or a metal straightedge to make a flat top surface.

9. Chill the charlotte in the refrigerator for several hours or overnight to set the mousse.

10. For the glaze, stir the gelatin into the cold water and let it soften. Heat the jelly in a butter melter, stirring occasionally until melted. Add the softened gelatin and stir until the gelatin dissolves. Pour into a small stainless steel bowl and let cool. Dip the bottom of the bowl in a larger bowl of ice water and stir until it begins to thicken very lightly. Remove the bowl from the ice water immediately. Pour the glaze on the top of the mousse and spread it quickly with a soft pastry brush to make a thick, even coating of glaze, letting the excess flow over the sides of the ring and being careful not to damage the surface of the mousse. Refrigerate to set the glaze.

11. Place the chilled charlotte on a bowl or cake pan taller and slightly smaller in diameter than the ring. Using a blow dryer, quickly and evenly warm the outside of the ring to just melt the mousse touching the ring near the top. Carefully slip the ring down off the charlotte. Transfer the charlotte to a serving plate.

12. Serve the charlotte accompanied by the *crème anglaise* flavored with the curaçao.

NOTE: If fresh blackberries are unavailable, you can use unsweetened frozen blackberries in the puree for the mousse and brushing. Defrost the berries before using.

STORAGE: In the refrigerator for up to 2 or 3 days.

Or, before glazing and unmolding, freeze for up to 2 weeks. Once frozen, cover the top of the charlotte airtight with plastic wrap. Remove the plastic wrap and defrost overnight in the refrigerator, then glaze and unmold as usual.

Mango Charlotte

The sweet, unctuous flesh of the mango makes a luxurious mousse that is set off beautifully by the slight bitterness of Seville oranges in the slices of *joconde*-marmalade roll lining this charlotte. You mold it in a round cake pan, which makes the assembly exceptionally easy. A *crème anglaise* sauce flavored with white rum is the perfect accompaniment.

For 8 to 10 servings

EQUIPMENT:
Electric blender or food processor
10-inch (25-cm) round cake pan, 1½ inches (4 cm) deep,
    or 9-inch (24-cm) round cake pan, 2 inches (5 cm) deep
• brush with melted butter
• dust with granulated sugar
Electric mixer
9-inch (24-cm) foil board or matt board cake-decorating circle (page 467)
• cut to fit inside the cake pan

CAKE:

Joconde-orange marmalade roll (page 276)	One roll 10 inches (25 cm) long or two rolls 6 inches (15 cm) long

FILLING:

Ripe fresh mangoes	Two 1-pound (450-g) fruits
Superfine or extra fine sugar	2⅔ ounces (75 g); ¼ cup + 2 tablespoons
Fresh lemon juice, strained	2 tablespoons (3 cL)
Unflavored gelatin	3½ teaspoons (1.8 cL)
Heavy cream, well chilled	2 cups (4.8 dL)

BRUSHING-SYRUP MIXTURE:

Heavy syrup (page 452)	2 teaspoons (1 cL)
White Jamaican rum	2 teaspoons (1 cL)

GLAZE:

Unflavored gelatin	¾ teaspoon (4 mL)
Cold water	3 tablespoons + 1 teaspoon (5 cL)
Fresh orange juice, strained	3 tablespoons + 1 teaspoon (5 cL)
Superfine or extra fine sugar	1½ ounces (40 g); 3 tablespoons + 1 teaspoon

ACCOMPANIMENT:

Crème anglaise (page 436)	1½ cups (3.5 dL)
White Jamaican rum	1 tablespoon + 1 teaspoon (2 cL)

1. Using a chef's knife, cut from the *joconde*-marmalade roll (or rolls) twenty-four slices, each about ⅜ inch (1 cm) thick. Line the sides of the cake pan with the slices, placing them adjacent to each other. Arrange the remaining slices over the bottom of the mold. Refrigerate while you make the mousse.

2. Slit the skin all the way around each mango and peel off the skin. With a spoon, scrape off any of the flesh that clings to the skins. Slice the flesh off the pit of each mango. You should have about 1¼ pounds (570 g) of flesh. If you don't have enough, cut open another mango and add as much of its flesh as necessary. Puree the mango flesh with the superfine sugar and lemon juice in the blender or food processor. Strain the puree through a fine sieve to remove any bits of fiber from the mango.

3. Pour about one third of the mango puree into a heavy 2-cup (5-dL) butter melter and stir in the gelatin. Let the gelatin soften, then warm over low heat, stirring constantly, until the gelatin dissolves. Remove from the heat and pour into a stainless steel bowl. Stir in the remaining mango puree, and allow to cool, stirring occasionally. Do not allow it to set. While the mango puree is cooling, chill the bowl and the wire whip or beater of the mixer in the refrigerator.

4. Pour the heavy cream into the chilled mixer bowl and whip the cream at medium speed in the mixer using the chilled wire whip or beater until it is light and thick and holds soft peaks. Stop whipping.

5. Dip the bottom of the bowl of mango puree in a larger bowl of ice water, and stir with a rubber spatula until it just begins to thicken. Immediately remove the bowl from the ice water.

6. Continue whipping the cream at medium speed until it holds stiff peaks, then whip in the mango puree to finish the mousse.

7. Brush the inside of the *joconde*-marmalade slices lining the mold lightly with the rum brushing syrup. Scoop the mango mousse into the cake pan and spread it evenly to fill the cake pan. Smooth the top of the mousse and sweep off any excess with a large icing spatula or a metal straightedge to make a flat surface.

8. Chill the charlotte in the refrigerator for several hours or overnight to set the mousse.

9. Place the cake-decorating circle upside down on the charlotte, and place a wire rack upside

down on top of the cake pan. Turn the cake pan and wire rack upside down together to unmold the charlotte onto the wire rack. Lift off the cake pan.

10. For the glaze, stir the gelatin into the cold water and let it soften. Heat the orange juice and sugar in a butter melter, stirring occasionally, until the sugar is dissolved in the orange juice. Add the softened gelatin and stir until the gelatin dissolves. Pour into a small stainless steel bowl and let cool. Dip the bottom of the bowl in a larger bowl of ice water and stir until it begins to thicken very lightly. Remove the bowl from the ice water immediately. Brush the entire surface of the charlotte with the glaze until evenly coated and glistening. Refrigerate until the glaze is set.

11. Transfer the charlotte to a serving plate and serve accompanied by the *crème anglaise* sauce flavored with the white rum.

STORAGE: In the refrigerator for up to 2 or 3 days.

Or, before unmolding, freeze for up to 2 weeks. Once frozen, cover the top of the charlotte airtight with plastic wrap. Remove the plastic wrap and defrost overnight in the refrigerator before unmolding.

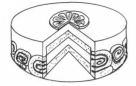

Blood Orange Charlotte

If you don't tell your guests that the mousse in this charlotte is made from blood oranges, the striking berry color will probably trick them into thinking it is anything but a citrus flavor. But once the secret is out, the orange flavor is unmistakable. This is a fun dessert for connoisseurs of taste.

For 8 to 10 servings

EQUIPMENT:

8¾-inch (22-cm) *vacherin* ring, 2⅜ inches (6 cm) deep
9-inch (24-cm) foil board or matt board cake-decorating circle (page 467)
• cut to fit inside the ring
Electric mixer

FILLING:

Fresh blood orange juice	2¼ cups (5.4 dL)
Superfine or extra fine sugar	3½ ounces (100 g); ½ cup
Fresh lemon juice	1 tablespoon (1.5 cL)
Unflavored gelatin	3½ teaspoons (1.8 cL)
Heavy cream, well chilled	1¾ cups (4.2 dL)

CAKE:

Joconde-orange marmalade roll (page 276)	One roll 6 inches (15 cm) long
Sponge cake (page 271)	Two 8¾-inch (22-cm) rounds

BRUSHING-SYRUP MIXTURE:

Heavy syrup (page 452)	¼ cup + 1 tablespoon (7.5 cL)
Curaçao liqueur	¼ cup + 1 tablespoon (7.5 cL)

DECORATION:

Heavy syrup	½ cup (1.2 dL)
Blood orange slice, reserved from the oranges juiced for the filling	One slice ⅛ inch (3 mm) thick

ACCOMPANIMENT:

Crème anglaise (page 436)	1½ cups (3.5 dL)
Curaçao liqueur	1 tablespoon + 1 teaspoon (2 cL)

continued

1. Stir together the blood orange juice, superfine sugar, and lemon juice. Pour about one third of the sweetened juice into a butter melter and stir in the gelatin. Let the gelatin soften, then warm over low heat, stirring constantly, until the gelatin dissolves. Remove from the heat and pour into a stainless steel mixing bowl. Stir in the remaining juice, and allow to cool, stirring occasionally. Do not allow it to set. While the sweetened juice is cooling, chill the bowl and the wire whip or beater of the mixer in the refrigerator.

2. Pour the heavy cream into the chilled mixer bowl and whip the cream at medium speed in the mixer using the chilled wire whip or beater until it is light and thick and holds soft peaks. Stop whipping.

3. Dip the bottom of the bowl of sweetened juice in a larger bowl of ice water, and stir with a rubber spatula until it just begins to thicken. Immediately remove the bowl from the ice water.

4. Continue whipping the cream at medium speed until it holds stiff peaks, then whip in the sweetened juice to finish the mousse.

5. Place the *vacherin* ring on a tray, with the cake-decorating circle on the bottom. Using a chef's knife, cut from the *joconde*-marmalade roll fourteen slices, each about ⅜ inch (1 cm) thick. Line the sides of the ring with the slices, placing them adjacent to each other in a single row. Using a wavy-edge bread knife, trim the sponge cake rounds to fit neatly inside the lined ring. Place one round on the bottom inside the lined ring, and brush it heavily with the curaçao brushing syrup. Lightly brush the inside of the *joconde*-marmalade lining slices with the curaçao syrup.

6. Scoop half of the blood orange mousse into the ring, spread it evenly, and smooth the surface. Heavily brush the second round of sponge cake with the curaçao syrup, turn it upside down, and place it on top of the mousse. Heavily brush the top side with curaçao syrup as well. Scoop the remaining blood orange mousse on top of the second sponge cake round and spread it to fill the ring. Smooth the top of the mousse and sweep off any excess with a large icing spatula or a metal straightedge to make a flat top surface.

7. Chill the charlotte in the refrigerator for several hours or overnight to set the mousse.

8. Place the heavy syrup and the blood orange slice for decoration in a heavy butter melter and bring to a simmer. Reduce the heat to low and continue simmering gently until the orange rind changes from opaque to translucent, 20 to 30 minutes. Transfer the orange slice and syrup to a small bowl and allow the slice to cool to room temperature in the syrup. When cool, cover airtight until ready to use.

9. Place the chilled charlotte on a bowl or cake pan taller and slightly smaller in diameter than the ring. Using a blow dryer, quickly and evenly warm the outside of the ring to just melt the mousse touching the ring near the top. Carefully slip the ring down off the charlotte. Transfer the charlotte to a serving plate.

10. Drain the candied blood orange slice thoroughly and place it on the center of the charlotte.

11. Serve the charlotte accompanied by the *crème anglaise* flavored with the curaçao.

NOTE: If you prefer to eliminate the alcohol from the brushing syrup, substitute blood orange juice for the curaçao liqueur and omit the curaçao liqueur from the *crème anglaise*.

STORAGE: In the refrigerator for up to 2 or 3 days.

Or, before glazing and unmolding, freeze for up to 2 weeks. Once frozen, cover the top of the charlotte airtight with plastic wrap. Remove the plastic wrap and defrost overnight in the refrigerator, then unmold and decorate as usual.

Gâteau au Fromage Blanc

(FRENCH CHEESECAKE)

The French-style cheesecake is actually based on a mousse made with a fresh, skim milk cheese called *fromage blanc* ("white cheese"). Like many of the other mousses in this chapter, it is assembled in a *vacherin* ring, with sponge cake lining the inside of the ring and sponge cake rounds on the bottom and top of the mousse. We also add a layer of sour cherry jam on the bottom sponge cake layer and glaze the top with cherry jelly. The texture is much lighter and creamier than the somewhat heavy and pasty cheesecakes we Americans are accustomed to.

The cheese we use for this dessert is the *fromage blanc* made by Vermont Butter & Cheese Company. It has 0 percent fat content. If you can't find this cheese or another lowfat *fromage blanc* in your area, you can make the mousse with ricotta (pureeing it in a blender to make it smooth), though the taste of the ricotta is rather insipid by comparison.

For lining the *vacherin* ring you will need a sheet of *joconde* with a wavy design combed in cigarette cookie batter. We like to tint the cigarette batter with burgundy food coloring to give a rich color contrast. The presentation is very elegant and sophisticated. An excellent alternative is to fingerpaint a swirling design in the cigarette batter. Either way, you need a band of the decorated *joconde* only for lining the ring. To minimize the number of sheets of sponge cake you must bake, we suggest using the rest of the sheet of *joconde* for rounds inside the cheesecake. However, if you make these desserts often you will probably want to reserve the decorated *joconde* for the bands lining the ring and use plain *joconde* for the rounds inside.

For 8 to 10 servings

EQUIPMENT:

8¾-inch (22-cm) *vacherin* ring, 2⅜ inches (6 cm) deep

9-inch (24-cm) foil board or matt board cake-decorating circle (page 467)

• cut to fit inside the ring

Electric mixer

CAKE:

Joconde with wavy design combed in burgundy-tinted cigarette cookie batter (page 278)	One 13 × 20-inch (33 × 50-cm) sheet or two 12 × 16-inch (30 × 40-cm) sheets (only one of them with design)

FILLING:

Heavy syrup (page 452)	½ cup (1.2 dL)
Large egg yolks	4
Unflavored gelatin	2 teaspoons (1 cL)
Cold water	2 tablespoons (3 cL)
Fromage blanc	10½ ounces (300 g); 1¼ cups
Heavy cream, well chilled	1½ cups (3.6 dL)
Sour cherry jam	8 ounces (225 g); ½ cup + 3 tablespoons

BRUSHING-SYRUP MIXTURE:

Heavy syrup	¼ cup (6 cL)
European kirsch	¼ cup (6 cL)

GLAZE:

Unflavored gelatin	1 teaspoon (5 mL)
Cold water	⅓ cup (8 cL)
Sour cherry jelly	3½ ounces (100 g); ⅓ cup

1. Cut two bands, each 2 inches (5 cm) wide and with total length at least 28 inches (72 cm), from the sheet of *joconde*. Cut three 8-inch (20-cm) rounds from the remaining *joconde*. Try to get at least one of the rounds (for the bottom layer) in one piece, but you will definitely need to piece the *joconde* together to get three rounds out of one large sheet or two small sheets of *joconde*. The alternative is to bake another sheet of *joconde* without the combed design, in which case you can easily get three rounds in one piece.

2. Bring the heavy syrup to a simmer in a butter melter and whisk it into the yolks. Strain the mixture into a 1-quart (1-L) stainless steel bowl or the top of a small double boiler, and set it over a saucepan of simmering water. Cook for about 30 minutes, scraping down the sides of the bowl every few minutes. Meanwhile, stir the gelatin into the cold water and let it soften. When the egg yolk mixture has thickened and heated to about 180° F (82° C), remove it from the heat and stir in the softened gelatin. Pour into the bowl of the mixer and whip at medium speed until light, thick, and cool. This is a bombe batter.

3. Scoop the *fromage blanc* into a mixing bowl and beat with a wooden spatula to soften it. Beat it into the bombe batter.

4. Using a clean bowl and wire whip or beater (chilled in the refrigerator if you have a second set), whip the heavy cream in the mixer at medium speed until it is light and thick and holds stiff peaks. Whip the *fromage blanc* mixture into the whipped cream to finish the mousse.

5. Place the *vacherin* ring on a tray, with the cake-decorating circle on the bottom. Line the ring with the bands of *joconde*, trimming the ends so they fit tightly together with no overlap. Place a round of *joconde* on the bottom inside the lined ring and brush it heavily with the kirsch brushing syrup. Lightly brush the inside of the *joconde* lining band with the kirsch syrup.

6. Spread the cherry jam over the round on the bottom of the ring. Place a second round of *joconde* inside the ring on top of the jam and brush it heavily with the kirsch syrup.

7. Scoop the cheese mousse into the ring and spread it evenly to fill the ring to the top of the *joconde* lining strips (about ⅜ inch = 1 cm below the top of the ring). Heavily brush the third round of *joconde* with the kirsch syrup, turn it upside down, and place it on top of the mousse. Fill the ring to the top with the remaining mousse and sweep off the excess with a large icing spatula or a metal straightedge to make a flat surface.

8. Chill the cheesecake in the refrigerator to set the mousse.

9. For the glaze, stir the gelatin into the cold water and let it soften. Heat the jelly in a butter melter, stirring occasionally until melted. Add the softened gelatin and stir until the gelatin dissolves. Pour into a small stainless steel bowl and let cool. Dip the bottom of the bowl in a larger bowl of ice water and stir until it begins to thicken very lightly. Remove the bowl from the ice water immediately. Pour the glaze on the top of the mousse and spread it quickly with a soft pastry brush to make a thick, even coating of glaze, letting the excess flow over the sides of the ring and being careful not to damage the surface of the mousse. Refrigerate to set the glaze.

10. Place the chilled cheesecake on a bowl or cake pan taller and slightly smaller in diameter than the ring. Using a blow dryer, quickly and evenly warm the outside of the ring to just melt the mousse and glaze touching the ring near the top. Carefully slip the ring down off the cheesecake.

11. Refrigerate the cheesecake until ready to serve.

VARIATION: You can use black currant jam instead of sour cherry jam, replace the kirsch in the brushing-syrup mixture with crème de cassis, and glaze the top with black currant jelly instead of cherry jelly.

STORAGE: In the refrigerator for up to 2 or 3 days.

Or, before glazing and unmolding, the cheesecake can be frozen in the ring for up to 2 weeks. Once frozen, cover the top surface airtight with plastic wrap. When ready to finish the cheesecake, remove the plastic wrap and let it defrost overnight in the refrigerator. Then glaze and unmold as usual.

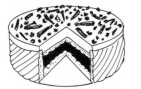

Nelusko

Nelusko was a character in Meyerbeer's opera *L'Orientale*. The name has long been associated with a frozen dessert, *bombe nelusko*, made from a chocolate *parfait* encased in *praliné* ice cream. In recent decades, *nelusko* has been generalized to many other desserts which contain chocolate and *praliné*. This mousse cake pairs two creamy mousses, the bottom layer chocolate and the top *praliné*, and wraps them in a band of diagonally piped sponge cake. Chocolate shavings on top supply a casual decorative touch.

Depending on your taste, you can brush the sponge cake with either Cognac or bourbon syrup.

For 8 to 10 servings

EQUIPMENT:

8¾-inch (22-cm) *vacherin* ring, 2⅜ inches (6 cm) deep
9-inch (24-cm) foil board or matt board cake-decorating circle (page 467)
• cut to fit inside the ring
Electric mixer

CAKE:

Diagonally piped sponge cake (page 228)	One 13 × 20-inch (33 × 50-cm) sheet or two 12 × 16-inch (30 × 40-cm) sheets

FILLINGS:

Unflavored gelatin	1½ teaspoons (8 mL)
Cold water	1 tablespoon (1.5 cL)
Milk	¾ cup (1.8 dL)
Superfine or extra fine sugar	7 ounces (200 g); 1 cup
Large egg yolks	6
Heavy cream, well chilled	2¼ cups (5.4 dL)
Heavy cream, heated to lukewarm	¼ cup (6 cL)
European bittersweet chocolate, melted	3½ ounces (100 g)
Praliné (page 446)	3 ounces (85 g); ¼ cup + 1 tablespoon

BRUSHING-SYRUP MIXTURE:

Heavy syrup (page 452)	¼ cup (6 cL)
Cognac or bourbon	¼ cup (6 cL)

continued

DECORATION:

Chocolate shavings (page 423)   1½ ounces (40 g)

Chocolate cigarettes (page 424, optional)   A few

Confectioners' sugar for dusting

1. Cut two bands, each 2 inches (5 cm) wide and with total length at least 28 inches (72 cm), from the sponge cake. Cut two 8-inch (20-cm) rounds from the remaining sponge cake. Try to get at least one of the rounds (for the bottom layer) in one piece, but you may need to piece the sponge cake together to get two rounds out of one large sheet.

2. Stir the gelatin into the cold water and let it soften. In a heavy 1-quart (1-L) saucepan, combine the milk with ¼ cup + 2 tablespoons (75 g) of the superfine sugar. Bring the milk and sugar to a simmer. Combine the remaining superfine sugar with the egg yolks in a small mixing bowl and beat with a wire whisk until lemon-colored. Whisk in the simmering milk. Strain the mixture through a fine sieve back into the saucepan and cook over low to medium heat, beating constantly with the wire whisk, until the mixture thickens and barely comes to a simmer. Remove it from the heat and stir in the softened gelatin. Pour into the bowl of the mixer, and whip at medium speed until light, thick, and cool. This is a bombe batter.

3. Whip the heavy cream at medium speed in the mixer, using a clean (and chilled if you have two sets) bowl and wire whip or beater until it is light and thick and holds stiff peaks. Then whip in the bombe batter to make the mousse. Stop whipping as soon as the bombe batter and cream are uniformly mixed.

4. Divide the mousse in half.

Gradually stir the lukewarm heavy cream into the melted chocolate. Take about ½ cup (1.2 dL) of mousse from one half and beat it into the melted chocolate using a wire whisk. Fold the chocolate mixture back into the remainder of this half of the mousse using the wire whisk.

Place the *praliné* in a small mixing bowl. Take about ½ cup (1.2 dL) of mousse from the other half and gradually beat it into the *praliné* with a wire whisk (you can use the same whisk as for the chocolate mousse) to make it smooth, with no lumps of *praliné*. Fold the *praliné* mixture back into the second half of the mousse using the wire whisk.

5. Place the *vacherin* ring on a tray, with the cake-decorating circle on the bottom. Line the ring with the bands of sponge cake, trimming the ends so they fit tightly together with no overlap. Place a round of sponge cake on the bottom inside the lined ring and brush it heavily with the Cognac or bourbon brushing syrup. Lightly brush the inside of the sponge cake lining band with the syrup.

6. Scoop the chocolate mousse into the ring and spread it evenly, filling the ring about halfway. Smooth the surface. Heavily brush the second round of sponge cake with the Cognac or bourbon syrup, turn it upside down, and place it on top of the mousse. Heavily brush the top side with syrup as well. Scoop the *praliné* mousse on top of the second round of sponge cake and spread it to fill the ring. Sweep off the excess with a large icing spatula or a metal straightedge to make a flat surface.

7. Chill the *nelusko* in the freezer for several hours or overnight to set the mousse.

8. Place the chilled *nelukso* on a bowl or cake pan taller and slightly smaller in diameter than the ring. Using a blow dryer, quickly and evenly warm the outside of the ring to just melt the mousse touching the ring near the top. Carefully slip the ring down off the *nelusko*. Place the *nelusko* back on the tray and let it defrost in the refrigerator.

9. Scatter the chocolate shavings, and some small chocolate cigarettes if you have them, over the top of the *praliné* mousse.

10. Refrigerate the *nelusko* until ready to serve. Then lightly dust confectioners' sugar over the chocolate shavings on top.

HOWS AND WHYS: Freezing the *nelusko* before unmolding makes the ring come off more cleanly, without smearing mousse on the side of the piped sponge cake lining the ring.

STORAGE: In the refrigerator for up to 2 or 3 days.

Or, before unmolding, the *nelusko* can be kept in the freezer for up to 2 weeks. Once frozen, cover the top surface airtight with plastic wrap. When ready to unmold the *nelusko*, remove the plastic wrap and proceed as usual.

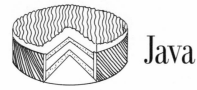

Java

Java is the main island of Indonesia, and under Dutch colonial rule it was a major producer of fine coffee. During the colonial period, its full-bodied beans were held in such high esteem that the word "java" entered the English language as slang for coffee.

This is a charlotte for lovers of caffè latte. Like *nelusko*, the mousse is based on a bombe batter, but here it is flavored with coffee. The coffee is incorporated from the outset by steeping coarsely crushed espresso beans in hot milk, then straining out the beans.

The lining for the ring is a band of *joconde* with a design combed in chocolate cigarette cookie batter.

For 8 to 10 servings

EQUIPMENT:

8¾-inch (22-cm) *vacherin* ring, 2⅜ inches (6 cm) deep
9-inch (24-cm) foil board or matt board cake-decorating circle (page 467)
• cut to fit inside the ring
Electric mixer

CAKE:

Joconde with diagonally striped design combed in chocolate cigarette cookie batter (page 278)	One 13 × 20-inch (33 × 50-cm) sheet or two 12 × 16-inch (30 × 40-cm) sheets (only one of them with design)

FILLING:

Espresso coffee beans, coarsely crushed in a mortar and pestle	1¾ ounces (50 g); ¾ cup
Milk	¾ cup (1.8 dL)
Unflavored gelatin	2 teaspoons (1 cL)
Cold water	2 tablespoons (3 cL)
Superfine or extra fine sugar	6 ounces (175 g); ¾ cup + 2 tablespoons
Large egg yolks	5
Heavy cream, well chilled	2¼ cups (5.4 dL)

BRUSHING-SYRUP MIXTURE:

Heavy syrup (page 452)	¼ cup (6 cL)
Double-strength brewed espresso (page 456)	¼ cup (6 cL)

1. Cut two bands, each 2 inches (5 cm) wide and with total length at least 28 inches (72 cm), from the *joconde*. Cut two 8-inch (20-cm) rounds from the remaining *joconde*. Try to get at least one of the rounds (for the bottom layer) in one piece, but you may need to piece the *joconde* together to get two rounds out of one large sheet.

2. Combine the crushed coffee beans with the milk in a small saucepan and bring to a simmer. Remove from the heat, cover, and let steep for 10 minutes. Stir the gelatin into the cold water and let it soften. Strain the milk through a fine sieve into a heavy 1-quart (1-L) saucepan, stir in ¼ cup + 2 tablespoons (75 g) of the sugar, and bring to a simmer. Combine the remaining superfine sugar with the egg yolks in a small mixing bowl and beat with a wire whisk until lemon-colored. Whisk in the simmering milk. Strain the mixture through a fine sieve back into the saucepan and cook over low to medium heat, beating constantly with the wire whisk, until the mixture thickens and barely comes to a simmer. Remove it from the heat and stir in the softened gelatin. Pour into the bowl of the mixer, and whip at medium speed until light, thick, and cool. This is a bombe batter.

3. Whip the heavy cream at medium speed in the mixer, using a clean (and chilled if you have two sets) bowl and wire whip or beater until it is light and thick and holds stiff peaks. Then whip in the bombe batter to make the mousse. Stop whipping as soon as the bombe batter and cream are uniformly mixed.

4. Place the *vacherin* ring on a tray, with the cake-decorating circle on the bottom. Line the ring with the bands of *joconde*, trimming the ends so they fit tightly together with no overlap. Place a round of *joconde* on the bottom inside the lined ring and brush it heavily with the espresso brushing syrup. Lightly brush the inside of the *joconde* lining band with the espresso syrup.

5. Scoop half of the coffee mousse into the ring and spread it evenly, filling the ring about halfway. Heavily brush the second round of *joconde* with the espresso syrup, turn it upside down, and place it on top of the mousse. Heavily brush the top side with espresso syrup as well. Scoop the remaining coffee mousse on top of the second round of *joconde* and spread it to fill the ring. Sweep a long wavy-edge bread knife across the top of the ring, using an undulating motion to take off the excess mousse and make a decorative pattern on top of the mousse.

6. Chill the *java* in the freezer for several hours or overnight to set the mousse.

7. Place the chilled *java* on a bowl or cake pan taller and slightly smaller in diameter than the ring. Using a blow dryer, quickly and evenly warm the outside of the ring to just melt the mousse touching the ring near the top. Carefully slip the ring down off the *java*. Place the *java* back on the tray and let it defrost in the refrigerator.

HOWS AND WHYS: Freezing the *java* before unmolding makes the ring come off more cleanly, without smearing mousse on the side of the *joconde* lining the ring.

STORAGE: In the refrigerator for up to 2 or 3 days.

Or, before unmolding, the *java* can be kept in the freezer for up to 2 weeks. Once frozen, cover the top surface airtight with plastic wrap. When ready to unmold the *java*, remove the plastic wrap and proceed as usual.

Turin

A band of finger-painted *joconde* wrapped around a luscious chestnut mousse filling gives this mousse cake a striking presentation. Turin, the capitol of the Piedmont region in northern Italy, is famous for its chestnuts.

For 8 to 10 servings

EQUIPMENT:

8¾-inch (22-cm) *vacherin* ring, 2⅜ inches (6 cm) deep

9-inch (24-cm) foil board or matt board cake-decorating circle (page 467)

• cut to fit inside the ring

Electric mixer

CAKE:

Joconde with swirling design finger-painted in chocolate cigarette cookie batter (page 278)	One 13 × 20-inch (33 × 50-cm) sheet or two 12 × 16-inch (30 × 40-cm) sheets (only one of them with design)

FILLING:

Cold water	3 tablespoons (4.5 cL)
Heavy syrup (page 452)	3 tablespoons (4.5 cL)
Unflavored gelatin	1½ teaspoons (8 mL)
Heavy cream, well chilled	2¼ cups (5.4 dL)
Dark Jamaican or Haitian rum	2 tablespoons (3 cL)
Chestnut spread (*creme de marron,* page 498)	Two 8¾-ounce (250-g) cans, or one 17½-ounce (500-g) can

BRUSHING-SYRUP MIXTURE:

Dark Jamaican or Haitian rum	¼ cup (6 cL)
Heavy syrup	¼ cup (6 cL)

DECORATION:

Confectioners' sugar	½ ounce (12 g); 2 tablespoons
Heavy cream	½ cup (1.2 dL)
Marron glacé (optional)	1

1. Cut two bands, each 2 inches (5 cm) wide and with total length at least 28 inches (72 cm), from the *joconde*. Cut two 8-inch (20-cm) rounds from the remaining *joconde*. Try to get at least one of the rounds (for the bottom layer) in one piece, but you may need to piece the *joconde* together to get two rounds out of one large sheet.

2. Chill the bowl and the wire whip or beater of the mixer in the refrigerator. Combine the water and heavy syrup in a butter melter, and stir in the gelatin. Let the gelatin soften, then warm over low heat, stirring constantly, until the gelatin dissolves. Remove from the heat and pour into a small stainless steel bowl.

3. Pour the heavy cream into the chilled mixer bowl and whip the cream at medium speed in the mixer with the chilled wire whip or beater until it is light and thick and holds soft peaks. Stop whipping.

4. Stir the rum into the chestnut spread, then stir in the dissolved gelatin with a wire whisk to mix thoroughly. Continue whipping the cream at medium speed until it holds stiff peaks, then whip in the chestnut spread mixture to finish the chestnut mousse.

5. Place the *vacherin* ring on a tray, with the cake-decorating circle on the bottom. Line the ring with the bands of *joconde*, trimming the ends so they fit tightly together with no overlap. Place a round of *joconde* on the bottom inside the lined ring and brush it heavily with the rum brushing syrup. Lightly brush the inside of the *joconde* lining band with the rum syrup.

6. Scoop half of the chestnut mousse into the ring and spread it evenly, filling the ring about halfway. Heavily brush the second round of *joconde* with the rum syrup, turn it upside down, and place it on top of the mousse. Heavily brush the top side with rum syrup as well. Scoop the remaining chestnut mousse on top of the second round of *joconde* and spread it to fill the ring. Sweep off the excess with a large icing spatula or a metal straightedge to make a flat surface.

7. Chill the *turin* in the freezer for several hours or overnight to set the mousse.

8. Place the chilled *turin* on a bowl or cake pan taller and slightly smaller in diameter than the ring. Using a blow dryer, quickly and evenly warm the outside of the ring to just melt the mousse touching the ring near the top. Carefully slip the ring down off the *turin*. Place the *turin* back on the tray and let it defrost in the refrigerator.

9. Sift the confectioners' sugar into the bowl of the mixer, stir in the heavy cream, and refrigerate for about an hour. Chill the wire whip or beater of the mixer as well. Whip the cream at medium speed in the mixer. When the cream holds soft peaks, slow down to avoid overbeating. Continue whipping until the cream is light and thick and holds stiff peaks.

10. Scoop the whipped cream into the pastry bag and pipe ten or twelve rosettes around the circumference of the mousse cake. Pipe a rosette on the center and four teardrops pointing out from the center. Place the optional *marron glacé* on the rosette in the center.

HOWS AND WHYS: Freezing the *turin* before unmolding makes the ring come off more cleanly, without smearing mousse on the side of the *joconde* lining the ring.

STORAGE: In the refrigerator for up to 2 or 3 days.

Or, before unmolding, the *turin* can be kept in the freezer for up to 2 weeks. Once frozen, cover the top surface airtight with plastic wrap. When ready to unmold the *turin*, remove the plastic wrap and proceed as usual.

CHAPTER SEVEN

Logs and Loaves

In bygone days many traditions developed around the custom of burning a large log in the hearth throughout Christmas Eve. This *bûche de Noël* (literally "Christmas log") was poked occasionally by whoever was tending the fire, and in the French countryside it was sprinkled with various beverages, the choice of which depended on the region, to enhance the scent of the fire. The ashes of the Christmas log, which we call a yule log in English, were supposed to have magical properties.

Sometime around the end of the nineteenth century, Parisian pastry chefs began making a gâteau in imitation of the form of a log. It became symbolic of the traditional yule log and was dubbed *bûche de Noël*. Soon everyone had to have this new gâteau to serve at the midnight feast following Christmas Eve mass. Today, the mention of a *bûche de Noël* in Paris is probably more likely to evoke the image of the gâteau than of a real log in a fireplace.

While a few other log-shaped gâteau are occasionally made in France, the *bûche de Noël*, which we will refer to as the yule log, is the only one that is widely known. You can assemble this gâteau in one of two ways. Either you can roll up a sheet of sponge cake (we use *joconde*) with a buttercream filling to make the yule log, or for a less rich yule log you can bake sponge cake in a special trough-shaped yule log mold, then slice it in half and fill the center with a layer of buttercream. Whichever method you choose, you then cover the log with buttercream using a pastry bag to simulate the bark of a tree, and adorn it with meringue mushrooms and almond-paste holly berries and leaves. The yule log is a splendid party dessert and makes a truly luxurious gift. Decorating it can be a very entertaining family project during the holiday season.

Although the yule log mold was originally intended for baking, you can also use it as a form for assembling gâteaux. The increasing popularity of gâteaux filled with light mousses rather than rich buttercreams, combined with the desire to use those yule log molds throughout the year, has inspired the development of the mousse log. For these gâteaux, you line the yule log mold with a band of sponge cake or slices of a *joconde*-jam sandwich or roll, fill it with a mousse, and then place a band of sponge cake on top of the mousse to eventually become the bottom of the gâteau. After unmolding, you can glaze or frost the outside of the log.

Depending on your inclination, you can take the mousse log in a variety of directions. One is to use it for a yule log, frosting it using a pastry bag. (In fact, this is the only presentation for which you frost a log.) For this purpose the best frosting to use is Italian meringue, since it keeps the dessert light. A totally different option is to line the mold with slices of a *joconde*-jam roll or sandwich and fill it with a fruit mousse, as you would for a charlotte, then brush it with a clear jelly glaze after unmolding.

The size of the yule log mold can be both a benefit and a problem. The one we recommend is 20 inches (50 cm) long. It makes a truly grand holiday dessert, but it may not fit on any platter you own. This problem can be surmounted by cutting the gâteau in half to make two desserts. Since these gâteaux freeze well, this option offers a nice degree of flexibility for your entertaining needs.

Assembling a gâteau based on a sponge cake (such as génoise) baked in a loaf pan has much in common with assembling one based on a sponge cake baked in a yule log mold. As you already know, the loaf shape is quite standard for simple cakes such as pound cake. However, for more elaborate gâteaux, the loaf is used infrequently in France. The reason is almost certainly that assembling a layered gâteau in a loaf shape can be a bit awkward in comparison with a round gâteau. Nonetheless, loaf-shaped gâteaux add variety to the repertoire, and, like log-shaped gâteaux, they are quite easy to cut and serve.

CAKE SIZES

To minimize the number of molds you need, we have standardized all of the recipes in this chapter to use either a yule log mold 20 inches (50 cm) long and 2¾ inches (7 cm) wide, or a 6-cup (1.5-L) loaf pan. When used for baking génoise, both of these molds require the same amount of batter as our standard 9-inch (24-cm) round cake pan. For mousse logs, the amount of mousse you will need for the yule log mold is half of the amount you would use for a charlotte assembled in an 8¾-inch (22-cm) *vacherin* ring. These equivalences allow you to switch back and forth between presentations very easily.

Preparing and Filling Yule Log Molds and Loaf Pans

①

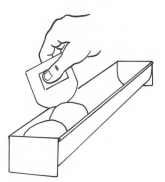

②

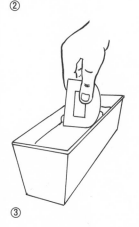

③

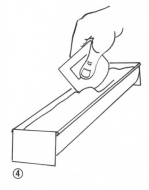

④

Brush the inside of the yule log mold or loaf pan with melted butter ①, and let the butter set. Then spoon some flour into the mold, and gradually tilt, rotate, and shake the mold to distribute an even coating of flour over the butter on the bottom and sides of the mold. Invert the mold and tap it to dislodge the excess flour.

Transfer the batter to the yule log mold or loaf pan by pouring and scraping it from the mixing bowl into the mold or by scooping up the batter with a bowl scraper and depositing it in the mold a little at a time ②. Using the curved edge of the bowl scraper or rubber spatula, smooth the surface of the batter ③. Ideally, you want the top surface of the cake to be flat when it comes out of the oven. Some (but not all) batters have a tendency to dome in the center during baking. If the batter is thick enough, you can reduce this tendency and get a cake with a flatter top by smoothing the batter from the center up the sides of the mold, making a depression in the center ④.

Unmolding Logs and Loaves

When the cake comes out of the oven, loosen the edges by sliding the tip of a paring knife or small icing spatula between the edge of the cake and the side of the mold; this allows the cake to settle evenly and makes it easier to unmold. Slide the mold onto a wire rack, and let the cake rest and begin to cool for 5 minutes.

Unmold the cake onto a wire rack. Sometimes you can do this by turning the mold on its side and sliding the cake out. More often it is easier to place a wire rack upside down on top of the mold and turn the mold and rack upside down together, then lift off the mold. Either way, you must turn the cake upside down again. The side that was on the bottom in the oven must be against the wire rack during cooling because this side will become the top of the finished gâteau and must remain flat for a loaf or level for a log. Also, the surface of the cake that was on top in the oven tends

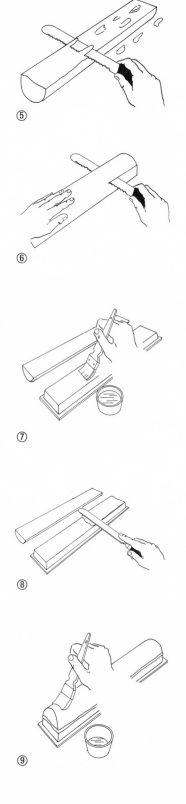

to stick to the wire rack if the cake is allowed to cool with that side down. For logs and loaves it can be awkward to turn the unmolded cake upside down between two racks (as we do for round cakes and sheets). We find it easier to carefully roll over a log on the rack or to turn a loaf first onto its side and then onto its flat top surface.

Let the cake cool on the wire rack.

CARDBOARD BASES

As for round and rectangular gâteaux, assembling the gâteau on a cardboard base will make it easier to decorate and move without damage. Cut the cardboard base from a sheet of matt board with a silver or gold foil surface (available from framing and art supply stores, see page 467). You may also be able to find rectangular foil board lids (page 467) for aluminum foil take-out containers in a size appropriate for loaf-shaped gâteaux.

For yule logs, which can be very awkward, an even better alternative is a rectangular foil board catering platter (page 467). These platters are about the size of a large place mat—14 × 21 inches (35× 53 cm) and the cardboard is thicker and more rigid than matt board. They have scalloped edges and can even be used as serving platters in a pinch. Cut them to size with a utility knife (with disposable razor blade), using a metal straightedge as a guide. As a final (and much less elegant) alternative for yule logs, you can cut a piece of heavy corrugated cardboard to size and cover it with aluminum foil.

ASSEMBLING YULE LOGS AND LOAF-SHAPED GÂTEAUX

We use the rolled log assembly method in only one recipe, our coffee yule log (page 348), and the method is described there.

Yule logs and loaf-shaped gâteaux based on molded sponge cakes are very similar to each other in construction, though very different in proportions and decoration. Cut a rectangle of matt board or foil board about ⅜ inch (1 cm) larger in length and width than the sponge cake so that it will provide a guide and support for frosting. If the bottom of the sponge cake isn't flat, cut off just enough of the uneven bottom with a wavy-edge bread knife to level it ⑤. Turn the sponge cake right side up and cut the sponge cake horizontally into two (for a yule log ⑥) or three (for a loaf ⑩) layers

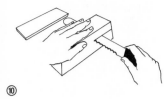

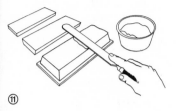

with the bread knife. Place the first layer on the matt board or foil board rectangle, centering it carefully.

Brush the top of the first layer and the bottom of the second layer of sponge cake heavily with flavored syrup to moisten and flavor them ⑦. Spread a thin layer of filling over the first sponge cake layer ⑧, ⑪, then place the second sponge cake layer on top, brushed side down. For a yule log, brush the entire outside of the sponge cake lightly with flavored syrup ⑨. For a loaf, brush the top of the second layer and the bottom of the third layer of sponge cake heavily with the flavored syrup ⑫. Spread a thin layer of filling over the second sponge cake layer and place the third sponge cake layer on top. Brush the top and sides of the sponge cake lightly with the syrup.

FROSTING A YULE LOG

Whether rolled or assembled from a molded génoise, yule logs are frosted by piping buttercream or Italian meringue over the surface to simulate the bark of a tree. The method is described in each recipe.

FROSTING A LOAF-SHAPED GÂTEAU

Conceptually, frosting a loaf isn't much different from frosting a round gâteau. However, in practice it is much more awkward.

First spread frosting over the top of the loaf ⑬ using an icing spatula with a blade about 10 inches (25 cm) long. Then spread frosting over all four sides, leaving a rim of frosting around the top edge ⑭. Do not lift the gâteau off the countertop—it will not balance easily on your fingertips.

Next, sweep the icing spatula over the top of the gâteau ⑮ to smooth the frosting and cut off the excess. Start with the icing spatula at the right side of the gâteau with the face of the blade at an angle of about 30° relative to the top surface. Sweep the blade across the top, keeping the edge of the blade at a fixed height and turning the face of the blade. When you reach the left side of the gâteau, the face of the blade should have rotated through about 90°. As you continue the right to left motion past the left side of the gâteau, sweep the blade up to avoid dropping the excess frosting. This motion spreads the rim of frosting across the gâteau and smooths the surface. Clean off the blade on the rim of the bowl of frosting. If the top of the

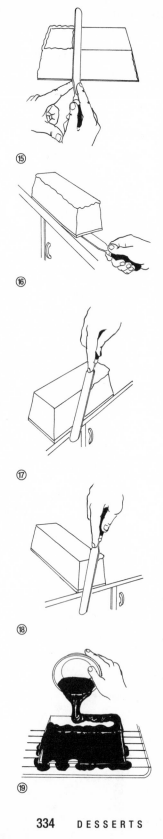

gâteau isn't quite smooth, repeat the motion, this time moving from left to right and rotating the blade of the icing spatula in the reverse direction. Take off just enough frosting to get a level surface.

When the top of the gâteau is smooth, use the icing spatula to slide the gâteau to the edge of the countertop ⑯. One side at a time, line up the edge of the matt board rectangle under the gâteau with the edge of the counter-top. Place the blade of the icing spatula against the side of the gâteau, with the face of the blade nearly parallel to the surface. Using the matt board as a guide, sweep the edge of the blade across the side of the gâteau to smooth the surface and clean off the excess frosting ⑰. As you do so, draw the blade downward and turn the face of the blade toward you. Clean off the blade on the rim of the bowl, and repeat as many times as necessary to smooth the frosting on the side you are working on. Then rotate the gâteau with the icing spatula to line up the next side at the edge of the countertop, and repeat ⑱ until you have smoothed all four sides of the gâteau. When you have worked around all four sides, clean up the frosting at the corners.

Do not expect the frosting to be perfect, and don't worry about any unevenness. You will mask the imperfections by glazing the loaf or enrobing it in almond paste.

GLAZING A LOAF-SHAPED GÂTEAU

The only glaze we use for loaf-shaped gâteaux is chocolate. As for any other gâteau, melt the chocolate and temper it (see page 538 for details). The temperature of the chocolate must be between 86° and 91°F (30 to 33°C). Bring a little clarified butter to room temperature. Beat it with a wooden spatula to make it smooth and creamy, then stir it into the chocolate to thin it. Allow plenty of extra chocolate so that it can flow over the entire surface easily. You don't want to spend much time spreading the glaze with an icing spatula, because it will begin to set quickly and you will leave smudge marks.

Place the gâteau on a wire rack, with a large tray underneath to catch the excess glaze. Pour the chocolate glaze over the top of the gâteau in a rectangle just inside the perimeter so that some of it flows naturally over the edges ⑲. Quickly smooth the top surface with an icing spatula to cover the top with a thin layer of glaze and make the excess flow evenly down the sides ⑳. Try to make the glaze cover all sides of the gâteau. If there are any bare or uneven spots around the sides, pour additional chocolate glaze over

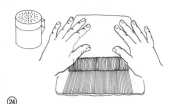

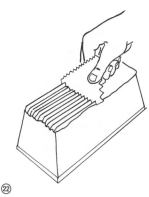

the sides that need it, and tilt the wire rack and tap it on the tray to be sure the chocolate flows evenly over all four sides. Smooth the glaze over any remaining bare or uneven spots with the edge of the icing spatula. Work as quickly as you can because once the glaze begins to thicken you will no longer be able to spread it smoothly.

Allow the chocolate to thicken and begin to set. Then use a paring knife or a small icing spatula to clean off any chocolate glaze that has accumulated around the base of the gâteau ㉑. Slide a large icing spatula under the gâteau and transfer it to a clean tray or serving platter. Allow the chocolate glaze to set.

A variation on this procedure is to glaze only the sides of the loaf. To do this, cut a rectangle of kitchen parchment to precisely the size of the top of the loaf. Lay it on top, carefully lining up the edges and pressing gently to secure it in place. Pour the glaze over the edges of the parchment so that it flows directly down the sides of the loaf, with as little on top of the parchment as possible. Let the chocolate begin to set, then peel off the parchment and clean off the bottom edge as usual.

A nice touch if you are glazing only the sides of the loaf is to make a decorative pattern in the frosting on top using a cake-decorating comb ㉒ (page 465). If you want to do this, spread the layer of frosting ¼ inch (6 mm) thick on top and comb the pattern into it before you smooth the frosting on the sides of the loaf.

Enrobing a Loaf-Shaped Gâteau with Almond Paste

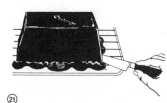

Covering the outside of the loaf with textured sheets of almond paste is a very decorative way to mask the imperfections in the frosting. Form the almond paste into a rectangular pad. Dust the pad and your countertop with confectioners' sugar. Use a plain rolling pin to roll out the almond paste into a rough rectangle ㉓ a little more than ⅛ inch (3 mm) thick, dusting with more confectioners' sugar as needed to prevent sticking. Then roll a textured (ribbed, checkerboard, or basketweave) rolling pin over the sheet of almond paste to impress the texture in it ㉔. Or you can texture the sheet of almond paste on a textured surface, such as a ribbed sheet of vinyl floor mat (page 480) or a Lego assembly board. Dust the sheet of almond paste with confectioners' sugar and turn it upside down on the textured surface. Roll your plain rolling pin over the almond paste to impress the texture. Then carefully lift the almond paste off the surface; or,

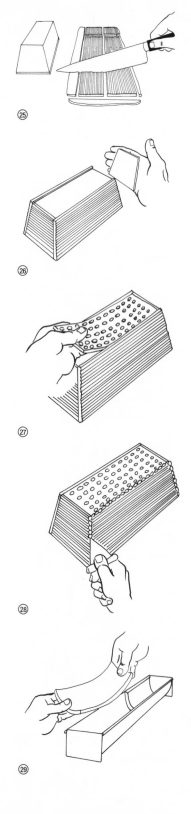

if it was rolled on a sheet of ribbed vinyl, turn the sheet right side up and peel off the vinyl.

Measure the length and width of the base of the loaf, and the height of the loaf along the sloping side. Cut from the sheet of almond paste two bands, each as wide as the loaf is high. From each band cut two rectangles ㉕, one as long as the length of the loaf and the other as long as the width of the loaf.

One at a time, press the rectangles of almond paste against the sides of the loaf, carefully lining up the top and bottom edges ㉖; then trim the vertical edges with a scissors so they don't extend past the corners of the loaf.

Gather together the almond paste trimmings (discarding any that have frosting on them), form them into a rectangular pad, and roll the pad out into another sheet a little more than ⅛ inch (3 mm) thick. Impress a texture in the sheet of almond paste using either a textured rolling pin or a Lego assembly board. Measure the length and width of the top of the loaf (inside the almond paste sides), cut a rectangle of almond paste to these dimensions, and carefully place it on top of the loaf ㉗.

You can get particularly handsome effects by combining different textures in the almond paste. For example, you can use a horizontal ribbed texture around the sides and a checkerboard or basketweave on top; or use the checkerboard or basketweave on the sides and the ribbed texture on top. Either way, you need to mask the seams where the rectangles of almond paste meet. To do this, scoop a little of the excess frosting into a parchment decorating tube, and pipe a continuous bead of teardrops over each seam ㉘. If you prefer, you can use royal icing (page 419) instead of frosting to mask the seams.

Another alternative for decorating the top of the loaf is to omit the rectangle of almond paste on top and instead make a decorative pattern in the frosting on top using a cake-decorating comb, just as you would when glazing only the sides of the loaf with chocolate.

ASSEMBLING A MOUSSE LOG

Brush the inside of the yule log mold with melted butter and dust it with granulated sugar. This will make the unmolding very easy.

For the most basic mousse log, you line the mold with a sheet of

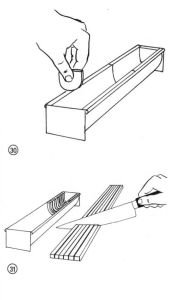

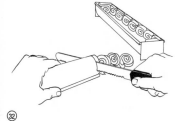

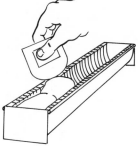

joconde. Cut two bands of *joconde* just wide enough to wrap around the inside surface of the mold. For our 2¾-inch- (7-cm-) wide yule log molds, the width of the band must be about 5⅛ inches (13 cm). You will need the combined length of the two bands to be 19¾ inches (50 cm), which is just a little larger than you can get in one piece (unless you bake on commercial size baking sheets). Turn each band upside down and carefully drape it down into the mold ㉙, lining up the long edges with the sides of the mold and butting the two bands together to cover the entire length of the mold. If the log will be glazed with chocolate, you can line the ends of the mold with two small pieces of *joconde* ㉚. However, this step is optional. If you plan to cut the log in half to make two gâteaux, you can cut two more end pieces, insert them back to back in the center of the mold, and slit the *joconde* lining at the center to mark where you will cut.

When you will be filling the log with a fruit mousse, you can create beautiful presentations by lining the yule log mold with slices of a *joconde*-jam sandwich or roll instead of a simple band of *joconde*. Slice the roll or sandwich ⅜ inch (1 cm) thick. If you are using a *joconde*-jam sandwich, cut the slices into 5⅛-inch (13-cm) lengths ㉛. You will need about four of these pieces. One at a time, carefully drape each piece into the mold, arranging the stripes crosswise and butting the pieces together to cover the entire length of the mold. Leave the ends of the mold unlined. On the other hand, if you are using a *joconde*-and-jam roll, start by lining each end of the mold with a slice of the roll. Then arrange a row of slices on each side of the mold ㉜ so that the spirals all run in the same direction, with the tail at the top of the mold, and the slices are butted against each other. (Obviously the slices of the roll will not cover the entire surface of the mold.) If you plan to cut the log in half to make two gâteaux, insert two more slices back to back with a piece of kitchen parchment separating them in the center of the mold.

Brush the inside surface of the *joconde* lining or the lining slices with flavored syrup to moisten and flavor them ㉝. If you have lined the mold with slices of *joconde*-jam sandwich or roll, be especially careful to brush them lightly so they don't soak through.

Scoop the mousse into the lined mold ㉞. Fill it almost to the rim and smooth the surface, leaving enough space to accommodate the thickness of another band of *joconde*. Measure the width inside the band of *joconde* or the slices lining the mold, and cut another band of *joconde* (again it will need to

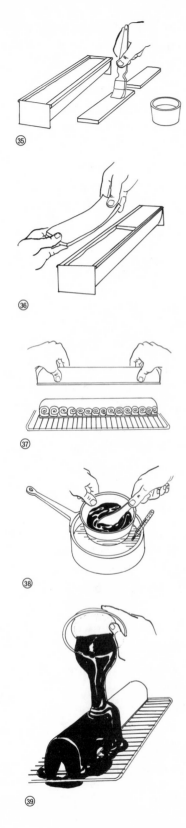

be in two pieces) to fit. Brush the top of the *joconde* with flavored syrup ㉟. Turn it upside down and insert it into the mold on top of the mousse to fill the mold to the rim ㊱.

Refrigerate the log until the mousse is set so that the log will hold its shape. Chill it for at least 2 hours.

If you will be glazing the log, cut a rectangle of matt board or foil board to just fit inside the top of the mold. If you will be frosting the log, cut the rectangle of matt board or foil board about ⅜ inch (1 cm) larger in length and width than the log. Place the rectangle upside down on top of the log. Place a wire rack upside down on top of the yule log mold and turn the mold and wire rack upside down together. The log may slip right out. If not, warm the mold with a blow dryer until the log releases and you can remove the mold ㊲. Return the log to the refrigerator to firm the mousse.

GLAZING A MOUSSE LOG

Before glazing, the mousse must be cold and set so that the glaze won't melt the mousse. If you are cutting the log in half to make two gâteaux, do that after the mousse is set and before glazing.

If you lined the yule log mold with plain *joconde*, you can glaze it with chocolate (thinned with a little clarified butter), with no frosting. Melt the chocolate and temper it ㊳ (see page 538 for details). The temperature of the chocolate must be between 86° and 91°F (30° to 33°C). The clarified butter must be at room temperature. Beat the clarified butter with a wooden spatula to make it smooth and creamy, then stir it into the chocolate. As for loaf-shaped gâteaux, allow plenty of extra chocolate so that it can flow over the entire surface easily. Place the log on a wire rack, with a large tray underneath. Pour chocolate over the top and let it flow down the sides ㊴. Pour additional chocolate glaze over any areas that may need it, and tilt the wire rack and tap it on the tray to be sure the chocolate flows evenly over the entire surface. Allow the chocolate to thicken and begin to set. Then use a paring knife to clean off any chocolate glaze that has accumulated around the base of the log. Slide a large icing spatula under the log and transfer it to a clean tray or serving platter. Allow the chocolate glaze to set.

If you lined the yule log mold with slices of a *joconde*-jam sandwich or roll, then you must glaze it with a clear orange juice glaze. If you lined the mold with plain *joconde*, you can also glaze it this way. Warm the glaze to melt it, then cool it until it barely begins to thicken. Brush the glaze over the surface of the log ㊵ until the entire surface, including both the lining

slices and any exposed mousse, is lightly and evenly coated and glistening. Clean off any excess glaze around the base of the log, and return the log to the refrigerator to set the glaze.

Storage

Gâteaux that are filled and topped with buttercream, ganache (chocolate cream filling), or mousse can be kept in the refrigerator, on a covered cake platter if you have one, for up to 2 days.

These cakes can also be frozen before glazing, enrobing with almond paste, frosting with Italian meringue, or decorating. Once the cake is frozen, cover it airtight with plastic wrap or in a plastic bag and store in the freezer for up to 3 weeks. The day before serving, remove the plastic wrap or bag and defrost the cake overnight in the refrigerator. Then finish the preparation.

Génoise Log

. . . .

The easiest way to prepare génoise for log-shaped cakes is to bake it in a trough mold, called a yule log mold. As the name suggests, this mold is used primarily for yule logs. The quantity of batter in this recipe is about the same as you need for a 9-inch (24-cm) round cake pan. Since the log is less versatile, we have given the recipe for baking just one and adjusted the proportions to require integral numbers of eggs and yolks.

For one log 20 inches (50 cm) long

EQUIPMENT:
Electric mixer
Yule log mold 20 × 3 × 2 inches (50 × 7 × 5 cm)
• brush with melted butter
• dust with flour
Large, heavy baking sheet

BATTER:

Large eggs, at room temperature	4
Large egg yolk, at room temperature	1
Granulated sugar	4½ ounces (125 g); ½ cup + 2 tablespoons
All-purpose flour	3½ ounces (100 g); ½ cup + 3½ tablespoons
Potato starch	⅓ ounce (10 g); 1 tablespoon
Unsalted butter, melted	½ ounce (15 g); 1 tablespoon

Preheat the oven to 375°F (190°C).

1. Combine the whole eggs, yolk, and sugar in a stainless steel mixing bowl, break up the yolks with a wire whisk, and beat until smooth. Set the bowl over a saucepan of simmering water and stir with the whisk until warm (about 100°F=40°C), frothy, and pale yellow.

2. Remove the bowl from the simmering water, and whip at medium speed in the mixer until the batter has risen and cooled, becoming light and thick and almost white in color. It should coat your finger very thickly and form very slowly dissolving ribbons when dropped from the whip.

3. Sift the flour with the potato starch onto a sheet of wax paper. A little at a time, dust the mixture over the batter and fold it in very gently but thoroughly. When the flour and potato starch are completely incorporated, slowly pour the melted butter over the batter and continue folding until the butter is uniformly mixed into the batter.

4. Scoop the batter into the prepared yule log mold, filling it to three fourths of its height. Smooth the surface of the batter and make a slight depression down the center. Place the mold on the baking sheet.

5. Bake until the top of the génoise is lightly browned and firm to the touch but not crusty, about 15 to 18 minutes. The tip of a paring knife inserted in the center of the cake should come out clean.

6. Remove the cake from the oven and slide the tip of a paring knife or small icing spatula between the edge of the cake and the pan to loosen the edge. Let the génoise rest in the pan for about 5 minutes. Unmold the génoise log onto a wire rack. Turn it upside down and let cool to room temperature.

STORAGE: Covered airtight with plastic wrap, for up to 2 days in the refrigerator.

Or freeze for as long as 2 months. If frozen, defrost overnight in the refrigerator, and unwrap the cake at least 2 hours before using to allow condensation produced by defrosting to evaporate.

Almond Génoise Loaf

You can bake any of our génoise recipes from chapter 2 in a loaf pan. The one we use most is almond génoise. Here we give a slightly different recipe which is less fragile and bakes better in a deep loaf pan than the almond génoise batter we use in a round cake pan (page 86).

For one 6-cup (1.5-L) loaf

EQUIPMENT:
Electric mixer
6-cup (1.5-L) loaf pan
• brush with melted butter
• dust with flour
Heavy baking sheet

BATTER:

Large eggs, at room temperature	4
Granulated sugar	2⅔ ounces (75 g); ¼ cup + 2 tablespoons
All-purpose flour	3½ ounces (100 g); ⅔ cup + 1 tablespoon
Almond-and-sugar powder (page 442)	3½ ounces (100 g); ¾ cup
Unsalted butter, melted	½ ounce (15 g); 1 tablespoon

Preheat the oven to 350°F (175°C).

1. Combine the eggs and sugar in a stainless steel mixing bowl, break up the yolks with a wire whisk, and beat until smooth. Set the bowl over a saucepan of simmering water and stir with the whisk until warm (about 100°F = 40°C), frothy, and pale yellow.

2. Remove the bowl from the simmering water, and whip at medium speed in the mixer until the batter has risen and cooled, becoming light and thick and almost white in color. It should coat your finger very thickly and form very slowly dissolving ribbons when dropped from the whip.

3. Sift the flour onto a sheet of wax paper, then mix with the almond-and-sugar powder. A little at a time, dust the mixture over the batter and fold it in very gently but thoroughly. When the flour and almond-and-sugar powder are completely incorporated, slowly pour the melted butter over the batter and continue folding until the butter is uniformly mixed into the batter.

4. Scoop the batter into the prepared loaf pan, filling it to three fourths of its height. Smooth the surface of the batter. (Don't make a depression in the center.) Place the loaf pan on the baking sheet.

5. Bake until the top of the génoise is lightly browned and firm to the touch but not crusty, about 35 to 40 minutes. The tip of a paring knife inserted in the center of the cake should come out clean.

6. Remove the cake from the oven and slide the tip of a paring knife or small icing spatula between the edge of the cake and the pan to loosen the edge. Let the génoise rest in the pan for about 5 minutes. Unmold the génoise loaf onto a wire rack. Turn it upside down and let cool to room temperature.

STORAGE: Covered airtight with plastic wrap, for up to 2 days at room temperature.

Or freeze for as long as 2 months. If frozen, defrost overnight in the refrigerator and unwrap the cake at least 2 hours before using to allow condensation produced by defrosting to evaporate.

Alhambra Sponge Cake

. . . .

This is a chocolate and hazelnut sponge cake designed for the gâteau called *alhambra*.

For one 6-cup (1.5-L) loaf

EQUIPMENT:
Electric mixer
6-cup (1.5-L) loaf pan
• brush with melted butter
• dust with flour
Heavy baking sheet

BATTER:

Large egg yolks, at room temperature	6
Superfine or extra fine sugar	4½ ounces (125 g); ½ cup + 2 tablespoons
Large egg whites, at room temperature	3
Cream of tartar (optional)	⅛ teaspoon (a pinch)
All-purpose flour	1¾ ounces (50 g); ¼ cup + 2 tablespoons
Unsweetened cocoa powder (Dutch processed)	1 ounce (25 g); ¼ cup
Nut-and-sugar powder (page 442) made with roasted hazelnuts (page 444)	3½ ounces (100 g); ¾ cup
Unsalted butter, melted and very hot	1¾ ounces (50 g); 3½ tablespoons

Preheat the oven to 350°F (175°C).

1. Combine the egg yolks with ½ cup (100 g) of the sugar in the mixer and beat at medium speed until the mixture whitens. Pour the mixture into a large mixing bowl.

2. Using a clean wire whip and bowl, whip the egg whites in the mixer at low speed until they start to froth. If you are not whipping the whites in a copper bowl, then add the cream of tartar. Gradually increase the whipping speed to medium-high, and continue whipping until the whites form very stiff peaks and just begin to slip and streak around the side of the bowl. Add the remaining sugar and continue whipping at high speed for a few seconds longer to incorporate the sugar and tighten the meringue.

3. Sift the flour and cocoa powder together over the egg yolk mixture. Scoop about one third of the meringue on top and quickly and thoroughly mix it in with a rubber spatula. Add the remaining meringue and gently fold it into the batter. When almost completely incorporated, add the hazelnut-and-sugar powder and continue folding until completely mixed. Slowly pour the melted butter over the batter and fold it in.

4. Scoop the batter from the mixing bowl into the loaf pan, filling it to three fourths of its height. Smooth the surface and make a slight depression down the center. Place the loaf pan on the baking sheet.

5. Bake until the top of the cake is dry and firm to the touch but not crusty, about 35 to 40 minutes. The tip of a paring knife inserted in the center of the cake should come out clean.

6. Remove the cake from the oven and slide the tip of a paring knife or small icing spatula between the edge of the cake and the pan to loosen the edge. Let the cake rest in the pan for about 5 minutes. Unmold the cake onto a wire rack. Turn it upside down and let cool to room temperature.

STORAGE: Covered airtight with plastic wrap, for up to 2 days at room temperature.

Or freeze for as long as 2 months. If frozen, defrost overnight in the refrigerator, and unwrap the cake at least 2 hours before using to allow condensation produced by defrosting to evaporate.

Pecan Mousseline

. . . .

We devised this variation on a classic recipe to take advantage of the availability of superb pecans in the United States. Pecan *mousseline* can also be baked in a round cake pan or cake ring and used just like génoise in round gâteaux.

For one 6-cup (1.5-L) loaf

EQUIPMENT:
Electric mixer
6-cup (1.5-L) loaf pan
• brush with melted butter
• dust with flour
Heavy baking sheet

BATTER:

Large eggs, separated, at room temperature	4
Nut-and-sugar powder (page 442), made with pecans	7 ounces (200 g); 1½ cups
Pure vanilla extract	⅛ teaspoon (a few drops)
Cream of tartar (optional)	⅛ teaspoon (a pinch)
Superfine or extra fine sugar	1 ounce (25 g); 2 tablespoons
All-purpose flour	2½ ounces (70 g); ½ cup

Preheat the oven to 350°F (175°C).

1. Combine the yolks with the pecan-and-sugar powder and beat at medium speed in the mixer until light and cream-colored. Beat in the vanilla extract.

2. Using a clean wire whip and bowl, whip the egg whites in the mixer at low speed until they start to froth. If you are not whipping the whites in a copper bowl, then add the cream of tartar. Gradually increase the whipping speed to medium-high, and continue whipping until the whites form very stiff peaks and just begin to slip and streak around the side of the bowl. Add the sugar and continue whipping at high speed for a few seconds longer to incorporate the sugar and tighten the meringue.

3. Sift the flour over the egg yolk mixture. Scoop about one third of the meringue on top and quickly and thoroughly mix it in with a rubber spatula. Add the remaining meringue and gently fold it into the batter.

4. Scoop the batter from the mixing bowl into the loaf pan, filling it to three fourths of its height. Smooth the surface and make a slight depression down the center. Place the loaf pan on the baking sheet.

5. Bake until the top of the cake is lightly browned and firm to the touch but not crusty, about 35 to 40 minutes. The tip of a paring knife inserted in the center of the cake should come out clean.

6. Remove the cake from the oven and slide the tip of a paring knife or small icing spatula between the edge of the cake and the pan to loosen the edge. Let the cake rest in the pan for about 5 minutes. Unmold the cake onto a wire rack. Turn it upside down and let cool to room temperature.

STORAGE: Covered airtight with plastic wrap, for up to 2 days in the refrigerator.

Or freeze for as long as 2 months. If frozen, defrost overnight in the refrigerator, and unwrap the cake at least 2 hours before using to allow condensation produced by defrosting to evaporate.

Coffee Yule Log

(BÛCHE DE NOËL CAFÉ)

· ·

Bûche de Noël is the traditional French Christmas cake. If you lived in France, you would not dream of making one at home. On Christmas Day, you would stroll down to your local *pâtisserie,* where you had placed your order well in advance, to pick up the grand finale of your Christmas dinner.

In the United States, you would be hard-pressed to find a pastry shop open on Christmas Day. While you may be able to order a yule log for Christmas Eve, you can almost certainly make a better one at home—and have fun doing it. We have never seen such joy and pride on our students' faces as when they put the finishing touches on their first *bûche de Noël.*

In this recipe, you spread the buttercream filling on a rectangular sponge cake sheet and roll it up into a long cylinder. You could use génoise, but we prefer *joconde* because it is thinner and doesn't make as fat a log as does génoise, and because it is more moist and flavorful. You cover the outside of the cake by piping adjacent ribbons of buttercream to resemble bark on a log, then decorate it with meringue mushrooms and almond paste holly berries and leaves.

EQUIPMENT:

Rectangle of foil board or silver or gold matt board (page 467)
• **at least as long as the *joconde* sheet and about 4 inches (10 cm) wide**
Small pastry bag fitted with
• **⁷⁄₁₆-inch (12-mm) plain pastry tube (Ateco #5)**
Large pastry bag fitted with
• **small fluted pastry tube (Ateco #0)**
Rolling pin

	For 8 to 10 servings	For 12 to 15 servings
CAKE:		
Joconde (page 224)	One 12 × 16-inch (30 × 40-cm) sheet	One 13 × 19-inch (33 × 50-cm) sheet

BRUSHING-SYRUP MIXTURE:

Double-strength brewed espresso (page 456)	¼ cup (6 cL)	¼ cup + 2 tablespoons (9 cL)
Heavy syrup (page 452)	¼ cup (6 cL)	¼ cup + 2 tablespoons (9 cL)

FILLING AND FROSTING:

Coffee buttercream (page 390)	12¾ ounces (360 g); 2 cups	1 pound + 1 ounce (480 g); 2⅔ cups
French buttercream (page 384)	3 ounces (85 g); ½ cup	3 ounces (85 g); ½ cup

DECORATION:

Chopped pistachios, or substitute chopped blanched almonds tinted pale green with food coloring	⅓ to ¾ ounce (10 to 20 g); 1 to 2 tablespoons
Meringue mushrooms (page 204)	8 to 10
Almond paste (page 432)	2 ounces (50 g)
Red, green, and yellow food colorings	
Confectioners' sugar for dusting	

1. Place the sheet of *joconde* on your counter, with the paper on which it was baked underneath. Neatly trim all four edges of the *joconde*. Brush the top with the espresso brushing syrup. Spread about ⅔ cup (120 g) for a small sheet or 1 cup (180 g) for a large sheet of the coffee buttercream over the *joconde* using a large icing spatula. Then use the paper under the *joconde* to lift one long edge of the sheet and begin rolling it up. Once the roll is started, let go of the paper and continue rolling the *joconde* into a log about either 15 inches (38 cm) or 19 inches (48 cm) long, depending on the size of the sheet of *joconde*. Lightly brush the outside of the log with espresso syrup. Cut from the foil board or matt board a rectangle about ½ inch (12 mm) larger in length and width than the log. Carefully roll the log onto this rectangle, then slide it onto a tray or a long serving platter.

2. Scoop the unflavored French buttercream into the small pastry bag. Pipe a circle of buttercream ½ inch (12 mm) thick on each end of the log. Pipe four or five mounds of buttercream, each 1 inch (2½ cm) in diameter, on the upper half of the log ①. Each mound will become a "knot."

3. Scoop the remaining coffee buttercream into the large pastry bag. Pipe some coffee buttercream in the center of the circle of plain buttercream on each end of the log ②. Then, starting at the bottom of one side of the log, pipe continuous ribbons of coffee buttercream back

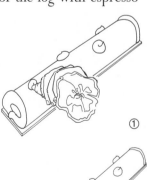

and forth over the length of the log ③. After the first two or three ribbons, pipe some ribbons only part of the length before reversing direction so that you make an irregular pattern like the bark on a tree. Stop when you reach the top of the log, rotate the platter, and pipe buttercream over the other side in the same fashion. Cover the entire surface of the log, including the knots, with coffee buttercream, with no gaps between adjacent ribbons.

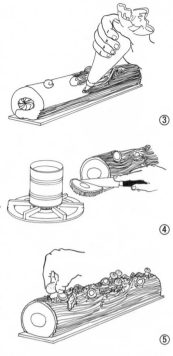

4. Refrigerate for at least 1 hour to make the buttercream firm.

5. Heat the blade of a paring knife. Cut off each end of the log with the hot blade ④, slicing through the buttercream to get a bull's-eye pattern. Heating the blade before each cut, slice off the tops of the knots, giving them a slightly concave surface and exposing the plain buttercream in the center.

6. Sprinkle some chopped pistachios in a few spots on the log to simulate moss. Arrange the meringue mushrooms on the log ⑤.

7. On your countertop, work the almond paste with the heel of your hand to make it smooth. Tint about one tenth of the almond paste a rich red with food coloring and form it into six to eight "holly berries." Add a drop each of green and yellow food colorings to the remaining almond paste to tint it a pale green. Roll about one quarter of the green almond paste under your palm into a thin string, and cut it into two or three "twigs." Dust your countertop and the rest of the green almond paste with confectioners' sugar. Roll out this green almond paste into a sheet about ³⁄₃₂ inch (2 mm) thick with the rolling pin, dusting with more confectioners' sugar as needed to prevent sticking. Cut from it four to six "holly leaves" and score the top of each leaf with the tip of your paring knife to resemble the veins of the leaf.

8. Arrange the almond paste twigs on the log. Bend each holly leaf in a gentle arch and arrange the leaves around the twigs. Place a bunch of three or four holly berries next to each twig.

STORAGE: In the refrigerator for up to 2 days. Once the buttercream is firm, you can cover the yule log loosely with wax paper to protect it.

Before decorating, freeze for up to 2 weeks, being careful to support the entire length of the log so that the frosting doesn't crack. Once frozen, cover airtight with plastic wrap. Remove the plastic wrap and defrost overnight in the refrigerator, then decorate as usual.

Chocolate Yule Log

(BÛCHE DE NOËL CHOCOLAT)

The disadvantage of rolling up a sheet of sponge cake with buttercream to make a yule log is that it requires a large amount of buttercream, making an extremely rich cake. We actually prefer to make the yule log by baking génoise in a special yule log mold. We slice the cake in half horizontally and fill it with a single layer of buttercream, then cover the outside of the cake with buttercream and decorate it with meringue mushrooms and almond paste holly berries and leaves, just as for a rolled yule log. Since not everyone has a yule log mold, we give both methods, and we have chosen to make the coffee yule log in the previous recipe by the rolled method, while we make the chocolate yule log in this recipe using the molded génoise. For either flavor, it is easy to switch methods simply by using the quantities of sponge cake, buttercream, and brushing-syrup mixture called for in the method you want to use, but substituting the flavor you want for the one we have specified.

For 10 to 15 servings

EQUIPMENT:
Rectangle of foil board or silver or gold matt board (page 467)
• **cut about ¼ inch (6 mm) larger in length and width than the génoise log**
Small pastry bag fitted with
• **⁷⁄₁₆-inch (12-mm) plain pastry tube (Ateco #5)**
Large pastry bag fitted with
• **small fluted pastry tube (Ateco #0)**
Rolling pin

CAKE:

Génoise (page 340)	One log 20 inches (50 cm) long

BRUSHING-SYRUP MIXTURE:

Heavy syrup (page 452)	⅓ cup (8 cL)
Dark Jamaican or Haitian rum	2 tablespoons + 2 teaspoons (4 cL)
Water	2 tablespoons + 2 teaspoons (4 cL)

FILLING AND FROSTING:

Chocolate buttercream (page 388)	12 ounces (340 g); 2 cups
French buttercream (page 384)	3 ounces (85 g); ½ cup

continued

DECORATION:

Chopped pistachios, or substitute chopped blanched almonds tinted pale green with food coloring	⅓ to ¾ ounce (10 to 20 g); 1 to 2 tablespoons
Meringue mushrooms (page 204)	8 to 10
Almond paste (page 432)	2 ounces (50 g)
Red, green, and yellow food colorings	
Confectioners' sugar for dusting	

1. Slice the génoise log in half horizontally with a wavy-edge bread knife, and place the bottom layer on the foil board or matt board rectangle. Brush the cut faces of both layers of génoise with the rum brushing syrup. Spread about ½ cup (85 g) of the chocolate buttercream over the bottom layer using an icing spatula. Add the second layer, cut side down, and lightly brush the outside of the log with the rum syrup. Slide the log onto a tray or a long serving platter.

2. Scoop the unflavored French buttercream into the small pastry bag. Pipe a circle of this buttercream ½ inch (12 mm) thick on each end of the log. Pipe four or five mounds of buttercream 1 inch (2½ cm) in diameter on the upper half of the log ①. Each mound will become a "knot."

3. Scoop the remaining chocolate buttercream into the large pastry bag. Pipe some chocolate buttercream in the center of the circle of plain buttercream on each end of the log ②. Then, starting at the bottom of one side of the log, pipe continuous ribbons of buttercream back and forth over the length of the log ③. After the first two or three ribbons, pipe some ribbons only part of the length before reversing direction so that you make an irregular pattern like the bark on a tree. Stop when you reach the top of the log, rotate the platter, and pipe buttercream over the other side in the same fashion. Cover the entire surface of the log, including the knots, with chocolate buttercream, with no gaps between adjacent ribbons.

4. Refrigerate for at least 1 hour to make the buttercream firm.

5. Heat the blade of a paring knife. Cut off each end of the log with the hot blade ④, slicing through the buttercream to get a bull's-eye pattern. Heating the blade before each cut, slice off the tops of the knots, giving them a slightly concave surface and exposing the plain buttercream in the center.

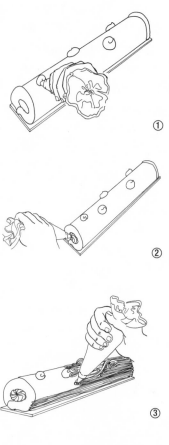

① ② ③

④

6. Sprinkle some chopped pistachios in a few spots on the log to simulate moss. Arrange the meringue mushrooms on the log ⑤.

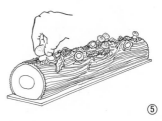

⑤

7. On your countertop, work the almond paste with the heel of your hand to make it smooth. Tint about one tenth of the almond paste a rich red with food coloring and form it into six to eight "holly berries." Add a drop each of green and yellow food colorings to the remaining almond paste to tint it a pale green. Roll about one quarter of the green almond paste under your palm into a thin string, and cut it into two or three "twigs." Dust your countertop and the rest of the green almond paste with confectioners' sugar. Roll out this green almond paste into a sheet about 3/32 inch (2 mm) thick with the rolling pin, dusting with more confectioners' sugar as needed to prevent sticking. Cut from it four to six "holly leaves" and score the top of each leaf with the tip of your paring knife to resemble the veins of the leaf.

8. Arrange the almond paste twigs on the log. Bend each holly leaf in a gentle arch and arrange the leaves around the twigs. Place a bunch of three or four holly berries next to each twig.

STORAGE: In the refrigerator for up to 2 days. Once the buttercream is firm, you can cover the yule log loosely with wax paper to protect it.

Before decorating, freeze for up to 2 weeks, being careful to support the entire length of the log so that the frosting doesn't crack. Once frozen, cover airtight with plastic wrap. Remove the plastic wrap and defrost overnight in the refrigerator, then decorate as usual.

Lemon Meringue Yule Log

This is a mousse log with a yule log presentation. The lemon meringue flavor combination is very appealing and the light filling and frosting make for a much less rich gâteau than the more usual buttercreams.

For 10 to 15 servings

EQUIPMENT:

Electric mixer

Yule log mold 3 inches (7 cm) wide and 20 inches (50 cm) long

• brush with melted butter

• dust with granulated sugar

Rectangle of foil board or silver or gold matt board (page 467)

• cut about ¼ inch (6 mm) larger in length and width than the top of the mold

Small pastry bag fitted with

• ⁷⁄₁₆-inch (12-mm) plain pastry tube (Ateco #5)

Large pastry bag fitted with

• small fluted pastry tube (Ateco #0)

Rolling pin

Propane torch (see precautions on page 480)

CAKE:

Joconde (page 224)	One 12 × 16-inch (30 × 40-cm) or 13 × 20-inch (33 × 50-cm) sheet

FILLING:

Fresh lemon juice, strained	1½ tablespoons (2.3 cL)
Heavy syrup (page 452)	1½ tablespoons (2.3 cL)
Unflavored gelatin	¾ teaspoon (4 mL)
Heavy cream, well chilled	1 cup + 2 tablespoons (2.7 dL)
Lemon curd (page 393), at room temperature	4½ ounces (130 g); ½ cup

BRUSHING-SYRUP MIXTURE:

Lemon syrup (page 453)	¼ cup (6 cL)
Water	¼ cup (6 cL)

FROSTING:

Italian meringue (page 184)   9½ ounces (270 g); 4½ cups

Confectioners' sugar for dusting

DECORATION:

Chopped pistachios, or substitute   ⅓ to ¾ ounce (10 to 20 g); 1 to 2 tablespoons

    chopped blanched almonds tinted

    pale green with food coloring

Almond paste (page 432)   2 ounces (50 g)

Red, green, and yellow food colorings

Confectioners' sugar for dusting

1. Cut two rectangles of *joconde* 5⅛ inches (13 cm) wide, with a total length of 20 inches (50 cm). Line the yule log mold with these rectangles, leaving the centers of the end faces unlined. Cut two bands of *joconde* about 2 inches (5 cm) wide, with a total length of 20 inches (50 cm).

2. Chill the bowl and the wire whip or beater of the mixer in the refrigerator. Combine the lemon juice and heavy syrup in a butter melter, and stir in the gelatin. Let the gelatin soften, then warm over low heat, stirring constantly, until the gelatin dissolves. Remove from the heat and pour into a small stainless steel bowl.

3. Pour the heavy cream into the chilled mixer bowl and whip the cream at medium speed with the chilled wire whip or beater until it is light and thick and holds soft peaks. Stop whipping.

4. Stir the lemon curd into the dissolved gelatin to mix thoroughly. Continue whipping the cream at medium speed until it holds stiff peaks, then whip in the lemon curd mixture to finish the lemon mousse.

5. Brush the *joconde* lining the yule log mold and the top of the 2-inch- (5-cm-) wide bands of *joconde* with the lemon brushing-syrup mixture.

6. Scoop the lemon mousse into the mold to fill it almost to the top, leaving just enough room for the *joconde* bands. Tap the mold firmly on the countertop to eliminate any air spaces. Turn the *joconde* bands upside down, and place them end to end on top of the mousse, between the ends of the rectangles of *joconde* lining the mold. Place the foil board or matt board rectangle upside down on top.

7. Cover the top of the yule log mold with plastic wrap and chill in the refrigerator for several hours or overnight to set the mousse.

8. Turn the yule log mold upside down onto a tray. Warm the outside with a blow dryer, then lift off the mold. Chill the log again before frosting.

9. Scoop about ½ cup (30 g) of the meringue into the small pastry bag. Pipe a mound of meringue ¾ inch (2 cm) wide and ½ inch (12 mm)

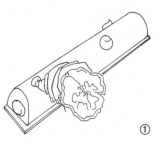

①

thick on each end of the log. Pipe four or five mounds of meringue ¾ inch (2 cm) in diameter on the upper half of the log ①. Each mound will become a "knot."

10. Scoop the remaining meringue into the large pastry bag. Pipe a circle of meringue around the mound of meringue on each end of the log ②. Then, starting at the bottom of one side of the log, pipe continuous ribbons of meringue back and forth over the length of the log. After the first two or three ribbons, pipe some ribbons only part of the length before reversing direction so that you make an irregular pattern like the bark on a tree ③. Surround each knot with a circle of meringue and pipe the ribbons tight against these circles. Stop when you reach the top of the log, rotate the platter, and pipe meringue over the other side in the same fashion. Cover the entire surface of the log with meringue, with no gaps between adjacent ribbons.

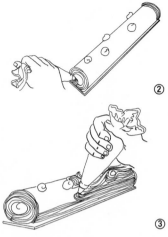

11. Dust the outside of the log with confectioners' sugar. Use a propane torch to lightly brown the ridges in the meringue bark, leaving white meringue still showing in the grooves in the bark.

12. Sprinkle some chopped pistachios in a few spots on the log to simulate moss.

13. On your countertop, work the almond paste with the heel of your hand to make it smooth. Tint about one tenth of the almond paste a rich red with food coloring and form it into six to eight "holly berries." Add a drop each of green and yellow food colorings to the remaining almond paste to tint it a pale green. Roll about one quarter of the green almond paste under your palm into a thin string, and cut it into two or three "twigs." Dust your countertop and the rest of the green almond paste with confectioners' sugar. Roll out this green almond paste into a sheet about 3/32 inch (2 mm) thick with the rolling pin, dusting with more confectioners' sugar as needed to prevent sticking. Cut from it four to six "holly leaves" and score the top of each leaf with the tip of your paring knife to resemble the veins of the leaf.

14. Arrange the almond paste twigs on the log. Bend each holly leaf in a gentle arch and arrange the leaves around the twigs. Place a bunch of three or four holly berries next to each twig.

NOTES: The amount of mousse required for this presentation is half of what you use in an 8¾-inch (22-cm) *vacherin* ring.

The length of this log makes it easy to cut and serve, but awkward to present unless you have a very long serving platter. To make it less unwieldy, you can cut it in half before frosting and make two small gâteaux.

STORAGE: In the refrigerator for up to 2 days.

Before unmolding, freeze for up to 2 weeks. Once frozen, cover the top of the log airtight with plastic wrap. Remove the plastic wrap and defrost overnight in the refrigerator, then unmold and finish as usual.

Marronnier

A *marronnier* is a chestnut tree. Our mousse log is filled with chestnut mousse and glazed with chocolate mixed with roasted chopped almonds. For decoration you model almond paste into chestnut shapes and glaze them with chocolate. Lined up in a row on top of the log, they give this gâteau a unique and luxurious appearance.

Because the length of the log is unwieldy, we have recommended cutting it in half before glazing to make two gâteaux. The gâteau keeps much better before glazing, so glaze and decorate one gâteau at a time.

For 12 to 15 servings

EQUIPMENT:
Electric mixer
Yule log mold 3 inches (7 cm) wide and 20 inches (50 cm) long
• brush with melted butter
• dust with granulated sugar
Rectangle of silver or gold matt board (page 467)
• cut to fit inside the top of the mold
Chocolate thermometer or pocket digital thermometer

CAKE:
Joconde (page 224)	One 12 × 16-inch (30 × 40-cm) or 13 × 20-inch (33 × 50-cm) sheet

FILLING:
Cold water	1½ tablespoons (2.3 cL)
Heavy syrup (page 452)	1½ tablespoons (2.3 cL)
Unflavored gelatin	¾ teaspoon (4 mL)
Heavy cream, well chilled	1 cup (2.4 dL)
Kentucky bourbon	1 tablespoon (1.5 cL)

Chestnut spread (*crème de marron*,
    page 498)
	One 8¾-ounce (250-g) can,
	    or half of a 17½-ounce (500-g) can

BRUSHING-SYRUP MIXTURE:
Kentucky bourbon	¼ cup (6 cL)
Heavy syrup	¼ cup (6 cL)

continued

Almond paste (page 432)	2⅔ ounces (75 g)
Confectioners' sugar for dusting	

GLAZE FOR EACH GÂTEAU:

European bittersweet chocolate, melted	10 ounces (285 g)
Clarified butter (page 449), at room temperature	1 ounce (30 g); 2 tablespoons
Blanched almonds, roasted (page 444) and chopped	2 ounces (60 g)

1. Cut two rectangles of *joconde* 5⅛ inches (13 cm) wide, with a total length of 20 inches (50 cm). Line the yule log mold with these rectangles, leaving the centers of the end faces unlined. Cut two bands of *joconde* about 2 inches (5 cm) wide, with a total length of 20 inches (50 cm).

2. Chill the bowl and the wire whip or beater of the mixer in the refrigerator. Combine the water and heavy syrup in a butter melter, and stir in the gelatin. Let the gelatin soften, then warm over low heat, stirring constantly, until the gelatin dissolves. Remove from the heat and pour into a small stainless steel bowl.

3. Pour the heavy cream into the chilled mixer bowl and whip the cream at medium speed with the chilled wire whip or beater until it is light and thick and holds soft peaks. Stop whipping.

4. Stir the bourbon into the chestnut spread, then stir into the dissolved gelatin to mix thoroughly. Continue whipping the cream at medium speed until it holds stiff peaks, then whip in the chestnut spread mixture to finish the chestnut mousse.

5. Brush the *joconde* lining the yule log mold and the top of the 2-inch- (5-cm-) wide bands of *joconde* with the bourbon brushing syrup.

6. Scoop the chestnut mousse into the mold to fill it almost to the top, leaving just enough room for the *joconde* band. Tap the mold firmly on the countertop to eliminate any air spaces. Turn the *joconde* bands upside down and place them end to end on top of the mousse, between the ends of the rectangles of *joconde* lining the mold. Cut the matt board rectangle in half crosswise and place the two halves upside down on top.

7. Cover the top of the yule log mold with plastic wrap and chill in the refrigerator for several hours or overnight to set the mousse.

8. Turn the yule log mold upside down onto a tray or wire rack. Warm the outside with a blow dryer, then lift off the mold. Cut the log in half to make two gâteaux and place each on a wire rack. Chill the logs again before glazing.

9. On your countertop, work the almond paste with the heel of your hand to make it smooth. Take about 1 ounce (25 g) of the almond paste and dust it and the countertop with confectioners' sugar. Roll it out into a sheet about ⅛ inch (3 mm) thick with your rolling pin, dusting with more confectioners' sugar as needed to prevent sticking. Cut from the sheet five rounds about 1⅜ inch

(3.5 cm) in diameter using the back end of a pastry tube (Ateco #7), a small round cookie cutter, or a paring knife. Combine the trimmings with the remaining almond paste, roll all of this almond paste back and forth under your hands to make a cylinder, and cut it into five equal lengths. Roll each piece into a ball, then form it into the shape of a chestnut with your fingertips.

10. If you did not melt the chocolate for the glaze in a stainless steel bowl, transfer it to one. Temper the chocolate as follows: Dip the bottom of the bowl of chocolate in a larger bowl of cold water and stir the chocolate until the temperature drops to between 80° and 84°F (26.5° to 29°C) and it begins to thicken. Immediately remove from the cold water and dip the bottom of the bowl of chocolate in a larger bowl of hot water. Stir over the hot water just long enough to warm the chocolate to between 86° and 91°F (30° to 33°C) and make it more fluid again. Then remove from the hot water immediately. Beat the clarified butter with a wooden spatula to make it smooth and creamy, then stir it into the chocolate.

11. One at a time, insert a skewer into the pointed end of each almond paste chestnut and dip it in the chocolate glaze up to about ³⁄₁₆ inch (1.5 mm) from the tip, leaving the tip unglazed. Place each chocolate-glazed chestnut with the tip pointing up on a sheet of wax paper, remove the skewer, and let the chocolate set. Pinch the tip of each to close the hole left by the skewer. Meanwhile, do not let the bowl of chocolate glaze cool below 82°F (28°C). As needed, dip the bottom of the bowl of chocolate in a larger bowl of hot water and stir the chocolate to gently warm it and keep it between 82° and 86°F (28° to 30°C).

12. Stir the roasted chopped almonds into the remaining tempered chocolate. Pour the chocolate over the top of one of the logs and use the edge of an icing spatula to make it flow evenly down the sides. Pour additional chocolate glaze over any areas that may need it, and tilt and tap the wire rack to be sure the chocolate flows evenly over the entire surface. Touch up any uneven areas around the sides with the edge of the icing spatula. Allow the chocolate to thicken, then use a paring knife or small icing spatula to clean off any excess chocolate around the bottom edge.

13. Before the chocolate sets, arrange the five rounds of almond paste on top of the log in a line down the center, spacing them evenly. Dab the bottom of each chestnut in chocolate, and stand it tip up on the center of one of the rounds. Transfer the gâteau to a serving plate and let the chocolate glaze set.

14. Refrigerate the gâteau until ready to serve.

NOTES: The amount of mousse required for this recipe is half of what you use for a mousse cake in an 8¾-inch (22-cm) *vacherin* ring.

The proportion of clarified butter in the chocolate glaze for *marronnier* is lower than usual because we want a slightly less fluid glaze to coat the almond paste chestnuts and to hold the chopped almonds on the surface of the log.

STORAGE: In the refrigerator for up to 3 days.

Before glazing, freeze for up to 2 weeks. Once frozen, cover each log airtight with plastic wrap. Remove the plastic wrap and defrost overnight in the refrigerator before glazing.

Pomone aux Poires

This mousse log is lined with a sheet of *joconde*, filled with a bavarian cream flavored with pear brandy, and studded with morsels of fresh pear. After unmolding, the *joconde* is brushed with orange juice glaze for a glistening but understated presentation. The name derives from the French spelling of Pomona, the ancient Roman goddess of fruit trees.

For 10 to 12 servings

EQUIPMENT:
Electric mixer
Yule log mold 3 inches (7 cm) wide and 20 inches (50 cm) long
• brush with melted butter
• dust with granulated sugar
Rectangle of silver or gold matt board (page 467)
• cut to fit inside the top of the mold

FRUIT:

Fresh pear, peeled and poached in light syrup (page 454)	1 small

CAKE:

Joconde (page 224)	One 12×16-inch (30×40-cm) or 13×20-inch (33×50-cm) sheet

FILLING:

Unflavored gelatin	1¼ teaspoons (6 mL)
Cold water	1 tablespoon (1.5 cL)
Egg yolks, lightly beaten	1½ tablespoons (2.3 cL); about 1⅓ large yolks
Superfine or extra fine sugar	1¼ ounces (35 g); 2½ tablespoons
Dry white wine	3 tablespoons (4.5 cL)
Poire william (pear brandy)	¼ cup (6 cL)
Heavy cream, well chilled	1 cup + 2 tablespoons (2.7 dL)

BRUSHING-SYRUP MIXTURE:

Heavy syrup (page 452)	¼ cup (6 cL)
Poire william (pear brandy)	¼ cup (6 cL)

GLAZE:

Unflavored gelatin	¾ teaspoon (4 mL)
Cold water	3 tablespoons + 1 teaspoon (5 cL)
Fresh orange juice, strained	3 tablespoons + 1 teaspoon (5 cL)
Superfine or extra fine sugar	1½ ounces (40 g); 3 tablespoons + 1 teaspoon

1. Drain the pear, cut it in half, and core it. Cut the flesh of the pear into ⅜-inch (1-cm) dice.

2. Cut two rectangles of *joconde* 5⅛ inches (13 cm) wide, with a total length of 20 inches (50 cm). Line the yule log mold with these rectangles, leaving the centers of the end faces unlined. Cut two bands of *joconde* about 2 inches (5 cm) wide, with a total length of 20 inches (50 cm).

3. Chill the bowl and the wire whip or beater of the mixer in the refrigerator. Stir the gelatin into the cold water and let it soften.

4. In a 2-cup (5-dL) butter melter, whisk together the egg yolks and superfine sugar until lemon-colored. Whisk in the white wine and 1 tablespoon (1.5 cL) of the *poire william*. Bring just to a simmer, whisking constantly. Remove from the heat, add the softened gelatin, and stir until dissolved. Strain through a fine sieve into a small stainless steel bowl and let cool. Stir in the remaining *poire william*.

5. Pour the heavy cream into the chilled mixer bowl and whip the cream at medium speed in the mixer using the chilled wire whip or beater until it is light and thick and holds stiff peaks. Then whip in the *poire william*–flavored custard to finish the bavarian cream. Fold the pear dice into the bavarian cream.

6. Brush the *joconde* lining the yule log mold and the top of the 2-inch- (5-cm-) wide bands of *joconde* with the *poire william* brushing-syrup mixture.

7. Scoop the bavarian cream into the mold to fill it almost to the top, leaving just enough room for the *joconde* bands. Tap the mold firmly on the countertop to eliminate any air spaces. Turn the *joconde* bands upside down, and place them end to end on top of the mousse, between the ends of the rectangles of *joconde* lining the mold. Place the matt board rectangle upside down on top.

8. Cover the top of the yule log mold with plastic wrap and chill in the refrigerator for several hours or overnight to set the mousse.

9. Turn the yule log mold upside down onto a tray. Warm the outside with a blow dryer, then lift off the mold. Chill the log again before glazing.

10. For the glaze, stir the gelatin into the cold water and let it soften. Heat the orange juice and sugar in a butter melter, stirring occasionally, until the sugar is dissolved in the orange juice. Add the softened gelatin and stir until the gelatin dissolves. Pour into a small stainless steel bowl and let cool. Dip the bottom of the bowl in a larger bowl of ice water and stir until it begins to thicken very lightly. Remove the bowl from the ice water immediately. Brush the entire outside of

the log with the glaze until evenly coated and glistening, being careful not to damage the surface of the *joconde*. Then refrigerate to set the glaze.

NOTES: The amount of mousse required for this presentation is half of what you use in an 8¾-inch (22-cm) *vacherin* ring.

The length of this log makes it easy to cut and serve, but awkward to present unless you have a very long serving platter. To make it less unwieldy, you can cut it in half before glazing and make two small gâteaux.

STORAGE: In the refrigerator for up to 2 days.

Before unmolding, freeze for up to 2 weeks. Once frozen, cover the top of the log airtight with plastic wrap. Remove the plastic wrap and defrost overnight in the refrigerator, then unmold and glaze as usual.

Cranberry Mousse Log

. . . .

We thought it would be fun to make a mousse log with a distinctive American flavor, and here it is—cranberry mousse with bourbon brushing syrup on the slices of a *joconde*-jam roll lining a yule log mold. The perfect dessert to serve at Thanksgiving!

For 10 to 12 servings

EQUIPMENT:

Electric blender or food processor

Electric mixer

Yule log mold 3 inches (7 cm) wide and 20 inches (50 cm) long

• brush with melted butter

• dust with granulated sugar

Rectangle of silver or gold matt board (page 467)

• cut to fit inside the top of the mold

FILLING:

Unflavored gelatin	1¾ teaspoons (9 mL)
Cold water	3 tablespoons (4.5 cL)
Fresh cranberries	¾ pound (340 g)
Granulated sugar	7 ounces (200 g); 1 cup
Heavy cream, well chilled	1 cup (2.4 dL)

CAKE:

Joconde-orange marmalade roll (page 276)	One roll 10 inches (25 cm) long or two rolls each 6 inches (15 cm) long
Joconde (page 224)	Two rectangular bands, each 2 inches (5 cm) wide and with a combined length of 19 inches (48 cm), cut from a large sheet

BRUSHING-SYRUP MIXTURE:

Kentucky bourbon	1½ tablespoons (2.3 cL)
Heavy syrup (page 452)	1½ tablespoons (2.3 cL)

continued

GLAZE:

Unflavored gelatin	¾ teaspoon (4 mL)
Cold water	3 tablespoons + 1 teaspoon (5 cL)
Fresh orange juice, strained	3 tablespoons + 1 teaspoon (5 cL)
Superfine or extra fine sugar	1½ ounces (40 g); 3 tablespoons + 1 teaspoon

ACCOMPANIMENT:

Crème anglaise (page 436)	1 cup (2.4 dL)
Kentucky bourbon	1 tablespoon (1.5 cL)

1. Chill the bowl and the wire whip or beater of the mixer in the refrigerator. Stir the gelatin into 1 tablespoon (1.5 cL) of the cold water and let it soften.

2. Combine the cranberries, sugar, and the remaining 2 tablespoons (3 cL) of water in the blender or food processor and puree them coarsely. The pieces of cranberry skin should be fairly large so that they can be strained out easily later. Pour the pureed berries into a heavy 2-quart (2-L) saucepan and bring to a simmer over medium heat, stirring constantly with a wooden spatula. Reduce the heat to low and continue cooking, stirring occasionally, until the cranberry puree is very soft and a uniform red color, 5 to 7 minutes. Strain the hot puree through a fine sieve to remove the skins. Stir the softened gelatin into the hot, strained cranberry puree and let cool, stirring occasionally. Do not allow it to set.

3. Pour the heavy cream into the chilled mixer bowl and whip the cream at medium speed with the chilled wire whip or beater until it is light and thick and holds soft peaks. Stop whipping.

4. Dip the bottom of the bowl of cranberry puree in a larger bowl of ice water, and stir with a rubber spatula until it just begins to thicken. Immediately remove the bowl from the ice water.

5. Continue whipping the cream at medium speed until it holds stiff peaks, then whip in the cranberry puree to finish the cranberry mousse.

6. Cut from the *joconde*-marmalade roll twenty-four slices, each about ⅜ inch (1 cm) thick. Line the yule log mold with the slices: Place one slice in each end of the mold, with the tail of the roll on top; then arrange eleven slices in a row, all spiraling in the same direction with the tail of the roll at the top, on one side of the mold. Arrange the remaining eleven slices on the other side of the mold in the same way.

7. Lightly brush the slices of the *joconde*-marmalade roll with the bourbon brushing syrup and brush the top of the *joconde* band heavily with the bourbon syrup.

8. Scoop the cranberry mousse into the mold to fill it almost to the top, leaving just enough room for the *joconde* band. Tap the mold firmly on the countertop to be sure that the mousse fills the spaces between the slices of the *joconde*-marmalade roll. Smooth the mousse up the sides, making a depression to accommodate the *joconde* band. Turn the *joconde* band upside down and place it on top of the mousse, between the tops of the slices of the *joconde*-marmalade roll. Place the matt board rectangle upside down on top.

9. Cover the top of the yule log mold with plastic wrap and chill in the refrigerator for several hours or overnight to set the mousse.

10. Turn the yule log mold upside down onto a wire rack. Warm the outside with a blow dryer, then lift off the mold. Chill the log again while you prepare the glaze.

11. For the glaze, stir the gelatin into the cold water and let it soften. Heat the orange juice and sugar in a butter melter, stirring occasionally until the sugar dissolves. Remove from the heat, add the softened gelatin, and stir until the gelatin dissolves. Pour into a small stainless steel bowl and let cool. Dip the bottom of the bowl in a larger bowl of ice water and stir until it begins to thicken very lightly. Remove the bowl from the ice water immediately. Brush the entire outside of the log with the glaze until evenly coated and glistening, being careful not to damage the surface of the mousse. Then refrigerate to set the glaze.

12. Serve the mousse log accompanied by the *crème anglaise* flavored with the bourbon.

NOTES: The amount of mousse required for this recipe is half of what you use for a charlotte in an 8¾-inch (22-cm) *vacherin* ring.

The length of this log makes it easy to cut and serve, but awkward to present unless you have a very long serving platter. To make it less unwieldy, you can cut it in half before glazing. If you plan to do this, allow two extra slices of the *joconde*-marmalade roll and stand them back to back (with a circle of kitchen parchment in between) at the center of the yule log mold to make a sort of partition. Cut the matt board rectangle in half before placing it on top. After you unmold the log, divide it in half by cutting between the two slices of *joconde*-marmalade roll at the center and remove the circle of parchment.

STORAGE: In the refrigerator for up to 2 or 3 days.

Before unmolding, freeze for up to 2 weeks. Once frozen, cover the top of the log airtight with plastic wrap. Remove the plastic wrap and defrost overnight in the refrigerator, then unmold and glaze as usual.

Blueberry Mousse Log

Blueberries have a fabulous color and flavor. They also create a dilemma: Much of their taste and color is in the skin, but the texture of the skin does not enhance a smooth, creamy mousse no matter how finely you puree it. We offer a simple trick: Coarsely puree the berries with sugar and some lemon juice to preserve their color, then bring to a simmer before straining out the skins. This allows you to extract the desirable flavor and color from the skins, without damaging the fresh blueberry taste. Now look at the skins that you are about to discard—still loaded with color and flavor. Combine them with heavy syrup and water, simmer, and strain again to make a deep, dramatically blueberry syrup for brushing.

For 10 to 12 servings

EQUIPMENT:

Electric blender or food processor
Electric mixer
Yule log mold 3 inches (7 cm) wide and 20 inches (50 cm) long
• brush with melted butter
• dust with granulated sugar
Rectangle of silver or gold matt board (page 467)
• cut to fit inside the top of the mold

FILLING:

Unflavored gelatin	1¾ teaspoons (9 mL)
Cold water	1 tablespoon (1.5 cL)
Fresh blueberries	12 ounces (340 g); 1 pint
Granulated sugar	1¾ ounces (50 g); ¼ cup
Fresh lemon juice, strained	2½ teaspoons (1.3 cL)
Heavy, cream, well chilled	1 cup (2.4 dL)

BRUSHING-SYRUP MIXTURE:

Heavy syrup (page 452)	2 tablespoons (3 cL)
Water	¼ cup (6 cL)

CAKE:

Joconde-raspberry jam sandwich (page 274)	One sandwich 11½ to 12½ inches (29 to 32 cm) long, 1¾ to 2 inches (4.5 to 5 cm) high, and at least 2 inches (5 cm) thick
Joconde (page 224)	Two rectangular bands, each 2 inches (5 cm) wide and with a combined length of 19 inches (48 cm), cut from a large sheet

GLAZE:

Unflavored gelatin	¾ teaspoon (4 mL)
Cold water	3 tablespoons + 1 teaspoon (5 cL)
Fresh orange juice, strained	3 tablespoons + 1 teaspoon (5 cL)
Superfine or extra fine sugar	1½ ounces (40g); 3 tablespoons + 1 teaspoon

ACCOMPANIMENT:

Crème anglaise (page 436)	1 cup (2.4 dL)
European kirsch	1 tablespoon (1.5 cL)

1. Chill the bowl and the wire whip or beater of the mixer in the refrigerator. Stir the gelatin into the cold water and let it soften.

2. Combine the blueberries, sugar, and lemon juice in the blender or food processor and puree them coarsely. The pieces of blueberry skin should be fairly large so that they can be strained out easily later. Pour the pureed berries into a heavy 2-quart (2-L) saucepan and bring to a simmer over medium heat, stirring constantly with a wooden spatula. Strain the hot puree through a fine sieve to remove the skins. Stir the softened gelatin into the hot, strained blueberry puree and let cool, stirring occasionally. Do not allow it to set.

3. Combine the skins strained out of the puree with the heavy syrup and water in a small saucepan and bring to a simmer. Reduce the heat to very low and cook 5 minutes. Strain through a fine sieve, pressing down firmly to extract as much syrup as possible, to obtain a dark blueberry syrup with a strong flavor of berries. Discard the skins.

4. Pour the heavy cream into the chilled mixer bowl and whip the cream at medium speed with the chilled wire whip or beater until it is light and thick and holds soft peaks. Stop whipping.

5. Dip the bottom of the bowl of blueberry puree in a larger bowl of ice water, and stir with a rubber spatula until it just begins to thicken. Immediately remove the bowl from the ice water.

6. Continue whipping the cream at medium speed until it holds stiff peaks, then whip in the blueberry puree to finish the blueberry mousse.

7. Cut from the *joconde*-jam sandwich five slices, each about ⅜ inch (1 cm) thick. (If the sandwich is less than 2 inches = 5cm high, you may need an extra slice; or you can leave a space between the ends of the mold and the first and last slices.) Cut from each slice two rectangles, each 5⅛ inches (13 cm) long. Line the yule log mold with the slices, starting at one end and arranging the slices with the stripes running crosswise. Leave the centers of the end faces unlined.

8. Lightly brush the slices of the *joconde*-jam sandwich with the blueberry syrup and brush the top of the *joconde* band heavily with the blueberry syrup.

9. Scoop the blueberry mousse into the mold to fill it almost to the top, leaving just enough room for the *joconde* band. Tap the mold firmly on the countertop to eliminate any air spaces. Turn the *joconde* band upside down, and place it on top of the mousse, between the tops of the slices of the *joconde*-jam sandwich. Place the matt board rectangle upside down on top.

10. Cover the top of the yule log mold with plastic wrap and chill in the refrigerator for several hours or overnight to set the mousse.

11. Turn the yule log mold upside down onto a wire rack. Warm the outside with a blow dryer, then lift off the mold. Chill the log again while you prepare the glaze.

12. For the glaze, stir the gelatin into the cold water and let it soften. Heat the orange juice and sugar in a butter melter, stirring occasionally until the sugar dissolves. Remove from the heat, add the softened gelatin, and stir until the gelatin dissolves. Pour into a small stainless steel bowl and let cool. Dip the bottom of the bowl in a larger bowl of ice water and stir until it begins to thicken very lightly. Remove the bowl from the ice water immediately. Brush the entire outside of the log with the glaze until evenly coated and glistening, being careful not to damage the surface of the mousse. Then refrigerate to set the glaze.

13. Serve the mousse log accompanied by the *crème anglaise* flavored with the kirsch.

NOTES: The amount of mousse required for this recipe is half of what you use for a charlotte in an 8¾-inch (22-cm) *vacherin* ring.

The length of this log makes it easy to cut and serve, but awkward to present unless you have a very long serving platter. To make it less unwieldy, you can cut it in half before glazing. If you plan to do this, cut the matt board rectangle in half before placing it on top.

STORAGE: In the refrigerator for up to 2 or 3 days.

Before unmolding, freeze for up to 2 weeks. Once frozen, cover the top of the log airtight with plastic wrap. Remove the plastic wrap and defrost overnight in the refrigerator, then unmold and glaze as usual.

Alhambra

Here is one of the gâteaux that was a favorite of Paul's as a child. It is made from a chocolate-hazelnut sponge cake baked in a loaf pan, filled and frosted with ganache, and glazed with chocolate. The Alhambra was the ancient palace of the Moorish monarchs of Granada in southern Spain. However, we suspect that the inspiration for the name of this gâteau was a famous music hall called Alhambra, on the *place de la République* in Paris, where Mistinguett and Maurice Chevalier frequently performed.

For 10 to 12 servings

EQUIPMENT:

Rectangle of silver or gold matt board or foil board (page 467)
• cut about ¼ inch (6 mm) larger in length and width than the *alhambra* sponge cake
Chocolate thermometer or pocket digital thermometer
Parchment decorating cone (page 416)

CAKE:

Alhambra sponge cake (page 344)	One 6-cup (1.5-L) loaf

BRUSHING-SYRUP MIXTURE:

Heavy syrup (page 452)	⅓ cup (8 cL)
Dark Jamaican or Haitian rum	2 tablespoons + 2 teaspoons (4 cL)
Water	2 tablespoons + 2 teaspoons (4 cL)

FILLING AND FROSTING:

Ganache *clichy* (page 400)	13 ounces (370 g); 1½ cups

GLAZE:

European bittersweet chocolate, melted	12 ounces (340 g)
Clarified butter (page 449), at room temperature	1¾ ounces (50 g); 3½ tablespoons

DECORATION FOR TOP OF GÂTEAU:

Heavy syrup, heated to lukewarm	1 tablespoon (1.5 cL)
Unsweetened chocolate, melted	½ ounce (15 g)
Gold leaf (page 517, optional)	1 sheet

continued

1. Slice off the bottom of the cake with a wavy-edge bread knife to make it flat. Turn it right side up and cut it horizontally into three layers. Place the bottom layer on the matt board or foil board rectangle. Brush the top of this layer heavily with the rum brushing syrup. Spread ¼ cup (65 g) of the ganache over it with an icing spatula. Brush the bottom of the middle cake layer with rum syrup, turn it right side up, and place it on the first layer of ganache. Brush the top of this layer heavily with rum syrup and spread it with ¼ cup (65 g) of the ganache. Brush the bottom of the third cake layer heavily with rum syrup, turn it right side up, and place it on the second layer of ganache. Lightly brush the outside of the loaf with rum syrup.

2. Spread the top and then the sides of the loaf with ganache, leaving a rim of ganache around the top edge of the loaf. Sweep the icing spatula across the top to take off the excess ganache and make it smooth. Slide the loaf to the edge of your countertop and sweep the icing spatula over the side to take off the excess ganache and make it smooth. Rotate the gâteau and repeat with each side in turn until the entire outside of the gâteau is coated with a smooth layer of ganache.

3. Transfer the gâteau to a wire rack and chill it in the refrigerator until the ganache is firm, at least 1 hour.

4. If you did not melt the chocolate for the glaze in a stainless steel bowl, transfer it to one. Temper the chocolate as follows: Dip the bottom of the bowl of chocolate in a larger bowl of cold water and stir the chocolate until the temperature drops to between 80° and 84°F (26.5° to 29°C) and it begins to thicken. Immediately remove from the cold water and dip the bottom of the bowl of chocolate in a larger bowl of hot water. Stir over the hot water just long enough to warm the chocolate to between 86° and 91°F (30° to 33°C) and make it more fluid again. Then remove from the hot water immediately. Beat the clarified butter with a wooden spatula to make it smooth and creamy, then stir it into the chocolate.

5. Pour the chocolate on top of the gâteau in a rectangle just inside the perimeter so that some of it flows naturally over the edges. Quickly smooth the top surface with an icing spatula to cover the entire top with a thin layer of glaze and make the excess flow evenly down the sides. Pour additional chocolate glaze over any areas that may need it, and tilt and tap the wire rack to be sure the chocolate flows evenly over the entire surface. Touch up any uneven areas around the sides with the edge of the icing spatula. Let the chocolate begin to thicken, then clean off any excess chocolate around the bottom edge. Transfer the gâteau to a serving plate and let the chocolate glaze set.

6. Gradually stir the heavy syrup into the melted chocolate. The chocolate will thicken and will probably seize, becoming thick and granular. Keep adding heavy syrup until the chocolate becomes smooth and fluid again. Add only as much syrup as necessary to make this "writing chocolate" smooth and soft enough to pipe from a parchment decorating cone.

7. Spoon 1 tablespoon (1.5 cL) of the writing chocolate into the parchment decorating cone, fold over the back end to close it, and cut the tip. Pipe a scroll pattern around the rim of the gâteau and write *Alhambra*, or an inscription of your own choice, across the center.

8. Refrigerate the gâteau until the writing chocolate inscription has set. Lift the front sheet of paper off the sheet of gold leaf and turn it upside down. With the gold leaf still attached to the back sheet of paper, press a bit of it on one spot on the surface of the chocolate glaze and then lift the sheet away from the gâteau, leaving a flake of gold on the surface. Repeat in several other spots, including some on the inscription. Do not go overboard. At most, you should use about one quarter of the sheet of gold leaf.

STORAGE: In the refrigerator for up to 2 days.

Before glazing, freeze for up to 2 weeks. Once frozen, cover airtight with plastic wrap. Remove the plastic wrap and defrost overnight in the refrigerator, then glaze and decorate as usual.

Trianon Framboise

The Grand Trianon and Petit Trianon are two buildings on the grounds of the palace at Versailles. Perhaps some chef thought that the profile of a loaf-shaped gâteau resembled that of the mansard roof on the Grand Trianon.

Whatever the origin of the name, gâteaux named *trianon* are invariably loaf-shaped. This one is filled and frosted with raspberry buttercream, and the sides are glazed with chocolate.

For 10 to 12 servings

EQUIPMENT:

Rectangle of silver or gold matt board or foil board (page 467)
• cut about ¼ inch (6 mm) larger in length and width than the génoise loaf
A U-notch glue spreader (page 487) or cake-decorating comb (page 465)
Kitchen parchment
Chocolate thermometer or pocket digital thermometer
Rolling pin
Parchment decorating cone (page 416 , optional)

FILLING AND FROSTING:

French buttercream (page 384)	8½ ounces (240 g); 1⅓ cups + 1 tablespoon
Raspberry jam	4¼ ounces (120 g); 6 tablespoons
Framboise (raspberry brandy)	1 tablespoon (1.5 cL)
Red food coloring	

CAKE:

Almond génoise (page 342)	One 6-cup (1.5-L) loaf

BRUSHING-SYRUP MIXTURE:

Heavy syrup (page 452)	⅓ cup (8 cL)
Framboise (raspberry brandy)	2 tablespoons + 2 teaspoons (4 cL)
Water	2 tablespoons + 2 teaspoons (4 cL)

GLAZE FOR SIDES OF GÂTEAU:

European bittersweet chocolate, melted	10½ ounces (300 g)
Clarified butter (page 449), at room temperature	1¾ ounces (50 g); 3½ tablespoons

DECORATION FOR TOP OF GÂTEAU:

Almond paste (page 432)   3 ounces (85 g)

Red food coloring

Confectioners' sugar for dusting

OPTIONAL DECORATION:

Heavy syrup, heated to lukewarm   1 tablespoon (1.5 cL)

Unsweetened chocolate, melted   ½ ounce (15 g)

1. Beat the buttercream into the raspberry jam in a mixing bowl using a wooden spatula. Then beat in the *framboise* and a drop or two of red food coloring to give it a rich pink color.

2. Slice off the bottom of the génoise with a wavy-edge bread knife to make it flat. Turn it right side up. If it was not baked in a loaf pan with vertical sides, trim the sides to make them vertical and trim the matt board or foil board rectangle accordingly. Cut the génoise horizontally into three layers. Place the bottom layer on the matt board or foil board rectangle. Brush the top of this layer heavily with the *framboise* brushing syrup. Spread ¼ cup (45 g) of the raspberry buttercream over it with an icing spatula. Brush the bottom of the middle cake layer with the *framboise* syrup, turn it right side up, and place it on the first layer of buttercream. Brush the top of this layer heavily with the *framboise* syrup and spread it with ¼ cup (45 g) of the buttercream. Brush the bottom of the third cake layer heavily with the *framboise* syrup, turn it right side up, and place it on the second layer of buttercream. Lightly brush the outside of the loaf with the *framboise* syrup.

3. Spread the top and then the sides of the loaf with buttercream, making the layer on top about ¼ inch (6 mm) thick and leaving a rim of buttercream around the top edge of the loaf. Sweep the icing spatula across the top to take off the excess buttercream and make it smooth. Then make a wavy pattern from one end of the top to the other using the glue spreader or cake-decorating comb. Slide the loaf to the edge of your countertop and sweep the icing spatula over the side to take off the excess buttercream and make it smooth. Rotate the loaf and repeat with each side in turn until the entire outside of the loaf is coated with a smooth layer of buttercream.

4. Transfer the gâteau to a wire rack and chill it in the refrigerator until the buttercream is firm, at least 1 hour.

5. Cut a piece of parchment the size of the top of the gâteau and place the parchment on top, carefully aligning the edges. Press gently to secure the parchment on the buttercream around the edges and cut off any overhanging parchment if necessary.

6. If you did not melt the chocolate for the glaze in a stainless steel bowl, transfer it to one. Temper the chocolate as follows: Dip the bottom of the bowl of chocolate in a larger bowl of cold water and stir the chocolate until the temperature drops to between 80° and 84°F (26.5° to 29°C) and it begins to thicken. Immediately remove from the cold water and dip the bottom of the bowl of chocolate in a larger bowl of hot water. Stir over the hot water just long enough to warm the chocolate to between 86° and 91°F (30° to 33°C) and make it more fluid again. Then remove from the hot water immediately. Beat the clarified butter with a wooden spatula to make it smooth and creamy, then stir it into the chocolate.

7. Pour the chocolate over the edges of the parchment on top of the gâteau so that it runs evenly down all four sides of the loaf. Use the edge of an icing spatula as needed to make the chocolate flow off the parchment. Pour additional chocolate glaze over any areas that may need it, and tilt and tap the wire rack to be sure the chocolate flows evenly over the entire surface. Touch up any uneven areas around the sides with the icing spatula. Let the chocolate begin to thicken, then carefully lift off the parchment and clean off any excess chocolate around the bottom edge. Transfer the gâteau to a serving plate and let the chocolate glaze set.

8. On your countertop, work the almond paste with the heel of your hand to make it smooth. Tint it pink with a drop or two of red food coloring. Dust your countertop and the almond paste with confectioners' sugar. Roll out the almond paste into a sheet about ⅛ inch (3 mm) thick, at least 2 inches wide, and a little longer than the length of the gâteau using the rolling pin. Dust with more confectioners' sugar as needed to prevent sticking. Cut from the sheet of almond paste three long strips, one ¾ to 1 inch (2 to 2.5 cm) wide and two ⅜ inch (1 cm) wide. Cut the wide strip to the length of the top of the gâteau and place it on top of the gâteau, running down the center. Twist each narrow strip into a long spiral, and cut each spiral to the length of the top of the gâteau. Lay one spiral on either side of the strip down the center of the gâteau, spacing them evenly between the center strip and the side of the gâteau.

9. Optional: Gradually stir the heavy syrup into the melted chocolate. The chocolate will thicken and will probably seize, becoming thick and granular. Keep adding heavy syrup until the chocolate becomes smooth and fluid again. Add only as much syrup as necessary to make this "writing chocolate" smooth and soft enough to pipe from a parchment decorating cone.

Spoon 1 tablespoon (1.5 cL) of the writing chocolate into the parchment decorating cone, fold over the back end to close it, and cut the tip. Pipe an inscription (such as the name of the gâteau, "Happy Birthday," or anything else you like) on the wide strip of almond paste on top of the gâteau.

10. Refrigerate the gâteau until ready to serve.

STORAGE: In the refrigerator for up to 2 days.

Before glazing, freeze for up to 2 weeks. Once frozen, cover airtight with plastic wrap. Remove the plastic wrap and defrost overnight in the refrigerator, then glaze as usual.

Trianon Montmorency

In this variation on the *trianon* theme, the buttercream is flavored with kirsch and kirsch-soaked dried sour cherries are added to the filling. Montmorency is a variety of sour cherry. While dried cherries are American rather than French, the idea of soaking them in a brandy and using them in a gâteau is directly parallel to the common French practice of using rum-soaked raisins for this purpose.

For 10 to 12 servings

EQUIPMENT:

Rectangle of silver or gold matt board or foil board (page 467)
• cut about ¼ inch (6 mm) larger in length and width than the génoise loaf
Rolling pin
Ribbed rolling pin or sheet of ribbed vinyl floor mat (page 480)
Basketweave or checkerboard rolling pin or Lego assembly board
Parchment decorating cone (page 416)

FILLING AND FROSTING:

Dried sour cherries	2½ ounces (70 g); ¼ cup + 3 tablespoons
European kirsch	3 tablespoons (4.5 cL)
French buttercream (page 384)	12 ounces (340 g); 2 cups
Red food coloring	

CAKE:

Almond génoise (page 342)	One 6-cup (1.5-L) loaf

BRUSHING-SYRUP MIXTURE:

Heavy syrup (page 452)	⅓ cup (8 cL)
European kirsch	2 tablespoons + 2 teaspoons (4 cL)
Water	2 tablespoons + 2 teaspoons (4 cL)

DECORATION FOR SIDES AND TOP OF GÂTEAU:

Almond paste (page 432)	9 ounces (250 g)
Red, green, and yellow food colorings	
Confectioners' sugar for dusting	

continued

1. Place the dried cherries in a strainer and steam them over simmering water until they just begin to soften, about 5 minutes. Transfer the cherries to a glass jar and pour 2 tablespoons (3 cL) of the kirsch over them. Cover airtight and let steep in the kirsch for at least 2 hours and preferably overnight. When ready to make the gâteau, drain the cherries thoroughly and cut them into halves or quarters if they are large.

2. Flavor the buttercream with the remaining 1 tablespoon (1.5 cL) kirsch. Beat in a drop or two of red food coloring to give it a rich pink color. Set aside about 2 tablespoons (25 g) of the kirsch buttercream for decorating.

3. Slice off the bottom of the génoise with a wavy-edge bread knife to make it flat. Turn it right side up and cut the génoise horizontally into three layers. Place the bottom layer on the matt board or foil board rectangle. Brush the top of this layer heavily with the kirsch brushing syrup. Spread a thin layer of the kirsch buttercream over it with an icing spatula. Scatter half of the cherries over the buttercream. Spread just enough kirsch buttercream over the cherries to fill the gaps between them and barely cover them to make a layer of uniform thickness. Brush the bottom of the middle cake layer with the kirsch syrup, turn it right side up, and place it on the first layer of buttercream. Brush the top of this layer heavily with the kirsch syrup and spread it with a thin layer of the kirsch buttercream. Scatter the remaining cherries over the buttercream, and barely cover them with an even layer of buttercream as with the previous layer. Brush the bottom of the third cake layer heavily with the syrup, turn it right side up, and place it on the second layer of buttercream. Lightly brush the outside of the loaf with the kirsch syrup.

4. Spread the top and then the sides of the loaf with kirsch buttercream, leaving a rim of buttercream around the top edge of the loaf. Sweep the icing spatula across the top to take off the excess buttercream and make it smooth. Slide the loaf to the edge of your countertop and sweep the icing spatula over the side to take off the excess buttercream and make it smooth. Rotate the loaf and repeat with each side in turn until the entire outside of the loaf is coated with a smooth layer of buttercream.

5. Transfer the gâteau to a wire rack and chill it in the refrigerator until the buttercream is firm, at least 1 hour.

6. On your countertop, work the almond paste with the heel of your hand to make it smooth. Set aside about one quarter of the almond paste. Tint the remaining three quarters pink with a drop or two of red food coloring. Dust your countertop and the pink almond paste with confectioners' sugar. Roll out the pink almond paste into a sheet a little thicker than ⅛ inch (3 mm), at least 6 inches (15 cm) wide, and about 12 inches (30 cm) long using the plain rolling pin, dusting with more confectioners' sugar as needed to prevent sticking. Roll the ribbed rolling pin down the length of the sheet of almond paste to impress the ribbed texture on it. (Or dust the almond paste with confectioners' sugar, turn it upside down on the sheet of ribbed vinyl, and roll the plain rolling pin over it to impress the texture. Then carefully peel the sheet of almond paste off the vinyl and turn it textured side up on your countertop.) Measure the height of the loaf along the sloping side and cut two bands of almond paste as wide as the loaf is high. From each band cut two rectangles, one as long as the base of the loaf and the other as long as the width of the loaf. One at a time, press each rectangle against the frosting on one side of the loaf and cut off the excess at the ends using scissors. Gather together the clean almond paste trimmings and work them into a smooth pad. Dust with confectioners' sugar and roll out this pad of almond paste into a rough rectangle a little thicker than ⅛ inch (3 mm) and at least as large as the top of the loaf. Roll a textured rolling pin (preferably a basketweave or checkerboard one) down the length of the sheet to impress the texture. (Or dust the almond paste with confectioners' sugar, turn it upside down on the Lego assembly board, and roll the plain rolling pin over it to impress the texture. Then carefully peel the sheet of almond paste off the Lego assembly board and turn it textured side up on your countertop.) Cut out a rectangle the size of the top of the loaf and place it on top to finish covering the outside.

7. Divide the untinted almond paste in half. Work a drop each of green and yellow food coloring into one half to tint it a pale green. Roll the green almond paste into a sheet about ³⁄₃₂ inch (2 mm) thick and cut from it a few leaf shapes. Form the remaining untinted almond paste into a rose (see page 430).

8. Spoon the reserved buttercream into the parchment decorating cone and cut the tip. Pipe a decorative bead of buttercream over all the seams where the rectangles of almond paste meet. Arrange the rose and leaves on top of the loaf, sticking them in place with a little buttercream.

9. Refrigerate the gâteau until ready to serve.

NOTE: If you prefer, you can pipe a decorative bead of royal icing (page 419), instead of buttercream, over the seams where the sheets of almond paste meet.

STORAGE: In the refrigerator for up to 2 days.

Before covering with almond paste, freeze for up to 2 weeks. Once frozen, cover airtight with plastic wrap. Remove the plastic wrap and defrost overnight in the refrigerator, then finish as usual.

Bourbon Chocolat

Although this gâteau utilizes two distinctly American ingredients, pecans and Kentucky bourbon, it is clearly French in style. The cake layers are pecan *mousseline*.

For 10 to 12 servings

EQUIPMENT:

Rectangle of silver or gold matt board or foil board (page 467)
• cut about ¼ inch (6 mm) larger in length and width than the génoise loaf
Chocolate thermometer or pocket digital thermometer
Small pastry bag fitted with
• fluted decorating tube (such as the Ateco #17 open star tube)

FILLING AND FROSTING:

Coffee buttercream (page 390)	11 ounces (315 g); 1¾ cups
Pecans, finely chopped	1 ounce (25 g); 3 tablespoons

CAKE:

Pecan *mousseline* (page 346)	One 6-cup (1.5-L) loaf

BRUSHING-SYRUP MIXTURE:

Heavy syrup (page 452)	⅓ cup (8 cL)
Kentucky bourbon	2 tablespoons + 2 teaspoons (4 cL)
Water	2 tablespoons + 2 teaspoons (4 cL)

GLAZE:

European bittersweet chocolate, melted	12 ounces (340 g)
Clarified butter (page 449), at room temperature	1¾ ounces (50 g); 3½ tablespoons

DECORATION FOR TOP OF GÂTEAU:

Pecan half	1

1. Set aside about ¼ cup (45 g) of the coffee buttercream for piping on top of the gâteau.

2. Slice off the bottom of the pecan *mousseline* loaf with a wavy-edge bread knife to make it flat. Turn it right side up, and cut the loaf horizontally into three layers. Place the bottom layer on the matt board or foil board rectangle. Brush the top of this layer heavily with the bourbon brushing syrup. Spread ¼ cup (45 g) of the coffee buttercream over it with an icing spatula and scatter half of the chopped pecans over the buttercream. Brush the bottom of the middle cake layer with the bourbon syrup, turn it right side up, and place it on the first layer of buttercream. Brush the top of this layer heavily with the bourbon syrup, spread it with ¼ cup (45 g) of the buttercream, and scatter the remaining chopped pecans over the buttercream. Brush the bottom of the third cake layer heavily with the bourbon syrup, turn it right side up, and place it on the second layer of buttercream. Lightly brush the outside of the loaf with the bourbon syrup.

3. Spread the top and then the sides of the loaf with coffee buttercream, leaving a rim of buttercream around the top edge of the loaf. Sweep the icing spatula across the top to take off the excess buttercream and make it smooth. Slide the loaf to the edge of your countertop and sweep the icing spatula over the side to take off the excess buttercream and make it smooth. Rotate the loaf and repeat with each side in turn until the entire outside of the loaf is coated with a smooth layer of buttercream.

4. Slide the gâteau onto a wire rack and chill it in the refrigerator until the buttercream is firm, at least 1 hour.

5. If you did not melt the chocolate for the glaze in a stainless steel bowl, transfer it to one. Temper the chocolate as follows: Dip the bottom of the bowl of chocolate in a larger bowl of cold water and stir the chocolate until the temperature drops to between 80° and 84°F (26.5° to 29°C) and it begins to thicken. Immediately remove from the cold water and dip the bottom of the bowl of chocolate in a larger bowl of hot water. Stir over the hot water just long enough to warm the chocolate to between 86° and 91°F (30° to 33°C) and make it more fluid again. Then remove from the hot water immediately. Beat the clarified butter with a wooden spatula to make it smooth and creamy, then stir it into the chocolate.

6. Pour the chocolate on top of the gâteau in a rectangle just inside the perimeter so that some of it flows naturally over the edges. Quickly smooth the top surface with an icing spatula to cover the entire top with a thin layer of glaze and make the excess flow evenly down the sides. Pour additional chocolate over any areas that need it, and tilt and tap the wire rack to be sure the chocolate flows evenly over the entire surface. Touch up any uneven areas around the sides with the edge of the icing spatula. Let the chocolate begin to thicken, then clean off any excess chocolate around the bottom edge. Transfer the gâteau to a serving plate and let the glaze set.

7. Scoop the reserved buttercream into the pastry bag, and pipe a row of overlapping teardrops around the rim of the gâteau. Pipe one rosette on the center and four teardrops pointing out from the center. Place a pecan half on the rosette in the center.

8. Refrigerate the gâteau until ready to serve.

STORAGE: In the refrigerator for up to 2 days.

Before glazing, freeze for up to 2 weeks. Once frozen, cover airtight with plastic wrap. Remove the plastic wrap and defrost overnight in the refrigerator, then glaze and decorate.

Components

CHAPTER EIGHT

Fillings and Frostings

· ·

In this chapter we focus primarily on those fillings and frostings that are easiest to prepare in quantities larger than you will need for a single dessert and that store very well. Many of them are versatile enough that you can use them in a variety of desserts. We also include a few preparations that are used frequently and deserve a little more detailed explanation than we can include in the recipes for the desserts. For example, brief instructions for making whipped cream (*crème chantilly*) are included in the recipe for each dessert that requires it, and more extensive instructions and options for variations are included in the whipped cream recipe in this chapter.

We do not differentiate here between fillings and frostings. Most of the preparations can be used as either, and often as both in the same dessert. The only real exception is Italian meringue, which is used alone as a frosting but never as a filling. However, you can make several fillings by mixing this light meringue with something else, such as creamed butter. Italian meringue can also be baked as a batter, and the recipe for it is included in chapter 4, Meringues (see page 184).

French Buttercream

· ·

Buttercream was one of the great developments in French pastry made during the middle of the nineteenth century. It is claimed to have been developed by Remondet, who was chef to the prince of Joinville. The taste and texture of buttercream are essential features of countless gâteaux.

There are several methods for making buttercream, but they all rely on a variety of egg-yolk-and-sugar preparations into which butter is incorporated. The yolks are always cooked with the sugar in some way, and then the mixture is whipped as it cools to make it light. In French, this egg-yolk-and-sugar preparation is called a *pâte à bombe*, because it is also used as the base for the interior of the elegant frozen desserts called bombes in both French and English. There is no English term for *pâte à bombe*, so we will just use a direct translation and call it a "bombe batter." For example, to make the classic French buttercream you first whip a hot firm-ball sugar syrup into egg yolks to cook the yolks, then continue whipping the mixture as it cools to make a light, thick preparation, which is the bombe batter. Finally you beat in softened butter to transform the bombe batter into the finished buttercream. The result is a velvety smooth, rich, stable, and versatile filling that, when combined with cake layers (in particular génoise), becomes a building block for innumerable classic gâteaux.

While this classic method produces the most elegant of the standard buttercream recipes, it has become common practice among French pastry chefs to "improve" it in various ways. For example, while the buttercream itself is rich without being heavy, it can be made even lighter (as well as slightly sweeter) by the addition of a little Italian meringue. On the other hand, for some cakes it is too firm and rich, and in these cases it can be made softer and less rich (but also heavier) by mixing it with French pastry cream. In a professional pastry kitchen where all of these components are readily available, such refinements are easy to make. But for the home cook they are unrealistic.

We have developed a new method of preparing buttercream which shares the good qualities of the classic French buttercream and tastes identical to it, but is at once lighter, softer, and creamier and requires only a single preparation. It also eliminates the risk of producing lumps of scrambled egg yolk when adding the hot sugar syrup—a common problem for cooks making buttercream for the first few times.

One variable in our new method is the number of egg whites. With a few notable exceptions, two egg whites give the best result. However, if you will be flavoring the buttercream with chocolate or *praliné*, then three whites are preferable. Also, if you are not experienced in working with hot sugar syrup and meringue, then you may find the recipe slightly easier to use with three whites rather than two.

For 2 pounds + 4 ounces (1,000 g); about 6 cups

EQUIPMENT:

Large bowl of cold water or candy thermometer
Electric mixer, preferably a stand mixer equipped with both wire whip and flat beater

Granulated sugar	12¼ ounces (350 g); 1¾ cups
Water	½ cup (1.2 dL)
Large egg whites (see note), at room temperature	2 (standard) or 3 (for flavoring buttercream with chocolate or *praliné*)
Cream of tartar (optional)	⅛ teaspoon (a pinch)
Large egg yolks, at room temperature	5
Unsalted butter, softened	1 pound + 2 ounces (500 g); 2¼ cups

1. Combine the sugar and water in a heavy 1-quart (1-L) saucepan or caramel pot and stir to thoroughly moisten the sugar. Bring to a boil over medium heat. Moisten a pastry brush with cold water and wash down the sides of the saucepan to dissolve any sugar crystals that form there. Continue boiling over medium heat without stirring, washing down the walls of the saucepan as needed to dissolve sugar crystals, until the sugar reaches the high end of the firm-ball stage (see pages 535–36). When you pluck a little syrup from the saucepan and immerse it in the bowl of cold water, you will be able to roll the syrup into a firm ball that holds its shape and is no longer sticky. The temperature of the syrup will measure 248°F (120°C) on the candy thermometer.

2. Meanwhile, when the sugar comes to a boil, start whipping the egg whites in the mixer at low speed until they start to froth. If you are not whipping the whites in a copper bowl, add the cream of tartar at this point. Gradually increase the whipping speed, and continue whipping at medium to high speed until the whites form very stiff peaks and just begin to slip and streak around the side of the bowl. Adjust the speed at which you whip the whites (lowering the speed if necessary) and the rate at which you cook the sugar so that they are ready simultaneously.

3. Pour the syrup into the egg whites in a steady stream while you whip the whites at high speed ①. Try to pour the syrup directly into the whites, but in a mixer with a steep-sided bowl you will probably need to pour the syrup down the side of the bowl in order to avoid pouring it onto the whip and splattering syrup around the inside of the bowl. The meringue will rise and become very light. When you have added about three quarters of the syrup, set the pot of syrup aside momentarily and pour in the egg yolks all at once ②. Then quickly pour in the remaining syrup.

4. Reduce the whipping speed to medium and continue whipping until the mixture is cool and still very light. This is the buttercream base.

5. Before adding the butter, remove any sugar syrup that has solidified on the side of the bowl using a bowl scraper.

6. Gradually beat in the softened butter at medium speed, using the flat beater if your mixer has one ③. When all of the butter has been added, beat the buttercream vigorously to make it as light as possible.

7. Use the buttercream right away, or refrigerate it for later use.

NOTE: If salmonella in eggs is a problem in your area, then it is important to pasteurize the eggs. The eggs in the buttercream base are partially cooked by the heat of the sugar syrup. Unfortunately, while the heat of the syrup is, in principle, sufficient to raise the temperature of the eggs above 160°F (71°C) and pasteurize them instantly, the mixing bowl quickly absorbs heat from the meringue and (depending on the size of the bowl, number of eggs, and speed of adding the syrup) may prevent the temperature of the buttercream base from actually reaching the pasteurization point.

The solution to this problem is to warm the mixer bowl and the egg whites before whipping.

To warm the bowl and egg whites, first turn the mixer bowl upside down in your sink and run hot tap water over it to heat it quickly. While the bowl is being warmed, pour some hot tap water into a bowl or saucepan large enough to set your mixer bowl in. Adjust the temperature of the water in the bowl to 120°F (50°C), and adjust the level of the water so that it is high enough to surround the bottom of the mixer bowl but not so high that the mixer bowl will float and tip over. Set the heated mixer bowl in the hot water bath, be sure that it is dry inside, and pour in the whites. Stir the whites occasionally with a wire whisk while you are bringing the sugar syrup to a boil. If the temperature of the hot water bath starts to drop below 120°F (50°C), add more hot water to keep the temperature there. When the syrup comes to a boil, remove the mixer bowl from the hot water bath and whip the whites as instructed in the recipe. Pour the hot sugar syrup into the whipped whites quickly, immediately followed by the egg yolks and the remaining hot sugar syrup so that the heat of the syrup will raise the temperature of the eggs all at once, before too much heat drains off into the mixer bowl.

NOTE ON QUANTITY: This recipe produces a fairly large quantity of buttercream. Unfortunately, it would be very difficult to prepare a smaller quantity of the buttercream base. If you do not have a stand mixer with a fat beater, you may want to divide the buttercream base in half and process each half separately following step 6 with half of the butter.

STORAGE: Covered airtight for up to 1 week in the refrigerator. Before using, let the buttercream soften at room temperature. Then beat it vigorously with a wooden spatula or the flat beater of the mixer to make it smooth, spreadable, and light.

Or divide the buttercream into quantities suitable for the desserts you expect to make and freeze for up to 3 months. A typical gâteau requires 1½ to 2½ cups (260 to 425 g) of buttercream for filling and frosting. Defrost overnight in the refrigerator, then proceed as for refrigerated buttercream.

NOTE ON SOFTENING REFRIGERATED BUTTERCREAM: If you forget to remove the buttercream from the refrigerator in advance, you can warm and soften it quickly in a stainless steel bowl. Briefly warm the bottom of the bowl over direct heat, stirring constantly and cutting the buttercream into pieces with a wooden spatula. Remove it from the heat and beat it vigorously with the wooden spatula. Return it to the heat and repeat as often as necessary to make the buttercream smooth and spreadable. Do not warm the buttercream too quickly or it will be lumpy.

If you do not warm the buttercream enough while softening, it may become grainy and deflate. This can also result from adding too much liquid flavoring or the right amount of flavoring in too soft a buttercream. If this happens, continue warming the buttercream and beating it vigorously with a wooden spatula until it is soft. Then beat it with a stiff wire whisk or in the mixer using the flat beater to make it light again. If the buttercream still doesn't look right, melt about one tenth as much butter as you have buttercream and beat the melted butter into the buttercream with the wire whisk or flat beater of the mixer to make it light and smooth again.

Chocolate Buttercream and Praliné Buttercream

· ·

When you flavor buttercream with chocolate or *praliné*, the flavoring has an unfortunate tendency to distort the beautiful texture of the buttercream. The standard response to this problem is to add only a small proportion of chocolate or *praliné*, so that the buttercream texture isn't altered too much. With our new, improved French buttercream we can now offer a more satisfactory resolution: If you prepare our French buttercream with 3 egg whites, rather than the standard 2 whites, then you can add 50 percent more chocolate or *praliné* to the buttercream without sacrificing the texture of the buttercream. The rule of thumb we use is that with the 3-egg-white buttercream recipe you can add an amount of unsweetened chocolate equal to 15 percent of the weight of the buttercream, or an amount of *praliné* equal to 30 percent of the weight of the buttercream. As an example, we give the proportions needed to make 1 pound (450 to 460 g) of chocolate or *praliné* buttercream.

As an added bonus, when you beat our flavored buttercreams they will become even lighter than our basic French buttercream. How light depends on how long you beat them and on the temperature of the buttercream. To get maximum lightness, the buttercream must be cool enough that the butter does not melt, and it must stay cool or it can deflate.

For 1 pound (450 to 460 g); about 2⅔ cups

EQUIPMENT:
Electric mixer, preferably a stand mixer equipped with both wire whip and flat beater

CHOCOLATE BUTTERCREAM:

Unsweetened chocolate, melted	2 ounces (60 g)
French Buttercream (page 384, 3-egg-white version)	14 ounces (400 g); 2¼ cups

PRALINÉ BUTTERCREAM:

Praliné (page 446)	3½ ounces (100 g); ⅓ cup
French Buttercream (3-egg-white version)	12 ounces (350 g); 2 cups

1. Place the melted chocolate or the *praliné* in a small stainless steel mixing bowl and gradually beat in about one quarter of the buttercream using a wooden spatula ①.

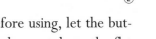

If the chocolate seizes when you have added a small amount of buttercream, gently warm the bowl with the chocolate and continue beating in buttercream until the chocolate is melted and smooth again. Then remove from the heat and beat in more buttercream.

If there are lumps in the *praliné* when you have added a small amount of buttercream, mash them with the wooden spatula and be sure the mixture is smooth before adding more buttercream.

2. When you have mixed about one quarter of the buttercream into the chocolate or *praliné*, beat the flavored portion of the buttercream back into the remaining unflavored buttercream ②.

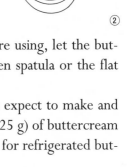

3. To make the chocolate or *praliné* buttercream as light as possible before using, scoop it into the bowl of the mixer and beat, with the flat beater if your mixer has one, until the color of the buttercream lightens noticeably.

STORAGE: Covered airtight for up to 1 week in the refrigerator. Before using, let the buttercream soften at room temperature. Then beat it vigorously with a wooden spatula or the flat beater of the mixer to make it smooth, spreadable, and light.

Or divide the buttercream into quantities suitable for the desserts you expect to make and freeze for up to 3 months. A typical gâteau requires 1½ to 2½ cups (260 to 425 g) of buttercream for filling and frosting. Defrost overnight in the refrigerator, then proceed as for refrigerated buttercream.

For notes on softening refrigerated buttercream, see page 387.

Coffee Buttercream

. . . .

For this buttercream, the buttercream base is a *crème anglaise* (English custard), but prepared with an unusually high proportion of egg yolks and sugar or, equivalently, a very low proportion of milk. The proportions make the preparation more delicate than an ordinary *crème anglaise,* and the result is a hair less elegant than our French buttercream. However, this method makes it possible for you to incorporate coffee flavor in a way that is superior to anything possible with other types of buttercream.

The problem is that to add sufficient coffee flavor to buttercream after the fact requires a very strong coffee extract in order to avoid adding too much water, which would make the buttercream curdle. The only practical way to make such a strong extract is to dissolve instant coffee in the minimum possible amount of boiling water. It should come as no surprise that the resulting buttercream tastes like instant coffee as opposed to real coffee.

With the custard buttercream base, you can incorporate the coffee flavor from the outset by steeping coarsely crushed coffee beans in the milk before straining the milk and using it in the custard. The result is a buttercream with a freshly brewed coffee taste.

The custard buttercream base also has a second advantage. If you feel uncomfortable about working with hot sugar syrups, then this method may be a less threatening alternative. If you prefer to prepare your basic buttercream using the custard base method, simply follow this recipe, eliminating the coffee and step 1 and reducing the quantity of milk to ¾ cup (1.8 dL).

For 2 pounds + 6½ ounces (1,080 g); about 6 cups

EQUIPMENT:

Mortar and pestle
Electric mixer, preferably a stand mixer equipped with both wire whip and flat beater

Espresso coffee beans	1¾ ounces (50 g); ¾ cup
Milk	1 cup (2.4 dL)
Granulated sugar	10½ ounces (300 g); 1½ cups
Large egg yolks, at room temperature	8
Unsalted butter, softened	1 pound + 5 ounces (600 g); 2⅔ cups

1. Coarsely crush the espresso beans in a mortar and pestle ①, processing in small batches so that none of the coffee is crushed finely. Combine the crushed espresso beans with the milk in a small saucepan and bring to a simmer. Remove from the heat, cover, and let steep for 10 minutes. Strain through a fine sieve, pressing down on the beans to extract as much milk as possible. You should have about ¾ cup (1.8 dL) of espresso-flavored milk. If necessary, add a little milk to get back up to ¾ cup (1.8 dL). Discard the coffee grounds and rinse out the sieve so it will be ready to use again for straining the custard.

①

2. Combine the espresso-flavored milk with ¼ cup (50 g) of the sugar in a heavy 1-quart (1-L) saucepan and bring to a simmer.

3. Meanwhile, combine the egg yolks with the remaining sugar in a mixing bowl and beat with a wire whisk until smooth and lemon-colored. Pour in about half of the hot milk, whisking constantly. Pour this mixture back into the saucepan and stir until thoroughly blended.

②

4. Place the saucepan over medium heat and, stirring constantly with a wooden spatula, bring the custard almost to a simmer. Reduce the heat to low and cook, stirring constantly with the spatula ②, until the custard thickens and coats the spatula heavily. (When you draw a line across the back of the custard-coated spatula with your fingertip, the custard should not flow back over the line ③). Reduce the heat to the lowest possible setting (moving the saucepan to the side of the burner as needed) and keep the mixture hot, again stirring constantly, for 4 minutes to pasteurize it.

③

5. Immediately strain the custard through the fine sieve into the bowl of the mixer. Beat the custard with the wire whip at medium speed until it is light and cool. This is the buttercream base.

6. Gradually beat in the softened butter at medium speed, using the flat beater if your mixer has one ④. When all of the butter has been added, beat the buttercream vigorously to make it as light as possible.

7. Use the buttercream right away, or refrigerate it for later use.

④

NOTE ON QUANTITY: This recipe produces a fairly large quantity of buttercream. Unfortunately, it would be very difficult to prepare a smaller quantity of the custard base. If you do not have a stand mixer with a flat beater, you may want to divide the custard base in half and process each half separately following step 6 with half of the butter.

STORAGE: Covered airtight for up to 1 week in the refrigerator. Before using, let the buttercream soften at room temperature. Then beat it vigorously with a wooden spatula or the flat beater of the mixer to make it smooth, spreadable, and light.

continued

Or divide the buttercream into quantities suitable for the desserts you expect to make and freeze for up to 3 months. A typical gâteau requires 1½ to 2½ cups (260 to 425 g) of buttercream for filling and frosting. Defrost overnight in the refrigerator, then proceed as for refrigerated buttercream.

For notes on softening refrigerated buttercream, see page 387.

Lemon Curd

. . . .

Lemon curd is not a common filling in French desserts. This recipe is an English lemon custard that Paul adapted for use in lemon charlottes.

For 1 pound + 9 ounces (700 g); 2⅔ cups

Fresh lemons	**4 small or 3 medium-size**
Large eggs	**4**
Granulated sugar	**9 ounces (250 g); 1¼ cups**
Unsalted butter, softened	**6 ounces (170 g); ¾ cup**

1. Finely grate the aromatic yellow zest from the outsides of the lemons. Juice the lemons and strain the juice. You should have about ½ cup (1.2 dL) of lemon juice.

2. Combine the eggs and sugar in a small mixing bowl and beat with the wire whisk until well mixed. Beat in the lemon zest and juice. Pour the mixture into a small, heavy saucepan.

3. Place the saucepan over medium heat and bring to a simmer, stirring constantly with a wooden spatula ①. Reduce the heat to very low and continue cooking, stirring constantly, until the mixture coats the spatula heavily. Do not boil or the custard will curdle.

4. Pour the mixture into a bowl and stir in the softened butter, one tablespoon (15 g) at a time. Let cool to room temperature.

STORAGE: Covered airtight for up to 1 week in the refrigerator.

Or freeze for up to 1 month. Defrost overnight in the refrigerator before using.

①

French Pastry Cream

Called *crème pâtissière* in French, this is a stove-top custard thickened with eggs, flour, and potato starch. The combination of starches gives it both stability and a refined texture. It is dense and smooth, but not very rich.

Pastry cream is used in many French pastries. However, in gâteaux it is used only occasionally, and then usually mixed with another filling to make it lighter.

For 1 pound + 8 ounces (680 g); 2⅔ cups

Milk	**1½ cups (3.6 dL)**
Vanilla bean	**½**
All-purpose flour	**1¼ ounces (35 g); ¼ cup**
Potato starch	**1¼ ounces (35 g); 3 tablespoons**
Large eggs	**2**
Large egg yolks	**2**
Granulated sugar	**5¼ ounces (150 g); ¾ cup**
Unsalted butter, softened	**2½ ounces (70 g); ¼ cup + 1 tablespoon**

1. Pour the milk into a small, heavy saucepan. Slit open the vanilla bean lengthwise and scrape out the seeds into the milk ①. Add the pod to the milk as well. Bring to a simmer, being careful not to let the milk boil over.

2. Meanwhile, sift together the flour and potato starch onto a sheet of wax paper. Combine the whole eggs, egg yolks, and sugar in a mixing bowl and beat with a wire whisk until smooth and lemon-colored. Whisk in the flour and potato starch. Pour in about half of the hot milk, whisking constantly. Pour this mixture back into the saucepan and stir until thoroughly blended and smooth.

3. Place the saucepan over medium heat and bring the pastry cream to a boil, stirring constantly with the wire whisk. Reduce the heat to low and continue boiling, stirring constantly and vigorously

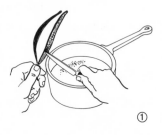

①

②

with the whisk ②, until the pastry cream no longer tastes of raw flour and develops a more velvety consistency, about 3 minutes. It will be very thick and smooth.

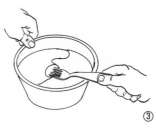

4. Strain the pastry cream through a fine sieve into a stainless steel bowl and stir in ¼ cup (55 g) of the butter. Rub the remaining 1 tablespoon (15 g) of butter over the surface of the pastry cream ③ to prevent a skin from forming on top. Then let cool to room temperature.

STORAGE: Covered airtight for up to 1 week in the refrigerator. Before using, let the pastry cream soften at room temperature. Then beat in the butter coating the surface using a wire whisk.

Crème Mousseline

(LIGHT PASTRY CREAM)

The classic buttercreams are very rich, which is fine when they are used in thin layers between light, airy sponge cakes or meringues. However, in cakes that require thick layers of filling, the richness of buttercream can be too much of a good thing. The usual alternatives are pastry creams (soft and heavy) and mousses (light and fluffy). But there is another possibility. *Crème mousseline* is basically a cross between buttercream and pastry cream. In fact, the recipe many professionals use for it simply mixes two parts buttercream with one part pastry cream—very convenient and flexible in a pastry shop where these two components are always available. But in most home kitchens, such is not the case, and it is more natural to prepare the *crème mousseline* as a component in its own right. Taking this approach also allows you to see clearly that *crème mousseline* is really just a pastry cream with an unusually high proportion of butter added. When you beat the cold pastry cream, that butter content allows you to incorporate more air than in a standard pastry cream. So *crème mousseline* becomes very light relative to classic pastry cream, and hence its name. Unfortunately, that evocative (but vague in its reference) name has deceived some rather distinguished pastry chefs into thinking it is lighter than buttercream. Not so! *Crème mousseline* is definitely softer and less rich than buttercream, but it is actually at least 10 percent heavier than buttercream. You can't have everything.

Yet another way to view *crème mousseline* is as a *crème anglaise*–based buttercream (see our coffee buttercream recipe, page 390), with the *crème anglaise* replaced by pastry cream and the butter content greatly reduced. With the *crème anglaise* base, the high butter content was essential to keep the buttercream from curdling. In contrast, the flour and starch in the pastry cream base for *crème mousseline* make the lower butter content possible.

For 2 pounds + 1 ounce (925 g); about 4½ cups

EQUIPMENT:
Electric mixer, preferably a stand mixer equipped with flat beater

Milk	**1½ cups (3.6 dL)**
All-purpose flour	**¾ ounce (20 g); 2⅓ tablespoons**
Potato starch	**¾ ounce (20 g); 2 tablespoons**
Large egg	**1**
Large egg yolks	**7**
Granulated sugar	**7 ounces (200 g); 1 cup**
Unsalted butter, softened	**10½ ounces (300 g); 1¼ cups + 1 tablespoon**

1. Bring the milk to a simmer in a small, heavy saucepan.

2. Meanwhile, sift together the flour and potato starch onto a sheet of wax paper. Combine the whole egg, egg yolks, and sugar in a mixing bowl and beat with a wire whisk until smooth and lemon-colored. Whisk in the flour and potato starch. Pour in about half the hot milk, whisking constantly. Pour this mixture back into the saucepan and stir until thoroughly blended and smooth ①.

①

3. Place the saucepan over medium heat and bring the pastry cream to a boil, stirring constantly with the wire whisk. Reduce the heat to low and continue boiling, stirring constantly and vigorously with the whisk, until the pastry cream no longer tastes of raw flour and develops a more velvety consistency, about 3 minutes. It will be very thick and smooth.

4. Strain the pastry cream through a fine sieve into a stainless steel bowl and stir in ¼ cup (50 g) of the butter. Allow to cool, stirring occasionally.

②

5. Cream the remaining butter in the mixer, using the flat beater if your mixer has one. Gradually beat in the pastry cream at medium speed to make the *crème mousseline* ②. After all the pastry cream has been added, beat vigorously with the flat beater to lighten the *crème mousseline*.

6. Use the *crème mousseline* right away, or refrigerate it for later use.

NOTE ON QUANTITY: This recipe produces a fairly large quantity of *crème mousseline*. Unfortunately, it would be very difficult to prepare a smaller quantity of the pastry cream base. If you do not have a stand mixer with a flat beater, you may want to divide the pastry cream base in half and process each half separately following step 5 with half of the butter.

STORAGE: Covered airtight for up to 1 week in the refrigerator. Before using, let the *crème mousseline* soften at room temperature. Then beat it vigorously with a wooden spatula or the flat beater of the mixer to make it smooth and spreadable.

Or freeze for up to 3 months. Defrost overnight in the refrigerator, then proceed as for refrigerated *crème mousseline*.

Whipped Cream

· ·

In France, sweetened whipped cream is called *crème chantilly*. It was supposedly invented by Vatel when he was maître d'hotel to Nicolas Fouquet, a former minister of finance under King Louis XIV. Supposedly *crème chantilly* was first served on August 17, 1661, at a banquet that Fouquet gave at his estate, Vaux-le-Vicomte, to honor the king. Actually the banquet was just part of a grand festival that included a comedy-ballet, *Les Facheux* by Molière, and inspired poetry by Jean de La Fontaine. As a result of this party and Fouquet's other activities (which included assembling a private army and building a fortified castle on the Breton coast), the king decided that he was, perhaps, too ambitious and had him arrested three weeks later.

Vatel then went to work for Louis II de Bourbon, Prince of Condé. The princes of Condé belonged to a branch of the French royal family and owned the castle of Chantilly.

The only secret to making whipped cream is that the cream and the whipping utensils should be cold. It can be made with pasteurized heavy cream or whipping cream or with crème fraîche, which is more flavorful. Heavy cream is easier to whip than whipping cream because it has a higher butterfat content. Because crème fraîche is very thick, it is easier to overwhip than heavy cream. To reduce the risk of overwhipping, thin it first with a little ice-cold milk.

For 1 pound + 2½ ounces (530 g); 4 cups

EQUIPMENT:
Electric mixer or wire whisk

Confectioners' sugar	1¾ ounces (50 g); ⅓ cup + 4 teaspoons
Either heavy cream	2 cups (5 dL)
Or crème fraîche (page 451),	1¾ cups (4.5 dL)
thinned with ice-cold milk	¼ cup (6 cL)
Either vanilla bean	¼
Or dark Jamaican or Haitian rum, European	
kirsch, Grand Marnier, or other liqueur	2 tablespoons (3 cL)

1. Mix the sugar with the heavy cream or the thinned crème fraîche in the bowl of the mixer and, if possible, chill the cream for an hour or so while the sugar dissolves. This makes the whipped cream lighter. Chill the whisk or beater you will be using to whip the cream as well.

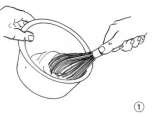

2. If you want a vanilla-flavored whipped cream, slit open the vanilla bean lengthwise and scrape out the seeds into the cream. Reserve the pod for another purpose (such as a *crème anglaise*).

3. Whip the cream at medium speed in the mixer or with a wire whisk ①. Slow down when the cream holds soft peaks to avoid overbeating. Continue whipping until the cream is light and thick and holds stiff peaks. Do not overbeat or the cream will curdle.

4. If you want to flavor the whipped cream with liqueur, gently fold it in with a rubber spatula ②.

STORAGE: Best used right away, but keeps for a short time in the refrigerator if necessary. After about 2 hours it will begin to separate. When that happens you can beat the cream with a wire whisk for a few seconds to pull it back together, but it will no longer be as firm and light as when it was first made. Or you can reduce the separation problem by placing the whipped cream in a cheesecloth-lined strainer over a bowl, so that excess liquid drains from it while it chills in the refrigerator.

Ganaches

(CHOCOLATE CREAM FILLINGS)

. . . .

A ganache is a rich filling made from cream and chocolate. According to the 1984 edition of the *Larousse Gastronomique*, it was invented at the Pâtisserie Siraudin in Paris sometime around 1850. Originally it was used only in chocolate bonbons, especially chocolate truffles. Books published at the end of the nineteenth and beginning of the twentieth century refer to it as *crème ganache*. In *L'Art Culinaire Moderne*, first published in 1936, Henri-Paul Pellaprat (the great cookbook author and teaching chef at the École du Cordon Bleu in Paris) recommended it for filling *petits fours*, but he made no mention of using it in larger desserts.

Today, ganache is one of the preeminent chocolate fillings for gâteaux of all sizes, as well as remaining, by far, the most important filling in chocolate bonbons. The consistency of the ganache is determined by the ratio of chocolate to cream. The more chocolate, the firmer the ganache. Also, a ganache made from chocolate with a higher cocoa butter content will be firmer than one made from a low cocoa butter chocolate. Whatever the proportions, ganache is a dense, rich filling, and this is the way we like it. However, some chefs like to make it lighter by whipping it to incorporate air when it begins to thicken.

Aside from the proportions, the quality of the ganache will be strongly influenced by the quality and character of the ingredients you use. The texture of a ganache made with a velvety smooth European bittersweet chocolate will be velvety smooth. The character of a poor quality chocolate will be readily apparent in a ganache made with it. We advise using a bittersweet chocolate with a relatively low sugar content in order to make a ganache that isn't too sweet. The quality of the cream is also important. Real pasteurized heavy cream will produce a better flavor than ultra-pasteurized cream. Even better is crème fraîche, which adds its characteristic nutty-sour note to the ganache and modulates the sweetness of the chocolate.

The basic ganache we use for filling gâteaux is ganache *clichy* (which is used in the rectangular gâteau called *clichy*, page 239). For gâteau where we want an alcohol-based flavor accent with the chocolate, we substitute a little rum or Grand Marnier for part of the cream in ganache *clichy* to make rum ganache or Grand Marnier ganache.

For 1 pound + 1¼ ounces (490 g); 2 cups

	GANACHE CLICHY	RUM GANACHE OR GRAND MARNIER GANACHE
European bittersweet chocolate (see notes), chopped	10 ounces (285 g)	10 ounces (285 g)
Heavy cream or crème fraîche (page 451)	1 cup (2.4 dL)	¾ cup + 1 tablespoon (2 dL)
Dark Jamaican or Haitian rum, or Grand Marnier	—	2 tablespoons + 2 teaspoons (4 cL)

1. Place the chocolate in a small stainless steel bowl. In a small, heavy saucepan, bring the cream just to a simmer, between 165° and 185°F (73° and 85°C). Reduce the heat and sterilize the cream by simmering it for at least 2 minutes, stirring constantly with a wire whisk to prevent the cream from boiling over.

2. Gradually pour the hot cream into the chocolate, stirring constantly with a wire whisk ①. Continue stirring with the whisk until the chocolate is completely melted and the ganache is smooth. (If all of the chocolate does not melt, dip the bottom of the bowl of ganache in a bowl of hot water and stir until the ganache is smooth.) Then stir in the rum or Grand Marnier if required.

①

3. Allow the ganache to cool, stirring occasionally. Use the ganache when it thickens, but before it sets. Or store the ganache for later use.

NOTES: If you choose a chocolate that is very low in sugar or very high in cocoa butter, you may want to increase the quantity of heavy cream in the ganache slightly so that it won't be too firm.

Sterilizing the cream makes the ganache less perishable, which is important for chocolate bonbons. While it isn't absolutely necessary for gâteaux that will be refrigerated for at most a few days or frozen, we think it is a good habit to get into.

STORAGE: Covered airtight, for up to 1 week in the refrigerator. Remove the ganache from the refrigerator 1 hour before using. When it has warmed to room temperature, place it in a stainless steel bowl and briefly warm the bottom of the bowl over direct heat, stirring constantly with a wooden spatula. Remove it from the heat and beat it vigorously with the spatula. Return it to the heat and repeat as often as necessary to make the ganache smooth and spreadable but not runny.

Or freeze for up to 3 months. Defrost overnight in the refrigerator, then proceed as for refrigerated ganache.

Chestnut Buttercream

. . . .

This is an extremely luxurious filling based on pureed chestnuts and butter. You can look at it as a buttercream with the bombe batter replaced by chestnut puree. The chestnut puree used for this filling in France is made from *debris de marrons glacés*—the debris of broken, candied chestnut pieces that is a by-product of manufacturing *marrons glacés* (glazed chestnuts). Unfortunately, you won't find this product (called *pâte de marrons glacés*) on your supermarket shelves, and the sweetened chestnut puree (called chestnut spread) that you will find is too soft and doesn't have enough chestnut flavor. To make it possible for you to make this wonderful filling, we have devised an excellent substitute by simmering peeled chestnuts (available canned) in sugar syrup, then pureeing them with the chestnut spread.

For 2 pounds + 10 ounces (1,200 g); 6⅔ cups

EQUIPMENT:
Food processor
Electric mixer, preferably a stand mixer equipped with both wire whip and flat beater

Granulated sugar	14 ounces (400 g); 2 cups
Water	1½ cups (3.6 dL)
Pure vanilla extract	2 teaspoons (1 cL)
Whole chestnuts (peeled)	One 10-ounce (283-g) can, well drained
Chestnut spread (*crème de marrons*)	One 17½-ounce (500-g) can
Kentucky bourbon or dark Jamaican or Haitian rum	3 tablespoons (4.5 cL)
Unsalted butter, barely softened	12 ounces (350 g); 1½ cups
Water, heated to a boil	3 tablespoons (4.5 cL)

   1. Combine the sugar and water in a 2-quart (2-L) saucepan and stir to thoroughly moisten the sugar. Bring to a boil to dissolve the sugar.

   2. Reduce the heat to medium and add the vanilla and the drained chestnuts. Bring the syrup barely to a simmer, then reduce the heat to very low and simmer very gently for 30 minutes, turning the chestnuts in the syrup occasionally.

   3. Drain the chestnuts on a wire rack and let them cool to room temperature. If you like, you can strain the syrup through several layers of moistened cheesecloth, then save it to use instead of heavy syrup in the brushing syrup mixture for gâteaux filled with chestnut buttercream.

4. Process the chestnuts in the food processor, with the feed tube open. When they start sticking around the sides of the processor bowl, gradually add some of the chestnut spread until you reach a consistency that the machine can process continuously. Continue processing to puree the chestnuts to a smooth consistency, adding more chestnut spread as needed to facilitate processing. Then without turning off the machine, pour in the remaining chestnut spread through the feed tube and process until the mixture is well blended and smooth. This is the chestnut paste. It will be warm.

5. Pour the chestnut paste into a stainless steel bowl, cover the bowl with a damp kitchen towel to prevent it from drying out, and let cool to room temperature.

6. You will have about 1 pound + 8¾ ounces (700 g) of chestnut paste. Place it in the mixer and beat it at low speed with the flat beater to break it up and make it smooth, adding a little of the bourbon or rum to soften it if necessary. Gradually beat in the softened butter. (Or, if your mixer doesn't have a flat beater, take half of the chestnut paste and gradually beat in half the softened butter, starting with a wooden spatula and then switching to the mixer as soon the mixture is soft enough for the beater to work. Repeat with the second half of the chestnut paste and butter.) When all of the butter has been added, beat vigorously (still using the flat beater if your mixer has one) to make the mixture light and smooth. In order to get a light buttercream, the temperature of the buttercream must be kept between 59° and 63°F (15° to 17°C). If the mixture gets warmer and becomes too soft, cool the mixture as you beat it either by rubbing ice cubes over the outside of the bowl of a stand mixer or by dipping the bowl in a larger bowl of ice water for a handheld mixer. Then beat in the bourbon or rum. If you are not using the chestnut buttercream right away, stop at this point.

7. Beat the chestnut buttercream in the mixer using the wire whip or beater and gradually pour in the boiling water. The chestnut buttercream will become lighter and creamier. Beat a little longer to make it as light as possible. Use the chestnut buttercream right away, or refrigerate it for later use.

STORAGE: Preferably before adding the boiling water. Covered airtight for up to 1 week in the refrigerator. Before using, let the chestnut buttercream barely soften to about 60°F (15°C). Then beat it vigorously with a wooden spatula or the flat beater of the mixer to make it smooth and light, being sure to keep the temperature below 63°F (17°C). Then proceed with step 7 of the recipe. For smaller quantities, use 1 tablespoon (1.5 cL) boiling water for each 14 ounces (400 g) of chestnut buttercream. If you have already added the boiling water, do not add any more; just whip it in the mixer with the wire whip to make it as light as possible.

Or divide the chestnut buttercream into quantities suitable for the desserts you expect to make and freeze for up to 1 month. Defrost overnight in the refrigerator, then proceed as for refrigerated chestnut buttercream.

Keep the syrup from poaching the chestnuts covered airtight in the refrigerator for up to 2 weeks.

Finishing Touches

How a gâteau tastes depends mainly on what is inside—the cake, brushing syrup, filling, and frosting. How it looks is determined by what is on the outside—the finishing touches. You can glaze the outside of the gâteau to make it shiny, provide a contrasting color, and sometimes add a flavor element. You can cover the surface of the gâteau with a sheet of almond paste for an altogether different surface texture and an element of richness. And whether the cake is glazed, covered with almond paste, or simply frosted, you can complete the decoration with piped designs or inscriptions or with garnishes made of chocolate or almond paste. Finally, many desserts are enhanced in both taste and appearance by an accompanying sauce.

This chapter gives detailed explanations of many of the techniques used to provide finishing touches in the recipes throughout the book. Our recipes illustrate the full range of these techniques. Of course, once you have mastered how each technique is used, you can vary the presentations of your gâteaux to suit your own tastes.

GLAZES

One way to give a cake a more finished look is to glaze it, giving it a shiny surface. There are different types of glazes for different types of cakes. Simple cakes call for a simple glaze, most often a brushing of apricot jam, followed by a second brushing of a confectioners'-sugar-and-water paste that we call confectioners' sugar glaze. You will use chocolate glaze and fondant on round, rectangular, and log- and loaf-shaped gâteaux, usually over a buttercream or ganache frosting. Chocolate glaze can also be used directly on some of the simple cakes. Jelly glazes fit best with the charlottes and mousse logs.

You will apply the glazes to the surfaces of the cakes in one of two ways. For chocolate glaze or fondant, you melt a large quantity of glaze and pour it over the top of the dessert, letting the excess flow off the sides. For the other glazes, you brush the glaze on the surface.

Chocolate Glaze

· ·

A dark, smooth, glossy coating of bittersweet chocolate over the outside of a gâteau is nothing short of seductive. The layer of chocolate glaze should be thin so that it doesn't overwhelm the dessert, and not too crisp or it will be difficult to cut and serve.

By itself, bittersweet chocolate is too thick and viscous when melted to spread easily in a thin layer, and it is too crisp when set. Adding cocoa butter (or, equivalently, using the high cocoa butter covering chocolate that the French call *couverture*) makes the chocolate more fluid when melted but also more crisp when set, so this is not a good choice. We think the best alternative is to add clarified butter to the melted chocolate after tempering. The clarified butter is very effective at thinning the chocolate, does not make it more susceptible to fat bloom (as vegetable oil can), and isn't very perishable, so the chocolate glaze stores well. When set the glaze is less brittle than pure bittersweet chocolate, and it has a subtle butter flavor that enhances the flavor of the chocolate.

We add an amount of clarified butter equal to 15 percent of the weight of the chocolate. If you are using a chocolate especially high in cocoa butter and find that this thins the chocolate too much, you can reduce the proportion of clarified butter to 10 percent. The recipe below is sufficient to glaze any of our round or rectangular gâteaux.

An interesting variation is to replace the clarified butter with browned butter (*beurre noisette*, page 450), which adds a more distinctive, nutty quality to the flavor of the chocolate.

For ¾ pound (340 g); 1½ cups

EQUIPMENT:
Chocolate thermometer or pocket digital thermometer
Bowl of cold water
Bowl of hot water

European bittersweet chocolate (see note), melted	10½ ounces (300 g)
Clarified butter (page 449), at room temperature	1½ ounces (45 g); 3 tablespoons

1. If you did not melt the chocolate in a stainless steel bowl, transfer it to one. Temper the chocolate as follows: Dip the bottom of the bowl of chocolate in a larger bowl of cold water and stir the chocolate until the temperature drops to between 80° and 84°F (26.5° to 29°C) and it begins to thicken. Immediately remove from the cold water.

2. Dip the bottom of the bowl of chocolate in a larger bowl of hot water ①. Stir over the hot water just long enough to warm the chocolate to between 86° and 91°F (30° to 33°C) and make it more fluid again. Then remove from the hot water immediately.

3. Beat the clarified butter with a wooden spatula to make it smooth and creamy, then stir it into the chocolate. The chocolate glaze is now ready to use.

NOTE: To select chocolates best suited for use in our chocolate glaze, see page 502. Avoid chocolates very high in cocoa butter (which will make the glaze too thin) or very low in sugar (because they will make the glaze less shiny).

STORAGE: After you have glazed a gâteau with chocolate, there will always be excess chocolate glaze. To keep it in temper and retain its smooth, uniform consistency, collect the excess chocolate glaze, pour it onto a sheet of wax paper, and spread it in a thin layer with an icing spatula. Then put it in a cool place (or briefly in the refrigerator if necessary) to set the chocolate. Peel the wax paper away from the chocolate, break the chocolate into pieces, and consolidate the pieces in an airtight container. Keep for up 2 weeks in a cool place or in the refrigerator for up to 2 months.

You can reuse the chocolate glaze in two ways. One is to melt and temper it, then add it to the next batch of chocolate glaze you make. Since the chocolate glaze has already been thinned, you cannot use its consistency to judge when it reaches each stage in the tempering process. Also, the temperature for each stage will be reduced by about 4°F (2°C) and you must scrupulously control the temperature at each stage. In other words, tempering the chocolate glaze will now become more treacherous than tempering pure bittersweet chocolate, especially if you have used a chocolate very high in cocoa butter. We find that the best way to temper leftover chocolate glaze is the shortcut tempering method (page 540), melting the chocolate glaze and then dropping in a solid piece of pure bittersweet chocolate to stir around as the melted glaze cools. When the glaze reaches a temperature between 82° and 87°F (28° to 31°C), remove what is left of the chunk of chocolate.

A much easier alternative (and the one we prefer) is to use the leftover chocolate glaze in a ganache (page 400), substituting the chocolate glaze ounce for ounce (gram for gram) for part of the bittersweet chocolate called for in the recipe. Since the percentage of clarified butter in the chocolate glaze is small, and since you will be substituting the chocolate glaze for only a fraction of the bittersweet chocolate in the ganache, this substitution will make very little difference in the ganache—probably less difference than substituting one bittersweet chocolate for another.

Fondant

. . . .

The name of this familiar creamy glaze is also the French word for "melting," which is precisely what it does when you put it in your mouth. Fondant is actually just sugar (with a little water) that has been crystallized in a controlled way to make the sugar crystals so small that there is no trace of graininess.

To make fondant, you need a large work surface, preferably one made of marble because it cools the fondant more quickly, requiring less time and effort and producing a smoother texture. Unless your work surface is very large, you will also need a set of fondant rails—four steel rails that you arrange on the work surface to make a rectangle of variable size to contain the fondant and keep it from flowing off the work surface. We recommend 18 × 1-inch (45 × 2.5-cm) steel angle irons (available at hardware stores), seasoned with oil to prevent rust. Alternatively, rails specifically made for preparing fondant are sold by some baking supply companies.

We give the recipe for the quantity of fondant required to glaze a 9-inch (24-cm) round gâteau or a large rectangular gâteau. If you prefer, you can easily prepare the fondant in a larger quantity and store it to have on hand when needed.

For 1 pound (450 g); 1⅓ cups

EQUIPMENT:
Bowl of cold water or candy thermometer
Large marble slab (optional)
Set of 4 fondant rails
Dough scraper or nylon bowl scraper

Sugar	14 ounces (400 g); 2 cups
Water	⅔ cup (1.6 dL)
Light corn syrup	4 teaspoons (2 cL)

1. Combine the sugar and water in a heavy 1-quart (1-L) saucepan or caramel pot and stir to thoroughly moisten the sugar. Bring to a boil over medium heat. Moisten a pastry brush with cold water and wash down the sides of the saucepan to dissolve any sugar crystals that form there. Add the corn syrup and continue boiling over medium heat without stirring, washing down the walls of the saucepan as needed to dissolve sugar crystals, until the sugar reaches the high end of the soft-ball stage (page 535–36). When you pluck a little syrup from the saucepan and immerse it in the bowl of cold water, you will be able to roll the syrup into a very soft, small ball that flattens when you lift it. The temperature of the syrup will measure 239°F (115°C) on the candy thermometer.

2. While the sugar is cooking, wipe the marble slab or your countertop with a cold wet cloth to moisten it, and arrange the fondant rails on the work surface to contain a rectangle about 8 × 10 inches (20 × 25 cm). (For a larger quantity of fondant, make a proportionately larger rectangle.)

3. Pour the hot syrup onto the work surface ① and sprinkle it lightly with cold water ②. Allow the syrup to cool to about 150°F (65°C), then begin stirring it constantly with a wooden spatula in one hand. Use the dough scraper in the other hand to scrape the syrup from the work surface and gather it to the center of the rectangle ③. Gradually the fondant will become very thick, white, and opaque. When it solidifies into a dull white, dry mass and is barely warm, stop working it.

4. Gather the fondant together, cover it with a damp cloth, and let cool to room temperature.

5. Scrape the fondant from the work surface. Take a small amount of fondant at a time and work it on the marble slab or countertop by repeatedly flattening it with the heel of your hand ④ and folding it onto itself until it becomes a smooth, coherent mass.

6. Gather the pieces of fondant into a ball ⑤ and place the ball in a small mixing bowl. Cover the surface of the fondant with a damp cloth and cover the bowl with plastic wrap so that the fondant won't dry and form a crust on top. Allow the fondant to rest for at least 24 hours before using.

STORAGE: Covered airtight, at room temperature for up 2 weeks or refrigerated for up to 2 months.

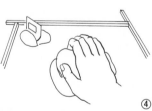

ABOUT USING FONDANT: When you are ready to use the fondant, warm it in a heavy saucepan over very low heat, stirring constantly with a wooden spatula until melted. The correct temperature for glazing with fondant is 100° to 105°F (38° to 40°C); when you touch it to the back of your index finger, it should feel warm but not hot. At this temperature the fondant should be fluid and have just enough body that it flows easily without being runny—similar to heavy cream or a light *crème anglaise*. If the fondant is too hot, it can

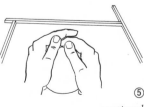

continued

melt a frosting (such as buttercream) over which it is poured, and it will become dull when it sets. On the other hand, if the fondant is too fluid (or fluid at too low a temperature), it can drip before setting.

You will almost certainly need to adjust the consistency of the fondant, probably by thinning it, to reach the required consistency. If the fondant is too thick, gradually stir in some heavy syrup (page 452) to thin it. (It is not unusual to require one part syrup for three parts fondant.) On the other hand, if it is too fluid, stir in some confectioners' sugar to thicken it.

If you accidentally overheat the fondant, dip the bottom of the saucepan in cold water and stir until the fondant has returned to the proper temperature.

Jelly Glazes

. . . .

A crystal clear layer of jelly on the surface of a charlotte or other mousse dessert makes a glittering finish without disguising the dessert underneath. If the mousse in the dessert is made from a red fruit, the jelly should be made from a red fruit. On the other hand, for pale fruits a glaze with less color, based on orange juice, looks best. In either case, the glaze needs a little unflavored gelatin added to make it set perfectly, and it must be diluted with water to reduce the sugar content so the sugar doesn't inhibit setting.

For ½ cup + 2 tablespoons (1.5 dL)

FRUIT JELLY GLAZE:

Unflavored gelatin	¾ teaspoon (4 mL)
Cold water	¼ cup + 1 tablespoon (7.5 cL)
Red currant, sour cherry, black currant, or elderberry jelly	3½ ounces (100 g); ¼ cup + 1 tablespoon

ORANGE JUICE GLAZE:

Unflavored gelatin	1 teaspoon (5 mL)
Cold water	¼ cup (6 cL)
Fresh orange juice, strained	¼ cup (6 cL)
Superfine or extra fine sugar	1¾ ounces (50 g); ¼ cup

1. Stir the gelatin into the cold water and let it soften.

2. Heat the jelly or the orange juice and sugar in a butter melter, stirring occasionally, until the jelly is melted or the sugar is dissolved in the orange juice. Remove from the heat and stir in the softened gelatin. The gelatin should dissolve. If necessary, stir the mixture over low heat to finish dissolving the gelatin.

3. Allow the glaze to cool. Use it before it sets, or store for later use.

STORAGE: Covered airtight in the refrigerator for up to 2 weeks. When ready to use, warm the glaze over low heat, stirring occasionally, until melted.

Strained Apricot Jam

You will use strained apricot jam as the first step of a two-stage glazing process on many of the simple cakes. You can also use it occasionally as an ingredient, for example, in a *salpicon* filling in some gâteaux, and as a glaze on fruit *tartes*.

We recommend straining an entire jar of jam at once so that you will always have it on hand. But if you prefer, you can strain the amount you need for each recipe, remembering that you will lose some of the jam to the strainer and must start with more jam than the recipe requires.

For any quantity

EQUIPMENT:
Wooden pestle, or use a rubber spatula

Apricot jam or preserves

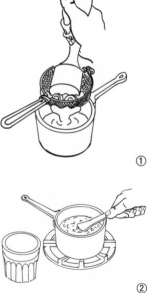

1. Melt the apricot jam over low heat in a small, heavy saucepan, stirring occasionally with a wooden spatula until melted.

2. Force the jam through a fine sieve with the pestle (or a rubber spatula if you don't have a pestle) to puree the pieces of fruit ①. Work as much of the fruit through the sieve as you can. Discard any dry, fibrous pieces that won't go through the sieve.

3. Stir the jam to make it more homogeneous. If the jam is runny when it cools, return it to the saucepan and simmer it gently to reduce the excess liquid ②. The strained jam should now be thick but still soft enough to spread easily with a pastry brush. Use it while still hot, or cool and store for later use.

STORAGE: Covered airtight at room temperature or in the refrigerator for up to several months. If you strain an entire jar of jam at once, you can store the strained jam in the same jar. Clean the jam jar and sterilize it with boiling water before pouring the hot strained jam into it.

Mold is more likely to start growing on top of the jam at room temperature than in the refrigerator. If this happens, scoop off and discard the jam with the mold on top. On the other hand, sugar is more likely to crystallize from the jam if it is stored in the refrigerator.

Confectioners' Sugar Glaze

The French name of this very simple glaze is *glace à l'eau*, which translates literally as "water glaze." Actually it is a mixture of confectioners' sugar and water, and the defining ingredient is the sugar. So, for lack of a better name, we call it confectioners' sugar glaze in English.

You will brush this glaze over apricot jam on the top of a simple cake, then return the cake to the oven briefly to dissolve the sugar and make the glaze more transparent. Usually you will flavor confectioners' sugar glaze with an alcohol such as rum or curaçao liqueur to emphasize the flavor in the cake. Always add the alcohol to the sugar first to provide the desired flavor, then add as much water as necessary to achieve the required consistency.

The quantity of confectioners' sugar glaze required for one cake is small, and the procedure is so easy that we recommend preparing it as called for in each recipe. The sample recipe below makes a quantity that would be more than sufficient for any of our cakes.

For about 2½ tablespoons (4 cL)

Confectioners' sugar	1 ounce (30 g); ¼ cup
Curaçao liqueur, dark Jamaican or Haitian rum, or other liqueur (optional)	1½ teaspoons (8 mL)
Cold water	As needed

1. Sift the confectioners' sugar onto a sheet of wax paper ①. Transfer it to a small bowl.

2. Stir in the optional alcohol with a wooden spatula ②. Very slowly stir in cold water until the mixture becomes smooth and creamy. It should be just fluid enough to spread easily with a pastry brush. If you add too much water and it becomes runny, stir in more sifted confectioners' sugar.

STORAGE: Prepare and use as needed. Storage is more trouble than it is worth.

①

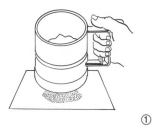

②

①

PIPED DECORATION

You can embellish many gâteaux by piping or writing on them in decorative shapes and patterns. You can pipe buttercream and whipped cream frostings from a pastry bag, usually with a fluted pastry tube. Occasionally you can pipe Italian meringue and ganache in the same way. For writing inscriptions and piping fine designs, you use writing chocolate, royal icing, or occasionally buttercream with a parchment decorating cone.

Piping with a Pastry Bag

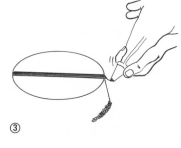

②

When you are piping with a pastry tube, the frosting must have the proper consistency. Whipped cream and Italian meringue must be stiff in order to hold a precise shape, but they must not be at all grainy. Buttercream and ganache must be softened so they can be piped, but they must still have enough consistency to hold their shape.

ROPES.

The simplest is to pipe a fluted rope of frosting. Fluted ropes are often used to divide the top of a gâteau into quadrants, which are then decorated with a repeated piping motif.

To pipe a rope, hold the pastry bag at a 60° angle with respect to the top of the gâteau, with the tip of the tube a little above the surface ①. Press firmly and evenly on the pastry bag, and move the tip of the tube in a straight line at uniform speed to get a straight rope of uniform thickness ②. When you get to the end, release the pressure on the bag, stop moving the tube, and terminate the rope with a quick flick of the tip of the pastry tube, up and slightly backward ③, ④.

③

ROSETTES AND ROSACES.

These are small, stylized flowerlike shapes piped from a fluted decorating tube or a small- to medium-size fluted pastry tube. At a nontechnical level, the two words rosace and rosette share a common meaning in both French and English. But to the professional pastry chef, rosaces is the correct term for all such piped decorations. The round, swirled piping we refer to as rosettes are merely a particular type of rosaces.

④

To pipe a rosette, hold the pastry bag nearly vertical, with the tip of the pastry tube just above the surface of the gâteau you are decorating. Press on the pastry bag and when the frosting spreads around the tip of the tube,

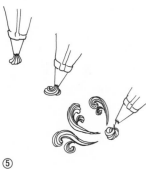

slowly lift the tube at the same time as you move it in a tight circle to make an upward spiral ⑤. Finish the rosette by releasing the pressure on the pastry bag and sweeping the tip of the tube to the center of the rosette and up. Adjust the pressure on the pastry bag, the rate at which you move the pastry tube, and the size of the circle you traverse to get a round swirl of frosting with well-defined fluting.

There is a second form of rosace that we use frequently, namely the teardrop. To pipe a teardrop, hold the pastry bag at an angle of about 60° with respect to the surface of the gâteau, with the tip of the pastry tube touching the surface. Press gently on the pastry bag, start moving the tip of the pastry tube up and away from you, and then quickly move the tip in a small loop—up, back toward you, and down onto the surface again. Finish by releasing the pressure on the pastry bag and drawing the tip of the pastry tube toward you to make the point of the teardrop ⑥. Adjust the pressure on the pastry bag (greatest at the beginning and middle of the motion, then decreasing quickly through the second half of the loop) and the rate at which you move the pastry tube (slowly at first, more quickly as you loop up and back down, then slowly again at the end) to get a teardrop with well-defined fluting.

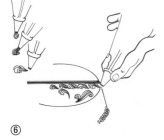

Sometimes you will want to pipe a continuous line of overlapping teardrops on top of a gâteau. To do this, do not draw out the tail to terminate each teardrop. Instead, when you get to the narrow part of each teardrop, stop moving the pastry tube toward you and increase the pressure on the pastry bag to begin the next teardrop. Pipe the teardrops with a rhythmic, repeating motion to move across the top of the gâteau in a straight line or circle.

You can also make a large variety of rosaces by varying these methods. For example, you can make a curving teardrop by moving the pastry tube in a horizontal arc, and elongating the teardrop as you draw it out toward the point. Once you have mastered the simple shapes, you can experiment with more complicated ones, always remembering to lift the tip of the tube so that it doesn't drag through the frosting, and to adjust the pressure on the bag and the speed of moving the tube to get constant or uniformly tapering shapes with well-defined fluting.

Piping with a Parchment Decorating Cone

You will use a parchment decorating cone for writing inscriptions and very fine decorative work, where even a small pastry bag with a decorating tube

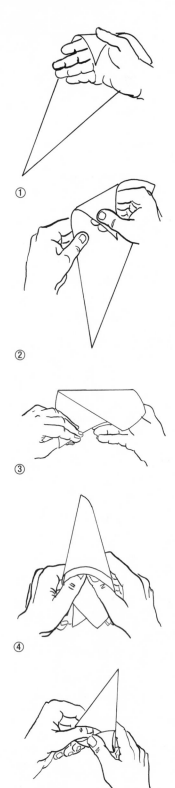

would be too large. Called a *cornet* in French, the parchment decorating cone was invented in 1808 by a pastry chef in Bordeaux named Lorsa.

You can easily make a parchment decorating cone from a piece of kitchen parchment. While you are at it, make at least four of them so you can master the technique more quickly and won't need to fumble with the parchment each time you need a decorating cone.

TO MAKE FOUR PARCHMENT DECORATING CONES.

Cut a rectangle of parchment 10 inches (25 cm) long from a roll 15 inches (38 cm) wide. Cut each rectangle in half crosswise to make two 7½ × 10-inch (19 × 25-cm) rectangles, and cut each of these in half along the diagonal to get four right triangles, one for each cone. Lay one triangle on your countertop with the 10-inch (25-cm) side on the bottom and the 7½-inch (19-cm) side on the right. Turn your right hand palm up and grasp the upper right corner of the triangle between the thumb and index finger of your right hand ①, with your thumb under the corner of the parchment. Rotate your right hand toward you ② to roll up the upper half of the triangle into a tight cone, with the point of the cone near the center of the hypotenuse of the triangle and the corner of the parchment on top of the center of the long side ③. Grasp the corner and the center of the long side between your right thumb on the inside of the cone and the index and middle fingers of your right hand on the outside of the cone. Lift the cone, point up, and wrap the free corner of the triangle around the outside of the cone with your left hand. The corner of the parchment on the outside of the cone should overlap the inside corner slightly, with a single layer of parchment in between. Grasp the corners between both thumbs inside the cone and your index and middle fingers outside the cone ④, and slide them in opposite directions to tighten the cone and give it a sharp point. The corners of the parchment triangle will extend below the base of the cone. Fold the corners up inside the cone to secure the finished decorating cone ⑤.

TO USE A PARCHMENT DECORATING CONE.

Spoon about 1 tablespoon (1.5 cL) or less of the preparation to be piped into the cone ⑥. Press the open end of the cone flat, with the edge of the parchment down the center (rather than at the side), to enclose the contents. Fold over the corners, and then fold over the center in the opposite direction as the corners to secure the closure. Holding the decorating cone tip up, cut off the tip to make a tiny hole ⑦. (The hole must be just large enough to allow the contents to flow easily but not run out the tip.) Grasp

the folded end of the decorating cone between the thumb and the index and middle fingers of one hand, turn it tip down, and press gently with your fingertips to make the contents flow through the hole and drop onto the top of the cake you are decorating. When you want to stop the flow, release the pressure and turn the cone upside down. When finished, empty and discard the decorating cone.

Writing inscriptions and drawing designs with a parchment decorating cone is more or less like writing with a pen and ink ⑧ except that you must control the flow of writing material to get lines of uniform width. However, you can also use the thickness of the writing material to create more three-dimensional designs. For example, you can make a beaded border design by piping adjacent dots, and you can get a similar effect by repeatedly looping backward, up, forward, and down with the tip of the cone as you pipe the line of a border design. Finally, you can do calligraphy with the decorating cone by varying the pressure you apply and the speed at which you move the tip to control the thickness of each stroke.

Writing Chocolate

This is a chocolate paste that is used almost exclusively for writing. It has a very dark color and does not need to be tempered. The quantity in our recipe is quite small, but it should be sufficient for decorating several gâteaux.

For about 3½ tablespoons (70 g)

Heavy syrup (page 452) heated to lukewarm	**2 tablespoons (3 cL)**
Unsweetened chocolate, melted	**1 ounce (30 g)**

1. A little at a time, stir the heavy syrup into the melted chocolate ①. The chocolate will thicken and probably seize, becoming thick and granular ②. Keep adding the syrup until the chocolate becomes smooth and fluid again, with a satiny sheen. Add only as much syrup as necessary to make the chocolate smooth and satiny and soft enough to pipe from a parchment decorating cone.

2. Spoon 2 to 3 teaspoons (1 to 1.5 cL) of the writing chocolate into a parchment decorating cone and use it right away. Let the excess cool to room temperature and save it for later use.

STORAGE: Covered airtight, in a small container, for up to 1 week at room temperature. When ready to use, melt the writing chocolate just like ordinary chocolate. If necessary, add a little warm heavy syrup to get the writing chocolate back to the required consistency.

Royal Icing

In England, royal icing is commonly used as a glaze on cakes and pastries. A few French pastries—such as *conversation* and *alumettes*—are glazed with royal icing before baking, but in cake making it is reserved almost exclusively for piping inscriptions and designs with a parchment decorating cone.

For 6 ounces (175 g); ¼ cup + 2 tablespoons

Confectioners' sugar	3½ ounces (100 g); ¾ cup + 4 teaspoons
Reconstituted powdered egg whites (page 511)	2 tablespoons (3 cL)
Distilled white vinegar	⅛ teaspoon (a few drops)

1. Sift the confectioners' sugar onto a sheet of wax paper ①. In a small bowl, stir the sugar into the egg whites to make a smooth paste ②. Beat the paste vigorously with a wooden spatula until it whitens and stiffens.

2. Beat in the vinegar to whiten the royal icing still more and make it drier. It should be just soft enough to pipe easily from a parchment decorating cone.

3. Spoon 2 to 3 teaspoons (1 to 1.5 cL) of the royal icing into a parchment decorating cone and use it right away. Save the excess for later use.

STORAGE: Cover the surface of the royal icing with a damp cloth to keep it from drying and forming a skin on top. Cover airtight with plastic wrap and keep for up to 3 days in the refrigerator. Beat vigorously with a wooden spatula before using.

①

②

CHOCOLATE DECORATION

Depending on your point of view, working with chocolate can be either immensely satisfying or incredibly aggravating. Or perhaps it would be more accurate to say it depends on your temperament and the temperature of your kitchen. The reason is that good chocolate is very easy to work with provided it is at the right temperature. Getting the chocolate to the right temperature is what takes patience, and keeping it at the right temperature depends on the temperature of your kitchen.

Let's deal with the kitchen temperature first. If your kitchen is hot, you will have problems with chocolate no matter how experienced or skillful you are because chocolate melts easily and sets slowly in a warm environment. You don't want the kitchen to be too cold either, but in the American home kitchen this is unlikely to be a problem. For chocolate work we strongly advise you to keep your kitchen temperature around 70°F (21°C), and definitely below 75°F (24°C).

We have already covered chocolate glaze and writing chocolate earlier in this chapter. In this section we focus on shaping chocolate into ribbons, petals, curls, cigarettes, sheets, and strips. We almost always use bittersweet chocolate for these decorations. Occasionally we use the same techniques with white chocolate. However, since white chocolate is excessively sweet and insipid, we use it very sparingly.

Ribbons and petals require tempering the chocolate, which is explained in detail in the reference on General Techniques (page 538). For curls, cigarettes, sheets, and strips, you begin by spreading a thin layer of chocolate on a baking sheet (page 462) and then letting it begin to set.

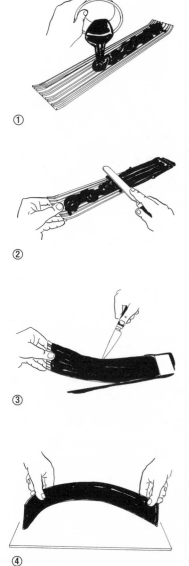

① ② ③ ④

Ribbons

Wrap a shiny strip of chocolate around the side of a round gâteau, and you have something special. Make it a ribbed ribbon of chocolate and you will dazzle even the professionals. Yet these techniques are very easy, provided your cake was baked in a pan with vertical sides or in a cake ring. The key is sheet polyester from an art supply store (page 483) or ribbed vinyl floor mat from a hardware store (page 480). Cut a strip of either material a little wider than the height of the gâteau and a little longer than the circumference of the gâteau. (You can clean and reuse these strips.)

Lay out the strip of polyester or vinyl on your countertop (ribbed side up for vinyl floor mat). Pour tempered chocolate down the length of the

⑤

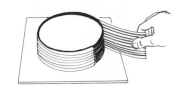

⑥

⑦

⑧

strip ① and spread the chocolate over the strip in an even layer about ¹⁄₁₆ inch (1.5 mm) thick ②. Carefully lift the chocolate-covered strip by one end and clean any excess chocolate off the edges ③. Bend the strip into a gentle arc and stand it on edge on a tray ④. Put it in a cool place (or briefly in the refrigerator) until the chocolate thickens and barely begins to set. It must remain flexible, so do not let the chocolate solidify. Wrap the chocolate-covered strip around the side of the chilled gâteau ⑤ with the chocolate on the inside and the ends overlapping. Gently press the strip against the side of the gâteau to make the chocolate adhere to the frosting. Refrigerate until the chocolate sets. Then carefully peel off the strip of polyester or vinyl ⑥, and trim the chocolate at the end with a hot knife to eliminate the overlap.

If you used a strip of polyester, the chocolate will have a high gloss. With ribbed vinyl floor mat, the chocolate will not be as glossy, but it will have grooves (you can make them horizontal, vertical, or even diagonal) from the ribs in the floor mat.

If you become enamored of this technique, you can adapt it to make larger sheets of chocolate (ribbed or not) for the tops of round or rectangular gâteaux, the sides of loaves, or the curved surfaces of logs.

It is quite easy to include designs in ribbons made on strips of sheet polyester. Temper a little white chocolate and spoon it into a parchment decorating cone (page 416). Pipe your design on the strip of polyester ⑦. (Or make a combed design.) Let the white chocolate begin to set. Then cover the strip with bittersweet chocolate and proceed as usual. When you peel off the polyester strip, the white chocolate design will be embedded in the dark chocolate ⑧.

Spreading Chocolate on a Baking Sheet

In the traditional method for making chocolate curls, cigarettes, and sheets, you spread a thin layer of tempered chocolate on a marble slab using an icing spatula, then wait until the chocolate begins to set and gets to just the right consistency. The problem with this method is that you have little control over how fast the chocolate cools, and if you don't catch it at just the right moment, you must scrape the chocolate off the marble and start from scratch. Very aggravating!

A more modern approach is to spread the tempered chocolate on a baking sheet, still using an icing spatula. Since the baking sheet is made of metal, you can cool it quickly by placing it in the refrigerator, or warm it quickly using a blow dryer. This method gives you much greater control but it still requires tempering the chocolate, a step that can be a bit tedious and would be nice to avoid.

①

The most modern and easiest approach eliminates the tempering step altogether. You heat your baking sheet in a preheated 250°F (120°C) oven. Place the hot baking sheet on your countertop (with a kitchen towel underneath if necessary to protect your countertop) and rub a large block of bittersweet chocolate over the surface of the baking sheet to melt the chocolate directly onto it ①. Work quickly so that you melt the chocolate rapidly, cooling the baking sheet and continually mixing barely melted chocolate with the warmer chocolate already on the baking sheet. This makes it possible to avoid scorching the chocolate that melts on the baking sheet first. (It also keeps the chocolate in temper by constantly seeding the melted chocolate with stable cocoa butter crystals from the block of chocolate. See page 538.) Use the edge of the block of chocolate to move the melted chocolate around and mix it at the same time as the edge of the block itself is melting and to smooth the surface so that you get an even thickness of chocolate across the entire surface of the baking sheet. Stop when you have melted a sufficient quantity of chocolate and achieved an even thickness. The thickness depends on which decorations you are making. If you want the chocolate to roll up onto itself for curls, cigarettes, or shavings, use a relatively thin coating of chocolate—a total of 3½ ounces (100 g) of chocolate for a 12 × 16-inch (30 × 40-cm) baking sheet or 4¾ ounces (135 g) of chocolate for a 13 × 20-inch (33 × 50-cm) baking sheet. On the other hand, for strips or sheets you want the chocolate you lift off the baking sheet to be thicker and more substantial; use 5¼ ounces (150 g) of chocolate for a 12 × 16-inch (30 × 40-cm) baking sheet or 7 ounces (200 g) of chocolate for a 13 × 20-inch (33 × 50-cm) baking sheet.

(Note that in order for this method to work, you should use a heavy baking sheet that is enclosed on all four sides. If the baking sheet is too light, it may cool before you melt enough chocolate. If you don't have a heavy baking sheet, you must use the method of spreading tempered chocolate on a cool baking sheet. If you use a cookie sheet, which is not enclosed on all four sides, you must be careful not to let the chocolate flow over the sides.)

Once you have spread the chocolate on the baking sheet, place it in the refrigerator to cool the baking sheet and the chocolate quickly. Let the chocolate start to set in the refrigerator. This should take 5 to 10 minutes.

As soon as the surface of the chocolate loses the high gloss sheen of molten chocolate, remove it from the refrigerator and place it on your countertop for a few minutes to give the temperature a chance to even out. The warmth beneath the surface of the chocolate will probably melt the surface again. Return the baking sheet to the refrigerator and repeat once or twice more until the chocolate is uniformly cooled and no longer liquid but not yet firm. Be very patient when you are adjusting the consistency of the chocolate. If you work slowly and patiently, the chocolate will gradually reach the right consistency and will maintain this consistency long enough to give you plenty of time to make your decorations. (If the chocolate becomes too firm, you can always warm the back of the baking sheet very gently and slowly with a blow dryer to make the chocolate a little softer and more pliable. However, it is tricky to do this evenly, so it is better to let the chocolate cool gradually.)

The way to test the consistency of the chocolate is to see how it behaves when you scrape a little of it off the baking sheet. If the chocolate shatters or cracks, then it is too cold and you need to let it warm up a little more. On the other hand, if the chocolate is soft and doesn't hold its shape, then it is too warm and you need to cool it slightly.

You will make the decorations by scraping chocolate off the baking sheet with a drywall knife (for shavings, cigarettes, strips, or sheets) or a plain round cookie cutter (for curls). On a French black steel baking sheet, you can use metal utensils. On a tinned steel or aluminum baking sheet you must use plastic utensils to avoid damaging the surface of the sheet.

Shavings

The easiest decorations to scrape off the sheet are shavings. The idea is to make shapes like the shavings you take off a piece of wood with a plane. To do this, use a drywall knife with a very flexible blade about 1½ inches (4 cm) wide (a putty knife).

Score the surface of the chocolate on the baking sheet crosswise to mark the width of the shavings ②. Start scoring at the right side of the baking sheet and make the separation between the first two score marks equal to the width of the blade of the drywall knife. The separation between the remaining score marks across the sheet can be smaller if you like.

Start from the far edge of the baking sheet at the right side. Hold your drywall knife at a shallow angle with respect to the surface of the chocolate with the edge of the blade about ¾ inch (2 cm) in from the edge of the bak-

③

ing sheet and with its left side lined up with the score mark in the chocolate. Push the knife forward to shave off the chocolate to the far edge of the baking sheet. The chocolate should come off in one piece, curling up slightly. If the chocolate comes off the baking sheet in a dark curled shaving, then move back about ¾ inch (2 cm) and shave off the next length of chocolate ③. Repeat, moving back ¾ inch (2 cm) at a time until you reach the near end of the baking sheet. Now go back to the far edge of the baking sheet and shave off the chocolate up to the next score mark, ¾ inch (2 cm) at a time. Continue until you have shaved all the chocolate off the baking sheet or made as many shavings as you need.

Cigarettes

The method for cigarettes is very similar to that for shavings. Here you need a drywall knife with a slightly flexible blade 3 inches (8 cm) wide.

Score the chocolate crosswise on the baking sheet, separating the score marks by the width of the drywall knife. Start at the top right of the baking sheet. Place the edge of the blade on the chocolate about 1½ inches (4 cm) in from the far side of the baking sheet, and push the drywall knife forward to roll the chocolate into a cigarette. Lift the drywall knife, place the blade 1½ inches (4 cm) in from the new far edge of the chocolate, and repeat. Continue rolling up cigarettes ④, working quickly and rhythmically down the baking sheet to the near side, then go back to the far side and work down the baking sheet between each successive pair of score marks until you have made all of the cigarettes you need.

④

Curls

This technique allows you to roll up very large curls of chocolate. The best tool to use is a plain round cookie cutter about 3 inches (7 cm) in diameter. Make a line lengthwise across the chocolate on the baking sheet to divide it into two equal bands about 6 inches (15 to 16 cm) wide. Starting at the right side of the baking sheet, place the far edge of the cookie cutter on the chocolate at the far side of the band nearest you, with the cookie cutter nearly flat on the baking sheet. Press down and draw the cookie cutter toward you all the way to the near side of the baking sheet, to roll up a curl ⑤. Move the cookie cutter back to the far side of the band nearest you, at the new right edge of the chocolate, and repeat. Continue working from right to left across the baking sheet, adjusting the angle of the cookie cut-

⑤

ter and the speed at which you move it to get curls as large as possible. Next, make more curls by pulling the cookie cutter toward you across the second band of chocolate, starting from the right side of the baking sheet and working across the baking sheet from right to left.

Strips and Sheets

The only difference between strips and sheets is the width. It is easier to keep these bands of chocolate manageable by working across the width of the baking sheet, but if you want very long strips, then you should work down the length of the baking sheet. Choose your drywall knife depending on how wide you want the bands to be—from a 1½-inch (4-cm) putty knife to a 5-inch (13-cm) joint knife. The blade should be very flexible.

Score the chocolate to mark the widths of the bands you want to make. Starting at the near side of the baking sheet, press the edge of the drywall knife under the chocolate and push it forward, holding the blade at a low angle, to start lifting up a band of chocolate. Gently lift the end of the band of chocolate above the blade with the fingertips of your free hand ⑥. Continue pushing the blade all the way across the baking sheet to the far side (or only partway across if you need a shorter band). Then let go of the drywall knife and lift the band with the fingertips of both hands ⑦ to move it to the gâteau you are decorating. Handle the chocolate gently, with as little pressure as possible, so that the warmth of your fingers doesn't melt it and it doesn't tear. Scoring the chocolate before lifting off the bands helps make straight bands and gives them sharp edges. If you want more ragged edges, then don't score the chocolate in advance.

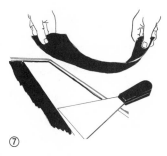

Other Methods for Making Shavings and Curls

You can scrape chocolate directly off a large block using a vegetable peeler or truffle slicer to make shavings or a plain round cookie cutter or a butter curler to make curls. However, if the chocolate is at room temperature, it will shatter and crack, producing curls or shavings with a pale, insipid look rather than the dark, rich color of the chocolate. Warming the chocolate slightly to just the right temperature would allow you to make beautiful curls or shavings, but adjusting the temperature of a thick block of chocolate so precisely can be quite an obstacle. If you can find a spot with just the right stable temperature—85° to 91°F (30° to 33°C), depending on the chocolate—go ahead and experiment.

Petals for Noëlla

Dabbing chocolate petals on a sheet of wax paper using a small, flexible icing spatula is fun but time consuming just because they are relatively small and you need so many of them. These petals are designed to decorate the top of a beautiful round gâteau called *noëlla*, but if you want to be creative you can think of many other ways to use them. You can also use the same basic technique to decorate a round gâteau by dabbing big petals directly on the side of the gâteau with a larger icing spatula.

For about 100 petals

EQUIPMENT:
Chocolate thermometer or pocket digital thermometer
At least 3 large sheets of wax paper
Icing spatula with a very flexible blade 4 inches (10 cm) long

European bittersweet chocolate, melted	**3 ounces (85 g)**

1. If you did not melt the chocolate in a stainless steel bowl, transfer it to one. Temper the chocolate as follows: Dip the bottom of the bowl of chocolate in a larger bowl of cold water and stir the chocolate until the temperature drops to between 80° and 84°F (26.5° to 29°C) and it begins to thicken. Immediately remove from the cold water.

2. Dip the bottom of the bowl of chocolate in a larger bowl of hot water. Stir over the hot water just long enough to warm the chocolate to between 86° and 91°F (30° to 33°C) and make it more fluid again. Then remove from the hot water immediately.

3. Lay out the sheets of wax paper on your countertop, and put a dab of chocolate under each corner to hold them in place. Place the bowl of chocolate on the counter and tilt it by propping it up from one side so that you can easily dip the tip of the icing spatula in the chocolate. Lightly touch the face of the blade on the chocolate in the bowl, coating only about ¾ inch (2 cm) at the tip of the blade. Clean any excess chocolate off the edges of the blade by wiping them on the edge of the bowl. Make a petal on the sheet of wax paper by gently pressing the chocolate-coated face of the blade on it, flexing the blade slightly and pulling it toward you ①. The petal should be ¾ to 1 inch (2 to 2½ cm) wide, 1 to 1¼ inches (2½ to 3 cm) long, and about ¹⁄₁₆ inch (1.5 mm) thick, with the center thinner than the edges. Continue making petals in this fashion until there is no

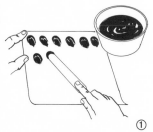
①

longer enough chocolate in the bowl to dip the icing spatula in. To keep the temperature of the chocolate between 86° and 91°F (30° to 33°C), dip the bottom of the bowl of chocolate in the bowl of hot water as needed, stirring the chocolate constantly to warm it evenly. Don't worry if the petals vary in size, since you can take advantage of this variation when you decorate with them. When you have finished, any chocolate remaining in the bowl can be saved for another purpose.

4. Put the petals in a cool place (or briefly in the refrigerator) to cool and set.

STORAGE: Cut the sheets of wax paper to the size of a tin cookie box or plastic storage container, and store the petals on the paper sheets in the box or container, covered airtight, so they don't get damaged. Keep at 60° to 75°F (15° to 24°C) for up to 2 months. When ready to use, carefully peel them off the wax paper.

DECORATING WITH ALMOND PASTE

Almond paste is like modeling clay. You can form or sculpt it in an infinite variety of ways, limited only by your imagination and artistic skill. We start by explaining some of the techniques most often used in cake decorating, and then give you the recipe for the almond paste at the end of this section (page 432).

How to Use Almond Paste

If a hard, dry crust has formed on the surface of the almond paste during storage, cut it off and discard it. Dust your countertop lightly with confectioners' sugar and place the almond paste on it. Work the almond paste on the counter with your hands, repeatedly flattening it with the heel of your hand ① and then folding it back onto itself to make it smooth. The almond paste must be firm, but smooth and malleable. If it is too firm or dry, soften it by working in a little heavy syrup (page 452) or an alcohol such as rum or curaçao liqueur if that is appropriate to the dessert you are making. On the other hand, if the almond paste is too soft, dust it with confectioners' sugar and work in the sugar with the heel of your hand to make it firmer. If the recipe for the gâteau you are making calls for it, add a drop or so of food coloring and work it into the almond paste to tint it uniformly.

Sheets

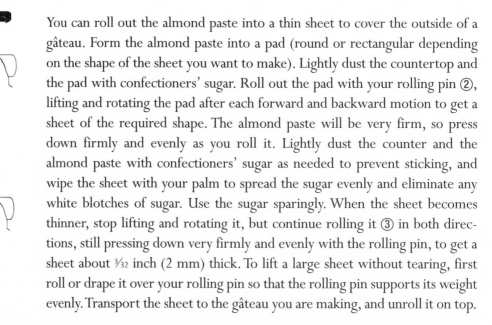

You can roll out the almond paste into a thin sheet to cover the outside of a gâteau. Form the almond paste into a pad (round or rectangular depending on the shape of the sheet you want to make). Lightly dust the countertop and the pad with confectioners' sugar. Roll out the pad with your rolling pin ②, lifting and rotating the pad after each forward and backward motion to get a sheet of the required shape. The almond paste will be very firm, so press down firmly and evenly as you roll it. Lightly dust the counter and the almond paste with confectioners' sugar as needed to prevent sticking, and wipe the sheet with your palm to spread the sugar evenly and eliminate any white blotches of sugar. Use the sugar sparingly. When the sheet becomes thinner, stop lifting and rotating it, but continue rolling it ③ in both directions, still pressing down very firmly and evenly with the rolling pin, to get a sheet about 3/32 inch (2 mm) thick. To lift a large sheet without tearing, first roll or drape it over your rolling pin so that the rolling pin supports its weight evenly. Transport the sheet to the gâteau you are making, and unroll it on top.

Textured Sheets

There are special rolling pins for giving sheets of almond paste a variety of textures such as ribbed, checkerboard, or basketweave. If you do a lot of decoration with almond paste, you will want to get one or more of these rolling pins (see page 480). Or you can get similar effects by rolling the sheet of almond paste on a textured surface, such as a piece of ribbed vinyl floor mat (page 480) or a Lego assembly board. For either method, you first roll out the almond paste into a sheet about ⅛ inch (3 mm) thick. The sheet should have the final width you need, but it can be slightly smaller in length because the final rolling to texture it will also elongate it. Dust the sheet with confectioners' sugar and wipe the sheet with your palm to spread the sugar evenly.

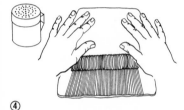

④

Using a textured rolling pin, roll the pin over the length of the almond paste sheet ④. Apply firm, even pressure to impress a uniform texture over the entire sheet, but do not press too firmly or you can make the sheet too thin or cut it.

With a textured surface, turn the sheet of almond paste dusted side down onto the surface. Roll your plain rolling pin over the almond paste to impress the texture in the underside. Carefully peel the almond paste sheet off the surface, or turn the surface upside down to remove the sheet.

Once you have a textured sheet, cut a piece of whatever size you need and lift it carefully, supporting its weight, to carry it to your gâteau.

Leaves

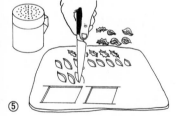

⑤

Tint the almond paste a pale green with food coloring and roll it out into a sheet ³⁄₃₂ inch (2 mm) thick. Cut the leaves from the sheet with the tip of your paring knife ⑤. Mark veins in the top of each leaf by pressing with the side of a small icing spatula, the back edge of a paring knife or the lines of fork, or impress the veins by pressing the leaf into a cake-decorator's leaf mold. Form each leaf into a gentle arch to make it look more realistic.

Ropes, Vines, and Twigs

Tint the almond paste with food coloring, green for vines or twigs, or any color you choose for ropes. Form the almond paste into a thick pad or ball. Roll the pad back and forth on the counter under the palm of one hand to

thin and elongate it into an even cylinder. As the cylinder gets longer, use both hands ⑥. Dust the almond paste very lightly with confectioners' sugar as needed to prevent it from sticking to your palms. By continuing to roll the almond paste under your palms, you can get a rope or string of whatever thickness you want. Cut it to the required length or lengths to make ropes, vines, or twigs for decorating the top of a gâteau. Use it right away so it doesn't dry and lose its flexibility.

Writing Cards

If you want to write an inscription on a gâteau that is not glazed or covered with a sheet of almond paste, you will need an almond paste writing card. Roll out a small piece of almond paste about ³⁄₃₂ inch (2 mm) thick, and cut from it a rectangle, a parallelogram ⑤, or a more fanciful shape with curved sides. Place this card on top of a gâteau and write on it the name of the gâteau or any message you like using writing chocolate (page 418) or royal icing (page 419).

Flowers

We will give a rose as an example. Depending on the color of your gâteau, you can either tint the almond paste a pale pink or peach color, or leave it untinted. You will need about 1¾ ounces (50 g) of almond paste. Take about one quarter of the almond paste and roll it into a ball between your palms. Place it on your countertop and rock the side of your hand back and forth over the center of the ball to make a dumbbell shape ⑦. Stand the dumbbell up vertically and flatten the bottom end to make a base. Shape the upper part of the dumbbell into a cone by pinching it gently on all sides to thin and elongate it. This will be the central support on which you assemble the petals. It should be about 1½ inches (4 cm) tall.

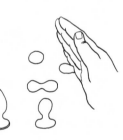

Roll out the remaining almond paste with your rolling pin into a sheet about ⅛ inch (3 mm) thick. Cut out four 1½-inch (4-cm) rounds using the back end of an ¹¹⁄₁₆-inch (18-mm) plain pastry tube (Ateco #9). Cut out three 1-inch (2.5-cm) rounds using the back end of a ⁵⁄₃₂-inch (4-mm) plain pastry tube (Ateco #0). Stack the rounds and cover them with a sheet of plastic wrap so they don't dry out while you are working.

Take one of the 1½-inch (4-cm) rounds and press it between your fingertips to enlarge it into an oval about 2 inches (5 cm) long with thin edges.

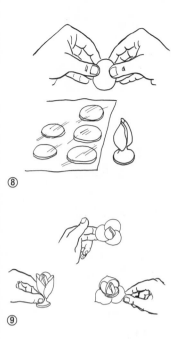

Wrap the oval around the central cone to make the first petal at the center of the rose. Pinch the petal at the bottom of the central cone to fix it in place and taper the bottom of the rose, and fold back the overlapping edge of the petal slightly. One at a time, press each of the 1-inch (2.5-cm) rounds between your fingertips to enlarge it into a round 1¼ to 1⅜ inches (about 3 cm) in diameter with thin edges ⑧. Wrap these petals around the central rosebud, each in turn overlapping the edge of the previous one, pinching the bottom of each to secure it. The three petals will completely surround the central cone. After that, take each of the remaining three 1½-inch (4-cm) rounds and press it between your fingertips to enlarge it into an oval 2 inches (5 cm) long with thin edges. Wrap these three petals around the previous three petals, each in turn overlapping the edge of the previous one, pinching the bottom of each to secure it ⑨. Turn back the upper edge of each of the outer three petals to give them a realistic look. This is a good place to stop. You want the rose to be a decorative accent, not the focus of the gâteau. Using a paring knife, cut the rose off the base.

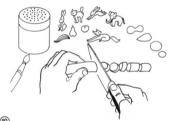

Other Decorations

Some of the easiest possibilities include fruits, animals, and cartoon characters ⑩.

Almond Paste

There are two types of almond paste. The simplest is raw almond paste, which is just a mixture of egg whites with almond-and-sugar powder. Raw almond paste is used in batters and sometimes as a sort of frosting.

The other possibility, which is the one we will be exploring in this section, is cooked almond paste, or confectioners' almond paste. The ingredients required are hot sugar syrup (which is what does the cooking) and blanched almonds, plus corn syrup (or glucose) to prevent crystallization of the sugar syrup and confectioners' sugar to absorb the oil given up by the almonds. The proportions depend on how the almond paste will be used. If it will be a filling for chocolate bonbons, then it must be soft and contain a high proportion of almonds. On the other hand, the almond paste recipe we give here is designed for decorating gâteaux. It contains more sugar than almonds, making it finer in texture, easier to model, and less perishable.

For 1 pound + 8 ounces (675 g)

EQUIPMENT:
Bowl of cold water or candy thermometer
Food processor

Granulated sugar	**10½ ounces (300 g); 1½ cups**
Cold water	**⅓ cup (8 cL)**
Light corn syrup	**¼ cup (6 cL)**
Blanched almonds	**7 ounces (200 g); 1⅓ cups**
Confectioners' sugar	**4¼ ounces (120 g); 1 cup**

1. Combine the granulated sugar with the water in a heavy 1-quart (1-L) saucepan or caramel pot and stir to thoroughly moisten the sugar. Bring to a boil over medium heat. Moisten a pastry brush with cold water and wash down the sides of the saucepan to dissolve any sugar crystals that form there. Add the corn syrup and continue boiling over medium heat without stirring, washing down the walls of the saucepan as needed to dissolve sugar crystals, until the sugar reaches the low end of the firm-ball stage (pages 535–36). When you pluck a little syrup from the saucepan and immerse it in the bowl of cold water, you will be able to roll the syrup between your fingertips into a ball the size of a pea that holds its shape ①. The temperature of the syrup will measure about 243°F (117°C) on the candy thermometer.

2. Meanwhile, combine the almonds and confectioners' sugar in the food processor. When the syrup is ready, turn on the food processor and pour the syrup through the feed tube in a thin stream ②. Continue processing until the almond paste is completely smooth. It will be hot.

3. Transfer the almond paste to a stainless steel bowl, cover it with a damp kitchen towel to prevent it from drying out, and let cool to room temperature. Form the cooled almond paste into a rectangular pad and cover it airtight with plastic wrap.

STORAGE: Covered airtight, at room temperature for up to 1 month.

Or divide the almond paste into quantities suitable for finishing individual desserts—typically 7 to 10 ounces (200 to 300 g) for most gâteaux. Wrap each piece of almond paste airtight in plastic wrap, enclose it in a small zippered plastic bag, and freeze for up to 6 months. If frozen, defrost overnight in the refrigerator and use within a few days.

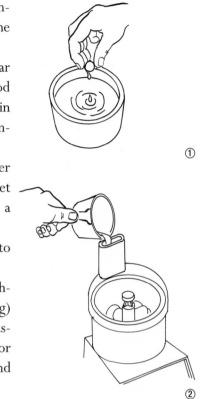

①

②

Sauces

Sauces are rather different from the other finishing touches in this chapter, since they aren't actually part of the construction of the dessert. Instead, they are served separately to accompany desserts such as charlottes, bavarians, *biscuit de savoie*, and pound cake. Of course a slice of one of these desserts surrounded by a pool of shimmering sauce can make a stunning individual presentation.

Chocolate Sauce

This is the classic sauce to serve with pears *belle hélène* or *profiteroles au chocolat*. We recommend serving it with our pear charlotte.

For 1½ cups (3.6 dL)

European bittersweet chocolate, finely chopped	8 ounces (225 g)
Boiling water	½ cup (1.2 dL)
Unsalted butter, softened	1 ounce (30 g); 2 tablespoons

1. Put the chopped chocolate in a small bowl and stir in the boiling water a little at a time using a wire whisk ①. When you have added all the water, continue stirring until the chocolate is completely melted and smooth. If necessary, gently warm the sauce (over a saucepan of simmering water) while stirring to finish melting the chocolate.

2. Add the softened butter and stir until it is melted and the sauce is smooth.

3. Serve the chocolate sauce while it is warm.

①

STORAGE: Covered airtight, for up to 3 days in the refrigerator. When ready to serve, place the sauce in a stainless steel bowl or the top of a double boiler and melt it over hot water.

Crème Anglaise

This delicate, egg-thickened custard sauce also serves as the basis for some mousses, such as bavarian cream, in which it is mixed with whipped cream. Unlike French pastry cream, it contains no starch and must not be boiled, or it can curdle. The more egg yolks you put in the *crème anglaise*, the thicker it will be. When it will be used as a sauce, it does not need to be too thick; for that reason, the recipe we give here has a relatively low egg yolk content. On the other hand, when the *crème anglaise* is to be used as the basis for a mousse, thicker is usually better because a thicker custard is less likely to deflate the whipped cream. There is even a variant of *crème anglaise* called a bombe batter that is very thick, and after cooking it is whipped while it cools to make it light as well. A *crème anglaise* made with a large number of yolks does require extra care in cooking since it will curdle more easily than one with a low egg yolk content.

For 3½ to 4 cups (8 to 10 dL)

Milk	**2 cups (4.8 dL)**
Vanilla bean	½
Large egg yolks	**6**
Superfine or extra fine sugar	**5¼ ounces (150 g); ¾ cup**

1. Pour the milk into a heavy 1½-quart (1.5-L) saucepan. Slit the vanilla bean lengthwise ①, scrape out the seeds into the milk, and add the pod to the milk as well. Bring to a simmer.

2. Meanwhile, combine the egg yolks and sugar in a mixing bowl and beat until smooth and lemon-colored. Slowly pour in about half the simmering milk, stirring constantly with the wire whisk ②. Pour this mixture back into the saucepan and stir until thoroughly blended.

3. Place the saucepan over low heat and, stirring constantly with a wooden spatula, bring the sauce almost to a simmer ③. Reduce the heat to very low and continue cooking, stirring constantly, until the custard coats the spatula and the bubbles that formed when you stirred the milk into the yolks have disappeared. Do not boil. The custard has thickened sufficiently when, if you draw

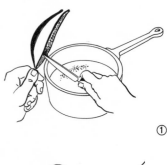

①

②

a line across the custard-coated spatula with your fingertip, the custard doesn't flow back over the line ④.

4. Remove from the heat and strain the *crème anglaise* through a fine sieve into a stainless steel bowl. Set the bowl over a larger bowl of ice water, and cool the *crème anglaise*, stirring occasionally. When the *crème anglaise* is cold, it is ready to serve.

HOWS AND WHYS: Cooling the *crème anglaise* quickly prevents bacteria from developing in it.

To recycle the pod of the vanilla bean, wash it after straining the *crème anglaise*, and let it air dry. Then store it with sugar in an airtight container to make vanilla sugar (page 527).

STORAGE: Best served the day it is made. Otherwise, pour it into a storage container, cover airtight, and keep for up to 2 days in the refrigerator.

Fruit Sauces

. . . .

The French call these sauces *coulis*. They are just sweetened fruit purees and are usually made from raspberries or strawberries. Blackberries also make a beautiful sauce, although for some reason very few chefs use it. Fresh fruits are best, but you can also use unsweetened frozen berries.

Like *crème anglaise*, these fruit sauces can also serve as the basis for mousses (see our charlotte recipes in Chapter 6).

For 2 to 2½ cups (4.8 to 6 dL)

EQUIPMENT:
Electric blender or food processor

RASPBERRY SAUCE:

Fresh raspberries	1 pound + 2 ounces (500 g); 1½ pints
Superfine or extra fine sugar	4½ ounces (125 g); ½ cup + 2 tablespoons
Fresh orange juice	3 tablespoons (4.5 cL)

STRAWBERRY SAUCE:

Fresh strawberries, hulled	1 pound + 4 ounces (560 g); 1⅔ pints
Superfine or extra fine sugar	3½ ounces (100 g); ½ cup
Fresh orange juice	3 tablespoons (4.5 cL)

BLACKBERRY SAUCE:

Fresh blackberries	1 pound (450 g); 1⅓ pints
Superfine or extra fine sugar	3½ ounces (100 g); ½ cup
Fresh orange juice	¼ cup (6 cL)

1. Puree the fruit with the sugar in the blender or food processor, adding the orange juice to enhance the fruit flavor and color.

2. Strain through a fine sieve to eliminate the raspberry or blackberry seeds or any hard, unripe pieces of strawberry.

STORAGE: Covered airtight, for up to 2 or 3 days in the refrigerator. Or freeze for as long as 2 or 3 months. If frozen, defrost overnight in the refrigerator before using.

Basic Preparations

· ·

This chapter is devoted to recipes for prepared ingredients that are called for repeatedly in cake making. Some add flavor or texture to cake batters, fillings, and frostings. Others enhance the appearance or taste of ingredients that will be used for decoration. A few are such versatile performers that it is difficult to pin them down to just one or two roles. One thing they all have in common is that they are not structural components.

For most of these recipes, you can either prepare the ingredients for each dessert as you need them, or prepare a larger quantity to keep on hand so that cake making will be easier and more efficient. We lean heavily toward the side of efficiency, but the choice is up to you. For some recipes, such as *praliné,* it is virtually impossible to make a quantity so small that you would use it up in one dessert. For these you must bite the bullet and prepare enough for several desserts.

Nut-and-Sugar Powders

. . . .

Many recipes in this book require a powder made by grinding together equal weights of blanched almonds and confectioners' sugar. Nut-and-sugar powders made with other nuts are prepared by the same method and with the same proportions, but are used less frequently. Since blanched almonds are used much more often than any other nut, we refer to the powder made with blanched almonds simply as almond-and-sugar powder. When raw almonds are required, we specify raw-almond-and-sugar powder. Normally, we use raw hazelnuts for making hazelnut-and-sugar powder, but once in a while we specify a hazelnut-and-sugar powder made from roasted hazelnuts. We have even included a cake made with pecan-and-sugar powder.

If you bake cakes often, we recommend preparing nut-and-sugar powders (particularly almond-and-sugar powder) in large batches to save repeating the same work. Also, if you are using large quantities of nuts, it is much less expensive to purchase them in bulk (for example, at a natural foods market or specialty store) than to buy the small packages sold in supermarkets.

The recipe below can be prepared in a standard 7-cup (1.7-L) food processor. If you have a much larger food processor, you may be able to prepare up to double this recipe in one batch.

For 12 ounces (340 g); about 2½ cups

EQUIPMENT:
Food processor

Nuts	**6 ounces (170 g)**
Confectioners' sugar	**6 ounces (170 g); 1¼ cups + 3 tablespoons**

1. Combine the nuts with half the confectioners' sugar in the food processor work bowl. Process the nuts and sugar, stopping to scrape down the sides of the bowl and break up any caking as needed, until the nuts are finely ground, but not so long that the mixture becomes oily. (Be especially careful with walnuts, which have a very high oil content.)

2. Sift through a medium sieve—with 1/16- to 3/32-inch (1.5- to 2-mm) mesh. Return the nuts that don't pass through the sieve to the food processor with the remaining confectioners' sugar and process until the nuts have been reduced to a fine powder.

3. Transfer all of the nut-and-sugar powder to a bowl, break up any caking with your fingertips, and mix thoroughly.

HOWS AND WHYS: This method is designed to produce the finest possible texture, while extracting the minimum amount of oil from the nuts. The food processor fluffs up the mixture as it grinds the nuts, minimizing compression and heat, which would extract more oil. The sugar in the powder absorbs the oil, helping to keep the powder from caking and turning into a paste.

STORAGE: Covered airtight for up to 1 month at room temperature.

Roasted Nuts

. . . .

Roasting nuts enhances their flavor and reduces their moisture content. We frequently call for roasted chopped almonds to decorate the bottom edges of round gâteaux, and roasted chopped almonds or hazelnuts can make a nice addition to some buttercream fillings. You can decorate the top and sides of a gâteau with roasted sliced almonds.

When you are using sliced almonds for decoration, we recommend tossing them with a little heavy syrup before roasting to sweeten them and enhance their browning.

For any quantity

EQUIPMENT:
Large, heavy baking sheet

Either almonds	Raw, blanched, sliced, or chopped
Or hazelnuts	Whole
Heavy syrup (page 452, optional)	1 teaspoon (5 mL) for each 1 ounce (60 g) sliced almonds

Preheat the oven to 350°F (175°C).

1. If you are roasting sliced almonds, toss them with the heavy syrup to coat them evenly.

2. Spread out the nuts loosely on the baking sheet. Roast them in the preheated oven, stirring occasionally to move the nuts from the edge of the baking sheet to the center and prevent the nuts from browning unevenly. Roast chopped or sliced almonds until lightly browned, about 10 to 12 minutes. Roast whole almonds or hazelnuts until lightly browned in the center, about 15 to 25 minutes, depending on the size and type of nuts; test one by cutting it in half. Be careful not to overcook the nuts or they will burn.

3. FOR HAZELNUTS ONLY: Pour the nuts into a large sieve and rub them against the mesh, using a kitchen towel to protect your hands, to remove most of their skins.

4. Pour the nuts out onto your countertop and allow them to cool.

STORAGE: Covered airtight for up to 1 week at room temperature.

Blanched Hazelnuts

For decorating gâteaux, hazelnuts usually look nicer if they are blanched—that is, their thin, papery skins are removed. While blanched almonds are widely available, blanched hazelnuts are not, so you must remove the skins yourself.

You will blanch hazelnuts by roasting them in a very hot oven to make the skins dry and loosen from their flesh without heating the interiors of the nuts enough to brown them. You can then rub off most of the skins easily. In other words, the technique is just like that for roasted hazelnuts except that you roast them in a much hotter oven for a much shorter time. Choose globular rather than elongated hazelnuts for blanching because their skins come off much more easily and their shape is more attractive.

For any quantity

EQUIPMENT:
Large, heavy baking sheet

Hazelnuts	Whole

Preheat the oven to 450°F (230°C).

1. Spread out the nuts loosely on the baking sheet. Roast them in the preheated oven, stirring once or twice to prevent the nuts nearest the edge of the sheet from burning, until their skins are dry and cracked and have darkened but not burned, about 4 to 6 minutes. The hazelnuts should remain pale inside.

2. Pour the nuts into a large sieve and rub them against the mesh, using a kitchen towel to protect your hands, to remove most of their skins.

3. Pour the nuts out onto your countertop and allow them to cool.

STORAGE: Covered airtight for up to 1 week at room temperature.

Praliné and Crushed *Pralin*

. . . .

Praliné is a fine, creamy paste made by pureeing a nut brittle (roasted almonds and/or hazelnuts embedded in caramel). It is exquisitely aromatic, and mixed with buttercream or a mousse it makes a rich, sensual filling for some luxurious gâteaux and mousse cakes. It is also used extensively in chocolates and to flavor ice creams.

To get crushed *pralin*, you sift out some of the ground almond brittle before it is reduced to a paste.

The origin of *praliné* goes back to the early seventeenth century when the chef of Marshal du Plessis-Praslin invented caramel-coated almonds. The Marshal, a minister of state under Louis XIV, liked to offer these sweets to the ladies in his circle. The ladies christened them *praslines* in his honor. In 1630 the Marshal's chef retired to Montargis, south of Paris near Orleans, and made his fortune selling *praslines* at a shop that he called the *Confiserie du Roy* (the "King's Candy Shop"). Montargis is still famous for his creation today.

Praslines became popular at the French court in the nineteenth century. Also during this period French pastry chefs began to pulverize them to make the flavoring we now call *praliné* (with the spelling modernized by deleting the silent "s" in the Marshal's name).

We offer two recipes for *praliné*. The first recipe works well for a small quantity and makes good crushed *pralin*; it calls for almonds, but for a more flavorful *praliné* you can substitute hazelnuts for half of the almonds. The second recipe is more convenient for a larger quantity and produces a slightly creamier texture, but it cannot be used to supply crushed *pralin*.

RECIPE 1: *PRALINÉ* AND CRUSHED *PRALIN*

For 12 ounces (340 g); 1 cup + 3 tablespoons *praliné*

• **Part of this amount can be made into crushed** *pralin*

EQUIPMENT:
Large baking sheet
• **coat it lightly with vegetable oil using a paper towel**
Large bowl of cold water or candy thermometer
Food processor

Granulated sugar	**7 ounces (200 g); 1 cup**
Water	**¼ cup (6 cL)**
Raw almonds	**7 ounces (200 g); 1⅓ cups**

1. Combine the sugar with the water in a heavy 3-cup (7.5-dL) to 1-quart (1-L) saucepan or caramel pot and stir to thoroughly moisten the sugar. Bring to a boil over medium heat. Moisten a pastry brush with cold water and wash down the sides of the saucepan to dissolve any sugar crystals that form there. Continue boiling over medium heat without stirring, washing down the walls of the saucepan as needed to dissolve sugar crystals, until the sugar reaches the thread stage (page 535). When you pluck a little syrup from the saucepan and immerse it in the bowl of cold water, it will form a long thread when stretched between your thumb and index finger. The temperature of the syrup will measure about 230°F (110°C) on the candy thermometer.

2. Add the almonds to the sugar syrup. Continue cooking, stirring constantly. The syrup will gradually thicken, forming progressively larger bubbles. Then it will become white and sandy as the sugar crystallizes.

3. Reduce the heat to low and continue cooking to melt the sugar and roast the almonds. The sugar will turn pale amber as it melts. Test the almonds by cutting one in half. They are ready when they are light brown in the center. There will still be a thin coating of white crystallized sugar on the almonds. Pour the almond-and-caramel mixture onto the oiled baking sheet and allow to cool.

4. Break the almond brittle into pieces and place in the food processor work bowl. Process until pulverized, then stop the machine and sift out some crushed *pralin* using a medium or coarse sieve (depending on how finely crushed you want it). Continue processing until the almond brittle is reduced to a smooth, creamy paste, with just a slight grittiness. This will take some time and the *praliné* will become hot.

5. Transfer the *praliné* to a stainless steel bowl and let it cool to room temperature.

STORAGE: Covered airtight, the *praliné* will keep for up to 3 months at room temperature or in the refrigerator. If some oil separates on top of the *praliné*, stir it back in before using.

Store the crushed *pralin* covered airtight at room temperature, also for up to 3 months.

RECIPE 2: *PRALINÉ*

For 1 pound + 11 ounces (775 g); 2⅔ cups *praliné*

EQUIPMENT:
2 or 3 large baking sheets
• coat 1 of them lightly with vegetable oil using a paper towel
Food processor

Raw almonds	7 ounces (200 g); 1⅓ cups
Hazelnuts	7 ounces (200 g); 1¼ cups + 3 tablespoons
Granulated sugar	7 ounces (200 g); 1 cup
Confectioners' sugar	7 ounces (200 g); 1⅔ cups

Preheat the oven to 350°F (175°C).

1. Spread out the nuts on the clean baking sheets and roast them, stirring occasionally, until brown in the center, about 20 minutes.

2. While the nuts are roasting, put the granulated sugar in a heavy 1-quart (1-L) saucepan or caramel pot and cook it over medium to high heat, without stirring. As soon as the sugar begins to melt around the sides of the pot, begin stirring with a wooden spatula. When the sugar becomes fluid, with small white lumps floating in the syrup, reduce the heat to low and continue cooking, stirring constantly and crushing the solid lumps with a wooden spatula, until the sugar is completely melted and turns a medium amber.

3. Stir the hot, roasted nuts into the caramel syrup. Continue heating, stirring constantly with the spatula, until the nuts and caramel are well mixed, with the caramel syrupy. Pour the nut-and-caramel mixture onto the oiled baking sheet and allow to cool.

4. Break the almond brittle into pieces and combine it with the confectioners' sugar in the food processor work bowl. Process to pulverize the almond brittle. Continue processing until the almond brittle is reduced to a smooth, creamy paste, with just a slight grittiness. This will take some time and the *praliné* will become hot.

5. Transfer the *praliné* to a bowl and let it cool to room temperature.

STORAGE: Covered airtight, the *praliné* will keep for up to 3 months at room temperature or in the refrigerator. If some oil separates on top of the *praliné*, stir it back in before using.

Clarified Butter

. . . .

You clarify butter by removing the residual milk solids. When melted, the clarified butter is clear yellow. In India, clarified butter is boiled to remove any remaining water and to sterilize the butter. The result is called *ghee*, and it can be kept, unrefrigerated (in India!), for a very long time.

Some cakes will stick to the cake pan when baked in a mold brushed with plain melted butter, but will not stick if the pan is brushed with clarified butter. So we recommend brushing cake pans and rings with clarified butter whenever sticking is a problem.

We also use clarified butter to thin bittersweet chocolate for our chocolate glaze (page 406).

For any quantity

Unsalted butter

1. Place the butter in a butter melter or small saucepan and melt it over low heat, without stirring. When the butter is melted, remove it from the heat and skim off the foam (which contains the whey proteins) that comes to the surface. Let rest for a few minutes to allow all of the milk solids to settle to the bottom.

2. Pour the clear yellow liquid—the clarified butter—through a very fine sieve into a bowl, leaving the milky residue (the protein casein and some salts) at the bottom of the saucepan.

STORAGE: Covered airtight for up to several weeks in the refrigerator or indefinitely in the freezer.

Browned Butter

Cooking melted butter browns the milk solids, imparting a nutty flavor to the butter and changing its color from yellow to brown. The browning must be done carefully in order to keep the milk solids from burning and producing a bitter flavor. The French name for browned butter is *beurre noisette*, or hazelnut butter. We suggest using it to thin chocolate when you want a chocolate glaze with a slightly nutty accent flavor.

For any quantity

Unsalted butter

1. In a heavy saucepan with a capacity about four times the volume of the butter, melt the butter and bring it to a boil. As the butter boils, a foam will form on top. When the foam collapses, stir to mix.

2. Continue to boil. Soon bubbles will start to form on the surface—first large bubbles and then progressively smaller ones. When the surface is covered with an opaque foam of tiny bubbles and the foam mounts in the saucepan, stir to deflate it.

3. Boil the butter until a new layer of tiny bubbles forms on top, then stir to deflate it again. Pour through a fine sieve into a bowl. This is the browned butter.

STORAGE: Covered airtight for up to 1 week in the refrigerator, or for several months in the freezer.

Crème Fraîche

. . . .

Crème fraîche, the French-style cultured heavy cream with a nutty and slightly sour taste, is now marketed in many areas of the United States. If the commercial product is unavailable in your local market, you can make a substitute for it at home by culturing ordinary heavy cream with a little buttermilk. The taste is not identical to real crème fraîche, since the bacteria in the cultures are not the same, but in most desserts it is an acceptable alternative. If you have some commercial crème fraîche, you can use it in the same way as buttermilk to culture your heavy cream and the result will have the authentic crème fraîche taste.

For 1 cup (2.4 dL)

Pasteurized heavy cream or whipping cream	**1 cup (2.4 dL)**
Cultured, pasteurized buttermilk	**1 teaspoon (5 mL)**

1. Stir together the cream and buttermilk in a small saucepan. Gently heat to between 85° and 90°F (30° to 32°C). Do not overheat or you will kill the culture.

2. Pour the cream into a glass or earthenware container, cover loosely, and let stand undisturbed at room temperature—65° to 85°F (18° to 30°C)—until thickened. Thickening will take from 6 to 30 hours, depending on the temperature of the room.

3. When thick, cover the crème fraîche airtight and chill it in the refrigerator.

NOTE: It is essential to use cultured, pasteurized buttermilk rather than pasteurized cultured buttermilk, since pasteurization after culturing the buttermilk kills the essential bacteria.

STORAGE: Covered airtight for up to 10 days in the refrigerator.

Heavy Syrup

· ·

This is *the* standard syrup for cake making. Because it has the ideal density (30° on the Baumé scale), it keeps almost indefinitely. A syrup with a lower concentration of sugar would ferment or become moldy eventually, and one with a higher concentration would crystallize.

In American volume measures the proportions are easy to remember: 2 cups sugar for each 1 cup water. (Or in metric measures, 1,700 g sugar for each 1 L water.) So you can prepare any quantity you like.

For 2 cups + 2⅔ tablespoons (5.2 dL)

Granulated sugar	**14 ounces (400 g); 2 cups**
Water	**1 cup (2.4 dL)**

1. Combine the sugar and water in the saucepan and bring to a boil, stirring occasionally to dissolve all the sugar.

2. Cover and allow the syrup to cool.

STORAGE: Covered airtight, for up to several months at room temperature. If some sugar crystals form in the syrup (indicating that some water has evaporated), strain them out before using.

Candied Lemon Slices and Lemon Syrup

You can poach lemon slices in heavy syrup to make an attractive garnish for gâteaux or charlottes. The poaching syrup becomes a strongly flavored lemon syrup, which you can use for brushing cake layers. Orange slices can be poached the same way, but they are used less frequently.

For 6 to 8 candied lemon slices and about 1 cup (2.4 dL) lemon syrup

Fresh lemon	**1 medium-size**
Heavy syrup (page 452)	**1½ cups (3.6 dL)**

1. Cut from the lemon six to eight thin slices, each about ³⁄₁₆ inch (4 to 5 mm) thick.

2. Place the lemon slices and heavy syrup in a heavy 1-quart (1-L) saucepan and bring to a simmer over medium heat. Reduce the heat to low and continue simmering gently until the lemon rind changes from opaque white to translucent, 20 to 30 minutes.

3. Remove from the heat and allow the lemon slices to cool in the syrup.

STORAGE: Keep the lemon slices submerged in the syrup in an airtight storage container for up to 1 week in the refrigerator.

Fruits Poached in Light Syrup

· ·

To soften and sweeten fruits (such as peaches, pears, apricots, and pineapple) that aren't quite ripe, you will poach them in light syrup. You can vary the sugar content of the syrup according to the ripeness and sweetness of the fruit. And you can flavor the syrup with a couple of tablespoons (a few cL) of an alcohol such as rum, curaçao, or kirsch, or by substituting wine for half of the water in the recipe. Dry white wine is especially good for enhancing the flavors of peaches and pears.

For about 2 pounds (1 kg) fruit in light syrup

Water	1 quart (1 L)
Granulated sugar	1 pound + 5 ounces to 1 pound + 12 ounces (600 to 800 g); 3 to 4 cups
Fresh lemon juice, strained	2 tablespoons (3 cL)
Vanilla bean, slit lengthwise	½
Fresh peaches, pears, apricots, pineapple, or other fruits	2 pounds (1 kg)

1. Combine the water, sugar, lemon juice, and vanilla bean in a large saucepan—capacity at least 4 quarts (4 L). Bring to a simmer to dissolve the sugar. This is the light syrup.

2. Prepare the fruits for poaching: Leave peaches and apricots whole. Peel pears and either leave them whole or core them and cut them in half. Peel, core, and slice pineapple.

3. Add the fruit to the simmering syrup. Choose a round wire rack or a smaller saucepan lid that will fit inside the large saucepan and place it on top of the fruits to keep them submerged. Bring the syrup back to a simmer, reduce the heat to low, and continue simmering very gently until the fruits are no longer hard and can be pierced easily with the tip of a skewer. They must still be a little firm, or they will become mushy by the time they have cooled. The cooking time can be anything from 5 to 30 minutes, depending on the ripeness and size of the fruit.

4. Remove from the heat and let the fruit cool in the syrup.

STORAGE: The poached fruit can be kept in the refrigerator, submerged in the syrup and covered airtight, for up to 3 or 4 days.

Fruit Salad

. . . .

A fruit salad is a nice accompaniment to some simple cakes such as *quatre quarts* (page 24) and *biscuit de savoie* (page 45), or it can be served as a dessert on its own. There is no special recipe, so we will just give you some general ideas and let you make it according to your own taste and the fruits available.

For any quantity

Fresh fruits, such as apples, pears, oranges, bananas, pineapple, peaches, strawberries, raspberries, blueberries, cherries, seedless grapes, or kiwis	At least 4 or 5 varieties
Superfine or extra fine sugar	To taste
Dark Jamaican or Haitian rum, curaçao liqueur, or kirsch	To taste
Either fresh lemon juice, strained	1 tablespoon (1.5 cL) for each 1 pound (500 g) fruit
Or fresh orange juice, strained	¼ cup (6 cL) for each 1 pound (500 g) fruit
Blanched almonds (optional)	To taste

1. Peel apples, pears, oranges, bananas, pineapple, peaches, and kiwifruit. Core apples, pears, and pineapple. Stone peaches. Hull strawberries. Cut the larger fruits into ½- to 1-inch (1.5- to 2.5-cm) dice. Divide oranges into segments. Slice bananas, and cut large strawberries into halves or quarters. Pit cherries. Leave grapes and small berries whole.

2. Place the fruits in a bowl and add a little sugar and alcohol to sweeten and flavor them. Toss with the lemon or orange juice, and add blanched almonds if you like.

STORAGE: Covered airtight for up to a day or two in the refrigerator.

Double-Strength Brewed Espresso

Brewing espresso double strength in your espresso maker produces a rich concentrate with an intensely attractive coffee taste. We mix it with heavy syrup to make brushing syrups for the cake layers in coffee-flavored gâteaux. The result has a much nicer coffee flavor than you would get by making a coffee concentrate from instant coffee.

We use a stove-top "moka" espresso brewer of the type first popularized by Bialetti. This is the least expensive, easiest to use, most low-tech machine you can get, and it works fine. If you want to use a fancier espresso machine, by all means do so. Be sure to use freshly roasted espresso coffee beans, finely ground. Resist the temptation to pack in more ground espresso than the machine calls for since that will make the steam take too long to penetrate the coffee and will produce a more bitter rather than stronger brew. The trick is to use only half the water that your machine calls for in relation to the amount of ground beans.

For any quantity

EQUIPMENT:
Espresso machine

Espresso beans, freshly roasted and finely ground	About ¼ cup (16 g) beans for each ⅓ cup (1.2 dL) brewed espresso
Cold water	Half the quantity specified by your machine for this quantity of beans

1. Place the ground espresso beans and cold water in your espresso machine and brew the coffee according to the manufacturer's instructions.

2. Allow the brewed espresso to cool before using.

STORAGE: Covered airtight, for up to 2 days in the refrigerator or 1 month in the freezer.

Caramel Food Coloring

. . . .

Make your own caramel food coloring to add a rich, natural tan color to fondants for glazing gâteaux flavored with coffee or *praliné*.

For about 1 cup (2.4 dL)

Granulated sugar	**7 ounces (200 g); 1 cup**
Water	**At least ½ cup (1.2 dL)**

1. Put the sugar in a heavy 3-cup (7.5-dL) to 1-quart (1-L) saucepan or caramel pot and cook over medium to high heat, without stirring. As soon as the sugar begins to melt around the sides of the pot, begin stirring with a wooden spatula. When the sugar becomes fluid, with small white lumps floating in the syrup, reduce the heat to low and continue cooking, stirring constantly and crushing the solid lumps with a wooden spatula. The sugar will melt completely and turn a medium amber, then it will begin to boil.

2. Continue cooking, stirring constantly. When the sugar begins to smoke and is very dark brown, pour in a little water. Stand back, because it will splatter. Continue heating, stirring constantly and gradually adding more water to thin the caramel to a fluid consistency. You will need to add about ½ cup (1.2 dL) of water altogether.

3. Remove from the heat and let cool to room temperature.

STORAGE: Covered airtight for several months at room temperature.

Reference

Equipment

· ·

Having the right tools and knowing how to use them makes the preparation of cakes easier and more enjoyable. This chapter provides a comprehensive glossary of the tools called for throughout the book, with detailed explanations to expand your understanding of some of the important basic tools and to introduce you to those which you may not have encountered before. We give mail-order sources for tools that you may not be able to purchase locally.

BAKING SHEETS

The baking sheet is the single most important piece of bakeware in your kitchen. You will bake meringues and sheet cakes directly on a baking sheet. When you bake cake batter in a ring, the ring must be placed on a baking sheet; and even when you are baking a cake in a mold, you will usually place the mold on a baking sheet for more even heat distribution and to catch any potential overflow of batter if you overfill the mold. Furthermore, the easiest way to do many types of decorative work with chocolate requires spreading melted chocolate on a baking sheet.

Your baking sheets should be large for maximum capacity, heavy-gauge (thick) to conduct heat well and promote even baking, and have a low rim on all four sides to contain the batter for thin sheet cakes. Cookie sheets (which don't have a rim on all sides) and deep jelly roll pans ① (which American bakers call sheet pans) are not the same as baking sheets. Cookie sheets are fine for baking a molded or piped cake batter, but they will not contain the batter for a sheet cake. On the other hand, a deep jelly roll pan will contain sheet cake batters but will make it difficult to spread the batters in the thin layers required in our recipes. Also, the high rim around the sides of the jelly roll pan will disrupt the air flow around molded and piped batters baked on it, making them bake unevenly.

①

The maximum size of your baking sheets will be determined by the size of your oven. For proper air circulation in the oven, there must be at least 1 to 1½ inches (2½ to 4 cm) between the baking sheet and the oven wall on all sides. Standard home ovens should accommodate at least a 12 × 16-inch (30 × 40-cm) baking sheet.

The best baking sheets are about 1/16 inch (1.5 mm) thick and are made from either black steel or aluminum. Lighter weight baking sheets have an unfortunate tendency to buckle when they get hot. If you are baking batter in a cake ring or *tarte* ring and the baking sheet under the ring buckles, the batter can leak out. We don't like tinned steel for baking sheets because the tin wears through easily and has a low melting point—about 450°F (230°C). Stainless steel baking sheets are not good for baking because they don't conduct heat evenly, but they are fine for chocolate work. However, you can get perfectly good results with both tinned steel and stainless steel baking sheets if you understand their limitations. The same cannot be said for air-cushion baking sheets. The air cushion is an insulator, so it eliminates bottom heat, which is essential for baking cakes properly.

French black steel baking sheets are our favorite. All four sides and corners of these baking sheets are enclosed by a gently sloping rim about ¼ inch (6 mm) high ②. They are available in two sizes suitable for home ovens—12 × 16 inches (30 × 40 cm) and 13 × 20 inches (33 × 50 cm). At the factory they are coated with oil to protect the surface during shipping. Before using a new baking sheet for the first time, wipe off this oil and season the baking sheet with a neutral vegetable oil as follows: Coat the entire surface (both top and bottom) of the baking sheet with oil using a paper towel. Heat it in a preheated 350°F (175°C) oven until the oil just begins to smoke. Then remove it from the oven right away, let it cool, and wipe off the excess oil with a paper towel. These baking sheets should never be washed, because they can rust easily. There should always be a thin film of oil on the surface to protect it and to help prevent cakes from sticking. After each use, scrape the baking sheet clean with a dough scraper. If food still sticks to the surface, remove it by using coarse kosher salt as an abrasive and rubbing it with a paper towel dipped in vegetable oil. Occasionally, the baking sheets should be seasoned again, following the same procedure as for a new baking sheet, to maintain a thin film of oil on the surface.

Sources: La Cuisine and Previn.

BLOW DRYER

A powerful hair dryer is a valuable tool in cake making. First, it is the most practical tool for heating rings and molds to unmold gâteaux, bavarians, charlottes, mousse cakes, and mousse logs ③. You can also use it to quickly warm the contents of the bowl of an electric mixer when you are creaming butter or beating a batter that is too cold.

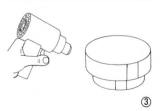

③

A collection of mixing bowls in various sizes is essential for cake making. We recommend stainless steel mixing bowls because they are durable and lightweight, don't react with foods, and transfer heat quickly. They are available in every size you could possibly need, from 1 cup (2.5 dL) on up. Surprisingly, the ones that are most difficult to find—and which few home cooks have in their kitchens—are the smallest ones. We find small stainless steel bowls (preferably heavy-gauge ones) indispensable for handling small quantities of batters and ingredients such as chocolate and jams.

Stainless steel mixing bowls come in three basic shapes. The U-shaped bowls, with vertical sides that curve in to meet a wide flat bottom, are versatile and stable on your countertop. Bowls with a roughly hemispherical shape (flattened at the bottom) are slightly better for whipping eggs or cream and, because they are relatively wide and shallow, they are good containers for hot or cold water to warm or chill the contents of a smaller bowl. However, as general-purpose mixing bowls they are less good because they spread the contents over too wide an area and because, with their narrow flat bottoms, they sit less stably on the countertop. The third shape has a trapezoidal cross-section, with straight sides that slope in to meet the flat bottom ④. This favorite of pastry chefs in France has the versatility and stability of the U-shaped bowl with the advantage that, unlike the U-shaped bowl, it nests well with no risk of two of them getting stuck together.

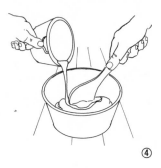

④

For whipping egg whites, a copper bowl is best, but not a necessity (see *Copper Bowls*).

This tool is similar to a rubber spatula (see *Spatulas*), but doesn't have a handle. The only ones worth buying are made of nylon. They are roughly rectangular, with two short straight edges, one long straight edge for smoothing flat surfaces, and one long, convex curved edge for scooping and scraping ⑤. While you can almost always use a rubber spatula (or sometimes an icing spatula) when we call for a bowl scraper, nylon bowl scrapers are superior to spatulas for scooping up ingredients and batters, for scraping out bowls, and for smoothing batter in a cake pan. The size to get is about 4½ inches (12 cm) wide by 3½ inches (9 cm) high.

⑤

Sources: J. B. Prince, La Cuisine, and Previn.

BREAD KNIFE

See *Knives*.

BRIOCHE PARISIENNE MOLD

This deep round mold with deeply fluted, sloping sides is designed for baking brioche ⑥. In this book we use it for baking *biscuit de savoie* (page 45). The size you will need is 8 inches (20 cm) in diameter and about 3¼ inches (8.5 cm) deep.

    Sources: La Cuisine and Previn.

⑥

BROWN WRAPPING PAPER

This is the best paper to use for lining loaf pans for baking fruitcakes and some other pound cakes. Brushed heavily with melted butter, it seals the bottom and sides of the cake after baking and prevents the cake from drying out.

BUTTER MELTERS

See *Saucepans and Butter Melters*.

CAKE-DECORATING COMBS

Used for combing designs in the frostings on gâteaux, these are plastic triangles ⑦ and squares—usually 3 to 4 inches (7 to 10 cm) on a side—with notched, scalloped, or wavy edges. A notched glue spreader (page 487) can be used for the same purpose. For larger surfaces there are 12-inch (30-cm) rulers with one notched edge, but you can get even prettier effects by using a long wavy-edge bread knife.

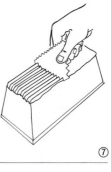

⑦

CAKE PANS

You will bake many cake batters in round cake pans. French ones, called *moules à manquer*, have sloping sides ⑧ and are about 1½ to 1¾ inches (4 to 4.5 cm) deep. French tinned steel cake pans are available in diameters ranging from 6 to 12 inches (16 to 30 cm), including a 9½-inch (24-cm) diameter. American household-style cake pans are very similar to the French ones, with sloping sides and a depth of 1½ inches (4 cm). Good aluminum cake pans are widely available in diameters of 8 and 9 inches (20 and 23 cm). To minimize the number of pans you need, we have used a 9- to 9½-inch (23- to 24-cm) round cake pan as the standard size in all of our round cake recipes. The 9½-inch (24-cm) French cake pan is slightly larger than the 9-inch (23-cm) American pan, but the difference is so small that we treat them as identical. For simplicity, we specify a 9-inch (24-cm) round cake pan in our equipment lists, using inches for the American size and cm for the French size because that is how they are described by their respective manufacturers.

American professional-style cake pans have vertical sides, with a depth of 2 inches (5 cm). They are too deep for baking French cakes, but you can use this type of pan for molding our mango charlotte (page 312).

Do not use black steel cake pans or aluminum cake pans with a dark anodized finish in our recipes, since a dark cake pan would cause the bottom and sides of the cake to cook too quickly and brown excessively.

CAKE RINGS

Called *entremet* rings in France, these stainless steel rings are 1⅜ inches (3.5 cm) deep. We use them for baking sponge cakes, especially génoise, and for assembling round gâteaux by molding in the ring ⑨. The size we require in all of our recipes is 8¾ inches (22 cm) in diameter. Many other sizes are available, with diameters spaced at ¾-inch (2-cm) intervals. We have included guidelines for adjusting our recipes to use different size rings.

Sources: La Cuisine and Previn.

CARAMEL POT

An unlined copper saucepan with a pouring spout ⑩, made specifically for cooking sugar syrups and caramel. Since the quantities of sugar syrup you will normally be cooking at home are small, you want a small caramel pot so that there will be enough depth of syrup in the pot to test the temperature easily. The sizes we find most useful are 4¾ inches (12 cm) and 5½ inches (14 cm) in diameter, with capacities of .85 quart (.8 L) and 1¼ quarts (1.2 L), respectively. Clean with coarse kosher salt and vinegar in the same way as copper mixing bowls (see *Copper Bowls*).

Sources: La Cuisine, Previn, and J. B. Prince.

The corrugated cardboard cake-decorating circles sold in the United States are totally inappropriate for use in French cake making. They are difficult to cut to the precise size you need, their thickness distorts the visual proportions of gâteaux, and when you cut a gâteau to serve it the thickness of the cardboard contributes a cheap, tacky note to an otherwise elegant presentation.

What you want are the foil board lids for aluminum-foil take-out containers, or, equivalently, the cake-decorating cardboards imported from France. These are made of a single layer of white cardboard with foil on one side. They are thin, they have just enough rigidity to support a cake, and the foil is moistureproof. You should be able to get silver foil board lids at a local catering or party supply store. They are inexpensive, but unfortunately they are sometimes sold in packages of 500, so you may want to share them with a group of cake-making friends. The largest sizes generally available are 9-inch (23-cm) circles and 7 × 9½-inch (18 × 24-cm) rectangles, the latter intended as the lid for a 5-pound (4-kg) loaf pan. Occasionally we have seen 9½ × 11-inch (24 × 28-cm) rectangles. The cake-decorating cardboards imported from France have a gold foil surface and are available in 9½-inch (24-cm) circles. As for round cake pans, we specify 9-inch (24-cm) cake-decorating circles in our equipment lists, using inches for the standard American size and cm for the standard French size.

An equally good alternative is a sheet of matt board with a silver or gold foil surface. It comes in 32 × 40-inch (80 × 100-cm) sheets, which you can cut to any size you want to fit your cakes ⑪. Obviously, a foil surface is preferable because it is not absorbent. While matt board is slightly less convenient for round gâteaux because it is not already cut 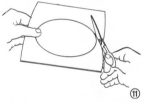 in circles, for other shapes it is much more versatile. It has the added advantage that it is a little thicker and stiffer than are the foil board lids, so it makes cakes easier to handle. Matt board is sold in framing and art supply stores.

For yule logs and large rectangular gâteaux you may prefer an even stiffer cardboard than matt board. Foil board catering platters are the perfect material. They have scalloped edges and measure 14 × 21 inches (35 × 53 cm)—large enough to cut out cake cardboards for three or four yule logs. The cardboard is too thick to cut easily with scissors. Instead, cut it with a utility knife (with disposable razor blades) using a metal straightedge as a guide. If you don't have a cake platter large enough for a yule log or other large gâteau, you can also use a foil board catering platter as a serving platter. Foil board catering platters are sold in catering and party supply stores.

Source for French Cake-Decorating Circles: Previn.

CHARCOAL LIGHTER

Designed for lighting charcoal briquettes for the barbecue, this device is an electric heating element in the form of a loop, with an insulating handle at the end where the power cord is attached (12). We find it does an excellent job of caramelizing sugar to decorate the top of a gâteau. You want one with a loop that has straight sides and is as small as possible (not the style with a large, bent heating element designed for a barbecue kettle) so that it will be easy to manipulate. When burned sugar sticks to it during use, clean the burned sugar off the hot heating element by rubbing it on the metal grate of a burner on your cooktop. After it has cooled, clean it with a dry wire brush.

(12)

COOLING RACKS

When you remove cakes from the oven, you should transfer them from the mold or baking sheet to a wire cooling rack (13) to cool them quickly, prevent condensation between cake and mold or baking sheet (which would make them soggy on the bottom), and avoid sticking. A few cakes are too fragile to remove from the baking sheet while hot, so these are left on the baking sheet and the baking sheet is placed on a wire rack to speed cooling. You will also place gâteaux and charlottes on wire racks for glazing.

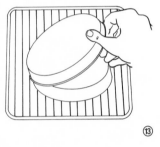

(13)

For rectangular sheets of cake we suggest that you have two or three rectangular wire cooling racks at least as large as your baking sheets. Round wire racks are often more convenient for unmolding cakes baked in round cake pans or loaf pans and for glazing round gâteaux and charlottes. We recommend having at least two of them with a diameter of 10 to 12 inches (25 to 30 cm).

Both rectangular and round cooling racks can be made of tinned, chrome-plated, or non-stick-surfaced steel wires spaced about ½ inch (12 mm) apart. The wires can be parallel straight lines or, for round cooling racks, they can form a spiral out from the center. The frame should have feet to hold the rack at least ½ inch (12 mm) above the countertop.

COPPER BOWLS

For whipping egg whites, a copper bowl is even better than stainless steel (see page 176). Bowls designed for whipping whites with a wire whisk have a hemispherical shape, which allows you to incorporate air most efficiently. If you have one of KitchenAid's heavy-duty electric mixers, we recommend the optional copper liner bowl made for these machines by Atlas Metal Spinning.

To clean a copper bowl, first wash it thoroughly with hot water. Clean the surface with a small amount of coarse kosher salt moistened with distilled white vinegar, which removes oxidation. Rinse out the bowl with cold water, then wipe it dry with a paper towel.

Sources: La Cuisine and Dean & DeLuca.

DOUGH SCRAPER

The baker's dough scraper is a flat, rectangular steel blade—typically about 3 × 6 inches (7½ × 15 cm) and not sharp—with a thick handle along one long edge ⑭. You will use it for working fondant and softening almond paste on your countertop, for cutting up ingredients such as butter, and for scraping your countertop and black steel baking sheets clean. It is also referred to as a pastry scraper or block scraper.

⑭

DREDGE

This cylindrical metal container with a perforated lid is the ideal tool for dusting confectioners' sugar and cocoa powder ⑮. To dust with a dredge, flick it forward horizontally at the same time as you tilt it forward, throwing a sprinkling of powder onto a cake or your countertop. This gives you better control than turning it upside down and shaking it. Return the dredge to the vertical position between each forward motion so that the confectioners' sugar or cocoa powder will drop back to the bottom of the container.

Sources: La Cuisine and Sweet Celebrations.

⑮

DRYWALL KNIVES

The triangular blades of these tools are great for decorative chocolate work ⑯. Small ones 1½ inches (4 cm) wide are called putty knives; large ones 6 inches (15 cm) wide are taping knives; and there is a full range of spackling and finish knives in between. The blades can be very flexible (called "full elastic"), slightly flexible ("half elastic"), or stiff. The size and flexibility you choose depends on what shapes you are making—for example, a full elastic putty knife for chocolate shavings or a half elastic 3-inch (7-cm) finish knife for chocolate cigarettes (see

⑯

pages 423–25 for more details.) The best drywall knives, especially the "full elastic" ones, are made by Embee.

If you do chocolate work on an aluminum or tinned steel baking sheet, use only plastic drywall knives because metal ones will scrape metal off the baking sheet. These are considered disposable, but for our purposes they can be washed and reused many times.

Drywall knives are sold at paint supply and hardware stores.

ELECTRIC MIXER

An electric mixer is an indispensable labor-saving device for creaming butter, whipping eggs and cream, and beating batters, fillings, and frostings. With rare exceptions, there are only two basic mechanisms used for electric mixers, planetary action and the eggbeater.

The best and most versatile electric mixers available are the heavy-duty, planetary-action stand mixers made by KitchenAid and Kenwood. They employ a single beater rotating on a vertical axis at the same time as the axis itself (mounted on the perimeter of a wheel) revolves around the bowl. The planetary-action mechanism ensures that the beater constantly moves around the entire interior of the bowl. These mixers are equipped with three types of beaters: a wire whip for whisking ⑰, a flat beater for mixing batters and creaming butter ⑱, and a dough hook for mixing pastry doughs and bread doughs. KitchenAid has two models, the 4½-quart (4.5-L) K45 and the 5-quart (5-L) K5. Kenwood also makes two models, the 5-quart (5-L) Chef and the 7-quart (7-L) Major (currently sold under the Rival Select brand name as the Chef and Chef Excel). They all have deep, beehive-shaped bowls with a dimple in the bottom. The planetary action moves the bottom of beater around in the circular depression surrounding the dimple, making these mixers equally effective with both small and large quantities.

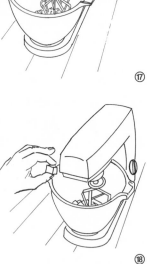

⑰

⑱

Most of the other electric mixers on the market employ the eggbeater mechanism. The eggbeater has two beaters that rotate on fixed axes in opposite directions. When beating a liquid, this mechanism sets up two whirlpools that circulate the liquid around the bowl and draw it between the beaters. Unfortunately, if the liquid becomes too viscous (as it does when you whip egg whites or heavy cream), then the circulation breaks down. With a handheld electric mixer, you can remedy this problem by moving the beater around the bowl. However, in a stand mixer the beaters will reach only part of the mixture in the bowl when it becomes too thick. Despite this basic design flaw, you can use an eggbeater-type stand mixer to do the early phase of the whipping for heavy cream or egg whites; then when the liquid starts to become too viscous, you should finish the whipping by hand with a wire whisk.

FOOD PROCESSOR

The food processor ⑲ is a close second to the electric mixer in its versatility for cake making. It is excellent for pureeing fruits, and it is without equal for preparing nut-and-sugar powders, almond paste, and *praliné*. In most recipes the quantities required demand a full-size, direct-drive food processor, with a work bowl capacity of at least 7 cups (1.7 L). We use the French food processors manufactured by Robot Coupe. Two other excellent brands are KitchenAid and Cuisinart.

⑲

GLUE SPREADER

See *Trowels and Glue Spreaders*.

GRATER

Grated orange and lemon zests are important flavorings in French cakes. It is easiest to grate the zest directly off the whole fruit. We have tried three different grater designs that are excellent for this purpose. A two-piece round cheese grater has a large, slightly domed grating surface over a stainless steel bowl; it should have two interchangeable grating surfaces. A related design uses a rectangular plastic container with an interchangeable flat grating surface on top; these models can have three different grating surfaces to choose from. Finally, the box grater is open at top and bottom, with a handle at the top and a different grating surface on each of the four sides. Whatever the design, you want a grating surface with small, round or oval holes that are sharp and raised on one side only. In a grating surface with four sharp spikes around each hole, the grated zest is difficult to remove from the grater.

ICE CREAM SCOOP

A spade-type ice cream scoop with antifreeze inside is our favorite tool for scraping frozen buttercream and other fillings from their freezer containers when we have neglected to defrost them in advance.

ICING SPATULAS

The icing spatula has a flat, narrow blade with straight, parallel edges and rounded end ⑳. It is one of the most versatile tools in the pastry chef's arsenal. You will use icing spatulas for spreading and smoothing batters, fillings, and frosting, for moving cake layers, for lifting gâteaux, and for a variety of decorating tasks.

For all but decorating, you need an icing spatula with a blade 10 to 12 inches (25 to 30 cm) long. The 12-inch (30-cm) blade is best for spreading and smoothing the batter on a baking sheet. The blade of the icing spatula should be flexible, but its base should have enough rigidity to allow you to lift a gâteau. The handle should be slender and smoothly rounded for fingertip control. The straight sides of the blade should extend for most of its length, then taper sharply to meet the handle. And the balance point should be in the tapering section of the blade.

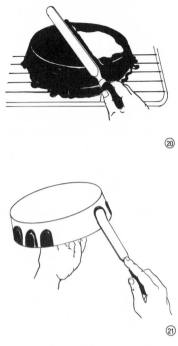

On the other hand, for decorative work you want an icing spatula with a very flexible blade 4 to 6 inches (15 cm) long. A 4-inch (10-cm) icing spatula is also useful for loosening the edges of cakes that are clinging to the pan after baking. For dabbing chocolate petals on the side of a round gâteau, an icing spatula with a very flexible 8-inch blade (20-cm) is ideal ㉑.

The American icing spatulas we have tried are fine as lifting and spreading tools, but are too clumsy for elegant decorative work or for spreading and smoothing the frosting on a round gâteau. For such icing spatulas you must look to European manufacturers, and only a few are available. The French icing spatulas from Matfer are well proportioned and balanced. They have blades in lengths from 6 to 12 inches (15 to 30 cm), with forged rat-tail tangs. The Swiss-made Victorinox icing spatulas are not quite as elegantly proportioned, but are still excellent and come in 8-, 10-, and 12-inch (20-, 25-, and 30-cm) lengths. For both the French and Swiss icing spatulas we advise getting the largest size, with a blade 12 inches (20 cm) long and about 1⅝ inches (4.2 cm) wide, in order to have a long enough straight edge to sweep the frosting on the tops of round gâteaux and a large enough blade for spreading batters.

To find a 4-inch (10-cm) icing spatula with a flexible blade you will probably need to look in the artist's supply department. Ateco makes an artist's palette knife which has precisely the same shape as an icing spatula and a more flexible blade than any culinary spatula we have found in this length.

Wusthof-Trident and F. Dick make luxurious forged icing spatulas that are very different from the classic French ones. Both have blades 10 inches (25 cm) long and 1⅜ inches (3.5 cm) wide. While not as efficient for spreading large amounts of batter as the wider 12-inch (30-cm) Matfer and Victorinox icing spatulas, these German icing spatulas are outstanding for assembling and decorating gâteaux. They have slim bolsters and full tangs, which make them heavier but lower their balance points to the base of the blade so the blades feel weightless. The superb balance of these icing spatulas gives you extraordinary control for smoothing the outside of a round gâteau.

The blades have exceptionally long, straight edges for their size, and extremely flexible tips, but their bolsters give them plenty of rigidity at the base of the blade for lifting.

At the opposite end of the spectrum, Ateco makes an extra-large icing spatula that deserves special mention. Its blade is 2 inches (5 cm) wide and 14 inches (36 cm) long. While this spatula is too clumsy for smoothing the frosting on a round gâteau, its enormous blade makes it even better than the 12-inch (30-cm) French and Swiss spatulas for spreading batter on a baking sheet.

Sources: La Cuisine, Previn, and J. B. Prince.

KITCHEN PARCHMENT

We use this strong, stiff, greaseproof paper to line baking sheets and cake pans and to make parchment decorating cones. For lining baking sheets and cake pans, it is roughly equivalent to brushing with butter and then dusting with flour. The parchment has the advantage of making it easier to unmold some fragile cakes without damage. While parchment is supposed to be a nonstick lining paper, some cakes do stick to it nonetheless. Frequently we find it advantageous to brush the parchment lining a baking sheet or mold with melted butter to reduce sticking to an absolute minimum.

Rolls of parchment come in several different widths, from 12 to 15 inches (30 to 38 cm) wide. For making parchment decorating cones (see directions on page 416), we are in the habit of using the 15-inch (38-cm) width. For lining baking sheets, choose a roll the same width as your baking sheets to simplify cutting it to size; or, if you can't get the exact width, buy one larger than your baking sheets. You can also purchase parchment in large rectangular sheets and in precut rounds for lining cake pans.

KNIVES

The important knives for cake making are the chef's knife, paring knife, and wavy-edge bread knife. We like the high-carbon stainless steel knives made in Solingen, Germany, by F. Dick and by Wusthof-Trident; they have comfortable handles, good balance, are easy to keep sharp, and don't pit or rust.

You use the chef's knife ㉒ for chopping nuts and chocolate and sometimes for cutting gâteau. We suggest a chef's knife with a 10-inch (25-cm) blade. The paring knife ㉓ is for cutting fruits and decorating; it should have a blade 3 to 3½ inches (7½ to 9 cm) long.

The best knife for slicing both breads and cake layers is a bread knife with a wavy or scalloped (rather than serrated) edge ㉔. This knife can also be used for making a decorative pattern in a frosting and for sawing through a chocolate glaze without shattering it. The standard bread knife is only 8 inches (20 cm) long—too short for slicing a 9-inch (24-cm) round of génoise, for example. Try to get a wavy-edge slicing knife with a blade 10 to 12 inches (25 to 30 cm) long.

Sources: La Cuisine, Dean & DeLuca, and J. B. Prince

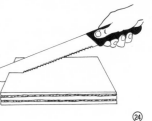

LEMON REAMER

To juice a lemon quickly, cut off both ends with a knife and then ream out the inside from one end to the other with this fluted, conical tool ㉕. Lemon reamers are available in wood or plastic.

LOAF PANS

French and American loaf pans are both rectangular with sloping sides, but the proportions are quite different. The French loaf pans are relatively narrow and deep ㉖, while the American ones are wider and shallower. We always specify the size of the loaf pan by volume in our recipes so that you can use either style, and we have designed the quantities so that all of our recipes use one size, a 6-cup (1.5-L) loaf pan. Choose tinned steel or aluminum loaf pans. We do not recommend black steel or anodized aluminum with a dark surface because it can produce excessive browning with our recipes.

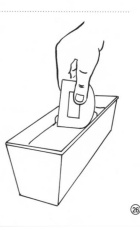

MARBLE PASTRY SLAB

While a marble work surface has a great advantage in pastry making, for cakes the main place where marble's ability to absorb heat is important is in making fondant. The marble should be ¾ to 1 inch (2 to 2.5 cm) thick and as large as possible without being unwieldy. An 18 × 24-inch (45 × 60-cm) slab will work nicely.

A marble slab can also make a very elegant platter for presenting a yule log.

Source: Ranier Devido Stone & Marble Company.

MEASURING CUPS AND SPOONS

You need two types of measuring cups, one for liquids and the other for dry ingredients. The reason is that liquids have a surface tension which makes the surface of the liquid curved rather than flat; in contrast, the surface of a dry ingredient can be swept flat.

When you measure dry ingredients, you fill the measuring cup above the rim and then sweep off the excess using an icing spatula or other implement with a straight edge so that the cup is filled level with the rim. Measuring spoons are generally designed for dry ingredients and are used in the same way. Dry measure cups and spoons are almost always made of metal or opaque plastic, since there is no reason to see through the side of the measuring implement.

Liquid measure cups are transparent and have graduations marked on the side. The curved surface of the liquid in the cup is called the meniscus. For water and for many other liquids found in the kitchen, the meniscus is concave. Liquid measure cups are designed to measure the volume based on the level of liquid at the bottom (center) of the meniscus. We prefer the tall, narrow glass liquid measure cups sold as bar supplies because the narrower the measuring cup, the more accurately you can read the height of the liquid.

Measuring liquid in a dry measure cup or spoon is more tricky. If you underfill the cup slightly, then the liquid will reach the top of the cup at the rim, but the surface will form the same concave meniscus as in a liquid measure cup. However, it is also possible to overfill the cup without spilling the liquid. In this case the surface tension of the liquid makes its surface become convex (just as it does with water droplets on a flat surface) and the liquid domes above the rim of the cup.

For both liquid and dry measure cups and spoons, we advise against purchasing cheap, generic-quality tools. Poor-quality measuring utensils are sometimes calibrated very inaccurately, rendering them worse than useless.

MICRO TORCHES

See *Propane Torches and Micro Torches*.

MICROWAVE

If you have a microwave, you can use it to melt ingredients (such as chocolate, butter, and jams) and components (chocolate glaze and writing chocolate), to soften butter and fillings (such as buttercream and ganache), and to heat heavy syrup and cream, as well as to defrost components that have been stored in the freezer. The microwave is especially good when fast but gentle warming is required and it is very convenient for small quantities of ingredients that can be contained in a small ramekin or custard cup. Always use nonmetallic containers and cycle the microwave at reduced power (following the manufacturer's instructions and your experience with the particular microwave), stopping to stir as often as necessary to melt, soften, or heat the ingredients evenly.

OVENS

The most common oven in home kitchens is an electric or gas "roasting" oven. In a roasting oven, the heat is generated by a heating element just above (for electric) or below (for gas) the oven floor, and food is cooked on racks that can be positioned at three or four different heights inside the oven cavity. Our cake recipes are designed for use in a roasting oven. Other ovens, such as convection ovens and deck ovens, have very different baking characteristics.

Within the cavity of your roasting oven, heat is circulated by radiation (infrared light waves emitted by the oven floor, walls, and—for electric ovens—the heating element) and by natural convection (air circulation produced by differences in pressure between air masses at different temperatures). Heat flows from the bottom of the oven to the top, because the heating element is at the bottom of the cavity and because hotter air is lighter than cooler air. The hottest air is at the top of the oven, and the greatest amount of radiant heat is at the bottom of the oven. The higher the oven temperature, the more radiant heat is generated by the heating element, and the greater the differential between the heat at the bottom and top of the oven.

Most home ovens have two racks, but it is usually best to bake on only one rack at a time. The vertical position of the oven rack is a major determining factor in how a cake will bake. Choosing a lower rack position will make the bottom of the cake cook more quickly and the top more slowly. Conversely, a higher rack position will make the bottom cook more slowly and the top more quickly. Generally cakes will bake most evenly on one of the middle rack positions. Unless otherwise specified, use a middle rack position in all of our recipes.

Regardless of the rack position, always allow at least 1 to 1½ inches (2½ to 4 cm) between your baking sheet and the oven walls on all sides. Positioning your baking sheets too close to the oven wall forces air currents to travel too quickly between the oven wall and the edge of the baking sheet, producing greater heat transfer and excessive browning near the edge of the baking sheet.

Horizontal heat circulation in a roasting oven is very poor. When you bake on two oven racks simultaneously, you disrupt the flow of heat in the space between the baking sheets. As a result, the bottoms of cakes on the upper baking sheet and the tops of the cakes on the lower baking sheet will cook slowly, while the tops of the cakes on the upper baking sheet and the bottoms of the cakes on the lower baking sheet will cook quickly. In a medium or hot oven, where the differential between bottom heat and top heat is an important factor, this is a disaster. On the other hand, in a low oven the heat is much more uniform and the baking is slower overall. For these reasons, the problems created by baking on two racks simultaneously are less serious in a low oven and can be compensated for by switching the baking sheets between top and bottom rack positions partway through the baking period.

The oven temperature determines not only how long a cake will bake but also the cake's characteristics and quality. Baking a cake melts butter; makes air bubbles in the batter expand and water evaporate; coagulates proteins and gelatinizes starches, making the batter set; and, finally, caramelizes sugar, giving the surface an appealing brown, beige, or golden color. For most cakes you want to minimize the evaporation of water from the batter so that the interior of the cake will be moist. To do this, we make the baking temperature as high as possible without overbrowning the surface of the cake before the inside is finished baking. On the other hand, for meringues the baking temperature must be low enough to allow the interior to dry out before the surface browns too much, but not too low or they will not expand enough and will be dry, hard, and heavy.

Preheating the oven is essential. The initial oven heat makes the batter rise quickly before it starts to set, making it lighter. How long the oven needs to preheat depends partly on the oven temperature and partly on the characteristics of your particular oven. As a rule of thumb, always let it preheat for a minimum of 15 minutes. Most ovens will preheat to even a high temperature within this time. For a hot oven, 30 minutes of preheating is even better. The oven thermostat cycles the heating element off and on, as the oven temperature rises and falls around the temperature you select. It can take one or two full cycles for the oven to reach the point where this pattern is established and the oven temperature is not overshooting the range it is designed to operate within.

You should expect the oven temperature to fluctuate within a range of about 25°F (15°C) around the temperature you set, provided the thermostat is properly calibrated. Unfortunately, oven thermostats drift over time, so even if properly calibrated at first, they can eventually become inaccurate. It is a good idea to check your oven thermostat regularly with an oven thermometer. Position the thermometer at the center of the oven cavity, and read it several times over the course of at least one cycle. If you find that the thermostat is inaccurate, then have it corrected (you may be able to do this yourself, following the manufacturer's instructions) or compensate for the inaccuracy by adjusting the oven temperature you set accordingly.

PAPER DOILIES

In France, it is customary to present cakes on paper doilies because they add a nice decorative touch. Choose a doily that will give you a 1- to 1½-inch (2.5- to 4-cm) border on all sides of the cake.

PASTRY AND DECORATING TUBES

Pastry tubes are large—about 2 inches (5 cm) long. They are used with large pastry bags for piping batters, fillings, and frostings. Decorating tubes are much smaller—usually about 1⅛ inches (3 cm) long—and are used with small pastry bags for decorative piping of frostings. To our knowledge, Ateco is the only American manufacturer that produces a complete range of pastry tubes. We use their numbering system in our recipes, in addition to the size and shape of each tube. The tubes we use for cakes have plain or fluted round openings.

The plain tubes ㉗ are numbered from 0 to 9, with openings ranging from ⁵⁄₃₂ to ¹¹⁄₁₆ inch (4 to 18 mm) in diameter. We use them mostly for piping cake batters and occasionally for fillings and frostings.

There are two sets of fluted pastry tubes ㉘, depending on the

㉗

number and size of the teeth. The basic fluted tubes, numbered from 0 to 9 in increasing size, have wide, deep teeth. They are used to make deep, distinctive fluting or for frostings that aren't fine enough to hold a very delicate shape. B-series, "French-style," fluted pastry tubes are numbered from 0B to 9B and have short, narrow teeth; they are used when you want fine, shallow fluting in a frosting that will hold a very precise shape.

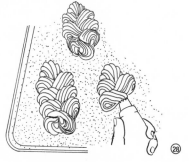

French-made pastry tubes differ from most of those made by Ateco (as well as other American manufacturers) in that they have a rolled rim at the back end of the tube. The French supplier Matfer produces pastry tubes in an even larger range of shapes and sizes than does Ateco, but the numbering system is completely different.

The assortment of shapes of the openings of decorating tubes is mind-boggling. However, for the type of decorating we do in this book, you need only one decorating tube, an open star tube with a ³⁄₃₂-inch (2-mm) opening and six teeth (Ateco #17).

Couplers are made to permit changing the pastry or decorating tube without emptying the pastry bag. Unfortunately, the largest coupler on the market will not accommodate any pastry tubes larger than an Ateco #5.

Sources: Sweet Celebrations, La Cuisine, and J. B. Prince.

PASTRY BAGS
....

You will use pastry bags to pipe batters and frostings. The pastry bag can be made of canvas with a plastic-coated interior or of nylon. We prefer the canvas because it isn't slippery when it gets wet. The advantage of nylon bags is that they dry quickly after washing, but they are slippery when wet.

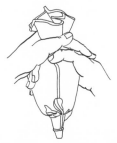

For piping batters or large quantities of frostings, you need a large pastry bag ㉙. Refilling the bag is a minor nuisance, so it is best to have one large enough to hold all the batter at once. On the other hand, if the pastry bag is too large, it becomes unwieldy. For home use, the most convenient sizes are 16 and 18 inches (40 and 45 cm) long. If possible, get one of each size so you have a choice and, when a recipe calls for piping batter with two different tubes, you can switch without stopping to clean out the bag, change the tube, and refill. To accommodate the largest pastry tubes, cut off the tip of the pastry bag with a scissors (page 547) to enlarge the opening to ¾ inch (2 cm) wide. Don't make the hole any larger than that or the smaller pastry tubes can fall through.

For decorating, you must have a smaller pastry bag. Not only would a large pastry bag be clumsy for small amounts of decorative piping, but a small decorating tube would fall through the hole in the tip of the large pastry bag. A 10-inch (25-cm) pastry bag is about right for decorating.

Sources: La Cuisine, Sweet Celebrations, and J. B. Prince.

PASTRY BRUSH

Indispensable for coating baking sheets and molds with melted butter and for glazing cakes with apricot jam and confectioners' sugar glaze or mousse desserts with jelly glaze. The brush should have natural boar bristles (called Chinese bristles) rather than nylon, which melts if it gets hot. Pastry brushes are made in two shapes, flat and round. The flat, paintbrush type is the most versatile ㉚. For brushing glazes on desserts and for buttering molds, use a flat brush 1 to

㉚

1½ inches (2.5 to 4 cm) wide. For buttering baking sheets, a 2-inch (5-cm) flat brush works well. If you are buttering several baking sheets at a time, using an even larger brush—for example, 4 inches (10 cm) wide—will be much faster.

To clean a pastry brush, wash it thoroughly by hand with detergent and hot water, working the detergent between the bristles with your fingers, then rinse thoroughly. (A dishwasher will ruin the wood handle.) Shake out the excess water, then press the bristles between towels to remove as much moisture as possible. Hang the brush, bristles down, to finish drying. Don't hang it bristles up or moisture will stay inside the ferule and eventually rot the base of the bristles.

Sources: La Cuisine, Dean & DeLuca, Previn, and J. B. Prince.

PROPANE TORCHES AND MICRO TORCHES

For quickly caramelizing the top of a gâteau, we like a propane torch with a large tip. For finer decorative work, you can switch to a smaller tip (such as a pinpoint tip) with a more focused flame.

Regardless of which tip you are using, when you point the flame down on a cake, the flame has an annoying tendency to go out because tipping the propane bottle changes the pressure to the tip. To avoid this, get a torch with a hose (rather than one that attaches directly to the propane bottle) so that you don't have to tip the bottle. Propane torches are sold in hardware stores.

Micro torches are designed for various types of craft and hobby work. Compared with a propane torch, a micro torch is much more compact, with a smaller, more focused flame. Rather than attaching to a propane bottle, the micro torch is self-contained, with a small refillable butane fuel cartridge. We like a micro torch for burning decorative designs in confectioners' sugar on top of cakes. They are sold in craft and hobby shops, hardware stores, and cookware shops. Some cookware shops have been promoting micro torches for caramelizing the tops of desserts, but they have too small a flame to do this effectively.

A compromise between the propane torch and the micro torch is the BernzOmatic Lightweight Mini Torch (model ST900S), which is designed for craft and hobby work and for small soldering tasks. It attaches to a propane bottle with a hose and has interchangeable pencil point and needle point tips available. While it won't caramelize a dessert as quickly as a full-size propane torch, it is probably less intimidating for cooks unaccustomed to using a propane torch.

Whenever you are using a torch, remember that it is not a toy. Follow the manufacturer's instructions and exercise appropriate caution. Keep the flame away from flammable materials such as clothing, drapes, and towels, and note that the tip of the torch will be very hot for some time after you extinguish the flame.

Source: McGuckin Hardware and J. B. Prince.

RIBBED VINYL FLOOR MAT

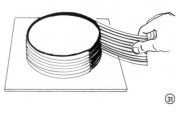

Manufactured by Warp Brothers under the trade name Plast-o-Mat, this clear ribbed vinyl is sold in hardware stores by the yard or prepackaged. We cut it into strips and use it to make ribbed ribbons of chocolate to wrap around the sides of gâteaux ㉛. You can also texture sheets of almond paste by rolling the almond paste out on the ribbed vinyl. Before you use the vinyl for the first time, wash it thoroughly with a solution of vinegar and water.

Source: McGuckin Hardware.

RING MOLDS

A standard American ring mold or a French "rice ring" mold, with two indentations running around the inside and outside near the bottom ㉜, is perfect for baking the old-fashioned cake called *trois frères* (page 48). You can also use a French *savarin* ring mold (a plain ring mold with no indentations) or the *trois frères* mold (page 487), which was created specifically for this cake. You will need one with a capacity of 5 to 6 cups (about 1.5 L). We use the same size ring molds in our recipes for bavarians in chapter 6.

ROLLING PINS

In cake making, rolling pins are used primarily for rolling out almond paste. We recommend a French-style rolling pin, which is a simple cylinder of hardwood (boxwood or beechwood) about 20 inches (50 cm) long and 2 inches (5 cm) in diameter with no handles ㉝. This is easy to maneuver and gives you a good feeling for the thickness of the almond paste you are rolling. Even better is a stainless steel rolling pin, which is actually just a length of stainless steel pipe (from your local steel yard) cut to the same size as the French rolling pin. The stainless steel is heavier and does more of the work for you; also, it has a higher thermal mass than does the wood, and as a result it stays cooler when you are working with it.

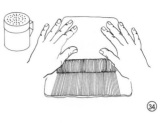

Plastic rolling pins with textured surfaces are designed to produce a textured surface on a sheet of almond paste. Ribbed (or grooved) ㉞, checkerboard (which produces a waffle texture), and basketweave patterns are the most common.

Sources: La Cuisine, J. B. Prince, and Sweet Celebrations.

SAUCEPANS AND BUTTER MELTERS

Stove-top cooking is a limited but important part of cake making. You must be able to prepare custards and sugar syrups, poach fruits, and melt butter, jams, fondant, and chocolate. These purposes call for saucepans and butter melters (which are really just small saucepans) in a variety of sizes.

Since the quantities of ingredients that you must heat for cakes are often quite small, it is important to have a small saucepan ㉟. As an example, you simply can't melt ¼ cup (6 cL) of jam properly in a 2-quart (2-L) saucepan. If you don't already have them, we recommend adding a 1-quart (1-L) saucepan and 2-cup (5-dL) butter melter plus some smaller butter melters to your collection of saucepans. Sets of butter melters in sizes ranging from ¼ to 1 cup (6 cL to 1.4 dL) are widely available in cookware shops.

Among the metals used for saucepans, copper and aluminum are by far the best heat conductors. Of the two, copper is the better conductor, but more important, it has a lower thermal mass, enabling it to react more quickly to changes in temperature. This feature is especially significant in cooking delicate sauces and sugar syrups, when you don't want heat stored in the pot to overcook the ingredients after you remove it from the burner. However, copper is heavy and expensive. Aluminum makes up for its higher thermal mass by being light in weight and considerably less expensive.

Whether a saucepan is made of copper or aluminum, the metal should be a heavy gauge to provide even heat distribution. The best thickness for both metals is about ⅛ inch (3 mm). Much thinner pots don't heat evenly and can warp, and thicker ones would be too heavy and have too much thermal mass.

Both copper and aluminum can interact chemically with certain foods. Some copper compounds are potentially harmful, and for this reason copper cooking utensils are always lined with another metal unless they will be reserved for a special purpose, such as cooking sugar or whipping egg whites.

The very best French copper saucepans are hammered for extra strength and lined with tin. Tin-lined copper pots should not be used for cooking sugar to the caramel stage because tin has a relatively low melting point and if you accidentally overcook the caramel, you can damage the tin lining. Copper pots lined with stainless steel don't have this drawback. However, since stainless steel is a poor conductor of heat, there is no advantage to a saucepan that is mostly stainless steel with only a thin layer of copper on the outside. Unlined copper saucepans, called caramel pots, are used for cooking sugar and melting chocolate (see *Caramel Pot*).

Aluminum can discolor eggs and foods containing acids. While these interactions aren't harmful, for aesthetic reasons it is undesirable to cook custards or fruits in bare aluminum saucepans. To prevent interaction with foods, aluminum saucepans can be lined or the surface of the aluminum can be anodized. The best material for lining is stainless steel because of its durability. Anodizing is an electrolytic process that chemically alters the surface of the aluminum to produce a durable surface that won't interact with foods. We think the stainless steel–lined aluminum saucepans made by All-Clad Metalcrafters are the best aluminum saucepans on the market.

SCALES

If you do much baking, a kitchen scale is an essential. The only accurate way to measure dry ingredients is by weight. This is particularly important for powders (such as flour and confectioners' sugar) and for ingredients in large pieces (such as nuts). Granulated sugars can be measured fairly accurately by volume, but this can be more cumbersome than weighing the sugar when fractional cup amounts are required. Measuring by volume is the superior method only for very small quantities that are below the level of sensitivity of the kitchen scales, typically ¼ ounce (7 g) and for some metric scales as low as 1 or 2 g.

Of course, an inaccurate kitchen scale is no advantage. Many of the spring balances made for kitchen use are very unreliable. Our preference is for a beam balance. A single-beam balance has two platforms—one for the ingredients and one for the balance weights—and one balance beam with a sliding weight for small increments. Even better (and much more convenient) is a double-beam balance, which has one large platform on top for the ingredients and two balance beams with sliding weights for small and large weight increments, respectively.

Digital kitchen scales can also be a good choice. While more fragile than beam balances, they can be quite accurate and are very easy to use. Be sure to choose one with a large capacity—at least 6 pounds (2.7 kg)—so you can weigh large amounts of ingredients, batters, and fillings and frostings in a bowl or pot.

While all of our recipes give both avoirdupois and metric weights, we urge you to get a metric scale and to use the metric system. No one likes to think in fractions of an ounce less than ¼, and we have never seen a kitchen scale calibrated in avoirdupois units with graduations finer than this. But metric scales calibrated in increments of 1 g are quite common, and the sensitivity they provide makes them much more desirable. We particularly recommend the metric double-beam balance made by Teraillon. Many digital scales allow you to switch between metric and avoirdupois weight at the touch of a button—a great asset if you aren't yet comfortable with metric weights.

Source: La Cuisine.

SHEET POLYESTER

Pastry chefs in France use crystal-clear sheets of polyester for forming glossy ribbons of chocolate to wrap around the sides of gâteaux. This sheet polyester is sold in art supply stores in the United States. You can buy material 7.5 mL thick in precut 18 × 24-inch (45 × 60-cm) rectangles, or 5-mL material by the yard from an 18-inch (45-cm) roll. Sheets of clear acetate are also available in art supply stores, but they are less durable than the polyester.

SIEVES AND SIFTERS

For straining liquids you need a sieve and for sifting dry ingredients you can use a sieve or a sifter. Sieves can have a bowl-shaped mesh set into a metal or plastic frame with a handle, a cone-shaped mesh in a metal frame with a handle (the French call this a *chinois* because it is shaped like a Chinese hat), or a large flat mesh set in a cylindrical frame with no handle (this is called a drum sieve in English or

tamis in French ㊱). An American flour sifter is just a sieve with a cylindrical metal frame, a flat or bowl-shaped mesh, and an agitator of some type.

More important than the style of the sieve is the fineness of the mesh. The mesh is graded according to the distance between two adjacent wires, measured center to center.

A fine mesh (less than ¹⁄₁₆ inch = 1.5 mm) is best for straining liquids. There are wonderful stainless steel strainers imported from Italy (and less expensive knockoffs from the Far East) that have a very fine, bowl-shaped mesh, about ³⁄₆₄ inch (1 mm). A boullion strainer (which the French call an *étamine* because it is as fine as muslin) has the finest mesh of all, about ³⁄₁₂₈ inch (0.5 mm). Except for the boullion strainer, which is usually cone-shaped, fine mesh strainers are bowl-shaped sieves or drum sieves.

For sifting flour, confectioners' sugar, and most other powdered ingredients (including almond-and-sugar powder), you should choose a flour sifter ㊲ or drum sieve with a medium mesh, ¹⁄₁₆ to ³⁄₃₂ inch (1.5 to 2 mm). The flour sifters with multiple screens sift slowly and are difficult to clean. Flour sifters with a wire rotor agitator operated by a crank and a single bowl-shaped screen contoured to the rotor are faster and more durable. For sifting almond-and-sugar powder and for large quantities of other dry ingredients, a 12-inch (30-cm) drum sieve is the most convenient and efficient.

Drum sieves with meshes much coarser than ³⁄₃₂ inch (2 mm) are used primarily for sifting chopped nuts.

A drum sieve we find particularly versatile is a stainless steel garden sieve (designed for sifting topsoil) with interchangeable meshes. The one we use has three meshes—³⁄₃₂ inch (2 mm), ³⁄₁₆ inch (4 mm), and ⁵⁄₁₆ inch (7 mm).

Always sift flour and other dry ingredients onto a large sheet of kitchen paper (either wax paper or, for larger quantities, freezer paper) so you can use the paper as a funnel for pouring.

Sources: La Cuisine, Dean & DeLuca, Sweet Celebrations, and J. B. Prince.

SILPAT BAKING MATS AND TEFLON PAN LINERS

Silpat baking mats are sheets of silicone-coated woven fiberglass designed to be a reusable nonstick replacement for kitchen parchment to line baking sheets. In fact, they are much more than that. Silpat can tolerate temperatures from −40° to 580°F (−40° to 305°C) and can be used up to 2,000 times. It is a thick, flexible, nonstick surface that can be used for chocolate and sugar work as well as for baking. We especially recommend it for baking *joconde* with combed, piped, or fingerpainted designs (page 278).

Silpat is the trademark used for these baking mats by their manufacturer Demarle. A very similar product called Exopat is made by Matfer. Both Silpat and Exopat are sold in sizes to fit commercial baking sheets—the French standard 16 × 24-inch (40 × 60-cm) black steel baking sheet and the American standard 18 × 26-inch (46 × 66-cm) full-size and 13 × 18-inch (33 × 46-cm) half-size sheet pans. Some home baking sheets, including a 13 × 20-inch (33 × 50-cm) French black steel baking sheet, will accommodate the half-size baking mat.

While much thinner and less substantial than Silpat or Exopat, reusable Teflon pan liners can also be used for baking *joconde* with embedded designs. The Teflon pan liners can be cut to the precise size of your baking sheets, and of course they can substitute for kitchen parchment in any other recipes that require lining the baking sheet wth parchment.

Sources: La Cuisine, Previn, and J. B. Prince.

SPATULAS

Depending on what you are using it for, you can choose among four different types of spatulas. Perhaps the most important for cake making is the icing spatula (see page 471).

A wide metal offset spatula or pancake turner is perfect for moving cake layers and particularly for removing them from baking sheets when they come out of the oven. While you can use a large icing spatula for this purpose, the width of a pancake turner often makes it a better choice.

You will use wooden spatulas for mixing batters and fillings and frostings. (See *Wooden Spatulas*.)

Because a wooden spatula is rigid, it isn't effective for scraping mixtures from the sides of bowls. So, for folding together delicate ingredients and for emptying a bowl of batter, a rubber spatula is a better tool. The blade of the rubber spatula must be flexible enough to conform to the contours of a round-bottomed bowl, but not too flexible. Our favorites are the rubber spatulas made by Rubbermaid Professional. There are two styles. Both have a heavy rubber blade with a long, rigid handle ③⑧. In the traditional-style spatula the blade is rectangular and flat—tapering from the thick, rigid center to the thinner, more flexible edges, with two of the corners curved. In the newer "spoonula" style the blade is similar but concave on one side so you can use it for scooping up batters more effectively.

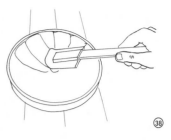

Sources: La Cuisine, Dean & DeLuca, and McGuckin Hardware.

STRAIGHTEDGES AND RULERS

We find a good straightedge or ruler, preferably made of stainless steel, invaluable for sweeping frosting smooth on the top of a round gâteau when we don't have an icing spatula with a long enough blade. We also use rulers for measuring everything from molds and rings to cake cardboards.

TARTE MOLD

Usually sold as deep quiche pans in the United States, these molds are round and about 1¾ inches (4.5 cm) deep, with steep, fluted sides and removable bottoms ③⑨. Their original use was for neither *tartes* nor quiches, but as cake pans. We use a *tarte* mold 8 inches (20 cm) in diameter for *pain de gênes* (page 38).

Legend has it that long ago a baker burned a cake that he had made in a *tarte* mold. To salvage it, he trimmed off the burned edges and transformed the cake into one with smooth sides. The new shape had some appeal and soon a round cake mold with no fluting was being made to produce it directly. This is the reason (probably apocryphal) that the French refer to a round cake pan as a *moules à manquer, manquer* meaning the "remainder" of the cake after trimming off the fluting.

Sources: La Cuisine and Previn.

TARTE RINGS

These short rings with no bottom are often called flan rings in the United States. They are designed for baking *tartes* (not flans), but we use them for some simple cakes as well. They are made of tinned steel or stainless steel with rolled edges ④⓪ (unlike cake rings and *vacherin* rings, which lack the rolled edge) and are available in many diameters and two heights—¾ inch (2 cm) and 1 inch (2.5 cm). The ones we require in our recipes are 8¾ inches (22 cm) wide and 1 inch (2.5 cm) deep.

Sources: La Cuisine, Dean & DeLuca, Previn, and J. B. Prince.

THERMOMETERS

Temperature plays an important role in many aspects of cake making, so accurate thermometers are great assets. Three thermometers are of particular importance.

As mentioned in the entry for ovens, you should monitor your oven thermostat by checking the oven temperature regularly with an oven thermometer. Extreme precision isn't necessary, since recipes are conventionally given with oven temperatures in 25°F (10° or 15°C) increments, and this is also about the range of fluctuation in oven temperature permitted by most oven thermostats. A mercury thermometer will be the most reliable.

For cooking sugar syrups, you can check the degree of cooking either by assessing its consistency or by measuring the temperature of the syrup. Candy thermometers are made for this purpose. Here we recommend either a mercury thermometer or a pocket digital thermometer. Since the consistency of the sugar syrup changes quite rapidly with increasing temperature, the thermometer should be calibrated in 2°F (1°C) gradations. Digital thermometers typically have a much finer resolution than that. Both types of thermometer should be designed in such a way that they can give an accurate reading for even a small volume of syrup. The sugar syrup must cover the bulb of a mercury thermometer or the sensor of a digital thermometer, so always choose the saucepan for cooking sugar syrups accordingly.

When you temper chocolate, you must accurately gauge the temperature at each stage of the process. While chocolate experts can do this by assessing the viscosity and appearance of the chocolate, for the rest of us the only way to be sure of the temperature is to use a chocolate thermometer. We especially like the convenience of a pocket digital thermometer. A mercury thermometer with a range from 25° to 125°F (−4° to 52° C) in 2°F (1°C) gradations will be slower but even more accurate.

For both cooking sugar syrups and tempering chocolate, we highly recommend the pocket digital thermometer model DT300 made by CDN (Component Design Northwest). The tip of the stem on this very compact thermometer must be inserted to a depth of at least ½ inch (1.2 mm) to get an accurate reading. In contrast, most other digital pocket thermometers require a depth of at least 1 inch (2.5 cm).

Since the whole point of using a thermometer is to get accurate temperature measurements, we suggest testing any new thermometer. The easiest way to do this is by measuring the temperature of ice water or boiling water. They should be 32°F (0°C) and 212°F (100°C)—at sea level—respectively. This test doesn't guarantee the accuracy at all temperatures, but it gives a good indication of the care taken by the manufacturer. If you buy a thermometer that can't pass this basic test, return it for another one.

Sources: La Cuisine, McGuckin Hardware, Sweet Celebrations, J. B. Prince, and Previn.

TRAYS

We frequently call for sliding a gâteau onto a tray before chilling it in the refrigerator or freezer. We use the word tray quite loosely for anything that has a flat surface large enough to accommodate one or more gâteaux and a low rim (or no rim at all) so that you can slide the gâteau on and off easily. For example, it could be a serving tray, a cafeteria tray, a French-style baking sheet, or an American cookie sheet. If you choose a tray or jelly roll pan with a tall rim, you may find it helpful to use it upside down to facilitate sliding the gâteau on and off. In our own kitchen, we use rectangular sheets of heavy-gauge aluminum in various sizes designed to fit on the shelves of our refrigerator or freezer. A local sheet metal shop can provide any size you want.

TROIS FRÈRES MOLD

This diagonally fluted ring mold was created for baking the cake of the same name. Its fluting is similar to a French kugelhopf mold, but the *trois frères* mold is much shallower ④. Its capacity and proportions are quite similar to an American ring mold. We use one with a diameter of 9 inches (23 cm) and a volume of about 5 cups (1.2 L).

④

Sources: La Cuisine and Previn.

TROWELS AND GLUE SPREADERS

We use these tools for combing cigarette cookie batter for decorative sheets of *joconde* and for combing frosting on the tops of gâteaux, just as we would use a cake-decorating comb.

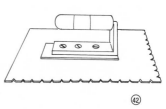

④

Trowels are designed for spreading floor adhesive. They are rectangular—typically 4 to 4½ inches (10 to 12 cm) wide and 9 to 10 inches (23 to 25 cm) long—with a handle attached to the back. You want a notched trowel. The notches can be U-shaped, V-shaped, or square, but the important thing is that the notches be narrow and widely spaced (that is, the teeth should be wide and blunt) ㊷. Use notched trowels for decorating large surfaces—an entire sheet of batter or the top of a large rectangular gâteau.

Glue spreaders are similar to trowels but about half the size and with no handle. They are almost identical in size and shape to bowl scrapers (page 464), with two short straight sides, one long straight side, and one long curved side. The long straight side is notched ㊸. Choose a glue spreader for smaller decorative work, where the large size of a notched trowel would make it too clumsy.

Source: McGuckin Hardware.

VACHERIN RINGS

These deep stainless steel rings ㊹ were originally intended for frozen desserts. We use them for molding charlottes and mousse cakes. They are 2⅜ inches (6 cm) deep, and the size we call for in our recipes is 8¾ inches (22 cm) in diameter.

Some springform pans can offer an acceptable alternative to a *vacherin* ring. You need only the outside ring, not the bottom of the springform. The ring must have rolled rims on top and bottom and an embossed rib to hold the bottom of the pan. If the bottom rim of the ring is turned in to hold the bottom of the pan, as many are, unmolding the charlotte will be difficult. The only springforms we think suitable are the German tinned steel ones from Dr. Oetker and Kaiser. Dr. Oetker makes one 2½ inches (6.5 cm) deep and 8¾ inches (22 cm) in diameter that is very close in size to an 8¾-inch (22-cm) *vacherin* ring.

Sources for Vacherin Rings: La Cuisine and Previn.

VOL-AU-VENT DISKS

These are tinned steel disks that are used for marking or cutting circles in all sorts of situations in French cake and pastry making. Each disk is slightly domed and has a hole in the center so that it can be lifted and positioned easily ㊺. *Vol-au-vent* disks are sold in sets of twelve sizes graduated from 4¼ inches (11 cm) to 9¾ inches (25 cm). They are expensive but very handy if you do a lot of baking.

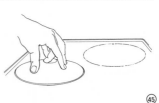

Sources: La Cuisine and Previn.

WAX PAPER

We like to measure out dry ingredients and sift them, when required, onto sheets of wax paper. To pour the ingredients, we lift two opposite edges of the sheet of paper and use it like a funnel. For larger quantities you can use freezer paper. Not only is using wax paper or freezer paper in this way very neat and efficient, it also saves on cleanup.

WHISKS

We use two distinct types of wire whisks, depending on the purpose and situation.

The balloon whisk is used for whipping cream and eggs. It has many thin, flexible wires arching up from the handle to enclose a space shaped like an incandescent lightbulb. The greater the number of wires, the finer and more flexible they are ㊻, and the larger the volume they enclose, the more efficient the whisk will be for whipping air into the cream or eggs. If you plan to do much whipping by hand, we advise you to invest in the best balloon whisk you can find, preferably 12 to 16 inches (30 to 40 cm) long with wire loops 3 to 4 inches (8 to 10 cm) across at the widest point.

㊻

You use a batter whisk for mixing and beating batters, butter, and other heavy materials, especially when rapid mixing is essential to keep the mixture smooth (as in making a pastry cream) or when it is important to beat in more air than you could with a wooden spatula (as in creaming butter). Here you need a whisk with a smaller number of stiffer wires ㊼ enclosing a smaller volume than the balloon whisk. The shape of the batter whisk is less bulbous than the balloon whisk. For making cakes at home, two convenient sizes are about 8 inches (20 cm) and 12 inches (30 cm) long.

㊼

Sources: La Cuisine, Dean & DeLuca, and Previn.

WOODEN SPATULAS

Shaped like a paddle, these flat spatulas are wonderful for mixing batters and creaming butter ㊽. They won't scratch your bowls or scrape the tin lining off the inside of a copper pot. And unlike rubber spatulas, they can be used to stir hot ingredients without damaging the spatula. Wooden spatulas are usually made of boxwood (the best) or beechwood. The sizes of interest for cake making range from 8 to 14 inches (20 to 35 cm) long.

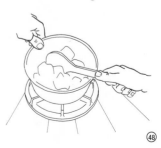

Sources: La Cuisine, Previn, and Dean & DeLuca.

㊽

WOOD GRAIN TOOL

This tool is just a convex rubber surface covered with concentric semi-circular ridges and mounted on a handle ㊾. The one we use, a Warner No. 16 Graining Tool, has a ridged surface 3 inches (7.5 cm) square plus one notched edge and one comb edge. We also have a French version in which the ridged surface and handle are molded from a single piece of rubber, with a comb edge at the back of the handle. Painters use the wood grain tool to make imitation wood grain effects on painted walls and furniture. We use it to make wood grain designs on the tops of gâteau in dark and white chocolate. It takes a little practice, but once you get the hang of it you can produce incredibly realistic effects. Use the ridged surface for heart grain, the notched edge for quartersawed, and the comb edge for vein grain. The two essential points to keep in mind when using this tool are that you must have the substance you are graining (whether paint or chocolate) sufficiently fluid but not runny and you must not allow it to build up on the face of the tool and clog the valleys between the semi-circular ridges.

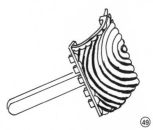

Source: McGuckin Hardware.

YULE LOG MOLD

This special trough-shaped mold is designed for making the classic *buche de Nöel* ㊿. We also use it for other log-shaped gâteaux. The one we call for in our recipes is 20 inches (50 cm) long and 2¾ inches (7 cm) wide.

Sources: La Cuisine and Previn.

Ingredients

U nderstanding your ingredients is more important in baking than in any other area of cook-ing. As for equipment, we summarize the ingredients used for French cakes in glossary form. Most of the ingredients required for French cakes are available in supermarkets, and you can find the remainder at gourmet food or wine shops. We provide mail-order sources for the few items that may be difficult to find in some parts of the country.

ALCOHOLS

A wide variety of alcohols are used in French cakes to flavor fillings and frostings, moisten and fla-vor cake layers, and soak dried and candied fruits. The alcohol can be the primary flavor in a gâteau, or it can be an accent flavor of varying degrees of subtlety.

The alcohols we use include: full-bodied rums from the Caribbean; the colorless eaux-de-vie (brandies) kirsch (cherry), *framboise* (raspberry), and *poire william* (pear); the grape brandies Cognac and Armagnac; the sweet liqueurs curaçao, Grand Marnier, maraschino, Cherry Marnier, crème de cassis, anisette, and Drambuie; and Kentucky bourbon. They are discussed in more detail under the individual entries.

ALMONDS

Almonds are one of the most important ingredients in French cakes. Whole, sliced, chopped, or powdered, they appear in many gâteaux. In cake batters, they often provide both flavor and tex-ture to give the cakes much of their richness and interest, especially in some of the simple cakes. In fillings and frostings, they supply flavor. And their roles in cake decorating run the gamut from a garnish of whole almonds to vines and leaves made of almond paste.

Two distinct types of almonds—sweet and bitter—can be used in baking. Bitter almonds are mildly toxic and cannot legally be sold as food in the United States. We use only sweet almonds in cakes. Sweet almonds contain a high percentage of oil (typically about 54 percent) as well as proteins (19 percent) and carbohydrates (20 percent). The almond is covered with a thin, papery skin which can be removed by blanching (plunging the almonds first in boiling water, then in cold water, after which the skins slip off easily with a little pressure). Almonds with the skins intact are called raw (or sometimes "natural"); those with the skins removed are called blanched. Raw almonds have a more robust and less sweet flavor than blanched almonds.

Almonds are sold in a variety of forms, including whole raw almonds, whole blanched almonds, slivered blanched almonds, and sliced almonds. Sliced almonds are normally used for decoration. They may be raw or blanched, and sliced blanched almonds are preferable because they are more attractive.

Almonds must frequently be chopped or powdered in cake making, and they are sometimes roasted to brown them, reduce their moisture content, and intensify their flavor. They are also an ingredient in the roasted-nut-and-caramel paste called *praliné*. See Nuts in this section and the recipes for Nut-and-Sugar Powders, *Praliné,* and Roasted Nuts in Chapter 10.

ANGELICA

Candied angelica is made from the stalks of an aromatic herb. The stalks are large and can be sliced thin and cut into diamonds or triangles for use as decoration. Green *glacé* pineapple is a good substitute for this rather esoteric ingredient.

Source: La Cuisine.

ARMAGNAC

See *Cognac and Armagnac*.

BAKING POWDER

This is a chemical leavening composed of an alkali (almost always baking soda) and one or more acid salts, plus a starch (such as cornstarch) to absorb moisture and give the powder more volume. Most modern baking powders contain two acid salts and are called "double acting." One of these acid salts (such as cream of tartar or calcium acid phosphate) begins interacting with the baking soda to produce carbon dioxide gas as soon as the baking powder is mixed into the batter and moistened. This first interaction produces many small bubbles of carbon dioxide in the batter. The other acid salt (usually sodium aluminum sulphate) interacts with the baking soda when the batter is heated. This second interaction expands the gas bubbles produced by the first interaction. Since it occurs after the batter has begun to set, the second phase of the double action helps reduce the opportunity for the walls between gas bubbles to break down or for the gas to escape before the final structure of the cake is established.

While chemical leavening is a mainstay in American cake making, it is used only rarely in French cakes, and then only as an adjunct to the primary mechanical leavening produced by whipping air into eggs. When baking powder is included in a recipe, it should be sifted with flour before adding it to the other ingredients to be sure it is evenly incorporated.

BOURBON

While it is not at all classic, we think Kentucky bourbon is every bit as good as dark rum or Cognac for enhancing the flavors of chestnuts and chocolate. Bourbons are very fruity, with a taste of charcoal and caramel from the charred white oak barrels in which they are aged.

BUTTER

We use butter as an ingredient in cake batters and fillings and frostings (most notably buttercream) and for brushing baking sheets and molds to prevent sticking.

Butter is made by churning heavy cream until the butterfat solidifies. The mass of butterfat is the butter, and the remaining liquid is buttermilk. The butter is washed to eliminate most of the milk protein and lactose, which spoil more quickly than does butterfat, and then kneaded to eliminate excess water.

Nearly all butter sold in the United States is made from sweet cream. This gives it a delicate, slightly sweet taste. By law it must contain at least 80 percent butterfat; the remainder consists of water (about 18 percent) and milk solids (proteins, salts, and lactose).

French butters are made from matured cream that has been thickened and soured by culturing with bacteria that produce lactic acid. As a result, they have a rich, nutty aroma and a fuller but less sweet flavor than American sweet cream butters. Typically, they have a higher butterfat content (82 to 86 percent) and contain less water than do American butters.

A large proportion of American butter is salted to extend its shelf life. Most French cakes contain no salt at all, and using salted butter in them produces a noticeable and undesirable saltiness. Do not use salted butter in our recipes.

The USDA grades butter based on several characteristics, including aroma, taste, texture, body, and uniformity of color. Only grades AA and A are sold in most supermarkets. Land O' Lakes makes excellent Grade AA unsalted butter that is widely distributed.

The temperature of the butter can be an important factor in cake making. Butter is very firm at refrigerator temperatures. It begins to soften at about 59°F (15°C), and butterfat begins to melt at about 68°F (20°C). When the butter melts, the emulsion that holds the butterfat and water together starts to break down and the milk solids begin to separate.

In order to mix solid butter with other ingredients, it is frequently necessary to beat the butter to give it a smooth, creamy consistency. This step is called "creaming" and is explained in the General Techniques section, page 531.

For some purposes (brushing molds for certain cake batters, adding to bittersweet chocolate to make a glaze), it is necessary to clarify the butter, which means to remove the milk solids and proteins, leaving just the clear butterfat. See the recipe for clarified butter on page 449.

If you melt butter and don't clarify it, then when you continue to heat it the milk solids in the butter will brown. This imparts a nutty flavor to the butter and changes its color from yellow to brown. The result is called browned butter. See the recipe for browned butter on page 450.

Unsalted butter stores quite well provided it is kept cold and covered airtight to prevent it from picking up off odors. In the refrigerator it will keep for 2 to 3 weeks (provided it was fresh to begin with), and in the freezer it can last for up to 2 or 3 months. If frozen, defrost the butter overnight in the refrigerator before using.

CANDIED CITRON, LEMON PEEL, ORANGE PEEL

The candied peels of these citrus fruits are frequently used in French cakes for both flavor and decoration. They are preserved against bacteria by virtue of being cooked in sugar syrup (because bacteria cannot live in a high-sugar solution), but candied fruits are still somewhat perishable— especially the fine quality ones that contain a minimum of artifical preservatives. They can be kept in the refrigerator, covered airtight, for 2 or 3 months, or frozen for up to 6 months. After that they can dry and harden, or part of their sugar content can crystallize on the surface.

Good candied citrus peels should be firm but tender, with an appealing taste of citrus zest. Unfortunately, most of those sold in our supermarkets are hard and taste too much of artificial preservatives. For exceptional quality candied citrus peels, look for those imported from France and Switzerland.

Often the citrus zest must be chopped before it is added to a cake batter. To prevent the bits of chopped zest from sticking together, mix a little flour with them before chopping.

Sources: La Cuisine and Dean & DeLuca.

CHERRY MARNIER

See *Maraschino Liqueur*.

CHESTNUTS

Unique because of their high starch and low oil contents, chestnuts play a limited but special role in French desserts in general. We use them most often in fillings, including mousses and a sort of chestnut buttercream. We also offer an unusual cake batter that contains pureed chestnuts.

Unlike other nuts, they are always cooked or candied before being incorporated into a dessert. Peeling and cooking chestnuts is so tedious that we recommend using canned chestnut products imported from France.

Marrons glacés are whole candied chestnuts. They are sold in 7-ounce (200-g) cans and are extremely expensive. We use them primarily for decoration. *Pâte de marrons glacés* is a thick, dry chestnut paste made from chestnuts broken in the candying process. In France, this is the puree used for chestnut fillings. Unfortunately, you aren't likely to find it in the United States, so we have devised alternatives using *chestnut spread*, a sweetened puree called *crème de marrons* in French, and (canned) *whole chestnuts* (*marrons entiers*). *Marrons glacés, chestnut spread*, and *whole chestnuts* made by Clément Faugier are excellent and are available in supermarkets and specialty stores. Note that there is also a less sweet *chestnut puree* (called *purée de marrons* in French) that is not suitable for use in our recipes.

Sources: La Cuisine and Dean & DeLuca.

CHOCOLATE

The tropical cocoa tree is native to Central and South America and was first cultivated by the Maya, who used it to make a beverage. Hernando Cortés introduced chocolate to Europe in the sixteenth century, but it was not until three centuries later that someone had the idea of eating sweetened solid chocolate. Thus the use of chocolate in desserts is a surprisingly modern phenomenon.

The fruit of the cocoa tree is a pod 6 to 8 inches (15 to 20 cm) long that contains twenty to fifty beans. The pods are harvested when ripe, and the contents are removed and fermented to separate the beans from the pulp and develop the cocoa aroma. The beans are sun-dried and roasted at a low temperature to further develop their aroma. After roasting, they are cooled, crushed, and sifted to separate the shells from the kernels (called "nibs"). The crushed kernels are milled to produce a dark brown paste, which is called chocolate liquor. During milling, some of the fat content of the beans (called cocoa butter) is released.

A little more than half of the weight of the chocolate liquor is cocoa butter. The other constituents (proteins, carbohydrates, etc.) of the chocolate are suspended in the cocoa butter.

All types of chocolate are derived from the cocoa liquor. The quality of the chocolate is determined by the beans from which it is made and how they are processed, particularly the roasting (which brings out their aroma) and how finely the nibs are milled.

Unsweetened chocolate (also called baking chocolate) is the pure chocolate liquor, containing just over 50 percent cocoa butter. It has a strong, bitter taste, and it is always melted and mixed with other ingredients, for example, to flavor fillings.

Bittersweet and semi-sweet chocolate are produced by adding sugar and extra cocoa butter to the chocolate liquor, then kneading the mixture mechanically (a process called conching) to give it a smooth texture and to evaporate volatile acids to make the flavor more mellow. Vanilla (or the artificial substitute vanillin) is often added to enhance the chocolate flavor, and lecithin (an emulsifier) is added to keep the cocoa butter evenly distributed. In principle, semi-sweet chocolate should be sweeter than bittersweet, but in practice the distinction is blurred and the two terms are often used interchangeably. Typically bittersweet and semi-sweet chocolates contain about 50 percent sugar and 50 percent cocoa solids (the chocolate liquor plus any additional cocoa butter), with cocoa butter making up about one third of the total. Bittersweet chocolates with a much lower sugar content and cocoa solids in the 60 to 70 percent range are referred to as extra bittersweet.

Covering chocolates (also referred to by their French name, *couvertures*) are bittersweet chocolates with a higher cocoa butter content, usually close to 40 percent. The extra cocoa butter gives the chocolate more sheen and a firmer snap. It also makes the chocolate more fluid when melted, so it can be spread in a thinner layer.

Milk chocolate and sweet chocolate are made by adding powdered milk or extra sugar to the chocolate during conching. We never use them in French cakes because they are too sweet, the chocolate flavor is too diluted, and, in the case of milk chocolate, the color is too washed out.

White chocolate isn't actually chocolate at all, since it contains no chocolate liquor. It is a mixture of cocoa butter, sugar, milk solids, emulsifiers, and a little vanilla for flavor. White chocolate has a vague chocolate taste thanks to the cocoa butter. However, it contains sugar more than anything else and, lacking the bitter component of chocolate liquor, it is overly sweet and insipid. We think it is suitable only for decoration.

For flavoring a cake batter or filling with chocolate, we often choose either unsweetened chocolate or cocoa powder (see the entry on page 505). Since these forms have nothing added to the chocolate, they give the maximum chocolate flavor for a given amount of chocolate and they don't alter the sugar content of the batter. Nonetheless, we flavor some batters and fillings with bittersweet chocolate (preferably extra bittersweet) because it is easier to use and can provide a more refined texture.

On the other hand, for glazing and decorating gâteaux we use bittersweet chocolate. For these purposes you want a chocolate that is very smooth, has good sheen, and is quite fluid when melted.

We also use bittersweet chocolate for the rich chocolate cream filling called ganache. Since the chocolate is diluted with cream here, ideally we prefer an extra bittersweet chocolate with a higher chocolate liquor content (and correspondingly lower sugar and cocoa butter contents) than we would use for glazing or decoration. Not surprisingly, the smoother the chocolate, the more velvety will be the texture of the ganache.

STORING CHOCOLATE

When properly stored, chocolate (both unsweetened and bittersweet) will last for over a year. Chocolate should be kept in a cool place—60° to 75°F (15° to 24°C)—and covered airtight to prevent it from absorbing odors. If the temperature is any warmer than that, some of the cocoa butter can migrate to the surface and form fat bloom. Chocolate should not be stored in the refrigerator because refrigeration can cause drops of water to condense on the surface of the chocolate. The water dissolves sugar in the chocolate, then evaporates, leaving sugar crystals on the surface. This is called "sugar bloom."

EUROPEAN BITTERSWEET CHOCOLATES

COMPONENT BREAKDOWN AND AVAILABLE BAR AND BLOCK SIZES

CHOCOLATE BRAND & DESIGNATION	COCOA SOLIDS	SUGAR	COCOA BUTTER	BAR/BLOCK SIZE
VALRHONA *Extra Noir*	53%	46.5%	29.8%	3 @ 2.2 pounds (1kg)
VALRHONA *Equatoriale Noir*	55.5%	44%	37.4%	3 @ 2.2 pounds (1kg) and 14 ounces (400g)
VALRHONA *Le Noir*	56%	44%	37.5%	3½ ounces (100g)
VALRHONA *Caraque*	56%	43.5%	37.1%	3 @ 2.2 pounds (1kg)
VALRHONA *Le Noir Gastronomie*	61%	39%	40%	8¾ ounces (250g)
VALRHONA *Extra Bitter*	61%	39%	40%	3 @ 2.2 pounds (1kg)
VALRHONA *Manjari*	64.5%	35%	40%	3 @ 2.2 pounds (1kg)
VALRHONA *Pur Caraibe*	66.5%	33%	40.6%	3 @ 2.2 pounds (1kg)
VALRHONA *Extra Amer*	67.5%	32%	37.9%	3 @ 2.2 pounds (1kg)
VALRHONA *Guanaja*	70.5%	29%	42.5%	3 @ 2.2 pounds (1kg)
VALRHONA *Le Noir Amer*	71%	29%	42.5%	3½ ounces (100g)

SELECTING CHOCOLATE

Chocolates vary enormously from one brand to another. In general, European bittersweet chocolates are milled more finely and conched for a longer time (up to 3 or 4 days) than American chocolates, which are usually conched for only a few hours. As a result, the European chocolates are appreciably smoother and richer than their American counterparts. Each brand has its own blends of beans and roasting procedures, and combines different proportions of chocolate liquor, cocoa butter, sugar, and other ingredients in its bittersweet chocolates.

We feel that for smooth, creamy texture and rich, elegant taste, the finest chocolates are those made by Valrhona in France and Lindt in Switzerland. Some other excellent brands are Tobler from Switzerland, Perugina from Italy, and Chocolove from Belgium and France. You will find these chocolates sold in three size ranges: small bars weighing 3 to 3½ ounces (85 to 100 g); larger

CHOCOLATE BRAND & DESIGNATION	COCOA SOLIDS	SUGAR	COCOA BUTTER	BAR/BLOCK SIZE
LINDT Surfin	52.5%	47.5%	34%	3 ounces (85g) and 13 ounces (370g)
LINDT Swiss Bittersweet	50%	50%	33%	10½ ounces (300g)
LINDT Excellence 70%	70%	30%	42.5%	3½ ounces (100g)
LINDT Excellence Dark Couverture	54%	46%	37%	2 @ 2.2 pounds (1kg)
LINDT Surfin Vanilla Couverture	49%	51%	34%	2 @ 2.2 pounds (1kg)
TOBLER Tradition	52%	48%	33%	3 ounces (85g)
PERUGINA Extra Bittersweet	65%	35%	35%	3 ounces (85g)
CHOCOLOVE Dark	55%	45%	37%	3¼ ounces (90g)
CHOCOLOVE Rich Dark	65%	35%	40%	3¼ ounces (90g)
CHOCOLOVE Strong Dark	70%	30%	40%	3¼ ounces (90g)
CHOCOLOVE Extra Strong Dark	77%	23%	40%	3¼ ounces (90g)

bars (sometimes called "family size") weighing 9 to 14 ounces (250 to 400 g); and blocks weighing 2.2 pounds (1 kg) and sold two or three to a package (which some gourmet shops break down to more managable sizes for home cooks). Many of the bittersweet and covering chocolates from these makers are listed in the accompanying tables. The first table lists their proportions of cocoa solids, sugar, and cocoa butter as well as the sizes of the bars and blocks available. The second table gives recommendations for which chocolates to use for which purposes and provides an approximate evaluation of their sweetness—determined by the ratio of sugar to cocoa particles (the nonfat portion of the cocoa solids)—and intensity—the percentage of cocoa particles. These tables will help you select the chocolate you want to use for each recipe.

For most purposes, we like the small bars of European bittersweet chocolate because the size

European Bittersweet Chocolates

RECOMMENDED USES AND SWEETNESS AND INTENSITY EVALUATIONS

CHOCOLATE BRAND & DESIGNATION	CHOCOLATE GLAZE	GANACHE	MOUSSES & BATTERS	DECORATIONS (BAKING SHEET)	RIBBONS & PETALS	SWEETNESS (SUGAR/COCOA PARTICLES)	INTENSITY (% COCOA PARTICLES)
VALRHONA *Extra Noir*		R	R		R	2.0	23.2%
VALRHONA *Equatoriale Noir*		R	R	R		2.4	18.1%
VALRHONA *Le Noir*		R	R			2.4	18.5%
VALRHONA *Caraque*		R	R	R		2.3	19%
VALRHONA *Le Noir Gastronomie*		R	R	R		1.9	21%
VALRHONA *Extra Bitter*		R	R	R		1.9	21%
VALRHONA *Manjari*		R	R	R		1.4	24.5%
VALRHONA *Pur Caraibe*		R	R	R		1.3	25.9%
VALRHONA *Extra Amer*	R	R	R		R	1.1	29.6%
VALRHONA *Guanaja*		R	R	R		1.0	28%
VALRHONA *Le Noir Amer*		R	R			1.0	28.5%

is very convenient for our recipes and they are designed to break easily into small squares. The squares make it easy to measure out the weight you need, even if you don't have a kitchen scale. These bars are available in most supermarkets and gourmet shops.

For some purposes, such as melting chocolate directly onto a baking sheet for decorating, you need a large bar or block of chocolate, and small bars from the supermarket just won't do. Large blocks can also be much more economical. They are available from professional suppliers and gourmet shops.

European unsweetened chocolates are more difficult to come by than the bittersweets. Of

CHOCOLATE BRAND & DESIGNATION	CHOCOLATE GLAZE	GANACHE	MOUSSES & BATTERS	RECOMMENDED (R) FOR: DECORATIONS (BAKING SHEET)	RIBBONS & PETALS	SWEETNESS (SUGAR/COCOA PARTICLES)	INTENSITY (% COCOA PARTICLES)
LINDT *Surfin*	R			R	R	2.6	18.5%
LINDT *Swiss Bittersweet*	R			R	R	2.9	17%
LINDT *Excellence 70%*		R	R			0.7	27.5%
LINDT *Excellence Dark Couverture*	R			R	R	2.7	17%
LINDT *Surfin Vanilla Couverture*	R			R	R	3.4	15%
TOBLER *Tradition*	R				R	2.5	19%
PERUGINA *Extra Bittersweet*	R	R	R			1.2	30%
CHOCOLOVE *Dark*		R	R			2.5	18%
CHOCOLOVE *Rich Dark*		R	R			1.4	25%
CHOCOLOVE *Strong Dark*		R	R			1.0	30%
CHOCOLOVE *Extra Strong Dark*		R	R			0.6	37%

American brands sold in supermarkets we prefer Baker's unsweetened chocolate. Even better is the unsweetened chocolate made in a convenient wafer form by Guittard and sold through professional sources. If you can get a European brand, such as the Valrhona, so much the better. Chocolove has recently begun marketing a French unsweetened chocolate in 3.2-ounce (90-g) bars that is a welcome addition to the market.

For white chocolate, we recommend Lindt's Blancor, which is available in 3-ounce (85-g) and 13-ounce (370-g) bars, and Valrhona's Chocolat Blanc Ivoire, which is sold in packages of three 2.2-pound (1-kg) blocks.

One other form of chocolate we occasionally use for cakes is sprinkles, which the Europeans call chocolate vermicelli. The ones on the supermarket shelf are mostly sugar and vegetable shortening with a little cocoa powder. Much better quality chocolate sprinkles are available from gourmet shops. For visual appeal, choose long, slender sprinkles over short, squat ones.

Sources for Chocolates: La Cuisine, Swiss Connection, and Dean & DeLuca.

COCOA BUTTER

Cocoa butter is a shiny yellowish white, with a mild aroma and flavor of cocoa. At room temperature it is quite hard, almost brittle. One of the most important virtues of cocoa butter is that it does not go rancid quickly.

Cocoa butter is a very pure fat. However, it can solidify in four distinct crystalline forms. Each crystal type, referred to by a Greek letter, has a different melting point. They are

γ melting point = 63°F (17°C)
α melting point = 70° to 75°F (21° to 24°C)
β' melting point = 81° to 84°F (27° to 29°C)
β melting point = 95°F (34° to 35°C)

The β form is stable, but the other three are not. After chocolate solidifies, if any of the three unstable forms is present it transforms to the β form at differing rates. γ and α crystals are very unstable and make the transition quickly. The β' form makes the transition gradually.

The chocolate you purchase has been prepared in such a way that the cocoa butter is in the stable β form. However, after you melt chocolate, it will not necessarily return to the β form when it cools and solidifies. Even after the chocolate solidifies, it still contains some liquid cocoa butter. How much depends on how it was cooled, how long it has been since the chocolate set, and the ambient temperature. Furthermore, if γ and α crystals are present, they can melt again at room temperature. When there is unstable liquid cocoa butter in the chocolate, it can move around in the semi-solid chocolate. Gradually the liquid cocoa butter comes into contact with stable β type seed crystals and solidifies in the stable form, making the β crystals grow larger, both inside the chocolate and at the surface. Large β crystals result in a coarse, irregular texture in the chocolate and dull gray streaking on the surface. The dull gray streaks are called fat bloom. Fat bloom is a potential problem for glazing and decorations, where the chocolate is not mixed with other ingredients and the appearance of the chocolate is important. The problem is avoided by a process called tempering; see page 538 in the General Techniques section for details.

COCOA POWDER

Much of the cocoa butter can be removed from chocolate liquor by means of a hydraulic press. What remains is formed into cakes, dried, pulverized, and sifted to make cocoa powder. Unsweetened cocoa powder still contains between 10 percent and 25 percent cocoa butter. Since it has a higher percentage of cocoa particles than does unsweetened chocolate, cocoa powder produces a stronger flavor and darker color when used to flavor a cake batter. Generally when cocoa powder is used in a cake batter, it is sifted with the flour called for in the recipe.

In Europe cocoa powder is "Dutch processed" by treating either the cocoa beans or the chocolate liquor with alkaline carbonates or ammonia. This process makes the cocoa powder less bitter, gives it a deeper reddish brown color, and makes it more soluble in water. Our recipes are designed to use Dutch-processed cocoa powder. Some of the best brands are Lindt from Switzerland and Valrhona, Cacao Barry, and Poulain from France. Droste cocoa powder from the Netherlands is also quite good and is widely available in supermarkets.

American cocoa powders, which are not Dutch processed, have very different baking characteristics from the European ones. They are mildly acidic, and the acidity needs to be compensated for by an alkaline ingredient such as baking soda in order to bring out the color and flavor of the cocoa. For this reason, American cocoa powders cannot be used interchangeably with European Dutch processed ones. Sweetened cocoa powders are suitable only for making hot cocoa, not for baking.

Sources for Cocoa Powders: La Cuisine and Dean & DeLuca.

COFFEE

This is an important flavoring in fillings and frostings, fondant, and syrups.

The coffee bean is the seed of a shrub believed to have originated in Ethiopia and to have spread from there through the Middle East to Europe.

As a beverage, coffee is a subject of enormous complexity and interest. Its quality and character depend on the climate and soil in which it is grown, the details of its roasting, and the care taken in its blending. However, most of the subtleties that distinguish different types and qualities of coffee are lost in cake making, where it is heavily sweetened and must be intensely concentrated in order to produce a rich coffee taste in the finished dessert.

The easiest way to get a very concentrated coffee flavoring is to use instant coffee. Professional French pastry books often call for Nescafé, which is ubiquitous in France and has become almost a generic name for instant coffee there. Unfortunately, cakes flavored with instant coffee usually end up tasting like instant coffee.

We have taken an aggressive approach to making cakes with real coffee taste. First, we always select espresso coffee beans for maximum intensity of flavor. We use double-strength brewed espresso (page 456) whenever this provides a sufficiently intense flavor, for example in coffee syrups to brush the cake layers in gâteaux and mousse cakes. On the other hand, for fillings and frostings (in particular coffee buttercream and coffee mousse), we take the more direct approach of brewing a very concentrated coffee with coarsely crushed coffee beans as an integral part of the recipe, then straining out the coffee beans.

COGNAC AND ARMAGNAC

These are the finest French grape brandies, both distilled under strictly controlled methods and aged in oak casks. Cognac can be a good accent flavor with chocolate. Armagnac, which is stronger in flavor and more scented than Cognac, is a classic flavoring in cakes that contain prunes.

CORNSTARCH

See *Potato Starch*.

CORN SYRUP

This syrup is produced from cornstarch by using enzymes or acids to break down the starch molecules into simple and complex sugars. It contains dextrose plus some maltose as well as more complex carbohydrates. When corn syrup is added to sucrose syrups, the dextrose helps inhibit crystallization of the sucrose. In addition, the larger carbohydrate molecules inhibit crystallization by surrounding the sucrose molecules and preventing them from joining together.

Since we use corn syrup only for the purpose of inhibiting crystallization, not for flavor, we always call for light corn syrup.

CREAM

Cream is an essential ingredient in many fillings, including whipped cream, ganache, bavarian cream, and all of our mousses.

The cream that floats to the top of unhomogenized milk is relatively high in butterfat. At the dairy, a centrifugal separator is used to produce even richer creams. They are classified from light to heavy in direct proportion to their butterfat content. The higher the butterfat content, the thicker the cream and the easier it will be to whip. However, since butterfat is lighter than water, heavy cream actually weighs less than light cream. We always use cream with a high butterfat content, either heavy cream (minimum 36 percent butterfat) or whipping cream (at least 30 percent butterfat, which is considered the minimum for whipping).

Like milk, cream is almost always pasteurized to kill harmful bacteria. Pasteurized heavy cream will last for about 1 week in the refrigerator, but the sooner you use it, the sweeter it will be.

To make cream less perishable, the dairy industry came up with the process of ultra-pasteurization, a high-temperature sterilization process. Unfortunately, ultra-pasteurized cream is devoid of the wonderful fresh, sweet taste of real pasteurized cream. It also contains artificial emulsifiers added to restore the whipping properties of the cream, which are destroyed by the ultra-pasteurization. If pasteurized heavy cream is unavailable, you can use crème fraîche in place of the heavy cream.

Whipping incorporates tiny air bubbles into cream, increasing its volume and viscosity. You can whip cream with an electric mixer or a wire whisk. If you are using a whisk, choose a round-bottomed mixing bowl. Cream whips best if it is at least 1 day old and at a temperature of 40°F (5°C), so always chill the cream, the bowl, and the whisk before whipping. Whip the cream at medium speed at first, then slow down when it forms soft peaks to avoid overbeating. Continue whipping until the cream is light and thick and holds firm peaks. It should expand to double its original volume. Do not overbeat or the cream will become grainy, then curdle, and eventually turn to butter.

CREAM OF TARTAR

This potassium salt of tartaric acid can supply the acid needed in several baking situations. Most important for cakes, adding a little cream of tartar when you are whipping egg whites is the next best thing to whipping the whites in a copper bowl in order to reduce the risk of overbeating (see Chapter 4, page 177 for details). Also, cream of tartar provides one of the acid components in baking powder and can inhibit crystallization in sugar syrups.

CRÈME DE CASSIS

A specialty of Dijon and the Côte d'Or in Burgundy, this sweet liqueur is made by macerating black currants in alcohol. Black currants were originally planted in Burgundy by monks who used the leaves for medicinal purposes. Cultivation of the fruit in the Côte d'Or expanded in the mid-eighteenth century when black currant liqueur was perfected and then again in the nineteenth century when many vineyards in Burgundy were destroyed by phylloxera and the vintners began growing black currants to make liqueurs and syrups.

We use crème de cassis in desserts flavored with black currants.

CRÈME FRAÎCHE

American-style sweet cream is called *crème fleurette* in France. Crème fraîche (literally "fresh cream") is actually a cream that has been matured by culturing it with special bacteria. It has a nutty and slightly sour taste, and it is much thicker than ordinary (sweet) heavy cream. The name came about in the days before refrigeration and rapid transportation when naturally occurring bacteria soured the cream before it got from the farm in the country to the market in Paris. Parisians developed a taste for crème fraîche, and today the cream is matured under controlled conditions to give it the desired flavor.

Crème fraîche has become popular in the United States only recently, but it is now marketed nationally. The butterfat content is not standardized. Some producers, such as Alta Dena, market crème fraîche with a butterfat content comparable to that of ordinary heavy cream. Others, such as Vermont Butter & Cheese and Santé, have a higher butterfat content of about 40 percent and are correspondingly more expensive. You can make a substitute for crème fraîche at home by culturing ordinary pasteurized heavy cream with a little buttermilk (see the recipe on page 451).

Crème fraîche can be used whenever heavy cream is called for. Because it is so thick, it is easier to overwhip than ordinary heavy cream. To reduce the risk of overwhipping crème fraîche, thin it with about ¼ cup (6 cL) of cold water or milk for each 1¾ cups (4.2 dL) of crème fraîche before whipping.

Crème fraîche will last for at least 10 days, and up to several weeks if it was cultured commercially.

CRYSTALLIZED VIOLETS

Whole candied flowers that you can use as decoration on gâteaux. They are hard, sugary, and expensive.

Source: La Cuisine.

CURAÇAO LIQUEUR

A sweet orange-flavored liqueur of medium proof extracted from orange peels by steeping them in alcohol. Originally it was produced by the Dutch from the skins of the green oranges grown on the island of Curaçao off the coast of Venezuela. This liqueur has an intense orange flavor with a slight edge of bitterness, making it ideal for flavoring fillings and frostings.

Grand Marnier is a proprietary curaçao-type liqueur made by the Cognac house Marnier-Lapostelle in France. It has a Cognac base and is the most elegant of the orange liqueurs, but it is less bitter and intense than curaçao and so gives less pizzazz to your desserts.

DRAMBUIE

A proprietary sweet liqueur based on Scotch whiskey with the addition of heather honey and herbs. It is produced on the Isle of Skye in Scotland by the Mackinnon family. We like its distinctive smoky character as an accent to caramel.

DRIED FRUITS

Raisins and currants are by far the most commonly used dried fruits in French cakes. Prunes are a distant third, but they are an essential ingredient in a few classic desserts.

Dried sour cherries are an American specialty that is a natural addition to the list of ingredients for French cakes. You can use them in the same ways as raisins, either including them directly in cake batters or steaming them and soaking them in alcohol before adding them to the filling in a gâteau. Dried sour cherries soaked in kirsch are every bit as interesting as raisins soaked in rum.

EAU-DE-VIE

The French term for brandy, eau-de-vie translates literally as water of life. You will find the phrase eau-de-vie on French bottles of the *alcools blancs*, the clear, colorless brandies distilled from fresh fruits such as cherries (kirsch), raspberries (*framboise*), and pears (*poire william*). These brandies are aged in glass or pottery. They are dry, high in alchohol (80 to 90 proof), and very aromatic. The best examples are produced in France, Switzerland, and Germany. The French ones typically have more of the perfume of the fresh fruit. See also *Framboise, Kirsch*, and *Poire William*.

Brandies made from grapes (such as Cognac and Armagnac) are aged in wood, which gives them a caramel color. They are very different from the *alcools blanc*. See also *Cognac and Armagnac*.

EGGS

Eggs are the most versatile ingredient in cake making. They provide structure, thickening, or lightness through their coagulating or foaming abilities.

Eggs contain proteins, both saturated and unsaturated fats, all essential amino acids and vitamins (except C), and most essential minerals. They are low in carbohydrates and contain only about 80 to 100 calories per large egg. About 11 percent of the egg's weight is in the shell, which has uses in cooking but not for cakes. Of the remainder, a little more than one third of the weight is in the yolk and slightly less than two thirds is in the white. Overall, the egg is 70 to 75 percent water.

The yolk contains about 51 percent water, 16 percent protein, and 30 to 33 percent lipids (fats and related compounds, including the emulsifiers lecithin and cholesterol). Water and fat are not soluble in each other. In the yolk, microscopic globules of fat are surrounded by molecules of lecithin which, in turn, bond loosely with water molecules, thus keeping the fat globules suspended in the water. The mixture is called an emulsion. The yolk contains more lecithin than it needs to keep itself emulsified, so it can stabilize other fat-in-water emulsions. This emulsifying ability is particularly important in sauces, but it also helps keep the butterfat distributed in some batters. Cholesterol, on the other hand, is particularly effective in stabilizing water-in-fat emulsions. Butter is an example of a water-in-fat emulsion stabilized, in part, by cholesterol. Cholesterol also plays a role in stabilizing the emulsion in fillings and frostings, such as buttercream, which contain butter and eggs but very little water.

The egg white consists almost entirely of water (about 88 percent) and proteins (about 11 percent) and is called the albumen. It is made up of four layers, alternating thick and thin. The first layer of albumen contains two thin, twisted, opaque white filaments—the chalazas—that connect the yolk to the inner membrane of the egg shell and keep the yolk anchored near the center of the egg.

The egg shell consists of two parts. The outer shell is the hard, porous, calcified part which the word shell calls to mind. Its exterior surface is protected by a film of albumen. The inner shell is really a pair of membranes separated by a thin layer of air. At the top, wide end of the egg, the cushion of air is thicker and is called the "air cell." As the egg gets older, moisture slowly evaporates through the shell and the air cell gets larger. For this reason, while a freshly laid egg will sink in cold water, a four-day-old egg will rise to the surface and a two-week-old egg will float, lying on its side.

Perhaps the most important property of eggs for cooking generally, and for baking in particular, is the ability of egg proteins to coagulate, turning from liquid to solid. Egg whites begin to coagulate at about 145°F (60 to 65°C). Heating whites above 160°F (71°C) toughens them. Yolks coagulate at about 155°F (70°C). The coagulation temperature of the yolks can be raised by diluting them with water or adding sugar. In *crème anglaise*, which contain yolks and both water and sugar, the temperature must reach 175° to 185°F (80° to 85°C) before coagulation occurs. For both whites and yolks, as the protein coagulates it absorbs liquid in the mixture. This thickens pastry creams and sauces such as *crème anglaise* and gives structure to cake batters as they bake.

Adding acids (such as lemon juice or cream of tartar) to a mixture containing eggs can promote or inhibit coagulation. If the initial pH is alkaline (as it is in egg whites), adding an acid promotes coagulation. On the other hand, if the initial pH is neutral or acidic, adding an acid slows coagulation.

If eggs are heated above their coagulation temperature, the protein molecules can shrink and lose some of their capacity to hold liquid. This is what happens when, for example, a *crème anglaise* curdles. In baking, on the other hand, the excess water evaporates as a soft, moist cake batter develops into a cake that is, at least relatively, firm and dry. Egg whites, which contain no fat, lose their softness when overheated and eventually become rubbery. For that reason, meringues are always cooked at low temperature.

Yet another important property of eggs is their ability to form foams when whipped. The foams are formed by trapping air bubbles in the liquid. Most frequently we think of this property in terms of whites, but whole eggs and egg yolks can also be whipped to frothy lightness. If the foam is cooked, then the egg protein coagulates, and it is this combined foaming and coagulation that is behind the preparation of all French cake batters.

Eggs are graded by the USDA according to both quality and size. The higher the quality grade, the thicker and more viscous the white and the firmer and plumper the yolk. Only the highest grades—AA and A—are sold in most retail markets.

Sizes are graded from small to jumbo, corresponding to a minimum weight of 18 to 30 ounces (510 to 850 g) per dozen. We always use large eggs, which weigh about 2 ounces (57 g) each in the shell. Be aware, however, that the grading system actually specifies only a minimum size, so if a producer has, say, a surplus of size extra-large eggs and a shortage of large eggs, they can sell the extra-large eggs as large.

Fresh eggs have thicker whites, firmer yolks, and better flavor than old eggs. Starting from the moment the egg is laid, its pH increases. The yolk starts off slightly acidic, but within a few days it is nearly neutral. The white begins with a slightly alkaline pH and rises to very alkaline. At the same time, the yolk membrane weakens because it is stretched as the yolk absorbs water from the white. Also the proportion of thick albumen in the white decreases, and the white becomes more runny. Eggs can be kept for up to 1 month in the refrigerator before they actually spoil, but their quality declines so much that we recommend using them within 7 to 10 days. Store the eggs upright (that is, large end up so the air cell is on top) in the coldest part of the refrigerator. Keep them in their carton to minimize absorption of odors and escape of moisture through the shell.

Occasionally, we use egg whites in a preparation that is not cooked. Because of the possibility of salmonella in the fresh whites, you should use powdered egg whites in such recipes. These products, such as Just Whites, are made from pure pasteurized egg whites. They are sold in supermarkets. Reconstitute the powdered whites by stirring in warm water according to the instructions on the package.

FILBERTS

Another word for hazelnuts. See *Hazelnuts*.

FLOUR

Flours are milled from a variety of grains. By far the most important is wheat, and whenever the word flour is used alone it refers to wheat flour. In French cakes we use wheat flour almost exclusively.

The wheat kernel is composed of three parts. The bran is the outer envelope and is rich in vitamins and minerals, but it is tough and papery. The germ is the embryo, which contains proteins and fats. And the endosperm is the farinaceous (starchy) body of the kernel.

Only the endosperm is used in white flour. The process of milling breaks the kernel and separates the endosperm from the other components by bolting—a process of sifting through successively finer sieves.

All of our recipes call for white flour. Whole-wheat and bran flours, which contain all or part of the germ and/or bran of the wheat, have textures totally incompatible with French cakes.

The endosperm contains primarily starch, water, and protein. The proportions of starch and protein depend on the type of wheat (typically, winter wheats have a lower protein content than spring wheats) and how the flour was milled (the proportion of protein is greater in the peripheral part of the kernel than in the center). Wheats high in protein are called hard, those low in protein soft.

After milling, flour has a yellowish color and poor baking qualities. Aging lightens the color, improves the flour's ability to absorb fats, and neutralizes (by oxidation) components of the flour (called thiol groups) that interfere with the development of elasticity in doughs and batters. Similar results can also be achieved by chemical bleaching. Flours that have been aged naturally are called unbleached, those that have been bleached chemically are called bleached.

Starch makes up the largest share (typically 73 percent to 78 percent) of the flour. The starch molecules are distributed in the flour in the form of granules. Starch is important in cake batters, sauces, and pastry creams because of its ability to absorb water without dissolving. If the granules are damaged, they can absorb cold water, but intact granules do not absorb water until the temperature of the batter or sauce reaches 140°F (60°C). At that temperature, the starch granules absorb water and swell up all at once. This makes the batter or sauce thicker and more viscous, and we say the starch has gelatinized. In addition, since the starch molecules do not dissolve in the water, they help give structure to cakes. When the batter or sauce cools, the water remains trapped in the starch granules, and the viscosity of the batter or sauce increases. The presence of sugar or acids reduces the thickening power of starches, and excessive heating overstretches the granules, reducing the amount of water they can hold.

The protein content of white flours ranges from about 7 percent for cake flour to 12 or 13 percent for bread flour, with all-purpose flour in the middle at around 10 percent. About 85 percent of the protein is made up of two types of protein molecules, gliadin and glutenin. These two proteins are not soluble in water, but they can absorb up to twice their own weight of water. Furthermore, when mixed with water they form an elastic complex called gluten, which is essential to the structure of both flaky pastry doughs and breads. However, in cake making the elasticity of gluten can cause toughness if there is too much protein in the flour or the cake batter is not handled properly.

Starch is much more important than gluten in cake batters because these batters contain a relatively large amount of liquid. The flour proteins are dispersed in the liquid and their concentration is too low to form a strong gluten fiber network. Also, the flour is usually folded in gently at the end of the mixing process to avoid activating the gluten so that the cake will be tender. Nonetheless, the protein in the flour does contribute an essential element to the structure of many cakes.

Four basic types of white flour are widely available in the United States, namely unbleached all-purpose flour, bleached all-purpose flour, cake flour, and bread flour. Some brands, such as Gold Medal and King Arthur, are marketed nationally while others are available regionally. The packaged flour on your supermarket shelf is labeled with the approximate contents of carbohydrate (mostly starch), protein, fat, and sodium. (Unfortunately, the new federal labeling law has made the information provided so vague that it is useless.) The remainder is primarily water and a small amount of ash (natural minerals from the wheat). The water content varies slightly as the flour loses moisture by evaporation during storage. By law, white flours must be enriched to replenish vitamins and minerals removed in milling and in aging or bleaching.

Both unbleached and bleached all-purpose flours are blends of soft and hard wheats with medium protein content. They are intended for use in everything, including cake batters, pastry doughs, breads, and sauces.

Cake flour is a very fine textured, soft (low-protein) flour that has been bleached with chlorine. Unlike the bleaches used for all-purpose flours, the chlorine bleach does not improve the flour's ability to develop gluten, and, in fact, inhibits development of gluten by raising the acidity of the flour. While cake flour is designed for use in cakes, we think it an unacceptable alternative. Cakes made with cake flour have a fine, loose crumb that its proponents characterize as "velvety" but which actually feels like sawdust in the mouth. Also, cake flour contributes an unpleasant astringent taste because of its acidity.

Bread flour is a high-protein (12 to 13 percent) flour made from hard wheats. It is usually bleached and treated with potassium bromate to improve its capacity to develop gluten. Its protein content is too high for cakes.

We used Gold Medal unbleached all-purpose flour in developing our recipes. It contains about 10.5 percent protein and 77 percent carbohydrate. Gold Medal's bleached all-purpose flour has the same proportions of protein and carbohydrate and so can be used interchangeably with the Gold Medal unbleached. If you use another all-purpose flour with different proportions of protein and carbohydrate, you may have to alter our recipes to compensate for their different baking characteristics. Unbleached all-purpose flours marketed regionally in the northeastern United States often have a higher protein content than Gold Medal. Southern all-purpose flours have a lower protein content. (For accurate protein and carbohydrate percentages, telephone the manufacturer. Do not rely on the vague package label.)

As an example of how to compensate for a flour with different protein content, we will use King Arthur unbleached all-purpose flour. The King Arthur all-purpose flour has a protein content of about 11.7 percent, which is too high for cake making. King Arthur also makes an unbleached white pastry flour, called Round Table pastry flour, which has a much lower protein content (about 9.2 percent) than all-purpose flour. To compensate for the higher protein content of King Arthur unbleached all-purpose flour compared with Gold Medal, we recommend two possible substitutions. For each 7 ounces (200 g) of all-purpose flour called for in one of our recipes, use:

- either 3½ ounces (100 g) King Arthur unbleached all-purpose flour
  plus 3½ ounces (100 g) Round Table white pastry flour
- or 6¼ ounces (180 g) King Arthur unbleached all-purpose flour
  plus ⅓ ounce (10 g) potato starch

Sift the all-purpose flour together with the pastry flour or potato starch. The remainder of the recipe will be unchanged.

When thickening with flour, it is essential to keep the starch granules separated in order to produce a smooth result. If you mix flour directly into a hot liquid, it will form lumps—dry inside and surrounded by a layer of moistened starch granules that prevent water from penetrating the interior of the lump. The classic methods of thickening are designed to avoid this, and if you follow the instructions in our recipes, you will never have a problem with it. Also, raw flour has an unpleasant, starchy taste, so any starch-thickened filling must be thoroughly cooked during its preparation.

Store flour covered airtight to prevent loss or absorption of moisture. You can keep white flour for up to 2 or 3 months before it begins to deteriorate in quality.

Source for King Arthur Flours: The Baker's Catalogue.

FOOD COLORINGS

These make it possible to enhance the natural colors of some ingredients and to greatly enlarge the range of colors available for decorating desserts. They must be used sparingly to avoid strident or garish effects.

We use food colorings primarily to tint fondant, buttercream, and almond paste. We prefer paste food colorings because they are easier to use and give greater intensity than do liquid food colorings. The color is chosen according to the flavor of the dessert (for example, pink or peach for raspberry or orange flavors and green for kirsch) or for decorative representation (green for almond paste leaves). Sometimes we use caramel food coloring (page 457) to give a rich, natural tan color to fillings flavored with coffee or *praliné*.

FRAMBOISE

The French word for raspberries, it is often used as an abbreviation for *eau-de-vie de framboise*, the clear, colorless brandy distilled from fresh raspberries. In German it is called *himbeergeist*. *Framboise* is dry and has a heady perfume of fresh raspberries. About 9 pounds (4 kg) of raspberries are required to produce one botttle of brandy, and it is very expensive. Sweet raspberry liqueurs are considerably cheaper (though still not inexpensive), but they are insipid compared with the eau-de-vie. See also *Eau-de-Vie*.

FRUITS

The most important role of fresh fruits in French cakes is in the fruit mousses. We also use fresh fruits in a few special gâteaux, where they contribute their unique textures as well as flavors. And citrus zests and juices are indispensable ingredients in many cake batters, fillings, and frostings.

Fruits also find their way into cakes in several other guises, including candied and glacé fruits, dried fruits (especially raisins and currants), and jams and jellies.

While we almost always prefer to use fresh fruits in season, poaching them when necessary, sometimes canned or frozen fruits can be acceptable substitutes. The best canned fruits are those that can stand up to poaching without too much alteration of flavor or texture, for example, pineapple, apricots, and peaches. Canned fruits in heavy syrup are generally preferable to those in light syrup for use in cakes because they are sweeter and have better flavor and texture.

Very fragile fruits such as berries should never be poached, and the canned ones are not successful. However, frozen berries (without sugar) work well in fruit mousses and sauces where they are pureed.

GELATIN

The protein gelatin is a transparent, colorless, odorless, and tasteless solid that is extracted from the connective tissues (bones, cartilage, and tendons) of animals. We use gelatin as a mechanical stabilizing agent in mousses, bavarian creams, and jelly glazes.

The key property of gelatin in cooking is its ability to increase the viscosity of liquids by absorbing water from its surroundings. When soaked in cold water, gelatin absorbs water and swells. Heating then dissolves the gelatin in the water. Cooling the solution increases its viscosity and, if there is sufficient gelatin, causes the mixture to set, or gel. This makes it possible for mousses containing gelatin to hold their shape after molding. If the right proportion of gelatin is used, the mousse can, at the same time, keep a soft, fragile consistency. Too much gelatin, however, will make the filling rubbery.

Acids, sugar, and enzymes in some fruits (such as pineapple) can affect the thickening ability of gelatin. Sugar in excess will inhibit setting by taking water away from the gelatin and by surrounding the gelatin proteins so that they have less opportunity to connect with each other. Too much acid can damage the gelatin protein molecules. Fresh pineapple contains bromelain, an enzyme that breaks down gelatin and destroys its setting capacity. Poaching fresh pineapple destroys the enzyme, as does the cooking required in canning pineapple.

There are two standard forms of gelatin: packets of powdered gelatin and transparent sheets of leaf gelatin. The powdered form is the standard in the United States, but in France leaf gelatin is the norm. Both were developed in order to make accurate measurement of small quantities of gelatin easy and reliable.

Before adding hot liquid or cooking, gelatin must always be softened in cold liquid to prevent it from lumping when heated. For powdered gelatin, you stir the gelatin into the cold liquid (either part of the liquid in the recipe or else cold water) and let the gelatin soften in the liquid for at least 5 minutes. For leaf gelatin, you let the sheets soften in a bowl of cold water for about 10 minutes, then remove the sheets from the water and squeeze out the excess water with your fingers.

After softening, you must heat the gelatin to dissolve it. Depending on the recipe, you can add it to a cold liquid and heat it until dissolved, or dissolve the gelatin in a hot liquid. Either way, the gelatin must be completely dissolved and no longer solid or grainy. If the gelatin has not dissolved, then the mixture won't set. However, excess heat damages the gelatin protein. Remove a mixture containing gelatin from the heat when steam begins to rise from the surface. When softened gelatin is stirred into a hot liquid, the temperature of the liquid should be below 180°F (80°C).

After the gelatin has dissolved, you cool the mixture to room temperature. At this point it will still be fluid. Then you chill it to make it set. For mousses, the mixture is lightened by incorporating whipped cream. To avoid deflating the cream, combine it with the gelatin mixture after that mixture begins to thicken.

We specify (unflavored) powdered gelatin in our recipes, and we assume that you will use the Knox brand because it is *the* standard in American home cooking. If you prefer to use leaf gelatin, substitute 2 sheets of leaf gelatin for each 1 teaspoon (5 mL) of Knox unflavored gelatin. The equivalence is the same for all leaf gelatins, regardless of the weight or thickness of each sheet, because all leaf gelatins are standardized in such a way that one leaf has a fixed thickening power.

If you use a powdered gelatin other than Knox, you will need its Bloom rating (which is a measure of its thickening power) to calculate how much to use in our recipes. The Bloom rating for Knox unflavored gelatin is 235. Divide the quantity of Knox gelatin by the Bloom rating of your gelatin and multiply by 235 to find the quantity of gelatin you need.

Sources for Leaf Gelatin: La Cuisine and Sweet Celebrations.

GLACÉ FRUITS

Fruits that are preserved by cooking them in sugar syrup, then glazing them with syrup, are called glacé (from the French word for glazed). The ones we see most often in the United States are cherries, pineapple slices, and, to a lesser extent, apricots. Glacé pears and peaches are also available, and in the luxury food shops of Paris you can find everything from plums and citron to whole glacé melons and pineapple. Glacé fruits are sold primarily in the fall and winter, especially around the holidays.

Unfortunately, many of the glacé fruits sold in our supermarkets taste too much of sugar and preservatives and not enough of fruit. On the other hand, the fine-quality glacé fruits imported from France and Switzerland are luxurious delicacies. Excellent glacé fruits are also available from Australia. Look for fine imported glacé fruits in gourmet food shops.

We use glacé cherries, pineapple, and apricots as decoration and to add texture and flavor to cake batters and fillings. For decoration, cherries and apricots can be left whole or cut in halves; and pineapple is cut into decorative shapes. For other purposes pineapple and apricot should be diced and cherries can be either quartered or left whole.

Like candied citrus peels, glacé fruits can be kept in the refrigerator, covered airtight, for 2 or 3 months or frozen for up to 6 months. If stored longer, they dry out and harden, and sugar can crystallize on the surface.

If you can't find glacé apricots, you can make a substitute by simmering dried apricots (choose the large, plump ones from Turkey) very gently in heavy syrup (page 452) to sweeten and tenderize them. Add a little water to the saucepan from time to time to replenish water lost by evaporation. Test the apricots for tenderness by piercing them with a fork. When they begin to get tender, take one out, let it cool, and taste it. Keep cooking until the apricots are tender and sweet enough for your taste, then let them cool in the syrup. The apricots are only partially candied at this point, but they are excellent for use in gâteaux. Store them in the syrup for up to several weeks, and drain them well before using. If the syrup crystallizes (indicating that you let too much water evaporate), add a little water and simmer the apricots in the syrup again just long enough to dissolve the sugar crystals; then cool in the syrup again.

When you are adding glacé fruits to a filling in a gâteau, we recommend soaking them in an alcohol (such as rum, kirsch, or curaçao) first to give them more flavor and integrate them with the flavor of the dessert. Cut the fruits into ¼-inch (6-mm) dice, then place them in a small container and add enough alcohol to almost cover. Press the dice down in the alcohol, cover airtight, and let steep overnight or longer. Immersed in the alcohol, the candied fruits can be stored at room temperature for months.

Sources: La Cuisine and Dean & DeLuca.

GOLD LEAF

A few flakes of real gold leaf on the chocolate glaze of a gâteau add sparkle and a sense of luxury well beyond the cost of the gold. Twenty-three karat gold leaf is available from suppliers to the jewelry trade as well as a few shops specializing in deluxe cooking supplies. It is edible, and it may even help prevent rheumatoid arthritis.

This thin, fragile gold comes in packages of twenty-five 3-inch (7.5-cm) square sheets with layers of paper separating and protecting them. To apply the gold leaf to the glaze on a gâteau, lift off the front sheet of paper and turn the gold leaf upside down. With the gold still attached to the back sheet of paper, press a bit of it on the surface of the (already set) chocolate glaze. The gold leaf will cling to whatever it touches, so when you lift the sheet away from the gateau it will leave a flake of gold on the glaze. Don't touch the gold directly with your fingers or it will cling to your skin and will be very difficult to transfer to the gateau.

We have suggested using gold leaf as an optional part of the decoration for our *alhambra* (page 369). Once you have purchased a package of it, don't hesitate to experiment with it for decorating other gâteaux glazed with chocolate as well. The amount of gold leaf that you will use for each gâteau is less than a quarter of a sheet, and the actual cost per cake is under 50 cents.

Source: La Cuisine.

GRAND MARNIER

See *Curaçao Liqueur*.

HAZELNUTS

The sweet flavor of the hazelnut is more assertive than that of the almond but not so aggressive as the walnut. It is a distinctive flavoring in numerous gâteaux and it marries well with chocolate. We also use whole hazelnuts for decorating the tops of gâteaux and chopped hazelnuts for finishing the bottom edges of round gâteaux and for adding to buttercream fillings.

Like almonds, hazelnuts have a thin, papery skin that can be removed by blanching. The method requires roasting briefly at high temperature rather than plunging in boiling water as for almonds. (See the recipe for blanched hazelnuts, page 445.) Unlike almonds, hazelnuts are almost always marketed raw (that is, with skins on). You will find two totally distinct shapes of hazelnuts, globular and elongated. They don't taste any different, but in our experience, globular hazelnuts can be blanched easily while elongated ones cannot. So we recommend selecting globular hazelnuts whenever you have the choice.

Sometimes hazelnuts are roasted (at a lower temperature and for a longer time than in blanching) to brown them and enhance their flavor (see the recipe for roasted nuts, page 444). After roasting, the skins are removed by rubbing the hot nuts against the mesh of a sieve.

JAMS AND JELLIES

We use jams (also referred to as preserves) for fillings in gâteaux. The most important ones for this purpose are raspberry (always with seeds) and apricot jams, Seville orange marmalade (always thin cut), and, to a lesser extent, black currant and sour cherry (with whole cherries) jams. We also use raspberry jam and orange marmalade in the *joconde*-jam rolls (page 276) and sandwiches (page 274) that are sliced for lining charlottes and strained apricot jam (see recipe on page 412) as a glaze on gâteaux.

Jellies are great for making glazes (page 411) for charlottes and other desserts that contain mousses. Sour cherry and red currant jellies are good for mousses made from red fruits that aren't too dark; black currant and elderberry jellies are preferable with darker-colored mousses such as blackberry.

The best jams and jellies to choose for use in cakes have a firm, not runny, texture and taste like sweetened fruit. Cheap, poor-quality jams taste more of citric acid and sugar than they do of fruit, and should be avoided. Among the standard brands sold in supermarkets and gourmet stores, some that we particularly like are: the Bonne Maman (especially their apricot jam and red currant and black currant jellies) and Madame Tartine (including sour cherry and apricot jams) lines from France; Arran (spectacular raspberry and black currant preserves), Scotts (excellent raspberry preserves, apricot jam, and thin cut Scottish "breakfast" marmalade), Robertson's (including Golden Shred orange marmalade), and Denrosa (Seville orange marmalade with honey, red currant and elderberry jellies, and black currant jam) from Scotland; Wilkinson's (morello cherry jam, black currant and red currant jellies) from England; and Clearbrook Farms (wonderful Michigan tart red cherry jam and apricot preserves) from the United States.

If your jam is a little runny, rather than well set and firm, then it will be too liquid to use for a filling or glaze. In this case, the jam should be simmered very gently in a heavy saucepan over low heat, stirring occasionally, to reduce its moisture content. Do not reduce it too much or it will become rubbery when cool. Jellies, on the other hand, never need to be reduced for use in our jelly glazes.

KIRSCH

Kirschwasser (cherry brandy in German) is the correct name for this clear, colorless brandy distilled from cherries. Kirsch gives a subtle cherry flavor to many cakes. It is a natural accent flavor for gâteaux that contain cherries or cherry jam, and it pairs well with the flavor of *praliné* in several classic gâteaux.

The kirsch brandies produced in the United States are a pale reflection of the elegant and very expensive originals from France, Switzerland, and Germany. The only one of the less expensive kirsch brandies that we recommend for use in cakes is the kirsch distilled in the Netherlands by Bols. See also *Eau-de-Vie*.

LEMONS

The juice and the zest of this citrus fruit supply two distinct flavoring elements. The juice, with its high acid content, gives piquancy to desserts. On the other hand, the zest—which is the thin outer surface of the skin—is oily and aromatic and gives a more subtle and seductive flavor to cake batters and fillings that contain it. The zest is usually required in finely grated form, which is most easily obtained by rubbing the whole lemon across a very fine grater. The white inner part of the skin is the pith, which is bitter and is not used except when the peel is candied (see *Candied Citron, Lemon Peel, Orange Peel*).

MARASCHINO LIQUEUR

This sweet liqueur is distilled from fermented Marasca sour cherries. At one time, these cherries grew only in Dalmatia and the liqueur was produced in the city of Zadar in what is now Croatia. Today maraschino is produced in Italy as well as Croatia. In contrast to kirsch, the stones of the cherries are crushed in the process of making maraschino. This, and the fact that maraschino is sweet, makes it very different from kirsch.

Cherry Marnier is an altogether different type of cherry liqueur produced by macerating cherries in sweetened Cognac. Like its cousin Grand Marnier, it is produced by the Cognac house Marnier-Lapostelle in France. Cherry Marnier is sweeter than maraschino liqueur with a slightly lower alcohol content and a more recognizable cherry flavor.

We use milk in pastry cream, bavarian cream, *crème anglaise*, and the bombe batter that is the base for some fillings and mousses.

Milk contains primarily water (about 87 percent), with the remainder comprised of butter-fat (about 3½ percent), proteins, and carbohydrates (including the sugar lactose). Always use whole milk (never skim milk) in our recipes.

To kill harmful bacteria, milk is pasteurized by heating it to either 145°F (63°C) for at least 30 minutes or 161°F (72°C) for a least 15 seconds, after which it is cooled rapidly.

Most milk is also homogenized. Before homogenization, the butterfat, which is lighter than water, rises to the surface to form a layer of cream on top. Homogenization breaks up the milk fat into globules so tiny that they are kept separated and dispersed throughout the milk by bouncing off water molecules (Brownian motion).

Milk sours by a process of slow fermentation in which bacteria convert the lactose into lactic acid, making milk lose its fresh, sweet taste. You can keep fresh pasteurized milk refrigerated for over a week before it goes sour, but during that time its flavor deteriorates gradually.

When you cook milk, choose a heavy saucepan and rinse it out with cold water immediately before pouring in the milk to help prevent the milk from sticking. To avoid scorching or forming a film on top, cook the milk over low to medium heat, stirring occasionally. Do not boil, since that would alter the milk's taste and make it overflow the saucepan. Heat the milk only to the point at which it begins to simmer—about 180°F (80°C).

Botanically, a nut is a dry, hard fruit with one seed, which is the nutmeat or kernel. It develops inside a fibrous hull, which opens to release the fruit when ripe. The kernel is the edible portion and is usually covered with a brown, paperlike skin.

However, in common English usage the word "nut" is applied to any edible kernel surrounded by a hard shell. Of the six nuts—almonds, hazelnuts, pistachios, walnuts, chestnuts, and pecans—we use in this book, only hazelnuts and chestnuts qualify as true nuts according to the botanists. Almonds, pistachios, walnuts, and pecans are the seeds of drupes, which, like their cousins the peach, apricot, and plum, have both soft and hard layers surrounding the seed.

Nuts are typically high in proteins and fats, as well as vitamins and minerals. The fat content may be polyunsaturated (in almonds, walnuts, and pecans, for example) or saturated (in cashews and macadamias).

For the large quantities of nuts used in French cakes, you will want to purchase shelled nuts. The most economical way to buy them is in large packages or in bulk. If your supermarket only carries small packages, try a natural foods market or specialty store. Do not use salted, smoked, or flavored nuts.

Almonds, hazelnuts, pistachios, walnuts, and pecans are to some extent interchangeable and are often handled by the same methods. In particular, these nuts are frequently chopped, powdered, or roasted. Chestnuts are in a class by themselves because of their low fat and high carbohydrate contents.

You can chop nuts with a chef's knife on a cutting board, in a wooden chopping bowl, or in a food processor. The food processor is too uneven and difficult to control, so we prefer to chop the nuts by hand. It is impossible to get bits of uniform size, and some of the nuts will be reduced almost to a powder. Sift out the nuts that are chopped too finely using a medium or coarse sieve, depending on how finely you want the nuts chopped. We frequently use chopped nuts to decorate the bottom edges of gâteaux, and we occasionally add them to fillings in gâteaux.

When nuts are powdered, they are usually mixed first with an equal weight of confectioners' sugar to absorb the oil they give up in the process. This trick was developed around 1845 by a pastry chef in Bordeaux named Gazeau. We give the recipe for nut-and-sugar powders on page 442.

Nuts can be roasted to enhance their flavor, to brown them, and to reduce their moisture content. The procedure for roasting nuts is explained on page 444. Pistachios are not roasted because it is desirable to preserve their green color.

Store shelled nuts sealed in their original container if vacuum packed or covered airtight in a plastic bag. At room temperature or, better yet, in the refrigerator, they will keep for weeks. Before opening, vacuum-packed nuts will keep for months. Hazelnuts and pistachios are especially perishable and should always be kept refrigerated. If the oil in the nuts goes rancid, it will be apparent in their smell and taste.

ORANGE FLOWER WATER

This fragrant liquid is distilled from neroli, an oil obtained from orange blossoms. It is the classic flavoring for some cakes, including *biscuit de savoie* (page 45), but must be used very sparingly. Orange flower water is sold in gourmet shops and some upscale supermarkets.

Source: La Cuisine.

ORANGES

As with lemons, both the juice and zest of oranges contribute to flavoring cakes. Orange juice lacks the piquancy of lemon juice and, with rare exceptions, it doesn't have enough intensity to be used alone. However, in combination with the zest it often gives a more balanced flavor than does the zest alone. The zest is the thin outer surface of the peel. It is oily and aromatic, with the strong scent characteristic of oranges. When grated zest is required, the whole orange should be rubbed across a fine grater to remove the zest but not the bitter white pith beneath it. The orange peel can be used in candied form (see *Candied Citron, Lemon Peel, Orange Peel*); and orange liqueurs (see *Curaçao Liqueur*), which derive their flavor from orange peels, are frequently used in cakes as well.

PECANS

The French rarely use pecans for anything, but they are a perfectly good nut to use in French cakes. As a decoration, you can substitute them for walnuts or hazelnuts; and you could use them instead of raw almonds and/or hazelnuts in *praliné*. Used in a nut-and-sugar powder, they can make an interesting alternative to hazelnuts in cake batters. As an example, we have used them in our recipe for pecan *mousseline* on page 346.

PISTACHIOS

Like almonds, pistachios are the seed of a stone fruit. Their oval kernels are a pale yellowish green and are split into two halves. Nutritionally, pistachios are almost identical to almonds, but their color and subtle yet seductive flavor give them a unique appeal.

We use pistachios most often as a garnish on gâteaux. They play a larger role in frozen desserts and in fillings for chocolate bonbons.

Use only unsalted, raw pistachios in desserts. Shelled raw pistachios are very perishable, so keep them in an airtight plastic bag in the refrigerator.

Source: La Cuisine.

POIRE WILLIAM

Short for *eau-de-vie de poire william*, this clear colorless brandy is distilled from the Williams pear, which is equivalent to the American Bartlett. It has a beautiful scent of fresh pears— closer to the fresh fruit than any of the other *alcools blancs*. Some producers bottle *poire william* with a whole pear inside the bottle, a trick accomplished by attaching the bottle over the blossom when it forms on the tree and letting the pear develop inside the bottle. As with *framboise*, do not try to substitute cheaper, but insipid, sweet pear liqueurs for the eau-de-vie. See also *Eau-de-Vie*.

POTATO STARCH

This is an almost pure starch that the French use in cake batters and for thickening sauces. It has twice the thickening power of flour and gives sauces a more refined texture than does flour. Used in place of part of the flour in a cake batter, it produces a more tender cake.

Cornstarch is a much more common starch in the United States, and many cookbooks say that it is equivalent to potato starch. We disagree. Potato starch is a root starch that swells and gels at a lower temperature than cornstarch, which is a grain starch. Potato starch also has considerably more thickening power than cornstarch, so you need less of it, and it lacks the cereal taste of cornstarch. In a cake batter, potato starch thickens the batter earlier in the baking period and allows the cake to finish baking at a lower temperature. The result is a moister cake without the pasty texture and raw taste associated with underbaked cornstarch.

Cakes made with American all-purpose flour are sometimes too coarse and not tender enough because the flour contains too much gluten-forming proteins. We have developed a simple rule of thumb to remedy the problem using potato starch: For 1 ounce (25 g) all-purpose flour substitute ⅓ ounce (10 g) potato starch plus 1 large egg yolk. The potato starch replaces the starch in the flour and the proteins in the egg yolk are a non-gluten-forming replacement for the proteins in the flour. The result is invariably a cake with finer crumb and moister and more tender texture. If replacing 1 ounce (25 g) of flour isn't enough, try replacing 2 ounces (50 g) or more of flour following the same substitution rule. We have used this substitution with great success in the classic pound cake *quatre quarts* (page 24) and in génoise (page 82). Always scale the original recipe to the quantity you need before making the substitution in order to get an improved recipe that doesn't require fractional quantities of egg yolks.

While potato starch is not as widely used as cornstarch in the United States, it is sold in most supermarkets in the kosher section. Potato starch is also available in Asian markets and in the oriental sections of some supermarkets.

Source: Sweet Celebrations.

RAISINS AND CURRANTS

These are both dried grapes and, in fact, currants are just a specific variety of raisin. We use raisins for baking in some simple cakes and for scattering over the buttercream filling in several gâteaux. The varieties we recommend most often are golden raisins (which the French call *raisins de smyrne* and the English call sultanas) and currants (*raisins de corinthe* in French).

In the United States, golden raisins are made from Thompson seedless grapes that are treated with sulfur dioxide to preserve their color and then dried artificially. If the same grapes are sun-dried, without the sulfur dioxide treatment, they darken and are called sun-dried seedless raisins. The reason we choose golden raisins is for their more attractive color.

Currants are made from a smaller seedless grape.

Muscat, or malaga, raisins are dark raisins made from muscat grapes. They are large and sweet and have a nicer flavor than the Thompson seedless variety. If you want to use them instead of seedless raisins in cakes, be sure to buy seeded ones and cut them into halves or quarters so they aren't too large.

When raisins are used in a filling, you should steam the raisins to soften and plump them. After steaming we recommend soaking the raisins in an alcohol (usually dark rum) to give them more flavor. Fill a saucepan to a depth of 1 to 2 inches (2.5 to 5 cm) with water and bring to a simmer. Put the raisins in a strainer over the saucepan. Cover and let the raisins steam over the simmering water until they just begin to soften, about 5 minutes. Pour the raisins into a small glass jar and add dark rum to almost cover. Press the raisins down in the rum, cover airtight, and let steep for at least a few hours and preferably overnight. Immersed in the rum, the raisins can be kept for months at room temperature. Drain them before using.

RUM

Distilled from molasses or from sugarcane juice, rum is a by-product of refining sugarcane that originated in the Caribbean islands. We frequently flavor cake batters and fillings and frostings with the rich, heavy, pungent rums from Jamaica, Haiti, Martinique, and Guadeloupe. We also like to soak raisins in these rums to make them more exciting. Jamaican and Haitian rums are much more widely available in the United States than rums from the French islands. One of our favorites is Barbancourt from Haiti. The flavor of the dry, light-bodied Puerto Rican rums is too weak to use in desserts.

SUGAR

Sugars are a large class of carbohydrates, but only a few of them are of interest in cooking. The most basic structurally are the simple sugars, or monosaccharides, composed of one sugar unit, $C_6H_{12}O_6$. These include dextrose (also called glucose) and fructose.

The double sugars, or disaccharides, are composed of two simple sugar units joined together. A water molecule is dropped in the process, so the formula for the common double sugars sucrose, lactose, and maltose is $C_{12}H_{22}O_{11}$.

Only simple and double sugars taste sweet. Starches are polysaccharides, consisting of many simple sugar units joined together.

Ordinary sugar is 99.8 percent pure sucrose, refined from sugarcane and from sugar beets. It is by far the most common sweetener used in baking, and sucrose is an essential ingredient in every cake. Sucrose is a hard, white, crystalline solid that is very soluble in water, but insoluble in alcohol. In baking it has several important properties. The simplest are its ability to enhance other flavors and to contribute a rich color via caramelization.

At a deeper level, sugar raises the coagulation temperature of eggs, giving batters more time to rise before setting. It is hygroscopic, meaning that it absorbs water from its environment. This combination of properties makes it possible to obtain a moist, soft cake without sogginess. Since the sugar retains moisture after baking, it retards drying and helps keep cakes fresh. Also, since the sugar competes with starch and gluten for available moisture, it reduces starch gelatinization and gluten formation and thus makes the cake's structure more tender.

In whipped eggs sugar becomes part of the cell walls of foam. It gives strength and rigidity to the structure by absorbing moisture from the foam, thus firming the eggs. This is especially apparent in meringues where, added at the end of the whipping, sugar prevents graininess and smooths and stabilizes the meringue.

The simple sugars dextrose and fructose are not nearly as important as sucrose is in cake making, but they are used occasionally in small amounts because of their special properties. Both of these simple sugars are more hygroscopic than sucrose. Fructose, which is found in ripe fruits and in honey, is about 50 percent sweeter than sucrose and more soluble in water than is sucrose. It is very difficult to crystallize because of its high solubility.

Dextrose is the sugar that is used as fuel by the cells in our bodies. It is the predominant sugar in sweet corn and is also an important constituent in honey. Like sucrose, dextrose is very soluble in water, but it is less than half as sweet as sucrose. Dextrose does not crystallize itself and inhibits the crystallization of sucrose.

Lactose is the sugar in milk and contributes to cakes only incidentally through the small percentage contained in milk and milk products. Maltose plays no significant role in cake making.

Sucrose is marketed commercially in many different forms. Here are the ones we use in cake making:

GRANULATED SUGAR. *The* standard sugar, in which the crystals have been broken down into small granules. Use granulated sugar in syrups and in other mixtures that have a relatively large proportion of liquid to dissolve the sugar. However, its crystal size makes it too coarse for many batters where it doesn't dissolve quickly enough and can produce a grainy texture.

SUPERFINE SUGAR. Sold in 1-pound (454-g) boxes, this sugar has the smallest crystals of any granular form of sugar. As a result, it dissolves more quickly than ordinary granulated sugar. Also, the smaller crystals are better for aerating creamed butter because they have more sharp edges to interrupt the crystals of butterfat. This is the best sugar to use for many cake batters. Unfortunately, it has become difficult to find in some areas of the country.

EXTRA FINE SUGAR. The size of its crystals is between that of granulated and superfine sugars. It is the best alternative to use when superfine sugar is unavailable.

CONFECTIONERS' SUGAR. This powdered sugar is produced by milling granulated sugar. A tiny amount of cornstarch is added to prevent caking. Confectioners' sugar dissolves more quickly than superfine. However, it doesn't have crystals with sharp edges, so it is less effective for aerating creamed butter. It is also used to dust cakes for decoration.

CRYSTAL SUGAR. This is a sugar with very large crystals—about $\frac{1}{16}$ inch (1.5 mm). Used for decoration, it gives a sparkling, jewel-like appearance.

SANDING SUGAR. With crystals about $\frac{1}{32}$ inch (1 mm) in size, this sugar stands between crystal sugar and granulated. It is used for decorating when crystal sugar would be too coarse and crunchy.

Source for Crystal Sugar and Sanding Sugar: Sweet Celebrations.

While vanilla is probably the most widely used and important flavor in desserts, in French cakes its use is limited to flavoring a few simple cake batters, whipped cream, and *crème anglaise* and to accenting the flavors of chocolate and pears.

The vanilla bean is derived from the pod fruit of a climbing vine in the orchid family. Vanilla is native to Mexico, but today it is grown in tropical regions around the world. Of about seventy species of vanilla, the only one of culinary interest is *Vanilla planifolia*. The best beans for desserts come from Mexico, the east coast of Madagascar, and the island of Réunion in the Indian Ocean, with Madagascar being the largest producer. Vanilla beans from Réunion, Madagascar, and other neighboring islands are called Bourbon vanilla beans because the French first planted vanilla on the Île de Bourbon (the old name for Réunion), and then later transplanted the vanilla to its other tropical islands.

The vanilla pods contain many tiny black seeds in an aromatic pulp. The pods open when ripe, releasing the seeds and pulp, so they must be harvested before they reach maturity. Initially the beans are yellow and have no vanilla taste because their principal flavor component, vanillin, is linked to glucose in the pulp. The beans must be cured in a fermentation process that lasts for three to six months. During the fermentation, enzymes in the pod release the vanillin, and the color of the pod changes to a very dark brown. The beans are then aged for up to 1 or 2 years to produce a richer and fuller flavor.

While vanillin is the dominant component of the vanilla flavor, by itself it is rather monochromatic. There are many secondary flavor components that contribute to the complexity and subtlety of the full vanilla flavor. The most important of these is piperonal, which has a scent of heliotrope.

Good vanilla beans are shiny, almost black, thin, and typically about 8 inches (20 cm) long. The very best beans are covered with a "frost" of white vanillin crystals, indicating that they were well cured and aged.

Tahitian vanilla, which is currently enjoying a certain vogue, is not actually true *Vanilla planifolia* but rather a different species (*Vanilla tahitiensis*) descended from the Bourbon vanilla vines that the French planted in Tahiti in the nineteenth century. Tahitian vanilla beans are plumper and wetter than Bourbon or Mexican beans, and they have an overwhelming fragrance more strongly scented of heliotrope. Traditionally they have been regarded as inferior for use in desserts and primarily suited only to making perfumes.

Vanilla extracts are produced by steeping vanilla beans in a mixture of alcohol and water. The standard intensity, called "one fold" vanilla extract, uses 13.35 ounces of vanilla beans per gallon of liquid. A "two fold" extract is twice as strong, and so on. Nearly all of the vanilla extracts sold for the retail market are one fold. We particularly like Nielsen-Massey's Bourbon vanilla extract.

To get the full complexity of the vanilla flavor, it is best to use vanilla beans. This works very well when you are flavoring a liquid, for example, a custard. Split the bean in half lengthwise, scrape out the aromatic pulp and seeds, and add the pod, pulp, and seeds to the liquid before cooking. After cooking, strain the liquid to remove the pod. Rinse and dry the pod thoroughly, then cover it with superfine or extra fine sugar in an airtight container. Within a few days, the sugar will take on the vanilla flavor and is called vanilla sugar. To keep a steady supply of vanilla sugar, replenish the sugar as needed and add more used vanilla beans when you have them. The vanilla sugar will last for years.

Unfortunately, it is not convenient to use whole vanilla beans to flavor most cake batters. There are several alternatives available. The most convenient is to use vanilla extract. The disadvantage to using vanilla extract is that it can lose some of its intensity as the cake bakes and the extract evaporates. To partially remedy this disadvantage and for the sake of economy, pastry chefs like to powder the dried vanilla beans they have preserved in vanilla sugar after flavoring a liquid, and add this powder to their batters. This procedure is more difficult to standardize in home baking, but if you want to try it you should grind the dried beans to a powder in a coffee grinder, then sift the powder through a fine strainer. Powdered vanilla is also available in some specialty food stores, and can be substituted for vanilla extract following the manufacturer's instructions. Yet another alternative is to substitute vanilla sugar for part or all of the ordinary sugar called for in the recipe. Again, this is difficult to standardize in home baking, since the intensity of the vanilla sugar depends on how the beans were first used, the ratio of beans to the sugar in which they are stored, and how long the beans were stored in the sugar.

Sources for Vanilla Beans and Extracts: La Cuisine and Dean & DeLuca.

VINEGAR

You will use this acetic acid solution for cleaning copper (see *Copper Bowls*) and as an ingredient in royal icing (page 419). We recommend distilled white vinegar because it is neutral in flavor and inexpensive.

WALNUTS

During the Middle Ages walnuts were an important food in some parts of France, but today they play a limited role in French cooking. We use them primarily for decorating gâteaux.

There are two common varieties of walnut, the English walnut and the black walnut. The English walnut is native to the region from southeastern Europe and Asia Minor to the Himalayas. Today California, Oregon, and the region of France around Grenoble are among the most important producers of English walnuts. The black walnut is native to North America. It has a stronger taste than the English walnut.

We use only English walnuts in French cakes. Shelled walnuts are sold in halves (which separate naturally in the shelling process) or in pieces. The halves make an especially nice garnish on the tops of some gâteaux. English walnuts have a higher oil content—about 64 percent—than do almonds.

General Techniques

. . . .

There are several general techniques in cake making that deserve a more detailed explanation than we can supply in other chapters. Some of these have to do with the subtleties involved in using fundamental ingredients, especially eggs, butter, sugar, and chocolate. Others are methods for using basic pieces of equipment, including baking sheets, molds, spatulas, and pastry bags. For detailed descriptions of the equipment and ingredients, see the reference chapters on these topics.

Eggs

Of the ingredients in cake making, eggs are among the most important and the most subtle. How they are separated, whipped, mixed with other ingredients, even their temperature and how quickly you heat them can have important consequences.

To Separate Eggs

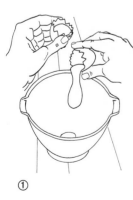

It is easiest to separate eggs when they are cold because the whites and yolks have greater viscosity and surface tension. Fresh eggs are easiest because they have stronger membranes around their yolks. Always crack the side of the eggshell on the countertop, rather than on the edge of a bowl, which can force a sharp edge of the cracked shell to puncture the yolk. Hold the egg vertically over a bowl, insert the tips of your thumbs in the crack, and pry the shell open. Let the bulk of the white drop into the bowl ①, then pour the yolk back and forth between the halves of the shell until the remainder of the white has separated from the yolk and dropped into the

①

bowl as well. Separate the chalazas from the yolk by running your fingertip over the edge of the shell. Add the chalazas to the rest of the white. If a speck of yolk gets in the white, remove it with the edge of the shell or blot it up with the corner of a paper towel. Carefully drop the egg yolk into a second bowl, trying not to puncture it on the edge of the shell if possible. After separating each egg, pour the white into a third bowl. That way if you puncture a yolk and too much drops into the bowl with the white you will lose only one white. After separating, you can store the whites in an airtight container for up to 4 or 5 days in the refrigerator, but the sooner you can use them the better. Unbroken yolks can be covered with cold water and stored in an airtight container in the refrigerator for at most 2 days, but usually this is more trouble than it is worth.

A Few Precautions

For many purposes it is best to bring the eggs to room temperature. This is particularly important if they are to be whipped. Remove the eggs from the refrigerator and take them out of their carton at least 45 minutes in advance. If you forget to take out the eggs in advance, you can warm them quickly by immersing them in warm water for 5 to 10 minutes, then drying the shells thoroughly before cracking.

Do not cook or beat eggs in bare aluminum saucepans or bowls because direct contact with aluminum discolors eggs. However, cake batters can be baked in bare aluminum because the butter brushed on the mold or baking sheet provides a barrier between the metal and eggs.

When using eggs to thicken a pastry cream or sauce, it is essential to raise the heat of the liquid evenly. Use a heavy saucepan and stir constantly. We recommend that you cook pastry creams and custard sauces over direct heat. You can always reduce the heat quickly by lifting the saucepan if the mixture is cooking too quickly. When the egg-thickened mixture has reached the required consistency, remove it from the heat and pour it into a bowl. Do not leave it in the saucepan because heat stored in the metal of the pan can continue to cook the mixture after you have removed it from the heat.

Always be careful when you mix eggs with flour or potato starch. If there isn't enough liquid in the mixture, these carbohydrates can dehydrate and "burn" the eggs, making them grainy. This is a potential problem in pastry creams, where you should not mix the starches with the eggs too long before adding the hot milk.

Whipping Eggs

Whole eggs, yolks, and whites can be whipped to produce thick, light foams. Whip eggs with an electric mixer or by hand with a wire whisk. Use a nonporous, round-bottomed bowl. Stainless steel is excellent, and glass is also all right; for whipping whites, copper is best (see page 176). Both bowl and whisk should be clean, dry, and at room temperature. To incorporate the most air and get maximum volume, eggs should be at room temperature before whipping and at least 3 days old. Fresher eggs have too much viscosity. The point at which you add sugar to the eggs is chosen to make whipping as easy and effective as possible. For whole eggs and yolks, add sugar at the beginning of the whipping. For whites, add the sugar at or near the end (see page 178).

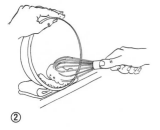
②

Always start whipping at low speed to incorporate many small air bubbles in the eggs. If you are whipping by hand, tilt the bowl and sweep the whisk around the bottom in a rhythmical circular motion ②. Each revolution should lift the entire mass of egg and incorporate air in the process. Whether you are whipping by hand or with a mixer ③, gradually increase the whipping speed as the eggs get foamy.

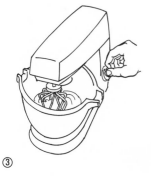
③

As you continue whipping, the thickness, volume, and color of the eggs will change in ways that depend on the proportions of whole eggs, whites, and yolks and on how much sugar (as well as almond-and-sugar powder) has been incorporated and at what stage of the whipping it was added. We address the different possibilities for whipping whole eggs and mixtures of whole eggs and yolks in the introductions to Chapters 1 (pages 15–18) and 2 (page 64). We cover the whipping of egg whites in great detail in the introduction to Chapter 4 (pages 174–182).

Always remember that once the eggs are whipped, they are fragile and must be used fairly quickly or they will deflate. Some meringues can hold up for 20 minutes or so before baking, but if there are yolks in the whipped eggs, the fat in them makes the egg foam much less stable. Our advice is don't press your luck. Use the whipped eggs right away.

BUTTER

Creaming Butter

Before you mix solid butter with other ingredients, you must "cream" the butter by beating it to give it a smooth, creamy consistency. If the quantity of butter is small, you can do it by hand. For the larger quantities required

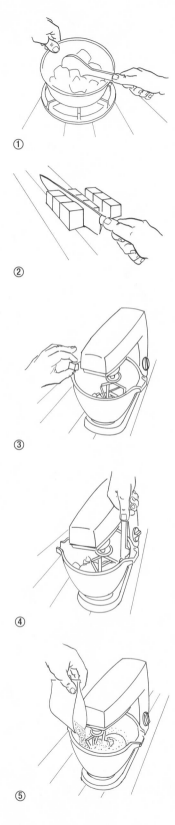

in many pound cake batters, you should cream the butter in an electric mixer. Creaming butter will be easiest if you first soften it by letting it warm at room temperature to about 59°F (15°C). The butter will soften more quickly and uniformly if it is cut into small pieces.

To cream butter by hand, place the softened butter in a stainless steel bowl and beat it with a wooden spatula until soft and smooth. If necessary, briefly warm the bottom of the bowl over very low direct heat while you beat and mash the butter with the spatula ①, but do not let the butter warm above 60° to 63°F (15° to 17°C). Continue beating the butter vigorously until it is smooth, white, and creamy. When creamed in this way, the French call it butter *en pommade*.

To cream butter with an electric mixer, use the flat beater if the mixer has one. Cut the butter into pieces 2 to 4 tablespoons (25 to 50 g) in size ②, and place them in the mixer bowl ③. Turn on the mixer and beat the butter at medium speed until the butter is soft, smooth, and creamy. Even if the butter wasn't thoroughly softened before you started beating, the energy supplied by the machine will warm and soften it as it works. If your mixer does not have a flat beater, use the eggbeater; in this case you should soften the butter uniformly in advance to enable the mixer to do the job, and move the beater around the bowl constantly to cream the butter evenly. Either way, stop the mixer and scrape down the sides of the bowl as needed to be sure all of the butter is creamed uniformly ④.

For batters in the pound cake family, you will add sugar to the creamed butter ⑤ and beat it for a longer time (usually about 5 minutes), still using the flat beater if your mixer has one. Beating with the sugar incorporates air bubbles into the butter, making the mixture much lighter. After 5 minutes of beating, the mixture will look almost white because it contains so much air. If your kitchen is warm, this prolonged beating will warm the butter significantly and can easily melt it. Melted butter will not hold air bubbles well. To minimize warming the butter, it helps to start with cold butter and chill the sugar before adding it. If the butter begins to get too soft, you can cool it as you cream it by rubbing ice cubes over the outside of the bowl of a stand mixer or, for a handheld mixer, by setting the mixer bowl in a larger bowl containing ice water.

Melting Butter

For coating molds and baking sheets with butter and for mixing small amounts of butter into batters, you need to melt the butter. If you don't melt the butter carefully, the milk solids in the butter will separate from the butterfat. Clumps of separated milk solids on a mold or baking sheet will make it more likely that a cake baked in it will stick; and adding separated butter to a light batter can partially deflate the batter.

Ideally, choose a small saucepan or butter melter so that the butter will fill it about halfway. Try to remember to take the butter out of the refrigerator in advance to soften it so that it will melt more evenly, and avoid melting butter direct from the freezer. Warm the butter gently over low heat and stir it often (or better yet constantly) to keep it from separating. The butter should be warmed only enough to just melt it. Hot butter is more likely to deflate a batter, it takes much longer to set when brushed on a mold or baking sheet, and it is more likely to separate. If you choose to melt butter in a microwave, stir it several times during the melting process and be careful not to overheat it.

Sugar

Sugar can be cooked either dry or after moistening it with water to make a syrup.

Cooking Sugar Dry

When cooked dry, sucrose melts at 320°F (160°C), forming a clear, nearly colorless liquid. As the temperature increases, it takes on a yellowish cast, and at about 335° to 338°F (168° to 170°C) it begins to break down and caramelize, turning pale amber and developing a richer and less sweet flavor. This light caramel stage is used for *praliné*. The caramel gradually turns a deeper shade of amber as the temperature increases. At 355°F (180°C) the sugar loses one sixth of its weight by evaporation of water in the sugar molecules themselves and begins to boil. The caramel will be a medium amber and have a very rich caramel taste. Like sugar itself, caramel is water-soluble, but unlike plain sucrose it is noncrystalline.

As the temperature continues to increase, the caramel darkens and gives off a faint burnt odor. At around 375°F (190°C) it begins to smoke and turns dark brown, almost black. At this point it is very bitter and suitable only as a brown food coloring. At 410°F (210°C) the sugar decomposes completely, leaving only carbon.

Cooking Sugar Syrup

Sugar syrups are prepared by moistening sugar with water, heating to completely dissolve the sugar, and then gradually boiling off the water and raising the concentration of sugar in the syrup. The syrup goes through a succession of well-defined stages by which you can recognize its density and temperature. For most purposes, you can judge the temperature with sufficient accuracy by touch and color, and we feel that this is much more convenient than using a candy thermometer, especially for small quantities of syrup. The stages that are of primary interest for cake making are the soft-ball, firm-ball, and hard-crack stages, plus the degrees of caramelization discussed earlier.

Choose the size of the saucepan (or, better yet, a copper caramel pot with a spout for pouring) for cooking the sugar so that it will be about half to two thirds full. Measure the sugar into the saucepan and add the water. Use at least ¼ cup (6 cL) of water for each 1 cup (200 g) of sugar. Stir to thoroughly moisten the sugar ①. Then stop stirring, place the saucepan over medium heat, and bring to a boil. (Stirring the sugar while bringing it to a boil would splash syrup on the sides of the saucepan, and the syrup on the sides would dry to form unwanted sugar crystals.)

At the moment when the syrup comes to a boil, the impurities in the sugar will rise to the surface and appear as a white foam or scum. Most sugar sold for domestic use in the United States is quite low in impurities. However, even slight impurities can cause the sugar to crystallize, so it is a good idea to skim the foam or scum off the surface of the syrup with a spoon. This is especially important if you are cooking sugar above the hard-ball stage.

Right after the syrup has come to a boil, it will have a tendency to foam up and can boil over if the heat is too high or the saucepan is too small. Adjust the heat so the syrup cooks quickly without foaming up. Never stir the syrup after it has come to a boil since stirring can lead to crystallization of the sugar.

At this point, you have two choices. The simplest is to cover the saucepan loosely while you continue cooking the syrup. The water vapor that condenses inside the lid will dissolve sugar crystals forming on the sides of the saucepan. The saucepan should be kept covered (except for occasional observation) until enough water has evaporated that the syrup no longer splatters on the sides of the pot.

If you choose not to cover the saucepan, then sugar crystals will form on the sides of the saucepan, and you must wash down the sides with a

③

④

⑤

⑥

⑦

moistened pastry brush to dissolve them ②. Use as little water as possible so you don't slow the cooking. You will need to do this at the early stage of cooking, right after the syrup comes to a boil. After that, no more sugar crystals should form on the sides of the saucepan.

If you use too large a saucepan, then in washing down the sides of the saucepan you will add too much water to the syrup. Also, if the level of syrup is too low, cooking will be irregular and it will be difficult to test the temperature of the syrup, especially if you are using a candy thermometer.

As you continue cooking the syrup, the water in it evaporates and its temperature increases. Below 293°F (145°C), that's all that is happening, so if you heat the syrup above the required temperature, you can always reduce the temperature (and correspondingly the concentration of the syrup) by adding a little hot water.

Testing the Stages of Cooking

If you are not using a candy thermometer, then after the syrup stops foaming up and splattering on the walls of the saucepan you must start testing it to check the stage of cooking. Have a large bowl of cold water next to the saucepan. Dip your hand in the cold water ③, quickly dip the tips of your thumb and index finger in the syrup to pluck out a little syrup ④, then immediately immerse them in the cold water again ⑤. (Don't worry, you won't get burned. The cold water will protect your fingers—so they will feel warm but not hot. However, if this procedure makes you too nervous, you can spoon a few drops of the syrup into the cold water instead.) Feel the syrup between your thumb and index finger. At first it will be watery and will dissolve immediately in the cold water. Repeat this test every minute or so. Gradually the syrup will become viscous and won't dissolve so quickly. When you take some syrup between your thumb and index finger and pull your fingers apart, the sugar will stretch out in a long thread ⑥. The syrup has reached the thread stage, at 230°F (110°C). Soon you will be able to roll it between your fingertips into a small, very soft ball that flattens when you lift it ⑦. This is the soft-ball stage, which corresponds to a temperature of 234° to 239°F (113 to 115°C). For fondant, the sugar is cooked to the soft-ball stage.

When the syrup reaches about 243°F (117°C), the ball you form between your fingertips will be about the size of a pea and, while still soft, it will hold its shape ⑧. This is the beginning of the firm-ball stage. It is used for almond paste and for classic French buttercream.

⑧

Cook the syrup a little longer and, when you test it in cold water, you will be able to roll the cooled syrup into a slightly larger ball that is no longer sticky. This is the high end of the firm-ball stage and the temperature of the syrup is about 248°F (120°C). This is the best stage to use for Italian meringue and our improved French buttercream.

If you did not wash down the sides of the saucepan carefully at the outset, then, when you test the syrup for the soft-ball or firm-ball stage, it will feel grainy because it contains undissolved sugar crystals. Do not use a grainy syrup because it will produce a grainy fondant, buttercream, or Italian meringue. If the crystals are transparent, add more water to the syrup to lower the temperature and dissolve the crystals. Then continue cooking, bringing the syrup back to the soft-ball or firm-ball stage. However, if the crystals are white and opaque, you cannot dissolve them, and the only way to use the syrup is to cook it further and make a caramel or *praliné*.

Above 250°F (121°C), the syrup becomes progressively more viscous. From 250° to 265°F (121° to 130°C) it is in the hard-ball stage and will form a very firm, but still malleable ball when tested in cold water. Beginning at 275°F (135°C) it is in the soft-crack stage and can no longer be rolled into a ball; instead, it forms hard threads or sheets that bend before breaking. If you bite a piece of the cooled sugar, it will stick to your teeth.

In making a blond caramel, a few drops of acid (such as lemon juice) are frequently added to the syrup during the hard-ball or soft-crack stage to help prevent crystallization.

At 293°F (145°C), the syrup has lost all of its water by evaporation. However, as long as there are no crystals on the sides of the saucepan, it will remain liquid even though this is below the melting point of sucrose.

From this point on, be especially careful not to cook the sugar beyond the required temperature, because, as you raise the temperature still higher, the structure of the sugar will change and you can't reverse the process by adding water and cooling it. When the sugar reaches the desired stage, immediately plunge the bottom of the saucepan into a large bowl of cold water to stop cooking. Then quickly remove it from the cold water so you don't lower the temperature of the syrup, and wait briefly until any bubbles in the syrup rise to the surface and disappear.

Next is the hard-crack stage. It corresponds to a temperature of 300° to 320°F (150° to 160°C). When you test the syrup in cold water, it forms hard sheets and threads that shatter easily. If you bite a piece of the cooled sugar, it no longer sticks to your teeth.

At 320°F (160°C), the true melting point of sucrose, the sugar yellows very slightly. The syrup should be transparent, and if you cooled it to room temperature, it would form a glassy mass and no longer crystallize.

As you continue cooking the sugar, it will gradually turn golden at about 330°F (165°C) and then amber, and will go through the same stages of caramelization as sugar cooked dry. In practice, the sugar will probably be slightly darker than the color appropriate to its temperature because syrup around the edge of the saucepan cooks more quickly than syrup in the center of the saucepan, especially if the flames on a gas burner lick the sides of the saucepan.

When you have cooked sugar a few times, you will be able to anticipate the stages of cooking as they come along and remove the saucepan from the heat before the syrup reaches the desired temperature. Be careful not to let the heat stored in the saucepan raise the temperature of the syrup above what you are aiming for. This is especially important for cooking caramels, since there the structure of the sugar is changing irreversibly.

To clean a saucepan in which sugar has been cooked, fill it about two thirds full of water and boil to dissolve the sugar clinging to the inside of the saucepan.

Changes at High Altitude

When you cook sugar syrups at high altitude, the syrup reaches a given concentration at a lower temperature than it would at sea level. The reason is that the boiling point of water is reduced by the lower atmospheric pressure at high altitude. This affects the correlation between the temperature and density of the sugar syrup from the boiling point of water up to 293°F (145°C), at which point all of the water in the syrup has evaporated. Within this range, the temperature required to reach any given concentration of sugar is reduced by 1.8°F (1°C) for each 1,000 feet (300 meters) above sea level. Altitude has no effect on cooking sugar syrups above 293°F (145°C) and for cooking sugar dry.

CHOCOLATE

Melting Chocolate

Never melt chocolate over direct heat because it scorches easily. Choose a method that warms the chocolate gently and evenly. For example, you can melt chocolate in a double boiler over hot (not boiling) water, under an infrared heat lamp (with the distance between the lamp and the chocolate adjusted to avoid overheating), in a microwave oven, or by putting the bowl of chocolate in a warm place (such as a gas oven with only the pilot light on). Whatever method you choose, first chop the chocolate or, if your heat source is gentle enough, you can simply break up small bars of chocolate along the divisions in the bars. Place the chocolate in a bowl and then warm it gently, stirring occasionally with a wooden spatula to make it melt evenly ①. The temperature of melted dark chocolate should be between 122° and 131°F (50° to 55°C) in order to completely melt not only the cocoa butter (which actually has a much lower melting point) but also any traces of other fats present as impurities. The cocoa solids will not actually scorch at temperatures below 140°F (60°C). However, since it is difficult to be certain how uniformly the chocolate is melting, even with an accurate thermometer it is important to keep the chocolate within the specified melting range. White chocolate, which scorches more easily than dark chocolate because it contains milk solids, should be melted to between 113° and 118°F (45° to 48°C).

①

Do not allow any water to get into melted chocolate. The addition of a tiny amount of water (even a little steam) can make the chocolate become thick and granular, rather than fluid and smooth. When this happens the chocolate is said to "seize." Unsweetened chocolate is particularly susceptible to this problem because, unlike most bittersweet chocolates, it contains no emulsifier to help keep it fluid. The reason chocolate seizes is that the cocoa particles absorb the water that they come in contact with. If there is not enough water, the moistened cocoa particles stick together in lumps. Once chocolate has seized, the only way to fix the problem is by adding more liquid, stirring in just enough to dissolve the cocoa particles and make the chocolate smooth again.

Tempering Chocolate

When bittersweet chocolate or white chocolate will be used for glazing or making decorations, it must be tempered after melting to prevent fat bloom from forming on the surface and to ensure that the chocolate will set quickly and have a smooth texture and good snap. There are several methods for tempering, but they are all designed to supply enough stable β type seed crystals to make the cocoa butter crystallize in stable form. (See page 504 for a discussion of cocoa butter crystallization and fat bloom.)

In the process of tempering, you slowly cool melted chocolate to a temperature that is well below the melting point of the stable β form of cocoa butter, to begin creating stable seed crystals. The chocolate will still be fluid because the cocoa butter crystals need time to grow before the chocolate will set. Normally the temperature is dropped to between 80° and 84°F (26.5° to 29°C) for dark chocolate. In this temperature range, unstable β' crystals can begin to form and the chocolate will start to thicken. Before the chocolate has a chance to set, you warm it back up slightly to melt any unstable β' crystals that have formed without melting the stable β seed crystals, always stirring constantly to keep the stable seed crystals evenly distributed throughout the chocolate. Dark chocolate should have a temperature between 86° and 91°F (30° to 33°C) to get the ideal working consistency—just fluid enough to spread easily and coat thinly. Within that temperature range, a professional chocolate maker would choose the precise optimal temperature depending on the particular chocolate and on the purpose he was using it for. In a home kitchen, you don't need that much precision. The best choice is to play it safe by aiming for the middle of the temperature range.

If the chocolate has been well tempered, then when you put it in a cool place it will set very quickly because the evenly distributed β seed crystals serve as centers of crystallization for the remaining cocoa butter. It will have a shiny surface with no fat bloom and its texture will be smooth. To minimize the possibility of fat bloom developing later, it is also best to let the chocolate cool slowly.

There are several methods for carrying out the tempering process. For the small quantities of chocolate you will be using at home, here is the procedure we recommend. For the moment we will limit ourselves to dark chocolate. Melt the chocolate by whatever method you like best. If the melted chocolate is not already in a stainless steel bowl or a metal pot, transfer it to one. (A metal bowl or pot will transfer heat to or away from the chocolate quickly.) Dip the bottom of the bowl of melted chocolate in a larger bowl containing cold water and stir the chocolate constantly with a rubber spatula ②, scraping it away from the bottom and sides of the bowl, until the temperature drops below 84°F (29°C). Always be careful not to let water get in the chocolate and, unless you are expert at judging the temperature of the chocolate by feel, use an accurate thermometer. The chocolate will begin to thicken and lose its glossy sheen. Do not let the temperature drop below 80°F (26.5°C) or it can set and you will have to melt it again. Remove the bowl of chocolate from the cold water and dip the bottom of the bowl of chocolate in a larger bowl containing hot water. Stir over the hot water ③ just long enough to make the chocolate fluid

②

③

again. The temperature of the chocolate must be between 86° and 91°F (30° to 33°C). Remove the bowl of chocolate from the hot water. The chocolate now is ready to use. If the chocolate gets above 92°F (33°C), you will have to repeat the tempering—cooling the chocolate until it starts to thicken, then warming it until fluid again.

For white chocolate, the tempering procedure is the same except that the temperatures are slightly lower. You must lower the temperature of white chocolate to between 77° and 80°F (25° to 26.5°C), then warm it back up to a working temperature between 84° and 86°F (29° to 30°C).

If you buy chocolate in large blocks, rather than in the small bars sold in supermarkets, there is another method that is even easier than the one we have just described and which produces results almost as good. We will call it shortcut tempering. Set aside about 20 percent (one fifth) of the chocolate in one solid piece. For example, for 9 ounces (250 g) of chocolate, set aside 1¾ ounces (50 g). Melt the remainder of the chocolate by whichever method you prefer. Then drop the reserved piece of chocolate into the melted chocolate and stir it around constantly. The chunk will gradually melt as the melted chocolate cools. Keep stirring until the melted chocolate reaches working temperature, that is between 86° and 91°F (30° to 33°C) for dark chocolate or between 84° and 86°F (29° to 30°C) for white chocolate. (Be sure to use an accurate thermometer to verify the temperature.) Then remove what is left of the chunk of the chocolate before the melted chocolate cools any further. (With this method you do not have to drop the temperature lower and then raise it back to working temperature.) The (tempered) solid chocolate constantly seeds the melted chocolate with stable β cocoa butter crystals as it melts, ensuring that the melted chocolate reaches working consistency in a well-tempered state. If anything, it is too effective in seeding the melted chocolate, producing so many seed crystals that the chocolate may not be quite as fluid as we would like when it reaches working temperature. The other minor drawback to this method is that, because the chunk of chocolate is not heated above 122°F (50°C), some impurities in the cocoa butter from the chunk may not melt, remaining as solid particles in the melted chocolate. The result is that chocolate tempered by this method may not be quite as smooth or shiny after setting as chocolate tempered by the more standard method. For some cooks, the difference in level of perfection is a small price to pay for the ease and simplicity of the shortcut tempering method. There is one circumstance when shortcut tempering is actually preferable. If you want to reheat leftover chocolate glaze (page 406) for glazing another gâteau, tempering it by the conventional method is difficult because it has been thinned with clarified butter. The better choice is to melt all of the leftover chocolate glaze, then temper it by the shortcut method, using a fresh chunk of bittersweet chocolate. The more effective seeding produced by this method will make it much easier to get the chocolate glaze to working consistency. As a final note on shortcut tempering, the reason you need a chunk of chocolate from a large block rather than a piece from a small bar is that the thin bar will break up into small pieces which can be difficult to remove from the melted chocolate when it reaches working temperature.

Regardless of which method you use to temper chocolate, you must maintain its temperature in the specified range to keep it at the proper working consistency until you are finished using it. For glazing a gâteau this is not usually a problem since you pour the glaze over the top of the gâteau all at once. However, making some chocolate decorations can be a little time consuming, and the tempered chocolate will cool quickly unless you do something to prevent it. The easiest remedy is to have on your countertop a bowl of warm water at the upper end of the temperature range you want for the tempered chocolate. You can then keep the temperature of the chocolate where you want it by dipping the bottom of the bowl of chocolate in the warm water bath as often and for as long as necessary.

PREPARING MOLDS AND BAKING SHEETS

One of the most aggravating occurrences in baking is when a cake sticks to the baking sheet or mold it was baked in. If the baking sheet or mold is properly prepared with butter, butter and flour, or kitchen parchment, this should never happen. Which mold preparation you use will also determine the surface texture and taste of the cake.

Nonstick molds have become popular because they are easy to use and don't require coating with any fat. We do not like them for baking cakes because they don't produce a desirable surface texture, and of course they don't contribute at all to the flavor of the cake. If you think you are reducing your fat intake and saving calories by using nonstick molds for cakes, you are fooling yourself because the amount of butter that ends up on the surface of the cake is minuscule. You would be better off cutting your slices of cake $\frac{1}{32}$ inch (1 mm) thinner and savoring them.

We do not like nonstick cooking sprays either. While it is certainly easier to spray a mold with one of these products than to coat the mold with butter, the result leaves something to be desired. At the urging of one

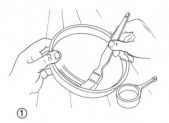

①

②

③

④

⑤

of our assistants, we experimented with a few of the most popular sprays on the market, some that contain flour and some that don't. None of them made unmolding the cakes easier than the conventional methods, and the taste that they left on the surface of the cake was unpleasant. Don't believe us? Bake a cake in a mold prepared with one of these products and then taste the crumbs left in the mold or the surface layer of the cake. When we finished our baking and tasting tests of nonstick sprays and had no more use for them, we offered the nearly full containers to the assistant who had advocated their use. She declined to take any of them! You just can't match butter.

Coating with Butter

The easiest and fastest way to coat molds and baking sheets with butter is to melt the butter and brush it onto the surface of the mold ① or baking sheet ② with a pastry brush. The butter will coat the metal best if it is liquid but not hot. This method gives you complete control over the thickness and uniformity of the butter coating. (The alternative is to take a piece of softened butter on your fingers and rub it over the surface to be coated.) For buttering molds, it is often best to use clarified butter, since the milk solids in the butter can cause sticking for some cakes. We specify buttering molds with clarified butter whenever we think it is advisable. Clarified butter must be melted and applied with a pastry brush.

How heavily the mold or baking sheet needs to be buttered depends on what kind of batter you are baking (the more butter in the batter, the less likely it is to stick and the less butter the mold or sheet requires) and the shape of the mold (a deep mold with sharp corners requires more butter than a shallow, smooth one).

Dusting with Flour

You will frequently need to dust molds and baking sheets with flour after brushing with melted butter. For molds, the flour fixes the butter so it won't run down the sides during baking. On baking sheets, the flour prevents batter from sliding around when it is spread or piped. The flour also forms a light crust on the surface of the cake when baked. Always let the butter set before dusting with flour so that too much flour doesn't stay in the mold.

Scoop the flour into the mold or onto the baking sheet, adding more than will be needed to coat it ③. For baking sheets, scatter the flour around

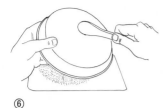
⑥

the baking sheet ④ rather than dropping it in one spot. Then tilt, shake, and tap the mold ⑤ or sheet to distribute the flour and coat the butter evenly. Once a thin layer of flour is on the butter, no more flour will adhere. Invert the mold ⑥ or baking sheet ⑦ and tap it firmly to dislodge the excess flour. You can tap the back of the mold or sheet with a wooden spatula or the plastic handle of a dough scraper. For molds, you can tap the rim of the upside-down mold on your countertop.

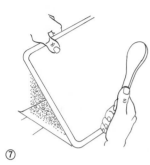
⑦

Lining with Kitchen Parchment

Lining baking sheets and molds with parchment is more or less equivalent to brushing with butter and dusting with flour. The reason for choosing parchment is usually logistical—it is simply easier to slide a fragile sheet of cake off a hot baking sheet if it is on a sheet of parchment. Although the parchment is supposed to be a nonstick surface, we find that sheets of cake (such as génoise or *joconde*) do not always release from it perfectly. To remedy this defect, and to supply the butter flavor that parchment lacks, we often brush the parchment lightly with melted butter.

⑧

To line a baking sheet with parchment, first brush the edges and diagonals of the baking sheet with melted butter ⑧. Place the sheet of parchment on the baking sheet, and smooth it out with your hands to eliminate any wrinkles and make it stick to the butter ⑨. On a French black steel baking sheet, if the parchment was not cut exactly to size you can trim off the excess by running the back edge of your chef's knife over the paper on the edge of the baking sheet ⑩ so that the edge of the baking sheet cuts the paper. For other baking sheets it is easier to cut the parchment exactly to size before you put it on the baking sheet. Either way, for some cakes we recommend brushing the parchment with melted butter to prevent the cake from sticking to the parchment.

⑨

Lining molds with parchment is cumbersome, and since it has little or no advantage over butter and flour (which is easier and cheaper), we rarely do it. The primary exception to this rule is for baking in rings, where a combination method is easiest because the ring rests on a baking sheet. To avoid dusting all or part of the baking sheet with flour, cut a square of parchment slightly larger in width than the diameter of the ring. Brush melted butter on the baking sheet in a square of the same size as the parchment—actually, brushing either the outline or the diagonals of the square will suffice ⑪. Place the square of parchment on the buttered square ⑫. Then brush the parchment with melted butter (clarified if required). That

⑩

leaves the ring itself. Brush the inside of the ring with melted butter ⑬, and let the butter set. Hold the ring vertically and spoon some flour onto the inside of the ring at the bottom ⑭. Gradually rotate and tap the ring to distribute an even coating of flour over the butter on the inside of the ring, adding more flour as needed. Tap the ring on your countertop to dislodge the excess flour, then place the ring on the baking sheet, centering it on the square of parchment. Or you can line the buttered ring with a strip of parchment (cut slightly wider than the ring is high and a little longer than the circumference of the ring) rather than dusting it with flour. Place the buttered ring on the baking sheet, centering it on the parchment square, and wrap the strip of parchment around the inside of the ring, allowing the end of the strip to overlap the beginning ⑮. Then brush the parchment inside the ring with melted butter. Lining the ring with parchment takes a little more time, but it simplifies the decorative technique of dusting just the top of a cake (not the sides) with confectioners' sugar. You simply wait until after dusting to peel off the parchment.

Lining Loaf Pans with Brown Wrapping Paper or Kitchen Parchment

You will bake some pound cakes, especially fruitcakes, in loaf pans lined with brown wrapping paper. You brush the paper heavily with melted butter, and after baking you leave the paper on the cake to seal it and prevent it from drying out until you're ready to serve it. Since the paper is saturated with butter, the bottom and sides of the cake are sealed airtight. For these cakes the top is sealed (and decorated) by glazing with apricot jam and confectioners' sugar glaze. Another presentation that we use less frequently requires peeling off the paper after baking, turning the cake upside down, and glazing both top and sides. In this case, kitchen parchment is preferable to brown wrapping paper because it peels off more cleanly.

Lining the loaf pan is easy if you follow a simple step-by-step procedure. Turn the loaf pan upside down on your countertop. For both the length and width, carefully measure the distance from the rim, up the side, across the bottom, and down the opposite side to the rim again. Cut a rectangle of brown wrapping paper (or parchment) slightly larger in length and width than your measurements. Turn the loaf pan right side up and center it on the rectangle of paper. Lightly sketch the outline of the bottom of the pan with a nontoxic pencil ⑯. Turn the loaf pan on its side. One side at a time, line up the bottom edge of the loaf pan with the corresponding side

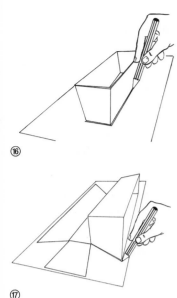

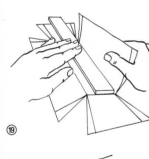

of the center rectangle (the sketched outline of the bottom of the pan) and sketch the outline of the side of the pan from the center rectangle out to the edge of the sheet of paper ⑰. When you have finished all four sides, you will have the outline of the bottom and sides of the pan on the paper. From both ends of the outline of each side of the pan, measure 1 inch (2.5 cm) toward the closest corner of the paper rectangle and make a mark. Draw a straight line from each of these marks to the nearest corner of the center rectangle. This last set of eight lines outlines a wedge at each corner of the paper. Cut out these four wedges ⑱. Next, fold the paper along each of the lines outlining the central rectangle ⑲. The paper will now fit nicely inside the loaf pan. Drop the paper inside and press the center rectangle down to the bottom of the loaf pan. Press the flaps on each side against the corresponding sides of the pan, creasing them where they meet the corners of the pan and overlap. Remove the paper from the mold and make a sharp fold at each crease. Brush the inside of the pan with melted butter ⑳. Drop the paper inside the pan again and press it against the bottom and side so that it adheres to the butter. At each corner, arrange the overlap of the sides of the paper so that the short sides are outside of the long sides. Brush the paper lining heavily with melted butter, making sure that the paper stays tight against the bottom and sides of the mold. Cut off any corners of the paper that stick up above the rest of the paper lining.

If you want to line the loaf pan with kitchen parchment instead of brown wrapping paper, the procedure is the same.

FOLDING

Folding is a method of combining two mixtures, at least one of which is light and fragile. The light element is most frequently whipped cream or eggs. The other mixture can be a heavy batter, a dry ingredient, or a second light mixture. The rule of thumb is that you always fold light mixtures into heavy ones and dry ingredients into light mixtures.

Usually the best tool to use for folding is a rubber or wooden spatula. Of the two, the rubber spatula is slightly preferable because it conforms better to the shape of the bowl. For large quantities of batter many professionals prefer to use their hands to get the most intimate feel of the batter. The essential feature of folding is the method, not the tool, and you should choose the tool that will combine the mixtures uniformly while deflating the light mixture as little as possible. In some situations, folding with a rubber spatula deflates the mixture too much because it takes too long, and it is actually better to use a stiff batter whisk (always folding gently) because it can accomplish the mixing more quickly and deflate the light component less.

If the second mixture is a heavy batter, you should first stir about one third of the light mixture into the batter to lighten it. Mix quickly and thoroughly using a wooden or rubber spatula or, if the batter is unusually thick, a batter whisk. Next, scoop the rest of the light mixture on top. To begin the folding operation, insert the edge of the spatula blade in the center of the bowl and cut down vertically to the bottom. Turn the blade horizontally and move it toward you across the bottom of the bowl. Finally bring the blade up to lift the batter from underneath onto the top. The motion is roughly circular. Rotate the bowl and repeat this motion. Continue, working gently so you don't deflate the light component, until the two mixtures are thoroughly blended and homogeneous.

To fold dry ingredients into the light component, the motion is the same, but the dry ingredient should be dusted or sifted over the light one either as you are doing the folding or by alternately dusting and folding. If you add a large amount of the dry ingredient at once it tends to lump, and you end up deflating the mixture before you get it smooth.

If both mixtures are light and fragile, then scoop either mixture on top of the other one in a large mixing bowl and mix gently using the same folding motion.

How to Use a Pastry Bag

The pastry bag is just a canvas funnel that will accommodate metal tips—the pastry tubes—of various shapes and sizes. It is one of the most powerful tools in the pastry chef's arsenal, yet it is also one of the least expensive. This simple device makes it possible to form batters, fillings, and frostings into a staggering array of shapes quickly and easily.

Like so much of traditional French cake making, the pastry bag is actually an innovation developed in the mid-nineteenth century. The parchment decorating cone had already been invented in 1808 by the pastry chef Lorsa in Bordeaux, but it was not until the great mold inventor Trottier produced metal pastry tubes that another pastry chef named Aubriot could perfect the pastry bag.

There is nothing particularly difficult about learning to use a pastry bag, just a few basic techniques that require a little practice. The same techniques are used over and over whether you are piping a meringue batter, decorating the top of a gâteau with buttercream, or, for that matter, filling deviled eggs. In the long run, the time you spend mastering the pastry bag will be amply repaid in the effort it saves you in all areas of baking and culinary decoration.

Trimming the Tip of the Pastry Bag

The opening at the tip of a new pastry bag will be quite small and you will need to enlarge it to accommodate all but the smallest pastry tubes. Take the largest pastry tube you expect to use with that particular pastry bag and drop it into the tip of the bag. Press the tube firmly in place. Using a pencil, mark a circle on the bag about ¼ inch (6 mm) up from the tip of the pastry tube. Then remove the pastry tube and cut off the tip of the pastry bag at this line.

Selecting the Pastry Tube

Choose the size of the pastry tube according to the shape to be piped and the consistency of the batter or frosting. If the opening is too large, you will find it difficult to control the batter, but if the opening is too small, it will require more effort to pipe the batter and the extra pressure you apply may soften or deflate it. We specify the pastry tube that we find ideal in each recipe. However, using a pastry tube of the next size up or down makes only a small difference, and you can compensate for a larger or smaller pastry tube by applying less or more pressure on the bag or by moving the tip of the pastry tube more quickly or more slowly.

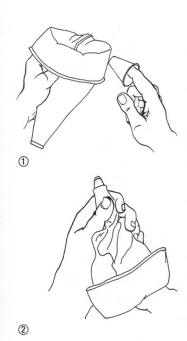

①

②

Fitting the Pastry Tube

Fold over the wide end of the pastry bag to form a large cuff ①. The length of the cuff should be about one third of the total length of the pastry bag. In other words, for a pastry bag 16 to 18 inches (40 to 45 cm) long you want a cuff 5 to 6 inches (13 to 15 cm) long; for a bag 10 to 12 inches (25 to 30 cm) long you want a cuff 3 to 4 inches (8 to 10 cm) long.

Hold the pastry tube tip down, drop it into the pastry bag, and slide it tightly into the opening at the bottom of the bag ②. Twist the bag just behind the pastry tube, and press the twisted fabric down into the back of the tube. This tightens the grip of the bag on the tube and at the same time blocks the tube, so that the batter won't run out through the tube while you are filling the pastry bag.

Filling the Pastry Bag

Take the pastry bag in one hand as though you were holding a drinking glass, with the tip of the bag pointed down and the cuff draped over your thumb and fingers to support the bag and hold it open like a funnel. Alternatively, you can place the pastry bag inside a large plastic drinking cup, draping the cuff over the rim of the cup to hold it open. For a large pastry bag, you will need a 1-quart (1-L) cup with a top diameter of about 4 inches (10 cm).

③

Filling the pastry bag is especially easy with a bowl scraper, but you can also use a large rubber spatula. Scoop up some batter from your mixing bowl and drop it into the bag ③. Scrape off the bowl scraper or spatula on the inside rim of the cuff ④, and repeat until all of the batter is in the bag, but do not fill it above the rim.

When you become more adept at handling the pastry bag, you can start with more of the bag draped over your hand to make filling the bottom of the bag easier. Then gradually drop the bottom of the bag down relative to your hand until only one quarter to one third of the bag overlaps your hand and the bag is filled to the rim of the funnel.

④

Closing the Pastry Bag

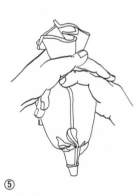

Unfold the cuff and press the batter down to the bottom of the pastry bag ⑤. You can do this either by pinching the bag between your fingers and sliding them down the bag or by laying the bag on your countertop and sliding the handle of a dough scraper or the side of your hand down the bag behind the batter. Twist the bag immediately behind the batter to enclose the batter securely ⑥. Then wrap the thumb and index finger of one hand around the twisted fabric to hold it closed. You will apply pressure to the batter in the bag with the palm and the other fingers of the hand holding the bag; and as the batter is piped out you will gradually twist the fabric behind the batter tighter to push the batter down toward the tube.

⑤

Opening the Pastry Tube

Hold the pastry tube in the fingertips of your free hand. This hand will guide the tube as you are piping. Always hold the pastry tube near the back end where the pastry bag overlaps it. If you hold the tip of the tube, you will work the tube loose from the grip of the pastry bag.

⑥

If the batter is very soft and runny, you can use your index finger as a tap to open and close the opening in the pastry tube. In this situation, you should cover the tube with your index finger at the start so none of the batter drips out.

To unblock the pastry tube, pull it and untwist the fabric behind it. Gently press on the pastry bag from the top with your other hand until the batter reaches the tip of the tube ⑦. You are now ready to pipe.

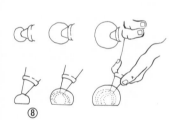

⑦

Whenever you want to stop the flow of batter, release the pressure on the pastry bag, and cover the tip of the pastry tube if necessary. If you need a free hand, turn the bag upside down, with the tip of the tube pointing up, so the batter won't drip out the tube.

General Piping Techniques

Piping is accomplished by squeezing and releasing the pastry bag with one hand to control the flow of batter, while guiding the tip of the pastry tube with the other to produce different shapes. There are three distinct basic ways to move the pastry tube and manipulate the batter. We call them *spreading, dropping*, and *dragging*. Sometimes you must use a combination of these motions to make a single shape, but isolating them makes them easier to understand.

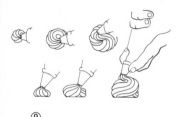

⑧

You will use the spreading method to pipe domes with a plain pastry tube and rosettes with a fluted pastry tube. Hold the tip of the tube just above the baking sheet or the dessert you are piping on, with the pastry bag at an angle of about 60° with respect to the surface. Press on the bag and, when the batter begins to spread around the tip of the tube, gradually raise the tip of the tube in a smooth, continuous motion without lifting it out of the mound of batter. To make a simple dome, raise the tube straight up, allowing the batter to spread around the tip of the tube in a dome of increasing height and width ⑧. The tip of the tube should remain inserted in the batter so that you are inflating the dome from the inside rather than dropping batter on top of it. To make a rosette (which is just a

⑨

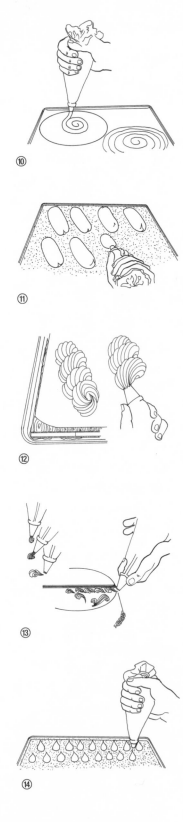

fluted dome), move the tip of the tube in a tight circle at the same time as you lift it ⑨.

To pipe spirals or long ropes of batter or wreaths, you will use the dropping method. Start with the tip of the pastry tube ¾ to 1½ inches (2 to 4 cm) above the baking sheet or dessert, and hold the pastry bag at a 60° angle with respect to the surface. Press on the pastry bag and let the batter drop onto the baking sheet, moving the tip of the tube to trace out the shape you want to pipe ⑩. Adjust the pressure on the bag and the speed at which you move the tube to get a uniform rope of batter.

You can use the dragging method to produce a variety of ribbons, fingers, and teardrops. Place the tip of the pastry tube on or just above the baking sheet or dessert you are piping on and draw the tip of the pastry tube across the surface as you press on the pastry bag ⑪. This produces a ribbon of batter. If you hold the pastry bag nearly vertical, you will make a thin, wide ribbon, whereas if you hold the bag close to horizontal, you will make a ribbon that is more cylindrical and rope-shaped. Most often you should hold the pastry bag at an angle of about 60° with respect to the surface on which you are piping. By varying the pressure on the bag and the speed at which you move the tube, you can vary the width of the ribbon to get more complicated shapes. For example, to make a figure eight or a corkscrew ⑫, the pressure and speed should be constant to get a uniform width. To produce a teardrop you must vary the pressure and speed, pressing firmly and moving the tube slowly at the beginning to form the wide end of the teardrop, and then gradually reducing the pressure and moving the tube more quickly to draw out the tip of the teardrop ⑬.

Terminating

You can terminate the piping motion in one of two ways, depending on the result you are looking for. Always release the pressure on the pastry bag a little before you reach the size and shape you want since the batter will continue flowing for a moment.

If you continue the same motion of the pastry tube after releasing the pressure, then you will draw out a tapering tail of batter ⑭. You can control the shape of the tail by the speed and direction of the motion of the pastry tube. This is how you finish a round of batter, a mushroom stem, or a teardrop, for example. With the exception of teardrops and mushroom stems, the terminating tail follows the contour of the piped shape as it disappears.

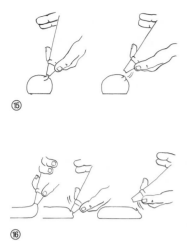

On the other hand, for domes and some other shapes you don't want a tail, and the termination should be almost invisible. To terminate the batter with no tail, you must cut the batter with a quick lateral motion of the tip of the pastry tube, so that the edge of the tube severs the connection between the piped shape and the batter in the tube. For domes, you accomplish this by a semi-circular flick with the tip of the pastry tube ⑮. If the batter was piped by the dragging method, you stop the piping motion and flick the tip of the tube in the reverse direction ⑯. In either case the tip of the pastry tube must just skim the surface of the piped batter. If the tube is too low it will drag the batter, damaging the piped shape; and if it is too high it can draw out an unwanted tail.

Refilling the Pastry Bag

If you need to refill the pastry bag, first squeeze out any batter remaining in the pastry tube. Twist the bag just behind the tube and press the twisted fabric into the back of the tube just as you did after fitting the tube into the bag at the outset. Scrape down the batter on the inside of the bag with a bowl scraper or rubber spatula, then fill the bag in the usual way.

Cleaning the Pastry Bag

When you have finished using the pastry bag, empty it and remove the pastry tube. Wash the bag thoroughly with hot water and dishwashing liquid, scrubbing with a brush both inside and out to remove any residue of butter, chocolate, or other fat. Turn the bag right side out and hang it up to air dry. Wash and dry the pastry tube separately.

CONTROLLING THE TEMPERATURE OF COMPONENTS

For many components and ingredients in cake making (including cake batters, fillings, frostings, butter, eggs, and chocolate) the temperature of the mixture or ingredient can be very important at one or more stages of its preparation or use. To some degree, you can control the temperature by how far in advance you take something out of the refrigerator or freezer and by the temperature of the kitchen itself. However, it is often necessary to be able to warm or cool a mixture or ingredient quickly as you are working with it. Some examples are tempering chocolate (which requires both cooling and warming), preparing pound cake batters (which should be kept cool while you are creaming the butter and sugar and beating in the eggs), and getting buttercream and ganache fillings to the correct working temperature and consistency. For both warming and cooling, you should always use stainless steel mixing bowls which respond to and conduct changes of temperature quickly. Glass, ceramic, and plastic mixing bowls are insulators that are ill-suited to conveying rapid changes of temperature.

The quickest warming tool is usually your cooktop, but this is not always convenient and, in addition, it may be too aggressive. A more gentle alternative is to dip the bottom of your mixing bowl in a hot or warm water bath as you stir or beat the contents of the bowl. When you are whipping a batter or filling in an electric mixer, an even more elegant alternative is to use a blow dryer. By aiming the blow dryer directly at the contents of the bowl as you continue whipping, you can adjust the temperature of the mixture quickly without overheating the mixing bowl before the heat can be transferred to its contents, and then having the heat stored in the bowl continue to warm the mixture even after you have removed the heat source (e.g., the hot water bath or the burner on your cooktop). When the mixture reaches the required temperature, you simply switch off the blow dryer.

For quickly cooling the contents of a mixing bowl, you can dip the bottom of the bowl in cold water or ice water (depending on how much and how quickly you want it cooled) as you stir or beat the contents. If you are using a stand mixer, then it may be more convenient to rub ice cubes over the outside of the mixer bowl while the machine is whipping. (Be sure to have a kitchen towel handy to mop up the water that drips around the bottom of the bowl as the ice melts.)

These warming and cooling tips may seem like trivial, commonsense advice. However, we cannot emphasize too much the importance of paying attention to temperatures of ingredients and components and being prepared to adjust temperatures quickly.

Measurement and Equivalences

. . . .

Cake making requires accurate measurement of ingredients for dependable results. The tools of measurement—namely, measuring cups and spoons and kitchen scales—are discussed in the Equipment chapter. Here we focus on equivalences between weight and volume methods of measurement and on the peculiarities inherent in measuring particular ingredients. We also include a conversion table for American, metric, and British units of measurement.

It is usually most accurate and convenient to measure dry ingredients by weight and liquid ingredients by volume. Nonetheless, we realize that not all home cooks have a kitchen scale, never mind an accurate one. Furthermore, there are exceptions to this general guideline. We therefore give approximate volume equivalences to the weights of dry ingredients in our recipes whenever possible. And we give weight equivalences for the volume measurements of some very viscous liquids.

Dry ingredients consisting of powders (such as flour and confectioners' sugar) or large pieces (such as nuts) are particularly difficult to measure accurately by volume because the amount of air included with the ingredient in a measuring cup is hard to control. On the other hand, most granulated forms of sugar have a density that does not vary significantly and can therefore be measured quite well by volume. Also, the tiny amounts of some dry ingredients (especially baking powder, gelatin, and cream of tartar) called for in recipes are often too small to measure with a kitchen scale; in this case a measuring spoon is preferable.

Particularly for powders, the method used to measure dry ingredients by volume can have a major effect on their density. The method we use for all dry ingredients except nuts is the "dip-and-sweep method." Before sifting, scoop the dry ingredient directly into a dry measure cup or measuring spoon, without packing it down. Then level the top by sweeping the straight edge of an icing spatula, a bowl scraper, or a ruler across the rim of the cup. Other methods (such as sifting powders into a measuring cup) give very different equivalences for powdered ingredients. However, most granulated sugars (except brown sugars) are not sensitive to the measurement method; for example, the equivalence will be the same if the granulated sugar is poured into the measuring cup and then swept level with the rim as it would be with the dip-and-sweep method.

We use nuts in a variety of forms in our recipes. The difficulty in measuring nuts by volume is that the size of the pieces is often large relative to that of the measuring cup. So the way the nuts are packed around the sides, bottom, and top of the cup affects the amount of nuts in the cup. If you must measure nuts by volume, we suggest filling the cup above the rim, shaking it to redistribute the nuts and eliminate any large air spaces, and then removing the nuts above the rim of the cup. We emphasize that measuring nuts by volume is very inaccurate, particularly for whole nuts and for sliced almonds. Chopped nuts and slivered almonds are less of a problem because they are smaller and tend to pack more regularly. Nut-and-sugar powders, like other powdered dry ingredients, should be measured by the dip-and-sweep method.

In home baking we normally measure eggs in integral units of whole eggs, whites, or yolks. All of our recipes call for large eggs, which weigh about 2 ounces (57 g) each, in the shell. Volume and weight equivalences are useful when a fraction of an egg is required or when eggs of different sizes are being substituted. In terms of volume, there are five large eggs or eight large whites or fourteen large yolks per cup (2.4 dL). Additional volume and weight equivalences are tabulated below. If you are using eggs other than large in size, convert the number of eggs in our recipe to volume or weight using these equivalences and then measure the required volume or weight of eggs.

VOLUME AND WEIGHT EQUIVALENCES FOR BAKING INGREDIENTS

INGREDIENT	VOLUME	WEIGHT
Granulated sugars (including superfine, crystal, and sanding)	1 cup	7 ounces (200 g)
Confectioners' sugar	1 cup	4¼ ounces (120 g)
Flour, all-purpose	1 cup	5 ounces (140 g)
Potato starch	1 cup	6¼ ounces (180 g)
Cornstarch	1 cup	4¾ ounces (135 g)
Cocoa powder, Dutch processed	1 cup	3¾ ounces (105 g)
Gelatin, powdered	1 tablespoon	.35 ounce (10 g)
Baking powder	1 tablespoon	.42 ounce (12 g)
Cream of tartar	1 tablespoon	.32 ounce (9 g)
Salt	1 tablespoon	.67 ounce (19 g)
Butter	1 cup	8 ounces (225 g)
Corn syrup	1 tablespoon	¾ ounce (20 g)
Jams and jellies	1 tablespoon	¾ ounce (20 g)
Raisins, golden or seedless	1 cup	160 g
Currants	1 cup	160 g
Almonds (shelled):		
Whole	1 cup	5¼ ounces (150 g)
Slivered	1 cup	4½ ounces (130 g)
Sliced	1 cup	3½ ounces (100 g)
Hazelnuts (shelled):		
Whole	1 cup	5 ounces (140 g)
Pistachios (shelled):		
Whole	1 cup	5 ounces (140 g)
Walnuts and pecans (shelled):		
Halves	1 cup	3½ to 4 ounces (100 to 115 g)
Nut-and-sugar powders	1 cup	4¾ ounces (135 g)
Praliné	1 cup	10 ounces (285 g)
1 large egg, in shell	—	2 ounces (57 g)
1 large egg, without shell	3 tablespoons + ½ teaspoon	1¾ ounces (51 g)
1 large egg white	2 tablespoons	1⅛ ounces (32 g)
1 large egg yolk	1 tablespoon + ½ teaspoon	⅔ ounce (19 g)

AMERICAN-METRIC-BRITISH CONVERSION TABLE

We give all measurements of ingredients, temperatures, and lengths in our recipes in both American and metric units, using the standard conventions for each system. British units are identical to the American ones except for the volume measures, for which we include the conversions below .

VOLUME:

1 quart
= 4 cups
= 0.95 liter (L)
= 33 British fluid ounces
= 32 American fluid ounces

1 cup
= 16 tablespoons
= 2.4 deciliters (dL)
= 8.3 British fluid ounces
= 8 American fluid ounces

1 tablespoon
= 3 teaspoons
= 1.5 centiliters (cL)
= 0.52 British fluid ounce
= 0.5 American fluid ounce

1 teaspoon
= 5 milliliters (mL)
= 0.17 British fluid ounce

1 L
= 10 dL
= 1.06 quarts

1 dL
= 10 cL
= 6.8 tablespoons

1 cL
= 10 mL
= 2 teaspoons

LENGTH:

1 inch
= 2.54 centimeters (cm)

1 cm
= 10 millimeters (mm)
= 3/8 inch

WEIGHT:

1 pound
=16 ounces
=454 grams (g)

1 ounce
= 28.4 g

1 kilogram (kg)
= 1,000 g
= 2.2 pounds

TEMPERATURE:
°F = °C x 9/5 + 32°

32°F = 0°C
212°F = 100°C

Sources for Equipment & Specialty Ingredients

Most of the equipment and ingredients needed for making our cakes should be available at local cookware, grocery, and gourmet shops. If you can't find an item locally, then we recommend these mail-order sources.

The Baker's Catalogue, PO Box 876, Norwich, VT 05055. Telephone: (800) 827-6386. American baking equipment and supplies. Electric mixers. Ingredients including King Arthur and Round Table flours, vanilla beans and extracts, glacé fruits, candied citrus peels, and dried sour cherries. Catalog available.

Dean & DeLuca, 560 Broadway, New York, NY 10012. Telephone: (800) 999-0306 or (212) 431-1691. European and American bakeware and cooking equipment. Ingredients including glacé fruits, cocoa powders, vanilla beans and extracts, *marrons glacés*, and *crème de marrons*. Catalog available.

J. B. Prince Company, 36 East 31st Street, New York, NY 10016. Telephone: (800) 473-0577; (212) 683-3553; fax: (212) 683-4488; www.jbprince.com. European bakeware and cooking equipment. Catalog available.

La Cuisine, 323 Cameron Street, Alexandria, VA 22314. Telephone: (800) 521-1176 or (703) 836-4435. Vast selection of French bakeware and European cooking utensils. Ingredients including Valrhona chocolates and cocoa powder, cocoa butter, chocolate vermicelli, vanilla beans and extracts, Swiss glacé fruits and candied citrus peels, shelled pistachios, *marrons glacés*, *crème de marrons*, and gold leaf. Catalog available.

McGuckin Hardware, 2525 Arapahoe Ave., Boulder, CO 80302. Telephone: (303) 443-1822. Hardware supplies including trowels and glue spreaders, propane torches, and ribbed vinyl floor mat. Kitchen machines and gadgets. American and European bakeware and cooking equipment.

Previn, 2044 Rittenhouse Square, Philadelphia, PA 19103. Telephone: (215) 985-1996. French bakeware, cake-decorating circles, and cooking equipment. Catalog available.

Ranier Devido Stone & Marble Company, 2619 New Butler Road, New Castle, PA 16101. Telephone: (412) 658-8518. Marble slabs.

Sweet Celebrations, P.O. Box 39426, Edina, MN 55439. Telephone: (800) 328-6722 or (612) 943-1508. American and some European baking equipment and supplies. Ingredients including cocoa butter, sanding and crystal sugars, vanilla beans and extracts, and leaf gelatin. Catalog available.

Swiss Connection, 501 First Street, Orlando, FL 32824. Telephone: (800) 537-9477 or (407) 857-9195. Lindt chocolate, chocolate vermicelli, and cocoa powder.

Bibliography

Bellouet, Gérard Joël. *La Pâtisserie: Tradition & Évolution*. Fontenay-le-Fleury, France: G. J. Bellouet, 1987.

Bianchini, F., and F. Corbetta. *The Complete Book of Fruits and Vegetables*. (English translation by Maurice Messegue.) New York: Crown, 1976.

Bilheux, Roland, and Alain Escoffier. *Traité de Pâtisserie Artisanale*. Paris: Éditions St. Honoré, 1984–87.

Bonnefons, Nicolas de. *Les Délices de la Campagne*. Paris, 1654.

Brécourt-Villars, Claudine. *Mots de Table, Mots de Bouche*. Paris: Éditions Stock, 1997.

Carême, Marie-Antoine. *Le Pâtissier Royal*. Paris: J. G. Dentu, 1815, and 3rd ed. Paris: Chez MM, 1841.

Castelot, André. *Le Petit Castelot Gourmand*. Cheux, France: Éditions S.A.C.N., 1995.

Chaboissier, D. *Le Compagnon Pâtissier*. 2nd ed. Paris: Éditions Jerome Villete, 1981.

Corréard, Marie-Hélène, and Valerie Grundy (editors). *The Oxford-Hachette French Dictionary*. Oxford: Oxford University Press, 1994.

Corriher, Shirley O. *Cookwise*. New York: William Morrow, 1997.

Curnonsky. *Cuisine et Vins de France*. Paris: Librairie Larousse, 1953.

Darenne, Émile, and Émile Duval. *Traité de Pâtisserie Moderne*. Nouvelle ed. Paris: Éditions L. Lambert, 1961. Originally published in 1909.

Dubois, Marguerite-Marie, et al. *Larousse Dictionnaire Moderne*. Paris: Librairie Larousse, 1960.

Dumas, Alexandre. *Le Grande Dictionnaire de Cuisine*. Paris: Alphonse Lemerre, 1873. Selections translated as *Dumas on Food* by Alan and Jane Davidson. London: Folio Society, 1978.

Encyclopedia Britannica. 11th ed. London: Encyclopedia Britannica Company, Ltd., 1910.

Fance, Wilfred J. *The New International Confectioner*. 5th ed. London: Virtue & Company Limited, 1981.

Fitzgibbon, Theodora. *Food of the Western World*. New York: Quadrangle/New York Times Book Co., 1976.

Flammarion (editors). *L'Art Culinaire Français*. Paris: Flammarion, 1976.

Franchiolo, P.-J. *L'Art Chez Le Pâtissier, Confiseur-Glacier*. Paris, 1958. Reprinted, Paris: Éditions Steff, 1979.

Gouffé, Jules. *Le Livre de Pâtisserie* (1873). Reprinted, Paris: Éditions Henri Veyrier, 1988.

Grimod de la Reynière. *Almanach des Gourmands*. Paris, 1803–1812. Reprinted, Paris: Valmer, 1984.

Healy, Bruce, and Paul Bugat. *Mastering the Art of French Pastry*. Woodbury, N.Y.: Barron's, 1984.

Healy, Bruce, with Paul Bugat. *The French Cookie Book*. New York: William Morrow, 1994.

Hermé, Pierre, and Marianne Comolli. *Secrets Gourmands*. Paris: Larousse, 1994.

Kamman, Madeleine. *The New Making of a Cook*. New York: William Morrow, 1997.

Kummer, Corby. *The Joy of Coffee*. Shelburne, Vt.: Chapters, 1995.

Lacam, Pierre. *Le Nouveau Mémorial de la Pâtisserie et des Glaces*. 8th ed. Crosnes, France: Chez Seurre-Lacam, 1949. Originally published as *Mémorial Historique de la Pâtisserie*, 1888.

Marin, François. *Les Dons de Comus ou les Délices de la Table*. Paris: Prault fils, 1739.

Massialot, François. *Le Cuisinier Roïal et Bourgeois*. Paris: Charles de Sercy, 1691.

McGee, Harold. *On Food and Cooking*. New York: Charles Scribner's Sons, 1984.

Minifie, Bernard W. *Chocolate, Cocoa, and Confectionary: Science and Technology*. 2nd ed. Westport, Conn.: AVI Publishing Company, 1980.

Montagné, Prosper. *Larousse Gastronomique*. Paris: Auge, Gillon, Hollier-Larousse, Moreau, et Cie (Librairie Larousse), 1938. English translation by Nina Froud, Patience Gray, Maud Murdoch, and Barbara Macrae Taylor. New York: Crown Publishers, 1961.
New edition compiled and directed by Robert J. Courtine. Paris: Librairie Larousse, 1984.
English translation edited by Jennifer Harvey Lang, New York: Crown, 1988.

Page, Edward, and P. W. Kingsford. *The Master Chefs*. New York: St. Martin's Press, 1971.

Partington, Angela (editor). *The Oxford Dictionary of Quotations*. 4th ed. Oxford: Oxford University Press, 1992.

Pasquet, Ernest. *La Pâtisserie Familiale*. Paris: Flammarion, 1974.

Pellaprat, Henri-Paul. *L'Art Culinaire Moderne*. Paris: Jacques Kramer, 1936.

Simon, André L., and Robin Howe. *A Dictionary of Gastronomy*. Woodstock, N.Y.: Overlook Press, 1978.

Stein, Jess, and Laurence Urdang (editors). *The Random House Dictionary of the English Language*. New York: Random House, 1966, 1967.

Stobart, Tom. *The Cook's Encyclopedia*. New York: Harper & Row, 1981.

Tante Line. *La Bonne Pâtisserie Française*. Paris: Guy Le Prat Éditeur, 1948.

Tante Marie's French Pastry. (English translation by Charlotte Turgeon.) New York: Oxford University Press, 1954.

Thuries, Yves. *Le Livre de Recettes d'un Compagnon du Tour de France*.
Tome I, *Pâtisserie Française*. Cordes-sur-Ciel, France: Sociétés Éditar, 1980.
Tome II, *Glaces, Petits Fours, Chocolats, Confiserie*. Cordes-sur-Ciel, France: Sociétés Éditar, 1982.
Tome III, *Nouvelles Pâtisserie, Pièces Montées, Travail du Sucre*. Gaillac, France: Sociétés Éditar, 1979.

Vence, Celine, and Robert Courtine. *Les Grands Maîtres de la Cuisine Française*. Paris: Bordas, 1972.

Wheaton, Barbara Ketcham. *Savoring the Past*. Philadelphia: University of Pennsylvania Press, 1983.

Guide to Pronouncing French Cake Names

Although we have tried to use American baking terminology whenever possible, this is after all a book on French cakes. To avoid sacrificing authenticity and becoming totally artificial, we have retained the French names of most cakes and a few components (such as *praliné*). We realize that many readers are not familiar with the French language and may be baffled by the pronunciation of some French words. This glossary is a simplified guide to pronouncing the French words used in the book. A few words in the French baking vocabulary (gâteau, génoise, ganache, etc.) have become sufficiently common in American cookbooks that they are considered part of the English language, and we have treated them accordingly throughout the book. Nonetheless, for the sake of completeness and for the benefit of those readers not yet familiar with them, we have included the pronunciation of these words as well.

abricotine	\a-brē-kō-tēn\	chocolatine	\shō-kō-lä-tēn\
anglais	\ãŋ-glä\	chocomel	\shō-kō-mel\
anglaise	\ãŋ-glez\	chocorêve	\shō-kō-rev\
ardechois	\är-de-shwä\	citron	\sē-trõ\
au, aux	\ō\	clafoutis	\kla-fü-tē\
biscuit	\bē-skwē\	clichy	\klē-shē\
blanc	\blõ\	colombier	\kô-lõ-bʸā\
bourbon	\bür-bõ\	crème	\krem\
breton	\brā-tõ\	croix	\krwä\
bûche	\büesh\	dauphinois	\dō-fēn-wä\
café	\ka-fā\	de	\d(ə)\
caraïbe	\ka-rīb\	délicieux	\dā-lē-sē-œ\
cassis	\ka-sēs\	des	\dā\
chanteclair	\shôn-tā-klār\	dijonnaise	\dē-zhō-nez\
chantilly	\shôn-tē-ʸē\	eau	\ō\
chocolat	\shō-kō-lä\	ébèniste	\ā-ben-ēst(ə)\

far	\fär\	polonaise	\pô-lô-nez\
fraîche	\fresh\	pralin	\pra-lē̃\
framboise	\främ-bwäz\	praliné	\pra-lē-nā\
framboisine	\främ-bwä-zēn\	progrès	\prô-grā\
frère	\frär\	pruneaux	\prũē-nō\
fromage	\frō-mäzh\	quarts	\kar\
ganache	\gä-näsh\	quatre	\ka-trə\
gâteau, gâteaux	\ga-tō\	rhum	\rôm\
gênes	\zhen\	roméo	\rô-mā-ō\
génoise	\zhen-wäz\	russe	\rũēs\
glacé	\gla-sā\	savoie	\sa-vwä\
grenoblois	\gre-nô-blwä\	stanislas	\stã-nē-släs\
janou	\zhä-nü\	succulent	\sũē-kũē-lã\
joconde	\zhô-kõd\	succès	\sũēk-se\
la	\lä\	thermidor	\ter-mē-dôr\
le	\l(ə)\	trianon	\trē-ã-nõ\
les	\lā\	trois	\trwä\
marguerite	\mar-ge-rēt(ə)\	truffes	\trũēf\
marronnier	\ma-rõ-nʸā\	vacherin	\va-shrē̃\
marrons	\ma-rõ\	vacherins	\va-shrē̃\
mascotte	\mas-kôt\	ventura	\vã-tũē-rä\
meringue	\mə-rẽg\	vie	\vē\
michounnet	\mē-shü-nā\		
moka	\mô-kä\		
montmorency	\mõ-mô-rẽ-'sē\		
mousseline	\mü-slēn\		
napolitain	\nä-pô-lē-tẽ\		
nelusko	\ne-lü-skō\		
Noël	\nō-el\		
noëlla	\nō-el-lä\		
noisettier	\nwä-ze-tʸā\		
noisettine	\nwä-ze-tēn\		
noix	\nwä\		
pain	\pẽ\		
paris	\pa-rē\		
pâtisserie	\pä-tē-srē\		
pâtissier	\pä-tē-sʸā\		
pavé	\pa-vā\		
poire	\pwar\		

Pronunciation Symbols

ə   about, system, circus

a   hat, plaid, catch

ā   late, break, pail

ä   father, heart, farm

e   any, head, best

ē   heat, queen, key

i   busy, ship, build

ī   bite, hide, guy

ŋ   sing, pink, tongue

ō   phone, show, toe

ô   caught, ball, law

œ   wolf, good, bull

œ̄   worm, squirm, purr

ü   rule, zoo, shoe

ǖ   close to the sound of the vowel in the word 'grew,' but with unrounded lips

ʸ   the adjacent character contains a sound close to English \y\ as in the word 'you';
e.g., French "chantilly' \shôn-tē-ʸē\

zh pleasure, television, mirage

~   nasalized sound

NOTE: In French, the last syllable of a word is generally stressed except in the case of optional final \ə\, as in the French word 'ébèniste' \ā-ben-ēste(ə)\, where the next to the last syllable is stressed.

Cross-Index of Components

· ·

Our recipes for many components produce larger quantites than you need to make a single cake. We have determined the quantities according to how often each component is used, how long it can be stored, and the economy of effort achieved by preparing a larger amount. Whenever you prepare components for future use, keep an inventory indicating the quantity and date prepared. Periodically replenish your supply of the components you use most frequently.

In the cross-index that follows, the components are grouped according to type, with cake layers and liners, fillings and frostings, meringue batters, glazes, sauces, decorations, and basic preparations listed separately. Each component is followed by the page numbers of the recipes in which it appears, with the recipe for the component itself listed first in **boldface** type. When a component appears in a variation on a recipe, the page number on which the variation begins is followed by the letter *V*.

A few components (whipped cream, confectioners' sugar glaze, chocolate glaze, jelly glazes, writing chocolate, and almond paste decorations) are normally prepared as part of the recipe for the individual dessert, either because they are exceptionally simple to make, or because they do not store well, or because the effort required to get the stored component to working temperature or consistency is comparable to that of preparing the component from scratch. While the components in question do not appear explicitly in the ingredient lists for the cakes, if you already have one of these components on hand, you can use it in a cake recipe and skip the corresponding ingredients and preparation. Whenever a component is implicit in a recipe, but not called for explicitly, this is indicated by listing the page number of the recipe followed by the letter *I*.

When you are planning to make a dessert, select components from your inventory and compare the listings below to see which cakes can be made by assembling these components. Then check the recipe for the cake you select to see if any additional components are required. Plan ahead whenever possible so that you can defrost your components or remove them from the refrigerator in time to reach the required temperature or consistency.

General Index

Page numbers in **boldface** type indicate the locations of recipes and of entries in the reference sections on Equipment and Ingredients.

Cakes for which there are color photos are indicated in **boldface** type, and the page number within the color insert is listed in brackets.

A

abricotine [10], **128–29**

alcohols, **494**. *See also* anisette liqueur; Armagnac; Cognac; crème de cassis; curaçao liqueur; Drambuie; eau-de-vie; *framboise;* Grand Marnier; kirsch; maraschino liqueur; *poire william;* rum

alcool blanc. See eau-de-vie

alhambra [29], 29, 344, **369–71**

Alhambra (music hall), 369

Alhambra (palace), 369

alhambra sponge cake (loaf), **344–45**

almond-and-sugar powder, **442–43**

almond cakes, 35, 38, 54, 56, 86

almond génoise, rounds, **86–87**, 342

almond génoise loaf, **342–43**

almond meringues. *See dijonnaise; russe; succès*

almond paste, **432–33**
  characteristics and proportions, 432
  enrobing a gâteau in, 77–78
  gâteau topped with, 233
  gâteaux enrobed in, 118, 121, 124
  topping a rectangular gâteau with, 335–36

almond paste, decorating with, 428–31
  flowers, 430–31
  garnishes on round gâteaux, 80
  holly berries, 329, 348, 351
  how to use, 428
  leaves, 329, 348, 351, 429
  other decorations, 431
  ropes, vines, and twigs, 429–30
  roses, 430–31
  sheets, rolled with rolling pin, 428

  textured sheets, 429
  writing cards, 430

almond paste, raw, 432

almond pound cake, **38–39**

almonds, **494–95**
  bitter, 494
  forms available, 495
  nut-and-sugar powders, in, 442
  sweet, 494–95
  uses, 494, 495
  See also almonds, blanched; almonds, raw; almonds, roasted; almonds, sliced; nuts

almonds, blanched, 495
  basic preparations containing, 432, 442, 455
  cakes containing, 35, 38, 54, 56, 86, 146, 224, 226, 342

almonds, raw, 495
  basic preparations containing, 442–43, 446–48
  cakes containing, 40, 148

almonds, roasted, **444**

almonds, sliced, 495

    roasted, **444**

angelica (candied), **495**

    cakes containing, 48, 131

anisettte liqueur, 90

    cakes flavored with, 35

apricot jam, strained, **412**

    glazing with, 21

apricot jam, whole, cakes

      containing, 128

apricots, glacé, 516

    cakes containing, 26, 35,

      128, 150

      substitution made from dried

        apricots, 516–17

apricots, poaching in light

    syrup, 454

Ardeche region, 106

ardechois, **106–7**

Armagnac, **506**

    cakes flavored with, 60, 233

    prunes, flavor to accompany,

      506

art form, French cakes as, 1–2

Aubriot (pastry chef), 546

Audran (musical composer),

    92

B

baking:

    meringues, 182–83

    pound cakes, 19

    sponge cakes, 19, 66

baking powder, **495–96**

    augmenting mechanical

      leavening, 11, 496

    chemical leavening

      mechanism, 495

    cream of tartar in, 495, 508

baking sheets, **462–63**

air-cushion, 463

aluminum, 463

black steel, 463

characteristics, 462

cookie sheets, contrasted

    with, 462

French, 463, 487

jelly roll pans, contrasted

    with, 462

seasoning black steel, 463

sizes, 462–63

stainless steel, 463

tinned steel, 463

uses, 462

baking sheets, preparing,

    136–37, 182, 213–14,

    541–44

    butter, coating with, 136–37,

      182, 213–14, 542

    flour, dusting with, 136–37,

      182, 215, 542–43

    kitchen parchment, lining

      with, 136–37, 213, 543

basic preparations, 440–57

    blanched hazelnuts, **445**

    browned butter, **450**

    caramel food coloring, **457**

    clarified butter, **449**

    crème fraîche, **451**

    crushed *pralin*, **446–48**

    double-strength brewed

      espresso, **456**

    fruit salad, **455**

    fruits poached in light syrup,

      454

    heavy syrup, **452**

    lemon syrup, **453**

    nut-and-sugar powders,

      442–43

    praliné, **446–48**

    roasted nuts, **444**

bavarian cream, 261, 360

    crème anglaise base, 261, 436

bavarians, 260–62, 282–93

    assembly, 262

    bavarian cream, 261

    brushing syrup for sponge

      cake, 262

    characterization, 261

    presentation, 262

    ring mold for, 261

    sauce for, 262, 434

    sponge cake for, 261–62

    storage, 270

    unmolding, 262

bavarians, charlottes, and

      mousse cakes, 260–327

bavarians, recipes for:

    orange bavarian, **285–87**

    peach bavarian, **282–84**

    romanov [27], **288–90**

    strawberry bavarian, **291–93**

beurre noisette, 450

biscuit, 15

biscuit chocolat [2], **40–41**

biscuit aux marrons, **51–53**

biscuit de savoie [3], 11,

    45–47, 434, 465

blackberries, recipes using, 309

blackberry charlotte, **309–11**

blackberry sauce, **438–39**

black currant jelly, 309, 320, 411

black currant preserves, cakes

    made with, 110, 320

black steel baking sheets,

    French, 463

    rectangular sheets of cake on,

      214

    seasoning, 463

    trays, using as, 487

    See also baking sheets; baking

      sheets, preparing

blanched hazelnuts, **445**

block scraper. *See* dough scraper

blood orange charlotte, 226, 276, **315–17**

bloom (on chocolate):
fat, 499, 504, 538, 539
sugar, 499

blow dryer, **463**
unmolding with, 75
warming ingredients and components with, 552

blueberries, 366

blueberry mousse log, **366–68**

bombe batter, 269, 324, 384, 402, 436

bombe nelusko, 321

Bonnefons, Nicolas de, 45

bourbon (Kentucky), **496**
cakes accented with, 106, 164, 321, 363, 378
fillings flavored with, 402

bourbon chocolat, **378–79**

bowls, **464**
ceramic, glazed, 176
copper, 176–77, 464
glass, 176
plastic, 176
shapes, 464
sizes, 464
stainless steel, 176, 464,554
for whipping egg whites, 175–77

bowl scraper, **464**

brandies. *See* Armagnac;
Cognac; eau-de-vie;
framboise; kirsch; *poire william*

bread knife, wavy edge, 473–74

Breton prune flan, **60–61**

brioche parisienne mold, 45, **465**

brioche polonaise, 132

Brittany, 60

browned butter, 406, **450**

brown wrapping paper, **465**
lining loaf pans with, 13, 544–545

bûche de Noël, 329, 490. *See also* yule logs

bûche de Noël café, **348–50**

bûche de Noël chocolat, **351–53**

Bugat, Marcel (pastry chef), 126, 156

Bugat, Paul, 29, 118, 156, 239, 369, 393

Butler, William, 297

butter, **496–97**
browned, 406, **450**, 497
clarified, **449**, 497
emulsion in, 496
grading, 496
matured cream, 496
melting, 532–33
en pommade, 532
salted, 496
sweet cream, 496
storage, 497
temperature, importance of in cake making, 14, 496, 532

butter, creaming, 14–15, 496, 531–32
aeration in, 14
electric mixer, in, 532
keeping cool, 532
pound cake batters, for, 14–15
sugar, beating with, 14–15, 532
temperature of butter for, 14, 532
wooden spatula, beating with, 532

butter, general techniques, 531–33
creaming. *See* butter, creaming
melting, 532–33

buttercream:
bombe batter for, 384
characteristics, 384, 388, 396
flavoring, 384, 388, 390
methods for making, 384
quantity, notes about, 386, 391
softening refrigerated, note about, 387

buttercream, recipes for:
chestnut, **402–3**
chocolate, 384, **388–89**
coffee, **390–92**
French, **384–87**
praliné, 384, **388–89**

butter melters. *See* saucepans and butter melters

C

cabinetry, 236

café noix, **152–53**

caffè latte, 324

cake, le [1], 11, **26–28**

cake au citron, **29–31**, 32

cake-decorating cardboards, **467**
circles, 20, 68–69, 72, 139, 264, 266, 268, 467
foil board catering platters, 332, 338, 467
foil board lids, 68, 72, 139, 216, 264, 266, 332, 467
French, 68, 72, 139, 467
matt board, 68, 72, 139, 216, 264, 266, 332, 338, 467
rectangles, 216, 332, 338, 467

clarified butter, 449

classic pound cake, **24–25**

clichy [20], **239–41**

Clichy, Louis (pastry chef), 168, 239

Clichy, Pâtisserie, 156, 239

cocoa butter, 498, **504**

 crystalline forms, 504, 538, 539, 540

cocoa particles, 501, 502–3

cocoa powder, 499, **505**

 American, 504

 cakes containing, 84–85, 222–23, 344–45

 Dutch processed, 505

 manufacturers, 505

cocoa solids, 499, 500–501

coffee, **505–6**

 as a beverage, 505

 cakes flavored with, 88, 93, 112, 152, 156, 158, 200, 236, 239, 252, 324, 348, 378

 espresso beans, 505

 history, 88, 324, 505

 instant, 505

 methods for flavoring with, 390, 456, 505–6

 See also double-strength brewed espresso

coffee buttercream, **390–92**

coffee yule log, **348–50**

Cognac, **506**

 as accent to chocolate, 506

 cakes accented with, 321

colombier, **35–37**

component approach, how to use to advantage, 4

components:

 analyzing, 2

preparing and assembling, 3–4

Condé, princes of, 398

confectioners' sugar, 525

 dusting gâteaux with, 20–21, 79–80

confectioners' sugar glaze, **413**

 glazing with, 21

Confiserie du Roy, 446

cookie cutter, round, 424

cookie sheets, 462, 487

cooling racks, **468**

 rectangular, 468

 round, 468

 sizes, 468

copper bowls, **468–69**

 cleaning, 176–77, 469

 liner for KitchenAid mixer, 468–69

 for whipping egg whites, 176–77, 468

cornstarch. *See* potato starch

corn syrup, **506**

cranberry mousse log, 276, **363–65**

cream, 398, **506–7**

 heavy, 398, 506

 light, 398

 pasteurization, 506–7

 ultrapasteurization, 507

 whipping, 507

 See also crème fraîche; whipped cream

cream of tartar, **508**

 in whipping egg whites, 177, 178

crème anglaise, 261, 262, 269, 294, 309, 312, 390, 396, **436–37,** 438, 510

proportion of egg yolks in, 436

 relation to bombe batter, 436

 vanilla in, 436–37, 526

crème chantilly, 194, 208, 398

crème de cassis, **507**

 cakes containing, 110, 320

 history, 507

crème fleurette, 507

crème fraîche, 32, 398, **451, 507–8**

 commercial, 508

 ganache, in, 400

 homemade, 451

 origin, 508

 whipped cream, in, 398

 whipping, 398, 508

crème mousseline, **396–97**

 characteristics, 396

 comparison with buttercream and pastry cream, 396

 methods for making, 396

crème pâtissière, 394

croix de lorraine [2], 11, **54–55,** 56

crosses, as symbols, 54

cross of Lorraine [2], **54–55**

crystallized violets, 194, **508**

curaçao liqueur, **508**

 basic preparations containing, 454, 455

 cakes accented with, 103, 309, 315

 cakes flavored with, 132, 198, 288, 291, 302

 See also Grand Marnier

currants, 523

 cake made with, 42

 See also raisins and currants

slip-and-streak stage, 16, 178
soft peaks stage, 177–78
sponge cake batter, for, 16
stiff-but-not-dry stage, 178
wire whisk, 176
egg yolks, 509–11
coagulation of proteins, 510
in egg white foams, 175
emulsifiers in, 509–10
nutritional makeup, 509
pH, 511
roles in batters, fillings, and
frostings, 509–10
whipping for sponge cake
batters, 16
elderberry jelly, 309, 411
electric mixer, **470**
beating butter, 14–15
cake batter, recommended
for, 12
eggbeater, 176, 177, 178,
470
flat beater, using, 14–15
handheld, 470
planetary action, 176, 180,
181, 470
pound cake batters, for,
14–15
sponge cake batters, for,
16–17
whipping eggs with, 470, 531
whipping egg whites with,
176, 177, 470
whipping heavy cream, 470
English cake, **42–44**
entremet rings, 466
entremets, 1
equipment, 460–90
basic list, 5–6
sources for, 558–59

espresso, double-strength
brewed, **456**
espresso beans, 324, 456, 505
espresso beans, chocolate, 158,
206
espresso machine, 456
Exposition Culinaire of 1903,
Paris, 239

F
far, 11, 60
far breton, **60–61**
clafoutis, similarity to, 60
muscat raisins in, 60
origin, 60
prunes in, 60
Fauvel (pastry chef), 38
filberts. *See* hazelnuts
fillings and frostings, 382–493
about, 383
fillings and frostings, recipes for:
chestnut buttercream, **402–3**
chocolate buttercream,
388–89
coffee buttercream, **390–92**
crème mousseline, **396–97**
French buttercream, **384–87**
French pastry cream, **394–95**
ganache *clichy,* **401**
ganaches, **400–401**
Grand Marnier ganache, **401**
lemon curd, **393**
praliné buttercream, **388–89**
rum ganache, **401**
whipped cream, **398–99**
finishing touches, 404–439
almond paste decoration,
428–33
chocolate decoration, 420–27
glazes, 405–13

piped decoration, 414–19
sauces, 434–39
flan rings. *See tarte* rings
flans, 58–62
characterization of, 11, 12
storage, 23
flans, recipes for:
far breton, 60–61
clafoutis, 58–59
flour, **511–14**
aging, 512
all-purpose, 512, 513
bleached, 512, 513
bran, 511
bread, 512, 513
cake, 512, 513
choice of, 6–7, 513
endosperm of wheat, 511–12
gelatinization of starch, 512
gluten in, 512
Gold Medal, 6–7, 512, 513
hard, 512
King Arthur, 7, 512, 513, 514
milling, 511–12
pastry, 513
protein content, 511, 512,
513
regional all-purpose, 513
Round Table pastry, 513
selecting, 6–7
soft, 512
southern all-purpose, 513
starch content, 511, 512, 513
storage, 514
substitution formulas, 513
thickening with, 14
unbleached, 512, 513
wheat in, 511
white, 511–14
whole wheat, 511

folding, 545–46

fondant, **408–10**

    characteristics, 408

    coloring, 457

    glazing with, 76–77, 144,
        217–18

    marble slab for, 408, 474

    rails for, 408

Fontaine, Jean de la, 398

food colorings, **514**

    caramel, 457, 514

food processor, 471

Fouquet, Nicolas, 398

fraises romanov, 288

fraisier, gâteau, 230

framboise, **514**

    cakes accented with, 124,
        245, 294

    cakes flavored with, 242,
        372

    See also eau-de-vie

framboisine [8], 121, **124–25**

France:

    Ardeche, 106

    Brittany, 60

    Franche-Comté, 187

    Grenoble, 112

    Limousin, 58

    Paris, 1, 38, 48, 92, 97, 239,
        329, 369

    Provence, 35

    Savoy, 45, 187

Franche-Comté region, 187

François I, King of France, 224

freezer paper, 489

French buttercream, **384–87**

French cake names,
        pronunciation, 562–64

French cakes, 1–2

French cheesecake [26],
    318–20

French fruit cake [1],
    26–28

French pastry cream, **394–95**

    crème anglaise, comparison
        with, 436

fromage, **90–91**

fromage blanc, 318

fromage citron [16], **196–97**

frostings. *See* fillings and
    frostings; fillings and
    frostings, recipes for

fruit cake, French [1],
    26–28

fruits, **514–15**

    canned, 515

    frozen, 515

    poaching, 454, 514–15

    roles in cakes, 514

    See also candied citron, lemon
        peel, orange peel; dried
        fruits; glacé fruits; jams
        and jellies; *specific fruits*

fruit salad, **455**

fruit sauces, 262, 438

    blackberry sauce, **438–39**

    raspberry sauce, 294, 304,
        438–39

    strawberry sauce, 304,
        438–39

fruits poached in light syrup,
    454

G

ganaches, 400

    characteristics, 400

    chocolate in, 400

    cream in, 400

    crème fraîche in, 400

    ganache *clichy*, 400, **401**

    Grand Marnier ganache, 400,
        401

    history, 400

    rum ganache, 400, **401**

    uses, 400

Gasparini (pastry chef), 174

gâteau d'ambroisie, 38

gâteau anglais, **42–44**

gâteau au fromage blanc
    [26], **318–20**

gâteau de gênes, 38

gâteau de savoie, 45

gâteaux, definition, 2

gâteaux, rectangular, 212–58

    See also rectangular gâteaux;
        rectangular gâteaux,
        recipes for; rectangular
        gâteaux, sheets of cake for

gâteaux, round nut meringue,
    134–70

    See also round nut meringue
        gâteaux; round nut
        meringue gâteaux, recipes
        for

gâteaux, round sponge cake,
    62–133.

    See also round sponge cake
        gâteaux; round sponge
        cake gâteaux, recipes for

Gazeau (pastry chef), 521

gelatin, **515–16**

    Bloom rating, 516

    damaged by excess heat, 516

    dissolving, 515–16

    Knox unflavored, 516

    leaf, 515, 516

    methods for using, 515–16

    powdered, 515, 516

    setting inhibited by acids,
        sugar, enzymes, 515

    softening, 515

    substituting for Knox, 516

    thickening properties, 515

Julien brothers (pastry chefs), 48

Just Whites (powdered egg whites), 511

K

King Arthur flours, 6–7, 512, 513, 514

kirsch, **519**
  basic preparations containing, 454, 455
  cakes accented with, 90, 92, 114, 126, 128, 130, 297, 306, 318
  cakes flavored with, 38, 56, 58, 94, 150, 230, 282, 375
  fillings flavored with, 398
  See also eau-de-vie

kitchen parchment, **473**
  lining baking sheets with, 136, 213, 543
  lining molds with, 13–14, 543–45
  lining rings with, 14, 544
  Teflon pan liners, substituting, 484
  under rings, 13–14, 65

knives, **473–74**
  bread knife, wavy edge, 473–74
  chef's knife, 473
  German high-carbon stainless steel, 473
  paring knife, 473

Kourakine, Prince Alexander, 263

L

Lacam, Pierre (pastry chef), 54, 88, 90

ladyfingers and sponge cake rounds, 264, **271–73**, 297, 300

leavening:
  chemical, 11, 495–96
  mechanical, 11, 496

Lego assembly board, 335, 336, 375, 429

lemon, **519**
  cakes flavored with, 29, 32, 196, 304, 354
  juice, 474, 519
  zest, 471, 519
  See also candied citron, lemon peel, and orange peel

lemon charlotte, **304–5**

lemon curd, 304, **393**

lemon meringue yule log [31], **354–56**

lemon pound cake, **29–31**

lemon reamer, **474**

lemon syrup, **453**

Leonardo da Vinci, 224

Leszczynski, Stanislaus, 174

light pastry cream, **396–97**

Limousin cherry flan, **58–59**

Limousin region, 58

liqueurs, sweet. *See* anisette liqueur; Cherry Marnier; crème de cassis; curaçao liqueur; Drambuie; Grand Marnier; maraschino liqueur

loaf pans, **474**
  cakes baked in, 24, 26, 29, 32, 342, 344, 346
  choice of metal, 474
  lining with brown wrapping paper or kitchen parchment, 465, 544–45

preparation of, 12–13, 331, 541–45
  size and style, 474

loaf-shaped gâteaux, 328, 330–36, 339, 342–47, 369–79
  alhambra sponge cake (loaf) for, **344–45**
  almond génoise loaf for, **342–43**
  assembly, 323–33
  cake sizes, 330
  cardboard bases for, 332
  frosting, 333–34
  glazing, 334–35
  pecan mousseline (loaf) for, **346–47**
  preparing and filling molds, 331
  similarity to log-shaped gâteaux, 330
  storage, 339
  unmolding cakes for, 331–32

loaf-shaped gâteaux, recipes for:
  alhambra [29], **369–71**
  bourbon chocolat, **378–79**
  trianon framboise, **372–74**
  trianon montmorency [32], **375–77**

loaf-shaped pound cakes:
  cake, le, 26
  cake au citron, 29
  quatre quarts, 24
  week-end, 32

lobster *thermidor*, 97

log, génoise, **340–41**

logs and loaves, 328–79.
  See also loaf-shaped gâteaux; loaf-shaped gâteaux, recipes for;

rosaces, 414–15

rosettes, 414–15, 549–50

spirals, 550

strips, 550

teardrops, 415, 550

wreaths, 550

pastry brush, **479**

cleaning, 479

size and style, 479

pastry cream, French, **394–95**

crème anglaise, comparison
with, 436

See also pastry creams

pastry cream, light, **396–97**

pastry creams:

characteristics, 394, 396

crème anglaise, comparison
with, 436

crème mousseline, comparison
with, 396

thickening, 510

uses, 394

pastry scraper. *See* dough scraper

pastry shops, historical:

Canigou, Le, 126

Chiboust, Pâtisserie, 38

Clichy, Pâtisserie, 156, 239

Confiserie du Roy, 446

Janou-Michou, 126, 156

Julien, 48

Siraudin, Pâtisserie, 400

pastry shops, in Paris, visiting,
1–2

pâte à bombe, 384

pâtissier's repertoire, 1–2

pavé framboise, **245–47**

pavé aux pruneaux, **233–35**

peach bavarian, **282–84**

peaches:

cakes containing, 126, 282

poaching in light syrup, 454

pear brandy. *See poire william*

pear charlotte, **301**

sauce for, 435

pears:

cakes containing, 300, 360

poaching in light syrup, 454

vanilla as flavor accent to,
525

pears *belle hélène*, 435

pecan-and-sugar powder, 442

pecan *mousseline* (loaf),
346–47

pecans, **522**

cakes containing, 346, 378

See also nuts

Pellaprat, Henri-Paul (chef),
48, 400

Pentecost, 35

petals, chocolate, 78–79, 426

petals for *noëlla*, **426–27**

pie pans, cakes baked in, 58,
60

pineapple, cake containing,
130

pineapple, glacé:

cakes containing, 49, 56,
130

poaching in light syrup, 454

substitute for candied
angelica, 49, 495

See also glacé fruits

piped decoration, 414–19

parchment decorating cone,
how to use, 416–17

parchment decorating cone,
making, 416

parchment decorating cone,
piping with, 415–17

pastry bags, piping with,
414–15

ropes, 414

rosaces, 414–15

rosettes, 414–15

royal icing, **419**

writing chocolate, **418**

pistachios, **522**

almonds, comparison with,
522

storage, 522

See also nuts

Plessis-Praslin, Marshal du, 446

plum cake, le, 26

plywood sheets, baking on,
202–3

poire william, **522**

cakes accented with, 300,
360

See also eau-de-vie

polyester, sheets of clear, 236,
483

Pomona, 360

pomone aux poires, **360–62**

potato starch, **523**

cornstarch, comparison with,
522–23

substituting for part of flour
in cake recipes, 24, 82,
221, 513, 523

pound cake, classsic, **24–25**

sauces for, 434

pound cakes, 11–12, 24–41

baking, 19

batters, preparation of,
14–15

characterization of, 11–12

glazing with apricot jam and
confectioners' sugar, 21

glazing with chocolate, 22

storage, 22–23

temperature, importance of,
14

unmolding, 19–20

preparing baking sheet,
213–14

removing the cake from the
baking sheet, 214–215

russe, 213, **226–27**

spreading batter on baking
sheet, 214

red currant jelly, 306, 411

Remondet (pastry chef), 384

ribbed vinyl floor mat, 166,
233, 335–36, 375, 429,
480

rice flour, 48

cakes containing, 48

ricotta, 318

ring molds, **480**

bavarians molded in, 282,
285, 291

cake baked in, 48

rings. *See* cake rings; *tarte* rings;
vacherin rings

roasted nuts, **444**

for decorating gâteaux, 444

in fillings, 444

in *praliné*, 446

rolling pins, **480**

rolling pins, plain, 118, 121,
124, 233, 335, 372, 375,
428, 480–81

rolling pins, textured:
basketweave, 233, 335–36,
375, 429, 481

checkerboard, 233, 335–36,
375, 429, 481

ribbed, 233, 335–36, 375,
429, 481

romanov [27], 262, **288–90,**
302

romanov, fraises, 288

Romanov imperial family, 288

romeo, **116–17**

round cake pans. *See* cake pans,
round

round nut meringue gâteaux,
134–70

adding extra layers, 143–44

assembly in a cake ring,
142–43

brushing rounds with syrup,
140, 142

cake sizes, 138

cardboard bases for, 139

choice of methods, 135–36

comparison with round
sponge cake gâteaux,
135–36

dusting and decorating the
outside, 145

dusting the top, 143

filling a cake ring, 142–43

filling the gâteau, 140

finishing the bottom edge,
144–45

glazing the top only, 143

glazing with chocolate or
fondant, 144

making the nut meringue
rounds, 136–38

spreading and smoothing the
frosting, 140–42

storage, 145

traditional freehand assembly
method, 140–42

trimming the rounds,
138–39

unmolding, 143

round nut meringue gâteaux,
recipes for:

café noix, **152–53**

chanteclair [13], **161**

chocolatine [13], **162–63**

chocorêve [15], **166–67**

janou, **156–57**

marie stuart [14],
164–65

michounnet, **156–57**

noisettine [13], **162–63**

paris [17], **168–70**

progrès [12], **154–55**

stanislas, **158–60**

succès kirsch [11], **150–51**

round sponge cake gâteaux,
62–133

adding extra layers, 75–76

assembly in a cake ring,
72–75

brushing the génoise with
syrup, 69–70, 73–74

cake sizes, 67–68, 72

cardboard bases for, 68–69,
72

choice of methods, 63–64

decorating, 80

dusting the outside, 78–79

enrobing in almond paste,
77–78

filling a cake ring, 74–75

filling the génoise, freehand,
70

finishing the bottom edge,
78

génoise for, 64–65

glazing with chocolate or
fondant, 76–77

making the sponge cake,
64–67

spreading and smoothing the
frosting, 70–72

storage, 81

traditional freehand assembly
method, 67–71

trimming and slicing the
génoise, 69, 73

round sponge cake gâteaux,
    recipes for:
  abricotine [10], **128–29**
  ardechois, **106–7**
  caraïbe, **103–5**
  cherry, **121–23**
  délicieux, **100–102**
  framboisine [8], **124–25**
  fromage, **90–91**
  génoise polonaise, **132–33**
  grand marnier, **118–20**
  grenoblois [7], **112–13**
  marguerite cassis [6], **110–11**
  marquis [9], **126–27**
  mascotte, **92–93**
  moka [4], **88–89**
  napolitain, **130–31**
  noëlla [5], **108–9**
  noisetier, **114–15**
  romeo, **116–17**
  succulent [7], **94–96**
  thermidor, **97–99**
royal charlottes. *See* charlottes,
    royal
royal icing, 80, 96, 336, 414,
    419, 430
  See also parchment decorating
    cone, piping with
rulers, 485
rum, **524**
rum, dark Jamaican or
    Haitian:
  basic preparations containing,
    454, 455
  cakes accented with, 97, 32,
    161, 326, 351, 369
  cakes flavored with, 26, 32,
    38, 42, 61, 116, 285
  fillings flavored with, 398,
    400, 402
rum, white Jamaican, 312

rum ganache, 400, **401**
russe, 213, 215, 216, **226–27**
russe au chocolat [23], **248–49**
russe grand marnier, **254–55**
russe praliné [23], **250–51**
Russia, 226
Russian charlottes. *See*
    charlottes, Russian
Russian-style table service, 263

S

saigon, le, **56–57**
Saigon cake, **56–57**
salon de thé, 1
salpicon filling, 131, 412
Sardou, Victorien (dramatist),
    97
saucepans and butter melters,
    481–82
  metals used for, 481–82
  sizes, 481
  See also caramel pot
sauces, 434–39
  blackberry sauce, **438–39**
  chocolate sauce, **435**
  crème anglaise, **436–37**
  fruit sauces, **438–39**
  raspberry sauce, **438–39**
  strawberry sauce, **438–39**
savarin ring mold, 48, 480
*savoie, biscuit de. See biscuit de
    savoie*
Savoy, counts of, 45
Savoy region, 187
Savoy sponge cake [3],
    45–47
scales, **482–83**
  beam balances, 482
  digital scales, 482
  importance of measuring by
    weight, 482

metric vs. avoirdupois units,
    482–83
scheduling cake making at
    home, 4
Schwehr, M. (pastry chef), 54
sheet polyester, 236, **483**
  acetate sheets, comparison
    with, 483
sieves and sifters, **483–84**
  chinois, 483
  coarse mesh, 484
  drum sieves, 483, 484
  fine mesh, 483
  flour sifter, 483
  garden sieve with
    interchangeable meshes,
    483
  kitchen paper, sifting onto
    sheet of, 484
  shapes, 483
  tamis, 483
  uses, 483, 484
  very fine stainless steel, 483
Silpat baking mats and Teflon
    pan liners, **484**
  Exopat, 484
  Silpat, 269, 278, 484
  Teflon pan liners, 269, 278,
    484
  uses, 484
simple cakes, 10–61
  baking, 19
  dusting with confectioners'
    sugar, 20–21
  filling molds and rings for, 18
  flans, 12
  glazing with apricot jam and
    confectioners' sugar, 21
  glazing with chocolate, 22
  home-style, Parisian, 11
  leavening, 11

processing, 526
Tahitian vanilla, 526
Vanilla planifolia, 526
vanilla sugar, 437, 527
Vanilla tahitiensis, 526
vanilla bean, 526–27
how to use, 526–27
recipes using, 194, 206, 208, 210, 394, 398, 402, 454
vanilla extract, pure, 526, 527
cakes containing, 24, 45, 48, 56, 108, 346
Vatel, 398
Vermont Butter & Cheese, 318, 508
vinegar, **527**
violets, crystallized, 194, **508**
vol-au-vent disks, **488**

W

walnuts, **527**
cakes containing, 112, 152, 252
See also nuts
Walton, Izaak, 297
wax paper, **489**
week-end [1], 11, **32–34**
weekend lemon cake [1], **32–34**
whipped cream, **398–99**
whisks, **489**
balloon, 489
batter, 489
whipping cream, 507
whipping eggs, 176, 177, 178, 531
white wine, dry, recipes containing, 288, 302, 360, 454
wire whisk. *See* whisks
wooden spatulas, **489**
wood grain tool, 236, **490**
making designs in chocolate, 236, 490
painters' use of, 490
writing chocolate, 80, 414, **418**, 430

See also parchment decorating cone, piping with

Y

yule log mold, 329, 330, 340, **490**
preparing and filling, 331
size, 330, 490
uses, 329–30
yule logs, 204, 329–30
assembly, 329, 332–333
brushing cake layers with syrup, 333
cardboard bases for, 332, 467
frosting, 333
génoise log for, **340–41**
traditions surrounding, 329
yule logs, recipes for:
chocolate [30], **351–53**
coffee, **348–50**
lemon meringue [31], **354–56**